U. S. Air Force in France 1950 - 1967

LTC Jerome J. McAuliffe, USAF Ret.

MILSPEC PRESS

To, COL Henry Poos,
Thank you for your USAF service in France.

Lt. Col. Jerome J. McAuliffe; USAF Ret.   6 October 2007

Published 2005
Milspec Press
2522 Cowley Way
San Diego, CA 92110
milspecpress@aol.com
jeromemcauliffe@aol.com

Printed in the United States of America

ISBN 0-9770371-1-8

overleaf photo: Aircraft formation over Chambley AB
Courtesy of Al Christensen

CONTENTS

Preface v

INTRODUCTION - MILESTONES 1

CHAPTER 1 HISTORICAL PERSPECTIVE 7

CHAPTER 2 BASE SELECTION AND MOVEMENT TO FRANCE 1950 - 1954 21

CHAPTER 3 CONSTRUCTION IN FRANCE 1951 - 1960 43

CHAPTER 4 MISSION READY 1955 - 1958 63

CHAPTER 5 REACTIVATION AND FINAL DISENGAGEMENT 1959 - 1967 87

COLOR PLATES - UNIT PATCHES 107

BASE OCCUPANCY TIMELINE 139

CHAPTER 6 BORDEAUX-MERIGNAC AIR BASE 143

CHAPTER 7 CHAMBLEY-BUSSIERES AIR BASE 165

CHAPTER 8 CHATEAUROUX-DEOLS AIR DEPOT 187

CHAPTER 9 CHAUMONT-SEMOUTIERS AIR BASE 219

CHAPTER 10 DREUX-LOUVILLIERS AIR BASE 257

CHAPTER 11 ETAIN-ROUVRES AIR BASE 283

CHAPTER 12 EVREUX-FAUVILLE AIR BASE 307

CHAPTER 13 LAON-COUVRON AIR BASE 329

CHAPTER 14 PARIS - USAF OPERATIONS 361

CHAPTER 15 PHALSBOURG AIR BASE 371

CHAPTER 16 TOUL-ROSIERES AIR BASE 387

CHAPTER 17 DISPERSED OPERATING BASES 411

CHAPTER 18 U.S. ARMY IN FRANCE 427

CHAPTER 19 RCAF BASES IN FRANCE 439

COMMON ACRONYMS 457

BIBLIOGRAPHY 461

PREFACE

This book is an attempt to fill a gap in the history of the United States' contribution to North Atlantic Treaty Organization (NATO) air power. From 1950 to 1967 the USAF set-up and maintained bases in France as part of NATO. Many current military aviation textbooks overlook this major effort made by the U.S. Air Force and U.S. Army to improve Western Europe's defensive strength. The swift buildup of this force in 1951-53 during the Korean War and our rapid exodus from France in 1966-67, amid the expansion of Vietnam hostilities, probably accounts for this oversight.

At peak strength, the U.S. Air Force had seventy-seven installations in France: nine tactical air bases, four dispersed operating bases (DOB), a major air logistics depot, eight off-base weapon storage sites, forty-nine radio relay sites, eleven radio navigational beacon sites, fourteen dependent schools, and twenty-seven hundred family housing units. These facilities supported up to four fighter-bomber wings, one light bombardment wing, three tactical airlift wings, and one tactical reconnaissance wing in France. The U.S. Army provided the infrastructure to support these air bases as required by the roles and missions defined in the National Defense Act of 1947.

As much as I am able, my goal is to relate the efforts made by the men of the U.S. Air Force during seventeen years of service and answer the question of why we were in France. I have tried to tell the story of the units involved, where they were stationed, their missions and activities, and what conditions were like at the bases. Included is a chapter giving a brief overview of the U.S. Army's sizeable effort and a chapter describing the service of the Royal Canadian Air Force as another contributor to NATO air power and a superb ally in France. We can't forget the many French civilians employed on our bases and our neighbors in the surrounding towns, who became friends and sometimes even family.

I want to acknowledge the help received from the staff at the USAF Historical Research Agency, Maxwell Air Force Base, Montgomery, AL; the USAF Museum Research Division, Wright Patterson AFB, Ohio; the National Archives and Records Administration Photo Archives, Washington, D.C.; the U.S. Army Military History Institute, Carlisle Barracks, PA; and the Air Force Safety Center at Kirtland AFB, New Mexico who assisted my searches through unit histories, photo archives, and accident reports.

A very special acknowledgement must go to the many patch collectors who dug deep into their keepsake boxes to provide me with their wing and squadron patches, particularly Mr. David Troutman and Mr. Ian Warner, patch collectors separated by an ocean, who generously shared their expertise and collections.

My greatest thanks goes to the men who served in France and their families, who have selflessly contributed information, photos, documents and reminiscences toward this project. Without your help this book would be lacking so much. I also want to thank the many veterans for their encouragement that kept me going for the years it took to complete this task. My apologies to men who feel details of their units are lacking. Many unit histories are still classified and were not available to me. Thank you all. It is your story; I hope that I have done it justice.

We went to France, endured extremely difficult peacetime living and working conditions, and have received little or no recognition for the job we performed. It was a time of frustration and hardship for most of us, but a time remembered fondly for the friendships and camaraderie that developed while "accomplishing the mission" in spite of it all.

This book is dedicated to the memory of the U.S. Air Force
men who gave their lives in service to their country
during the Cold War in France,
and
to my family for their encouragement and assistance,
particularly my wife Loralee and son Michael who lent their graphic expertise,
and my daughter Marianne who has done a masterful job of proof reading.

MILESTONES

1948 -1949

26 June 1948 to 30 September 1949 - Berlin Airlift conducted over fifteen months to prevent Soviet Union from forcing WWII Allies out of Berlin Zone of Occupation. Blockade convinces Allies of Soviet threat to Western Europe.

1949

4 April - North Atlantic Treaty formally signed by United States, Belgium, Canada, Denmark, France, Iceland, Italy, Luxembourg, the Netherlands, Norway, Portugal, and the United Kingdom.

29 August - Soviet Union detonated its first nuclear device, about four years ahead of U.S. estimates.

1950

25 June - North Korea invaded South Korea. U.S. mobilized for Cold War.

November-December - Negotiations underway between U.S. and France to establish air bases and station combat wings in France to meet NATO's defense needs.

1951

21 January - Twelfth Air Force activated to command all USAFE units assigned to NATO including those based in France.

27 February - Agreement signed to construct the Chateauroux Air Depot in central France.

July - 73d Air Depot Wing arrived at Chateauroux, France from CONUS; 150 officers and 1,440 airmen began the largest logistical air depot in Europe.

Spring-Summer - State Department and France negotiated for air basing rights in France. Airfield and tent camp construction began in fall at Bordeaux-Merignac, Chaumont-Semoutiers, Laon-Couvron, and Toul-Rosieres.

13 October - Agreement signed between French Air Force and USAFE to build ten main tactical air bases and six support installations in northern France.

Autumn - Air base construction began in French Zone of Occupation in West Germany in addition to air base construction in France. This action would remove all U.S. tactical air bases east of Rhein River.

7 December - 126th Light Bombardment Wing flying B-26B/Cs from Langley AFB, Virginia is first combat wing transferred to France. Arrived Bordeaux-Merignac AB, France tent camp on commercial airport.

10 December - Bordeaux-Merignac Air Base considered operational and assigned to Twelfth Air Force.

1952

10 January - 117th Tactical Reconnaissance Wing flying RB-26Cs and RF-80As from Lawson AFB, Georgia arrived Toul AB, France at unusable tent camp.

15 April - USAFE began Project 7019. Project 7019 was rotation of combat aircrews from France to Korea for sixty days of in-country combat experience.

13 May - 137th Fighter-Bomber Wing flying F-84Gs moved from Alexandria AFB, Louisiana into completed tent camp at Chaumont AB, France.

25 May - 126th Light Bombardment Wing, relocated north from Bordeaux AB to completed tent camp at Laon AB, France. Bordeaux AB remains a support base.

10 July - 48th Fighter-Bomber Wing activated at Chaumont AB with resources of 137th Fighter-Bomber Wing.

10 July - 10th Tactical Reconnaissance Wing activated at Toul AB with resources of 117th Tactical Reconnaissance Wing.

4 October - Final agreement signed between French government and USAF, listing several air bases and support facilities for use of USAFE in France. Locations were: Chalons area, Chambley, Chaumont-Semoutiers, Chenevieres area, Cherbourg area, Dreux-Louvillier area, Etain-Rouvres, Evreux-Fauville, Laon-Couvron, Phalsbourg-Bourscheid, Toul-Rosieres, Nantes area, Vitry-Brienne area, and Vouzier area. First listing of dispersed operating base locations.

1953

1 January – 38th Light Bombardment Wing activated at Laon AB with resources of 126th Light Bombardment Wing.

9 May - 10th Tactical Reconnaissance Wing departed Toul AB, France and moved into partially completed Spangdahlem AB, West Germany.

10 July - Project Native Son announced by Department of the Air Force. Policy would "employ native personnel" overseas in place of U.S. military personnel wherever possible to reduce costs.

1954

Winter - USAFE developed its aircraft dispersal program to survive Soviet nuclear attack. Objective was to base aircraft squadrons at least thirty miles (50 kms) apart.

2 April - 465th Troop Carrier Wing from Donaldson AFB, South Carolina arrived at still unusable Toul AB with C-119C Boxcars.

April - Project Caravan began. U.S. Army SCARWAF engineering units constructed trailer camps at, and delivered house trailers to bases in France, to solve severe family housing shortages.

May - First F-86F Sabres arrived in France at Chaumont AB and were assigned to 48th Fighter-Bomber Wing.

October - First programmed rotational tactical flying squadrons arrived in France for six-month tour of duty—a fighter squadron at Chaumont AB and troop carrier squadron at Evreux AB. This was first evaluation of dual-based operational concept to reduce NATO basing costs.

12 December - 388th Fighter-Bomber Wing arrived with F-86Fs from Clovis AFB, New Mexico at unusable Etain AB, France.

13 December - 21st Fighter-Bomber Wing from George AFB, California arrived with F-86Fs at incomplete Chambley AB.

1955

4 February - Phalsbourg AB accepted and activated. To reduce costs, programmed fighter wing did not deploy from CONUS. Phalsbourg placed in standby status.

May - First B-57B Canberras arrived Laon AB, France, assigned to 38th Bomb Wing.

23 May - 465th Troop Carrier Wing flying C-119Cs relocated to Evreux AB, France, from Toul AB.

Summer - All four dispersed operating bases (DOBs): Chalons-Vatry, Luneville-Chenevieres, Vitry-Brienne, and Vouziers-Sechault, France, became operational.

12 August - 322d Air Division (Combat Cargo) HQ, moved to Evreux-Fauville AB, France from Ramstein AB, West Germany.

22 September - 60th Troop Carrier Wing flying C-119Gs arrived at unfinished Dreux AB, France from Rhein-Main AB, West Germany.

1956

2 June - 309th Troop Carrier Group with C-123Bs arrived Dreux AB from Ardmore AFB, Oklahoma, and assigned to 60th TCWg.

17 July - 50th Fighter-Bomber Wing flying F-86Hs relocated to Toul AB from Hahn AB, West Germany.

November - First F-100D Super Sabres arrived in France at Chaumont AB assigned to 48th Fighter-Bomber Wing.

1957

17 April - 317th Troop Carrier Wing with C-119Gs arrived Evreux AB, from Neubiberg AB, West Germany.

8 July – 465th Troop Carrier Wing deactivated at Evreux AB; its three C-119G squadrons assigned to 317th TCWg.

10 December - 49th Tactical Fighter Wing flying F-100Ds activated at Etain AB with resources of 388th Tactical Fighter Wing.

31 December - After six years of preparation, USAFE reached peak combat strength in France with eight wings: one tactical bombardment wing, four tactical fighter wings, three troop carrier wings.

1958

1 February - Victor Alert program commenced in USAFE; this action placed twelve fighter aircraft

on fifteen-minute alert posture with nuclear weapons at several air bases. This alert program provided rapid response to emergencies at minimum costs.

8 February - 21st Tactical Fighter Wing deactivated at Chambley AB. Base placed in standby status. Action required by USAFE budget reductions.

May - First RF-101C Voodoos arrived in France at Phalsbourg AB assigned to 66th Tactical Reconnaissance Wing.

18 June - 38th Tactical Bombardment Wing deactivated at Laon AB. Action required by USAFE budget reductions.

10 July - 66th Tactical Reconnaissance Wing flying RF-84F Thunderflashes relocated to Laon AB, France from Sembach AB, West Germany.

25 September – 60th Troop Carrier Wing deactivated at Dreux AB by USAFE budget reductions; its three C-119G squadrons assigned to 322d Air Division.

25 September – 309th Troop Carrier Group with C-123Bs departed Dreux AB, returning to Ardmore AFB, Oklahoma. This action required by USAFE budget reductions.

25 September – 317th Troop Carrier Wing deactivated at Evreux AB by USAFE budget reductions; its three C-130A squadrons assigned to the 322d Air Division.

1 October - USAFE budget cuts closed Bordeaux-Merignac Air Base. Bordeaux-Bacalan Depot also closed. Property returned to French Air Force.

1959

10 July - USAFE instituted Project RED RICHARD (Rapid Relocation). RED RICHARD was result of France's President Charles de Gaulle's ultimatum that U.S. must remove all stored atomic weapons and delivery systems from French soil.

July - 10th Tactical Reconnaissance Wing began using Toul AB, France as forward operating location standing Echo Alert with their RB-66B/Cs, deploying from UK.

25 August - 49th Tactical Fighter Wing relocated to Spangdahlem AB, West Germany from Etain AB, France as required by Project RED RICHARD. Etain AB became a standby base.

1 September - Chenevieres and Vouziers-Sechault DOBs inactivated by USAFE.

25 October - Vitry-Brienne and Chalons-Vatry DOBs inactivated by USAFE.

10 December - 50th Tactical Fighter Wing returned to Hahn AB, West Germany from Toul AB, France as required by Project RED RICHARD. Toul AB became a standby base.

1960

15 January - 48th Tactical Fighter Wing moved to RAF Lakenheath, UK from Chaumont AB, France, as required by Project RED RICHARD. Chaumont AB became a standby base.

31 December - USAFE strength in France declined to one tactical reconnaissance wing, one fighter-

interceptor squadron, and six troop carrier squadrons. Only Evreux and Laon Air Bases considered fully operational.

1961

4 January – 10th, 11th, and 12th Troop Carrier Squadrons deactivated at Dreux AB by USAFE budget reductions. Dreux became a standby base.

12 August - East German government, with Soviet approval, began building a wall directly through Berlin and on East-West Zone border in Germany. This produced second Cold War crisis over Berlin. USAFE was immediately reinforced, France quickly approved use of standby air bases for tactical fighter aircraft.

5 September - To augment USAFE, Operation TACK HAMMER rapidly deployed eight fighter squadrons into France from CONUS. These TAC Composite Air Strike Force squadrons were relieved by STAIR STEP units.

30 October - Operation STAIR STEP began and saw movement of one-hundred-four F-84Fs, seventy-eight F-86Hs and twenty RF-84Fs from Air National Guard to France.

2 to 9 November - STAIR STEP units arrived in France. Chambley, Chaumont, Dreux, Etain, Toul, and Phalsbourg changed status from standby to main air bases.

1962

8 May - 366th Tactical Fighter Wing activated at Chaumont AB, France, to replace STAIR STEP units. This action kept Chambley, Chaumont, Etain, and Phalsbourg as active air bases after departure of STAIR STEP units.

30 July - All STAIR STEP units had departed France for CONUS home bases for early release from active duty by 20 August. Dreux and Toul air bases were changed to standby bases.

1963

13 March - 317th Troop Carrier Wing with three squadrons flying C-130As reactivated at Evreux-Fauville AB, France.

15 July - 366th Tactical Fighter Wing departed Chaumont AB, France, and transferred, with all its F-84Fs, to Holloman AFB, New Mexico. By this action Chambley, Chaumont, Etain, and Phalsbourg air bases again reverted to standby status.

1964

1 April - 322d Air Division HQ transferred to MATS and moved south from Evreux AB to Chateauroux Air Depot, France.

20 June - 317th Troop Carrier Wing with all C-130As departed Evreux-Fauville AB, France and moved itself to Lockbourne AFB, Ohio. Evreux AB became standby base.

1965

19 April - 26th Tactical Reconnaissance Wing activated at Toul AB, France. This reconnaissance wing would introduce new RF-4C to USAFE. Toul became an active air base.

24 September - 25th Tactical Reconnaissance Wing with two squadrons flying RB-66B/Cs activated

at Chambley AB. Chambley AB became an active air base.

31 December - USAFE strength in France was three tactical reconnaissance wings and two rotational troop carrier squadrons. Chambley, Laon and Toul air bases were operational; Chaumont, Dreux, Etain, Evreux and Phalsbourg were in standby status.

1966

7 March - President Charles de Gaulle announced France would withdraw from NATO military structure but remain in its political organization. All NATO forces and headquarters had to be removed from France by 1 April 1967.

6 April - 513th Troop Carrier Wing activated at Evreux AB, France. All its airlift squadrons would be TDY units rotated from CONUS.

1 July - 513th Troop Carrier Wing departed Evreux AB, France, and moved to RAF Mildenhall, UK as required by Project FRELOC.

10 July - EUCOM instituted Project FRELOC (Fast Relocation of Lines of Communications). This project would remove all USAFE personnel, aircraft, equipment, and supplies from French soil as quickly as possible. RCAF also had to depart their facilities in France.

1 September - 66th Tactical Reconnaissance Wing flying RF-101Cs relocated to RAF Upper Hayford, UK from Laon AB, France as required by Project FRELOC.

5 October - 26th Tactical Reconnaissance Wing flying RF-4Cs relocated to Ramstein AB, West Germany, from Toul AB, France, as required by Project FRELOC.

15 October - 25th Tactical Reconnaissance Wing deactivated at Chambley AB by Project FRELOC. All RB-66B/Cs returned to CONUS or sent to Southeast Asia.

1967

31 March - All air bases returned to French government.

23 October - Suippes Gunnery Range released to Military Liquidation Service in Paris. It was last USAFE installation in France. After sixteen years the USAF departed France.

1994

February - USAF aircraft deploy to France for first time in more than 20 years. Five KC-135 Stratotankers flew from Istre AB to refuel aircraft patrolling airspace over Bosnia-Herzegovina in Operation Deny Flight.

1999

In Kosovo, NATO forces engage in first NATO combat operations since its creation.

2004

17 December - NATO Operation Deny Flight terminated. USAF KC-135 and personnel depart France.

1

HISTORICAL PERSPECTIVE

To understand the reasons for basing a large portion of the United States Air Force in France over the period of 1950-67, one must return to Europe at the end of the Second World War and the five years immediately following—1945 through 1950. This background material may appear redundant to some readers, but realizing these events occurred almost sixty years ago I feel they should be included.

Post World War II Europe and the Formation of NATO

World War II ended in Europe on 8 May 1945 with most of Europe and the western Soviet Union in complete devastation. Germany surrendered unconditionally and was divided into four Allied Zones of Occupation. The 1945 Yalta agreement provided for Germany to be occupied by France, Great Britain, the Soviet Union, and the United States of America. This agreement also called for the four victors to occupy four separate zones in the capital city of Berlin. Berlin was located deep within the Russian Zone of Germany, 168 miles via autobahn from the nearest point in the U.S. Zone of Occupation, and 84 miles via autobahn from the closest point in the British Zone of Occupation. (Map 1.1) Austria was also divided into four zones, with its capital city of Vienna split four ways. Italy had surrendered in September 1943, but was not occupied or divided into zones after VE Day.

International optimism had never been higher; all the mistakes of post World War I would not be repeated in 1946! The newly formed United Nations would prevent future conflicts by peaceful resolution of problems, or if peaceful negotiations failed, a U.N. military force supplied by member nations would enter the fray and solve the disputes. Germany would be disarmed, changed into a democracy, and converted into a civilian industrial and agricultural economy. It was estimated that it would require from five to ten years to accomplish these goals.

Immediately after the war the primary mission of U.S. military forces in Europe was to disarm Germany, bring peace and economic stability to the German people, and depart as soon as practical. The mission of the United States Air Forces in Europe was to disarm and destroy all Luftwaffe air assets, dispose of excess USAAF property remaining in Europe, and provide airlift to remaining U.S. troops. American combat forces were demobilized as quickly as possible, and by December 1945 only two reduced Army divisions remained in Germany. The Army had completely departed France by 1946 except for a small group of Graves Registration Teams. Over 3.5 million U.S. military personnel had departed Europe and had been discharged from military service. Virtually all U.S. armed forces personnel had left except for the Occupation Forces in Germany, Austria, and a small number of Army troops in Italy to control the Trieste problem. By 1948 the U.S. Military Governor in Germany had grave concerns that there would be insufficient troops to enforce the peaceful transition in his zone.

As World War II ended, allied cooperation that had been forged by the common goal to defeat Hitler began to weaken. There were difficulties with the Soviet Union even before the end of the war regarding the postwar occupation zones in Germany, and by late 1945 serious disagreement began to develop between the Americans and Russians concerning the occupation zones in Berlin. The U.S. came to the realization that the Soviet Union was not planning to leave any of the occupied lands it had liberated in its westward march to capture Berlin. During 1946 the Soviet Union made it very obvious that it planned to stay in Latvia, Lithuania, Estonia, Rumania, Hungary, Bulgaria, Poland, Czechoslovakia, southern Finland, and Yugoslavia. Russian troop strength increased in the eastern nations during 1947-48 to enforce its occupation and produce a forward basing posture for attacking Western Europe. The "Iron Curtain" descended across the center of Europe, and the nations occupied by the Soviet Union became "Eastern Europe." To the west of Germany: France, Luxembourg, Belgium, Netherlands, Italy, Spain, and the United Kingdom became "Western Europe." Sweden and Switzerland remained neutral, with Switzerland providing a common meeting place for most international conferences. The Soviet Union's short-term goals were to force the three western nations out of Berlin and Vienna. Their

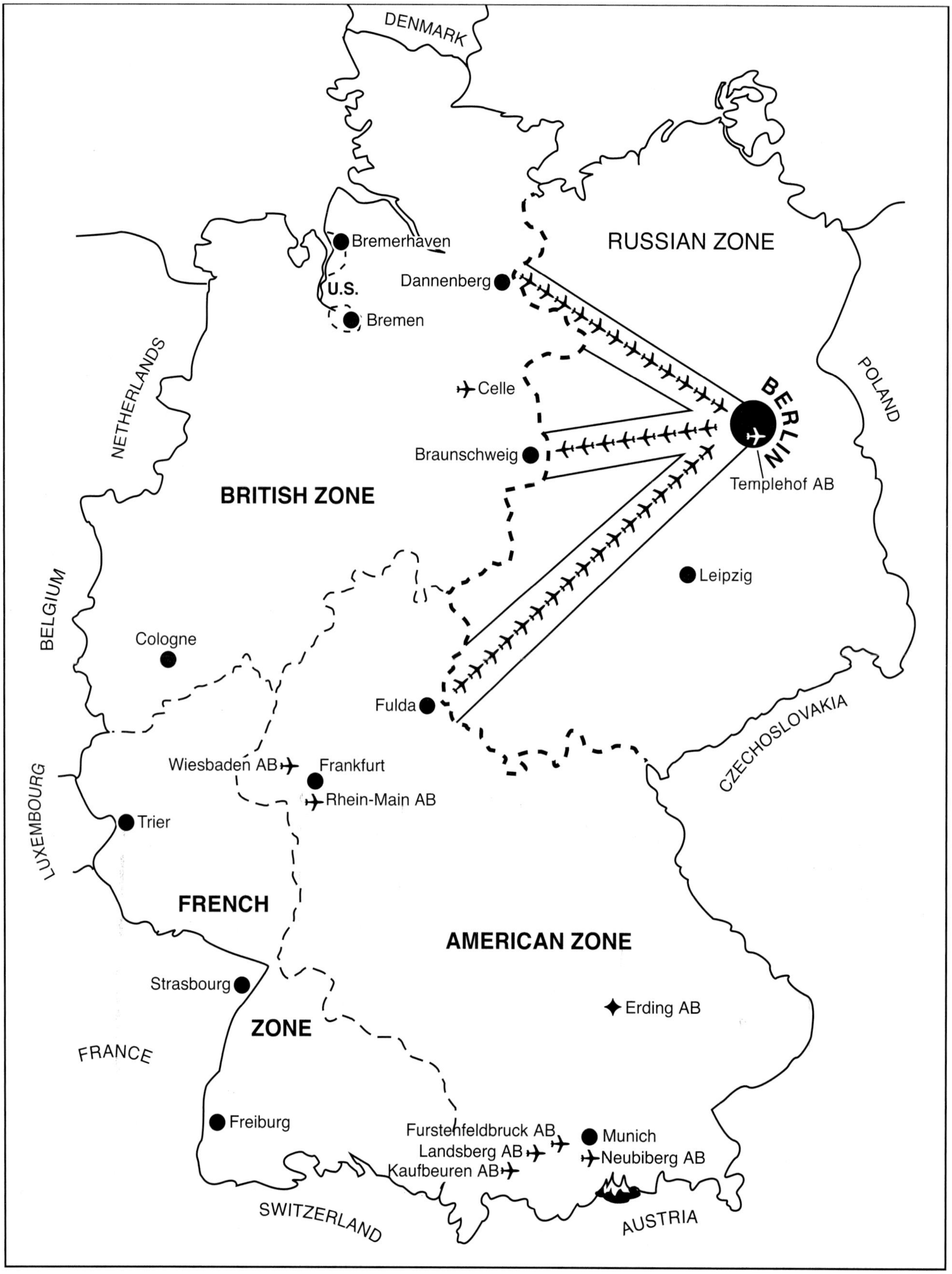

Map 1.1 Occupation Zones in Germany, Post World War II

intermediate goal was to conquer Turkey and Greece through civil wars, by supporting communists against capitalists and through military intervention. The longer term Soviet goal was to force the western powers completely out of Austria and West Germany, eventually making all Western Europe into communist states.

During 1947-49 the U.S. had serious concerns that the governments of France and Italy would be taken over by their internal communist political parties. The best option for preventing a communist takeover was to create strong, financially stable countries. To revive the economies of Europe, the United States offered a comprehensive economic aid program in June 1947 known as the "Marshall Plan" named after the Secretary of State, George C. Marshall. This plan was not related in any way with future military aid programs, i.e., the Military Assistance Program (MAP) or later the Mutual Defense Assistance Program (MDAP). The Marshall Plan achieved great success in Western Europe but the Soviets remained steadfast in their goal of communist domination.

By 1948 Germany had become a major pawn in our effort to prevent the westward march of Communism. The Russians curtailed Allied access to Berlin in June 1948. It appeared that the Soviet Union was willing to risk a third world war to dislodge the Allies from the city. West Germany's future depended upon keeping Berlin open as agreed at Yalta. To avoid war the Allies decided upon an airlift into the city to maintain their presence. This military action produced the Berlin Airlift that operated from June 1948 until September 1949. Through heroic effort on the part of the allies and the citizens of Berlin, the Soviet plan to isolate and starve the city into submission failed. The overwhelming success of the airlift forced the Russians to back down and once again grant the Allies unlimited access in May 1949. The airlift prevented a Soviet Union takeover of Berlin, but the U.S. and Allies realized they lacked the military power to prevent a determined Soviet takeover of not only Berlin but possibly all of Western Europe. Over the following forty years Berlin remained a flash point for the start of WWIII between the Soviet Union, and Western Europe and the United States.

The cold war that developed in Europe during 1946 and escalated into the attempted seizure of West Berlin by the Soviet Union in 1948 convinced the western European nations that they had to fashion some type of common defense organization. Discussions by Great Britain and other Western European nations led to a multinational defense agreement in March 1948 known as the Brussels Pact. The Brussels Pact consisted of a common defense treaty between Great

WWII bomb damage was still evident in many German cities. This was downtown Munich, May 1952.
Jerry McAuliffe

Britain, France, Belgium, Netherlands, and Luxembourg. This collective security plan was known as the Western Union. Realizing that economic and social conditions within the Western Union nations would prevent them from generating the required military power to counter the Soviet Union's capability, the U.S. proposed a North Atlantic military security system. By summer 1948 the U.S. Senate indicated that it would give approval to defensive alliances among the United States and North Atlantic nations. After Senate approval, U.S. representatives attended the Western Union Military Committee meetings in London. The fundamental concept of this North American and Western European alliance was the premise that an attack on one member nation should be regarded as an attack on all member nations. This concept later became codified as Article 5 in the NATO Treaty. (Appendix 1.1)

On 5 October 1948 the Western Union selected its first Commander in Chief (CINC), Field Marshall Montgomery of Alamein, and established defense headquarters at Fontainebleau, France. Discussions continued in Europe and in Washington with additional nations: Canada, Denmark, Iceland, Ireland, Norway, and Portugal. These led to a multinational defense agreement that became the North Atlantic Treaty Organization (NATO).

NATO documents were formally signed on 4 April 1949 in Washington, D.C. by representatives from Belgium, Canada, Denmark, France, Iceland, Italy, Luxembourg, Netherlands, Norway, Portugal, the United Kingdom, and the United States. Only Ireland declined to participate in NATO. Portugal would permit the use of its Lages, Azores air base, critically located in mid Atlantic Ocean. Iceland would not develop its own military force but would contribute the air base near Keflavik, seaport facilities at Reykjavik, and ground radar sites for NATO's use. The Treaty became effective on 24 August 1949 and signatories agreed to remain in NATO for twenty years, but could subsequently withdraw after giving one year's notice. Eleven of the twelve original nations agreed to expand Europe's military capability as quickly as forces were raised and facilities constructed. This was the first peacetime U.S. multi-national military agreement in our history. Eventually Greece, Turkey, Federal Republic of Germany and Spain also joined NATO.

The NATO scheme fit well into containment of International Communism that had become the primary goal of the Truman Administration. This policy was defined in National Security Council Memorandum 68 on 7 April 1950. NSC 68's goal was regional, multi-national, military alliances wherein the U.S. would supply the bulk of the military hardware with implementation beginning immediately. This policy became the MAP and MDAP programs that provided air, ground, and naval equipment free to all nations interested in opposing communism and maintaining their independence. Peacetime costs to the American taxpayer would be great if all proposed actions were undertaken. The first MAP funds authorized in 1949 were $1,314,000,000. The U.S. military budget would have to be doubled or tripled, and that remained the major problem.

Signing military agreements is easy; executing military agreements requires money and people, which in 1949 were not available. The U.S. defense budget for Fiscal Year 1951 (1 July 1950 through 30 June 1951) was the smallest postwar sum. Large reductions in personnel, equipment procurement, and training had already begun. Suddenly, on 25 June 1950 the North Koreans invaded South Korea. America completely changed its international military posture for the next fifty years—NATO would now become a reality!

NATO Organization and Strategy

The NATO Defense Committee had the primary task of planning and budgeting the strategy to be implemented as directed by the North Atlantic Council Ministers. The actual, detailed, military plans were developed by the Military Committee and delivered to the Defense Committee for approval and planning. In the first years of NATO, the planners knew that Soviet ground forces in East Germany and Czechoslovakia could overrun all of Western Europe. NATO could not fund or man ground forces to match or exceed Soviet forces; in fact from 1949 through 1989 Soviet and later, Warsaw Pact infantry and armored forces were always numerically superior. The first requirement was to create a sufficient force to prevent or deter a Soviet attack on the West.

NATO's primary defense strategy became the use of strategic and tactical airpower to offset the Soviet Union's numerical superiority of air and ground forces. Counter-air operations would destroy Soviet airpower as quickly as possible to gain air superiority; and nuclear weapons would be used on enemy airfields to maintain this superiority. Interdiction attacks on railroad systems and autobahn networks would halt or slow Soviet forces that relied on rail transportation for rapid mobility. The U.S. and United Kingdom would provide the strategic bomber forces equipped with atomic weapons. NATO would provide the tactical air power to conduct day and night counter-air and interdiction operations. As western ground forces were expanded, more planning was given to close air support operations provided by tactical aircraft. NATO would trade off the massive expense of combat ground forces for the less expensive option of tactical air power using nuclear weapons. Tactical air power combined with tactical nuclear weapons would be the lowest cost option. "More bang for the buck" in manpower and equipment would provide a very positive deterrence to attack, and have available massive nuclear retaliation in the event deterrence failed. Denmark objected to this strategy at the initial planning in 1949; later the French would object to having these weapons in their country and required their removal after they were able to build their own nuclear weapons and delivery systems. NATO's strategy of employing nuclear weapons continued up to 1989 when the Soviet Union disintegrated. Only the delivery methods changed slightly, from all tactical fighters and bombers to the addition of ground launched cruise missiles (GLCM) and short range ballistic missiles (IRBM).

NATO planning involved force quantities that were never achieved, but established cost and basing discussions. The Lisbon Conference held in February 1952 recommended 12,000 tactical aircraft and 90 army divisions be available thirty days after mobilization as directed by Supreme Allied Commander Europe (SACEUR). A 1954 Defense Committee planning document, DC-13, stated that NATO would require 90 army divisions, 2,324 naval vessels, and 11,940 aircraft within ninety days after a Soviet invasion of Western Europe. These estimates were extremely unrealistic and most military commanders understood it was political rhetoric. Ninety army divisions would require approximately 1,800,000 men! In 1952, F-84F tactical fighters cost $770,000 each. Typically, at 100 fighters per air base, about 120 air bases would be needed at an approximate cost of $40 million apiece! Then at least 1,500 airmen would be required to man each air base!

Another major limitation would be finding sufficient airfield real estate across Western Europe. New air base sites had to be found, construction started, and these bases readied for jet engine powered, high performance combat aircraft operations. Existing airfields would require major expensive improvements. The initial concept was to base tactical air defense fighter aircraft forward in West Germany, and fighter-bombers and light bombers with nuclear weapon delivery capabilities at greater distances in England, France, Italy, and Turkey. Tactical troop carrier and reconnaissance aircraft would be based still further west in England, France, and Belgium. Most NATO nations agreed to supply airfields; Denmark and Norway refused basing for other NATO nation's aircraft in peacetime, but would expand their air bases to meet NATO standards. The U.S. promised to make a major contribution of at least twenty-five tactical air wings to NATO airpower, and to supply 2,500 combat aircraft to NATO nations through the Mutual Assistance Program (MAP) by 1955. France agreed to provide approximately twenty air bases for NATO members' use, specifically Canada and the United States, and space for a new major air depot. The U.S. would eventually base combat aircraft in Belgium, England, France, Iceland, Italy, Netherlands, Portugal, Spain, Turkey and West Germany.

Next new major NATO support facilities, known as lines of communications (LOCS), would be constructed west of the Rhein River in Belgium, France, Luxembourg, Netherlands, and in southern Europe. France agreed to establish the primary support facilities for NATO ground forces, which included special maintenance depots, hospitals, seaports, fuel pipelines and storage tanks, and major ammunition depots. Much of this support infrastructure in France became the responsibility of the U.S. Army in Europe. France became a major force in NATO because of its geographical location and willingness to accommodate NATO tactical air bases and ground forces to support LOCS.

The major USAF command responsible for the basing, training and operation of U.S. tactical air units assigned to NATO was United States Air Forces in Europe (USAFE) headquartered at Wiesbaden Air Base, West Germany. USAFE established two numbered air forces; Third Air Force commanded units in the United Kingdom and Twelfth Air Force was assigned the command responsibility for all USAFE organizations in Belgium, France, Germany, Italy, and Netherlands. NATO commands were divided geographically into: Allied Forces Central Europe (AFCENT), Allied Forces Southern Europe (AFSOUTH), and Allied Forces Northern Europe (AFNORTH). NATO tactical airpower in Central Europe was commanded by Allied Air Forces Central Europe (AAFCE). The AAFCE commander was also the USAFE Commander. NATO's air units were further divided into various numbered Allied Tactical Air Forces (ATAF). Thus USAFE units based in France were normally assigned to AAFCE and 4th ATAF war planning. As one of our B-26 pilots stated to me after he attended some training at Wiesbaden, "If you really understood all the NATO acronyms and organizational charts you were bound to be promoted to Brigadier General!" All NATO commands consisted of a mix of commanders from the region's national military forces. The majority of NATO air and ground forces were based within their own nations but were ready to deploy into operations under NATO commands. Training and field exercises could be conducted in other member nations. The major exception was West Germany. Because of its post-WWII occupation status, it had Belgian, Canadian, British, French, and U.S. combat forces stationed throughout the country.

Two significant technological changes occurred to greatly enhance NATO's tactical airpower. First, the development of relatively lightweight, small, nuclear devices with increased yields that could be delivered by fighter-bomber aircraft. Second, constant improvement in fighter-bomber aircraft made it possible for them to carry heavier bomb loads at faster speeds and at longer ranges.

Beginning in 1952, all U.S. tactical jet aircraft assigned to USAFE's two air forces could be configured to deliver nuclear weapons. The first tactical atomic weapon was the American Mark 7 that could be carried by the F-84G fighter and B-45A light bomber. This weapon weighed 1,700 pounds (800Kg), was large—15 feet long, 32 inches in diameter, and had an estimated yield of 30 Kilotons. Later, the Mk 7 was supplemented by the low drag Mark 28EX weapon that weighed 2,000 pounds (910Kg), was 14 feet long, 20 inches in diameter and had a variable yield between 100 and 500 Kilotons. Both weapons could be delivered by almost all USAFE tactical bombers and fighter aircraft as well as Matador or Mace cruise missiles. All weapons were included in NATO war plans.

By 1954 the European nations began to lose enthusiasm for developing their military forces as planned by NATO ministers. This change of attitude was the result of the Korean War armistice and the death of Joseph Stalin, the Soviet Union premier. Western Europe was confident that the United States would not only allocate funds to defend them, but patiently suffer at times the wrath of their politicians and people when they condemned our presence and weapons. They preferred to spend on domestic social programs rather than self defense; the U.S. became the primary force to push or drag the NATO nations into programs to defend themselves from the Soviet Union and Warsaw Pact threat. Only West Germany supplied a modern military capability to meet its NATO obligations and support the U.S. air and ground forces based on its soil.

The sudden disintegration of the Soviet Union and Warsaw Pact nations during 1989 did not end NATO; to this very day the NATO force structure and strategy continues to be revised, expanded, and improved as more nations are added. The dependence upon nuclear weapons has greatly decreased over the past fifteen years and conventional forces are its mainstay. But the costs of conventional forces are about four to six times greater. This strategy has meant continuously decreasing combat capability as forces are cut to meet budgets. Tactical airpower has declined also but is still an important part of NATO war plans.

Many military and civilian personnel from NATO nations have been sent to CONUS for education and training, i.e., administrative, technical, medical, and flight training. Professional military education of NATO forces continues to the present time. The German Bundesluftwaffe conducts fighter pilot training today at Holloman AFB, New Mexico under NATO agreements.

USAFE/NATO in Germany

Air bases in the U.S. Zone of Occupation in Germany were selected in April 1945 when there were absolutely no requirements for tactical defensive planning. By 1948 it was obvious they were tactically untenable because of their proximity to the East German and Czechoslovakian borders. The two USAFE fighter bases, at Furstenfeldbruck and Neubiberg were within eighty miles of the east-west border. The USAFE air depot at Erding, West Germany, was approximately seventy miles from the border. Rhein-Main AB in Frankfurt was the primary passenger and air cargo terminal; the 60th Troop Carrier Wing was assigned. USAFE and Twelfth Air Force headquarters were located at Wiesbaden AB and in downtown Camp Lindsey Air Station. (Map 1.2)

By 1950, USAFE wanted its vulnerable fighter units moved west of the Rhein River to provide greater air defense warning time. France quickly agreed to provide air base sites within their zone of occupation in the Rhein-Palatinate as part of the NATO expansion program. These new sites would all be fifty miles or more west of the Rhein and most were located on rolling hilltops in rural settings. Land acquisition in the Rhein-Palatinate was rapid, and during 1951 construction began on seven new air bases. These bases were not funded by NATO, but by USAF money partially offset by German war reparation payments, and construction was performed by West German contractors. Completion was on time and the quality was high.

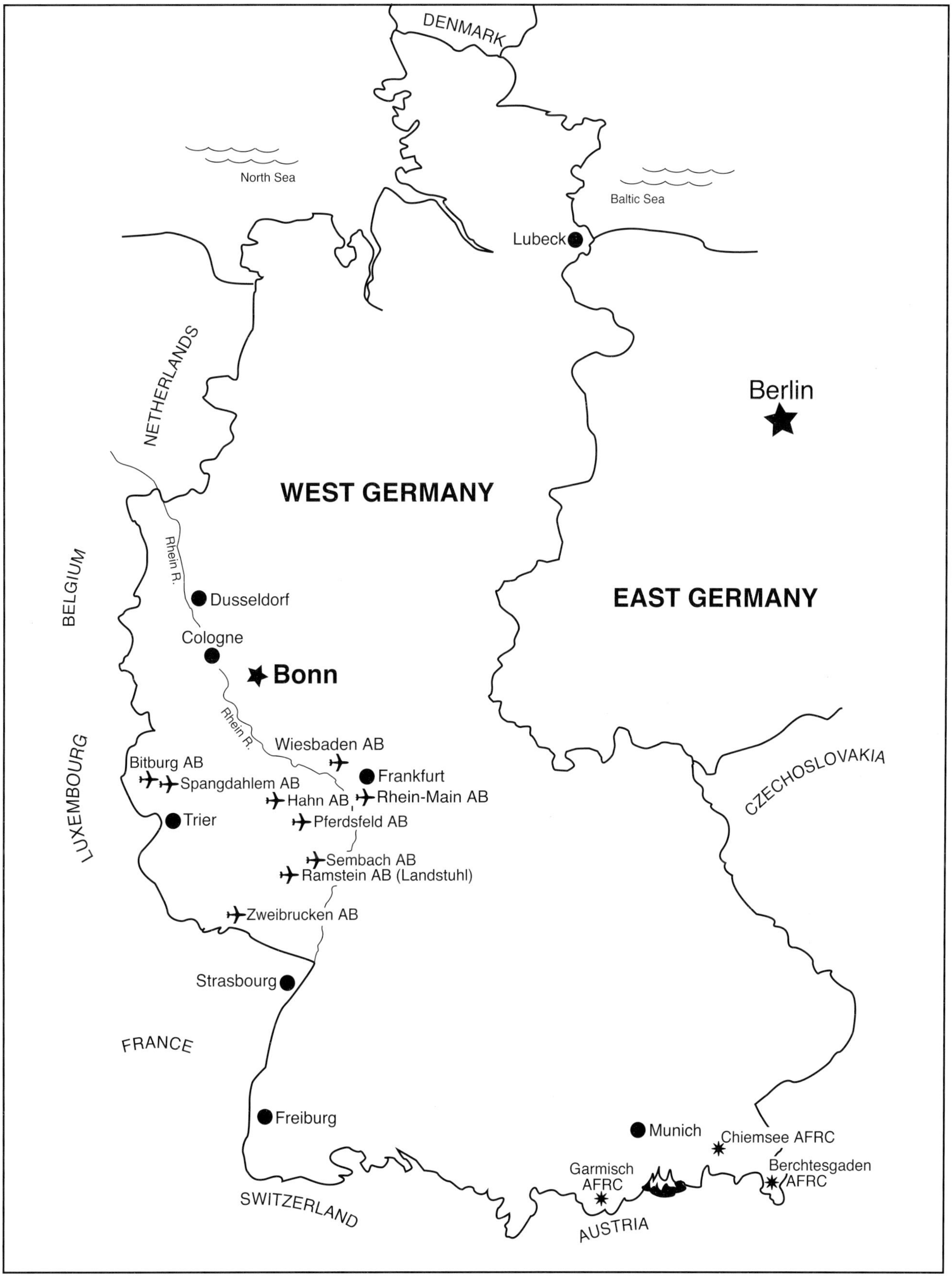

Map 1.2 USAFE Bases in West Germany 1954

These new air bases were in operation for forty years, primarily as sites for USAFE fighter operations: Bitburg, Hahn, Pferdsfeld, Ramstein (Landstuhl), Sembach, and Spangdahlem. A seventh site, Zweibrücken, was assigned to the Royal Canadian Air Force (RCAF) in 1952 as a fighter base. It remained a Canadian Forces base until 1976, and then was operated by USAFE. In Spring 2005, Ramstein, and Spangdahlem are still active U.S. air bases supporting operations in Iraq. Rhein-Main is scheduled for closure in 2005 and Sembach AS is a support facility for Ramstein Air Base. The remaining bases have been returned to Germany. About $600 million is now being spent to improve Ramstein and Spangdahlem Air Bases to extend their usefulness for twenty years or more.

The U.S. Army stationed all its combat ground forces within West Germany. Its 1950s peak strength consisted of two Army corps with three armored divisions, six mechanized infantry divisions, one airborne division, three armored cavalry regiments, and four artillery brigades, plus many combat support units. There were no U.S. Army combat forces based in France. Chapter 18 provides an overview of U.S. Army activities in France from 1950 through 1967.

USAF in the Cold War

The USAF was a shadow of its predecessor the United States Army Air Force, with manning at 20 percent of peak World War II strength. U.S. military conscription had ended in July 1947 and peacetime enlistments did not support the occupation of Germany and Japan, plus provide a viable strategic military force. At the end of the Second World War, USAFE manning had been reduced from a high of 450,000 personnel in April 1945 down to 33,037 by December 1946; airfields declined from 152 in April 1945 to 31 by December 1946.

Between 1947 and 1950 the USAF planned first for thirty-six wings, next forty, then forty-eight combat wings to meet all of its war plan tasking, but each fiscal year funding fell short. The USAF never achieved even this very limited strength. The 1948-49 Berlin Airlift taxed existing USAF resources of cargo aircraft, aircraft engines, skilled aircrews, and maintenance personnel. Unfortunately most citizens believed that the vast airpower created during WWII still existed within the new peacetime Air Force. This was a totally false assumption that would be proven during the Korean air war.

When the Korean War began 25 June 1950, the USAF had been an independent branch of the U.S. military establishment for less than three years, and was very small and ill equipped for its assigned worldwide missions. Air Force Chief of Staff, General Hoyt S.Vandenberg later stated that in the summer of 1950 we had "a shoestring Air Force." A serious shortage of combat aircraft began to develop by the fall of 1950.

Major expansion began after the start of the Korean War. This was deemed necessary to provide for U.S. defense, fight and win the Korean War, as well as expand USAFE-NATO airpower strength across Western Europe. Total USAF military personnel grew from 411,277 in 1950 to 977,593 in 1953. Air Force expansion goals from 1951 through 1956 called for increases in all areas.

1. The highest priority was assigned to Strategic Air Command; 1,800 new bombers (B-36, B-47, and B-52s) were procured, and SAC expanded its worldwide basing to ensure force survival. Strategic bombardment using large nuclear weapons would be the primary U.S. military option to settle serious international disputes.
2. A build-up of North America's air defense required approximately 4,000 new all-weather interceptors for Air Defense Command. ADC increased its air bases, and expanded aircraft control and warning radar systems with command/control sites throughout the forty-eight states (CONUS), Alaska, Canada, and Greenland.
3. Tactical Air Command forces were increased to support overseas commands in Europe and the Far East. Approximately 4,000 tactical fighter aircraft were procured.
4. Military Air Transport Service's worldwide strategic and tactical airlift capability was increased as approximately 1,200 new transport aircraft were purchased.
5. From July 1950 to June 1953 more than 146,000 Air Force Reservists, both in combat units or as individuals were called to active duty for twelve, twenty-one, or thirty-six months. Two AF Reserve combat wings were flying missions in Korea by October 1950. Over 46,000 Air National Guardsmen were ordered to active duty during the Korean War. Various wing, group, or squadron-sized units were federalized in the first year of the war from 10 October 1950 to 1 July 1951 for twenty-one months of Air Force service.

Congress quickly approved 143 USAF combat wings, but again only 137 wings were funded, and this decreased to 110 wings in 1955. At this time the Department of Defense (DOD) portion of the Federal budget was near $40 billion a year, which was a high of 64 percent in fiscal year 1953 (1 July 1952 thru 30 June 1953). This DOD funding represented 14.2 percent of the gross national product. The USAF portion of this FY 1953 DOD budget was approximately $15 billion. The DOD budget decreased to 10 percent of GNP in 1959. (Table 1.1)

In the early 1950s Europe received a higher priority for air power than Korea by the U.S. Administration and Department of Defense. Deterring the threat of a Communist takeover of Western Europe was considered more important to our long-term survival than a Communist victory in Korea. The USAF transferred thirteen combat wings from its Tactical Air Command plus one air depot wing from Air Material Command, and relocated the units to Europe from April 1951 through December 1954. Eight wings were regular Air Force wings, four wings were federalized Air National Guard units, and one wing was a mobilized Air Force Reserve unit. Four of these wings deployed to the United Kingdom, three into West Germany, and six wings were deployed to France. (Table 1.2) Chapter 2 will focus on this deployment to France. These wings gave NATO approximately 500 fighters, 100 light bombers, 100 tactical reconnaissance aircraft, 100 tactical airlift transports, and 18,000 personnel. These numbers exclude Strategic Air Command's bombers and tankers that were rotated through England on TDY commencing in 1947.

Table 1.3 depicts USAFE strength changes in aircraft and personnel from 1944 through 1970. Note the low point in 1947 just at the time the Berlin airlift demanded maximum effort. Many of the airlift's aircraft and personnel were assigned as temporary duty (TDY) and not carried on USAFE's strength records. Also, it clearly shows the sudden jump in strength from 1951 to 1953, peaking in 1955 then a very steady decline over the following fifteen years. A sudden jump occurs in 1961, which is the arrival and departure of STAIR STEP units responding to the second

Table 1.1 Defense Outlays
As a Share of Gross National Product

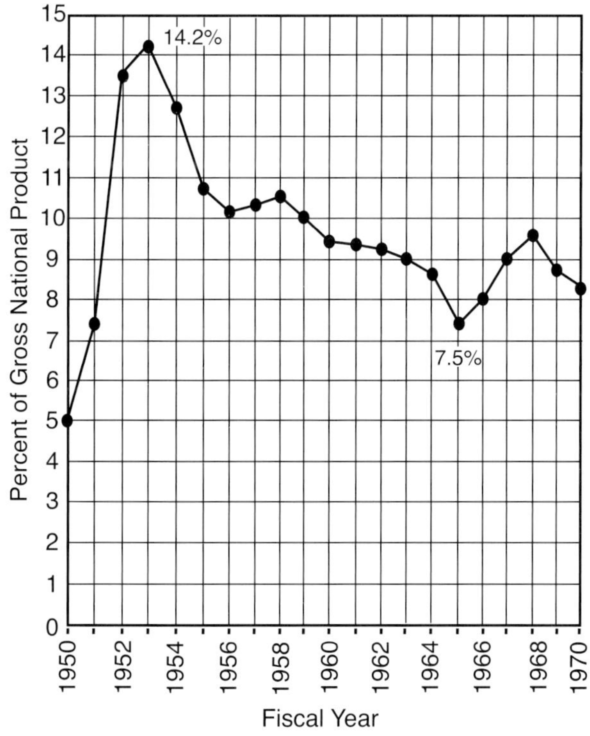

Source: U.S. Department of Defense

Table 1.2 U.S. Air Force Combat Wings Moved to Europe, 1951-1954

United Kingdom:	
81st Fighter-Interceptor Wing to RAF Bentwaters (F-86A)	AUG 1951
123d Fighter-Bomber Wing to RAF Manston (F-84E)	DEC 1951
47th Light Bomb Wing to RAF Sculthorpe (B-45A)	MAY 1952
20th Fighter-Bomber Wing to RAF Wethersfield (F-84G)	MAY 1952
Germany:	
433d Troop Carrier Wing to Rhein-Main AB (C-119B)	AUG 1951
66th Tactical Reconnaissance Wing to Sembach AB (RB-26C & RF-80A)	JULY 1953
50th Fighter-Bomber Wing to Hahn AB (F-86F)	AUG 1953
France:	
126th Light Bomb Wing to Bordeaux-Merignac AB (B-26B/C)	DEC 1951
117th Tactical Reconnaissance Wing to Toul-Rosieres AB (RB-26C & RF-80A)	JAN 1952
137th Fighter-Bomber Wing to Chaumont AB (F-84G)	MAY 1952
465th Troop Carrier Wing to Toul-Rosieres AB (C-119C)	APR 1954
21st Fighter-Bomber Wing to Chambley AB (F-86F)	DEC 1954
388th Fighter-Bomber Wing to Etain-Rouvres AB (F-86F)	DEC 1954

Table 1.3 U.S. Air Forces in Europe Personnel and Aircraft Strength*

Year	AF Personnel	Aircraft Assigned	Year	AF Personnel	Aircraft Assigned
1944	450,000	18,600	1958	66,568	1,011
1945	64,349	17,580	1959	66,923	1,635
1946	33,037	2,300	1960	64,330	1,338
1947	21,053	458	1961	77,478	1,595
1948	28,687	368	1962	62,905	1,426
1949	16,611	381	1963	60,609	1,254
1950	16,246	366	1964	56,982	1,079
1951	51,138	668	1965	56,127	985
1952	73,204	1,025	1966	58,212	884
1953	85,269	1,509	1967	56,503	730
1954	79,060	2,132	1968	51,572	730
1955	91,434	2,096	1969	50,338	730
1956	79,410	2,027	1970	44,437	770
1957	80,424	2,021			

*Statistics are as of 31 December of each year.

Source: USAF in Europe Historical Highlights, HQ USAFE

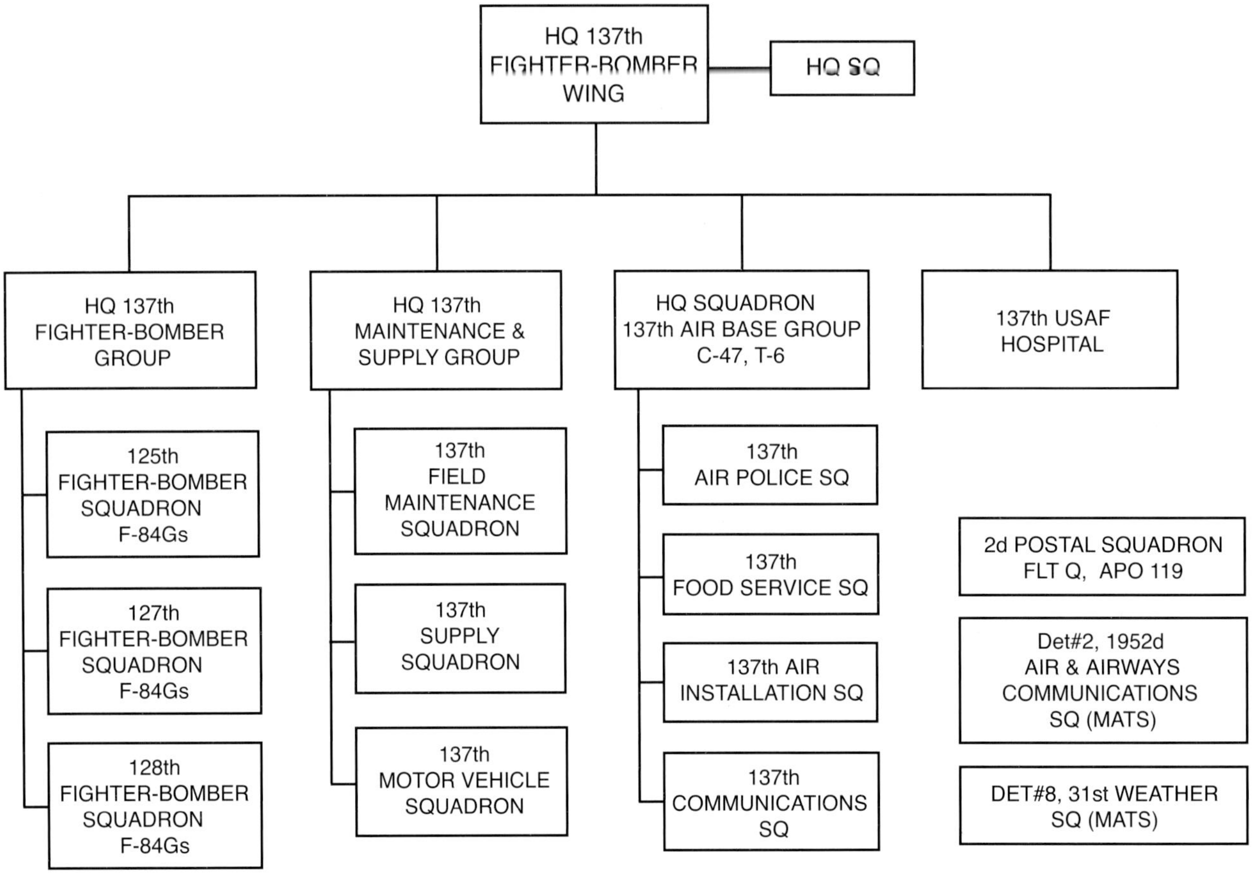

Figure 1.1 USAFE 137th Fighter-Bomber Wing/Base Organization, Chaumont AB, France, May 1952

Berlin Crisis. From 1966 through the 1970s, NATO's total strength steadily declined, as the U.S. reduced forces in Europe to fight a limited war in Vietnam for ten years.

At this time it may be appropriate to describe USAF wing organization to readers not familiar with its 1950-70 era structure. The USAF is organized into sections, flights, squadrons, groups, wings, air divisions, and numbered air forces in ascending order under their major commands. In 1949 the USAF developed a new wing-base plan for the USAF, the Hobsen Plan. The decision was made that the major commands: Strategic Air Command (SAC),Tactical Air Command (TAC), Military Air Transport System (MATS), Far East Air Force (FEAF), and United States Air Forces Europe (USAFE) would operate similar interchangeable flying organizations. The number of personnel in each wing would vary depending upon the assigned aircraft type and quantity, but the command structure would be identical. A wing consisted of groups and squadrons having from 1,000 to 1,800 officers and airmen assigned and operating from thirty to eighty aircraft. A fighter wing had seventy-five fighters and about 1,300 personnel. A light bomb or troop carrier wing had fifty-four aircraft and 1,500 personnel. In France a light bomb wing had forty-eight B-26 aircraft and a fighter wing had seventy-two F-86 fighters authorized, plus three to nine C-47, L-20, and T-33 support aircraft.

A combat wing is the fundamental USAF organization. It is a self-sufficient organization that can conduct combat operations and operate an air base for flight operations. It contains three squadrons flying the same type of aircraft, and all necessary support organizations to maintain its assigned aircraft and base facilities. A combat wing is divided into four groups: the combat operations group, a maintenance and supply group, the airbase group, and a medical group. The wing hosts three or more special support detachments at each base to provide postal, weather, and airway radio services. A Brigadier General or Colonel would command the wing; his group commanders would be Colonels or Lieutenant Colonels.

Figure 1.1 shows a typical fighter wing organizational chart, in this case the 137th Fighter-Bomber Wing at Chaumont AB, France, in 1952. The 137th Fighter-Bomber Wing operated F-84G aircraft. The flying group and its three squadrons performed the wing's combat flying mission. The flying group HQ was eliminated in 1957 to reduce manpower within USAFE and many Group jobs were moved up into Wing HQ. Later in 1959, the Air Base Group title was changed to Combat Support Group with the identical functions. Congress likes to fund combat units rather than airbase units! Air base maintenance is the mission of the wing's Air Installation Squadron. It is important to understand that a USAF combat wing organization is manned and equipped to maintain its base but cannot construct its own permanent base. This limited wing construction capability was not understood by DOD and NATO planners. USAF wings that moved to France in 1951 and 1952 experienced decreased mission readiness for several months while waiting for base completion.

The wings sent to the UK occupied RAF bases. Most had been upgraded since WWII. The bases in West Germany were either well established or completed quickly, but DOD and State Department officials greatly underestimated what was involved in the movement of combat wings to France and the unique problems they would face there. NATO had ambitious plans, little experience and a lot of bureaucracy. The USAF and U.S. Army that went into France in 1951 were the guinea pigs that felt the full brunt of these military and political shortcomings.

Appendix 1.1 NORTH ATLANTIC TREATY ARTICLES
Courtesy NATO online

The North Atlantic Treaty

Washington D.C. - 4 April 1949
The Parties to this Treaty reaffirm their faith in the purposes and principles of the Charter of the United Nations and their desire to live in peace with all peoples and all governments.
They are determined to safeguard the freedom, common heritage and civilization of their peoples, founded on the principles of democracy, individual liberty and the rule of law. They seek to promote stability and well-being in the North Atlantic area.
They are resolved to unite their efforts for collective defense and for the preservation of peace and security. They therefore agree to this North Atlantic Treaty:

Article 1
The Parties undertake, as set forth in the Charter of the United Nations, to settle any international dispute in which they may be involved by peaceful means in such a manner that international peace and security and justice are not endangered, and to refrain in their international relations from the threat or use of force in any manner inconsistent with the purposes of the United Nations.

Article 2
The Parties will contribute toward the further development of peaceful and friendly international relations by strengthening their free institutions, by bringing about a better understanding of the principles upon which these institutions are founded, and by promoting conditions of stability and well-being. They will seek to eliminate conflict in their international economic policies and will encourage economic collaboration between any or all of them.

Article 3
In order more effectively to achieve the objectives of this Treaty, the Parties, separately and jointly, by means of continuous and effective self-help and mutual aid, will maintain and develop their individual and collective capacity to resist armed attack.

Article 4
The Parties will consult together whenever, in the opinion of any of them, the territorial integrity, political independence or security of any of the Parties is threatened.

Article 5
The Parties agree that an armed attack against one or more of them in Europe or North America shall be considered an attack against them all and consequently they agree that, if such an armed attack occurs, each of them, in exercise of the right of individual or collective self-defence recognised by Article 51 of the Charter of the United Nations, will assist the Party or Parties so attacked by taking forthwith, individually and in concert with the other Parties, such action as it deems necessary, including the use of armed force, to restore and maintain the security of the North Atlantic area.

Any such armed attack and all measures taken as a result thereof shall immediately be reported to the Security Council. Such measures shall be terminated when the Security Council has taken the measures necessary to restore and maintain international peace and security .

Article 6
For the purpose of Article 5, an armed attack on one or more of the Parties is deemed to include an armed attack: on the territory of any of the Parties in Europe or North America, on the Algerian Departments of France (2), on the territory of or on the Islands under the jurisdiction of any of the Parties in the North Atlantic area north of the Tropic of Cancer; on the forces, vessels, or aircraft of any of the Parties, when in or over these territories or any other area in Europe in which occupation forces of any of the Parties were stationed on the date when the Treaty entered into force or the Mediterranean Sea or the North Atlantic area north of the Tropic of Cancer.

Article 7
This Treaty does not affect, and shall not be interpreted as affecting in any way the rights and obligations under the Charter of the Parties which are members of the United Nations, or the primary responsibility of the Security Council for the maintenance of international peace and security.

Article 8
Each Party declares that none of the international engagements now in force between it and any other of the Parties or any third State is in conflict with the provisions of this Treaty, and undertakes not to enter into any international engagement in conflict with this Treaty.

Article 9
The Parties hereby establish a Council, on which each of them shall be represented, to consider matters concerning the implementation of this Treaty. The Council shall be so organised as to be able to meet promptly at any time. The Council shall set up such subsidiary bodies as may be necessary; in particular it shall establish immediately a defence committee which shall recommend measures for the implementation of Articles 3 and 5.

Article 10
The Parties may, by unanimous agreement, invite any other European State in a position to further the principles of this Treaty and to contribute to the security of the North Atlantic area to accede to this Treaty. Any State so invited may become a Party to the Treaty by depositing its instrument of accession with the Government of the United States of America. The Government of the United States of America will inform each of the Parties of the deposit of each such instrument of accession.

Article 11
This Treaty shall be ratified and its provisions carried out by the Parties in accordance with their respective constitutional processes. The instruments of ratification shall be deposited as soon as possible with the Government of the United States of America, which will notify all the other signatories of each deposit. The Treaty shall enter into force between the States which have ratified it as soon as the ratifications of the majority of the signatories, including the ratifications of Belgium, Canada, France, Luxembourg, the Netherlands, the United Kingdom and the United States, have been deposited and shall come into effect with respect to other States on the date of the deposit of their ratifications.

Article 12
After the Treaty has been in force for ten years, or at any time thereafter, the Parties shall, if any of them so requests, consult together for the purpose of reviewing the Treaty, having regard for the factors then affecting peace and security in thc North Atlantic area, including the development of universal as well as regional arrangements under the Charter of the United Nations for the maintenance of international peace and security.

Article 13
After the Treaty has been in force for twenty years, any Party may cease to be a Party one year after its notice of denunciation has been given to the Government of the United States of America, which will inform the Governments of the other Parties of the deposit of each notice of denunciation.

Article 14
This Treaty, of which the English and French texts are equally authentic, shall be deposited in the archives of the Government of the United States of America. Duly certified copies will be transmitted by that Government to the Governments of other signatories.

2

BASE SELECTION AND MOVEMENT TO FRANCE 1950 - 1954

For the Air Force in Europe, this period was a time of grand planning, quick decisions, and arrival of the initial tactical forces to bring the plans made by the NATO Defense Committee to reality. Negotiations began during fall 1950 between HQ USAF teams and the French Defense Ministry to select air bases and determine the amount of construction funding needed to get a few bases operational at the earliest possible date. The prospect of a war in Europe was a grave concern of U.S. and NATO leaders. But, in the rush to provide a deterrence to Soviet aggression, the four wings that arrived during 1951-52 made the challenging flight across the North Atlantic to occupy bases that were far from ready for operation. In this chapter, I hope to convey how these decisions were made and what it was like to move a wing to France in the early 1950s.

Air Bases Selected

France was a nation rich in airfields after WWII. In 1938 France had 34 commercial airports, 82 military airdromes and approximately 115 private airstrips. During WWII another 76 primitive airfields known as auxiliary landing grounds (ALG) were rapidly constructed, and most prewar airfields were repaired and expanded by U.S. Army Engineer Aviation Battalions. With so many possibilities, site selection was not a simple task. Selection involved extensive discussions between the French Air Force; French departmental and city governments, and the French Civil Aviation Agency, with U.S. representatives from Department of State, Department of Defense, the Corps of Engineers, HQ USAF, and USAFE organizations to obtain final approval for each location. The U.S. team was badly divided; State Department's approach to obtaining air base leases was diametrically opposite USAF's concept of obtaining agreements. State wanted very detailed, lengthy discussions with a completed final treaty at minimum cost for all bases prior to the start of construction. This process would have consumed several years. Conversely, the USAF was under great pressure from the administration and DOD to get the real estate and begin construction at once with minimum cost analysis. Putting U.S. combat wings into Europe to lead NATO air power development by example was the driving force. DOD felt rapid action was required to demonstrate to the Soviet Union and our allies that the U.S. was able and ready to defend Western Europe. (Map 2.1)

Table 2.1 lists the preliminary locations selected and the useage proposed by USAFE. Twenty-one of the sites selected by the USAF team were World War II airfields that had been used from 1935 through 1945 by the French Air Force, the German Luftwaffe, and the U.S. Ninth Tactical Army Air Force. The WWII bases on the list had names familiar to many USAAF Eighth and Ninth Air Force's veterans. By 15 November 1950 the preferred base sites had been identified, and negotiations for land acquisition could proceed. At the same time the U.S. Army was negotiating for their logistical sites, and the Royal Canadian Air Force was seeking four additional fighter air base sites to add to the Rhine Air Defense Barrier in northeastern France. Air bases at Luneville and Marigny were opposed by the local population because of potential jet noise and the dangers of aircraft crashes. Airfields at Dreux, Lyon, and Lorient were opposed by department and city governments because of proposed commercial air development in the area.

Real estate purchases and site designs began in 1951, as soon as approvals were given. On 27 February 1951 an agreement was reached with the French to establish a major USAFE supply depot at Chateauroux-Deols airfield. Next, Fontainebleau was approved for the USAFE offices of Supreme Headquarters Allied Powers Europe (SHAPE). About 1 August 1951 permission was given to build temporary "interim" tent camps at Bordeaux-Merignac airdrome and at Chaumont, Laon, and Toul airfields. By February 1952 final permission was given by France to establish eight tactical air bases: Chambley, Chaumont, Dreux, Etain, Evreux, Laon, Phalsbourg, and Toul to be constructed with all permanent facilities. (Table 2.2)

The sites selected for the main air bases varied from open farmland to commercial airports. Bordeaux-Merignac was a well-developed international airport with concrete runways, taxiways, navigation

Table 2.1 Proposed Locations and Utilization of USAFE Bases in France

Proposed Location	Proposed Use
Bordeaux Airfield	Interim deployment air base, USAFE supply sub-depot, Airfield for gunnery training, Rotational troop carrier air base
Chaumont Airfield	Interim deployment air base, Fighter air base
Cherebourg-Maupertus Airfield	Rotational troop carrier air base
Cognac Airfield	Combat and technical center, Rotational fighter air base
Dreux Airfield	Troop carrier air base
Etain site	Fighter air base
Evreux Airfield	Troop carrier air base, Combat cargo command headquarters
Istres Airfield	Airfield for gunnery training, Rotational troop carrier air base
Laon-Couvron Airfield	Interim deployment air base, Light bomber air base, Air division headquarters
Lorient Airfield	USAFE depot air base
Luneville Airfield	Fighter air base
Lyon Airfield	USAFE major air depot air base
Chambley (Mars-la-Tour) site	Fighter air base
Melun Airfield	Administrative air base, USAFE HQ, MATS terminal for Europe, Hospital
Metz-Frescaty Airfield	Interim deployment air base
Nantes Airfield	Rotational troop carrier air base, USAFE sub-depot airfield
Damblain (Neufchateau) site	Fighter air base
Phalsbourg site	Fighter air base
Marigny (Sezanne) site	Light bomber air base
St. Dizier Airfield	Light bomber air base
Toul-Rosieres Airfield	Tactical reconnaissance air base, Tactical control center

aids, a control tower, utilities and an unused adjoining land parcel with two usable hangars and five usable structures immediately available. Chateauroux-Deols was a commercial airport with good grass runways, taxiways, utilities, and a very large aircraft factory available for rent. Near to this airport was another small military airfield, La Martinerie. It had ten small usable hangars and other buildings that were immediately available for development into a large supply depot. About 1,100 acres was the minimum area required for a modern air base with one runway. Chaumont, Etain, Evreux, Laon, and Toul had circa 1944 runways, limited parking aprons, and space for a tent camp. Phalsbourg was a 1938 grass auxiliary airstrip. These airfields were being farmed or grazed under leases that had to be canceled. The Chambley, Dreux, Grostenquin, and Marville sites were farms that had to be purchased from their owners, which required extra time. None of the sites chosen had adequate buildings, hangars or housing to accommodate a combat wing. Major construction would be required at all air bases to produce a usable facility to support bombers, transports, and jet fighters. Since dependents were not allowed to accompany U.S. military personnel in 1951-52, construction of family housing, schools, service clubs, and commissaries could be postponed. Bordeaux, Chaumont, Laon, and Toul were designated interim air bases to be developed in two steps. First a temporary bare-base tent camp was built in a relatively short time at minimum cost to support flying training missions. Then the final permanent base followed, often requiring about four years of major construction while the wing operated the base. Chambley, Dreux, Etain, Evreux, and Phalsbourg were planned as one-step bases that began with permanent construction. One-step construction started in 1952 but these bases were not ready for wing occupancy until late 1955. After the ten air bases were approved, follow-on negotiations were conducted to obtain additional real estate for support functions such as depot storage sites, communications buildings and radio towers, railroad spurs, pipeline routes, and family housing. (Map 2.2)

Several terms are used to describe USAFE air bases in France. Defining these will clarify the various types of bases. As mentioned, an interim air base was a two-step base that began as a temporary tent camp and permanent construction continued while a combat wing operated the base. It changed from an interim air base to a main operating air base at comple-

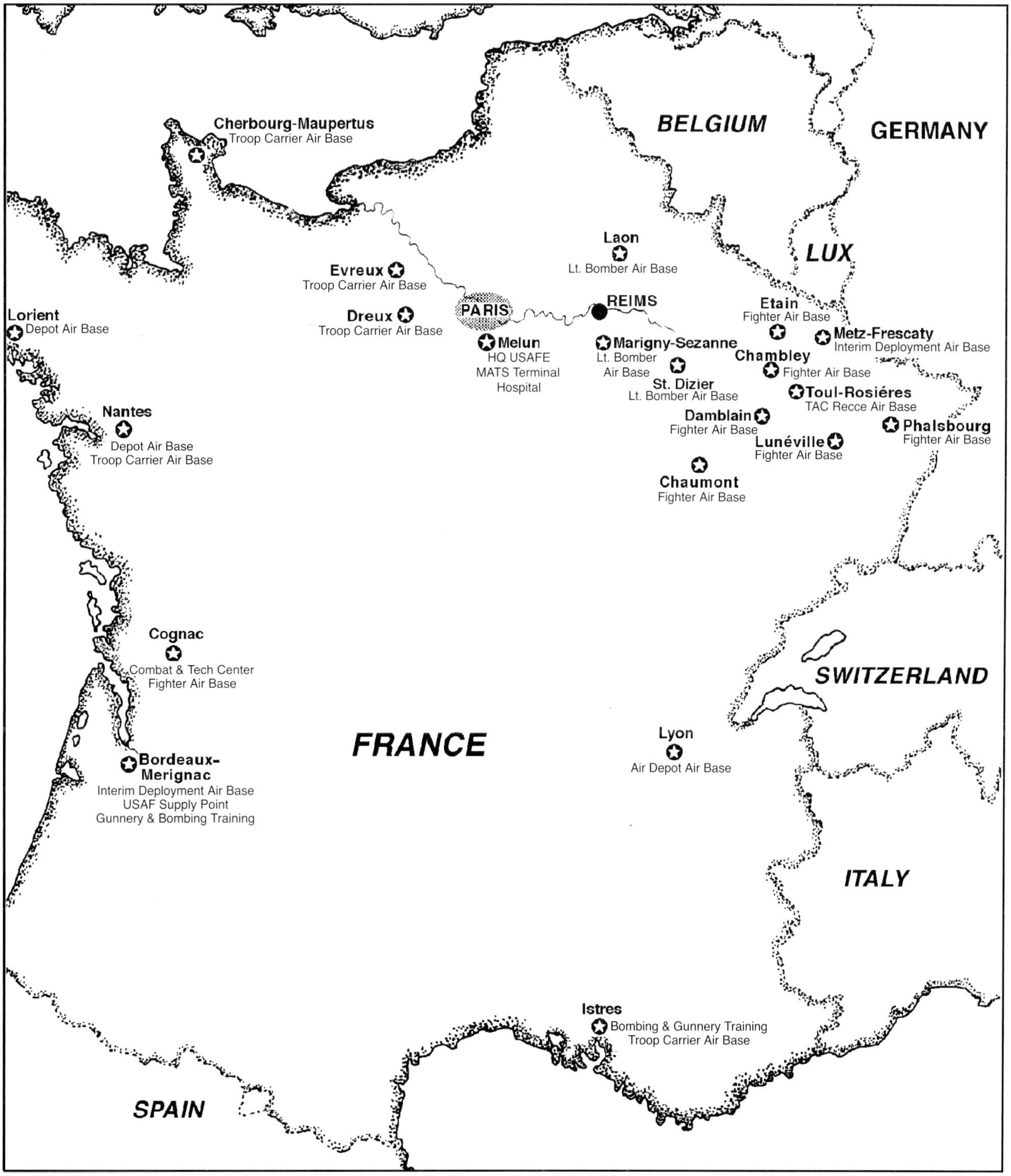

Map 2.1 Proposed Locations and Utilization of Bases in France

Table 2.2
Final Approved USAFE Air Base Site Locations 1952

Bordeaux-Merignac	a pre WWII commercial-military airdrome, 340 miles southwest of Paris
Chambley-Bussieres	a new site, on farmland, 190 miles east of Paris
Chateauroux-Deols	a commercial airport and military airdrome, 150 miles south of Paris
Chaumont-Semoutiers	a pre WWII military airfield,150 miles southeast of Paris
Dreux-Louvilliers	a new site, on farmland, 59 miles west of Paris
Etain-Rouvres	a pre WWII military airfield, 185 miles east of Paris
Evreux-Fauville	a pre WWII commercial and military airdrome, 61 miles west of Paris
Laon-Couvron	a pre WWII military airdrome, 66 miles northeast of Paris
Phalsbourg-Bourscheid	a pre WWII grass military airfield, 260 miles east of Paris
Toul-Rosieres	a WWII auxillary landing ground, 195 miles east of Paris
Two Additional Bases Were Selected and Designated for Royal Canadian Air Force Fighter Bases	
Grostenquin	a new site, forested farmland,195 miles east of Paris
Marville-Montmedy	a new site, open farmland,190 miles east of Paris

Note: The official base name was usually a combination of the nearest city as well as the local village.

tion of NATO phase-two construction when it would have capacity for one or two combat wings. A one step base remained unoccupied until NATO phase-two construction was completed. Only then did it receive its combat wing and become a main operating base. Eight main operating bases were completed in France for the USAF. A main base became a standby deployment base when the combat wing departed with its aircraft, and the base was operated by an air base squadron, or later, a combat support squadron or detachment. One or more squadrons could be flying from the standby air base, but because it did not have a wing commander, his staff, and all support squadrons, USAFE defined it as "standby." These standby bases were also known as reinforcement air bases because they were maintained in condition to immediately accept two flying squadrons from CONUS in case of a military build-up in Europe. The major USAFE depot, Chateauroux Air Depot (CHAD), had a very large airfield at Deols, but it was not considered a main operating base because a combat flying wing was never based there. Chateauroux-La Martinerie depot storage area was also known as an air station because its airfield was closed. Bordeaux-Merignac AB was unusual in that it was an interim air base, then a standby air base, next a depot base, and lastly it was expanded into a large reinforcement air base prior to closing. A dispersed operating base was a base with minimum facilities constructed specifically for aircraft dispersal from the main bases in the event of possible enemy air strikes. A forward operating location was usually an air base located in West Germany and used for Victor Alert aircraft operations.

Initial Deployment of USAF Into France, 1951-1952

The difficult decision facing HQ USAF was determining which wings were combat ready to transfer to France and which air bases would be sufficiently completed to accept them. The combat wings available for immediate movement to France were all federalized Air National Guard units activated on 10 October 1950 and 1 April 1951. HQ USAF wanted the wings moved to France as soon as possible after conversion into newer aircraft. At the end of their active duty tour, wing personnel, aircraft, and all equipment would be in place to easily redesignate them as regular USAF wings.

The first major USAF unit to move to France was the 73d Air Depot Wing from Kelly AFB, Texas, in July 1951. Many individually activated USAF reservists were assigned to this depot wing. Its mission was to establish and operate the largest depot in Europe to logistically support the USAFE theater of operations. It moved into the Chateauroux-Deols commercial airport and the La Martinerie storage site. This location had easy access to good highways, nearby seaports of Bordeaux and La Rochelle, and very good railroad service—prime criteria for an air depot. The Marcel Bloch aircraft factory on the west edge of the Deols airfield was leased by USAFE for depot level aircraft maintenance. La Martinerie, five miles to the southeast, became the depot headquarters, warehouse center, and troop housing area. France agreed to this depot complex on 27 February 1951. It was not on the original list but was a substitute for the suggested site

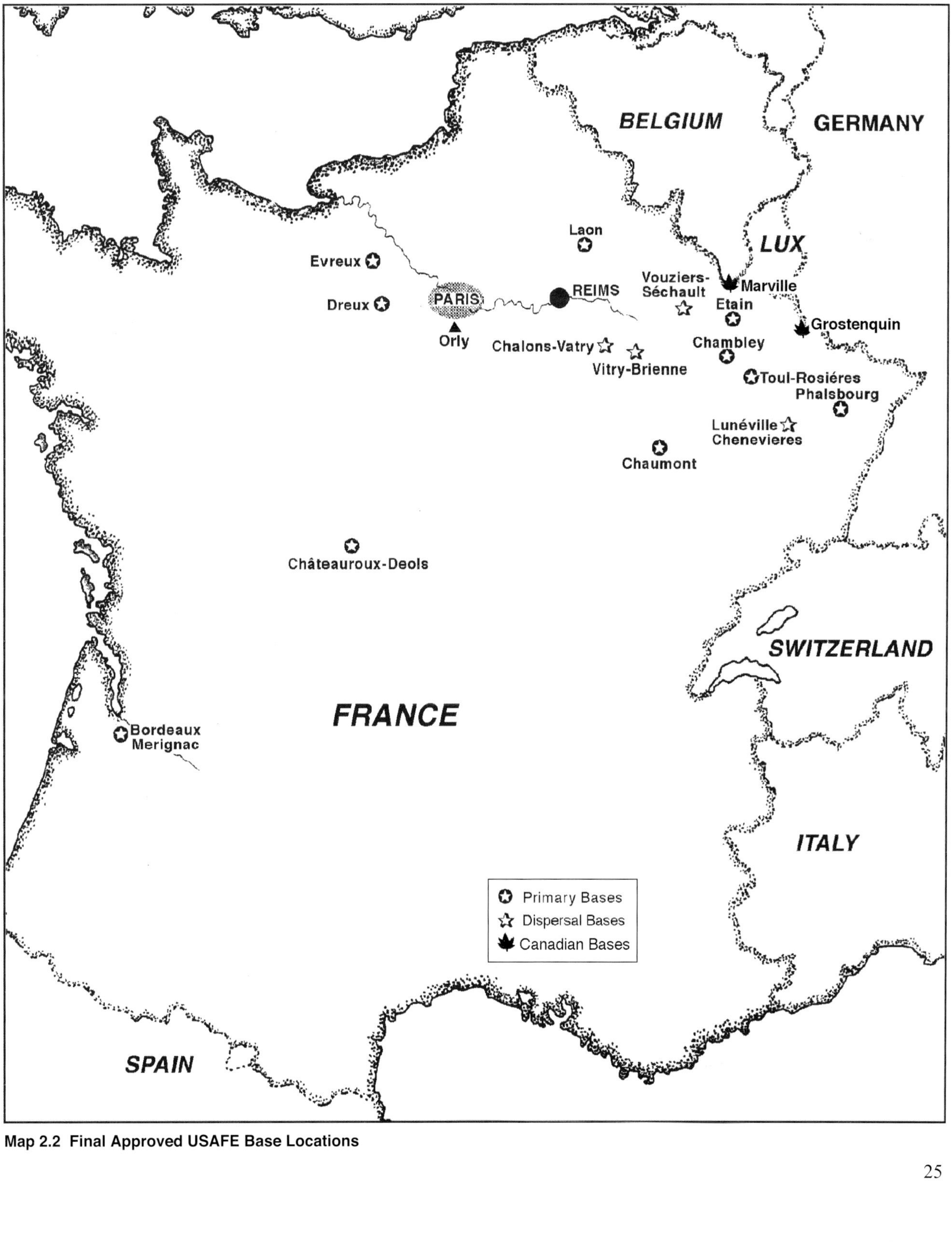

Map 2.2 Final Approved USAFE Base Locations

Tents in the mud, La Martinerie - October 1952. 866th Engineering Aviation Battalion's quarters while supervising base construction.
"History Central Air Materiel Area, Europe" via William Adamek

Luxembourg caserne near Toul AB, January 1952. 1870s barracks with boarded-up windows and no heat were the first home of the 117th TRWg.
Sam Whitworth

Tents at Chaumont AB, August 1952. Note drainage ditch on the right to catch the frequent rains.
Charles Radloff

Bordeaux AB, 1951. B-26s parked among remains of bombed out WWII hangars. These were hangars the 126th LBWg had been told were in usable condition!
Frank Casale

at Lyon, France. Later Chateauroux became the only USAFE air depot when it replaced both the depots at Erding AB, West Germany, and RAF Burtonwood, England. From 1952 through 1955 additional sub-depots were established in France and operated under the Chateauroux Air Depot command. Munitions sub-depots were constructed at St Mihel and Chize and a clothing sub-depot was set up at the Bordeaux-Bacalan Ford factory. A large vehicle sub-depot was organized at Moulins, France. The Chateauroux Air Depot continued to function from 1951 until its termination in 1967, the end of all U.S. bases in France. Chateauroux and its sub-depots are thoroughly described in chapter 8.

Several combat wings were considered for deployment to France; two were alerted for movement then canceled. In May 1951 the 116th and 136th Fighter-Bomber Wings were selected for France after converting into F-84Es, but increasing Korean War combat caused CINC FEAF to request their presence in Japan and South Korea. The 116th FBWg was ready to depart George AFB, California, for Bordeaux-Merignac in July 1951. The wing had shipped some equipment and dispatched its advanced echelon to Europe before it received cancellation of its orders for France and was sent to Japan instead. Its equipment had to be reshipped from France to Japan. The 136th FBWg was scheduled to move to Chaumont AB from Langley AFB, Virginia, but runway construction at Chaumont had not yet begun. France had not even completed the final agreement for base use! Consequently the 136th was sent to Korea.

The 126th Light Bomb Wing had been told it would exchange its older B-26B/C Invaders for new Canberra light bombers, but this new airplane was still at least three years away from production. Even the reworked "black" Invaders were unavailable because losses in Korea were consuming them faster than depot production. Therefore, the 126th Wing prepared for overseas deployment by 1 October 1951 with its WWII configured B-26s without night interdiction capability. It was initially considered for assignment to Korea to add its B-26 Invaders to the Fifth Air Force day interdiction program. But this movement was changed, resulting in the 126th Bomb Wing being the first combat wing to arrive in France on 7 December 1951 at Bordeaux-Merignac AB. A description of this base follows in chapter 6.

Next the 117th Tactical Reconnaissance Wing prepared to move to France after receiving reworked RB-26s and RF-80As. The 117th arrived at Toul-Rosieres AB in January 1952. The base was a disaster—after six months of construction it was a sea of mud and the wing commander considered it uninhabitable. The new runway was breaking up and could not support flying. Its three tactical squadrons, one with "black" RB-26Cs and two with RF-80As, had made the hazardous flight across the North Atlantic in January to be mission ready in France as soon as possible, then had to be deployed into West Germany at Furstenfeldbruck, Neubiberg and Wiesbaden for safe operations. About 900 wing personnel were stationed in old, substandard, French Army casernes. By June 1952 the flying squadrons returned to Toul, and the support units moved to the base preferring tents to the antique casernes. The base slowly became usable during the summer of 1952. A description of Toul AB follows in chapter 16.

In 1950 the 1630th Air Base Squadron had a team at Orly Airport, the major commercial airfield located south of Paris, to support the air transport needs of SHAPE and USAFE. A Military Air Transport Service (MATS) airlift terminal was established in January 1951 at Orly. This was a small, sixty-man unit whose initial mission was to support military and commercial transports moving U.S. Government officials and high-ranking military personnel to NATO offices in Paris and SHAPE Headquarters at Fontainebleau. Use of Orly Airport was strictly limited to VIP transport missions since tactical aircraft were not allowed to fly into the Paris airspace. The MATS terminal unit used buildings at Orly during the 1951-1954 period. A description of this air base follows in chapter 14.

In May 1952 the 137th Fighter-Bomber Wing arrived at its new home, Chaumont AB, after flying its factory-new F-84Gs across the North Atlantic to France. By April Chaumont's tent camp was completed and it was in good condition, much better than Toul. The French contractor had laid a new, macadam runway over an old one, and it supported the heavy F-84G fighters. The tent camp and all prefabricated wood buildings were completed. A description of this base follows in chapter 9.

These wings were the first to experience the primitive conditions at the interim bases in France. The urgency to place units in France and the bureaucracy encountered in obtaining land and building the bases resulted in substandard living and working conditions. Efforts of commanders and troops were focused on surviving the winters of 1951 and 1952, then organizing and training their units to improve combat capability. All the wings were deployed to France with serious shortages of authorized vehicles, aircraft support equipment, shop test equipment, and clothing. Also, they had not been authorized the additional equipment required for outdoor aircraft and vehicle maintenance. These living and working conditions created a serious morale problem, especially when the men compared their facilities to those in West Germany. No further combat wings were deployed into France until April 1954.

In 1953 construction began on three of the four dispersed operating bases (DOBs) built specifically for the USAF. Approximately ten additional DOBs were built in France for NATO's wartime use. These bases were almost uninhabited except during simulated wartime exercises. The DOBs were kept in a usable condition by small detachments from a combat wing's main base. A full description of these dispersed bases is in chapter 17.

Permanent construction proceeded at all bases. But, the one-step bases of Etain and Chambley were still incomplete when the 388th Fighter-Bomber Wing arrived at Etain and the 21st Fighter-Bomber Wing arrived at Chambley on 12 and 13 December 1954. Their F-86F flying squadrons had to operate at other air bases for about six months until moving into their new homes. These two fighter wings were the last TAC wings to depart CONUS and be stationed in France until 1961.

During Fiscal Year 1954, USAFE spent $762 million to operate and maintain forty-five squadrons flying 2,132 aircraft at fifty-three air bases with 116,284 officer and airmen personnel across Europe. The CONUS based fighter wing programmed for Phalsbourg AB in 1954 remained in the U.S., which reduced projected expenditures. Reasonable O&M cost estimates forecasted USAFE to be a $1 billion a year air force by 1955! But, reductions of the defense budget were already being planned by the U.S. administration.

Project 7019

Shortly after the 126th and 117th Wings arrived in France they were tasked to support USAF Project 7019 that began on 15 April 1952. The directive affected all combat wings in USAFE. The wings were required to rotate combat aircrews to FEAF on temporary duty for sixty days of combat operations in Korea to gain combat experience in the B-26, RF-80, and F-84s. When the 137th Fighter-Bomber Wing arrived in May, it was tasked as well. All three wings had to quickly complete aircrew training in France to meet this demand.

Each wing was levied three fighter pilots or three B-26 four-man aircrews every three months to support Project 7019. The crews consisted of three officers and one airman: pilot, navigator, bombardier, and gunner. The officers and airmen were generally volunteers for this combat duty and were rewarded with a fifteen-day leave in the U.S. after completion of their Korean tour, before their return to France. The project provided air war combat skills to the squadrons and wings in France, but its primary purpose was to solve the USAF problem of combat crew shortages in Korea. As the Korean War entered its third year, a very serious aircrew shortage developed in FEAF. Men were sent to Korea for one year or the completion of one hundred combat missions, whichever came first. Increased war operations meant many pilots and crew members completed their required number of combat missions long before their one year tour of duty was served. After two years at war, the USAF had still not developed the capability to produce one and a half air crew members for each aircraft assigned to the Korean theater. Also, aircrew casualties had increased during 1951, requiring more replacements.

An interesting situation was encountered by some of these USAFE aviators upon completion of their sixty-day combat tours. FEAF Command and wing personnel officers would try to keep them in Korea longer by insisting they had agreed to stay for one year! Heated discussions were often required to get these men back to their bases in Europe after ninety days TDY. The total time away from their wings in France, including travel and leave, was 90 to 110 days and resulted in fewer trained USAFE aircrews during 1952-53. Project 7019 ended in September 1953 after the Korean War armistice on 27 July 1953. A copy of 7019 orders can be found at the end of the chapter. (Appendix 2.1)

Project "Native Son" in France

It was immediately apparent that operating an air base in France would require much assistance, since there were very few Americans in the USAF who were fluent in French. When the 126th Bomb Wing arrived at Bordeaux there were no more than four officers and two airmen who were proficient in speaking and reading French. Many American high schools did not offer French in their language courses.

Early in 1951, USAFE authorized the hiring of French civilians as telephone operators, and to provide interpreter/translation services and civil engineering staffs during the base construction phase, similar to procedures in Japan and West Germany. Translators were essential to plow through the French documents necessary during base development. A bilingual French civil engineer who could interface with contractors and was able to answer questions and make additional drawings was a very important asset to avoid construction mistakes.

Upon arrival at Bordeaux in 1951, the 126th Bomb Wing was authorized 173 local workers. By February 1952 about eighty French workers were employed throughout the Mérignac air base. Employees were divided into two categories, schedules A or B. Schedule 'A' was unskilled labor, paid hourly. 'B' classified personnel filled administrative and clerical jobs and were paid monthly. Hourly workers received from 101 francs (thirty-five cents) to 136 francs (forty-five cents) per hour. Monthly wages ranged from 27,000 francs (seventy-eight dollars) to 57,800 francs (one hundred-sixty-five dollars). These were low wages by Bordeaux standards, and applicants were not plentiful. Employees were paid by the French Government who was then reimbursed by the U.S. Army. Pay was sometimes delayed by paperwork errors, but eventually hiring local workers became a very successful program and wages increased.

By the summer of 1952 many French workers were employed in the mess halls, producing very good meals and relieving airmen from mess hall (KP) duty. Employing local civilians allowed for more effective use of the troops stationed abroad. By freeing a technically skilled airman from extra duties such as interior guard, base clean-up, and KP, more man-hours could be spent doing the job he was trained to do. In addition, French civilians were employed in the non-appropriated fund activities on base, i.e., base exchanges (BX), snack bars, clubs, recreation centers, and auto service centers.

During 1951-52 the cost of overseas basing of USAF forces was criticized by the administration as being too expensive. As a way to reduce costs, Project "Native Son" was announced by the Department of the Air Force on 10 July 1953. This new worldwide policy would "employ native personnel" overseas in place of U.S. military wherever possible. It expanded the areas where civilians could be employed on base. In 1954 as "Native Son" was implemented, each air base employed approximately 350 men and women in many support areas, i.e., medical, civil engineering shops, communications center, base supply, vehicle operation and maintenance, food service, fire department, and security police. The positions filled by the French citizens were directly related to positions listed in the squadron's Unit Manning Document (UMD) that had specific job titles and skill requirements as defined by the Air Force Specialty Code (AFSC). These people were replacements for USAF personnel not an additional work force. (Fig2.1) They could not be placed in direct combat positions such as within the flying squadrons as aircraft mechanics, crew chiefs, armament and avionics maintenance, or in the operations/intelligence offices. By 1962, Laon AB had a total of 720 French employees. The Chateauroux Air Depot employed the greatest number of civilian personnel; about 3,900 men and women worked in various depot functions in addition to French maintenance contractors.

These workers were easily trained for their new jobs and became productive, efficient, and dependable employees. Most of the French workers enjoyed the opportunity to work on base and receive training never before available. Telephone operators were given thorough training on USAF/NATO communications procedures and emergency alert actions. At least one French operator was on duty at all times, day and night, to access the French telephone system in case of alerts. Some bases, such as Dreux in 1956, provided government transportation for these operators. Employee turnover was very low. Each native hired was estimated to save about $5,000 per man-year compared to USAF personnel. Many positions filled by French personnel involved rotating shifts and weekend duty assignments.

In Native Son there were two classifications of base personnel, local wage rate (LWR) and general schedule, depending upon the areas of employment. All employees were paid through the French Government twice a month, French taxes were withheld, and the workers paid into the French retirement system which meant they had benefits after employment was terminated in 1966-67 during Operation FRELOC. All employees were managed in accordance with USAF worldwide directives and in a manner similar to U.S.

Bilingual French telephone operators connected Etain AB to the outside world,1958.
Stan Thompson

Figure 2.1 Native Son Manning Principles - Letter from USAFE Deputy Chief of Staff/Personnel to 48th FBWg.
Daniel Buret

SL-MPO, 48th FBW, APO 119, USAF, dtd 27 Nov 57, Subj: LWR (French) Manning Authorizations

PMOP 1st Ind 18 December 1957

Hq United States Air Force in Europe, APO 633, USAF

TO: COMMANDER, 48th Fighter Bomber Wing, APO 119, USAF

1. Native space authorizations are not a bulk allotment. A definite relationship exists between the skill level of the AFSC authorized on the manning document and the skill level of the incumbent hired. This relationship will be achieved as outlined below.

2. It is the responsibility of the Civilian Personnel Office Classification Analyst to write and grade each position as presented by the operating official regardless of the manning document AFSC and grade.

3. It is at this point that close coordination and cooperation between Civilian Personnel and Manpower is absolutely essential. The Manpower Officer will review and coordinate with Civilian Personnel on the establishment of new positions, as well as the results of classification surveys of already established positions.

4. If the Manpower Officer does not agree that the positions are represented as his records reflect the organization, a review is necessary with the operating official to clarify the duties and responsibilities. This review will not be conducted so as to impair the Civilian Personnel annual classification survey requirement. The outcome of the Manpower Officer's study may result in further action by Civilian Personnel. If on the other hand the position is correctly stated but appears to be associated with a higher or lower AFSC than that stated on the UMD, then the Manpower Officer will reflect an adjustment on the manning document.

5. This procedure will provide for the review of positions prior to initial hiring or final survey action.

FOR THE COMMANDER-IN-CHIEF:

t/C.D. SONHKALB
Colonel, USAF
Assistant DCS/P

UNITED STATES AIR FORCES IN EUROPE

Certificate of Service

presented to

BURET Daniel

IN RECOGNITION OF 10 YEARS OF CIVILIAN SERVICE

THIS 30th DAY OF JUNE 1962

Figure 2.2 Certificate of appreciation that accompanied a silver medal for 10 years of service.

Daniel Buret

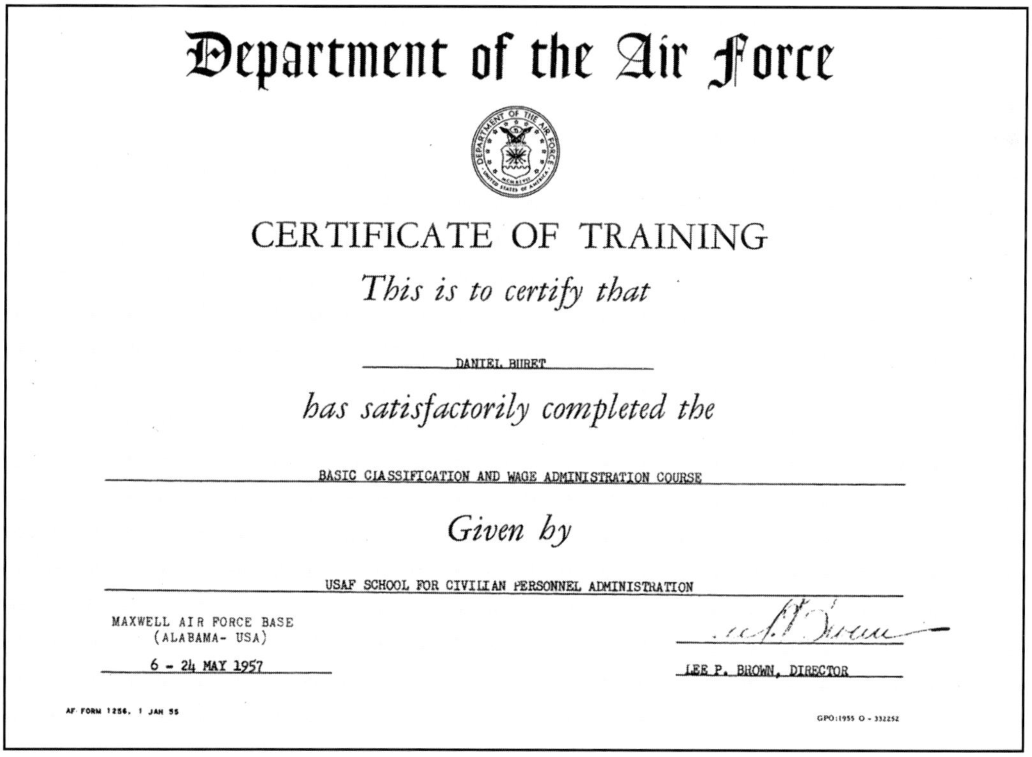

Department of the Air Force

CERTIFICATE OF TRAINING

This is to certify that

DANIEL BURET

has satisfactorily completed the

BASIC CLASSIFICATION AND WAGE ADMINISTRATION COURSE

Given by

USAF SCHOOL FOR CIVILIAN PERSONNEL ADMINISTRATION

MAXWELL AIR FORCE BASE
(ALABAMA- USA)

6 - 24 MAY 1957

LEE P. BROWN, DIRECTOR

AF FORM 1256, 1 JAN 55

GPO:1955 O - 332252

Figure 2.3 Certificate of completion of a personnel management course at Maxwell AFB.

Daniel Buret

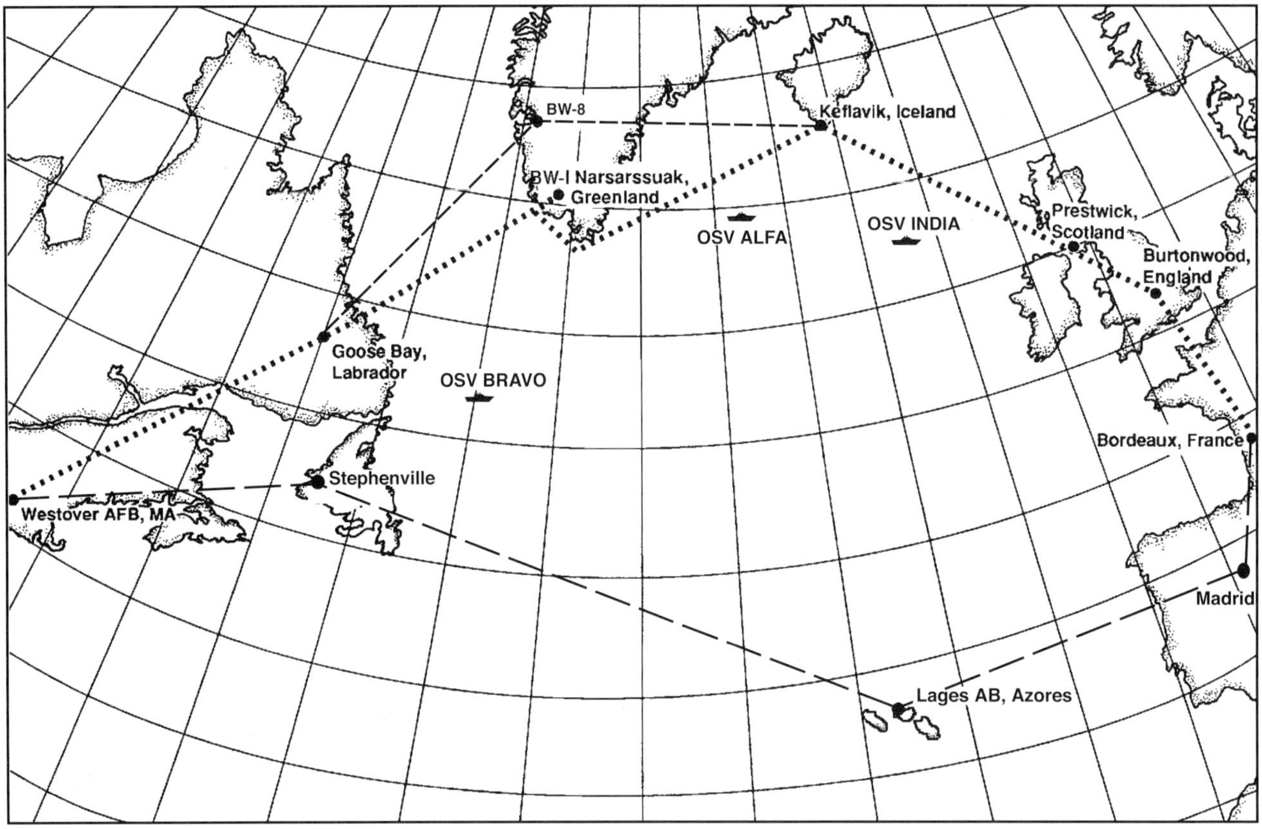

Map 2.3 North Atlantic Air Routes

Government Civil Service procedures. All employees participated in incentive and award programs that the USAF made available to encourage good performance. The value of the French personnel was recognized in letters of commendation from supervisors and medals awarded for longevity. A bronze medal was given for five years, silver for ten, and a gold medal for fifteen years of service. (Fig 2.2) Most French employees worked on the same air base during their ten to fifteen years of service to USAFE and provided a great deal of cohesiveness and job knowledge in their offices and shops. A few employees met USAFE recognition boards for evaluation of their outstanding service rendered to their squadron and base commanders in France. French civilian managers attended special schools and some were afforded the opportunity to acquire special USAF personnel management training in the U.S. (Fig 2.3) The French employees were very unhappy with President de Gaulle's decision to force the U.S. Air Force and Army out of France in 1967. At some bases they loudly protested the removal of our forces from France and the end to their employment. Some U.S. news correspondents reported their actions as anti-American when their protests were actually against President de Gaulle's ultimatum that the U.S. must leave France. One of the saddest days during base closures in January 1967 was the dismissal of the French base employees. At base closing ceremonies certificates of recognition were presented to the French employees signed by the base commanders as they said their final good-byes. But, more impressive than any certificate is the continuing bond of friendship and understanding that exists between many of these workers and the airmen and officers they worked with so many years ago. Some of the past employees have formed base associations and hold annual functions where former USAF service members and their families are warmly welcomed.

Movement, Planning and Preparations

The movement of USAF units from CONUS to France in 1951-54 closely followed WWII procedures. Every wing had movement identification numbers for all personnel, aircraft, and cargo. Almost all personnel were moved by Military Sea Transport Service (MSTS) troop ships. Cargo was moved by MSTS cargo ships or commercial freighters chartered by MSTS. All aircraft were flown overseas by squadron pilots and aircrews led by their wing commanders. Each wing movement was supported by MATS. The total time required to

Base Headquarters, Goose Bay Labrador, November 7, 1951.
Jerry McAuliffe

relocate a combat wing from its U.S. base to its new French air base was two to three months, excluding the time required for arrival of the rear detachments. Each wing dispatched a small advance echelon (ADVON) detachment of sixty to eighty men by MATS airlift to its future home about twenty days before departure of the aircraft. Several wings required two months to fly all assigned aircraft across the North Atlantic. Some crates containing essential unit property and vehicles arrived five months after departing by commercial truck from the unit's packing area at its CONUS base.

Aircraft Movements into France

The wings being assigned to USAFE used the same North Atlantic air route that had been used in 1941-45 to move bomber, cargo, and some fighter aircraft to and from Europe. By 1948 the route was busy again due to Berlin Airlift operations. These northern air bases were improved and operated by the Northeast Air Command (NEAC).

The last stop in the U.S. was usually Westover AFB, Massachusetts, or Loring AFB, Maine. The first stop on the North Atlantic route was Goose Bay, Labrador, 730nm northward into Canada. Fighters often used Loring AFB because it reduced the distance to 520nm. The next stop was 680nm across the Davis Strait to Bluie West One (BW-1), Narsarssuak, Greenland, and then 607nm to Keflavik AB, Iceland. The longest over-water flight leg was 746nm between Keflavik and Prestwick, Scotland. From Prestwick Airfield the aircraft flew to Burtonwood Air Depot, England, and on to France. An alternate route was from Goose Bay AB, 973nm to Bluie West Eight, Sondrestrom AB, Greenland. (BW-8 is located 470nm north of Narsarssuak.) The next stop was 610nm across Greenland direct to Keflavik. A third route that was developed later went 1,475nm from Newfoundland to Lages AB, Azores, then 1,120nm into Spain. Map 2.3 illustrates the three routes flown to and from Europe.

Ocean Station Vessels were located on the over water flight paths to supply communication and navigation service to civil and military aircraft; these ships remained in a constant position for several months at a time until relieved by a similar ship. The Ocean Station Vessels provided a non-directional radio beacon, weather reports, and served as airways communications centers. OSV ALFA was located midway between Greenland and Iceland, OSV BRAVO was located well south of the route between Labrador and Greenland, and OSV INDIA was located south of the airway between Iceland and Scotland.

Island hopping was necessary due to the short range of most of the aircraft and frequent storms that occurred both summer and winter. Because of the pressure to arrive as soon as possible, several wings flew the northern route from November through February when it was considered closed. The caution exercised by wing commanders to avoid the loss of aircraft and crews resulted in slow, careful flights to Europe. The first flights of the 126th Bomb Wing's B-26s departed Langley on 30 October 1951 and the last four invaders arrived at Bordeaux-Merignac on 26 November 1951. The 21st Fighter-Bomber's F-86Fs departed George AFB, California, on 12 December 1954 and their last two Sabres arrived at Toul AB on 24 February 1955. The B-26 aircraft were flown by a three-man crew consisting of pilot, navigator and crew chief. The C-119s were flown by a five-man crew: pilot, co-pilot, navigator, radio operator and crew chief. Of course, the F-84 and F-86 fighters held only the pilot. Out of 1,000 aircraft transferred over the years 1951-55, no more than four were lost enroute, all due to ground accidents, with zero fatalities.

Air-to-air refueling, standard equipment on today's military aircraft, was not available in this early build-up period. The F-84G had this capability, but there were only a few KB-29 and KC-97 tanker aircraft, and these were used primarily on the Pacific routes. Almost all the aircraft assigned to NATO (B-26s, B-45s, RF-80s, F-84Es, F-86A/Fs, C-47s, T-33s and C-119s) did not have air-to-air refueling systems. Most of these aircraft had a range of about 900 to 1,300 miles—adequate with zero headwinds if the weather remained good at the destination and alternate airfields. The real problem was that there were very few alternate airfields between Goose Bay, Labrador, and Prestwick, Scotland.

The most critical air base along the route was Bluie West One. The approach into the BW-1 runway is at the end of a 50-mile long fjord; a straight-in approach is impossible visually or on instruments. MATS minimum requirements for approach into BW-1 were a 5,000-foot ceiling and 10 miles visibility to enter the fjord. The normal approach was to let down offshore to about 1,000 feet and then fly down the fjord between the mountains. After some gentle turns the pilot would make a sharp 90 degree right turn onto a short final approach to a 6,500 foot-long runway. Fog along the shoreline or in the fjord would make landing impossible. After a 680nm flight from Goose Bay, the alternate, fuel permitting, was BW-8, 470nm to the north with a 5,800-foot runway. The final option was landing or ejecting on the icecap to await rescue aircraft from BW-1. BW-1 had two SB-17Gs complete with A-1 lifeboats assigned to the 6th Rescue Squadron to assist in rescue work. All pilots and aircrews flying the northern routes were required to wear a very uncomfortable orange rubber 23-pound survival suit (poopy suit) in case of bailout. One thing everyone knew, the

Maintenance support C-54 on the ramp at Bluie West One, Greenland, November 1951.
Jerry McAuliffe

Looking across the runway at Bluie West One, Greenland, November 1951.
Jerry McAuliffe

View of mountains and frozen lakes from C-54 flying across Greenland after departing Bluie West One, November 21, 1951.
Jerry McAuliffe

B-26 and jet fighters were not to be ditched—there is no record of them floating!

The 1952 era jet fighters had only one low frequency automatic direction finder (ADF) radio navigational system to find airfields and then the runway! Ground Control Approach (GCA) radar was available at all enroute air bases except BW-1. Crossing the North Atlantic during the 1950s and 1960s will always be remembered as an adventure by these airmen.

Each wing deployment to Europe required the support of six or seven MATS C-54 transports, two with each squadron. Some C-54s were U.S. Navy R5Ds assigned to MATS and flown by enlisted Chief Petty Officers. One C-54 was the lead aircraft. It would depart about two hours before the first tactical aircraft and report current enroute and destination weather conditions. If the weather reports were good, the squadron would begin launching flights of four aircraft. No aircraft was allowed to fly individually except the four-engine C-54s. The second C-54 was the logistical support aircraft carrying the squadron's enroute maintenance team. It took off after the squadron's last aircraft reached the halfway point.

Each wing formed enroute aircraft operations and maintenance teams to support their aircraft as they moved from CONUS to France. Flying squadrons selected team members with maximum expertise on their particular model aircraft, engine, and systems. These enroute teams were supported by the usual transient maintenance crews permanently stationed at every stopover air base. The light bomb squadrons and troop carrier squadrons had ten-man teams each, because each bomber or cargo plane carried a crew chief to maintain its aircraft. These teams were composed of an operations officer, maintenance officer, two aircraft specialists, two engine specialists, an aircraft radio repairman, an aircraft electrical specialist, a hydraulic specialist, propeller specialist, and supply clerk. Fighter wings had three, twenty-two to twenty-eight-man teams each containing the same specialists, minus the propeller specialist, plus about eighteen crew chiefs to support their aircraft. The operations officers coordinated aircraft movements to avoid having more than one squadron at each stop due to limited ramp space. The supply clerk managed the flyaway support kits that were carried in the C-54, or attempted to obtain required parts from base supply at each stopover. One or two spare engines were also carried in the C-54 plus special aircraft tools. The aircraft moved to France were in very good condition and required minimum unscheduled repairs.

The wings supplied an ADVON to assist the depot

Boarding the Troopship USNS General Eltinge for France.
USAF photo via Sam Roberts

detachment in opening the air bases. Advance parties were airlifted from CONUS directly to their air bases in France by MATS C-124, C-121, or C-97s, arriving at least thirty days prior to arrival of the wing's aircraft.

Later as replacement aircraft moved to France in 1952-58, they were delivered by MATS crews assigned to the 1708th Ferrying Group or by wing replacement crews. For example, after completion of Combat Crew Training School at Randolph AFB, Texas, B-57 pilots and navigators would pick up new B-57s at the factory or depot and fly the Canberras to Laon AB, France. Aircraft with greater ferry ranges like the B-57s would fly directly from Keflavik to Laon, France, without having to stop in the UK. These movements usually involved only four to six aircraft per month, but they were always flown in pairs. Extra fuel tanks were installed in C-47s and C-119s to increase their range for safety. After 1956 the fighters and bombers, e.g., B-66, F-100, and RF-101s, with air-to-air refueling systems could make a rapid, direct, one-day crossing of the Atlantic Ocean.

The large movement of personnel, aircraft and equipment to Europe for Operation STAIR STEP in October and November 1961 was a major improvement over the deployments to France in 1951-52; the USAF had improved all phases of rapid deployment to Europe.

Surface Movements, MSTS Ships, and Commercial Air Transport

The first step in moving a wing overseas was packing and crating all unit property. Each squadron was responsible for packing and crating its own support equipment, parts, and supplies. All crates were handmade to special sizes; no commercial crates were available. When the crates were fabricated, extra wood was added to use as construction material after the items were unpacked. Units that followed this advice from experienced WWII veterans were happy they did. The extra plywood was turned into excellent workbenches and shop shelving. Crating in this manner produced over 250 containers for each flying squadron. Standard steel shipping containers used in later movements were not in common use at this time. They would have saved a tremendous amount of time and labor during these moves to Europe. An important step in this procedure was preparing accurate packing lists and clearly identifying boxes to be able to unpack in an orderly fashion when setting up shops after arrival. One interesting problem was determining what equipment and parts could be packed beginning forty-five days prior to departure while still supporting a busy flying schedule.

Bunks on the troopship, USNS General Patch.
Dale Peotter

Once packing was complete, commercial trucks and trains then transported this impedimenta from the CONUS base to the Port of Embarkation (POE) where it was loaded on ships to begin its journey to France. The U.S. Army had established a major Port of Debarkation at La Pallice, France, near La Rochelle that duplicated the facilities at Bremerhaven. This became the sea terminal for most personnel and cargo moving into France. The Bordeaux-Bacalan port was also used for vehicles and cargo. Unit equipment could arrive at any of these three ports which made it difficult to trace items suspected of being lost. Upon arrival in France, U.S. Army truck companies hauled the Air Force material from La Pallice to the air bases in 2.5-ton trucks or 10-ton semi-trailers. The wings going to Toul and Chaumont used the French railroad to move their cargo from La Pallice to their bases.

Every wing being moved to France had its main troop contingent of approximately 1,000 to 1,200 officers and airmen transported on one troop ship. The ocean crossing took ten to fourteen days between ports. Ports of embarkation in the U.S. were the same as used in WWII, namely, New York, New Orleans, and Houston. Some of the MSTS ships were the USNS GEN Butner, GEN L. Eltinge, GEN Geiger, GEN W.G. Hahn, GEN H.F. Hodges, GEN A.M. Patch, and GEN Upsure. The journey began by traveling on train or bus from the CONUS base to the port. New York used Camp Kilmer, New Jersey, as a staging base and troops traveled by train to Brooklyn where they boarded their ship. Unassigned U.S. Air Force and Army personnel boarded along with wing personnel until the ship was filled with about 2,500 troops heading to Europe.

Lack of space and unsanitary conditions aboard the ships were a surprise for Air Force personnel. A typical 25 by 25 square-foot space held thirty men; there was little room for any activity except sleeping. All the USAF troops were very happy they had not joined the Navy. Bad weather in the winter often made the ocean crossing extremely difficult. The ships encountered very rough seas, and many of the troops were seasick for most of the voyage. All were exceedingly relieved to arrive at the port of La Pallice. A common recollection of these troops was their amazement upon seeing the size and strength of the 1941 German submarine pens located in the harbor. Once on shore, the men were loaded on French SNCF trains and then embarked on a one-day ride to their new bases in France. Upon arrival, they were shocked to see the tent cities that would be their home for two or more years. No one had briefed them on the conditions they would meet.

Replacement Individual Personnel and Dependents

After the complete wings were deployed to France, the normal process began of replacing individual officers and airmen as their tours of duty ended and they rotated back to CONUS for new assignments or separation from the Air Force. Between 1950 and 1954 individual unassigned and replacement personnel traveled to France by ship through Camp Kilmer, then to POE

Troopship USNS General Patch.
Jerry McAuliffe

in Bayone, New Jersey, usually direct to the port at Bremerhaven, West Germany. A personnel processing squadron at Bremerhaven would assign them to units depending upon their AFSCs to fill empty slots in particular wings and squadrons throughout USAFE.

Once dependents were allowed in France, families were transported in the same ships but had much better quarters, though mothers had to keep a sharp eye on their children at all times. WAC and WAF women traveling on board were allowed to volunteer to assist the families traveling with young children. Families frequently traveled unaccompanied since husbands were already stationed in France. They had to obtain housing before their families could make the trip.

In 1954 the USAF decided to move military personnel and families to Europe by transport aircraft, either MATS airlifters or civil air carriers under MATS contract. The cost of moving troops by MSTS ships was increasing. Also, the HQ USAF Director of Personnel realized that the Air Force was losing about three months of productivity out of a three-year overseas assignment due to the long voyages. Air transportation reduced this relocation time to less than three weeks. Rotating about 15,000 men per year to USAFE by surface ship resulted in approximately 3,600 man-years of lost labor! This lost time was felt most acutely in the critically needed jobs such as pilots, aircrew members, and aircraft maintenance personnel. Troop ships were not used again until the Vietnam war required large movements of men and their combat equipment from CONUS to SEA. Camp Kilmer ceased processing USAF personnel in 1956.

The major east coast air terminals serving Europe were New York International Airport (Kennedy) for contract airlines and McGuire AFB, New Jersey, or Westover AFB, Massachusetts for MATS military air transports. Whether departing or returning to New York, most USAF personnel were processed by the 2267th Personnel Processing Squadron (CONAC), and later HQ 3121st USAF Logistic Control Group (Atlantic) (AFLC) at Manhattan Beach Air Force Station in Brooklyn, New York.

The major USAFE air terminals were Orly Airport, Paris, France; Rhein-Main Airport, Frankfurt, Germany; and RAF Mildenhall, UK. The 7113th Personnel Processing Squadron was established, and it operated the USAF Air Traffic Coordination Center, Paris Air Passenger Center (PAPC) located in the Hotel Littre in Paris. It processed personnel to and from Paris Orly Airport and those by train from Germany. Three hotels in Paris were leased by the Air Force, the Hotel Littre (128 rooms), Hotel Powers (55 rooms), and Hotel Victoria Palace, all in the Montparnasse District. Families arriving in France were quartered at least one night in one of these hotels until met by their sponsor. The 7113th designator was changed to HQ 7415th Air Base Group in 1957.

Upon arrival at Orly, Air Force personnel were either processed there or bused to the Hotel Littre, processed, and dispatched by rail to their new duty stations in France. This presented some interesting problems as the troops tried to get information on how to proceed to their new base. Pronunciation of city and town names became critical. Mispronunciation when asking for directions put several men intending to go to Laon AB on the train bound for Lyon about 290 miles to the southeast instead of a short ride 65 miles to the northeast of Paris. Perhaps there may still be some very old airmen riding the trains around France looking for their assigned bases!

An Air Force wife, Nancy Brooks, relates her experience in 1960 as she traveled to France with three young sons:

> I began my trip in December 1960 on a commercial flight from San Francisco to New Jersey with three sons, ages four, two and nine months.
>
> We flew into one Chicago airport and had to go by helicopter to the other airport and found out that due to weather we would have to spend the night there, so I got very little sleep as I was on the phone checking possible flights. I had been told if I missed my flight to Paris I would not be able to come, so I was really panicked. Finally got to New Jersey and then had to go by bus to McGuire only to find out they were snowed in. What a mess, it was just packed. We had to sleep on benches in the airport. Have you ever tried to sleep in an airport with three children? But, they were so good on the trip that I do not remember having a problem. I can't remember how we ate.
>
> I had to have disposable diapers for the entire trip, plus formula. I had the boys plus diapers, and I had checked all our bags and forgot to change shoes, so I had on heels. We waited and waited. I had to keep sending telegrams to my husband telling him why we were delayed. There was a nursery that I could have had the children go to, but chose not to as I was afraid I would miss the flight, and good I didn't because all the children in the nursery got chicken pox and couldn't continue to Europe.
>
> Finally was told the flight was leaving. It was about eight p.m. and off to France we flew, but at the boarding gate three fellows were assigned to help with boarding the boys, whether or not they wanted to.
>
> Once on board I found out each child had to be strapped in, even the baby. His feet kept getting caught in the web seats. On board, I was on my own; no help. I was so tired, but of course the boys were not, so I had my hands full, and trying to get them to warm a bottle was almost impossible. I had purchased boxed food for all of us as there was no other food. We landed in Goose Bay to refuel and had to get off. Had someone to help with each boy and someone to help me (as I was in heels in Goose Bay in December). There was a playpen for the baby and the other two could run around in the terminal while we waited. Back on board I was just trying to get settled when I told someone, "I think I am going to faint," and out I went. They put me in a bed in the pilots' compartment and I found out later they gave each child to a single person to care for. I woke up just before we landed in Paris. A staff car brought my husband to the plane as they would not let me get off until he was there. When I gave my passport to the inspector, he asked me why I didn't have it signed...Too long a story for him to understand.
>
> We then went to a hotel in Paris. On the way I kept saying, "I can't believe I am here." In our bathroom one of the boys found something and said, "Look, mom, a bathtub just my size." Well, you know what that was, and we just laughed. So began our stay in France!

Appendix 2.1 Project 7019 Orders

Courtesy Henry S. Brown

RESTRICTED

HEADQUARTERS
126TH BOMBARDMENT WING (L)
APO 17, US Air Force

SPECIAL ORDERS
NO 221

24 September 1952

E X T R A C T

3. Folg-named offs, and amn, USAF, orgn as indicated, this sta, WP Frankfurt, Germany; thence to 6403rd Pers Proc Sq, APO 959, FEAF, CIPAP, o/a 1 Oct 52 for TDY w/5th AF Units (Project 7019) for a pd of aprx ninety (90) days—DPUO. Upon compl TDY WP 6403rd Pers Proc Sq for rtrn trans to proper orgn and sta. Trip to FEAF w/b by Embassy Route. Rtrn trip will be directed by FEAF. Pers will rept NLT 1900hrs on 2 Oct 52, to Project Off, Baseler Hof Hotel, Frankfurt, Germany, w/bag. Total of one hundred (100) pounds bag for ea person is authd. International immunization rcd w/b taken. Curr immunization required are Smallpox (not over six (6) mos old), Typhoid, Tetanus, Cholera (not over six (6) mos old), Typhus, Yellow Fever, and Shick Test for individuals under thirty-five (35) yrs of age. Immunization must be at least fifteen (15) days old. Passports are required, and visas as fol, Pakistan, India, French Indochina, Saudi Arabia, must be secured prior to dept. Indiv Pay Rcd w/b taken. AF Form 5 of Combat Crew w/b carried. Exch of currency as needed w/b accom prior to dept. "You will contact CO, 6403rd Pers Proc Sq, for rtrn priority to proper sta, upon compl TDY". Tvl by all means of trans authd. TDN. JTR 22 Dec 50, as amnd, will apply. Cy pd vou w/b furn the FIQE B, the Fiscal Off, 7100th Hq, Spt Wg, APO 633, c/o Postmaster New York, N.Y. ATTN: B&F Off. Chargeable to: 5733400 380-502 P481,8-02 S61-502 L150. Tvl in Germany chargeable to: G1022-53 890 S91-506 L150. Fund Res No: 10. Mailing Address: APO 959, c/o Postmaster, San Francisco, Calif. ATTN: Project 7019. Stf Off, Maj Willey, will rept to Hq, FEAF, Tokyo, Japan, prior to TDY w/5th AF Units. All pers w/clear through 6403rd Pers Proc Sq, APO 959, Prior to dept fr FEAF, upon compl TDY. Priority to FEAF: MEET 1D 7150 AFIO. Auth: Msg, Hq, USAF, AFPMP-1 56417, dt 3 Apr 52. Fifteen (15) days DEALVP is authd.

Hq. 126th Bomb Wg (L)

RANK	NAME	AFSN	AFSC	CLEARANCE
MAJ	CLIFFORD A. WILLEY (Stf Off)	9[illegible]A	1435	Top Secret

108th Bomb Sq (L)

RANK	NAME	AFSN	AFSC	CLEARANCE
1ST LT	HAROLD R. BUEHLER	[illegible]	1224 C	Secret
2ND LT	BENNY L. DAVIS	AO [illegible]	1534 P	Top Secret
2ND LT	WILLIAM R. HALL	AO [illegible]	1534 P	Top Secret
A/2C	CHARLES R. MC KINNEY	AF 1[illegible]	32351 F	Secret

RESTRICTED

168th Bomb Sq (L)

1ST LT	LEONARD O. COLLORD	AO [redacted]	1224 C	Secret
1ST LT	HENRY S. BROWN	AO [redacted]	1534 P	Secret
2ND LT	WILLIS S. SHELTON	AO [redacted]	1534 P	Secret
A/2C	RICHARD F. FEICHTINGER	AF [redacted]	32351 F	Secret

Par 3, SO 221, Hq, 126th Bomb Wg (L), APO 17, USAF, 24 Sep 52, Contd.

180th Bomb Sq (L)

RANK	NAME	AFSN	AFSC	CLEARANCE
1ST LT	CHARLES A. WAUGH	AO [redacted]	1224 C	Secret
1ST LT	DENNIS M. MERGO	AO [redacted]	1534 P	Secret
2ND LT	ROBERT D. HANSON	AO [redacted]	1534 P	Secret
A/3C	WILLIAM M. WRENN	AF [redacted]	32351 F	Secret

*** *** ***

BY ORDER OF COLONEL KENNEDY:

OFFICIAL:

Hugh J Ray

HUGH J. RAY
Major USAF
Adjutant General

HUGH J. RAY
Major USAF
Adjutant General

DISTRIBUTION "A" Plus:

30 ea Off concerned
30 ea Amn concerned
2 for 201 file

RESTRICTED

ACKNOWLEDGMENTS

I would like to thank the following people who contributed to this chapter:

William A. Adamek was a Chief Warrant Officer at Chateauroux AB from July 1957 to June 1960 and October 1962 to June 1966. He provided me with a pictoral history of the Chateauroux Air Depot, "History Central Air Materiel Area, Europe," where the photo of Chateauroux tents in the mud appeared.

Nancy Brooks is the widow of Captian Wesley J. Brooks, a pilot in the 18th TRSq, 66th TRWg stationed at Laon AB, France, in 1962.

Henry S. Brown was a navigator with the 168th LBSq at Laon AB in 1952 who flew in Project "7019."

Daniel Buret was chief of the French Civilian Personnel office and is a resident of Laon, France.

Frank Casale was a heavy equipment operator with the 862d U.S. Army Engineer Aviation Battalion preparing for the arrival of the 126th LBWg in 1951.

Dale Peotter was an aircraft crew chief in the 108th LBSq at Bordeaux and Laon AB, 1951-52.

Charles Radloff was in the 2nd Air Postal Squadron at Chaumont AB 1952-54 and in Paris from 1954-56.

Sam Roberts was assigned to the Operations Section as a Survival Training and Personal Equipment Specialist at Etain AB with the 563d Fighter-Bomber Squadron, 1954-58.

Stan Thompson was in the 388th Com Squadron at Etain from May 1957 to November 1959.

Sam Whitworth endured the winter of 1952 in the old Luxembourg barracks. He was in the 117th Wing HQ Squadron at Toul until moving to Evreux AB with the 465th in 1955.

Hotel Powers, Paris.
Jean-Marc Noval

3

CONSTRUCTION IN FRANCE 1951 - 1960

NATO infrastructure planning began in late summer 1951, when 131 air bases were being considered. The planning conferences developed the concept of a standard tactical air base, flexible enough to meet the operational requirements of fighter-bomber, fighter-interceptor, troop carrier, and reconnaissance wings. Also included in the design plan were underground utilities and as much dispersement of buildings as possible to reduce vulnerability. The air bases would be built in three phases:

Phase I was construction of roads, one runway, taxiways, hangars and aircraft parking, and installation of limited utilities.

Phase II was construction of the standard NATO buildings.

Phase III covered the nationally funded buildings and support facilities required for both military personnel and dependents.

NATO's Standard Air Base

First consideration was given to the runway. Each base was to have one standard aircraft runway 8,000 feet long, 150 feet wide and 2 feet thick, and a parallel 80-foot wide taxiway. The runway sites were usually clear and level, well-drained, grass covered soil; most runways were built with minimum earth moving. The runway length, with headings into prevailing local winds, dictated the real estate parcel size and shape. Because the parcels were small, about 1,100 acres, and located around the main runway, each air base had a unique layout. This required extra architectural and engineering time and increased costs. The requirement for a 2,000 foot-long aircraft over-run area at both ends of the runway was added later. In the late 1950s overruns were paved to extend the runway to accommodate the faster century series fighters. Runways usually took about nine months to complete.

Also approved were three aircraft hangars with their maintenance shops and aircraft parking hardstands, a base operations building, an aircraft engine and accessory maintenance shop, a communications center building, munitions storage, and on-base utilities. Base facilities considered for joint funding were the wing/base headquarters, aircrew personal equipment (parachute) shop, motor vehicle shops, interior security fences, the fuel storage system, and two supply warehouses. Joint funding meant about 50 percent NATO and 50 percent U.S. payments. Each nation had to fund all additional base support facilities 100 percent. These were airman and officers' quarters, mess halls, administration offices, two or three additional supply warehouses, small-arms firing ranges, and connecting roads. Extra warehouse space was required to store Project SEAWEED emergency war reserve vehicles and equipment in operational readiness. This material was stored at all the main air bases but had to be segregated in base supply warehouses. Support facilities also included recreational structures, i.e., the base exchange complex, commissary, chapel, movie theater, service club, library, gymnasium, and dependent school. There were no provisions for funding runway approach lighting, off base radio navigation aids, aircraft firing-in butts, underground fuel storage, covered outdoor supply storage, a jet engine test cell, and many other facilities considered standard requirements by the USAF. (Fig 3.1)

Construction of firing-in butts for ground testing aircraft machine guns was not just a funding issue at Chaumont, Chambley, Etain, and Toul. Nearby towns and the flat terrain surrounding the bases made it difficult to locate them safely. To cut costs, firing-in butts were not constructed at Dreux and Evreux where troop carrier wings were programmed, or at Laon, Phalsbourg and Chateauroux. Storing aircraft munitions on base was also a safety problem at some bases so they had to build off-base storage sites.

USAF wanted most of these facilities that it considered standard to be funded by NATO, but it was largely unsuccessful in getting even joint funding. Since the United States paid 44 percent of NATO infrastructure expenses at this time, DOD and the Administration insisted these nationally funded facility costs be kept to a minimum. This cost cutting resulted in building base structures that never had sufficient working space. Thus even before construction began, limitations existed that would make our main air bases in France inferior to USAF air bases in CONUS and West Germany!

Construction Management

The U.S. Army Corps of Engineers was the agency assigned to direct all U.S. military construction projects overseas. The usual process was to have regional Corps of Engineers supervising engineering officers, commercial Architectural and Engineering (A&E) firms, and builders under contract; and the end user providing project civil engineering officers on site. The Corps of Engineers was very involved in all phases of design and construction in France because of its experience in West Germany. Construction there had been so rapid immediately after WWII that many facilities were substandard. This resulted in abnormally high operation and maintenance (O&M) expenses–90 percent of the original construction cost was spent each year on building maintenance within two to five years after completion. Roofs, plumbing, electrical and heating systems were the major areas requiring repair. The largest single share of construction money, 42 percent of EUCOM's annual budget, was spent repairing dependent housing in West Germany. No one wanted to repeat this fiasco with the new facilities in France; they hoped to have high quality construction using good materials, and offset these costs with lower O&M expenses over the twenty or more years of occupancy.

The basic A&E designs for these bases and standard structures were performed in the U.S. by Gilboy, O'Dea and O'Malley under contract to the Corps of Engineers. These designs were then converted to metric dimensions, so the French contractor could prepare accurate bids. Base site plans were prepared in France once the real estate surveys were available. The RCAF followed their own A&E designs, which is why the two Canadian air bases looked completely different than the USAFE bases.

In the beginning two separate offices managed construction in France; the Air Force and Army were each responsible for their own widespread projects. Both established Paris offices in 1951 to direct their civil engineers at each construction site. After about

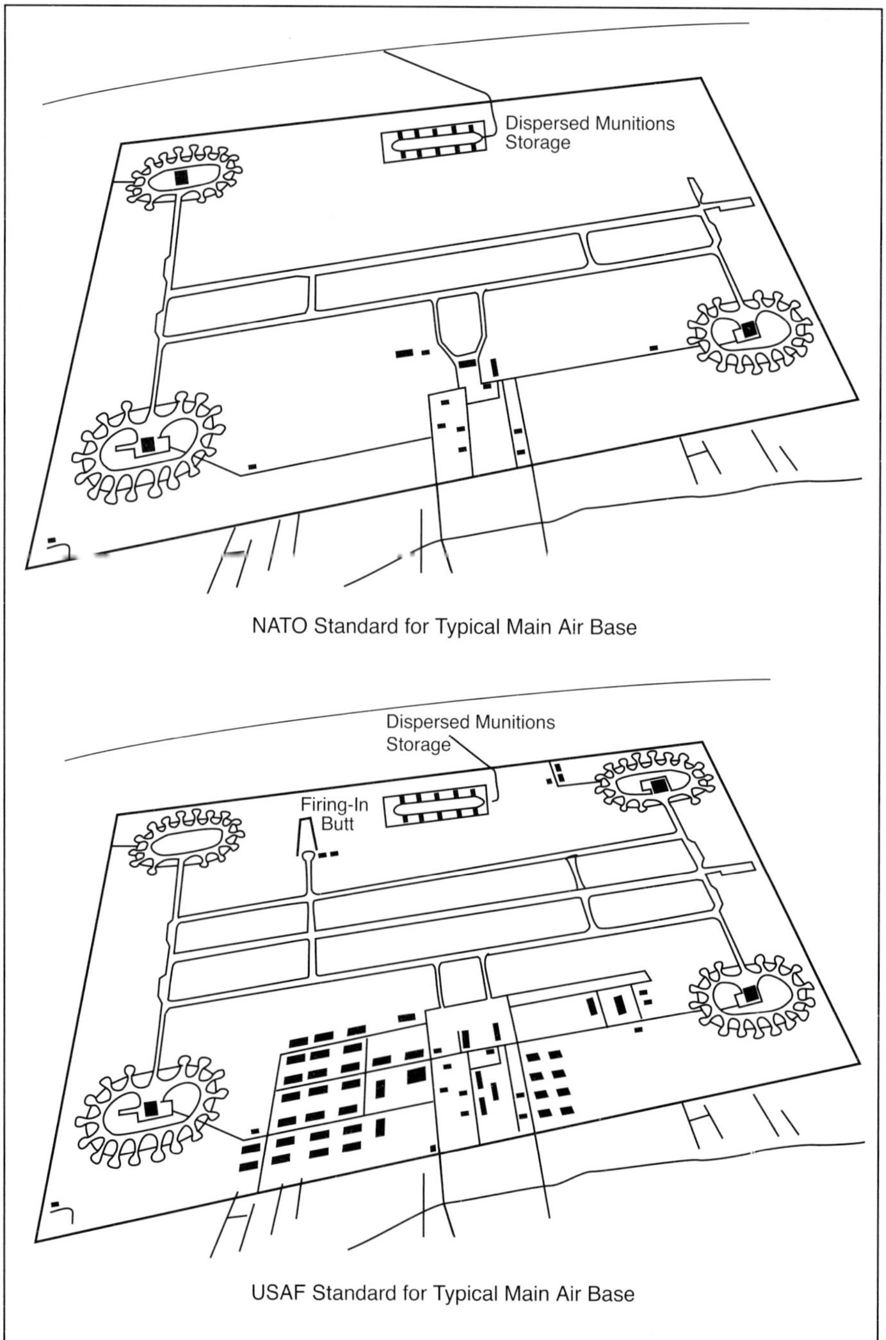

Source: USAF Aircraft Basing in Europe, North Africa, and the Middle East 1945 - 1980

Figure 3.1 NATO and USAF Standards for Air Base Facilities 1952

"Fighter Size" hangar and apron surrounded by a marguerite, 72d Fighter-Bomber Squadron, Chambley AB 1956. Note the revetment left front, it is possibly the only one built on the air bases in France.
Al Christensen

eighteen months the Pentagon became concerned that possible competition and conflict between the two services would be detrimental to completing the projects on schedule. Studies conducted during 1952, primarily by the Corps of Engineers, resulted in the formation of a joint agency to coordinate all Air Force, Army, and Navy construction in France. On 15 January 1953, the Joint Construction Agency (JCA) was established. It reported directly to CINCEUR, Deputy for Facilities.

The new JCA Central Office was established in Paris to command three regional offices. The JCA North District Office located just west of Paris in Boulogne-sur-Seine was the primary engineering center for most USAFE air base projects. The JCA Port District Office, located in Bordeaux, was the center for U.S. Army and Navy port construction. It also managed USAFE projects for Bordeaux-Merignac AB, the Chateauroux Air Depot and its Chize, Bacalan, Moulins sub depots, and the Cazaux Gunnery Range. The JCA Northeast District Office, located in Verdun, was the center for U.S. Army ADSEC lines of communications projects, and also supervised construction of the USAFE St. Mihiel sub-depot and Metz-Frescaty depot. The JCA took control of all construction efforts in France over the following five years until succeeded by the U.S. Army Construction Agency, France, in 1958. By this time the majority of USAFE construction had been completed; the remaining projects were 3,000 family housing units.

JCA offices and divisions were usually commanded by U.S. Army Corps of Engineer officers because most had higher rank than USAF project civil engineers. The USAF engineers were primarily captains and a few majors that had left the Army for the new Air Force in 1949-50.

Among the layers of French construction management was the Bureau des Ponts et Chaussees (Department of Bridges and Highways) usually with an office on each base to approve every detail of land use. Not a shovel of dirt could be dug without this bureau's approval.

Interim Tent Camps

Designs required for the tent camps at Bordeaux, Chateauroux, Chaumont, Laon, and Toul Air Bases were minimal and the interim bases were completed within five months. Whenever possible existing roads, ramps, and any existing structures were used although most required repairs. The major design challenge was insuring that the tent city would not interfere with future permanent base construction. The first step in construction was site grading, and ditching for drainage during the frequent rains. Gravel roads were constructed where needed. Next, water lines and sewage pipes were installed, then an overhead electrical sys-

French contractor building tent frames on wood floors. Bordeaux AB, November 1951. George Spencer

Tent canvas over wood frames on concrete floors. Chaumont AB, August 1952. Typical of all living quarters in France 1951-53. Charles Radloff

Airmen worked weekends to winterize their tents by adding wood and tar paper to the frames. Chaumont AB, October 1952. Charles Radloff

Winterized tents in the snow. Toul AB, January 1953. Sam Whitworth

tem with minimum capacity was installed throughout the camp. This site preparation required approximately sixty days.

About 230 medium-size wood tent frames and 25 large-size tent frames were constructed at each base. These took about sixty days to complete. The walls, doors, and rafters were wood. The floors were usually concrete pads such as those at Chaumont, Laon, and Toul, though the tents at Bordeaux and most of those at Chateauroux had wood floors. At Bordeaux the tent frames cost about $1,000 each. Concrete floors reduced the cost to $600 per tent structure. All bases used U.S. Army tents in two standard sizes: "Tent, General Purpose, Medium, 16 feet wide by 32 feet long" and "Tent, General Purpose, Large, 16 feet wide by 48 feet long." The GP medium tent was used for housing troops and officers. The GP large tent was used for supply storage, repair shops, squadron flight operations offices, and recreation rooms. Each medium tent could house eight to ten airmen. The limited base electrical system only allowed for two hanging lights in a 16 by 32-foot tent. Two coal or oil burning stoves provided heat in each tent during the winter. About five months was required to complete tent camp construction at each interim air base at a cost of $450,000 per base.

Prefabricated portable wooden buildings were erected for two mess halls, seven 200-man latrines, the wing hospital, communications center, and the base exchange. These prefabricated buildings could be assembled in a wide variety of layouts to fit the required function. Each interim base was provided with twenty-two prefabricated structures, except for Chateauroux. It was authorized sixty structures. The Base Exchange was usually a 2,800 square-foot, one-story structure; the mess hall would have 5,400 square feet in the usual "H" shape floor plan. Most prefab buildings were built on concrete slabs. The prefab

A fine example of a prefabricated wood building.
Mess Hall, Laon AB, November 1953.
USAFE History Office

Prefabricated wood building in the background is the latrine.
PSP pathways covered the mud, Toul AB 1954.
Sam Whitworth

panels were 8.2 feet high, and 4.1 feet wide or 8 feet wide, insulated and supplied with or without installed windows. Panels did not have any electrical or plumbing installed.

A serious international debate occurred over the use of the prefabricated wood buildings on the interim air bases. The prefabricated buildings were vigorously opposed by the French government because they were purchased in Germany by USAFE. This eliminated much local construction money. The EUCOM Commander opposed their use in France because the prefab buildings were purchased with West German Deutch Marks, money earmarked for Allied occupation that should not be taken out of Germany. These buildings had been used extensively on the new air bases under construction in the French Zone of Occupation in Germany, and USAFE was well satisfied with them. USAFE insisted that the prefabricated buildings be used in France in 1951 to speed use of the base and won the argument. Using these structures saved about two years of construction time in the early years, but between 1955-58 the buildings were removed and French contractors built permanent replacement structures. A few prefabricated buildings were still in use on USAFE air bases in Germany as late as 1998.

During this period of initial force build-up, the policy was to rent or lease indoor space rather than build new facilities, saving time and money. Monthly rents for two to four-year leases were very reasonable compared to new construction, at five to twenty cents a square foot per month. Indoor space was badly needed to store construction materials, building fixtures, military supplies, and for vehicle maintenance shops. Some bases such as Chambley, Dreux, and Etain were built in rural locations with no storage facilities nearby to rent or lease. The Chateauroux Air Depot was more fortunate in finding buildings to lease. The city of Chateauroux had been industrialized since the 1900s, and storage space was available for lease. Even hotels were leased for two years for officers' quarters while awaiting construction of the tents on base. The U.S. Army used portions of the pre-WWII Maginot Line bunkers for storage and living quarters; much of this fortification network was useable but without plumbing and electrical systems.

Permanent Base Construction

Standard building designs and construction methods were proposed for all the NATO air bases to save time and costs; some of these standard designs had been built on USAFE air bases in West Germany. The majority of the buildings were built with concrete block walls and poured concrete floors. Four standard NATO building designs are described: hangars, base operations, personal equipment shop, and wing/base headquarters.

Aircraft Hangars

U.S. air bases had three different types of aircraft hangars: fighter size, transport size and bomber size. These were always the largest buildings on the base and required the longest time to complete—thirty-six months. Three hangars were constructed at every air base except Dreux and Evreux. They had five large hangars for transport-size aircraft. Each hangar was intended to support a single flying squadron and provide shops and facilities for its organizational and field level aircraft maintenance. (Field level maintenance is now known as intermediate level maintenance.) Later a Base Shops building was constructed near the aircraft parking ramp for additional aircraft repair shops. The hangars were encircled by a taxiway leading to sixteen round aircraft parking hardstands that eliminated vulnerable wing-tip-to-wing-tip apron parking.

"Fighter Size" Hangar Chambley AB 1961.
USAF Historical Research Center, Maxwell AFB

"Transport Size" Hangar, Evreux AB 2002.
Still in use by the French Air Force at Evreux, with very few changes.
Jerry McAuliffe

"Bomber Size" Hangar Laon AB 1954.
National Archives

This circular design was called "marguerite" by the French because it resembled a daisy.

The most common hangar style was the 37,000 square-foot fighter size hangar. Three were constructed at each fighter base: Chambley, Chaumont, Etain, Phalsbourg, and Toul. The fighter-size hangar was large enough to also accommodate transport aircraft such as the C-47, C-54, and C-118.

Fighter-size hangars had six large 25 by 30-foot rolling outside doors that moved to both sides of center to provide an unobstructed opening 120 feet wide. The front wall above the sliding aircraft doors had a small, manually operated "tail door" to accommodate aircraft with a 40-foot high vertical stabilizer. This size hangar was considered ideal for the typical 1950 era jet fighters; its 13,200 square feet of open floor could provide space for ten F-86 fighters undergoing repairs. Two large translucent panels 8 feet by 110 feet were installed in the roof. The hangars were heated with forced hot air. Each of these hangars was surrounded on three sides by a single story, 16,000 square-foot concrete block lean-to building. It housed all flying squadron functions: headquarters, operations, briefing room, intelligence, personal equipment storage, aircraft supply rooms, and aircraft and engine component and systems maintenance shops. There were two truck entrances at the rear of the hangar to provide easy access to maintenance shops. Hangar floors were made of 25-inch-thick reinforced concrete designed to support 80,000 pounds per square-foot loading, which was adequate for the later, heavy F-100, RB-66, and RF-4C aircraft. Each marguerite hardstand was ninety feet in diameter and provided space for two fighters.

Dreux and Evreux had five larger transport-size hangars for their C-119G, C-123B, and C-130 airlifters. This second hangar design was taller than the fighter hangar and could hold two C-119s, three C-123s, or two C-130s. The large tail door would have to be raised to accommodate the C-130, and the Hercules was usually pushed in tail first. With the six hangar doors open, the opening measured 150 feet wide by 35 feet high. The hangar was 110 feet deep. Six translucent panels were installed in the roof. These hangars provided 16,500 square feet of floor space for aircraft maintenance. Large lean-to shops were constructed on both sides of the hangar structure.

Laon had three hangars of a unique design and size, called a "bomber-size" hangar. Its 19,500 square feet of floor space could hold seven B-26s or B-57s inside for aircraft maintenance. When the six hangar doors were open, the opening measured 170 wide by 35 feet high. The hangar was 130 feet deep. A single story concrete lean-to structure around the perimeter provided eighteen rooms for squadron administrative offices and aircraft maintenance shops. It also had two entrances on the rear hangar wall for vehicles. The Campenon-Bernard Company fabricated these three steel hangars, transported and then assembled them on Laon AB during 1953-54. This company supplied similar arched hangars at several French Air Force bases. The marguerites surrounding each bomber size hangar were eighty feet in diameter to hold one bomber each.

Base Operations Building

The base operations building was the second largest structure built on every main air base; it was located parallel to the main runway and adjacent to a five and one-half acre transient aircraft parking apron. This building contained the airfield control tower, flight operations center, airfield radio station, weather station, wing command post, flight simulator rooms, and base crash/fire station. It was five stories high at the control tower cab, three stories high in the fire station section, and two stories high in the operations wing. The building was 252 feet long and 50 feet wide overall. It usually required about twenty-four months to complete. The base weather station was on the first floor near the entry door; the flight simulator room, instrument school room, flight planning room, and flight center were usually down the hall. Wing command and operations post, wing operations staff offices, and the training office were normally on the second floor. Later, after 1957, a wing Combat Operations Center (COC) was constructed by modifying the second floor and eliminating two walls. The base operations portion of the structure was 32 feet wide and 110 feet long providing 6,600 square feet of office space.

The roof of the control tower cab was sixty feet above ground and offered the controllers a very good view of the runway, taxiways, and most aircraft parking areas. Control tower cabs were the highest point on the base with a good 360-degree view of the local flying area. Radio antennas were installed on the tower cab roof. Control tower radios sets, direction finders, and radar approach control centers were installed below on the third and fourth floor rooms of the core building.

The fire station occupied about one-half of the structure. The fire station portion was 38 feet wide and 120 feet long providing 4,100 square feet of indoor parking for fire equipment. The fire station had seven bays that could accommodate the largest USAF aircraft crash/fire trucks then being purchased. Typically each air base had the following vehicles: one R-2 crash rescue truck, four O-10A fire-crash trucks, (or later two O-11A and two O-11B fire-crash trucks) and two F-7 tanker foam trucks. Smaller 530-B fire trucks for structure fires were also housed here as it was the only fire station on base. Permanent living quarters for the forty-man crash and fire truck crews were on the second floor of the firehouse. Brass poles were installed to provide quick access to the first floor from the living quarters sixteen feet above. The seven fire truck bays had 13 by 16-foot rapid-acting overhead doors on both sides of the building.

Personal Equipment Shop

This building, usually located within 600 feet of the base operations building, was used to maintain pilots' and aircrews' personal flying equipment (PE). These were parachutes, life vests, one-man dinghies, helmets, flight suits, anti-G suits, jackets, gloves, oxygen masks, and survival radio beacons. This single story PE shop, although a small structure 70 feet long by 30 feet wide, was easily recognized because of its three-story elevator tower and very small upper windows. The tower was used for hanging and drying parachutes; an extended parachute is about forty-five feet long. After removal from the drying tower ropes, the parachutes were inspected, carefully folded, and repacked on special long tables, and then returned to PE rooms in the individual flying squadron's hangar. Other PE equipment was inspected, tested, and repaired if necessary at scheduled intervals, then returned to the flying units. It usually took fourteen months of construction to complete the personal equipment shop building.

Wing/Base Headquarters

The primary command and administrative center on each base was the Wing/Base Headquarters building, centrally located for easy access. Often this was the first building newly arriving military personnel and visitors entered. It was easily identified by the two tall flagpoles on the front lawn flying the American and French flags. These two flags could be seen from most locations about the base. Wing Headquarters was a large structure 180 feet long by 52 feet wide, built with concrete block walls and poured concrete floors. It was a two-story office building with 18,700 square feet of floor space, and contained the offices of

Above:
Base OPS Building nearing completion at Evreux AB 1955.
National Archives

Left:
Base OPS Building, Chaumont 1959. Looking toward the fire station wing.
Claude Ambraze

Left:
Makeshift Personal Equipment Building using damaged WWII building, Laon AB 1953.
National Archives

Right:
Personal Equipment Building, Laon AB 1954. Newly completed permanent construction.
National Archives

Above:
Permanent Wing/Base HQ Building, Toul AB 1955.
Norm Adams

Left:
Temporary Wing/Base HQ, Laon AB 1952.
Wing Commander's office in portable building, center.
Wing staff offices in tents, foreground.
Jerry McAuliffe

the wing and base commanders and their staffs. One large, 30 by 50-foot, theater-like conference/briefing room was on the first floor. The tactical group, i.e., the fighter-bomber commander's headquarters and staff were also located in this structure prior to elimination of this command function in 1957. The Wing/Base headquarters building required about twenty-six months to complete.

Base Logistics Facilities

The road network in France was adequate up to the main gates for the typical truck traffic required to support the bases. But all temporary roads on base had to be improved to accommodate heavy truck traffic during building construction. During Phase I and II construction, most supply deliveries were made by trucks or transferred to the base by trucks from a nearby town with a suitable railroad freight siding. Munitions were usually delivered by U.S. Army trucks directly to the storage sites. Railroad spur lines were completed during late 1951 and 1952 into Chaumont, Laon, and Toul air bases from nearby main rail lines; these spur track routes may have existed since WWII. Spur line construction into Dreux and Phalsbourg required about eighteen months. The French national railroad system, SNCF, provided excellent cargo delivery service to the air bases by building on-base rail sidings next to all base supply warehouses. Aviation fuels were the major products shipped into the bases by rail tank cars. The aviation gasoline or jet fuel was then pumped into refueling trucks for delivery to the flight line. The tank cars became handy storage tanks at the early air bases. Later, ten to twelve 100,000-gallon underground fuel storage tanks were installed, providing for 900,000 gallons of aircraft fuel and 300,000 gallons of vehicle fuels. Later after 1956, when the Army pipeline was completed across France, the POL products were delivered directly into the underground storage tank farms then on to the truck-fill stands. Truck-fill stands were the only above ground portion of the POL system.

Base Utilities

Utilities installed on each base had to accommodate a 50 percent load increase in the event of wartime expansion of up to 2,500 personnel. Originally it was hoped that natural gas, water and sewers would be supplied by local French utilities, but that was not the case. Most bases were located in rural areas and the small local systems would have been overloaded by the base population.

Potable water was the initial concern; France had a serious problem with contaminated drinking water because of extensive pollution that developed during WWII. U.S. Army engineers were successful in drilling water wells at several bases, which solved this critical problem. One of the first jobs on base was trenching for the installation of water distribution and sewage systems. These had to be installed before any paving began, but it took a long time to complete. Two bases required off-base annexes to properly site their sewage disposal plants. Sewage disposal pumps ran on electricity, making power outages a very serious problem. Water was stored in four to six underground storage tanks that held 50,000 gallons each, and was pumped throughout the base by electric pumps.

Inspecting the progress of digging a water well, Chaumont AB 1951.
Coleman Montero

Electrical power on base was always an issue. Commercial electrical service at all the air bases was obtained from the local utility, but the power companies required time to expand their service routes ten to thirty miles to supply this greater demand. Initially the tent camp load was only 175,000 watts, but the permanent base would require 2.5 million watts. All bases had two isolated, separate, above-ground electrical service routes to provide redundancy. The 15,000 Volt, 50 Hertz (cycles) service would go underground about one mile from the base. Electrical service was buried to insure survival in case of a bombing attack.

The difference in electrical power between Europe and North America has presented equipment operation problems over the last sixty years. Every base had back-up generators for mission critical electrical needs in the event of commercial power failure. A few air bases had two central standby generators installed in the central heating and power station to meet emergency requirements.

Telephone System

The base telephone system was installed by USAFE and wing personnel. An installation team from the 12th Communications Construction Squadron would work on the new base for about two weeks to install telephone poles and cables. A six-man team would dig and set about fifteen, thirty-foot long poles a day using two special USAF trucks. Next the wing's communications squadron would install the base switchboards and tactical telephones at all squadron headquarters, supply offices, flight line operations, and maintenance centers. French Poste, Telephone and Telegraphe (PTT) installed the underground trunk cable from the nearest town. This provided the base with at least six long distance lines into the base communications center.

Air Base Defenses

During this NATO construction program there were no provisions or funding for air base defenses in a conventional war other than undergrounding base utilities. No hardened shelters or earth revetments were created to protect parked aircraft. Additionally, at this time USAFE aircraft were either natural aluminum or painted in a silver finish, except for the black B-26s and B-57s. This made the parked aircraft very conspicuous and vulnerable. There were no U.S. Army anti-aircraft artillery (AAA) units located in France to defend our airfields. Anti-aircraft artillery facilities, i.e., gun pits, ammunition storage pits, missile launcher hard stands, and AAA radar director sites were not installed in France, unlike our air bases in West Germany and the United Kingdom. Bomb shelters, decontamination rooms, concrete defense fortifications or other hardened facilities for protection of base personnel were not constructed. The combat wings did train their air police squadrons to provide local base defense and site security. But the force was very small (eighty airmen, approximately the size of two infantry platoons) to defend the large area with many high priority targets. During the 1950s, base structures were painted white or cream making them very clear targets almost impossible to camouflage. During 1970-80 when the bases were operated by the French, they improved base survival by painting all structures olive drab and building earthen parking revetments around many hardstands.

Construction Problems

Lawrence Benson, author of an excellent study, *"USAF Aircraft Basing in Europe...,"* states very bluntly when describing base construction in France, "USAFE's expansion into France was slower and more difficult than in Germany or the UK due to extremely entangled diplomatic, economic, and political problems complicated by the NATO infrastructure process." The reader may get bored with frequent descriptions of the problems encountered when building our bases in France, but it is important that this history be remembered when entering future international military alliances. Today, when reviewing the development of USAFE facilities in France completed between 1951 and 1957, it's amazing that we accomplished as much as we did! A great debt is owed to the USAF Civil Engineers who served in France and attempted to direct this construction and produce usable facilities in spite of overwhelming obstacles. Inability to control costs, schedules, and quality frustrated them at every turn.

NATO air base development and construction was a struggle beginning with the initial agreements between the USAF, the French government, and the Department of State. Three major decisions affected the course of events in France over the next sixteen years. These decisions were:

(1) Only French commercial contractors could construct the NATO facilities,
(2) Only French building materials, labor and equipment could be used,
(3) USAF made the decision to deploy many tactical wings into France on an unrealistic schedule and expected them to maintain combat capability.

One clause in NATO basing agreements specified that foreign bases within each country be built with domestic labor and materials. France was still rebuilding its own infrastructure that had been destroyed during WWII, yet the NATO treaty stipulated that our resources, manpower and experience went untapped while local French contractors tried to accomplish these huge construction projects with outdated equipment and substandard material. By the end of WWII, France had lost 600,000 people, and had 70 percent of its railroads and its principal ports destroyed. It did not possess sufficient experienced contractors, labor, or heavy equipment to build all required NATO/USAFE facilities on the schedules proposed. Available building materials were often less than U.S. industrial grade, causing failure immediately after occupancy. Items such as doors, windows, pumps, transformers, motors, piping, insulation, interior hardware, and heaters failed frequently. Repairs to newly constructed facilities encountered long delays leaving the buildings unusable by the wings. BGEN David H. Tulley, U.S. Army, Assistant Chief of Engineers for Military Construction, voiced his frustration in the NOV/DEC 1954 issue of *The Military Engineer* as follows, "We are undertaking construction programs worth half a billion dollars in a country whose economy and capabilities can not and will not meet such demands within the time prescribed. Aside from the completely unfavorable construction environment which exists in France—environment colored by communist pressures, by lack of a dynamic construction industry, by absence of adequate national construction capacity, by complicated legal processes for real estate acquisition, by absence of any effective French governmental construction agency and reluctance to build one, and by the need for a stable government—the procedures which govern our construction operations are complicated and unique. Experience has proved these procedures to be time-consuming and mutually frustrating."

Another factor in using local contractors was financial. It is always very expensive to have American contractors build facilities in foreign countries. The logistics of working overseas and the increased costs for wages and per diem to attract skilled tradesmen considerably inflates the expense of a project. The USAF had recently been the brunt of congressional criticism due to high construction costs and delays at SAC's new air bases in French Morocco where it had used American contractors. It did not wish to repeat that experience. The prevailing attitude at the time was that U.S. companies would have built the air bases in less time but at many times the cost. When all the collateral expenses are considered though, that may not have been true. Several French contractors began projects, stopped work and then renegotiated a cost overrun increase or left the project completely, causing a complete recycle of the bidding process. Many construction budgets were increased 300 percent before completion.

During this period the USAF was authorized special heavy equipment construction units of the U.S. Army, Corps of Engineers known as U.S. Army Engineer Aviation Battalions. The USAF paid the personnel and equipment costs for these Special Category Army with Air Force (SCARWAF) units but did not control their training. In France these engineering units could not perform their primary construction missions since all major NATO construction projects had to be done by French contractors, but they performed much valuable work making improvements, alterations, and repairs to existing facilities. Anyone who has lived on base in France will remember SCARWAF for its development of trailer parks for on-base housing. A more complete description of the contributions made by SCARWAF troops will be found in chapter 18.

Permanent construction continuing at Chaumont AB, August 1953.
John Ibsen

Permanent barracks under construction Toul AB, 1955.
Norm Adams

Chaumont AB was one giant construction site in 1953.
John Ibsen

Going to work at the newly completed base shops building meant trudging through the dirt in 1954 at Toul AB. Norm Adams

Runway construction was always at the top of the complaint list; some new runways disintegrated immediately after completion and some were poured three times. Concrete spauling on the runways caused jet engine damage that resulted in excessive engine overhaul costs. In an attempt to minimize these problems, the French contractors were provided with large American built paving machines such as the Blaw-Knox rail mounted concrete spreaders/finishers needed for runway and taxiway construction. But they were not delivered on schedule, and without them other projects were delayed as well.

Lastly, winter weather played an important part in the construction delays. The winters of 1952-53 and 1953-54 were extremely wet in northern France, delaying completion of runways, underground utilities, and buildings. Mortar washed away almost as fast as it was troweled on the concrete block walls. Just keeping the network of base roads useable for construction vehicles was a full-time task.

Despite all the early problems, most base construction after 1954 was of good quality, and would serve USAFE well through 1967.

NATO Funding Procedures, "Slices"

The method of funding NATO infrastructure construction in France caused uncertainty and problems. All NATO nations agreed to share in financing the facilities required to support military forces across Europe. It was agreed that the nations would contribute money in proportion to their gross national product. America, of course, contributed the major amount, which varied from 45 percent of total NATO expenditures in 1951 to 39 percent in 1968. After the annual NATO military budget was determined by the NATO Defense Committee, they then prioritized construction projects. The result was an annual "slice" of funds earmarked for particular projects. Slice #1 began in 1950 and every year the slice digit increased. Choosing the projects and amount of funding for each project caused the most serious disagreement among the NATO allies. The cost of the 1952 slice had originally been estimated at $700 million but was drastically cut by lowering the standards of the facilities, and eliminating all facilities that could be delayed until 1953. Nearly 90 percent of that figure was for airfields. Some projects were underfunded or skipped-over in consecutive slices. There was no continuity of funding. Therefore, one slice might include funds for the runway but not the taxiway, with the following slice also omitting the taxiway. The USAF would then directly fund the taxiway to keep construction moving toward completion and hope for later reimbursement from a NATO slice. Funds from NATO sources and from USAFE sources were released to contractors at different intervals. This cycling of funds caused interruptions in construction. Contractors were repeatedly warned by the USAFE site civil engineer not to proceed beyond certain limits because they might have to wait a year or more for payment. This would probably bankrupt the French contractor's business and all work would stop. This "Slice" concept of funding made it impossible to support a crash construction program; it delayed progress and increased direct program costs to the U.S.

The U.S. Air Force created it's own problems by constantly changing its force structure plans from 1952 to 1958. Changes in mission and types of aircraft to be assigned to the bases resulted in changes in the layout and size of the buildings. At several bases buildings under construction were stopped because of design changes, or changes were made that increased costs not included in a currently funded "slice." DOD budget cuts frequently affected construction planning. Many construction projects at the Chateauroux Air Depot were canceled in 1954 when the USAF decided it could reduce the number of depot maintenance hangars needed by contracting depot work out to civil aviation companies within Europe. The USAF cancelled $8 million of construction at Chambley, Etain, and Toul in late 1957, though these facilities were built later during the STAIR STEP expansion period. All work at Chenevieres and Vouziers DOBs stopped in fall 1957. The microwave radio relay system program was cut $162,838 in May 1957, and another $7 million cut in July 1957, ending system construction. These cuts eliminated several relay stations. This resulted in decreased system reliability because longer radio paths would fade in and out at various times, depending on time of day and season of the year. The typical engineering motto of the day was, "Don't start vast projects with half vast ideas."

USAF leaders planned unrealistic construction schedules; they estimated eighteen to twenty-four months from "initial design" to "beneficial occupancy." This deadline would have been difficult to meet in the U.S. for projects of this size. Construction times in France were double these estimates. USAF officials refused to believe progress reports from civil engineers on site, and dispatched combat flying wings to Europe before their bases were ready for minimal operations. Air base construction had slipped one to two years behind schedule. This resulted in several combat wings programmed for arrival in France during 1952-53 arriving in 1954-55 at still unfinished bases. Their arrival meant construction of the bases was further delayed. Contractors were unable do their job efficiently, and had to reschedule work to accommodate the presence of 1,300 troops who required water, sewers, heating systems, useable barracks, and mess halls.

Construction of Dependent Housing

In 1950, in initial negotiations with the French Government, their officials attempted to exclude military dependents. The French team demanded that no dependents of U.S. military personnel be permitted to live in France, either on or off base. The government was concerned that Americans would inflate rental prices and drive the French out of their apartments and rental units. Housing in France was in great demand; 460,000 homes were completely destroyed, and 1,660,000 badly damaged in WWII. This was 20 percent of French real estate. Also, to discourage dependents from living in France, they proposed taxing base and post exchange sales as well as commissary sales, at 13 to 17 percent. France opposed the very large American BX, commissary, and housing complexes that were evolving in West German cities. While the U.S. never acquiesced to these demands, families were not permitted a permanent change of station (PCS) move to the new interim air bases in 1951-52, though a few families did arrive at Chateauroux and Bordeaux as tourists on a six-month visa. Suitable housing, even in the large city of Bordeaux, was difficult to find in January and February 1952.

The USAF Air Staff realized that making France an isolated tour of duty would create a continuous personnel rotation problem. Much negotiation was required with the French Government to settle this difficult issue. Agreements were reached in 1952-53 with France and NATO that produced the following rules: families would be permitted to reside in France under a status of forces (SOF) agreement, but family housing units could not be built on the bases. They were to be located a minimum of five to seven miles away from the air bases because France wanted to be sure that some money would be spent in the local economy.

As additional combat wings arrived, USAFE knew more families would require housing in the very rural areas of northeastern France. It would have to create new methods of funding family housing since the U.S. Congress did not want to authorize money for Permanent Military Construction (PMC) in Europe when an acute need for military housing existed within their home districts. Funding family housing in West Germany had never been an issue because construction costs were covered by German war reparations payments. By 1952, DOD, EUCOM, and USAFE established two unique methods of funding family housing construction in NATO nations; the first plan was called Guaranteed Rental Income Housing (GRI). Later, in 1955, Commodity Credit Housing (CCH) was added to the scheme. At a few bases GRI housing was also known as Rental Guaranteed Housing (RGH) but the financing arrangements were identical.

Guaranteed Rental Income Housing

GRI developments were planned communities of 200 single and duplex units built on one parcel of land near a large village or city for each main air base. France would purchase the land and transfer it to the USAF for these family housing annexes. The basic idea was that a French contractor would build these units, and upon their acceptance by JCA, the contractor would be guaranteed a rental income at a 95 percent occupancy rate for five years. Rents were computed based on housing allowance rates, at 30 percent occupancy by majors and 70 percent by technical sergeants. All married officers, and NCOs in the grades of master sergeant, technical sergeant, staff sergeant, and sergeants having four years or more of total service were authorized a family housing allowance as part of their total compensation.

While living in GRI units, officers and NCOs would forfeit their usual monthly housing allowance. All maintenance would be performed by the builders. In 1952 Congress authorized the JCA to award contracts to French contractors for U.S. Army housing. The first contract awarded was for 300 units to be built at Orleans during 1953. This original GRI program proved unsatisfactory because the homes were very small, the rents higher than programmed, and maintenance was poor. In December 1954, additional contracts were awarded to construct up to 234 duplexes in the Nancy, Poitiers, Metz, Ingrandes, La Rochelle, and Bordeaux areas. By this time most of the problems had been corrected. JCA also awarded contracts for USAF GRI housing projects in 1954. GRI housing was built in the vicinity of all the main air bases but one. Chambley was the only air base that did not receive a housing annex. The following bases received:

Chaumont—300 units	Dreux—260 units
Etain—110 units	Evreux—152 units
Laon—200 units	Phalsbourg—40 units
Toul—90 units.	

A 410-unit apartment complex, Cite de Touvent, was

"Cite Marquette" Open house at the GRI housing development at Laon AB in May 1956. The one pictured is a duplex unit. Families had been eagerly awaiting the opportunity to move to the modern homes.
National Archives

"Cite Brassioux" CCH small two bedroom house in 1998.
Jerry McAuliffe

"Cite Clark" GRI four-plex houses, Phalsbourg AB 1962.
Roger Warren

"Cite Lafayette" GRI homes built for Evreux Air Base are still in use in 2002.
This is an example of the large three bedroom home.
The homes are well maintained and retain their unique look with the distinctively American architecture.
Jerry McAuliffe

constructed about seven miles from the Chateauroux Air Depot under the GRI program in 1954. Approximately 1,800 GRI family housing units were built over the 1954-57 period, which helped ease the critical housing shortage in France.

Commodity Credit Housing

The second method of funding family housing in France began in August 1954 when Congress passed new legislation that raised the possibility of another solution—the creation of rent-free housing financed by the sale of surplus commodity products on the international market! In September 1955, EUCOM received orders to stop awarding GRI contracts and to begin building "surplus commodity housing." This new program involved a very complicated series of interactions among several independent agencies. The U.S. Department of Agriculture had accumulated a large surplus of agricultural products over several years, 1950-55, as a result of its subsidy programs to support American farm prices. The Commodity Credit Corporation, which handled these surpluses, made them available to specially selected commodities trading companies. These traders then sold the commodities on the international market, excluding the United States and France. Money obtained from these sales could then be used to finance housing for military dependents.

This very complex scheme proceeded as follows: work began on houses when the JCA contracting officer issued a payment certificate to a participating builder indicating the amount of money in dollars and French francs that he would receive for the project. The builder in turn submitted the certificate to the international commodity dealer, who paid the contractor from the commodity sales, after all expenses. U.S. military personnel lived in the homes rent free instead of receiving a housing allowance. Their allowance went directly to cover utilities and maintenance costs, and to repay the Commodity Credit Corporation for the commodities delivered to the dealer. (Figure 3.2)

Surplus commodity sales were lengthy processes with slow payments; commodity credits proved a very tedious solution to the still urgent need for housing in France. Negotiations between the U.S. military and the French over the payment procedures lagged. Both factors delayed JCA for one year in circulating an invitation for bids under the new program. In July 1956, JCA's North District Office solicited construction bids and received four viable responses. Negotiations with the bidders lasted until May 1957, when a consortium of the French construction firm Compagnie Immobiliere Marc Rainaut and the New York commodity trading firm, Bunge Corporation, signed a contract to start housing construction. By the time the contracts were in operation, JCA had been deactivated, and construction management fell to its successor organization, the U.S. Army Construction Agency, France. In total the surplus commodity program financed about 2,700 units in a score of French communities between 1957 and the early 1960s. Of these, the Air Force gained 1,600 additional housing units. (table 3.1) This strange concept produced funds for $1,309,000 worth of land purchases and $40,626,000 of house construction! There are no reports of either the French landowners or contractors not receiving full compensation for their property and building efforts

Both GRI and CCH housing was always in high demand with waiting lists as they were more comfortable and modern than houses rented on the economy. The housing constructed in France was similar to Capehart and Wherry projects built on USAF bases in CONUS. A few single, many duplex, and some triplex units were built in park-like settings with irregular street layouts that usually incorporated a large children's play area. The homes had a rectangular, single story layout, and four floor plans: small or large two bedroom and small or large three bedroom. Monthly rent in 1962 was $85 for the small two bedroom and $90 for the large two bedroom, $95 for the small three bedroom and $100 for the large three bedroom model. Energy costs were more expensive than in the U.S.

Table 3.1 Commodity Credit Housing

Air Force CCH Units			U.S. Army CCH Units			
Base	CCH Units	Name				
Chateauroux AD	615	Cite de Brassioux	Braconne	44	Orleans	131
Chaumont AB	108	Village Pershing	Bussac	52	Paris	40
Etain AB	382	les Clairs Chenes	Captieux	24	Poitiers	90
Evreux AB	175	Cite Layfatte	Chinon	42	Saumur	30
Laon AB	85	Cite Marquette	Fontainebleau	78	Toul	18
Toul AB	320	Toulaire	Fontenet	50	Verdun	146
			Ingrandes	88	Vitry le Francois	30

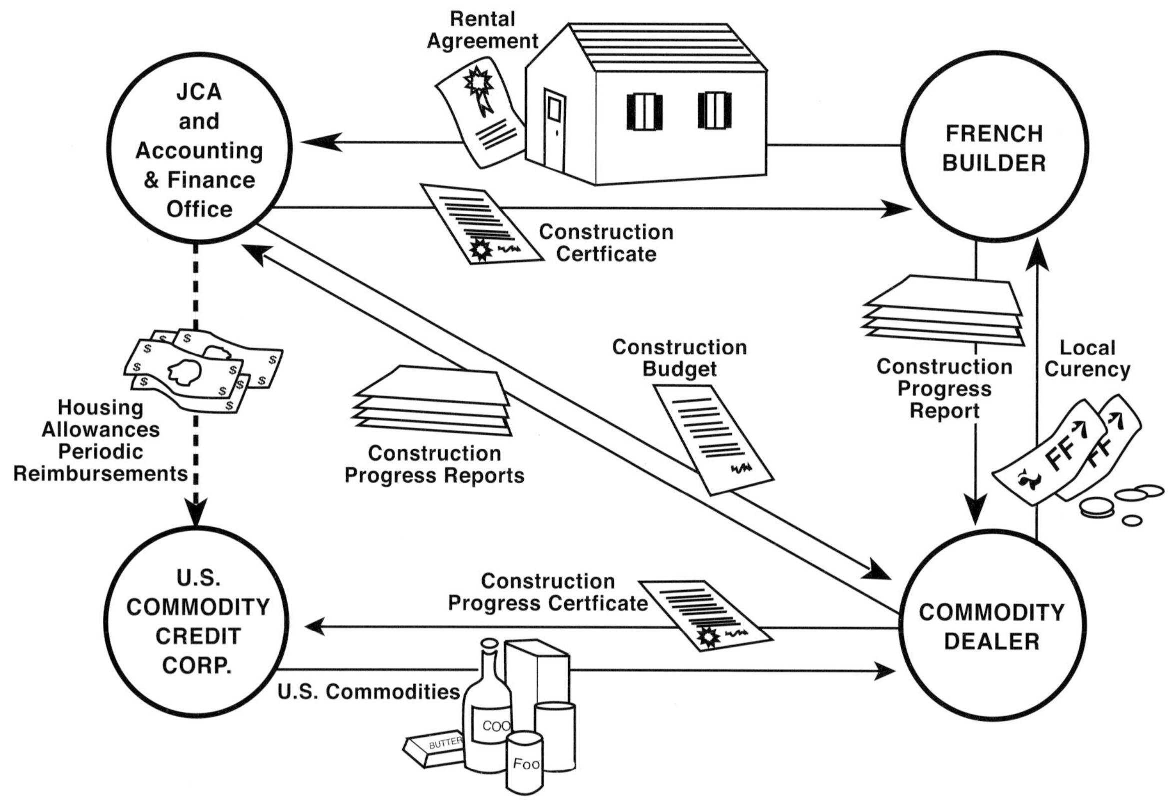

Figure 3.2 Surplus Commodity Family Housing Plan - France

averaging about $40 to $80 per month for electricity and fuel oil or gas. Many units had a side drive for off-street parking. A centrally located community center was constructed in the larger housing tracts. Some of the larger tracts had an on-site grammar school for grades one through six. These homes had one excellent feature that all families enjoyed and remember from the long damp winters in France. The floors were heated by hot water pipes in the concrete slabs. This energy efficient radiant heating system was installed in most CCH and GRI houses, and made it very comfortable for children playing on the floors. The homes came equipped with electric ranges, refrigerators, hot water heaters and oil burning furnaces. All appliances operated on commercial French electrical power, i.e., 220 volts alternating current, 50 cycles. Having appliances installed eliminated the expense of shipping them from CONUS and the need for power transformers to operate them.

House Trailers

Through Project Caravan, the EABn built trailer parks for 1,700 single-family trailers at the main air bases during 1954-55. Because the house trailers were located on base they were always in high demand with long waiting lists. Even though they were not as comfortable as GRI and CCH housing they were very convenient to all base facilities. The following numbers show the distribution of trailers among the bases. Bordeaux-Merignac was the only base that did not have family trailers.

Chambley—260	Chateauroux—75
Chaumont—128	Dreux—242
Etain—180	Evreux—317
Laon—218	Phalsbourg—76
Toul—243	

The house trailers supplied to the air bases in 1954 were eight feet wide, and between twenty-nine and forty-one feet long. Six different style trailers were procured for Project Caravan; the styles varied from simple, thirty-eight foot-long, rectangular metal boxes called "Spam Cans" to ornate models only twenty-nine feet long, but with seven windows, rounded ends, and curved roofs with overhangs. Most trailers had a double bed and two, short, "bunk" beds. They were intended for young families with small children and were very cramped for families with teens. All were well insulated to keep them comfortable in the

Official acceptance of completed trailer park built by the 862d U.S. Army Engineer Aviation Battalion.
USAFE History Office

winter but there was no cooling system for the summer. Portable butane gas tanks or oil heaters usually provided winter heating and every unit had electrical, water, and sewer services. Some trailer parks had telephone service through the base switchboard into the French telephone system. The trailers were parked on concrete pads with sidewalks and paved streets. Often sheds were added onto the trailers to increase badly needed storage space. Some men even built on an extra room or covered patio to expand their living area. Adjacent to the rows of trailers were community laundry rooms equipped with electric washers and dryers. The majority of the trailers were government owned, but a few privately owned trailers were also allowed in the park. Typical rents in 1957 were $35 per month for a small trailer and $60 per month for the larger trailers. Utilities were an additional expense paid once a month by the family to the base comptroller.

Construction Costs

The costs of NATO construction greatly exceeded 1951 estimates, which were probably wild guesses typical of emergency response programs. Some actual 1952 costs for each NATO air base were: runway-taxiways-aprons $3,500,000; utilities $500,000; tent camp $450,000; three standard NATO hangars $900,000; and fourteen standard NATO buildings $2,700,000. Total U.S. expenditures on air base construction in France approached $1 billion by 1953. The USAF and Joint Construction Agency allocated approximately $175 million per year from 1953 to 1957 and paid obligations of $150 to $200 million a year over this period.

ACKNOWLEDGEMENTS

I would like to thank the following people who contributed to this chapter:

Norm Adams was an avionics technician in the 465th Troop Carrier Wing stationed at Toul AB, April 1954 to May 1955. He then performed the same job at Evreux-Fauville AB, May 1955 to December 1955.

Claude Ambraze was the French Civil Engineer at Chaumont AB, 1951 to 1967.

Peter Brock is Battalion Chief of the City of Raleigh Fire Department and a military fire apparatus enthusiast.

Al Christensen was a Weather Officer in Detachment #10, 31st Weather Squadron, MATS, stationed at Chambley AB, 1955-1957.

John Ibsen was a jet engine mechanic with the 48th Field Maintenance Squadron at Chaumont AB from February 1953 to January 1956. His photos were kindly provided by his widow, Mauricette Ibsen.

Coleman Montero was in air force installations at Chaumont from October 1951 to November 1953. He acted as interpreter to coordinate activities with the French Ponts et Chaussees.

Charles Radloff was in the 2nd Air Postal Squadron at Chaumont AB 1952-54 and in Paris 1954-56.

George Spencer was an avionics technician in the 108th LBSq, 126th LBWg. He opened up Bordeaux AB in 1951 and Laon AB in 1952.

Sam Whitworth arrived at Toul AB with the 117th TRWg in January 1953. He was in the Headquarters Squadron at Toul and moved to Evreux AB with the 465th in 1955.

4

MISSION READY 1955 - 1958

The years from 1 January 1955 through 31 December 1958 were mostly positive for the USAFE in France. The usual creature comforts expected on an air base had been added, facilities for families had been expanded, and there was a constant improvement in aircraft tactical capabilities and improved nuclear weapons. But large budget reductions in 1957 caused serious problems for all USAF commanders. This chapter is divided into two parts, the advances made during this period to insure mission readiness, and a thorough description of life on and off the bases in France for both military and dependents once the permanent facilities were in place.

Accomplishments 1955-1958

Mission Readiness

Phalsbourg was the last air base completed and still waiting for its tactical fighter wing in early 1956. It would be in standby status until its first flying unit, the 23d Helicopter Squadron, arrived in October 1957. All combat wings had upgraded their mission aircraft, the 38th LBWg began conversion from its old B-26B/C Invaders to new B-57B/C Canberras in June 1955. By 1957 the F-86Fs and Hs were replaced by new F-100D Super Sabres. The tactical reconnaissance force was improved from RF-80As and RB-26s to RF-84Fs and RB-57As. The RB-66Cs arrived in Europe during 1957. The tactical airlift fleet was also improved by replacing the C-119Cs with C-119Gs, and the C-130A training program had started. The MK-7 nuclear weapon was being supplemented with the MK-28 external weapon to be carried on the F-100D Super Sabres standing alert duty in Europe.

USAFE achieved peak strength in France during the fall of 1957 with eight combat wings: the 21st, 48th, 50th, and 388th Tactical Fighter Wings; the 60th, 317th, and 465th Troop Carrier Wings; and the 38th Tactical Bombardment Wing. (Figure 4.1) U.S. military personnel in France in 1957 totaled approximately 14,000 USAF and 30,000 Army.

Major construction projects were finally completed during 1957, though some smaller projects remained at all air bases and at remote sites. USAFE facilities in France now consisted of one major European air depot with four sub-depots; eight main operating air bases, each capable of supporting a combat wing; and four dispersed operating air bases. Also construction had been completed at seventy-two smaller off-base sites that had been obtained from France. These facilities ranged from auto parts warehouses to sewage treatment plants. By 1955 the temporary PSP parking ramps had been removed, but a few bases required additional runway and taxiway repairs to improve operations. A microwave radio relay system was installed across France, and reliable com-

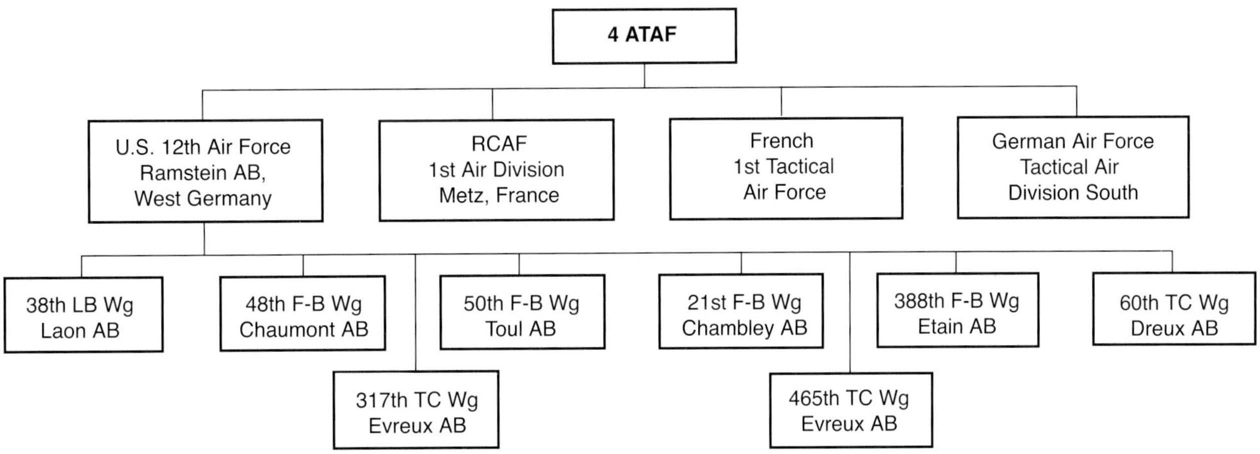

Figure 4.1 Fourth Allied Tactical Air Force, 4ATAF - 1 July 1957

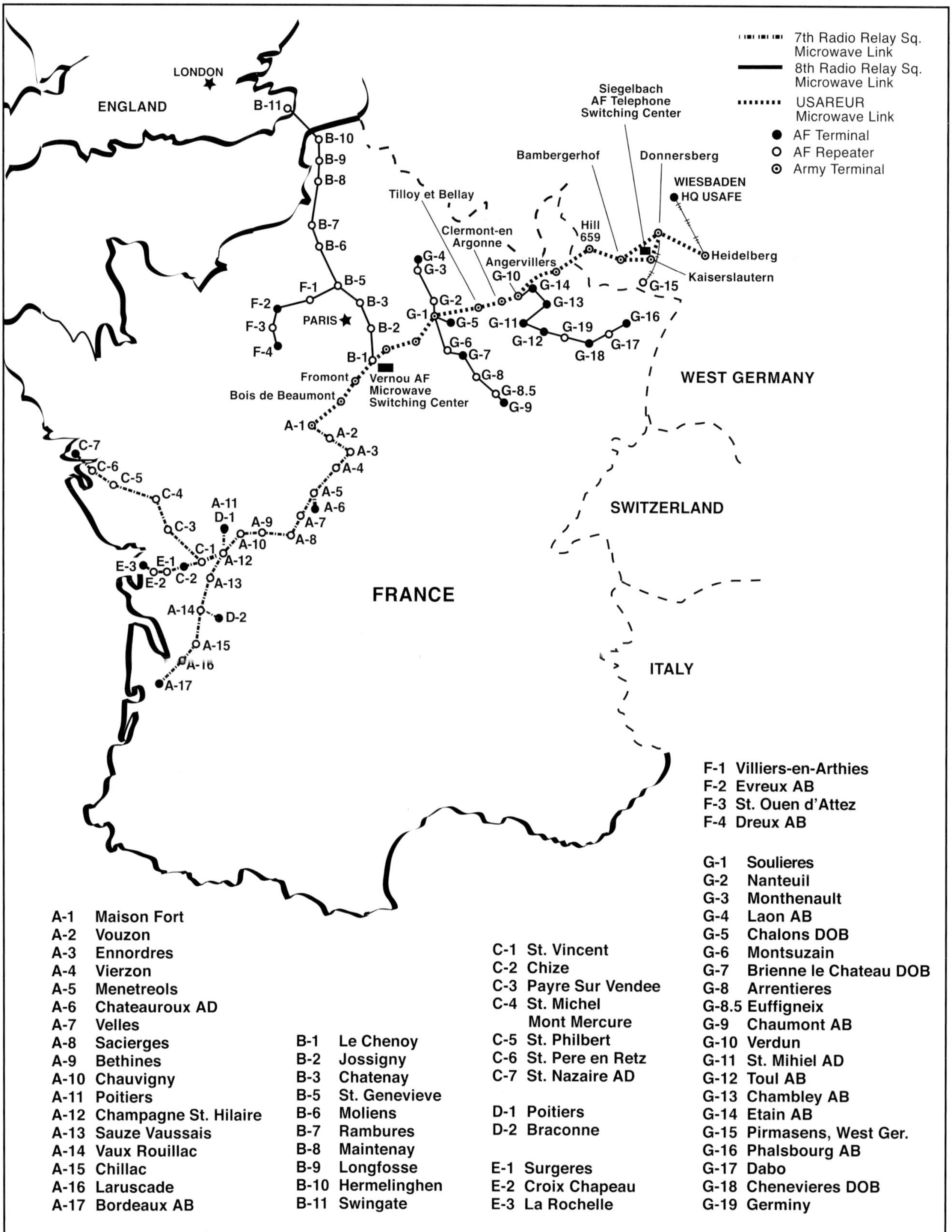

Source: Wayne Gors, 7th Radio Relay Squadron

Map 4.1 Air Force Radio Relay System - France

Radio Relay site Alpha-12 at Champagne St. Hilaire near Poitiers.
Jim Martin

munications existed from HQ USAFE at Ramstein, Germany, to all bases in France. USAFE and most of Western Europe had installed Ultra High Frequency (UHF) Command radio equipment to improve aircraft communications for flying safety. All tactical aircraft were now factory equipped with UHF radio sets and able to move out of the congested VHF radio band. Flying safety was improving throughout France as pilots and mechanics became more familiar with their new jet aircraft. Aircraft arresting barriers were installed at the fighter bases to reduce aircraft damage when braking was poor because of wet and icy runways. Aircraft losses in France were high due to flying in bad weather conditions, so the pilots warmly welcomed all airfield and navigation improvements. Navigation aids were gradually upgraded from on-base, low power, non-directional radio beacons to higher-powered off base NDBs to improve ADF approaches. Mobile GCA units or RAPCONs were installed and operating at the main air bases to improve night and bad weather approaches. By late 1957 TACAN (Tactical Air Navigation) ground stations were installed at most bases and the airborne TACAN radio sets were installed in all wing aircraft to improve flying safety.

Of course as all these NATO military objectives were finally being accomplished after seven difficult years, it became time to cut back, "build down" the force structure as the bills came due! During 1956 and 1957 much pressure was being applied throughout DOD to reduce personnel and operating expenses. USAFE took measures command-wide to reduce expenses. Almost all construction projects were cancelled, military personnel were reduced, and operation and maintenance funds were reduced 15 percent across the board. France became a good place to reduce forces. USAFE inactivated the 21st Tactical Fighter Wing at Chambley on 8 February 1958, and the base was reduced to standby status. The 38th Tactical Bomb Wing was inactivated on 18 June 1958 at Laon AB. Next on 25 September 1958 the 60th Troop Carrier Wing at Dreux and the 317th Troop Carrier Wing at Evreux were reduced to six flying squadrons and placed directly under command of the 322d Air Division. Additional savings were produced by closing Bordeaux-Merignac AB in 1958 after considerable permanent construction had been completed. This emergency staging base was returned to the French Air Force in 1959. These reductions eliminated approximately 9,600 USAFE military personnel, many of whom left the Air Force with early-out discharges.

In July the 66th Tactical Reconnaissance Wing relocated to Laon AB from Sembach AB, West Ger-

Golf-17 Dabo. Easternmost radio relay site in France, near Phalsbourg AB.
Tom Simundich

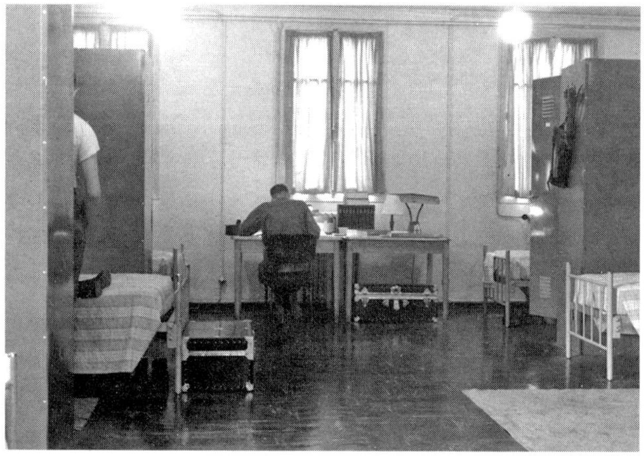

Crew living quarters.
8th Radio Relay site, Golf-17 Dabo.
Tom Simundich

8th Radio Relay Squadron Golf-17 Dabo station.
Directional parabolic antennas at top of tower.
Tom Simundich

8th Radio Relay Squadron Bravo-9 Longfosse station.
Next to last RRL site in France, working into England.
Located near Boulogne-sur-Mer on the English channel.
Larry White

Radio Relay site Alpha-12, Champagne St. Hilaire. Performing tests of the radio channels to insure system reliability.
Jim Martin

7th Radio Relay Squadron site Alpha-12, Champagne St. Hilaire. "Fly Swatter" reflectors.
Jim Martin

Alpha-10, Chauvigny, 7th RRL repeater site.
Jim Martin

Emergency power generator at Golf-17.
Tom Simundich

CMT-6 multiplex equipment on the left, Philco CLR-6 on the right. Champagne St. Hilaire, 7th Radio Relay Squadron Alpha-12 site.
Jim Martin

many, after phase-out of the 38th. This move from Sembach allowed USAFE to avoid anticipated protests about noise from the RF-101s programmed to arrive by the summer of 1958. The 66th TRWg had a record stay of eight years in France; it was based in France longer than any other combat wing.

USAFE Radio Relay System

A radio relay system (RRL) was constructed during 1954-55 to interconnect all USAFE facilities in France. This vital USAFE theater-wide system interconnected France, Germany, and United Kingdom air bases and supplemented the frequently intermittent national telephone systems. The RRL system crossed northern France and extended south to Bordeaux, west to La Rochelle, and north to Calais. By 1955 the radio relay system served all the main air bases, Chateauroux Air Depot, three sub-depots, three disbursed operating bases, and connected into nearby U.S. Army RRL stations in France. There remained only four or five USAFE sites in France not served by this system when RRL site construction was terminated in 1957 due to budget limitations. This state-of-the-art radio relay system provided constant USAFE/USAREUR/EUCOM/NATO command communications across France until decommissioned by Project FRELOC in 1967. (Map 4.1 and Appendix 4.1) The RCAF also operated its own RRL system in eastern France to interconnect its fighter wings.

The RRL system was operated and maintained by the 7th and 8th Radio Relay Squadrons. Headquarters of the 7th RRL Sq was located at Bordeaux-Merignac AB until late in 1957 when it moved to Chateauroux Air Depot. The 8th RRL Sq was headquartered at the Vernou site, Orly AB, and Dreux AB. RRL squadrons were divided into flights; each flight had an officer and a senior NCO supervising four to six RRL operating locations. The two squadrons had a total of approximately 24 officers and 780 airmen assigned to operate and maintain the radio relay system in France. The network used commercial microwave radio sets that provided around-the-clock voice and teletype services. This required each RRL site to be manned by approximately fourteen airmen, most of whom lived on the RRL site. Ground radio repairmen were kept busy performing routine maintenance and continual channel testing to insure very high quality voice and teletype circuits. Mobile truck-mounted RRL sets were available to immediately replace a damaged or destroyed fixed site. Microwave relay sets were installed at forty-nine off base sites and were easily recognized by their radio towers. Sites were spaced about thirty-two miles (50 kms) apart. Every site had one or two, eighty-foot high antenna towers with microwave antennas pointed in different directions toward adjacent stations. The RRL sites were installed on the highest hilltop available in the area and adjacent to a service road. Some were rather isolated but many airmen enjoyed the duty. Most sites were within walking distance of a small village. The RRL sites obtained their support, e.g., food, fuel, medical, base exchange, commissary, post office, and recreation facilities through host-tenant agreements with the closest USAFE base or U.S. Army post. Each site had at least one Air Force truck for transportation.

Tom Simundich who was stationed at Dabo relates an amusing tale of an event that occurred before he arrived, but clearly describes some of the benefits of RRL site isolation:

> A war story told about an event that occurred before I arrived at Dabo was about the Captain wanting to kick the complacency out of the troops who were smug about the presentability of the site after they had spent twelve hours getting it into inspection shape. The Captain walked into the equipment room, dirty; then the lounge area, messy; then the latrine, unsanitary; then the sleeping quarters, disgusting; and finally the kitchen, filthy! At that time the troops had pooled their money to hire a French woman of a certain age to cook and take care of the kitchen. When she heard the Captain's remark she let loose with her Gallic ire and lit into him saying, how dare he call the kitchen filthy! It was spic and span clean. The Captain cowered at this and left with his tail between his legs. He wound up having his complacency taken down a few pegs.

To add a little confusion, USAFE changed the RRL squadron designators in December 1962; the 7th RRL Sq became the 2058th Radio Relay Squadron and the 8th RRL Sq became the 2059th Radio Relay Squadron. The site detachment's numbers were also changed with no apparent numerical order. There was no change in mission or equipment and the network continued to function smoothly in France. In 1964 six sites were shut down south of the Chize sub-depot. These had provided a link to the now closed Bordeaux-Merginac AB and Bordeaux-Bacalan sub-depot. The RRL network operated through the summer of 1966 as the carefully planned system shutdown began in Project FRELOC. Usually RRL equipment shutdown and removal was the final step in closing an air base. All

RRL repeater sites were returned to France by early March 1967 after the equipment was removed. The RRL system was later reconfigured through Belgium to interconnect Third Air Force bases in the United Kingdom to USAFE Headquarters in West Germany.

The X-band microwave radio relay equipment operated over a frequency range of 7.125GHz up to 7.425GHz and used commercial Philco Corp. CLR-6 radio sets. The CLR-6 was also known by its USAF military nomenclature AN/TRC-30. This highly reliable equipment was off-the-shelf hardware developed in the 1950-54 period when there was a great expansion of microwave communication networks across the U.S. Each station could transmit and receive twenty-four telephone voice channels simultaneously, using Philco multiplex system CMT-4. This system could also handle teletype, facsimile, and digital data through its stations. Depending upon the station's position in the network, up to ten sets of equipment were installed; most sites had four sets. Every microwave radio receiver/transmitter and multiplex equipment in operation had a duplicate back-up set of equipment to assure 100 percent station reliability. The CLR-6 and CMT-4 were large and heavy fixed electronic sets; four racks of CMT-4 sets were 9 feet wide, 15 inches deep, 7 feet tall and weighed 1,300 pounds. Each CLR-6 microwave transceiver set was 2 feet wide, 32 inches deep, 8 feet tall and weighed 500 pounds. To improve system reliability every RRL site also had back-up emergency diesel powered electrical generators on-site, located in a separate power house. Philco Corporation technical representatives conducted training classes on CLR-6 and CMT-4 equipment at Dreux AB for newly assigned airmen who would man the RRL stations.

USAFE Navigation Aids Program

A brief overview of the USAFE radio navigation aids programs is presented here for the pilots and for MATS Air and Airways Communications Service (AACS) personnel who served in France. Early planning considered that France and NATO would supply the required aircraft navigation facilities at the air bases in France. France did have an airway system between major cities and adjacent nations using four-course, low frequency, radio ranges, and many marker beacons with compulsory reporting points and GONIO direction finders. Within France all airways communications used VHF voice radios. International airways used some VHF radio but preferred high frequency CW (Morse Code) radio. An excellent description of CW operation appears in the book *Departure Message* by Chuck Lunsford.

It was determined by winter 1951 that USAFE would have to supply all off-airways base navigation aids and local airdrome radio aids. Bordeaux-Merignac and Paris-Orly were the exceptions; all area, local, and ground control functions, as well as navigations aids were furnished by the French government. All other air bases would need equipment and operators supplied by the USAF and RCAF.

The interim air bases, Chaumont, Laon, and Toul, received their portable control towers and AACS personnel detachment by January 1952. Towers were operational on VHF 118.1 and 126.18 MCs by the end of the month, then the low frequency non direction, beacon navigation aid was set up on base at the end of the runway. The wing commander and wing operations officer would fly the C-47, and personally develop the instrument letdown procedures and publish the first IFR chart for their base! The NDB vertical antenna used a twenty-foot telephone pole giving about fifteen watts of effective power and useful signal out to about twenty miles. USAFE assigned the NDB frequencies and two letter identifiers: CU on 515KCs for Chaumont, CV on 344KCs for Laon, and TU on 477KCs for Toul. Voila! The air base was operational day and night, VFR and IFR, with weather minimums of 1,000 feet and three miles visibility. If conditions were less than this minimum, the aircrew would have to rough it overnight at Furstenfeldbruck or Burtonwood. Of course there was no approach, runway, or taxiway lighting, but that did not seem to be a serious problem for our WWII pilots. Rotating airport light beacons were operational upon runway completion.

In October 1952, Laon and Toul received their mobile GCA units, AN/MPN-1s. This important radar aid became operational in January after construction of an access road and parking pad. The GCA sets came equipped with their own diesel generators and operated from these units on a limited schedule until base power could be routed to their remote location. During the mid 1950s, the MPN-1s were replaced by new AN/CPN-4 or MPN-11 GCA units at every air base in France. Later, remote radar indicators were installed in the control towers to provide radar approach control facilities (RAPCONS).

In 1954 and 1955, NDB radio aids were upgraded with higher powered transmitters of 80 to 300 watts, and located off base about three to five miles to improve approach accuracy.

This relocation permitted taller antennas that increased NDB reception range. Additional property had to be purchased, a transmitter building constructed, and commercial electrical power routed to the site. Appendix 4.2 lists the location of these off-base sites. These real estate annexes were returned to the French government from October 1959 through March 1967.

In the 1954-56 period, Terminal VHF Omnidirectional Range (TVOR) navigation ground stations were installed on base at Dreux, Evreux, and Phalsbourg. only. Airborne VOR/ILS receivers were installed primarily in USAF bomber and cargo aircraft. There were no Instrument Landing Systems (ILS) installed on USAFE bases in France. ILS was available at the major French international civil airports, Bordeaux, Le Bourget, Marseille, and Orly.

During 1957-59, Tactical Air Navigation (TACAN) ground stations, AN/URN-3, were installed at all USAFE air bases in France except Dreux. Its installation was cancelled because the base was changing into standby status. Airborne TACAN UHF interrogators, which provided the pilot with bearing and distance data, became the U.S. standard worldwide aircraft radio navigation aid. It replaced the old low frequency (LF) Automatic Direction Finder (ADF) receivers. All the TACANs were installed on base, near the center of the airfield, except Toul. An off base site located in Rosieres, one mile north of the runway, was acquired to improve low altitude coverage. All ground radio navigation systems were operated and maintained by AACS personnel.

Life in France

USAFE Personnel

Following is a description of U.S. military personnel policies, 1950-67 and the USAF programs in particular that affected individual service during the Cold War. This material may help the reader understand the wide variations of service longevity and morale in France.

First, since its creation on 18 September 1947, all USAF personnel have been volunteers. But, most USAF personnel did not volunteer to serve in France, and had no choice in serving there. When notified of USAFE duty, their first thoughts were West Germany, next England or Spain, and lastly France. By 1953 the USAF community was well aware of the subnormal living and working environment that existed in France. Unfortunately, being forced to serve there created a bad attitude among some airmen toward France, the French people, and the USAF. Of course, a significant portion of the French citizenry did not want the USAF in their country, which aggravated the situation. The overall reenlistment rates in France seldom exceeded 5 to 8 percent of first term airmen, even after vast improvements in the middle 1960s.

After World War II, U.S. military plans were based on a regular military establishment of about 1.2 million personnel, and a larger reserve force of about 3.7 million, with 350,000 civil service civilians in the Departments of War and Navy. The active duty force would be divided about equally between U.S. and overseas basing. The reserve force would consist of 1.2 million paid and trained ready reservists assigned to units equipped with WWII stocks of aircraft, ships, weapons, and supplies; and 2.5 million unpaid standby reservists. Standby reservists had WWII service but the only connection with their former branch of service was annual notification of changes in address, family or health. The standby reservists would be mobilized as individuals depending upon their military jobs and rank. These reservists would be filler personnel for active duty units or activated ready reserve units, when needed for national emergencies. Whenever possible, base and depot support services would be contracted out to commercial companies to reduce military manning.

Prior to the end of military conscription in July 1947, a national debate ensued on how to maintain a peacetime force. Voluntary enlistments in the Army and Navy were not maintaining authorized postwar personnel levels. Congress refused pay raises that the Navy and War Department requested to increase enlistments. Between 1946-47 the U.S. considered Universal Military Training (UMT) for all males. The concept was, that after satisfactory completion of three months of UMT, a man would be offered an opportunity to enlist in the regular or ready reserve forces for four years. UMT never moved beyond Congressional studies and debate. Projected costs overcame serious consideration, and UMT was never enacted to meet U.S. defense manpower needs. Instead, Congress and the President chose conscription to solve the Army's manning shortages. The Selective Service Act was restored in July 1948 after a one-year suspension and continued until July 1973. The 1948 draft law affected only men eighteen to twenty-six years of age with no prior military service.

The new conscription law supplied men to fill the enlisted ranks of the Army for two years, but in effect, it provided men for all branches of the U.S. military, active duty and reserve. All Air Force, Marine Corp, and Navy enlisted personnel were four-year volunteers, but many were men who did not wish to serve two years in the Army. Amendments to the 1948 law stated that six years of service in a ready reserve component was acceptable service in lieu of serving two years as a draftee followed by six years in the standby reserve. This change solved the ready reserve's serious manning shortages in the three lowest grades; it brought most units up to 95 percent strength when the Korean War mobilization began. This law helped maintain the ready reserve forces at full authorized manning from 1950 until the draft ended in July 1973.

U.S. GO HOME scrawled on museum wall, Chateauroux 1958.
Ed Duquette

In France the U.S. Army enlisted ranks were primarily filled with drafted men whose tour of duty varied from twelve to twenty months depending on job assignments. Regular Army enlistees served thirty-six months. About 20 percent of U.S. Army enlisted personnel continued to be four-year volunteers.

The majority of USAF officers who were assigned to France during the first ten years were WWII veterans serving in regular or active reserve career status. Officers with no WWII service were volunteers drawn from a variety of commissioning programs, and had from two to six years of total obligated service. Sources of new USAF officers were the U.S. Military Academy–West Point (the Air Force Academy did not graduate officers until June 1958); Officer Candidate School; inter-service transfers; university level Reserve Officer Training Corps; pilot and navigator Cadet Flying Training; medical, dental, nursing, and veterinary schools; and mobilized individual USAF reservists.

Most officers who brought their family to France served an "accompanied" tour of duty of four to five years. Unmarried USAF officers usually served three years in France. Senior USAF enlisted NCO ranks contained many WWII veterans. Their tour in France was three years if they were single, but if they were married and accompanied by their family, they served for four or more years. The tour of duty in France for both married officers and NCOs was only two years if their families remained in CONUS; these men served "unaccompanied" tours of duty. Many officers and NCOs served in this status during 1951-54 due to the lack of family housing and dependent schools in France.

USAF airmen ranks were filled primarily with young, eighteen to twenty-three year old, high school graduates, single men, who were serving a four-year voluntary enlistment. Typically, an airman received five to ten months of basic training and technical schooling prior to assignment overseas. These airmen would then serve for three years in France. This resulted in a complete personnel turnover on base every three to four years. It was very unusual for an airman to be sent to Europe with less than three years remaining on his enlistment. Airmen and officers could extend their stay in France for one or two additional years if their duties and rank permitted.

Air Force Reserve and Air National Guard officers and airmen activated during the Korean War and Berlin Wall crisis served in France with their reserve units, or were assigned to regular USAF or AFRES units as filler personnel. The Korean War mobilization in 1950-53 was for a twenty-one month period resulting in fifteen or more months of service in France. The Berlin Wall Crisis activation, 1961-62, was a twelve-month service period, resulting in about ten months of service in France. All these reservists served unaccompanied tours of duty because the USAF would not pay for family moves for officers and NCOs serving less than three years in Europe. A few ANG and AFRES officers and airmen did bring their families to France as tourists at their own expense during 1952 and 1962.

There were very few female USAF officers and enlisted women based in France. From 1950 to 1955, the only female officer personnel were four or five USAF Nurses assigned to the Tactical Hospital in each combat wing. At the interim air bases, nurses worked in tents or the prefab hospitals and usually lived off base in nearby hotels. Later after 1955 when permanent base quarters were completed, authorization was increased to ten nurses. They were provided on-base quarters either in the hospital complex or in officer quarters. The Air Depot had up to thirty USAF nurses assigned to the 7373d USAF Hospital, including several flight nurses assigned to medical air evacuation duty.

In the 1950s, there were no Women in Air Force (WAF) assigned to combat wings. There were no WAF squadrons in France as there were in Germany, but the Chateauroux Air Depot did have six to ten WAF Officers assigned to administrative positions throughout the depot organization. Female officers were all single, and lived in women officer quarters (WOQ) at La Martinerie.

U.S. Civilians Working With USAFE

The largest group of U.S. female employees in France was the DOD school teachers. They were contract employees and did not have civil service or military status. The teachers were accorded officer status and had limited access to base services, but could live in government supplied quarters, though many chose to live on the economy.

Air Force Field Service officers were a group of female personnel working in France under USAFE supervision. They managed and directed activities at the on-base Service Clubs. Two or three women were employed at each air base except Chateauroux which had six club employees because of the large airmen population. These women were civilians hired in the U.S. and paid from non-appropriated funds. They had a three-year contract, were not civil service personnel, and usually lived off base on the French economy. These women supervised and directed the service club activities that provided excellent recreation services for military personnel and their dependents.

The American Red Cross (ARC) also stationed male and female representatives at each air base by 1955. Of course they were not in the military, but they received complete support from, and worked directly with, the base commander to provide emergency assistance to military personnel and their families. The ARC operated Red Cross Centers, similar to the service clubs, in some of the larger cities close to Air Force bases and Army posts. Chateauroux AD had a large staff of eight or more full time ARC field workers. They also operated a large downtown recreational center in Chateauroux. The ARC Hospital Unit trained "Gray Ladies" to assist hospitalized military personnel. The women they trained for this volunteer work were usually wives of base personnel. Red Cross employees were accorded officer status and had full access to all base services. They usually resided off base on the economy.

Two other categories of non-military U.S. personnel in France were Department of Air Force (DAF) and Department of Army (DA) civil service employees, both male and female, who had very special job skills. They had all voluntarily applied for job transfers from similar positions within CONUS, and usually worked in France for three or more years. Most of these Government Service (GS) employees were located at the Chateauroux Air Depot and at the JCA Field Offices as construction managers or inspectors. They could live in base quarters, in off base military housing, or on the French economy, and they were entitled to use all military services on base. The USAF paid for their relocation to and from France.

The final group of Americans working on base in France were civilian field technical representatives for U.S. manufacturers that supplied equipment to the Air Force, Army, and other NATO nations. These representatives worked under military contract clauses that specified this type of product support. Fairchild Aircraft, General Electric-Jet Engines, Hughes Radar Systems, Lockheed Aircraft, Martin Aircraft, North American Aviation, Philco Corp, Pratt and Whitney, RCA, Republic Aircraft and several other companies provided these highly trained field engineers. Their primary responsibility was conducting product training for officers and airmen, analyzing hardware failure, and providing technical feedback to company management. They were especially helpful when providing support on complex radio/radar electronic systems. These "tech reps" were very few in number—generally one man per corporation, usually based at the Chateauroux Air Depot or in Paris, and lived on the French economy.

All bases had an Emergency Plan for Evacuation of Noncombatants. This plan, required by USAFE, described the warning system, meeting locations, and list of very limited personal items allowed for rapid departure from France. The evacuation plan applied to dependents and American civilian employees in the event of war or political upheaval.

Military Life On Base

The duty and work of USAF personnel assigned to France was very similar to that in CONUS, with a few exceptions. Typical working hours were Monday through Friday, 0800 hours until 1700 hours and frequently a half day on Saturday. These hours varied within squadrons and shops; some activities were "round the clock" to keep the base in a ready condition for war. When the defense condition (DEFCON) within Europe was low, only about 20 percent of the workers were on a 24/7 schedule, and the aircraft were not in alert posture. When the DEFCON increased due to international tensions, all aircraft were placed on alert and pilots and crews as well as aircraft maintenance teams would be available around the clock. DEFCON alerts were practiced several times a year and involved extra duty hours for support functions throughout the base. The majority of the sixteen years in France, DEFCON was low. The alert teams deployed from France into West Germany worked much longer hours. Some sections regularly had longer working hours—many aircraft maintenance shops worked a 55 to 60-hour week because of personnel and parts shortages. Air police and crash/fire personnel also worked longer hours in France than in CONUS because of personnel shortages. Personnel turnover always required many overtime hours for on-the-job training.

During the early years in France military duties such as squadron and group formations, parades, flag retreats, inspections of personnel and quarters, guard duty, charge of quarters, and kitchen police were reduced to a minimum so maximum effort could be directed towards improvement of the base and the unit's combat capability. Native Son eliminated many of these additional military duties.

By 1955 permanent barracks were completed and living conditions had improved for officers and airmen. The primitive tent cities had been dismantled but many airmen preferred the old tents to the new barracks. The tents had offered more personal space and fewer rules, and some barracks were of such poor quality they were colder than the tents. The barracks accommodated ten to twelve airmen to an open bay, with each man having a standard steel cot, foot locker, and clothing rack or wall locker. The usual two-story building had four bays on each floor and could house about ninety men. Some barracks were configured into two-man rooms on the second floor for senior NCOs. Each barracks building had a day room and many squadrons installed washing machines. There were parking lots close to living quarters for privately owned vehicles (POV), but no garages.

The Bachelor Officer Quarters (BOQ) were the same size buildings but were divided into single and double rooms that shared a connecting bathroom. A BOQ room contained a bed, dresser, and closet for each man. Usually lieutenants and junior captains shared a double room, and senior captains and higher grades had single rooms. At most bases in France each officer had a single room because there was a shortage of officers and many lived off-base with their families.

Many air bases had one or two tactical flying squadrons located a half-mile or more away from the central base facilities. These men lived close to their work and aircraft but had to have transportation to the main base support services. A bus or truck was usually available, but it was often necessary to walk many miles to get around the base.

Most bases had hourly commercial or military bus/truck service into the closest towns or the centers of nearby cities, usually from 0800 until 2400 hours. Depending on which base you were stationed, missing that last bus could mean a long eight to twelve mile hike back in total darkness along French country roads.

Wing R&R Facilities

During the early years, 1952-54, the three combat wings established rest and rehabilitation (R&R) facilities to rotate men out of their harsh living and working conditions at the interim bases. Twelfth Air Force gave permission to the wing commanders to rent suitable resort buildings on the sunny Riviera. Villas were rented around Cannes in the fall of 1952. This was a great morale booster for the officers

Exterior of the newly completed barracks at Toul AB, 1954.
Norm Adams

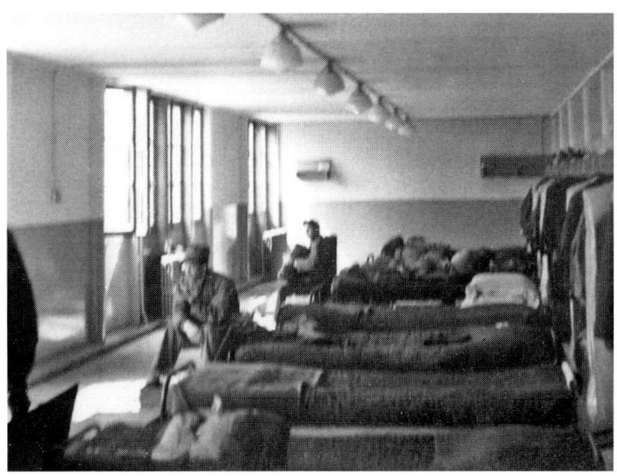

Interior of the newly completed barracks at Toul AB, 1954.
Norm Adams

and airmen who were selected from throughout the units to spend one week R&R leave. This was not deducted from the normal thirty days leave per year earned by every service member. The villas could accommodate twenty-five men per week and were free to airmen. Officers paid $2.00 per day for meals. Every Sunday C-47s from Chaumont, Laon, and Toul would fly the fortunate troops to the Nice, Cote d'Azur Airport.The base C-47s in France were well used; they flew up to 100 hours a month! Most men were able to get at least one R&R trip a year. The winter visits were a special treat; everyone really appreciated the clear sunny days on the beach after weeks of gray solid overcast in northern France. This R&R program continued until fall 1954 when the barracks were completed.

Unlike West Germany, airmen and officers in France could wear civilian clothes during off-duty hours, both on and off base, but there were advantages to wearing a uniform when traveling in France. Most French museums and monuments such as the Eiffel Tower and Arc d'Triomphe were free to uniformed personnel. After 1954 the majority of men traveled in civilian clothes in France. A coat and tie were required to get off base, which made Americans very obvious in the small towns. Class A or B uniforms were still mandatory in West Germany until 1955 when it became a sovereign nation.

Everyone stationed in France remembers being forced to convert his American currency into Military Payment Certificates (MPC). All U.S. military personnel stationed in Europe were required to use these certificates by the Uniform Code of Military Justice (UCMJ) authority from 1945 through 1959. MPCs were issued to prevent U.S. currency falling into Russian hands and being used to pay Soviet agents in America. The colors and markings were changed (without warning) every two or

Military Payment Certificates 1952
Jerry McAuliffe

1952 Ration Card, cigarette coupons on the left, hard liquor coupons on the right. Though the author did not smoke, he had buddies who were always happy to get extra cigarette ration coupons.
Jerry McAuliffe

three years to discourage black market activities and currency speculation. These paper bills were issued in denominations of five cents, ten cents, twenty-five cents, fifty cents, one dollar, five dollars, and ten dollars. This "monopoly money" or "funny money" was used at all military facilities, but could not be used off base. Pay and allowances were received in MPCs on the last day of the month. They could be converted to French francs as part of the pay process at a fixed rate of 350 FF to one U.S. dollar. Also, MPCs could be exchanged for American Express travelers checks for traveling in Western Europe, or for money orders in dollars to mail home. From 1951 to 1954 the franc varied from about 380 to 480 FF to one U.S. dollar in the international currency market. The fixed rate of 350 FF to $1 resulted in a 20 to 30 percent tax by France on off-base travel and purchases by military personnel. It was disappointing to see the 1952 American tourists in Paris cashing their U.S. traveler's checks at 455 FF to the dollar or receiving 485 FF for a dollar bill. Apparently tourist dollars did not cross east-west borders!

The last step before going home was converting MPCs back to U.S. dollars when departing from Bremerhaven, Rhein-Main, or Paris.

This low exchange rate noticeably increased military contracting procurement and construction costs relative to similar purchases in West Germany since the German Deutch Mark stayed constant at 4.2 DM to one U.S dollar. On 1 January 1959 de Gaulle converted the Franc to the "new Franc" decimal system, 490 old Francs became 4.9 Francs.

BX System

The Air Base Group was responsible for providing services for all base personnel. In addition to the base exchange (BX), the Air Force European Exchange System (AFEX) operated the movie theater, snack bar, service station, auto parts store, laundry, dry cleaners, barbershop, shoe repair shop, the "Stars and Stripes" newsstand and bookstore, and the Class VI and beverage shop. The AFEX in France grew into an excellent retail store network serving all USAF military personnel and dependents. It was managed by a few USAF officers and airmen of the 7480th Supply Sq (Special Activities) but was operated by American civilians and staffed primarily by French employees.

Each base tried to get a BX up and running as soon as possible so it usually started in a tent, then grew into a 2,500 square foot portable wood building, and finally into a 20,000 square-foot permanent building. This size BX at the eight main air bases would have a normal inventory of 11,000 items. The Chateauroux Air Depot had a very large 40,000 square-foot BX. Two large BXs and commissaries were operated in Paris at Rue Marbeuf and at Usine Louis Bleriot, Suresnes for local military and dependents. None of the AFEX stores in France equaled the large, department-store-like buildings found in Frankfurt and Munich that even included auto showrooms! BXs also had a full Sears & Roebucks catalog order service. Merchandise was usually delivered within three or four weeks by U.S. (APO#) mail. American and foreign automobiles and motorcycles could be ordered through the BX with deliveries made through local dealers or BXs in West Germany.

Very few items were rationed in France; only cigarettes and other tobacco products, liquors and spirits, and auto gasoline, to prevent black market dealing. We always questioned the concept of a black market for American liquors in France? Beer and wine were not rationed but hard liquor rationing was probably instituted to reduce AA membership among the troops that did not leave the base! Ration coupons were used to control purchases of these items. Each coupon was dated, and the ration booklet was issued in the pay line every three months. Cigarettes were limited to "fifteen packs of twenty cigarettes per pack." A carton of cigarettes cost $2.40 in 1956. Liquor was rationed to "one bottle of hard liquor per week." A forty ounce bottle of Seagram's VO cost $2.55 in 1952. BX sales had no federal, state, or local taxes. Cigarette and liquor rationing continues to the present day in EUCOM and USAFE.

The Class VI store sold beer, wine, liquors, and spirits, and was usually located in a building separate from the main BX. It carried a very wide, low-cost selection of excellent American, British, French, German, Italian, and Spanish liquors and wines. The troops learned to enjoy French and German fine wines while serving in France, but were surprised upon their return home to find almost no stores stocked them. They were ahead of the "wine" curve. The Class VI store was the place to buy common soft drinks also—a bottle of Coke cost five cents in 1954! "Class VI" is an old Army logistical definition of supply items used for "Personal Demand Items" (Non-military sales items). It's interesting to note that Class V is "Ammunition, all types."

By 1954 there was usually a laundromat in the BX complex. Prior to that, laundry service was provided by local French companies. The standard QM laundry washed and pressed most work clothes and cotton summer khaki uniforms. The BX tailor shop did

Permanent buildings at Phalsbourg AB 1962.
Barracks on the right, mess hall on the left.
Roger Warren

Base theater Chaumont AB.
John Ibsen

Giving some pointers to the little league team, Etain AB 1955.
David Alan "Davy" Crocket

Etain Pioneers vs Phalsbourg Falcons 1957.
Stan Thompson #26

Above - Christmas party held in the NCO club at Moulins Air Depot.
David Davis

Left - French orphans opening their gifts at a Moulins Air Depot Christmas party.
Most bases adopted a local orphanage and provided gifts and a Christmas party for them.
Ralph Spaulding

dry cleaning, pressing, and alteration of uniforms and civilian clothes. It was a favorite place to have stripes sewn on because they did such a great job. Also available was a large barbershop and shoe repair shop.

Of course, the usual USAF Clothing Sales Store was set up by 1954 on every air base to sell uniform items to officers and airmen. This store was not part of the BX organization, but was operated by the wing's supply squadron. In 1951-53 the clothing sales store was a semi-trailer van that visited the base about once a month from West Germany. Unusual items or sizes had to be ordered and picked up the following month when the van returned. Some common clothing items such as work shoes, OD coveralls, and blue dress shirts were in short supply as the USAF expanded during the Korean War.

The Snack Bar and Stars and Stripes bookstore were usually located in the large service club building and operated from 0800 to 2200 hours daily. Stars and Stripes provided an excellent selection of travel books and maps for planning vacation trips in Europe. It also stocked books for all age groups, especially for preschool children, and had a textbook ordering service for technical, scientific, aviation, and military history books. It was popular because it was the only place to buy printed material in English, except for two special bookshops in Paris.

Most auto service stations grew into buildings with six to eight service bays to provide POV maintenance. Repairs were usually performed five days a week and the gas pumps were open seven days a week and on holidays. Unusual American car parts that were not stocked could be ordered through the BX auto parts store. A common repair job was front-end alignment due to the very rough back-roads in Europe. This service station was separate from the base auto hobby shop where one could do their own auto repairs.

On-Base Recreation

Wing commanders felt it was important to provide enough activities to occupy the off-duty hours of the officers and airmen living on base. Even at the interim bases, snack bars and unit day rooms were set up immediately in tents. Theaters were set up in nearby towns whenever a suitable building to seat about 150 men could be rented. The next step was to build a theater on base in a sheet steel Fillod building. Service clubs were also organized in nearby towns in rented buildings large enough for a dance floor, game room, and snack bar. A base library was set up in a tent and stocked with books by fall 1952.

At air bases such as Chambley, Dreux, and Etain that were remote from large cities, providing recreational activities on base was a special concern of squadron commanders. On-base recreation was critical for that segment of the base population who did not wish to travel off base into a "foreign environment." Some airmen felt uncomfortable dealing with unfamiliar language, money, and food, and only left the base to travel to CONUS on one or two holiday leaves.

After permanent buildings were completed, many additional activities became available on base for all personnel including dependents and children. A large, 50,000 square-foot service club building replaced the off base club. It became the center of base socializing. The club had a large hall for dances, variety shows, and base-wide receptions; contained the base library with 15,000 or more books; meeting rooms for youth activities such as Boy Scout and Girl Scout programs, and a Teen Town. Many special activities were conducted here for dependents and French base employees.

Officer, NCO, and Airmen's Clubs, and Open Messes were very important meeting places throughout the week. These clubs served noon and evening meals to members and scheduled nightly entertainment, with bands and singers often coming from Paris shows. A bandstand, dance floor and large bars provided an off-duty gathering spot from 1700 to 0200 hours for Officers and NCOs. Many great parties were held at these clubs as people departed for CONUS.

Hobby shops were operated with non appropriated funds (MWR) raised by BX sales, and were well stocked. They offered arts and crafts classes, photo labs, and woodworking shops. Instructors were available to assist and educate, especially in the use of power tools. The most popular hobby shop on base was the automotive shop. It had all the important tools and machines needed to do extensive repairs, including alignment machines, hydraulic lifts, wheel balancers, welders, and a complete selection of hand tools. The auto shop supervisor was kept very busy advising on repairs for a wide variety of U.S. and foreign made vehicles. Repair parts could be purchased through the BX auto parts store, including parts for British and German autos.

Most bases developed a Rod and Gun club for hunting and fishing. Many French base employees also participated. Outdoor team sports became one of many tools used to maintain troop morale, and began during the summer of 1952 with inter-squadron games and expanded into USAFE-wide playoffs. Construction of a large base gym was a high priority so that indoor sports could be conducted during the long damp winters. Initially aircraft hangars were used for basketball games until the gym was completed. Chambley AB won the All Air Force in France title in 1955. The Chambley team went on to play Army as well as Air Force teams throughout EUCOM. Etain was named the top athletic base among the twenty-four installations competing for the Twelfth Air Force Commander's trophy in 1956, and won the Commander's trophy permanent award in 1958. Several base golf courses were constructed by self-help from officers and airmen, and special tournaments were held. Forty-seven players competed on 31 October 1957 at Chambley's last golf event prior to base closing. Baseball, football, softball, and soccer were popular outdoor sports. Football, of course, became the great fall event, sometimes played in very muddy fields after a typical Lorraine downpour. Local French citizens were always welcome at these games, and they enjoyed the unusual sports, foods, and their town names being used over the PA systems. Names of the inter-base teams were the Chambley Desert Rats, Laon Rangers, Bordeaux Red Devils, CAMAE Sabres, Toul Tigers, Dreux Plainsmen, Chaumont Mudhens, Evreux Normands, Phalsbourg Falcons and the Etain Pioneers.

Overall the commanders and troops did an excellent job of keeping active, and most importantly, bringing credit upon USAFE, their nation, and themselves.

Driving POVs in France

The first movement briefings for USAF personnel deploying to France were held in August and September 1951. They included the statement that POVs would not be allowed in France. That regulation was changed in mid October 1951, but it was too late for officers and airmen on their way to France, and the 126th and 117th air echelons. A personal auto could only be sold to another service member, not a French national, or France would impose a 90 percent sales tax. Special French registration was required for the new cars purchased in the BX. The new car faced the same restrictions as a used car brought into the country. It had to be sold to another military member or returned to CONUS with the owner when he departed France.

The author purchased a new 1952 MG TD sports car at Laon AB in July 1952 after a test drive on the base with an MG sales representative. I ordered it through the BX for $1,450 and could have picked it up at the MG factory or at the MG dealership in Paris. The MG came with the standard left hand drive. By mid 1949 British auto companies were supplying left hand drives to capture sales in the North American auto market. My workload did not allow me a seven-day leave to the Morris Garages, Abingdon-on-Thames, England, to tour the factory and drive the MG back to France. In place of a risky journey driving a new car on the left side of the English roads, I picked up the MG at the Paris dealer—Motor Comptoir, on Rue de Courcelles. The $1,450 price included amber headlight bulbs, French national vehicle registration, and the MG's passport. The passport or "Carnet de Passage" listed the auto's serial numbers and a complete list of its accessories. Every POV in France required its own "Carnet de Passage." A thorough inspection was made at every border crossing to be sure the auto agreed with its passport, and a tear-out page to certify this was left with the customs inspector. France

1952 red MG TD. Note the tourist "TT" license plates.
Jerry McAuliffe

The open road in France 1952 - just avoid the trees!
Jerry McAuliffe

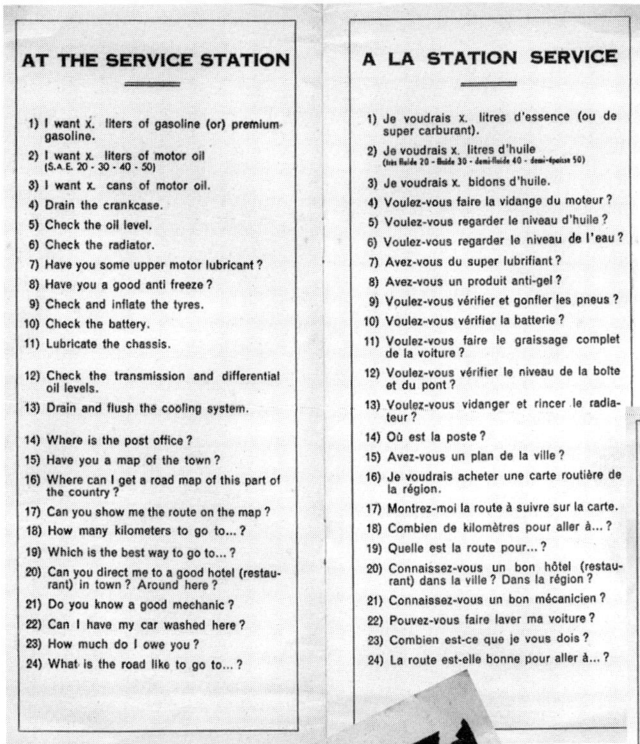

AT THE SERVICE STATION

1) I want x. liters of gasoline (or) premium gasoline.
2) I want x. liters of motor oil (S.A.E. 20 - 30 - 40 - 50)
3) I want x. cans of motor oil.
4) Drain the crankcase.
5) Check the oil level.
6) Check the radiator.
7) Have you some upper motor lubricant?
8) Have you a good anti freeze?
9) Check and inflate the tyres.
10) Check the battery.
11) Lubricate the chassis.
12) Check the transmission and differential oil levels.
13) Drain and flush the cooling system.
14) Where is the post office?
15) Have you a map of the town?
16) Where can I get a road map of this part of the country?
17) Can you show me the route on the map?
18) How many kilometers to go to...?
19) Which is the best way to go to...?
20) Can you direct me to a good hotel (restaurant) in town? Around here?
21) Do you know a good mechanic?
22) Can I have my car washed here?
23) How much do I owe you?
24) What is the road like to go to...?

A LA STATION SERVICE

1) Je voudrais x. litres d'essence (ou de super carburant).
2) Je voudrais x. litres d'huile (très fluide 20 - fluide 30 - demi-fluide 40 - demi-épaisse 50)
3) Je voudrais x. bidons d'huile.
4) Voulez-vous faire la vidange du moteur?
5) Voulez-vous regarder le niveau d'huile?
6) Voulez-vous regarder le niveau de l'eau?
7) Avez-vous du super lubrifiant?
8) Avez-vous un produit anti-gel?
9) Voulez-vous vérifier et gonfler les pneus?
10) Voulez-vous vérifier la batterie?
11) Voulez-vous faire le graissage complet de la voiture?
12) Voulez-vous vérifier le niveau de la boîte et du pont?
13) Voulez-vous vidanger et rincer le radiateur?
14) Où est la poste?
15) Avez-vous un plan de la ville?
16) Je voudrais acheter une carte routière de la région.
17) Montrez-moi la route à suivre sur la carte.
18) Combien de kilomètres pour aller à...?
19) Quelle est la route pour...?
20) Connaissez-vous un bon hôtel (restaurant) dans la ville? Dans la région?
21) Connaissez-vous un bon mécanicien?
22) Pouvez-vous faire laver ma voiture?
23) Combien est-ce que je vous dois?
24) La route est-elle bonne pour aller à...?

registered the auto and driver in international tourist status; the license plates were a distinctive red with white numerals combined with "TT" which indicated a tourist. So all the U.S. troops driving autos in France became tourists! American and German autos purchased through the BX were normally picked-up in Munich, West Germany. BX auto prices were excellent, a new 1952 VW "Beetle" cost $875, a Henry J Kaiser $685, a Jaguar XK-120 was $2,600, and the 1952 Porsche 356 was $5,200. Very few Porsches were seen on USAFE bases in the 1950s since $5,200

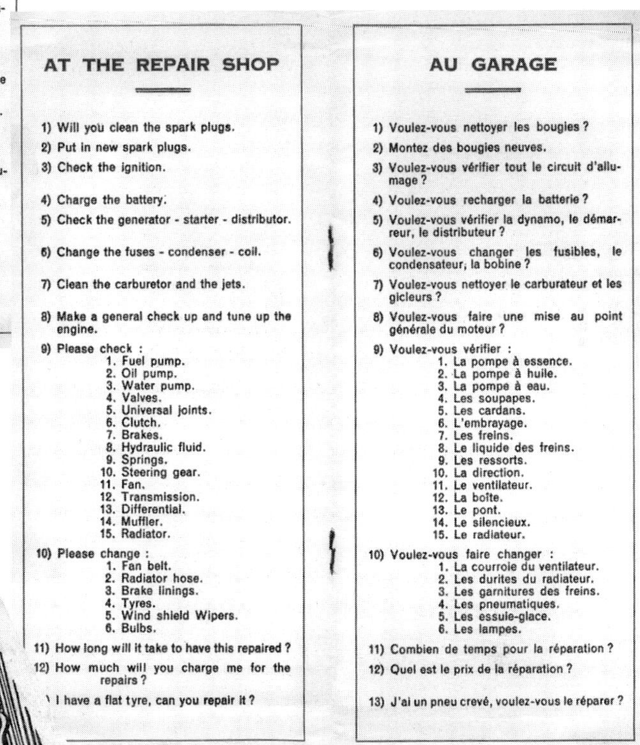

AT THE REPAIR SHOP

1) Will you clean the spark plugs.
2) Put in new spark plugs.
3) Check the ignition.
4) Charge the battery.
5) Check the generator - starter - distributor.
6) Change the fuses - condenser - coil.
7) Clean the carburetor and the jets.
8) Make a general check up and tune up the engine.
9) Please check:
1. Fuel pump.
2. Oil pump.
3. Water pump.
4. Valves.
5. Universal joints.
6. Clutch.
7. Brakes.
8. Hydraulic fluid.
9. Springs.
10. Steering gear.
11. Fan.
12. Transmission.
13. Differential.
14. Muffler.
15. Radiator.
10) Please change:
1. Fan belt.
2. Radiator hose.
3. Brake linings.
4. Tyres.
5. Wind shield Wipers.
6. Bulbs.
11) How long will it take to have this repaired?
12) How much will you charge me for the repairs?
13) I have a flat tyre, can you repair it?

AU GARAGE

1) Voulez-vous nettoyer les bougies?
2) Montez des bougies neuves.
3) Voulez-vous vérifier tout le circuit d'allumage?
4) Voulez-vous recharger la batterie?
5) Voulez-vous vérifier la dynamo, le démarreur, le distributeur?
6) Voulez-vous changer les fusibles, le condensateur, la bobine?
7) Voulez-vous nettoyer le carburateur et les gicleurs?
8) Voulez-vous faire une mise au point générale du moteur?
9) Voulez-vous vérifier:
1. La pompe à essence.
2. La pompe à huile.
3. La pompe à eau.
4. Les soupapes.
5. Les cardans.
6. L'embrayage.
7. Les freins.
8. Le liquide des freins.
9. Les ressorts.
10. La direction.
11. Le ventilateur.
12. La boîte.
13. Le pont.
14. Le silencieux.
15. Le radiateur.
10) Voulez-vous faire changer:
1. La courroie du ventilateur.
2. Les durites du radiateur.
3. Les garnitures des freins.
4. Les pneumatiques.
5. Les essuie-glace.
6. Les lampes.
11) Combien de temps pour la réparation?
12) Quel est le prix de la réparation?
13) J'ai un pneu crevé, voulez-vous le réparer?

ESSO folder with auto questions translated.

Below is the vital claim check to retrive my MG at the port of New York.

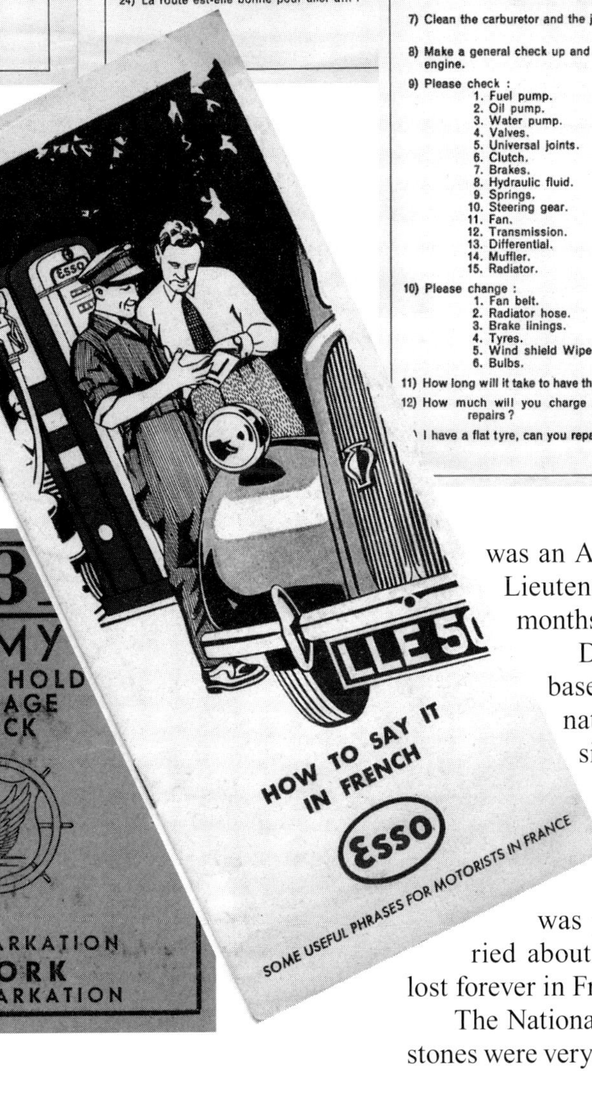

was an A2C's income for five years and a 1st Lieutenant's income for about twenty-five months.

Driving in France required some on base training to learn the laws and international road signs, including conversion from miles to kilometers. ESSO provided a handy folder with auto and route questions in English and the corresponding French. This was a great help; all the driver had to do was point to his question. I always worried about losing that ESSO folder and being lost forever in France.

The National Routes with their red-topped headstones were very good two lane highways. The Departmental Roads with yellow topped markers were narrow and winding, and at times rough, but ideal for sport car touring. Virtually all National Route intersections were in the center of cities and towns and looped around the Cathedral. Missing the desired exit sign just meant another swing around the Cathedral. In 1952-55, France was almost in total blackness at night. No road signs were illuminated, and with the amber headlights on LOW beam it was easy to miss a turn-off. Traffic was minimal after 2200hrs, so one could just select reverse, back-up past the missed intersection, turn onto the correct route and proceed onward. On three trips in fall 1952 from Paris to Laon at 0200hrs, I did not see a single auto in either direction for sixty miles on NR2.

Gasoline for POVs was limited to twenty gallons a month for small engine autos such as Henry Js, Volkswagons, MG TDs, and Simcas. Larger autos, primarily American, were allowed thirty gallons a month. Gasoline ration coupons were purchased in five-gallon increments in the monthly pay formation. In 1952 each auto gasoline coupon cost seventy-five cents (fifteen cents a gallon). By 1958, a gallon of gas cost twenty-six cents, and by 1966 it was thirty-three cents a gallon. This price was about five to seven cents less than the CONUS open market. Eastern Standard Seaboard Oil (ESSO) Corporation was selected by the Army Quartermaster to supply auto fuel in Western Europe; therefore, ESSO gasoline was sold on all U.S. military facilities and at selected service stations off base that accepted the ration coupons. ESSO issued special maps showing the location of these stations. They were not plentiful in France but were common on the German Autobahns. Drivers carried a small, five-liter can of gas in their cars as insurance. Gas stations in France closed by 2100hrs, and also no one wanted to run out of gas in a town that did not have an ESSO station that accepted ration coupons! Gasoline cost seventy-five to eighty cents a gallon on the French economy; it was heavily taxed to discourage auto ownership. European nations did not want their very limited highway networks overloaded.

Michelin maps were excellent, except the old versions covered so small an area that everyone had to have four to six maps in the glove box. Parking was no problem in Paris and other large cities. The MG had no door locks and nothing was ever taken from it.

Touring northeastern France on Sunday afternoons was great fun. The Marne and Aisne River Valley roads were terrific MG roads, and there were many WWI and WWII battlefields and monuments to visit. Many detours were encountered though, due to bombed out bridges and major road repairs. The touring day would end with a very long supper of excellent food and wine at a small roadside restaurant. The problem was to remember to stop before 1700hrs because by 1730hrs the door would be locked. Restaurants in France closed their doors early because they planned for one seating a night. Hotels operated on the same schedule except in small towns where they locked up for the night at 1630hrs! Of course the guests could come and go because they were given keys to the hotel's front door. I spent a few nights in the MG while learning the French schedules. Sleeping in the car was not frowned upon, but the parking lights had to be on all night if the car was parked on a street or in a public parking lot. Otherwise the Gendarme would ride up on his bicycle, wake you, and politely remind you to turn them on. It is amazing for me to drive across national boundaries today and see only unmanned border stations, and now, with the Euro there is not even a stop to pick up some different currency. We did live in a very different world just fifty-three years ago!

The final episode of my 1952 MG TD story is that I shipped it home through Bremerhaven, and it arrived safe and sound at the Brooklyn Navy Yard prior to my arrival at Camp Kilmer. The MG started smartly after twenty-eight days, and I drove it around New York City for a few days, and then finally back to Chicago, Illinois. The only problem I had was being stopped at least twice a day for having very strange license plates. Laying out the "Carnet du Passage" really impressed the Pennsylvania Turnpike police! I never got a traffic citation because of those "funny plates," but I drove in my Class A blues to help explain the whole story. The 1952 MG TD still sits in my garage awaiting restoration.

Many USAF veterans and their families have fond memories of driving around France and long trips to Garmisch, West Germany, and Switzerland. Unfortunately, as the autos increased in France during the late 1950s and through the 1960s, automobile and motorcycle accidents became a very serious problem for all commanders. Traffic fatalities and property damage increased alarmingly. Many safe driver training programs and vehicle inspections were instituted at every base to reduce this accident rate; an estimated 200 USAFE personnel and dependents were killed from 1950 to 1967 in automobile accidents.

Dependent Housing

Project Caravan provided the on-base trailers and the GRI and CCH developments gave the families comfortable homes, but many air force families decided to live off base on the French economy. This was also known as "going native." In many places it was the only housing available until a vacancy came up in GRI, CCH, or the on-base trailers. Military housing offices were established in the larger cities to list rentals and handle rental agreements. The offices employed a large number of translators to assist in the process. Housing varied from small apartments carved out of larger homes, to freestanding homes, but none had the conveniences Americans were used to. USAF personnel living off base, whether on the economy, in GRI, or CCH housing, were subject to a French house tax and auto tax that totaled about $100 per year. Usually all housing was unfurnished, except for the trailers. Household goods and POVs were shipped at government expense. During the 1952-55 period, goods arrived at the Port of Bremerhaven and later during 1955-1967, the port of La Pallice. POVs had to be picked up by their owners and driven to their new duty stations, but the Army Transportation Corps contracted with French moving companies to deliver the household goods. They unpacked the containers and carried the family's possessions into their new home. Some families were briefed on what to bring to France, what was unnecessary, and what would probably not function there; and then again, others never got any advice. Many U.S. electrical items such as television sets, phonograph players, clocks, timers, and some radio sets would not operate on French electrical power. Large appliances never operated properly on France's 50 Hz power. Normal shipping time for family autos and household goods was seven to ten weeks in each direction.

Living in France, whether in military housing or on the economy was a very interesting and unusual experience that most Air Force families will never forget, as one Air Force wife relates:

> Our first house was in the village of Champs about 25 miles from Laon AB. Getting our furniture into the house was a problem as the staircase had a curve and it was very hard to get box springs around the curve. Our couch had to be put through the front room window! When the movers saw what I was unpacking they thought we were rich! What a laugh! I had so many unique experiences living there. We could not drink the water, so we had to bring water from the base. We washed our produce in bleach water. We had to bring fuel for our heating stove from the base and had to take our garbage back there for disposal.
>
> There was no heat upstairs except for what they called a space heater, which was a freestanding heater that ran on kerosene. We had to keep it in the hall to give some heat to the boys' room and ours, and not asphyxiate us from the fumes. Had quite an experience with those stoves. To turn it on, you turned a valve and let the fuel run in for just a second and then lit the fuel in the bottom with a match. Well, for some reason I always forgot and when I lit it there was way too much fuel, and boy, did it do a little dance till the fuel burned down. Scared the heck out of me, but did I learn my lesson? No! I did the same thing with the one upstairs in the bathroom, but this time I did a dumb thing, I opened the small window just above it and the flames went shooting out the window. I quickly called the base for my husband, but he was flying. They sent out an airman to help me and by the time he arrived it was normal. He kept looking at me and I could not understand why. I thought he must think I was just a crazy housewife, but when I went upstairs I looked in the mirror and laughed. My face was covered in soot!
>
> We had a 16 yr old girl living with us who helped around the house. Our electric bill horrified her. She said it would be three months for her family. I finally figured out why. The utility man would look in the window, see my American refrigerator and electric stove that we could not use, and the washer and dryer; and just wrote down an amount!

Strong friendships developed between the local population and the American military community that exist to this very day. Americans frequently return to the old towns and villages to show their children, and even grandchildren, where they lived in France.

Dependent Education

Early in 1952 and through 1953, when there were few families, and before dependent schools were built, grammar school children attended French public schools and did surprisingly well. Young children who had spent a summer playing with neighbor children learned enough French prior to starting second or third grade to adapt. But by 1954, when dependents were allowed to move to France, it was necessary to build schools for the influx of children. The first schools were portable wood buildings with eight classrooms. These were replaced by single-story, concrete masonry buildings with twelve to fifteen classrooms to accommodate 360 students. Originally it was decided that only grades one through eight would be provided in France, and high school students would board at some of the large dependent high schools in West Germany.

All DOD schools were located on U.S. property, either on the air bases or the housing annexes. Tuition and books were free for dependents. Base motor vehicle squadrons provided school bus service to the housing annexes. DOD Dependent Schools hired American credentialed teachers qualified in various grade levels and employed them on one-year contracts. All DOD high schools were fully evaluated and accredited by the North Central Association of Colleges and Secondary Schools.

The high school situation was never satisfactorily solved. Most teenagers ended up as boarding students in Kaiserslautern and Mannheim, West Germany, or at the few high schools provided in France. DOD developed five high schools: Paris, Chateauroux (La Martinerie), Verdun (Desandrouins Hospital), and later Toul (Jeanne d'Arc Hospital), and on Dreux AB. Verdun and Toul high schools were located in the large, unused, U.S. Army war emergency hospital buildings.

Many of these school sites were too far from the student's home to be able to commute daily, so boarding was required. The air base provided transportation home on weekends or holidays, and some schools were too far for weekend family visits. The Kaiserslautern and Mannheim schools were 200 miles or more away from the air bases in France. Dreux High School was 165 miles from Laon AB and 220 miles from Chateauroux. Rather than have their teenagers board so far from the family, several officers and NCOs elected to serve a two-year unaccompanied tour of duty in France.

Almost all air bases had a kindergarten and a well staffed nursery for younger children. A monthly fee was charged for the kindergarten and an hourly rate for the nursery; DOD did not provide this service. Base day care centers were unheard of in the 1950s and 1960s.

Adult Education

Adult education was provided on base for military personnel, civil employees, and dependents. Education and training was always an important function of the USAF, both for personnel development and off duty enjoyment. Evening programs began in the summer and fall 1951 with Practical French Language courses usually taught by local bilingual French citizens in the mess halls after supper. Some instructors had a British accent so thick it was difficult to understand the English as well as the French. This was the start of language classes that eventually became mandatory two or four-week classes for our newly arrived personnel. This enabled most personnel to at least travel and survive in France. Finding large enough classroom space was a challenge in the early years, but after 1954 every main base had a designated Education Center that was open during normal duty hours and up to five nights a week. Also more classrooms became available as permanent building were completed.

Formal on-base evening classes began in the fall and winter 1952-53 when college level courses were presented by employees of the University of Maryland. EUCOM had contracts with U.S. universities to provide off-duty education to military personnel at either very low cost, or for only textbook charges. A wide variety of college and high school subjects were available with the goal of completing two years of college general education courses, or finishing high school. U.S. Armed Forces Institute provided group study for its correspondence courses in mathematics and science; all textbooks were supplied by USAFI. Another important on-base education program was group study of USAF Extension Course Institute professional military education correspondence courses. Groups met for Squadron Officer School, Command & Staff School, Air War College, and Industrial College of the Armed Forces to facilitate completion of these tedious courses required for officer promotion and retention. Officers serving in France were unable to attend the Air University resident courses due to their overseas assignment.

None of these excellent education programs reduced the GI Bill education benefits that became available to the service members upon separation from the USAF.

A few individuals were able to attend French schools in the larger cities and in Paris at their own expense. University level courses in the arts, language, and humanities were offered. A few were presented in English, but the majority required a high degree of proficiency in French. Art classes in Paris were a great opportunity for dependents. A one-hour train trip could deliver dependents from Dreux, Evreux, Fontainebleau, or Laon to their daily classes. Of course, military personnel and dependents stationed in the Paris area had unlimited options. This was a very enjoyable and unusual opportunity for Americans living in France.

AFN

Armed Forces Radio Network (AFRN), later known as Armed Forces Network (AFN), was an important part of life in France. Its AM and FM radio broadcasts provided many hours of entertainment. During the first six years a very limited range AM radio service at USAFE and Army facilities provided news, base/command announcements, and music for about ten hours a day, seven days a week. Wide area FM broadcasting began on 23 May 1958 when AFN France was reworked, and AFN Orleans began broadcasting to U.S. military personnel in Camp Des Loges, Dreux Air Base, and Orleans. AFN Poitiers joined the AFN France network on 20 November 1958, and AFN Verdun followed on 16 October 1959. AFN France grew into a collection of forty-seven FM radio transmitters. Television broadcast service was not established in France. Many young French students who lived close to our bases also enjoyed the AFN broadcasts. It was a very practical way of learning English while enjoying the music. AFN France was shut down in 1967 when France withdrew from NATO and moved with SHAPE to Chievres, Belgium, as part of FRELOC. AFN still operates in Europe with radio and television broadcast services.

Travel

Travel ranged from an evening bus trip into the nearest large town to a four week vacation across four or five different nations. Many of the base personnel traveled around France and Western Europe when off duty after adjusting to the language "problem." Their great fear was getting on the wrong train platform and getting lost in a "real" foreign town with a new foreign language. Metz and Verdun were popular day trips For those who preferred to travel in a group, several different low cost trips could be arranged through the base Special Services Office travel desk. They organized tours to Amsterdam, Brussels, London, and Madrid to name a few. Travel in NATO nations did not require a passport, only special orders and the USAF ID card. Within France airmen usually needed only their USAFE Senior Airman Pass. Family members required passports and had to have them prior to departing the U.S.

Leaves were often spent at Armed Forces Recreation areas in West Germany in the state of Bavaria. The facilities at Garmisch-Partenkirchen, Chiemsee, or Berchtesgaden offered a wide variety of activities, both indoor and outdoor, winter and summer. One of the great summer adventures in Garmisch was visiting the very top of Germany—taking a ride to the highest point on the Zugspitze mountain—2,966m (9,728 feet) above sea level with a breathtaking view of four countries! Well worth the $2.75 cost of the trip! The Casa Carioca Theater in Garmisch was a favorite entertainment spot. It presented a fabulous two-hour ice show every evening with talent from across

Sitting on top of the world 1952 - the Zugspitze, tallest mountain in Germany.
Jerry McAuliffe

Service club and theater, Armed Forces Recreation Center, Garmisch, West Germany. Garmisch was an inexpensive vacation spot. Jerry McAuliffe

Superbagneres, France in the Pyrenees mountains. Tours to "Super-bunny-ears" were the cause of many broken bones among the troops of the 126th. Jerry McAuliffe

Europe. Prices at all hotels were aimed at the lower ranking officers and enlisted men; food was served at the normal ration rates. In 1952 breakfast cost thirty-five cents, lunch was forty-five cents, and supper a big splurge at fifty-five cents. Quarters in the military inns cost one dollar for officers and fifty cents for enlisted men. All charges were paid with Military Payment Certificates and train travel was free until the occupation ended in 1955. (Note: all prices listed were for the summer of 1952, when the author first visited the EUCOM's playground.)

Of course, there was always Paris! Many of the airmen in France lost interest in visiting AFRC facilities in Germany because of strict uniform regulations and curfews for enlisted men. A three-day pass for a long weekend in Paris became more popular than a trip to Garmisch. The Armed Forces Information Center in Paris was located on 127 avenue Champs-Elysees. The snack bar window had an unbeatable view of the Arc de Triomphe; probably half a million photos were taken of the Arc by service personnel from that window! Young airmen hungry for a hamburger and other American food zeroed in on the snack bar at American Legion Post #1 located across from the Hotel Powers. The U.S. Army snack bar just off Champs-Elysees even had popcorn! For liquid refreshment there were bars aplenty, but some favorites were Two Ks near the American Embassy, Granadas where the Follies dancers went after work, and in Pigalle, Garlands and the Canada bar to name a few. Many men fondly remember sitting at an outdoor table at Deux Magots people watching, walking along the Seine, and visiting the museums, churches and restaurants of Paris. Whatever one's interest, the city provided something for everyone. It was a city that inspired love or hate in the Air Force people that visited, and almost everyone stationed in France was there at least once.

Most men, both single and those accompanied by their families, took advantage of their time in France and traveled as much as possible to see the sights, sample the culture, and learn more about the history that surrounded them.

Appendix 4.1 Radio Relay Site Numbers and Locations in France

ALPHA NET
- A-1 Maison Fort
- A-2 Vouzon
- A-3 Ennordres
- A-4 Vierzon
- A-5 Menetreols-sous-Vatan
- A-6 Chateauroux AD
- A-7 Velles
- A-8 Sacierges-St. Martin
- A-9 Bethines
- A-10 Chauvigny
- A-11 Poitiers (D-1)
- A-12 Champagne-St. Hilaire into C-1 & D-1
- A-13 Sauze-Vaussais
- A-14 Vaux-Rouillac into D-2
- A-15 Chillac
- A-16 Laruscade
- A-17 Bordeaux AB

BRAVO NET:
- B-1 Vernou-Le Chenoy
- B-2 Jossigny
- B-3 Chatenay-en-France
- B-4 Site not used
- B-5 St. Genevieve into F-1
- B-6 Moliens
- B-7 Rambures
- B-8 Maintenay
- B-9 Longfosse
- B-10A Hermelinghen
- B-11 Swingate, U.K.

COCOA NET:
- C-1 St. Vincent-la-Chatre
- C-2 Chize AD into E-1
- C-3 Payre sur Vendee
- C-4 St. Michel Mont Mercure
- C-5 St. Philbert-de-Grand Lieu
- C-6 St. Pere en Retz
- C-7 St. Nazaire AD

DELTA NET:
- D-1 Poitiers
- D-2 Braconne

ECCO NET:
- E-1 Surgeres
- E-2 Croix Chapeau
- E-3 La Rochelle (La Pallice port)

FOXTROT NET:
- F-1A Villers-en-Arthies
- F-2 Evreux AB
- F-3 St. Ouen d'Attez
- F-4 Dreux AB

GOLF NET:
- G-1 Soulieres
- G-2 Nanteuil-la-Foret
- G-3 Monthenault
- G-4 Laon AB
- G-5 Chalons Vatry DOB
- G-6 Montsuzain
- G-7 Brienne le Chateau DOB
- G-8 Arrentieres
- G-8.5 Euffigneix
- G-9 Chaumont AB
- G-10 Verdun
- G-11 St. Mihiel AD
- G-12 Toul AB
- G-13 Chambley AB
- G-14 Etain AB
- G-15 Pirmasens, West Germany
- G-16 Phalsbourg
- G-17 Dabo
- G-18 Chenevieres DOB
- G-19 Germiny

Source: Wayne Gors, 7th Radio Relay Squadron

Appendix 4.2 USAFE Navigation Aids Sites in France

NONSARD - Chambley AB: LF Radio Beacon Annex 288 KHz, "ME" 100W. NDB site was 4 km northwest of Nonsard village. 8.0nm at 30° to runway 03 on Chambley AB. Located 48° 56'N - 05° 47'E. NDB was to replace an on-base NDB 468 KHz, "ME", 20W. Nonsard installation was stopped February 1958.

LA CHAMPENOISE - Chateauroux AD: LF Radio Beacon Annex 466 KHz, "CX" 100W. NDB site was at La Champenoise, 5.2nm at 230° to runway 23 on Chateauroux AB. Located 46° 56'N - 01° 48'E.

MEURES - Chaumont AB: LF Radio Beacon Annex 515 KHz, "CU", 300W. NDB site was at Meures, 5.8nm at 192°, to runway 19 on Chaumont AB. Located 49° 11'N - 05° 04'E.

LAONS - Dreux AB: LF Radio Beacon Annex 250 KHz, "DE" 50W. NDB site was at Laons, 5.4nm at 237° to runway 24 on Dreux AB. Located 48° 42'N - 01° 10'E.

VILLE-EN-WOEURE - Etain AB: LF Radio Beacon Annex 358 KHz, "ER" 100W. NDB site was at Ville-en-Woeure, 0.7nm at 239° to runway 24 on Etain AB. Located 49° 14'N - 05° 41'E.

CHAMPENARD - Evreux AB: LF Radio Beacon Annex 486 KHz "KC" 100W. NDB site was at Champenard, 5.6nm at 226° to runway 23 on Evreux AB. Located 49° 06'N - 01° 20'E.

BOIS-les-PARGNY - Laon AB: LF Radio Beacon Annex 344 KHz "LC" 50W. NDB site was south of Pargny, 4.2nm at 208° to runway 21 on Laon AB. Located 49° 42'N - 03° 36'E.

ESCHBOURG - Phalsbourg AB: LF Radio Beacon Annex 486 KHz "PL" 50W. NDB site was at 4.6nm 245° to runway 24 on Phalsbourg AB. Located 48° 49'N - 07° 19'E.

ECROUVES - Toul AB: LF Radio Beacon Annex 477 KHz "DT" 50W. NDB site was near Ecrouves, 6.2nm at 040° to runway 04 on Toul AB. Located 48° 41'N - 05° 53'E.

DAMPIERRE-sur-BLEVY - Dreux AB: Radio Direction Finder Annex for Dreux AB

WINTERSBOURG - Phalsbourg AB: Radio Direction Finder Annex for Phalsbourg AB

ACKNOWLEDGEMENTS

I would like to thank the following people who contributed to this chapter:

Norm Adams was an avionics technician in the 465th Troop Carrier Wing stationed at Toul AB, April 1954 to May 1955. He then performed the same job at Evreux-Fauville AB, May 1955 to December 1955.

Nancy Brooks provided the story of living on the economy. She is the widow of Captian Wesley J. Brooks, a pilot in the 18th TRSq, 66th TRWg stationed at Laon AB, France, in 1962.

David Crockett spent two years at Etan AB as a security officer with the air police. He was voted most valuable USAFE baseball player in 1956.

David Davis was with the 75th Vehicle Repair Squadron at Moulins Air Depot from 1952-55. He was the base club manager in 1954.

Ed Duquette arrived at CHAD in March 1958 and was assigned to Det. #3, 11th Commaintron. He was an A/2C microwave technician/radio relay equipment operator 30450. He transferred to the 7th RRL squadron and was assigned to St.Vincent-la-Chatre, Cocoa #1 and Chize, Cocoa #2 until 1960.

Wayne Gors was a member of a tower crew with the 7th RRL Squadron. He helped build RRL towers at the Bordeaux, Toul, Chalons, Chambley and Etain sites from 1953 to 1957.

John Ibsen was a jet engine mechanic with the 48th Field Maintenance Squadron at Chaumont AB from February 1953 to January 1956. His theater photo was kindly provided by his widow, Mauricette Ibsen.

Jim Martin was with the 7th RRL Squadron at Chauvigny and Champagne St. Hilaire from 1957-60. I would also like to thank him for the abundant information he has provided on the 7th Radio Relay Squadron in France.

Sam Roberts was assigned to the Operations Section as a Survival Training and Personal Equipment Specialist at Etain AB with the 563d Fighter-Bomber Squadron, 1954 -1958, and is active in organizing Etain Pioneers reunions.

Tom Simundich was stationed at Dabo with the 8th RRL Sq from 1961-64. I would also like to thank him for providing much information about 8th RRL Squadron locations and operations.

Ralph Spaulding was stationed at Moulins Air Depot from 1952-54 and worked in motor vehicle repair.

Bob Strobel was assigned to the 7415th Air Base Group at Orly Airport and then the Paris Air Passenger Center in Hotel Littre between 1956 and 1960.

Stan Thompson was in the 388th Com Squadron at Etain from May 1957 to November 1959 and stationed at Toul AB until 1960. He was #26 on the Etain Pioneers basketball team.

Roger Warren was a SSGT in the 102d Tactical Fighter Wing at Phalsbourg in 1961-62 assigned to HQ 102d TFWg orderly room where he worked as mail clerk, First Sergeant, and various other jobs that needed to be done.

Larry White was with the 8th/2059th RRL Squadron, Det #16 stationed at the Longfosse RRL site from January 1963 to October 1965.

5

REACTIVATION AND FINAL DISENGAGEMENT 1959 - 1967

There were vast changes for the USAF in France between January 1959 and December 1967. There was almost constant instability with relocation of forces, then buildup of forces for a possible war, and finally complete disengagement from our facilities in France.

In November 1959, the Seventeenth Air Force at Wheelus Air Base, Libya, was transferred to Ramstein Air Base, West Germany. It was enlarged to assume command of all USAFE units in Western Europe, including all wings in France, taking on the mission of the Twelfth Air Force that had been deactivated in 1957.

All weather air defense, long a concern of USAFE leaders, had been upgraded in 1958 by the addition of three more F-86D squadrons to Europe. One squadron, the 513th Fighter-Interceptor Squadron operated at Phalsbourg AB from April 1958 to January 1961.

By 1959 USAFE forces in France were reduced to one tactical reconnaissance wing, six troop carrier squadrons, one air defense fighter squadron, and the air depot. But in two years, money and effort were again directed to improving and maintaining these bases. In 1961 fighter squadrons were rushed into France to counter the Soviet threat to West Berlin. When the Berlin Crisis ended in 1962, only four fighter squadrons remained in France, and they also returned to CONUS in mid 1963. Most of the air bases were in standby status, though two reconnaissance wings were added in 1965.

All the instability culminated in the 1966 decision of President Charles de Gaulle to end France's military association with NATO. This forced the U.S. completely out of France within one year. The abruptness of the notice left military personnel with great animosity toward the French government and a possible scorched earth reaction could have set in. Cooler heads prevailed and decided it was in our long-term political interest to be polite and return all facilities to the French in good condition so they would be usable in the event of another crisis in Europe. On 23 October 1967 our flags were furled, and after sixteen years all U.S. forces departed France. Prospects of relocating to better conditions in the United Kingdom or West Germany dampened anger; but many USAF veterans remember FRELOC and have never returned to France.

Relocation
Project RED RICHARD 1959

In 1958 and 1959 both economic and political forces combined to reduce USAFE's presence in France. DOD's budget was severely reduced by the Eisenhower administration in 1958. DOD's Project Clearwater dealt with the lingering gold flow problem by reducing manpower overseas. That resulted in USAFE taking a 14 percent budget cut and a 12 percent reduction of officer personnel, which made it necessary to reduce flying wings.

Pronouncements in 1959 by President Charles de Gaulle created the adverse political climate. He was still very unhappy about President Eisenhower's decision not to allow Britain, France, and Israel to take back the Suez Canal after its seizure by Egypt in October 1956. De Gaulle had decided upon two major, long-term, national goals. First, he desired to remove France from NATO's military command; he wanted the insurance policy NATO provided but didn't want to pay for it. Second, he wished to form a strong, political and economic bond with the Soviet Union independent of Western Europe. The first step toward removal was his refusal to cooperate in NATO naval exercises in March 1959. Next in April 1959 he demanded that no nuclear weapons could be stored in France unless they were under direct French control, including inspection and maintenance, with locks and keys held only by the French military. Relinquishing control of atomic weapons was antithetical to long standing U.S. weapons policy in effect since 1945. Finally, he demanded that all nuclear weapons and delivery aircraft be removed from French soil by July 1959.

When France withdrew permission for the U.S. to store atomic weapons on its soil, Chambley, Chaumont, Etain, Laon, Phalsbourg, and Toul air bases were rendered useless as tactical fighter or bomber installations. Since NATO strategy had continued to be "massive nuclear retaliation" using new, smaller weapons, this ultimatum meant all tactical fighter wings had to depart because all USAF fighter aircraft were now capable of delivering nuclear weapons.

In July 1959, the United States Commander in Chief, Europe (USCINCEUR) directed USAFE to implement Project RED RICHARD, the rapid relocation of the three tactical fighter wings remaining in France flying nuclear-capable F-100Ds. They were transferred to bases in the United Kingdom and West Germany because USCINCEUR did not want these wings removed from Europe and returned to the U.S. On 10 July, the 49th Tactical Fighter Wing left Etain for Spangdahlem, completing its move on 25 August 1959. To provide space for the 49th at Spangdahlem, the 10th Tactical Reconnaissance Wing relocated from Spangdahlem to RAF Alconbury, RAF Bruntingthorpe, and RAF Chelveston. Next the 50th Tactical Fighter Wing left Toul and returned to Hahn Air Base, West Germany, on 10 December 1959. Project RED RICHARD was completed on 15 January 1960 with the movement of the 48th Tactical Fighter Wing from Chaumont to RAF Lakenheath, England. Now the air bases at Chaumont, Etain, and Toul-Rosieres were reduced to standby status. At a time when USAFE was desperately trying to reduce expenses, Project RED RICHARD required the movement of 5,300 military personnel and equipment, expending $11 million in transportation costs.

President de Gaulle had scored a major victory in his goal of reducing U.S. influence in France; the first step toward evicting the U.S. military from France was accomplished. Commanders and troops considered all their efforts in France wasted as 1959 ended and the tactical fighter forces, the mainstay of NATO strategy, moved to other air bases in Europe.

Budget problems continued to confront USAFE forces. During 1960, its last year in office, the Eisenhower administration forced DOD to make more cuts to curb growing national deficits and a balance of trade "gold flow" deficit approaching $4 billion. To economize, President Eisenhower halted most movements of dependents to Europe, and ordered the return to CONUS of many dependents already stationed overseas. One example of these dependent related expenses was schooling: in October 1960 there were 9,400 USAFE dependent students attending grades one through twelve at base DOD schools in France. The administration also seriously considered withdrawing all the tactical fighter squadrons permanently based in Europe and replacing them with rotational TAC fighter units. United States economic policy had now become the driving force of NATO strategy.

After President Kennedy took office in January 1961, he canceled both the dependent return program and the planned rotation of combat squadrons to USAFE. The Kennedy Administration envisioned a change in U.S. military strategy around the world, and especially in Europe. The new strategy would be known as "Flexible Response" rather than "Massive Retaliation." Flexible Response meant more conventional ground forces would be made available to fight a conventional war for about thirty days duration, and if not resolved diplomatically within that time, the it would then escalate into nuclear war. Initially this change in NATO direction held great appeal until the costs of this new strategy were calculated. More conventional ground forces meant greatly increased costs and member nations would not spend the money. NATO further reduced its forces in Europe.

Dreux and Phalsbourg joined Chaumont, Etain, and Toul-Rosieres as standby bases. Standby bases were considered closed because the combat flying wings had departed. These bases were operated by a support squadron or support group. The concept was that a small contingent of USAF personnel and French employees would maintain the bases in operating condition should NATO require augmented airpower to cope with a European war. The number of personnel at each base varied widely depending on the workload generated by tenant units, off-base sites, housing units, dispersed operating bases, and TDY flying units. For instance, Dreux was very active in its role as home to the dependent high school. Toul became a forward operating base for Detachment #1 of the 10th TRWg. Phalsbourg and Toul became the temporary home of the 66th TRWg flying squadrons during the time their runway at Laon was undergoing major repairs. Two RF-101 Voodoo squadrons flew from Phalsbourg and two from Toul. Each base had to accommodate 650 officers and airmen of the 66th Wing from fall 1958 into spring 1960. A small flying unit, Detachment #12 Atlantic Air Rescue Center, moved into Chambley AB in late 1960. Detachment #12 flew six Kamen HH-43B Helicopters for search rescue and recovery missions across central Europe. Once these bases were reduced to standby status, all military construction and improvement projects were canceled; likewise communication systems programs were deleted. Equipment and funds were moved to improve air bases in West Germany.

Seventeenth Air Force manpower teams arrived to evaluate manning requirements to maintain these standby bases, and grossly underestimated the manpower necessary to keep the facilities in usable condition. Personnel they deemed excess were transferred to other bases in Europe or, the majority, were returned to the U.S. for discharge. A few months later when a total review was completed, Seventeenth Air Force realized the workload vs. manpower was totally unrealistic and authorized increases. For instance, they determined that Toul needed 138 additional men to maintain its facilities. But it was too late, the people were gone and it would take two years to fill these vacancies.

Reactivation
Operation STAIR STEP 1961

Berlin Crisis Two became the first test of the flexible response strategy. Premier Khrushchev decided that the Soviet Union would sign a peace treaty with the East German government. In effect the German Democratic Republic would control the Russian zone of Berlin and could end joint occupation of the city. This action was a clear violation of the Potsdam Agreement of 1945. Again the U.S. threatened war and Khrushchev backed down. Instead he began speaking out about restricting the West's aerial access to Berlin and preventing the entry of East Germans into the city. This possibility started an exodus of Germans from the eastern zone as they rushed to leave their sector and relocate in West Germany. Departures snowballed from a few dozen refugees daily to a flow of 4,000 per day by August 1961. On the night of 12 August 1961 the Soviet-backed East German government began erecting the Berlin Wall to prevent this flow of workers from communism, precipitating a new Cold War crisis that had been brewing for the previous twelve months. Berlin became a divided city. The response agreed to by the Kennedy Administration was to rapidly increase conventional tactical airpower in Europe during the summer of 1961.

Less than two years after the RED RICHARD realignments of 1959 USAFE had an immediate need for all its air bases in France, including those on standby. The French government agreed to allow the U.S. to use our standby bases during this crisis, providing the aircraft based there were armed with conventional weapons only. Seventeenth Air Force reactivated five primary air bases in France, Chaumont, Chambley, Etain, Phalsbourg, and Dreux. This emergency deployment definitely prolonged the USAF stay in France.

After three years of manpower reductions, this new international crisis required expansion of U.S. military forces. On 25 August 1961 DOD announced 148,000 reserve personnel would be called on 1 October for twelve months of active duty service—27,000 of these people would be from Air Force Reserve and Air National Guard flying squadrons and support units

Building the Berlin Wall in 1961.
ISN Parallel History Project

F-84F fighters at Harmon AB, Newfoundland, being towed to their takeoff position to conserve fuel for their flight to the Azores on their way to France.
USAF History Office, Maxwell AFB

to augment the Air Force, and 112,000 were Army reservists. Many Army reservists were sent to Europe to bring ground combat units up to full strength. The Air National Guard (ANG) was tasked to supply six tactical fighter wings and one tactical reconnaissance wing to expand USAFE. Also deployed to Europe was a complete ANG Tactical Control Group consisting of six Tactical Control Squadrons manned by 230 officers and 1,850 airmen having many tons of mobile ground radar and radio equipment for battlefield command and control of tactical air power. These tactical control units were dispersed throughout West Germany; none were assigned to France.

The Air Force responded with a two-phase deployment of reinforcements to Europe—the largest such overseas movement of aircraft since World War II. The first phase began on 5 September with Operation TACK HAMMER. Tactical Air Command launched eight F-100D squadrons from its Composite Air Strike Force to augment USAFE strength with 144 fighters. All TACK HAMMER fighters moved across the Atlantic Ocean with air tanker refueling enroute. The TACK HAMMER deployment was an interim measure until ANG units could relieve Tactical Air Command squadrons.

The second phase began with the movement of eleven Air National Guard squadrons in late October and November 1961. Operation STAIR STEP was the code name for the rapid aerial movement of the fighters to Europe. Aircraft supplied by ANG wings totaled one hundred four F-84Fs, twenty RF-84Fs, seventy-eight F-86Hs, and seventy-two F-104As. All the STAIR STEP fighters were flown to France except the F-104s. The majority of the fighters arrived on 4 November and amazingly had no losses enroute; the F-84Fs and F-86Hs were considered old and obsolete aircraft even though they were only seven to nine years out of the factory. The three F-104 squadrons were activated on 1 November 1961. They disassembled their Starfighters and loaded them into MATS C-124s which delivered them to air bases in Germany and Spain.

The STAIR STEP fighters were flown on one of three different air routes, depending upon aircraft type. The F-86Hs departed from Loring AFB, Maine, and used the standard North Atlantic route described in chapter 2 because they had no air-to-air refueling capability. Eight C-47s and sixteen T-33A support aircraft going to France flew this same route, but assembled at Westover AFB, Massachusetts. The four F-84F squadrons assembled at McGuire AFB, New Jersey, by 27 October. Next they flew 530nm northward, stopping at Harmon AB, Stephenville, Newfoundland. Then on 1 November they flew the longest

F-84F STAIR STEP fighters of the 141st TFSq from Chaumont AB, France.
USAF via Nick Scafidi

leg east, 1,480nm across the Atlantic Ocean to Lajes AB in the Azores. The twenty RF-84Fs flew from Bangor AFB, Maine, to Argentia NS, Newfoundland; then to Lajes AB. From there they flew 1,120nm to Moron and Torrojon Air Bases in Spain. The following day on 4 November, the Thunderstreaks proceeded to their five different bases in France. The last few aircraft arrived in France on 8 November.

All F-84Fs were equipped with air-to-air refueling systems, but they were not used for this trip. Instead, two full 450-gallon external tanks and very careful fuel management provided for the Harmon to Lajes route without midair refueling. KC-97 tankers were in position for emergency refueling if necessary. The RF and F-84F drop tanks were filled to capacity at Harmon by jacking up the aircraft's main wheels eighteen inches to increase the total internal and external fuel load from 1,560 to 1,650 gallons. Thus the slanted tanks allowed an additional forty-five gallons of JP-4 per tank. This technique was developed by the 141st Tactical Fighter Squadron maintenance officer. Aircraft tugs then towed the F-84Fs to the active runway and waited until the control tower notified the flight of four aircraft to depart. Engines were then started and they immediately departed for Lajes.

Most STAIR STEP personnel were moved to and from France by MATS military aircraft. This movement of approximately 9,900 men occurred within thirty days including the ADVONs, main units, and rear echelons. All flights departed from ANG home stations directly to their new air bases in France, West Germany and Spain; all personnel processing was accomplished at home bases prior to boarding. Critical unit supplies and equipment, primarily aircraft support gear and tools, were airlifted by MATS C-118s, C-121s, and C-135s. The usual time enroute was twenty-eight to thirty hours with one refueling stop.

MATS C-97s and C-124s transported the equipment. All STAIR STEP units had practiced TACs mobility concepts and prepared their own local plans, which proved to be an excellent M-Day exercise. All personnel arrived in Europe in excellent condition, ready to work, a major advancement compared to the fatiguing eleven-day ocean voyages. Upon arrival at the bases the MATS aircraft were rapidly unloaded by the passengers and base teams, then departed France within three hours.

Heavy equipment was transported by MSTS contracted shipping, which delivered most of the cargo to La Pallice and some to Bremerhaven. Shipment required about two months. CONEX shipping containers greatly reduced packing time, protected equipment, and prevented losses. The 152d Tactical Control Group shipped their truck and trailer mounted mobile radar sets and radio systems by ship. These tactical command-and-control units had over 590 M-series heavy military vehicles to transport their equipment.

The primary combat mission of the STAIR STEP units was air superiority and offensive tactical air support operations using conventional munitions to defend West Germany if a war developed over Berlin access. Upon arrival in France their missions consisted of command inspections, theater flying training, air-ground close support operations, gunnery training, photo missions, and air defense alert duty. Though equipped with conventional weapons, the STAIR STEP F-84F and F-86H squadrons maintained their proficiency to deliver nuclear weapons by practicing toss bombing.

Our standby air bases in France were very convenient for this emergency deployment. If the STAIR STEP fighters had to be added to our aircraft already in West Germany, the concentration of aircraft would have made a very vulnerable target. Also the four dispersed operating bases in France were still available for our use if further aircraft dispersement became necessary.

Again economic considerations, national debt and balance of trade "Gold Flow" limited the deployment of STAIR STEP wings into France. Only one-half of the available force departed CONUS. The remaining ten CONUS based fighter squadrons were prepared to fly to France within five days to reinforce their wings. Only Phalsbourg received a complete fighter wing. The 102d TFWg was the only complete combat wing to occupy Phalsbourg since its acceptance in 1955. STAIR STEP wings were sent to the locations shown in Table 5.1

Five wings were re-designated 7000 series Tactical Wings. The 7000 designator indicated an incomplete wing that would be disbanded after it completed the operation it was formed to accomplish. A 7000 wing had only a partial wing headquarters, partial support squadrons, and one combat flying squadron at its new air base. For example, the 108th Tactical Fighter Wing became the 7108th Tactical Wing. The remainder of the wing based at its ANG home station continued using its usual designators, i.e., the 108th Tactical Fighter Wing; McGuire AFB, New Jersey.

The 7117th Tactical Wing flying RF-84Fs was assigned to Dreux, but a serious problem developed immediately. French air traffic controllers prevented jet operation from Dreux by claiming it would conflict with high density commercial air traffic in the Paris region. De Gaulle stood behind the union's demand. Consequently, the 106th Tactical Reconnaissance Squadron was grounded until it moved RF-84F operations to Chaumont. But USAFE insisted that the 7117th Wing continue to operate and improve Dreux for possible use as a troop carrier base. The 106th was never able to operate their Thunderstreaks at Dreux. Many USAFE leaders felt this restriction was the second step in de Gaulle's planned total eviction of American forces from France.

USAFE worked overtime to prepare the standby bases in France for the TACK HAMMER and STAIR STEP forces. Additional personnel had to be sent TDY from Germany to assist in base renovation. The STAIR STEP deployment clearly demonstrated the difficulty of reactivating standby operating bases. The bases in France had deteriorated in the two years since being placed in standby status. The primary causes were a lack of skilled USAFE personnel to perform repairs, improper supervision of the French maintenance contractors, and shortage of funds to purchase repair parts. USAFE had not allocated sufficient funds or acknowledged that an unused building requires as much service as an occupied structure. Consequently all facilities slipped into disrepair, especially hangars and vehicles. In fall 1961, as these bases were returned to operating status for STAIR STEP units, 60 to 70 percent of the vehicles were inoperative. Lack of serviceable refueling trucks was a grave problem for the fighter squadrons.

Each STAIR STEP base required both minor and major repairs to its buildings, vehicle fleet, commu-

Table 5.1 STAIR STEP Wings Sent to France 1961

102d Tactical Fighter Wing	three F-86H squadrons at Phalsbourg AB
108th Tactical Fighter Wing	one F-84F squadron at Chaumont AB
117th Tactical Reconnaissance Wing	one RF-84F squadron at Dreux AB
121st Tactical Fighter Wing	one F-84F squadron at Etain AB
122d Tactical Fighter Wing	one F-84F squadron at Chambley AB
131st Tactical Fighter Wing	one F-84F squadron at Toul AB

The 163d TFSq found weeds on the marguerites and runway at Chambley AB when they arrived in 1961. The base had deteriorated in the two years it was in standby status.
USAF History Office, Maxwell AFB

nications systems, heating plants, and POL storage facilities that resulted in spending approximately $3.5 million per base! All base improvement projects had been suspended since 1958. Much equipment had been removed from the bases in the interim to meet other USAFE needs, but overall they were in fair condition after many repairs were completed on buildings and base utilities. No STAIR STEP personnel had to spend the 1961-62 winter in tents!

Another $3.5 million per base in emergency permanent construction funds had to be spent to meet new Seventeenth Air Force minimum requirements. Some of these funds were used for projects that had never been completed previously because of inadequate NATO funding, i.e., interior base fencing, supply storage sheds, emergency power generators, and expanded munitions storage shelters.

Overall, morale remained high during the eight months these units were in France and good U.S. French relations developed in the small towns surrounding the air bases. But, by March 1962 the Berlin crisis was subsiding, and plans were being made for departure of the ANG wings from France. Units were to return all personnel, equipment, and aircraft to CONUS by 1 September 1962 for early release from active duty. The bases would revert to standby status.

STAIR STEP units had not been allowed to bring dependents or POVs to France, which simplified the return to CONUS.

Deactivation plans were altered by USAF's decision to create a new fighter wing. Eighty F-84Fs were retained from the departing squadrons, and the 366th Tactical Fighter Wing with four squadrons was created at Chaumont on 8 May 1962. Wing Headquarters and one of its four squadrons, the 389th, was based there. The 390th operated at Chambley, the 391st at Etain, and the 480th at Phalsbourg. Activation of the 366th was an example of the Flexible Response strategy advocated by Secretary of Defense, Robert McNamara by increasing USAF tactical fighter wings.

The six STAIR STEP wings departed France in a timely manner using military air transportation; their 130 aircraft made the return flight via the North Atlantic route. Good weather and well coordinated support teams made the trip uneventful. The 102d TFWg and its F-86Hs, and the 7117th and 7131st Tactical Wings with their RF and F-84Fs, and all support aircraft returned to their ANG home bases between 8 and 20 July. The majority of personnel were released early from active duty on 20 August 1962 to save manpower funds.

Unfortunately, the Berlin Wall was built and a barbed wire fence with minefields extended the entire north-south length of a divided Germany. The wall effectively isolated East Germany for the next twenty-eight years. But the American, British, and French Zones still remained in Berlin and access to the city was not challenged again. TACK HAMMER and STAIR STEP forces had served their purpose; their rapid deployment to France had unequivocally demonstrated the United States' determination to defend Berlin. It's possible that the sudden appearance of 170 tactical fighters with nuclear weapon delivery capability changed Khrushchev's attitude toward his Berlin "settlement."

On 1 July 1962, USAFE had 101,207 assigned personnel, the largest manpower strength reached by the command throughout the 1960s and into the 1980s.

With the Berlin crisis settled, total USAFE strength decreased to 85,085 by December. Return of STAIR STEP personnel to CONUS accounted for most of this reduction. The 366th was the only tactical fighter wing still based in France. It was allowed to continue flying its F-84Fs with conventional weapons. On 15 July 1963 the 366th moved to Holloman AFB, New Mexico.

With the departure of the 366th, manpower assigned to France decreased about 50 percent as Chambley, Chaumont, Etain, and Phalsbourg once again became standby bases. Only three air bases were active: Evreux, Laon, and Toul. No tactical fighters or bombers remained in France. Instead fighter units from CONUS were rotated to France on TDY. Evreux was the support base for Dreux. Toul was still being used by the Det #1, 10th TRWg as a forward base for its RB-66B/Cs. The 66th TRWg with four squadrons continued operating its RF-101C Voodoos from Laon. By 1963, USAFE was reviewing the cost of maintaining seven standby air bases in France every six months. It would have preferred to close the bases in France and spend the money to improve air bases in West Germany and the United Kingdom.

Two tactical reconnaissance wings were activated in 1965, the 25th at Chambley and the 26th at Toul. The 25th TRWg was activated on 24 September 1965 with two squadrons, the 19th and the 42d. The 19th TRSq operated RB-66Bs for day and night photography, and the 42d TRSq performed tactical electronic warfare missions with RB-66Cs. These were the same RB-66s that had served with the 66th and 10th Tactical Reconnaissance Wings and had moved about Europe since being introduced in 1956. The 26th TRWg was activated at Toul on 24 September 1965 with the 22d and 32d Tactical Reconnaissance Squadrons. On 1 January 1966 its third reconnaissance squadron, the 38th, was added. The wing's mission was to receive the factory new RF-4Cs, learn to fly and maintain the Photo Phantom, then train other wings in order to upgrade NATO's day/night reconnaissance. These were the last USAF wings to be activated in France.

CINCUSAFE ordered a 10 percent reduction in Headquarters USAFE manpower on 15 October 1965 to free additional people for the Vietnam air war.

Relations between France and the United States continued to deteriorate during the summer of 1965. Several objections were being raised by France: air traffic control restrictions, aircraft noise levels, and lack of taxes on BX and Commissary sales. DOD began planning for possible withdrawal of our forces from France. Dual basing all flying squadrons was being programmed into the DOD five-year budget. But once again the dual basing concept was opposed by USAFE as well as SACEUR because of great concern that the air wings based in CONUS could not meet NATO war response times.

Also, during April 1965, the Soviet Union again began harassment in the Berlin air corridors by flying within 100 feet of air traffic. Russian jet fighters made supersonic passes below 300 feet altitude over West Berlin, especially during West German parliamentary meetings. The western nations continued using the Berlin Corridor but this period of renewed harassment was a poor time to reduce NATO defense strength.

Disengagement
Project FRELOC 1966 - 1967

After fifteen years of bad times and good, the end of USAFE basing in France was decided by French President Charles de Gaulle in 1966. Initially de Gaulle had talked about withdrawing from NATO in 1969 in accordance with the treaty that permitted termination-after twenty years of membership. Instead, in a letter to President Lyndon B. Johnson on 7 March 1966, he announced that France would withdraw from NATO's military structure, but would not leave the political organization. De Gaulle wanted France to become the major political force in NATO planning after the U.S. departed Europe.

France halted all participation in the integrated military commands of both SHAPE and AFCENT, and would no longer place French air and ground forces at the disposal of NATO commands. The withdrawal of French military personnel from NATO headquarters would become effective 1 July 1966. Interestingly, French Army forces were not removed from West Germany until 1992.

Next on 29 March 1966, President de Gaulle informed NATO ministers that NATO headquarters and all NATO forces and equipment had one year, until 1 April 1967, to leave France.

At first the Pentagon wanted to contest de Gaulle's decision as being illegal under the terms of the NATO treaty, but the State Department advised that nothing could be done to reverse his position. President Johnson agreed with State Department and gave the Joint Chiefs of Staff direct orders to clear out of France immediately at any cost. Johnson did not wish to waste his time with de Gaulle; there were more pressing problems in Vietnam. This eviction notice was a very serious setback for NATO defense strategy, but it came at a fortuitous time for the U.S. The expenses and manpower required to operate our force structure in France could be quickly diverted into the expanding war in Southeast Asia.

By spring 1966, USAFE operations in France were at a low ebb with only the Chateauroux Air Depot functioning at full strength. Four air bases were operational: Chambley, Evreux, Laon, and Toul. Chaumont, Dreux, Etain, and Phalsbourg Air Bases were in standby status with absolute minimum manning. Only two complete and one partial tactical reconnaissance wings remained in France. On 14 July 1966 DOD announced that all dependent movements into France would cease effective 1 August to avoid the cost of a second move within eight months.

HQ USAF announced on 15 June 1966 that seven tactical reconnaissance squadrons would be relocated from France within three months; four squadrons would be sent to the UK, two would be returned to CONUS, and one would be deactivated in place. No major construction projects had been approved for the air bases since Operation STAIR STEP. Several minor construction projects had been completed at Chambley, Chateauroux, and Toul since 1964. Leaving France was a giant undertaking for the U.S., and resulted in CINCEUCOM establishing Project FRELOC "Fast Relocation of Lines of Communication," which involved all the services in a single integrated effort. The first FRELOC action message was transmitted on 21 June 1966 and by March 1967 approximately 22,000 messages and directives had been transmitted by the FRELOC Group. Many major decisions about the move were not made until just three and one-half months prior to final eviction but de Gaulle's deadline was met through exceptional intra-service cooperation and efficiency.

The first action taken by USAFE as part of FRELOC was relocation of its tactical units out of France to other European countries to maintain combat capability. CINCUSAFE was very concerned that these reconnaissance wings would be ordered back to CONUS by HQ USAF to become dual based wings and then be dismantled to provide replacement aircraft and crews for the Vietnam War.

The 513th Troop Carrier Wing was activated at Evreux on 15 April 1966 to control TDY airlift squadrons being sent to USAFE to support Project FRELOC. USAFE had lost all its organic tactical airlift wings in 1964 after departure of the 317th TCWg from Evreux, but FRELOC created a new requirement for quick response, short-haul transport aircraft in Europe. The cheap solution was to activate HQ 513th Troop Carrier Wing. It could command one or two C-130B squadrons rotated TDY from CONUS to France for 90 or 180-day tours of European operations. On 1 July 1966 the 513th supervised the closing of Dreux and Evreux air bases and moved its 811 military personnel plus 1,373 dependents to RAF Mildenhall, England. The move was accomplished with minimum problems and the 513th continued its FRELOC support mission from the UK. The 5th Aerial Port Squadron at Chateauroux moved 59 military plus 66 dependents on 15 August 1966 to RAF Mildenhall to support the 513th. The 322d Air Division, also at Chateauroux, relocated to RAF High Wycombe, England. This involved moving 145 military, 316 dependents, and a small amount of cargo.

By September, after eight years at Laon, the 66th TRWg with two flying squadrons, the 17th and 18th, and their sixty RF-101s moved to a newly reactivated standby base at RAF Upper Heyford, England. Two serious problems were encountered with this relocation: there were immediate complaints about the Voodoo's J-57 engine noise, and there was a shortage of off base family housing. The small English towns were unable to accommodate the sudden influx of American families.

The 25th TRWg was inactivated in place at Chambley on 15 October 1966 after one year of service. Its phase-out began on 22 August when the 42d TRSq was deactivated and its ten RB-66Cs and aircrews were sent directly to Southeast Asia. The 19th TRSq was sent to Shaw AFB, South Carolina, about 1 August 1966, with sixteen RB-66Bs. It became another USAFE dual based squadron, but in reality the 19th evolved into an RB-66 combat crew training unit for the Vietnam War and did not return to Europe for exercises. Remaining 25th Wing personnel were transferred to the 7367th Combat Support Group at Chambley to shut down the base, and then were transferred to organizations in Germany.

The 26th Tactical Reconnaissance Wing was assigned to the 86th Air Division at Ramstein AB, West Germany. By 5 October 1966 the 26th at Toul, and two of its squadrons, the 38th and 22d and their thirty-two RF-4Cs departed Toul and relocated to Ramstein. Their move resulted in crowded base facilities and a shortage of family housing in the area. About one month later, the 22d moved to Mountain Home AFB, Idaho, with its sixteen RF-4Cs to become a dual-based squadron assigned to USAFE. The 38th TRSq remained at Ramstein. The third squadron, the 32d, was transferred without personnel and equipment from Toul to the 10th TRWg at RAF Alconbury on 15 August 1966. This was a paper transfer only as all personnel and equipment were moved to Southeast Asia

Table 5.2
Air Force Material Assets in France 1 April 1966
(In Dollars)

Asset	Value
181 Operational Aircraft	$ 327,717,104.00
Spare Parts, Aircraft	$ 67,427,667.00
Base Funded Supplies	$ 4,785,133.00
EAID Property	
Commissary Equipment	$ 57,805,172.00
Precision Measuring Equipment	$ 274,900.00
Laboratory Equipment (AFLC)	$ 1,500,000.00
2,994 Vehicles, All Types	$ 17,945,822.00
Fuels and Lubricants	$ 163,996.00
Aircraft War Consumables	$ 36,458,132.00
TOTAL:	$ 542,827,926.00

Ref: FRELOC After Action Report 1966-1967 USAREUR COM Z

to equip tactical reconnaissance units being expanded to fight the Vietnam War. Before their departure, 26th Wing personnel assisted the 7544th Combat Support Group in removal of property from Toul.

All flying organizations were relocated by 15 October 1966. Now began the major task of hauling out sixteen years of accumulated supplies and material spread across France! All NATO, U.S. and RCAF real estate, buildings and utilities had to be abandoned and turned over to France. The cost of relocating NATO installations would exceed one billion dollars! Headquarters SHAPE at Rocquencourt and other NATO command organizations had to be moved into completely new facilities in Belgium near Mons and in Brussels. Belgium offered a very good site for a new Supreme Allied Headquarters at Camp Casteau, north of Mons. A German contractor was selected and started construction immediately to provide these facilities in record time.

CINCEUCOM tasked the Commander in Chief, U.S. Army Europe to prepare the project plan and execute the operation to remove all material from France. An overall Program Evaluation Review Technique (PERT) system was established by COM Z for FRELOC and used by the Commanding General and all staff agencies. PERT had become the latest DOD management tool to solve all of mankind's problems; it grew out of the Polaris Submarine Launched Ballistic Missile program! The very first action at each installation was to take careful inventory of all removable buildings and structures, material, consumable supplies, vehicles, and communication systems. A description of the U.S. Army's FRELOC operation can be found in chapter 18.

The estimated dollar investment of USAFE inventory in France, of material assets other than real property, was $542,827,926. This estimate, dated 1 April 1966, included 181 operational aircraft, 160,992 line item spare aircraft parts; 32,835 types of equipment consisting of 248,267 individual items; over 7.7 million gallons of fuel; and 2,994 vehicles of all types. War consumables included 6,431 aircraft wing pylons, 16,848 auxiliary fuel drop tanks, and 9,390 tons of aircraft munitions. This material still existed after stocks were being consumed and not replaced in the five years since the departure of STAIR STEP units. Tables 5.2 and 5.3 illustrate the quantity of supplies that were located at Chateauroux Air Depot and the large amounts of ammunition still remaining at the three fighter bases. After inventory was completed, HQ USAFE decided that excess supplies be redistributed to bases within its command to eliminate ordering duplicate supplies from CONUS. The FRELOC Group obtained part-time use of Operations Command and Control Group's IBM 1401 Computer, and began issuing material directly from France to fill requisitions from all its organizations in Europe. This group issued 62,097 redistribution orders for base funded supplies valued at $2,806,608. This represented 60 percent of these items in France! The remaining items were shipped to air bases in Germany to be stored for future use. Many of these supplies were later used within Europe or transferred to Southeast Asia to meet war needs.

Large quantities of POL products worth $1.9 million were moved to other USAFE storage locations. The stockpile amounted to 6,438,000 gallons of JP-4, 1,286,000 gallons of 115/145 aviation gasoline, and 42,660 gallons of aircraft oil.

The long-term shortage of vehicles in France had been resolved as requirements declined when bases were changed to standby status after STAIR STEP. Of the 2,994 vehicles remaining in France in 1966, 1,585 were transferred to other USAFE bases across Europe. Many were driven to their new bases to save rail shipping costs. At least 291 newly purchased vehicles from the "FY 1965-66 Buy Program" that were enroute to France were diverted to other bases. RAF Chelveston, an interim UK storage site, received 889 vehicles that it stored for future needs. This resulted in only 520 vehicles being sold as surplus through Redistribution and Marketing. Disposition of vehicles was completed by 1 February 1967.

An excellent FRELOC decision made by USAFE that was approved by DOD in late December 1966 was establishment of interim storage sites outside of France. This allowed material to be dumped quickly, and then later as time and labor permitted, it could be identified, sorted, issued, stored, or returned to CONUS. This was the only solution possible to meet the 1 April 1967 deadline. The decision allowed critical assets to be removed immediately. USAFE shipments were five times the normal annual amount during the last six months of FRELOC! Three sites in the United Kingdom were opened to receive supplies and equipment: RAF Greenham Common, RAF Chelveston, and RAF Sculthorpe. Extraordinary efforts were necessary to prepare these sites for immediate receipt of shipments. Greenham Common and Sculthorpe had been in standby status for five years; buildings and storage areas required considerable rehabilitation. An airlift terminal was established at RAF Greenham Common to receive supplies. Special cargo handling equipment was pre-positioned on the ramp so aircraft could be efficiently unloaded and processed for rapid turn-around. Both permanent party and TDY personnel were repeatedly commended for their teamwork to accomplish this operation; USAFE did not want a repeat of the Chateauroux 1951-53 storage debacle.

Originally, when this plan was proposed it was assumed that permanent supply teams would be organized to operate the sites for several years until the property was consumed or returned to CONUS. Minimum manning levels requested by USAFE to HQ USAF were ninety-six personnel spaces for Greenham Common, seventy-six for Chelveston, and fifty-nine for Sculthorpe. This request was flat rejected by the Secretary of Defense, because he insisted these sites

Table 5.3
Air Force Material Assets Existing in France 1 April 1966 (By Tons)

Bases	General Supplies	AMMO	Base Property	Non Appropriated Funds	Misc.	Totals
Chambley	4,068.3	1,428.2	1,734.3	23.0	155.0	7,408.8
Chateauroux	12,133.1	2.5	20.8	188.1	907.1	13,351.6
Chaumont	6,802.7	1,030.1	674.3	16.7	1,008.6	9,532.7
Etain	5,667.9	1,013.3	786.8	25.6	0	7,493.6
Evreux/Dreux	3,111.7	14.0	678.5	190.0	83.3	14,077.5
Laon	7,427.0	474.7	1,145.6	177.9	71.6	9,346.8
Phalsbourg	3,739.2	206.8	340.9	52.4	347.2	4,686.5
St. Mihiel	317.7	5,144.7	0	0	0.5	5,462.9
Toul	9,702.9	74.1	2,879.4	143.8	119.3	12,919.5
TOTALS:	63,020.5	9,388.1	8,360.9	817.5	2,692.6	84,279.9

Source: FRELOCK After Action Report 1966-1967 USAREUR COM Z

SHAPE HQ at Rocquencourt, France in 1951 is representative of the vast NATO complexes in France that had to be abandonded in 1967.
NATO photos

were only for temporary storage and did not require personnel to operate them. This was a good example of the existing DOD management methods; the whiz kids liked to argue over the meaning of words rather than provide resources! They seemed to think this mass of supplies and equipment would distribute itself. Support units of combat wings based in the UK had to provide the labor to operate these large depots for the twenty years that it took to process this "temporary" material. When all FRELOC supplies, vehicles, and materials were completely moved into the UK from France, the huge amount of storage space required surprised USAFE. RAF Greenham Common needed 375,000 square feet of indoor storage and 110,000 square feet of outdoor storage for its newly acquired assets. RAF Chelveston used 143,260 square feet of indoor storage for war consumables and 171,000 square feet of outdoor storage for vehicles. RAF Sculthorpe was the smallest depot, and required 38,700 square feet of indoor storage and 119,000 square feet of outdoor storage for its supplies.

Another good decision was designating USAFE as executive agency for the removal of all 1,672 family house-trailers from France. Since Project Caravan began in 1954, USAFE had acquired more trailers than any other service in Europe and many of these were in France since no permanent on-base housing could be built. First it re-purchased the 263 trailers owned by U.S. military personnel in France. All the house trailers then became accountable U.S.Government property and could easily be processed out of France without being liable for taxation, which would have been the case if they were privately owned. Second, these trailers were offered to EUCOM units; 428 were transferred to the U.S. Army in Europe and 74 were accepted by USAFE. The Agency for International Development (AID) received 351 trailers for their needs in Southeast Asia. The remaining 802 were sold through disposal channels at an average price of $90 per unit. Bids ranged from $40 to $163 per trailer depending on its overall condition and whether or not parts had been removed. Cannibalization was authorized to obtain parts to repair U.S. Government trailers throughout Europe. Removal of trailers from France was completed by 11 March 1967.

Communication-Electronics (C-E) systems owned by the U.S. Government posed another interesting problem for FRELOC planners. Communication circuits were required to maintain contact between Germany and the people still working in France, yet these were extremely valuable items and USAFE wanted them removed as soon as possible. Ground radio navigation aids would be kept by France if not removed by 31 March 1967. This C-E equipment ranged from base telephone exchanges to long-haul wide band, multi channel radio that tied France to the UK and Germany. The radio relay system could not be shut down until the bases it served were cleared out. An early task was removal of HI-VALUE radio nav aids. Control tower radio sets, non-direction beacons, direction finders, GCA radars, VOR and TACAN beacons were able to shut down as soon as the flying units departed. After their departure, flight operations were reduced to cargo aircraft flying daylight VFR only.

Removal of C-E equipment required skilled personnel to carefully disassemble, preserve, pack, and identify the equipment for future installation. A shortage of these specialists existed in Europe at this time because similar equipment was being installed throughout Southeast Asia. This FRELOC removal work was performed by a USAFE unit known as European Ground Electronics Engineering and Installation Agency (EURGEEIA) that was part of Air Force Logistics Command. EURGEEIA was augmented by volunteer Air National Guard personnel sent to France for ninety-day tours of active duty. Many of these men were assigned to ANG GEEIA Squadrons and this work was part of their M-Day mission. Another source of assistance was the Electronics System Division—Site Activation Task Force (ESD SATF) sent TDY from AF Systems Command to set up new C-E facilities in Germany as the equipment arrived from France. Enormous effort was required to remove the C-E equipment in France and rapidly reconfigure networks in Germany to replicate the lost circuits into Spain, Belgium, Netherlands, and United Kingdom. Total rework of all Air Force and Army communications facilities in Europe required several years and considerable expense. For example, it cost the U.S. approximately $1.4 million in material and labor to reconfigure Defense Communication System circuits between Hillingdon, UK, and Feldberg, West Germany. EURGEEIA expended 42,900 man-hours, ANG GEEIA provided 38,400 man-hours, and ESD SATF invested 10,300 man-hours to accomplish the FRELOC C-E tasks. Together the teams removed $21.7 million worth of C-E equipment, all of which was later used by the USAF. All C-E systems were removed by 31 March 1967 with the exception of navigation aids at Evreux and Orly Airport as requested by the French Government. These were made available for the June 1967 Paris International Air Show; but the VOR and TACAN ground stations were removed immediately afterwards. The 85 officers, 1,879 airmen and 5 DAF civilians that had supported the C-E systems installed in France, and their 2,913 dependents, were reassigned within USAFE.

Buried communications cable, antenna towers, buildings, and utilities worth $200 million were not removed but left for negotiations between the United States and the French. There is no record of compensation received for these C-E fixed plant assets. The base telephone systems at Chambley, Chaumont, Dreux, Etain, Evreux, and Phalsbourg worth $1.4 million were NATO financed and left in place for NATO negotiators to settle. The Chateauroux depot telephone system manufactured and purchased in France was considered non-supportable and offered for direct sale.

The greatest challenge was removal of property and supplies at the Chateauroux air depot and its subdepots. NATO supplies and aircraft parts, as well as USAF material, had to be separated and shipped to several different storage sites. The Air Force Reserve, flying C-124s, provided extra airlift to remove all HIGH VALUE depot property to CONUS, especially aircraft engines, shop machinery, and precision measuring laboratory test equipment (PMEL). Vast quantities of supplies were moved from Chateauroux Air Depot to England and West Germany. At Captieux and Chize, munitions depots near the Atlantic coast, there were approximately 100,000 tons of ammunition.

Real estate transfer began on 31 January 1967 with the St. Mihiel Ammunition Depot becoming the first major installation returned to the French government through the MLS in Paris. Between 20 and 31 March 1967, USAFE released nine main air bases in France to MLS for disposal. By the end of March, USAFE had relocated about 33,000 Air Force personnel and their dependents, shipped over 85,000 tons of material, and closed 77 installations, including the forward operating office in Paris located at 22 Rue de la Tremoille. By 31 March 1967, the United States had met President de Gaulle's deadline. The Government of France took possession of Chambley, Chaumont, Dreux, Etain, Evreux, Laon, Phalsbourg, and Toul Air Bases, and the Chateauroux Air Depot on 1 April 1967. On 23 October 1967, USAFE released its final installation to the French government, the Suippes Ground Range property. Return of the air-to-ground gunnery range had been delayed at the request of France because thorough removal of unexploded ordnance required extensive labor by Explosive Ordnance Disposal (EOD) technicians.

Finally on 23 October 1967, our flags were furled, and after sixteen years, all U.S. forces departed France.

A small group of Air Force personnel remained behind with permission of the French Government to complete reimbursement negotiations. Settlement of real estate claims resulted in long delays. It was very difficult to agree on assessment values, property restoration costs, and general administrative procedures with all levels of French bureaucracy. The USAF and Army had invested over $4 billion on 350 parcels of French real estate, excluding their acquisition cost. It had been faster to move into France than to depart it. It took three to four years before disposition of some facilities was satisfactorily agreed upon; the bureaucrats continually found obstacles to accepting MLS estimates, or would refuse to reimburse the U.S. for improvements. The standard technique employed by the French government was to frustrate the U.S. negotiators until they accepted a quick settlement at minimum reimbursement.

The Department of State, Department of Defense, and HQ Air Force carefully managed the news about our departure from France, the decrease in tactical airpower, and the problems it created for an integrated NATO air defense of Western Europe. Negative comments by USAF personnel departing France were not permitted to be released to the media. Final relocation costs and lost infrastructure investments were never mentioned in press briefings and cannot be found up to the present day. Fortunately for State and DOD, the media was focusing on Vietnam so the removal of our forces from France went virtually unreported in the U.S. The few news releases by DOD concerning FRELOC were very vague and erroneous as to base locations and unit movements from France.

Project FRELOC had a positive effect on the U.S. International Balance of Payments (IBOP). USAFE estimated a net annual savings of $45,931,900 by eliminating operations in France. More than 10,280 Air Force personnel were transferred to CONUS and over 5,600 French employees' jobs were terminated. Additional savings not computed were the elimination of costs of Air Force personnel living off base on the economy, costs for transportation, base utilities, and forecasted major military construction projects required in France. The Army also saved a similar amount of money by departing France.

The FRELOC After Action Report optimistically states, "The movement out of France was made in a friendly manner which won admiration and friendliness from the French people. This was a wise policy which will aid in the attainment of the large and more permanent objectives." To most people this was putting a happy face on a situation that cost the United States dearly, but since there was no alternative to our departure, we at least could show the NATO nations that U.S. Forces in their countries were not there to occupy but to defend them, at their invitation.

All NATO tactical and logistics planning had to be dramatically revised because of FRELOC. LOCs through Belgium, Luxembourg and Netherlands were established but presented very attractive targets. Most supplies were poorly positioned for emergency use after removal from France. War Readiness Material (WRM) was widely separated from the combat wings. Lack of satisfactory storage locations for conventional aircraft munitions was a serious deficiency in war planning. The French Government insisted that the NATO and U.S. pipelines installed across France could be used in peacetime only; this was one of USAFE's greatest concerns and huge sums had to be spent on additional POL storage facilities in West Germany.

Most NATO military leaders and ministers thought France would return to NATO's military structure; especially in the event of a Soviet attack on Western Europe. France always remained in the NATO political structure and maintained a FAF liaison office on Ramstein AB.

The most serious result of FRELOC affecting NATO war plans was the loss of air bases in France to receive rapid reinforcement of tactical airpower from CONUS. USAF war plans consistently called for over 1,200 fighters and reconnaissance aircraft from TAC, ANG, and AFRES, to arrive in Europe within fifteen days after requested by SACEUR. Initial plans made after FRELOC called for TAC augmentation aircraft to arrive at the following bases: 111 TAC fighters at Chelveston, 115 at Sculthorpe, and 50 at Mildenhall. Later, additional air bases in the Netherlands and northern Germany were added to war plans for arriving fighters. By summer of 1968, USAFE commanders hoped they had fully absorbed the impact of Project FRELOC and another force reduction, Crested Cap; plus a withdrawal of forces from Europe to support Southeast Asia operations. They were concerned that further improvements in Europe would be deferred as long as fighting continued in Vietnam. Another threat to the security of the free world surfaced in August 1968 when the Soviets invaded Czechoslovakia; but NATO chose to treat this as an internal Iron Curtain matter. It watched apprehensively and hoped the invasion would not go beyond the borders of Czechoslovakia, because this time USAFE could not be reinforced to provide that deterrent "show of force." The hot war in Southeast Asia took precedence over the cold war in Europe.

USAF and U.S. Army forces have never again been stationed in France, but in February 1994 USAF aircraft deployed there for the first time in more than twenty years. Five KC-135 Stratotankers flew from the French air base of Istre to refuel aircraft patrolling airspace over Bosnia-Herzegovina in Operation DENY FLIGHT.

Common Problems Encountered in France

The following systemic problems were commonly reported in squadron, group, and wing histories submitted to HQ USAFE from the organizations based in France 1951-66. Some of these were peculiar to France and some were USAFE wide. The reason for describing these pervasive problems is to assure the reader that his individual unit, squadron, group, or wing was not unique in France, cursed by the gods of logistics, or somehow deficient in qualified leadership.

Lack of Communication

Lack of communication was a fundamental problem that affected all USAFE activities in France. We are not talking about the lack of communication equipment or system hardware, but the absence of simple verbal or written information! The problems began in 1950 and continued until our departure in 1967. Surprisingly this communication gap does not appear in the wing histories of units based in West Germany or the United Kingdom. As previously mentioned, the English-French language difference was problem enough, but added to this was the almost complete lack of information available from USAFE that definitely impaired our efforts in France.

The communications problem began with the French government's unwillingness to tell their people about France's commitment to NATO and what it would entail. There was no mention of the planned arrival of U.S. military forces to operate air bases and lines of communications across their nation. Local Communists took advantage of this lack of information by spreading hostile rumors and misinformation. "The American military would take over France, seize property, homes, businesses, and conscript them into forced labor." The communists had time to sell the concept that having U.S. troops in France would be a repeat of WWII German occupation. Prior to property surveys and land acquisition, the local population was not informed that owners would receive just compensation for their land. Neither their local newspapers nor political leaders told them what it would be like having many Americans stationed at these bases after construction was completed; they had no facts, only rumors. The Wing commander at Toul AB finally seized the initiative in 1953 and, against regulations, conducted a press conference on base with the local media for several hours. The information he provided defused a situation that had created open hostility toward his base and personnel.

The same communication gap existed among USAF combat wings as they prepared to depart their CONUS air bases for duty in France. Wing commanders could get little firm information from HQ USAFE with which to brief their staffs. A package of maps, photos, and written description of their new base would have been extremely helpful; the data was requested but seldom received. This basic information was not available through HQ USAF or HQ TAC.

Frustrated by this lack of information, the Commander of the 126th Bomb Wing dispatched two officers on a one-week trip to Bordeaux in October 1951 to investigate and report on conditions at the base. This was only two weeks prior to his ADVON's departure. They returned with the first hard facts, maps, and photos of Bordeaux-Merganic AB that existed in CONUS! The real shock came to the 126th Wing ADVON party upon arrival at Rhein-Main AB on 23 October 1951. When contacting HQ Twelfth Air Force at Wiesbaden; they were told the staff officer was not expecting the wing until after 15 January 1952. No one at Twelfth Air Force knew the wing was scheduled to arrive at Bordeaux by 10 December 1951! It didn't even know the wing was going to France; it had been told the wing was to be based at Rhein-Main! So much for the flow of information from higher headquarters.

From 1951 through 1954 France remained a great mystery; it appeared that no one was willing to report the truth about conditions there. Combat wings arriving later in 1954 received a little more information from Twelfth Air Force, but it was back to the communication gap as the STAIR STEP units prepared to move into France. TAC briefings in CONUS were erroneous. The information presented did not accurately describe the condition of base buildings, shop equipment, vehicle fleets, telephone systems, and shortages of office equipment. Nor did it prepare them for the major reorganizations they would have to make after arrival in France. This inadequate preparation by USAFE is very similar to the well-briefed fighter mission, "Kick the tire, light the fire, the first man off is leader, and we will brief the mission on squadron common while climbing outbound to the target."

When individual filler personnel were assigned to bases in France, they were not briefed on their destination. When processing through Camp Kilmer, McGuire AFB, or Manhattan Beach AFS, they only knew they were departing for "somewhere" in France. This presented some interesting problems as the troops were suddenly thrust into the French culture with no language ability, and only cursory information on how to proceed to their new base.

Roger Misgen recollects his experience as a newly arrived pilot in 1955.

> When I completed flight training at Goodfellow AFB I was assigned to Toul AB in France. After arriving at the port of Hamburg, I found my orders were changed from Toul to Evreux. I was put on a train in Germany but had to change trains as I crossed into France. Speaking no French, I thought I was told to get off the train at Pacy sur Eure. There I was, in a rainstorm, in a foreign country where I couldn't speak the language, and the inhabitants couldn't or wouldn't speak English. I was confused to say the least, a brand new 2d Lieutenant from a farm in Minnesota, and no way to find out where I was, or how to get to Evreux Air Base. My angel must have been watching because out of nowhere came a G.I. construction grader being towed by an open truck. I hailed the vehicle and found out it was the Army Engineers traveling fom Dreux AB to work on Evreux. The driver offered me a ride in the open truck. I tossed my B-4 bag up on the grader and climbed aboard. I arrived wet and disheveled, but happy to be there.

Airmen and officers in West Germany were dispatched to France without being told the base location or phone numbers, and without train arrangements or simple maps. During 1951 and 1952 even newly assigned civil engineering officers were sent out to their construction projects without maps, photos, or a briefing of project scope—not even local town names. It seemed no officials in the Army or Air Force thought to purchase a stock of Michelin road maps of France to assist these people. A classic case was finding Dreux-Louvilliers Air Base; the base was eighteen miles from Dreux and sixteen miles from Louvilliers. Bewildered newcomers would head for the city of Dreux to ask directions after searching the area, but the townspeople, unaware of our new base, directed them to Dreux-Vernouillet a WWII airdrome about five miles in the opposite direction. Had their supervisors told these struggling travelers that the villages of Crucey and Dampierre were very close to the new NATO air base they would have found it much sooner, with a lot less irritation.

Inadequate Electrical Power

Air base electrical power was primarily supplied by the French national electrical power grid, which in the rural regions was inadequate for all the new NATO facilities under construction during 1951-56. Electrical interruptions were frequent, often due to overloading. An on-base auxiliary power plant should have been part of the initial designs, but was not approved as a NATO infrastructure requirement, and became a nationally funded project instead. But USAF also refused to fund it. When a power failure occurred, operational capability was nil. The air base would lose all lighting, water pressure, building heat, runway/taxiway lights, fuel storage pumps, control tower radio sets, and radio navigation aids. Candles became the primary source of light! Fortunately by the early 1960s the French national power grid improved and power outages were greatly reduced.

The 1955-56 winter was unusually cold in northern France; in fact it was the coldest winter season during our sixteen-year stay. Inadequate electrical back-up for the heating system resulted in frozen water pipes in the buildings! Ice storms caused power lines to break, and when the electrical power failed, pumps that operated the hot water heating system stopped, causing broken pipes. The underground electrical systems on base did not fail, but the off base tower mounted supply lines did. The barracks were icy cold and without water. Much effort was directed toward providing for families during these cold spells. Getting heat and water service restored to the new trailers was a pressing problem because so many families had very young children. Roger Misgen remembers what it was like in the trailers at Evreux during the winter storms:

> During two winters that I was in residence at the Evreux trailer court we lost our electric power twice for about four or five days at a stretch due to the wires snapping during a historic cold spell. It was well below freezing in all of northern France. When wires get cold they tighten up, and when the base was wired the wires were strung too tightly causing them to snap during the very cold weather.
>
> With the loss of electricity, the heaters in the trailers didn't work. We piled everything we could on the bed at night and were especially concerned for our two month old baby. For light we had to use candles, flashlights, and an oil lamp we purchased on the French economy. The main part of the base was supplied electricity from an emergency generator so that the hang-

ers, base headquarters, the commissary, officers club, and other necessary buildings had electricity and heat. We spent time there whenever we could.

Along with the electrical problem came the water problem. The water was out, due to the cold. This meant no laundry, no bathing, and rationing what water we received from the tankers. The big tanker trucks plied the streets of the trailer court delivering potable water into everything we could find that would hold water. This gavc us drinking water and allowed us to wash and shave in cold water and to do some hand laundry. It was tough on those of us who had babies. Those were the days before disposable diapers!

It was toughest on those women whose husbands were off on a flight and had no help at all except from neighbors. Some couples were able to take leave and go somewhere that had electricity, heat, and running water, such as Germany.

Of course, being young and resilient we made it through the crisis. We had parties, played games and attended the Officers Club for some meals. Everyone would bring their children along. We didn't have much water but we had plenty of beer! Looking back, it was another of the very valuable growth experiences that Air Force service gave us, which perhaps toughened us and made us into the beings we are today.

These storms cost many man-hours and expensive replacement parts to rapidly restore service. The air installations squadron troops performed an outstanding job of restoring base utilities. The problem was partially solved by installing many small, gasoline-engine-driven, electrical generators for critical base functions. The inspection and maintenance of these power units required additional labor by the base air installations squadron. Of course all off-base electrical power line repairs were performed by the French utilities. Our new bases in France did survive this very unusual harsh winter but it strengthened the argument for greater on-base, emergency generation capacity.

An associated electrical problem that affected aircraft maintenance and operations was the difference in power line frequencies. U.S. equipment had North American standard 60 Hz electrical motors installed. They did not function correctly and would overheat when operated on the standard European commercial 50 Hz electrical power. Shop machinery rotated at slower speeds. The installation of a separate U.S. standard electrical system, i.e., three phase, 440Vac or 220Vac, 60 Hz, technical power service would have solved this problem. Here again, both NATO and USAF refused to fund this system. USAFE did fund procurement of frequency converters that were used in many base activities. This frequency incompatibility also caused destruction of the power supply in radio systems, test equipment, fluorescent lighting, and flight simulators. As late as 1961, aircraft flight simulators, vital for pilot proficiency training, were laying unused for eighteen months due to the lack of a suitable 60 Hz power converter. The USAAF was aware of this problem in WWII and every unit had many 60 Hz power generators available.

Vehicle Shortages

A persistent vehicle shortage plagued all wings and bases in France and was never solved. Initially, the vehicle fleet in France consisted of well-worn, WWII Army trucks, transferred from surplus stocks in West Germany. These were very inferior to vehicles the wings had left behind in CONUS—as directed by USAFE, who essentially unloaded junk on the new arrivals in France. These trucks were supposedly overhauled, but the overhaul consisted of nothing more than an air-force-blue paint job. The next step was to replace them with the new commercial vehicles common throughout the USAF at that time. Then, unfortunately, the number of vehicles allocated per base was reduced to meet budget limits not operational requirements. Special purpose vehicles such as crash rescue equipment, refueling tankers, and aircraft tugs were counted as part of the total base fleet. More importantly, the shortage of general purpose, small trucks adversely impacted aircraft maintenance. Virtually everyone was reduced to walking about the marguerites from the hangar shops; delays were inevitable. The last attempt to fill the need for trucks was purchasing a mix of French and German models to save money, but this created a logistics problem because all repair parts had to be purchased locally.

The total number of base vehicles would have been barely satisfactory if 100 percent had been kept in commission; but usually one-quarter of the fleet was inoperative (dead-lined). A backlog of dead-lined vehicles developed due to shortages of parts, tools, manuals, and skilled labor. Parts procurement was extremely difficult all across Europe; for instance, Ford and GM parts could only be found in Belgium. Motor vehicle squadrons would dispatch a truck and driver to pick up parts at the depot or distributor to eliminate the two or three-week delivery wait.

Aircraft refueling rigs were critical to the mission, but often one-third to two-thirds were inoperative because of repair-part shortages. The wings' director of maintenance requested depot support teams but received no response. Instead they had to dispatch people to the depot to pick up critically needed parts. The depot did not provide high priority shipping to the combat wings; it did not seem to appreciate the importance of keeping refueling rigs running. The obvious fact is, without fuel aircraft can't fly, and with many rigs inoperative, fewer planes could be turned around in the programmed time.

Assignment of Untrained Personnel

The problem of untrained personnel was Air Force-wide but especially felt in USAFE due to its lower personnel priority than SAC, ADC and FEAF. This resulted in 50 percent or more of the wing enlisted personnel being untrained, i.e., their Air Force Specialty Code (AFSC) and skill level did not match the unit manning document position to which they were assigned. Often airmen newly arrived from CONUS were direct duty assignees; they arrived in France after completing basic training only, with no technical schooling in a particular specialty. Many man hours were expended in training programs that diverted skilled technicians from their primary work. The more difficult the job the greater the shortage of trained airmen. Aircraft engine mechanics, airborne radar repairmen, airborne radio operators, and vehicle mechanics all required extensive on-the-job-training. This was usually conducted at the squadron shop level. There was little or no group or wing level organization to conduct training sessions. USAFE command-level training schools or teams should have been established for many career fields to remove some of this training burden from the individual wings. There was a persistent shortage of classrooms, tools, and shop space that prevented rapid training at the squadron level.

Hand Tool Shortages

This subject is a constant theme in wing histories. All tools were supplied from CONUS. What the wings did not take with them when they left CONUS remained a shortage for one or two years. Typically, six to eight months elapsed between submittal of a shop requisition to unit supply and receipt of the requested tool. This shortage of hand tools was increasing aircraft out-of-commission time during periodic inspections. Some repair shops record working out of two or three individual mechanics' tool kits. This really slowed production in a twenty-man section! Vehicle mechanics and civil engineering shops needed metric-sized hand tools for their trucks and equipment purchased in France and Germany, but they always had difficulty getting funds to purchase these tools locally. Time consuming procedures full of red tape were required for local purchases. It appears Chateauroux Air Depot could not procure metric tool kits for U.S. bases across Europe because there were no published Equipment Component Lists (ECL) for an individual or shop metric-sized tool kits, plus no USAF Stock Numbers for metric tools.

Aircraft Hardware Shortages

An inadequate supply of common aircraft hardware is described frequently in wing histories as another source of maintenance delays. Aircraft could not be returned to operational status during periodic inspections for lack of simple hardware. This included screws, nuts, bolts, washers, cotter pins, safety wire, rivets, gaskets, O-rings, hydraulic line fittings, and cushion clamps. Fasteners were often reused which was an unauthorized action in some repairs. There were many reasons for the problem: maintenance officers and NCOs inaccurately forecasting needs, a shortage of trained technical supply clerks and indifferent maintenance-supply liaison. A major problem was that hardware part numbers, originally in Army-Navy (AN) or National Aeronautical Standard (NAS) numbers, changed to Military Standard (MS) part numbers. Then in the late 1950s the USAF stock numbers changed to Federal Stock Numbers (NSN).

All aircraft hardware had to be supplied from CONUS through the Chateauroux Air Depot. It could not be purchased in Europe because of quality control standards for aeronautical dimensions and strengths. Even the UK had a different aviation hardware dimension system. Crew chiefs would scrounge, borrow, and steal needed items from hangar stock-bins to keep their aircraft in commission when stopping at bases in Germany and England.

Excessive TCTO Tasking

A Time Compliance Technical Order (TCTO) is a special directive issued to perform a one-time maintenance action on USAF equipment to improve or correct a newfound problem. This extra TCTO workload, when coupled with a shortage of trained airmen and hardware shortages, created a very real burden for the flying wings. Many of USAFE's aircraft were new deliveries, and after a year or two in operation they acquired a large number of TCTOs that varied from a

2-hour visual inspection to 180 hours of major repairs. TCTOs and other system improvements affected all USAF equipment: aircraft airframes, engines, and accessory systems, as well as vehicles and ground support equipment. Inadequate depot support pushed this workload on the wing maintenance organizations. It was very difficult to amend or revise depot maintenance contracts to include the indefinite cost increases and man-hours required to perform TCTOs, therefore the easy option was to let the wings solve their own TCTO problems. This extra workload greatly diminished aircraft in-commission rates. The reduced flying hours and aircrew training caused great concern to all wing commanders but they had no option but to have their squadrons perform these added tasks.

Summation

FRELOC began a bleak five year period during which USAFE lost 25 percent of its total strength. But in retrospect, the United States saved trillions of dollars by withdrawing its forces from France in 1967 instead of continuing to maintain them to the present day as we do in Germany. The Soviets did not put the vulnerability of our forces in West Germany to the test. Europe survived and thrived. The Soviet Union disintegrated, and former Warsaw Pact nations are now looking forward to becoming members of the very organization created to destroy them.

Efforts of the U.S. Air Force and Army men who served in France have been largely ignored, but they did their part to fight the Cold War, and none ever knew when it might have become a shooting war. Our forces were often victims of international political maneuvering and budget cuts, yet were always expected to perform their wartime mission.

The following chapters concentrate on the history of each base and the flying organizations that occupied them during our sixteen years in France.

Dedication ceremony at SHAPE HQ, Casteau, Belgium, 1967.
NATO photos

ACKNOWLEDGEMENTS

I would like to thank the following people who contributed to this chapter:

Roger Misgen was a C-119 pilot stationed at Evreux AB with the 465th Troop Carrier Wing in 1955-56.

Nicholas Scafidi was in the 108th Supply Squadron in the 108th Tactical Fighter Wing of the New Jersey Air National Guard that was activated for the Berlin Crisis in October 1961. He was stationed at Chaumont AB as part of Project STAIR STEP from 1961 to 1962.

International Security Network's Parallel History Project on NATO and the Warsaw Pact, www.isn.ethz.ch/php, by permission of the Center for Security Studies at ETH Zurich and the National Security Archive at the George Washington University on behalf of the PHP network, for the photo of building the Berlin wall.

COMMAND ELEMENTS, EUROPE 1950 - 1967

U.S. AIR FORCES
IN EUROPE

12th AIR FORCE

17th AIR FORCE

NATO

SUPREME HQ
ALLIED POWERS
EUROPE

FOURTH
ALLIED TACTICAL
AIR FORCE

ALLIED FORCES
CENTRAL EUROPE

U.S. ARMY
AVIATION ENGINEERS
SCARWAF

ROYAL CANADIAN 1st AIR DIVISION

U.S. ARMY
EUROPE COM Z

BORDEAUX AIR BASE, FRANCE

126th BOMBARDMENT WING, LIGHT

7 DECEMBER 1951 - 24 MAY 1952

126th
BOMBARDMENT WING,
LIGHT

108th BOMB
SQUADRON,
LIGHT

180th BOMB
SQUADRON,
LIGHT

168th BOMB
SQUADRON, LIGHT

CHAMBLEY AIR BASE, FRANCE

21st FIGHTER-BOMBER WING

12 DECEMBER 1954 - 8 FEBRUARY 1958

21st FIGHTER-BOMBER WING

72d FIGHTER-BOMBER SQUADRON

416th FIGHTER-BOMBER SQUADRON

531st FIGHTER-BOMBER SQUADRON

CHAMBLEY AIR BASE, FRANCE

7122d TACTICAL WING

7 NOVEMBER 1961 - 16 JULY 1962

122d TACTICAL FIGHTER WING

163d TACTICAL FIGHTER
SQUADRON

CHAMBLEY AIR BASE, FRANCE

25th TACTICAL RECONNAISSANCE WING

24 SEPTEMBER 1965 - 15 OCTOBER 1966

25th TACTICAL
RECONNAISSANCE WING

19th TACTICAL
RECONNAISSANCE
SQUADRON

42d TACTICAL
RECONNAISSANCE
SQUADRON

CHATEAUROUX AIR DEPOT, FRANCE

73rd AIR DEPOT WING

27 FEBRUARY 1951 - 20 MARCH 1967

CENTRAL AIR MATERIAL AREA, EUROPE

RADIO RELAY SQUADRONS, FRANCE

7th RADIO RELAY SQUADRON

(Approved 1955)

8th RADIO RELAY SQUADRON

(Approved 1954)

CHAUMONT AIR BASE, FRANCE

137th FIGHTER-BOMBER WING

13 MAY 1952 - 9 JULY 1952

137th FIGHTER-BOMBER WING

125th FIGHTER-BOMBER SQUADRON

127th FIGHTER-BOMBER SQUADRON

128th FIGHTER-BOMBER SQUADRON

CHAUMONT AIR BASE, FRANCE

48th FIGHTER-BOMBER WING

10 JULY 1952 - 15 JANUARY 1960

48th FIGHTER-BOMBER WING

492d FIGHTER-BOMBER SQUADRON

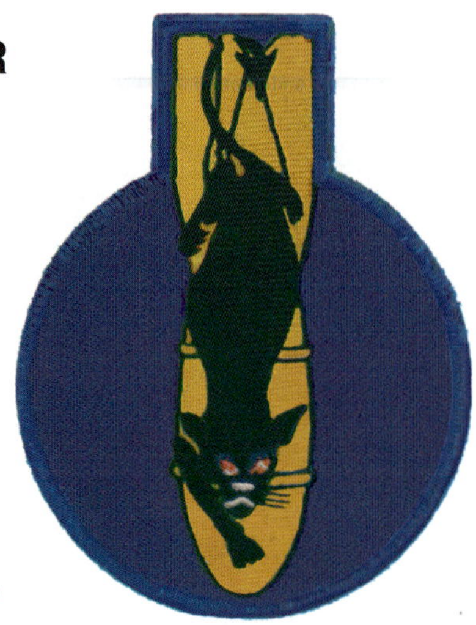

494th FIGHTER-BOMBER SQUADRON

493d FIGHTER-BOMBER SQUADRON

CHAUMONT AIR BASE, FRANCE

7108th TACTICAL WING

3 NOVEMBER 1961 - 20 JULY 1962

108th TACTICAL FIGHTER WING

141st TACTICAL FIGHTER SQUADRON

CHAUMONT AIR BASE, FRANCE

366th TACTICAL FIGHTER WING

8 MAY 1962 - 15 JULY 1963

366th
TACTICAL
FIGHTER WING

389th TACTICAL
FIGHTER SQUADRON

390th TACTICAL
FIGHTER SQUADRON

391st TACTICAL
FIGHTER SQUADRON

480th TACTICAL
FIGHTER SQUADRON

DREUX AIR BASE, FRANCE

60th TROOP CARRIER WING

15 OCTOBER 1955 - 25 SEPTEMBER 1958

60th TROOP CARRIER WING

10th TROOP CARRIER SQUADRON

11th TROOP CARRIER SQUADRON

12th TROOP CARRIER SQUADRON

DREUX AIR BASE, FRANCE

309th TROOP CARRIER GROUP (ASSAULT)

2 JUNE 1956 - 25 SEPTEMBER 1958

376th
TROOP CARRIER
SQUADRON
(ASSAULT)

NO
GROUP PATCH
APPROVED

377th
TROOP CARRIER
SQUADRON
(ASSAULT)

378th
TROOP CARRIER
SQUADRON
(ASSAULT)

31st WEATHER
SQUADRON

AACS AND
31st WEATHER SQ
HAD DETACHMENTS AT
ALL BASES IN FRANCE

AIR & AIRWAYS
COMMUNICATIONS
SQUADRON

DREUX AIR BASE, FRANCE

7117th TACTICAL WING

3 NOVEMBER 1961 - 22 JULY 1962

117th TACTICAL RECONNAISSANCE WING

106th TACTICAL RECONNAISSANCE SQUADRON

ETAIN AIR BASE, FRANCE

388th FIGHTER-BOMBER WING
12 DECEMBER 1954 -10 DECEMBER 1957

388th
FIGHTER-BOMBER
WING

561st FIGHTER-BOMBER
SQUADRON

562d FIGHTER-BOMBER
SQUADRON

563d FIGHTER-BOMBER
SQUADRON

ETAIN AIR BASE, FRANCE

49th FIGHTER-BOMBER WING

10 DECEMBER 1957 - 25 AUGUST 1959

49th
FIGHTER-BOMBER
WING

7th
FIGHTER-BOMBER
SQUADRON

8th
FIGHTER-BOMBER
SQUADRON

9th FIGHTER-BOMBER
SQUADRON

ETAIN AIR BASE, FRANCE

7121st TACTICAL WING

5 NOVEMBER 1961 - 16 JULY 1962

121st TACTICAL FIGHTER WING

166th TACTICAL FIGHTER SQUADRON

EVREUX AIR BASE, FRANCE

465th TROOP CARRIER WING

23 MAY 1955 - 8 JULY 1957

465th TROOP
CARRIER WING

780th TROOP
CARRIER SQUADRON

781st TROOP
CARRIER SQUADRON

782d TROOP
CARRIER SQUADRON

EVREUX AIR BASE, FRANCE

317th TROOP CARRIER WING

17 APRIL 1957 - 25 SEPTEMBER 1958
15 APRIL 1963 - 20 JUNE 1964

317th
TROOP CARRIER
WING

39th
TROOP CARRIER
SQUADRON

40th
TROOP CARRIER
SQUADRON

41st TROOP CARRIER
SQUADRON

EVREUX AIR BASE, FRANCE

513th TROOP CARRIER WING
15 APRIL 1966 - 1 JULY 1966

322d AIR DIVISION

EVREUX AB	CHATEAUROUX AD
12 AUGUST 1955 - 1 APRIL 1964	1 APRIL 1964 - 25 AUGUST 1966

LAON AIR BASE, FRANCE

126th BOMBARDMENT WING, LIGHT

25 MAY 1952 - 31 DECEMBER 1952

126th BOMBARDMENT WING, LIGHT

108th BOMB SQUADRON, LIGHT

180th BOMB SQUADRON, LIGHT

168th BOMB SQUADRON, LIGHT

LAON AIR BASE, FRANCE

38th BOMBARDMENT WING, LIGHT

1 JANUARY 1953 - 18 JUNE 1958

71st BOMB SQUADRON, LIGHT

405th BOMB SQUADRON, LIGHT

822d BOMB SQUADRON, LIGHT

LAON AIR BASE, FRANCE

66th TACTICAL RECONNAISSANCE WING

10 JULY 1958 - 30 AUGUST 1966

66th TACTICAL RECONNAISSANCE WING

17th TACTICAL RECONNAISSANCE SQUADRON

18th TACTICAL RECONNAISSANCE SQUADRON

32d TACTICAL RECONNAISSANCE SQUADRON

38th TACTICAL RECONNAISSANCE SQUADRON

PHALSBOURG AIR BASE, FRANCE

23d HELICOPTER SQUADRON

15 NOVEMBER 1956 - 8 JANUARY 1958

513th FIGHTER INTERCEPTOR SQUADRON

16 APRIL 1958 - 8 JANUARY 1961

PHALSBOURG AIR BASE, FRANCE

102d TACTICAL FIGHTER WING

7 NOVEMBER 1961 - 20 JULY 1962

102d TACTICAL
FIGHTER WING

101st TACTICAL
FIGHTER SQUADRON

138th TACTICAL
FIGHTER SQUADRON

131st TACTICAL
FIGHTER SQUADRON

TOUL AIR BASE, FRANCE

117th TACTICAL RECONNAISSANCE WING

10 JANUARY 1952 - 9 JULY 1952

117th TACTICAL RECONNAISSANCE WING

112th TACTICAL RECONNAISSANCE SQUADRON

157th TACTICAL RECONNAISSANCE SQUADRON

160th TACTICAL RECONNAISSANCE SQUADRON

TOUL AIR BASE, FRANCE

10th TACTICAL RECONNAISSANCE WING

10 JULY 1952 - 9 MAY 1953

10th TACTICAL RECONNAISSANCE WING

1st TACTICAL RECONNAISSANCE SQUADRON

32d TACTICAL RECONNAISSANCE SQUADRON

38th TACTICAL RECONNAISSANCE SQUADRON

TOUL AIR BASE, FRANCE

465th TROOP CARRIER WING

2 APRIL 1954 - 22 MAY 1955

465th TROOP
CARRIER WING

780th TROOP
CARRIER SQUADRON

781st TROOP
CARRIER SQUADRON

782d TROOP
CARRIER SQUADRON

TOUL AIR BASE, FRANCE

50th FIGHTER-BOMBER WING

17 JULY 1956 - 10 DECEMBER 1959

50th
FIGHTER-BOMBER
WING

81st FIGHTER-BOMBER
SQUADRON

417th FIGHTER-BOMBER
SQUADRON

10th FIGHTER-BOMBER SQUADRON

TOUL AIR BASE, FRANCE

7131st TACTICAL WING

13 NOVEMBER 1961 - 17 JULY 1962

131st TACTICAL FIGHTER WING

110th TACTICAL FIGHTER SQUADRON

TOUL AIR BASE, FRANCE

26th TACTICAL RECONNAISSANCE WING

1 JULY 1965 - 5 OCTOBER 1966

26th TACTICAL RECONNAISSANCE WING

22d TACTICAL RECONNAISSANCE SQUADRON

32d TACTICAL RECONNAISSANCE SQUADRON

38th TACTICAL RECONNAISSANCE SQUADRON

RCAF GROSTENQUIN, FRANCE

2 WING (F) ROYAL CANADIAN AIR FORCE

1 NOVEMBER 1952 - 1 JULY 1964

2 WING (F)

416th SQUADRON

421st SQUADRON

423d SQUADRON

430th SQUADRON

RCAF MARVILLE, FRANCE

1 WING (F) ROYAL CANADIAN AIR FORCE

1 MARCH 1955 - 1 APRIL 1967

1 WING (F)

410th SQUADRON

439th SQUADRON

441st SQUADRON

445th SQUADRON

Notes

The following chapters provide descriptions of activities at each of our main air bases, the Chateauroux Air Depot and its sub-depots, the four DOBs, the U.S. Army, and RCAF 1 Air Division. At the end of each chapter I have included tail numbers for each base. Collecting these was a daunting task. As my research progressed, it became a great challenge and consumed much time. Unfortunately most wing and squadron unit histories do not list assigned aircraft. I have had to search the microfilm Aircraft Record Cards at the USAF HRC, Maxwell AFB, AL. Reviewing 2,500 F-86D cards and 2,400 F-84F cards looking only for those in France may have produced a few errors! I would appreciate corrections and additions. The aircraft listings are as complete and error free as I can make them, but input from the reader is welcomed. Several veterans provided partial lists which proved of immense value to narrow the search. After twelve years of searching, the 38th Bomb Wing B-57B/C tail buzz letters are still not complete, help! Aircraft losses are also difficult to find and, unfortunately, my listings are not complete. The one line summaries I have included are an abbreviated description from the accident report of the event that caused loss of an aircraft that operated in, or was enroute to France.

For easier reading, I have deleted the AN/ "Army-Navy" prefix for the radio and radar equipment used in France. Dates are given in day, month, year sequence used in the U.S. military.

The bar chart on the following two pages gives a timeline of the U.S. wings and squadrons, and the aircraft they flew. Hopefully it will provide the reader with a clearer picture of the comings and goings over our sixteen years in France.

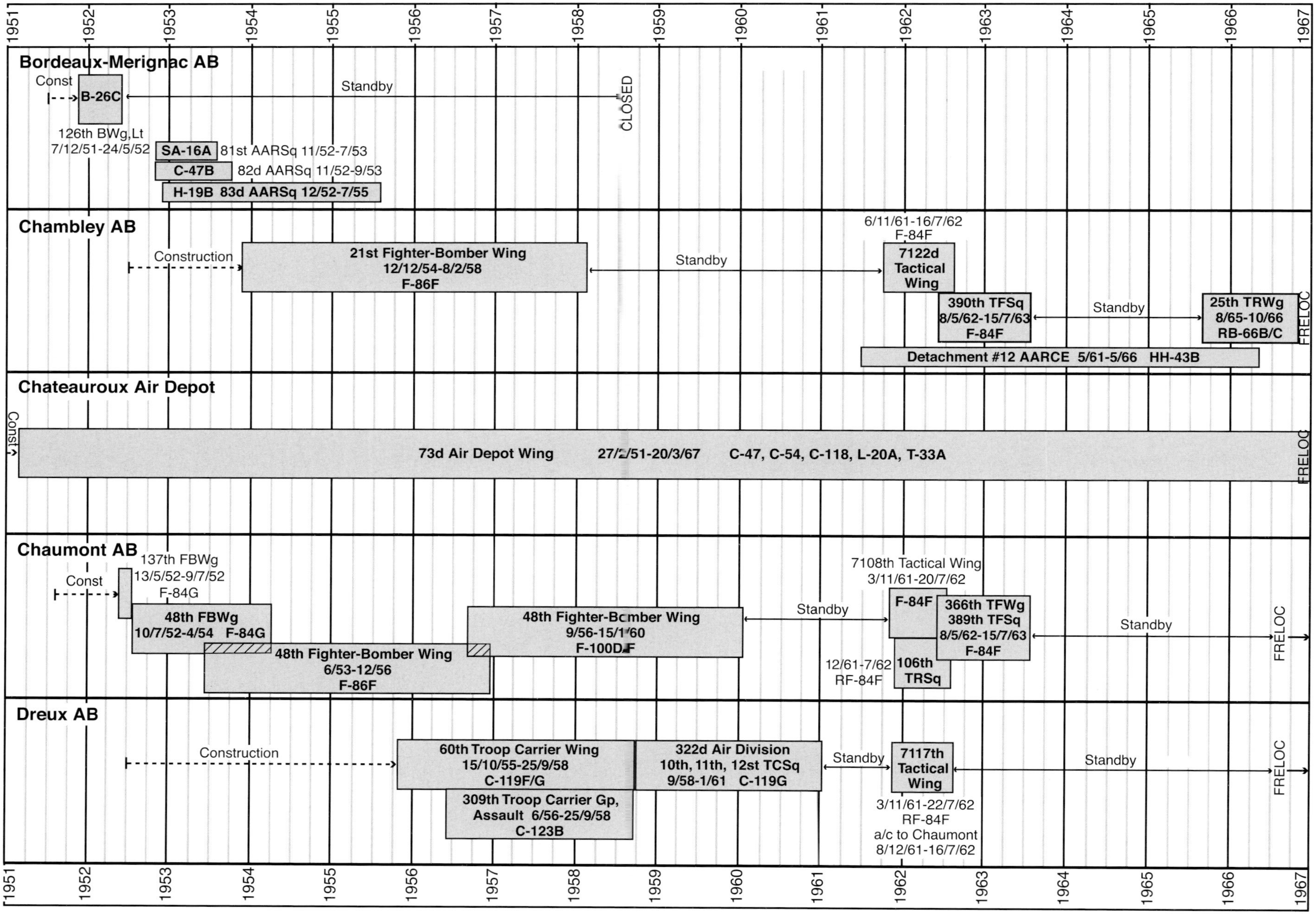
1951
1952
1953
1954
1955
1956
1957
1958
1959
1960
1961
1962
1963
1964
1965
1966
1967
Bordeaux-Merignac AB
Const
B-26C
Standby
CLOSED
126th BWg,Lt
7/12/51-24/5/52
SA-16A
81st AARSq 11/52-7/53
C-47B
82d AARSq 11/52-9/53
H-19B 83d AARSq 12/52-7/55
Chambley AB
Construction
21st Fighter-Bomber Wing
12/12/54-8/2/58
F-86F
Standby
6/11/61-16/7/62
F-84F
7122d
Tactical
Wing
390th TFSq
8/5/62-15/7/63
F-84F
Standby
25th TRWg
8/65-10/66
RB-66B/C
FRELOC
Detachment #12 AARCE 5/61-5/66 HH-43B
Chateauroux Air Depot
Const
73d Air Depot Wing
27/2/51-20/3/67
C-47, C-54, C-118, L-20A, T-33A
FRELOC
Chaumont AB
Const
137th FBWg
13/5/52-9/7/52
F-84G
48th FBWg
10/7/52-4/54 F-84G
48th Fighter-Bomber Wing
6/53-12/56
F-86F
48th Fighter-Bomber Wing
9/56-15/1/60
F-100D/F
Standby
7108th Tactical Wing
3/11/61-20/7/62
F-84F
366th TFWg
389th TFSq
8/5/62-15/7/63
F-84F
12/61-7/62
RF-84F
106th
TRSq
Standby
FRELOC
Dreux AB
Construction
60th Troop Carrier Wing
15/10/55-25/9/58
C-119F/G
309th Troop Carrier Gp,
Assault 6/56-25/9/58
C-123B
322d Air Division
10th, 11th, 12st TCSq
9/58-1/61 C-119G
Standby
7117th
Tactical
Wing
3/11/61-22/7/62
RF-84F
a/c to Chaumont
8/12/61-16/7/62
Standby
FRELOC

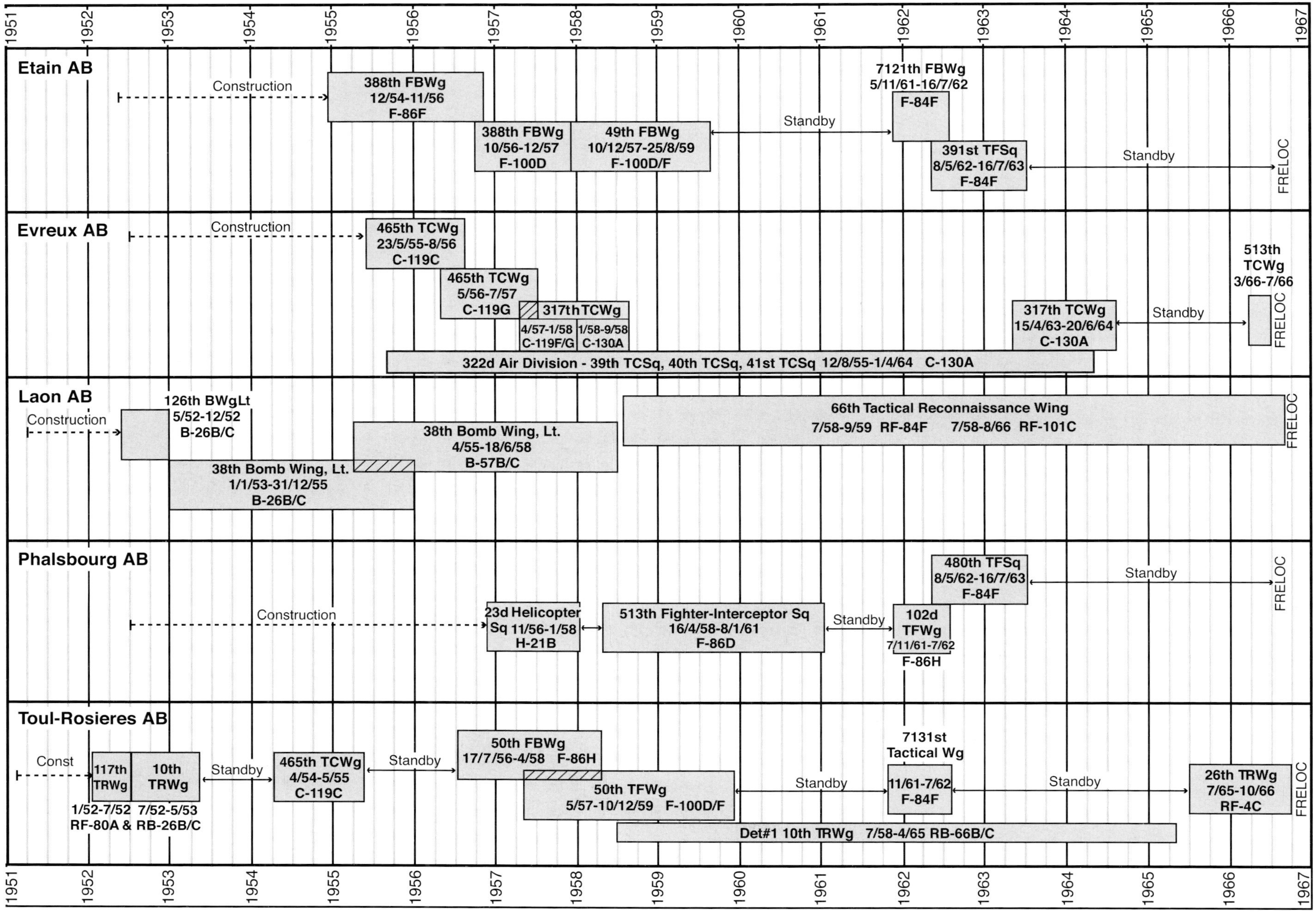
1951
1952
1953
1954
1955
1956
1957
1958
1959
1960
1961
1962
1963
1964
1965
1966
1967
Etain AB
Construction
388th FBWg
12/54-11/56
F-86F
388th FBWg
10/56-12/57
F-100D
49th FBWg
10/12/57-25/8/59
F-100D/F
Standby
7121th FBWg
5/11/61-16/7/62
F-84F
391st TFSq
8/5/62-16/7/63
F-84F
Standby
FRELOC
Evreux AB
Construction
465th TCWg
23/5/55-8/56
C-119C
465th TCWg
5/56-7/57
C-119G
317th TCWg
4/57-1/58
C-119F/G
1/58-9/58
C-130A
317th TCWg
15/4/63-20/6/64
C-130A
Standby
513th
TCWg
3/66-7/66
FRELOC
322d Air Division - 39th TCSq, 40th TCSq, 41st TCSq 12/8/55-1/4/64 C-130A
Laon AB
Construction
126th BWgLt
5/52-12/52
B-26B/C
38th Bomb Wing, Lt.
1/1/53-31/12/55
B-26B/C
38th Bomb Wing, Lt.
4/55-18/6/58
B-57B/C
66th Tactical Reconnaissance Wing
7/58-9/59 RF-84F 7/58-8/66 RF-101C
FRELOC
Phalsbourg AB
Construction
23d Helicopter
Sq 11/56-1/58
H-21B
513th Fighter-Interceptor Sq
16/4/58-8/1/61
F-86D
Standby
102d
TFWg
7/11/61-7/62
F-86H
480th TFSq
8/5/62-16/7/63
F-84F
Standby
FRELOC
Toul-Rosieres AB
Const
117th
TRWg
10th
TRWg
1/52-7/52 7/52-5/53
RF-80A & RB-26B/C
Standby
465th TCWg
4/54-5/55
C-119C
Standby
50th FBWg
17/7/56-4/58 F-86H
50th TFWg
5/57-10/12/59 F-100D/F
Standby
7131st
Tactical Wg
11/61-7/62
F-84F
Standby
26th TRWg
7/65-10/66
RF-4C
FRELOC
Det#1 10th TRWg 7/58-4/65 RB-66B/C

A standard WWII Douglas B-26C-35-DT #44-35549 flown by the 180th Light Bomb Squadron, 126th Bomb Wing (L) at Bordeaux-Merignac Air Base.
Air Force Historical Research Center, Maxwell AFB, AL

6

BORDEAUX-MERIGNAC AIR BASE

The city of Bordeaux is in the Gironde Department, 340 miles southwest of Paris. It was established by Celtic tribes and later developed by the Romans as a flourishing trading port. In the middle ages it was the capital of Aquitaine in the kingdom of France. Bordeaux came under British rule when Eleanor of Aquitaine married Henry II of England in 1152. During the 300 years of British rule it greatly expanded its trading market, and Bordeaux wines, long an important product of the region, acquired their international reputation.

Its maritime trade continued growing when Aquitaine was returned to France in 1453. In the 18th century it traded products as far away as America. In fact, when Thomas Jefferson visited Bordeaux in 1787, while ambassador to France, he was very taken with the architecture and the university, but mostly with the wine. He ordered 250 bottles for the Paris embassy, and after his return to the United States ordered Bordeaux wine for President Washington's table. Today Bordeaux is known as much for its industry and commerce as for it famous wine.

Bordeaux-Merignac Airport (44° 50' N - 00° 43'W, elevation 161 feet) is located six miles (10 km) west of the city. During the 1920s and 1930s it became a busy commercial-military field. Air France flew from Bordeaux throughout Europe and Africa, Marcel Bloch Aviation built aircraft, and L'Armee de l'Air used the field as a training center for airframe and engine specialists. In the mid 1930s, expansion of the French Air Force included construction of a bomber base in the southeast corner of the airfield, separate from the technical training center. This facility had concrete aprons, four large steel hangars, four small concrete operations buildings and a large administration building.

During WWII the German Luftwaffe K.G. 40 used the French air base for maritime reconnaissance, flying Fw 200C Kondors and later He 177A Griefs, to patrol the North Atlantic and locate allied shipping. The U.S. Eighth Army Air Force and the RAF bombed the field in 1943. Several hangars and aircraft were destroyed by these air raids, and the bomb damage remained in 1950 because this southeast corner had lain idle since 1945.

In 1950 NATO proposed developing the former French bomber base for four distinct purposes:

(1) an interim deployment base for tactical wings awaiting their permanent base completion in northern France,
(2) a USAFE supply point to be developed later into an air depot,
(3) an airfield from which to conduct aerial bombing and gunnery training, and
(4) an airfield for troop carrier units rotating from CONUS into Europe for training.

The Bordeaux-Merignac airdrome was a very active airfield when the USAF became its fourth tenant in 1951. The commercial terminal on the field's northern edge served Air France and British European Airways. West of the commercial terminal was the Dassault Aircraft factory where the new Ouragan jet fighter was being built and flight tested. The French Air Force training base was still being used for technical training; they only flew once or twice a day. Only the site of the former French bomber base had not been cleared or improved.

Evidence of the Luftwaffe's presence was found throughout the area: many warning signs in the hangars were in German, the perimeter was still mined, and aircraft munitions were scattered throughout the new base. Large quantities of concrete practice bombs were stacked along hangar walls. Bombed-out hangars remained with only two hangars usable.

Site construction for the NATO base started about 1 August 1951 when a French contractor built concrete roads that, added to the existing circa 1935 streets, were the beginning of a tent city. Detachment A of the 85th Air Depot Wing from Erding, West Germany, was sent to manage logistics as tons of material began to arrive. Water lines and sewage pipes were laid, and a limited electrical system was installed. A vital open drainage trench was dug to drain the base during Bordeaux's heavy winter rains. The tent configuration at Bordeaux was a little different than at the other interim bases. There were 225 GP medium tent frames and 20 GP large tent frames constructed with wood floors. The GP medium tents housed nine airmen or six officers. Squadron Headquarters, Unit Supply, Operations and aircrew Personal Equipment used the GP large tents. Fortunately Bordeaux's mild, wet, rarely freezing winters allowed for reasonable tent living. Prefabricated portable wooden buildings were erected for three large mess halls, seven large 300-man latrines, the hospital, communications center, and base exchange. The main entrance to the base was on the north side off highway D106 near the town of Beutre. There was a back road off the base leading into the small town of Pichey. Bordeaux Air Base's mailing address was APO 16.

126th Bombardment Wing, Light

The 126th Light Bomb Wing was assigned to occupy this site until completion of their interim base near Laon, France. The wing, consisting of approximately 305 officers and 1,360 airmen, was called to federal active duty on 1 April 1951 for a period of twenty-one months for the Korean War emergency. The wing had been flying Douglas B-26B and C Invader light bombers since late 1946 when the postwar National Guard was organized. It remained with the same mission and same aircraft type through 31 December 1952 when released from active duty.

The 126th LBWg originated as the WWII 344th Bombardment Group, Medium, flying Martin B-26s in the Ninth Air Force from England, France, Belgium, and Germany, earning a Distinguished Unit Citation (DUC). The 344th Bomb Group was redesignated the 126th Bomb Group, Light and allotted to the Illinois Air National Guard on 24 May 1946 as part of the postwar development of the reserve forces, keeping the heritage, insignia, and lineage of these former USAAF units. The 126th Bomb Group was expanded into the 126th Bombardment Wing, Light in October 1950.

When activated, the 126th consisted of four light bombardment squadrons and supporting units: the 108th based at Chicago Midway Airport, Chicago, Illinois; the 115th at the Lockheed Air Terminal, Burbank, California; the 168th at O'Hare International Airport, Park Ridge, Illinois; and the 180th at Rosecrans Municipal Airport, St. Joseph, Missouri. In May 1951 the 115th LBSq was transferred to the 47th Light Bomb Wing, which reduced the 126th to the usual three flying squadrons. By 15 July 1951 the 126th Wing had assembled at Langley AFB, Virginia, for three months of intensive combat aircrew training. Rumors persisted during this period that it would deploy to somewhere in France, Spain, or North Africa to expand NATO, even though a requirement existed for the wing in Korea. By 1 October 1951 the 126th began packing for movement to Bordeaux, France.

Commanders of the 126th LBWg during its time in France were BGEN Frank Allen from 1 April 1951 to 4 February 1952 and COL William J. Kennedy from 4 February 1952 to 31 December 1952.

Many of the B-26s required engine changes prior to overseas movement. USAFE did not want R-2800 engines with more than 500 hours total time to arrive in Europe because it had no depot engine overhaul capability at that time. Engines had to have less than 500 hours upon arrival in France or be replaced with zero time engines prior to overseas flights. This requirement resulted in forty-two engine changes within thirty days. About thirty-five man-hours were required for each engine replacement. Having to dispose of 1,200 gallons of used 100-weight engine oil was another problem created by the engine changes.

In preparation for the move, the wing dispatched an ADVON of fourteen officers and fifty-four airmen to France. The mission of the advance party was to assist Detachment A to set up the base and prepare for aircraft arrivals. Just prior to departure on 19 October, HQ, Tactical Air Command directed the ADVON and bomb wing to proceed to Rhein-Main AB, West Germany, not Bordeaux. Diplomatic problems with France had developed; France was still objecting to combat aircraft on its soil. At this time the Communist party was the major political party in Bordeaux and very much against the USAF being stationed there. The possibility of being based in Germany, not in France existed until 4 November.

The ADVON team departed Langley on 20 October and arrived in Europe the next day. They flew to Europe in a C-124A; it was the first one seen at Langley and the first one to arrive at Rhein-Main, and drew crowds of spectators at both bases. The ADVON's reception at Rhein-Main AB foretold future problems; a call to Twelfth Air Force HQ duty officer to advise him of the team's arrival revealed that nobody knew where they came from or why they had come to Europe! They had to wait eight days at Rhein-Main for final permission to enter France. Finally on 30 October the party flew into Bordeaux-Merignac in two C-82s to perform their job.

The first challenge the ADVON encountered was contacting the outside world. Commercial telephone connections were primitive; it was exceptional to have an uninterrupted conversation. They sometimes had to wait four to six hours to obtain a long distance line to Twelfth Air Force headquarters in Wiesbaden, West

Men from the U.S. Army 862d Engineer Aviation Battalion unloading pierced steel planking at Bordeaux AB, November 1951.
Frank Casale

Germany. Teletype messages intended for Bordeaux were routed to Chateauroux and then mailed to Bordeaux, which meant they didn't arrive for a week! Twelfth Air Force frequently requested the ADVON contact the 126th air or surface echelons to check on the progress of the wing's movement. They were concerned that the B-26 bombers would arrive in a dramatic show of force before all the diplomatic kinks had been smoothed out with the French. Contacting 126th Wing headquarters in Virginia would have been easy from West Germany but communication was nearly impossible from Bordeaux. It seems Twelfth Air Force didn't want to ask questions lest anyone realize how little they knew about the NATO operation in France. Consequently there was a total breakdown of command and control for at least thirty days during the air and sea movement.

Railcars filled with supplies began arriving at a siding near the airport. No one knew where the material originated, or if it was destined for the 126th Wing, but it had to be unloaded immediately to clear this small siding. Forty-five flat cars of World War II pierced steel planking (PSP) arrived one week and forty-one cars the following week, though there was no equipment for lifting or transporting the heavy bundles of PSP. Next, eleven carloads of telephone poles arrived. Fortunately the Army's 83d Engineer Construction Battalion from Bussac provided trucks and the 862d Engineer Aviation Battalion came from Rhein-Main AB to operate heavy lifting equipment. With everyone's help the material was eventually unloaded and stored.

The ADVON commander, LTC William C. Hoffman, quickly realized that his team should have had a minimum of 250 airmen. He could have used thirty to forty men just to meet base security needs. Theft of supplies and construction material was common. Sixty men were necessary to unload the rail cars, and thirty to forty men were needed to erect tents on completed frames and install stoves and fuel lines. Most obvious of all, with so much to do, his small ADVON should have arrived on 1 October not 30 October!

The most frustrating problem for the 126th ADVON and Detachment A people was the constant flow of visiting officers. Majors through Lt. Generals inspected the base, made design changes, and asked astounding questions. These late design changes delayed building completion and increased construction costs. Their questions showed a complete lack of understanding of the Air Force mission in France, such as, "Why are you here now? How long will you be here? How many men in a light bomb wing?" and the classic, "How many B-26s will be based here?" Their visits would last about three hours, after which they would return to Wiesbaden, or depart for Bordeaux where they stayed in downtown hotels. Not a single visiting officer spent a night on base in a tent. It sent a clear message to Bordeaux personnel that their base was a very undesirable place and not worth more than a cursory visit. As one 126th Wing major remarked sarcastically, "Bordeaux AB was too close to the front for the VIPs to risk being captured."

Back at Langley, wing commander BGEN Frank Allen was concerned that the B-26s would not have sufficient fuel for the winter flight across the North Atlantic. Long range, 675-gallon, bomb bay, ferry tanks were ordered from the depot for the Atlantic crossing. After unpacking and installation, the tanks were found to leak because of excessive corrosion from six years in outdoor storage. They were removed, repacked, and returned to the depot. This required extra work by aircraft mechanics just prior to departure. The wing

Bordeaux Air Base from the air, March 1952. White circles mark World War II bomb craters.
Ray DuCasse

commander decided to stick with the existing internal tanks (925 gallons total) and bet on reliable weather forecasting.

The air movement was conducted as described in chapter 2. The flight echelon consisted of forty-eight B-26s and two C-47s, flying the North Atlantic route. The 180th LBSq, led by the wing commander, was the first to depart Langley AFB on 30 October for Westover AFB, Massachusetts, followed by the 108th LBSq on 1 November, and the 168th LBSq on 2 November. The two C-47s flew together and departed ahead of the bombers but arrived much later because of their slower air speed. They carried airborne radio operators that maintained contact with the C-54s and ground airway stations. The wing did not set a record for speed in its crossing, but all aircraft and personnel arrived safely. One must remember that the WWII B-26s did not have anti-icing fluids, deicing boots, cockpit heaters, or windshield defogging systems.

In fact, bad weather between Iceland and Prestwick, Scotland, caused thirteen B-26s of the 108th Bomb Squadron to run dangerously low on fuel. The flight leader, COL Wilson V. Newhall, decided to land on what appeared to be an abandoned airfield spotted through thickening clouds. The formation let down and buzzed the airfield with no knowledge of their location. As they flew low to observe airfield conditions, a man cutting the grass along the runway jumped off his tractor in fright at the unexpected sight. He was the postmaster, maintaining the runway for the daily mail flight. After landing the men discovered they were on the Isle of Tiree off the coast of Scotland, on an airstrip used by the RAF Coastal Command in World War II. Tiree had no public facilities and was home to only seventy or eighty families. The officers departed in a C-54 while the postmaster made arrangements for the thirteen crew chiefs to stay with families. The Scots generously opened their homes and were disappointed they had only thirteen men to house. There is no record of them ever being reimbursed for their hospitality but their kindness made a big impression on the airmen who kept in touch with them for many years afterwards.

The following day a fully fueled C-54 was flown to Tiree from Prestwick, the fuel was transferred into drums, and about 100 gallons were hand pumped into each B-26. Following that, a C-54 brought out the pilots and navigators. They flew the B-26s off the island but left the crew chiefs behind. Knowing they too would soon leave, the islanders threw a farewell party for their guests. Some of them went by boat to the mainland to purchase enough spirits to ensure a

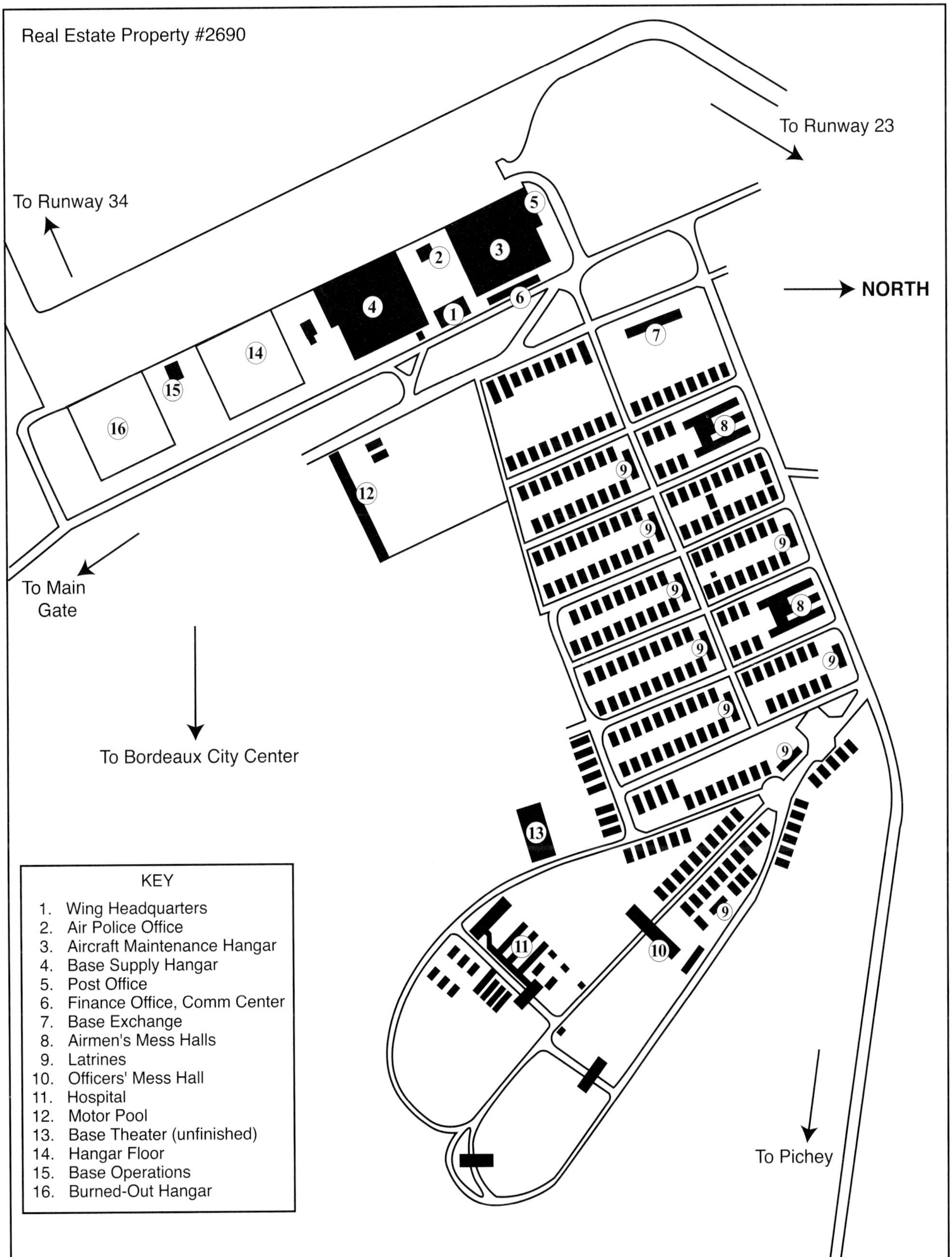

Map 6.1 Bordeaux-Merignac AB, France, January 1, 1952

Remains of a German He-177 in a bombed-out hangar.
Bordeaux-Merignac AB, November 1951.
Frank Casale

German cement practice bombs stored on floor
of destroyed hangar, November 1951.
Jerry McAuliffe

great party. Music and dancing continued until morning. The next day a C-54 flew to the island and picked up the sleepy crew chiefs. After a stop at Prestwick for immigration and customs, they continued on to Burtonwood Air Depot where they were served a late Thanksgiving dinner.

The enroute maintenance team following the bombers consisted of five officers and eighteen NCOs. Weather was the primary concern but a few minor problems were encountered; frequent inspection and thorough cleaning of engine oil filters was required on the newly installed R-2800 engines, many spark plugs had to be changed to platinum plugs to ease cold weather starting, and there were a few VHF radio tuning difficulties.

The only enroute accident occurred near Mont St. Michel, France, when two 180th LBSq bombers touched—a wing tip into the aft tail cone, causing minor damage. Forty-four Invaders arrived at Bordeaux AB on 22 November 1951. The last four Invaders arrived on 26 November after being delayed by weather and mechanical problems.

Lastly, the surface echelon departed Langley on 19 November by chartered buses for a daylong trip to Camp Kilmer in New Brunswick, New Jersey. The U.S. Army served them an excellent Thanksgiving Day dinner on 22 November. On 28 November, officers and airmen, with duffel bags over their shoulders, marched up the gangplank to board the troopship USNS General H.F. Hodges to set sail from the Brooklyn Navy Yard to La Pallice, France. A miserable eleven-day voyage ensued, with a North Atlantic winter storm system the whole way. Virtually all the men suffered from seasickness and fatigue. They were extremely happy to enter port and depart the ship for a train ride to Gazinet, a suburb of Bordeaux. From there they had a seven-mile ride to the air base in Army trucks and the shock of seeing their new base! It was not what they expected! Who would have imagined moving into a base with burnt and bombed-out hangars and row upon row of tents set on plots of bulldozed, raw, muddy earth! They didn't realize their first impression could have been worse! The advance party and flight echelon personnel had already made up beds, fired up the tent stoves, and organized the quarters by sections in anticipation of their arrival. Some of the men were so weak from the crossing they had to be helped down from the 2.5-ton trucks and wanted nothing more than to stretch out on a bunk that didn't rock! By 2400 hrs on 7 December all personnel were present and accounted for! The 126th Light Bomb Wing was back together again after fifty days.

On 7 December 1951 the 126th Wing with all personnel and aircraft at Merignac AB was transferred from Tactical Air Command to USAFE. It was the first combat wing assigned to NATO to arrive in France. It was also the first USAF combat unit to move back to France since WWII. And, it was the first to encounter all the problems of being based in France. Living and working conditions were unacceptable by peacetime USAF standards.

The 126th moved into Bordeaux-Merignac long before its infrastructure was able to support a wing. Working conditions for aircraft maintenance were totally inadequate. Expendable parts and some shop tools had been left behind in the states because higher headquarters assured the squadrons that the necessary supplies would be readily available in France. These did not exist, nor did the hangars and shops that were promised. This misinformation caused considerable hardship for the troops. Virtually all aircraft

126th's aircraft parked in front of bombed hangar .
This was their introduction to Bordeaux AB, November 1951.
Frank Casale

B-26 with its propellor and wheels sunk in the mud.
There was insufficent parking space on the ramp.
USAF History Office, Maxwell AFB

108th Sq tents with latrine in background, November 1951.
Jerry McAuliffe

108th Bomb Squadron radio shop tent.
George Spencer

maintenance work had to be done outdoors because of lack of hangar space. Only one hangar was available for aircraft work, and its roof had been perforated by bomb fragments, allowing rain to enter. The 1943 bombings destroyed two hangars, badly damaged a third, and did minor damage to the fourth. The best hangar was used as the base supply warehouse because it offered secure storage. The badly damaged hangar housed field maintenance squadron shops and was used primarily for major aircraft repairs

There was no wing level planning for maintenance shop sites, causing a scattered arrangement. Each maintenance section set up its own medium-size shop tent on any available spot . Pierced steel planking (PSP) was used as flooring in the shop tents to keep them from sinking into the mud. Electrical power was not always available, forcing some shops to operate their own small power generators. Radio shops had to generate their own 60 Hz ac power because French 50 Hz power would damage electronic test equipment. No thought had gone into the problems commercial French power would cause. There was a critical shortage of aircraft electrical ground power units, with only one per squadron. Some sections did not establish shops, but left their equipment packed until the next move.

Aircraft parking was a serious problem. Planes were parked wing-tip to wing-tip due to limited ramp space; some B-26s had to be parked on the ground and would sink into the mud with each rainfall. Extracating the planes required ingenuity and lots of manpower since there were no aircraft tractors (CLETRAC) available. Cables were attached between the main gear and 2.5-ton truck. This way no towing force was applied to the fragile nose gear. The heavy mud was shoveled by hand to create a ditch in front of the plane, then PSP ramps were placed in the ditch and the aircraft pulled carefully out of the pit.

The tents were heated with two standard World

Tent Christmas party, Bordeaux AB, December 16, 1951. Note the Sibley oil stove in the foreground.
Paul Douglas

The city of Bordeaux offered theaters and an opera house in 1951, as well as the service club.
Bob Gertner

War II QM Sibley stoves that burned a variety of fuels. At Bordeaux an extremely low-grade fuel oil was supplied that resulted in heavy greasy soot balls rolling around inside the tents and on the ground while producing very little heat. A new stove was designed in Germany and tried at Merignac. The infamous "dingbat" stoves burned hotter and one stove would heat a tent. A dingbat stove sounded similar to a little jet engine when the fuel was precisely adjusted. Dingbats would explode occasionally with great puffs of soot, and a few tents burned. One 300-man latrine building was burned to the ground in February because a dingbat overheated. Most of the soot and fumes were the result of poor quality fuel, not the stove design. The extremely damp weather and the fumes from the low-grade oil caused widespread respiratory illness. The base hospital used the same stoves for heating which just prolonged the problem for airmen sent there. Seriously ill personnel were airlifted by medevac C-82s to the 495th Station Hospital at Wiesbaden for long-term treatment. The solution was the arrival of spring and mild weather.

Trips began to the sunny shores of San Sebastian, Spain in January 1952.
Jerry McAuliffe

Life on base was not all hardship. There were no inspections in the tents, so life after work was a bit more relaxed than normal military standards. The men built furniture out of scrap wood to augment their G.I. bunks. Bottles of red wine were common in the tents. For pennies, children of the local farmers came round the tents and refilled the empty bottles from a wagon loaded with jars of homemade wine. Since it was Bordeaux perhaps it was good wine, but who knows, the airmen of 1951 were not connoisseurs; more likely, as they described themselves, kinda sewers! German mines still littered the base perimeter and everyone was warned to avoid the area. Mysteriously, these mines were occasionally detonated. Air police would arrive at the site to find no one knew anything about the explosion—so the activity surreptitiously continued!

Except for the World War II veterans, almost none of the airmen had been to a foreign country. There was no information booklet about the culture and language of France for these pioneers that was provided for later troops. Everyone realized they would hear only French, but it was always a shock to realize they couldn't communicate with the townspeople. Language classes were held, but there were too few teachers and most men didn't bother to crash the crowded classes. Eventually most learned enough French to get a great meal and make their way around the area.

Bordeaux had a strong communist faction at that time, and the airmen were warned to avoid confronta-

TB-26B #44-34597 undergoing periodic inspection outdoors at Bordeaux-Merignac AB, May 1952.
Ray DuCasse

tion. There were the expected "U.S. Go Home" posters in town, but no serious protests. The troops discovered later that the troublemakers were intimidated by the "Chicago Mobster" movie image. They were told that the Chicago guardsmen all carried guns and were tough gangster types. In an effort to have the French get to know their American neighbors, Special Services developed an enlisted club in Bordeaux and encouraged chaperoned young ladies to attend the dances. Special services also organized tours to show the men more of Europe: Superbagneres for skiing; Lourdes; San Sebastian, Spain; and Rome, Italy. No one seemed to need a tour arranged to find Paris!

Flight operations began slowly due to bad weather, inadequate VHF radio communication sets for civil airport/airways operation, and limited maintenance facilities. Pilots shook their head in disbelief at one unique obstacle. Flying was interrupted at least once a week to allow a local farmer to graze his sheep throughout the aircraft parking area. By February and March improved weather allowed increased flying activity and simultaneously improved wing morale.

Cross-country flights began to West Germany, mainly for radar calibration and interceptor exercises. Many new NATO ground control intercept (GCI) radar stations were being set up, requiring performance evaluation and director/operator training. From January through April, B-26s were being dispatched TDY to Furstenfeldbruck AB to provide radar and visual tracking training for the U.S. Army 34th AAA Brigade. These flights also enabled pilots and navigators to complete their AFR 60-2 training requirements.

The first major NATO exercises involving British, French, Italian, and U.S. Naval and Air Forces took place in February 1952. Operation GRAND SLAM deployed eighteen B-26 aircraft to FAF Istres AB near Marseilles. The exercise was conducted without aircraft accident or personnel injury.

The gunner training program in France was typical of the poor USAF decisions made during this time. When activated, the 126th Wing had approximately forty gunners who had accumulated several hours of actual turret firing, both air-to-air and air-

F-84E Skyblazers from Furstenfeldbruck with B-26 in background. Open House Airshow at Bordeaux in May 1952.
Jerry McAuliffe

The airshow held at Bordeaux in May 1952 was a popular success with the residents of the area.
Dale Peotter

to-ground, while in reserve status. Some men were WWII B-29 gunners with combat experience. After activation TAC ordered the gunners to be taken off flying status, stating that the B-26 gun turret system was obsolete. These gunners were then reassigned to other units throughout the USAF. In November 1951 the Air Force reversed this decision and decided that gunners would be assigned to the B-26 crews. Newly assigned personnel began to arrive to fill these vacancies. Unfortunately, these new gunners had virtually no flight training. Many had never been in a B-26 Invader. None of them had combat experience, therefore, the wing had to begin an intensive training program to develop their skills.

During January and February 1952, Operation VAMPIRE pitted FAF De Havilland Vampire jet fighters against our B-26 formations near Dax, France. The Vampire pilots needed the training with gun cameras, and the B-26 gunners badly needed the turret tracking experience. Our gunners were very surprised at how easily they tracked the fast jets after a few hours of training. General Electric's CF-6 remote control turret system still possessed rapid acting servo systems that could pose a threat to jet fighters if the gunner had a few hours of system operation.

Splash gunnery training was conducted in the Bay of Biscay during March and April 1952 with 16,000 rounds fired from the lower turrets. This was the first actual gun turret firing for many of the newly assigned gunners. Accuracy greatly increased with this training. Turret system mechanics enthusiastically welcomed this firing after almost a year of zero activity.

Operation VAMPIRE and the splash gunnery training were great opportunities to produce a completely trained combat crew, especially since the wing was tasked in April 1952 to supply crews for combat operations in Korea.

USAF Project 7019 sent the B-26 aircrews to FEAF on sixty-day tours to gain combat experience in night intruder operations. Wing and group operations officers also participated in this project; crews were assigned to the 3d or 17th Bomb Wings in Korea for combat training.

After surviving the Bordeaux winter and adjusting to difficult living conditions, a personnel policy decision struck the 126th Wing that adversely affected it throughout its stay in Europe. On 11 March 1952 HQ USAF announced a program of early release for Air Reserve officers and airmen. Simply stated, this policy decimated the wing's combat capability. The policy primarily affected enlisted men. By 16 March over 150 airmen were eligible for early separation. These were men whose reserve enlistments would expire before 31 December 1952 even though they had all agreed to serve until that date. These airmen departed Bordeaux by 1 April. Next, airmen who had WWII service were eligible for early release; these men were primarily skilled NCOs whose expertise wasn't replaced until 1953-54. Lastly "personnel non essential to the mission" were to be released as soon as possible. This stupid early release policy resulted in about 60 percent of the reserve airmen departing by 1 June 1952 after only six months at Bordeaux. I was very concerned the wing commander might declare himself "non-essential" and go home! Fortunately, regular Air Force filler personnel manned about 25 percent of the wing prior to departure from Langley, and they had to carry the mission burden. A few replacement personnel arrived, but most were new first term airmen with no maintenance experience. Very few replacements were received for armament, electronics, and engine maintenance. This resulted in the bomb squadron shops being 60 percent manned as the 126th was moving to Laon AB.

Air/ground operations with the U.S. Army in West Germany also began in April. This provided good training for the B-26 crews and air/ground liaison teams. One B-26 was a bit low while flying close air support. While attacking a column of armored vehicles, it struck one and dragged its bomb bay door across the vehicle causing engine and airframe damage but no injury to personnel. The pilot feathered the engine and made a successful emergency landing at Wiesbaden. Superior airmanship on the part of the 180th LBSq pilot saved the plane and crew. The Army was impressed with the attack realism!

The USAF transferred forty B-26 Invaders to France as part of MAP during 1951 and 1952. In February 1952 the 126th Wing was ordered to train FAF pilots to fly B-26s; they usually flew twenty to twenty-five hours for checkout. FAF Navigators/Bombardiers soon followed for ground and flight training. The objective was to train three to six crews per month. These French crews were excellent students and went on to fly Invaders in their Indochina war.

A serious operational problem developed as the 126th Wing began flying in European airspace. The basic problem was the very inadequate VHF Command radio set installed in the B-26. Almost all the B-26s were equipped with the 1942 SCR-522 VHF radio sets with four preset channels for pilot selection. A skilled radio repairman with test equipment was needed to change channel frequencies. The air traffic control system in Europe required as many as forty channels. The late WWII eight channel AN/ARC-3 was an absolute necessity for European IFR flying. Finally by February 1952, the B-26s began ARC-3 radio conversion, greatly improving the wing's operational capability. This program was done at Bordeaux by a mobile depot team from Erding AD. This radio upgrade required 110 man-hours per aircraft. Since the work had to be done outdoors, it was stalled whenever it rained. Consequently aircraft were also dispatched to the Erding and Burtonwood Depots, though the Burtonwood Depot conversions were unsatisfactory and created even more problems for the radio maintenance people at Bordeaux.

One example of the problems associated with depot maintenance at Burtonwood is both disturbing and humorous. While one of the B-26s was at the depot for ARC-3 conversion, Burtonwood performed a 100-hour inspection to train their mechanics to service B-26 aircraft. The inspection was not required and was done without the 126th's authorization. When the 126th crew arrived to bring the aircraft back to Bordeaux, they discovered that the nose gear down-latch-lock was maladjusted. The pilot and crew chief searched for jacks to correct the problem themselves, but neither jacks nor people were to be found—the depot had closed for the evening. The crew chief, being an inventive sort, discovered he could insert the long handled nose gear safety pin from inside the cockpit through a small gear inspection hole in the cockpit floor, so the pilot decided to proceed to Paris Orly as planned to drop off material at that base. The gear safety pin was installed for takeoff then removed when the plane was airborne. Enroute both generators and the radios failed—they had lost their electrical system! There was no way to contact Orly tower on that particularly dark night. The pilot pressed on and directed the crew chief to fire a red flare to declare an emergency as they approached the airport. The flare gun failed when the crew chief attempted to fire it, but he had the presence of mind to keep holding the gun in the canopy mount. The pilot quickly identified an approaching TWA Constellation from its unusual tail light configuration and followed at a close distance to land behind it at Orly. During the approach, the navigator held the flare gun while the crew chief reinserted the nose gear safety pin. The B-26 landed safely but the French air traffic controllers were quite upset at this unauthorized landing and dispatched airport police to meet the B-26. In the midst of being chastised in French, the flare gun finally discharged its red flare into the air and totally interrupted the police proceedings. The exasperated police gave up on reprimanding the crazy Americans and let them deliver the package to the MATS terminal personnel. The next day the B-26 proceeded on to Bordeaux. It was later determined that improperly adjusted voltage regulators caused the electrical failure.

By 20 April 1952, overhauled black B-26Cs with ARC-3s installed began arriving from the Hill AFB Depot, slowly replacing the wing's original B-26s. These black B-26s were extensively reworked, rewired, and had several improvements added for night operations. During this period many B model aircraft were reworked into C models, forever mixing up the tail serial numbers verses aircraft model.

The ARC-3 was capable of electronically self-tuning by just inserting the proper crystal; the navigator could do this frequency change. On some missions the crew carried a bag of four to ten additional crystals for in-flight channel frequency changes. By June 1952, each radio shop had inventories of 1,200 individual crystals, and occupied one radioman full time to keep track of which navigator had what crystals, and what channel frequencies were in each of the squadron bombers.

The first of April 1952 saw a worldwide major USAF personnel grade change as well. The first four enlisted grades changed from the old U.S. Army titles to new USAF titles. Unfortunately there were no pay increases. These changes were:

E-4 Sergeant (Sgt) to Airman First Class (A/1C)
E-3 Corporal (Cpl) to Airman Second Class (A/2C)
E-2 Private First Class (Pfc)
to Airman Third Class (A/3C)
E-1 Private (Pvt) to Airman Basic (A/B)

USAF NCO grades of E-5 Staff Sergeant (S/Sgt), E-6 Technical Sergeant (T/Sgt), and E-7 Master Sergeant (M/Sgt) remained unchanged. All USAF officer grade titles have retained the U.S. Army officer titles.

Flight operations began slowing down in late April as the wing started packing for Laon AB, 400 miles to the northeast. In anticipation of the 126th's departure to its permanent base, the 7413th Air Base Squadron was activated in April to operate Bordeaux-Merignac AB and the units assigned to the Bordeaux region.

Continual shortages of B-26 parts in Europe caused excessive numbers of out of commission aircraft and limited flying. These parts were typically high consumable items such as windshields, boost pumps, nose transparencies, and brakes. The classic example occurred during the move to Laon. In April, two squadrons at Bordeaux had three aircraft that needed hydraulic actuators and pumps. Over the next few weeks these planes in AOCP status became sources of parts for other squadron aircraft. But all planes had to be flown to Laon AB by 24 May! The solution was to fly three good B-26s from Bordeaux to Laon on 17 May; remove the parts needed for the AOCP airplanes, fly parts back to Bordeaux in another B-26, install these parts on the out of commission aircraft, and get all Invaders to Laon by 24 May. These Invaders were then stripped of these parts to restore the three B-26s back to flying status to keep the status reports correct. These three B-26s remained parked in AOCP status until September when they were prepared for their return flight to CONUS. Aircraft parts shortages persisted for the following two years. There's no record of the maintenance man-hours expended on these cannibalization actions; man-hour accounting, later required by AFR 66-1, was years away. Usual maintenance time for a B-26 was about thirty-two to forty maintenance man-hours per flight hour.

The bomb squadrons flew approximately 350 hours per month during their stay at Bordeaux. This was accomplished with no aircraft losses due to superior pilot skills and excellent maintenance in spite of continual, challenging obstacles. At no time during the six months at Merignac did the wing have a combat posture: there were no bombs or rockets on base, no bomb loading vehicles, no base emergency fuel supply, and no base defense. The wing did not possess authorized USAF refueling trucks for aircraft refueling, but was able to contract with the ESSO operator from the commercial air terminal. By the end of May 1952 the 126th Bomb Wing officially departed Bordeaux-Merignac AB. After departure of the 126th no other USAFE combat flying wing was based at Bordeaux.

Bordeaux-Merignac AB 1952-1961

In addition to Bordeaux-Merignac AB, several other sites around the city were used by the U.S. military. The 7480th Supply Squadron and the Army Corps of Engineers operated from the downtown area. The Bacalan Ford Plant and Bacalan WWII submarine pens were used by the 126th Wing for supply storage.

To the troops in France the 7480th Supply Squadron (Exchange Service) was probably the most important unit in all of Europe! Authorized by USAFE on 15 November 1951, its mission was the establishment and supervision of Air Force Base Exchanges (AFEX) in France. This special organization was activated on 1 January 1952 and was housed and operated in downtown Bordeaux but attached to Bordeaux-Merignac AB for its support. The 7480th Supply Squadron operated from 125 Quai Des Chatrons in a commercial office building. Its first order of business was to set-up offices for civilian buyers who began arriving in December 1951. Their primary task was procurement from French vendors and suppliers throughout Western Europe to stock the BXs in France and French Morocco. The squadron dispatched one, two, or three adventureous airmen to every new air base to set up its base exchange (BX). Exchanges were initially established in tents and then expanded into temporary buildings on each base. The 7480th's mission enlarged with the operation of the Class VI stores and all the USAFE movie theaters. By 1 October 1954,

Aircraft #44-35641. Black B-26s began arriving from CONUS, late April 1952.
Jerry McAuliffe

after AFEX absorbed the exchange operations in Austria, Germany, Italy, Libya, Netherlands, Spain, and UK, it was redesignated the 7480th Supply Group (Special Activities). By 1955, 1,020 French civilians were employed to operate the base exchanges; later several French workers were promoted to BX managers. The 7480th continued to operate in Bordeaux until 15 January 1955 when it moved to Mainz Kastle, Wiesbaden, West Germany, APO 633. Det #2, 7480th remained in Bordeaux for local procurement and supported the many U.S. Army exchanges in southeastern France. Det #2 managed the large AFEX depots at Chateauroux, La Rochelle and Paris. The BXs developed into an excellent retail store system in France, supplying the troops everything from British sports cars to German furniture.

The Corps of Engineers, U.S. Army, established a district engineering office in downtown Bordeaux in 1951. This office planned and contracted all construction for the U.S. Air Force, Army and Navy in the Bordeaux region. It also inspected and approved construction progress, and gave final approval for payments. French architectural and engineering firms under contract accomplished the construction design work. In January 1953 this office became known as the Joint Construction Agency Port District Office, Bordeaux.

The 126th Bomb Wing was typical of all 1950 flying wings in that it required attachment of three or more squadrons from other major air commands for base support functions. These small detachments had specialties not found in Air Force combat wings. Flight "M" 2d Air Postal Squadron operated the base Air Post Office (APO 16); Detachment #60, 18th Weather Squadron worked with the USAFE weather reporting system and supported flying operations; and Detachment #5, 1992d Airways and Air Communications Service Squadron provided communications for flight operations to HQ USAFE. The Merignac AACS detachment was very small because it did not operate the control tower or any navigation radio aids; the French aviation ministry provided this service since the airdrome was a civil airport. These detachments remained at Bordeaux after the 126th's departure but in 1952 and 1953 their designators changed to Detachment #60, 31st Weather Squadron; Detachment #12, 2d Air Postal Squadron (APO 16); and Detachment #31, 1992d AACS Squadron.

Considerable construction upgraded the facilities around Bordeaux in 1953 and 1954. In 1953 a grammar school for dependents was built on base, using Fillod buildings. In 1954 a 132-unit Guaranteed Rental Income family housing area was constructed at Pessac, about four miles southeast of the air base. A large Army-Air Force commissary that opened in 1954 was built at Camp Gradignan, located six miles southeast of Bordeaux AB.

New permanent buildings: a BX, mess hall, hospital, and AIO shops were completed in 1955. Base headquarters and base operations buildings were expanded from their 1935 structures. Both large hangars were extensively repaired and used until 1958. By 1956 the base had been vastly improved and lost its tent camp appearance. Many tenant units were based at

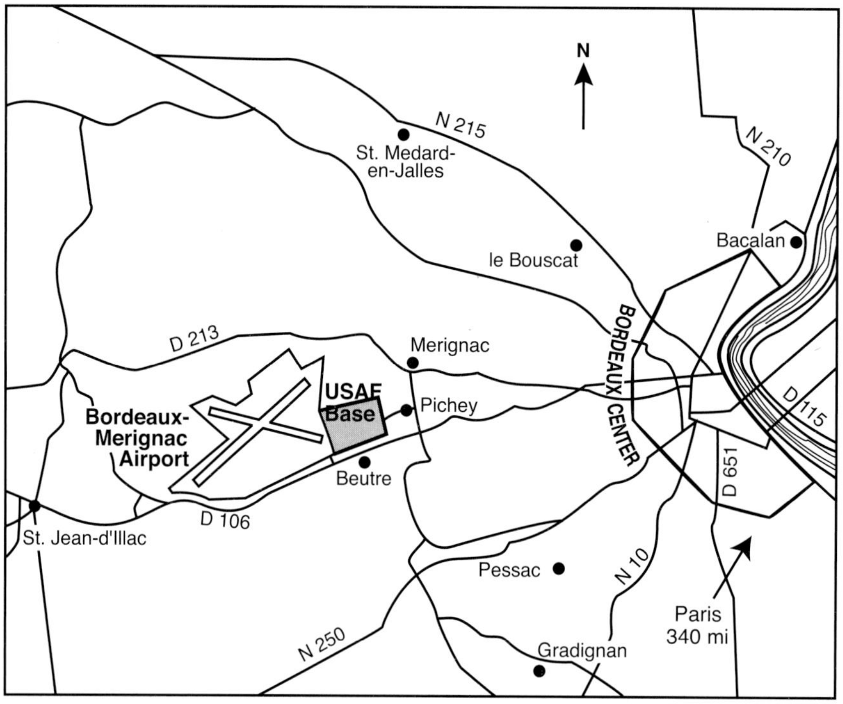

Map 6.2 Bordeaux-Merignac AB and Surrounding Area

Bordeaux during the 1950s while the 7413th Air Base Squadron was operating and maintaining the base.

Detachment #1, 4th Aerial Port Squadron was assigned to operate the large new air cargo terminal built in 1954.

The 12th Air Rescue and Recovery Service Group stationed the 81st, 82d and 83d ARRS Squadrons at Bordeaux-Merignac from 1952 to 1955. These squadrons operated SA-16 amphibians and H-19B air rescue helicopters. They practiced pilot recoveries at Lake Cazaux near Arcachon. The lake was ideal for water rescue training during the summer months.

In 1954, the 7th Radio Relay Squadron established its headquarters at Bordeaux-Merignac AB during installation of the RRL system and remained there until late 1957, when it relocated north to Chateauroux Air Depot.

Because the Erding Depot was being turned over to the German Air Force, the 1884th AACS Engineering and Installation Squadron moved permanently from Erding to Bordeaux AB. The advanced detachment set up their repair shops in November 1955. The complete squadron arrived in March 1956 to continue its work of installing and maintaining air traffic control communications and navigation electronic systems across Europe, Africa, and Middle East.

Bordeaux AB had surprise visitors in October 1956 during the Hungarian revolution. A SAC B-47 squadron unexpectedly flew in from Spain for two weeks in a show of force. The USAF increased its NATO presence whenever Soviet aggression in Europe raised concerns that the Russians may again try to limit access to Berlin. The base was able to accommodate these crews and aircraft; the newly expanded parking apron was very adequate.

A winter clothing sub-depot was established in the Bordeaux-Bacalan port area and was operated by the 7349th Supply Squadron, Depot, under the command of the Chateauroux Air Depot. This sub-depot used the old submarine pens and Ford warehouses in Bacalan. The cement hulks provided damp and chilly but secure storage, and the price was right—no rent was charged! The U.S. Army constructed a Bacalan seaport terminal adjacent to the sub pens consisting of barracks, offices, warehouses, and depot shops. This was an extension of their port system in France.

The 7413th Air Base Squadron was expanded to the 7413th Air Base Group in 1954 because of increased mission demands. Bordeaux had become a frequent refueling stop for F-84F and F-100 fighters flying from England to Wheelus AB, Tripoli, for gunnery practice.

Marseille-Marignane Airport

As the movement of USAFE aircraft increased in volume across France to the bombing/gunnery ranges in Libya and new U.S. air bases in French Morocco, a serious need developed for a convenient refueling stop

Tents being winterized by the 843d EABn at Bordeaux, November 1952. (After the 126th had left!)
Jerry McAuliffe

Bordeaux P.O. operated by Flight "M" 2d Air Postal Squadron, November 1951.
USAF History Office, Maxwell AFB

Base theater completed spring 1953.
National Archives

New BX and barbershop completed 1954. Original BX on left.
National Archives

Above:
Permanent construction progressing, 1955. The chapel, theater and mess hall (right side photo) have been completed.
Dan Martin

Above:
The air installations/civil engineering building completed in 1955.
National Archives

The enlarged and improved base operations building, 1955.
National Archives

Marseille-Marignane Airport, 1952.
Detachment #2 7413th Air Base Group established a flight operations office here in 1955.
Jerry McAuliffe

on the Mediterranean seacoast of southern France. Istres airdrome was considered in 1950 to perform this function, but by 1954 Istres was closed to USAF aircraft due to extensive test flying by the FAF. USAF aircraft stopped at several airports along the coast but the Marseille-Marignane Airport, a large commercial field with a flight service station and contract ESSO fuel service, became the most common destination. The flight service station stop allowed pilots to obtain weather data and file an instrument flight plan when returning into European airspace.

Detachment #2 of the 7413th Air Base Group at Bordeaux-Merignac was activated on 20 July 1955 to establish a flight operations office on the Marignane Airport. USAFE manpower limitations precluded another complete air base in this region. Detachment #2 was a small group tasked to set up and operate an air terminal and function ten hours a day to support the increased USAFE air traffic into North Africa. It consisted of twenty-four military personnel: four officers and twenty airmen. Their job specialties were commander, air operations officer, administrative specialists, air operations specialists, communications operators, supply specialists, aircraft mechanics, and weather observer. All detachment personnel lived off base in hotels on the local French economy. They were paid with French currency not military payment certificates. Even though these men were stationed approximately 385 miles from their main headquarters at Bordeaux, they enjoyed this remote location and the independent living among the French population.

Bordeaux-Cazaux Operations

During 1955-56 Bordeaux AB was being developed as a port of debarkation for aircraft, material, and personnel if required in an international crisis. The 850th Engineer Aviation Battalion expanded the aircraft parking apron to fifty-five acres at the cost of four million dollars. This extra ramp was constructed to accommodate up to three wings of fighters (225 aircraft). Forty-eight acres were graded and fenced for the storage of aircraft drop tanks and wing pylons (F-84, F-86 and F-100). Later someone discovered they were the wrong pylons and would not mate with the drop tanks; a logistical crisis ensued keeping people busy for several weeks.

By late 1953 Bordeaux had begun its third important mission, the establishment and support of a very badly needed gunnery range. The scarcity of peacetime gunnery ranges was a serious factor limiting the combat proficiency of the ten fighter wings based in Europe. The bombing and gunnery ranges in Libya were saturated with aircraft. In November 1953 a conference was held by USAFE Twelfth and Third Air Force to establish a fighter gunnery school at Cazaux, located thirty-four miles southwest of Bordeaux. The FAF operated Cazaux AB, a fighter field known as Base Aerienne #706. The airfield, located beside Lake Cazaux, had been a gunnery range and

The cargo terminal at Bordeaux-Merignac airport 1995.
As best I can determine, this building sits where the hangars were located on the old air base.
Jerry McAuliffe

armament test center since the late 1920s. It offered the USAFE both air-to-air and air-to-ground ranges. The air-to-air range was six nautical miles off the coast in the Bay of Biscay; the air-to-ground range was on the base and a portion of the lake. Detachment #1, 7413th was organized to assist in range support, maintenance, and to operate two 24-foot crash boats. Three H-19Bs were assigned to Cazaux airdrome for rescue work. Chateauroux Air Depot assigned Detachment #1, 1992d AACS Sq to operate the range control radio net. Fighter squadrons deployed to Bordeaux AB for one week to use the ranges. Having Cazaux AB adjacent to the range allowed fighters to land, refuel, and rearm for maximum utilization of their range time. Unfortunately because of air traffic congestion at Merignac Airport, plus population growth around Cazaux and Arcachon, as well as the increasing lethality of USAFE weapon systems, the air-to-air range was discontinued in January 1957 and the ground range closed in August. The entire operation was returned to the FAF on 30 October 1957.

The beautiful Cazaux area containing pine forests and great sand dunes was not abandoned; a Boy Scouts of America outdoor camp was constructed for use by scouts from all the U.S. bases in France. Former scouts from Dreux, Laon, and Chateauroux still have fond memories of their days at this camp.

After seven years of use, Bordeaux Air Base and all depot facilities closed in 1958 to reduce USAFE expenses and manpower. All Bacalan sub-depot activities ceased and were relocated to Chateauroux. Most equipment was distributed to air bases in France or returned to depot stocks. The U.S. Army continued to operate the port facilities, including the submarine pens. The family housing project constructed in Pessac was transferred to the U.S. Army. Bordeaux AB was returned to the FAF and removed from USAF real estate records in June 1961.

The former base site has been engulfed by Bordeaux's commercial airport. Though nothing remains of the air base, the city of Bordeaux (Michelin #335 Local) can be visited by train from Paris' Montparnasse station.

Appendix 6.1 Permanent Change Station orders 126th LBWg

Comm. Officer

311.24 081700Z RESTRICTED

FROM: CG TAC LANGLEY AFB VA

PRIORITY

TO: JEPLG/CG 126TH BOMB WG (L) LANGLEY AFB VA

JEDWP/CG AMC WP AFB OHIO

XXXX ZEN/CINCUSAFE WIESBADEN GER

JESBN/CG WRAMA ROBINS AFB GA

JWFMB/DEPUTY INSP GEN USAF KELLY AFB TEX

CO 47TH BOMB WG L LANGLEY AFB VA

CMDR MATS ANDREWS AFB MARYLAND

INFO:

UECBE/CG NYPE BROOKLYN NY

UECBE/USAF PORT AIR REPR NYPE BROOKLYN NY

TNOPC 0256 PD THIS IA WARNING ORDER PD THE FOLLOWING UNITS ARE ALERTED FOR A PERMANENT CHANGE OF STATION FOR FOREIGN SERVICE IN ACCORDANCE WITH SR 55-720-1/AFR 75-37 PAREN POM PAREN

UNIT	SHIPMENT NUMBER	PRESENT STATION	APPROX STR OFF	AMN	TO&E
HQ&HQ SQ	1455-A	LANGLEY AFB	33	70	1-1021T 14APR50
126TH BOMB		HAMPTON VA			W/CH 1 18 JAN 51
WG L					1XCOLM 5 SEC II
HQ 126TH	1455-B	LANGLEY AFB			1-1122T 4MAY 50
BOMB GP L		HAMPTON VA			1XCOLM 5 SEC II
108TH BOMB	1455-C	LANGLEY AFB			1-1123 24MAR 48
SQ L		HAMPTON VA			1XCOLM 5 SEC II&III
168TH BOMB	1455-D	LANGLEY AFB			1-1123 24MAR 48
SQ L		HAMPTON VA			1XCOLM 5 SEC II&III
180TH BOMB	1455-E	LANGLEY AFB			1-1123 24MAR 48
SQ L		HAMPTON VA			1XCOLM 5 SEC II&III

2. A. TENTATIVE READINESS DATE IS 30 OCT 51 PD

B. ADVANCE PARTY IS AUTHORIZED PD

3. A. UNITS WILL BE PROCESSED FOR A MILD TEMPERATURE ZONE IN ACCORDANCE WITH T/A 21 PEACE PD

B. REQUEST CINCUSAFE SUBMIT TO CG TAC AT EARLIEST A LIST OF DISCRETIONARY ITEMS OF INDIVIDUAL CLOTHING AND EQUIPMENT AVAILABLE FOR THESE UNITS UPON ARRIVAL AT OVERSEA DESTINATION PD

4. A. UNITS WILL MOVE WITH ALL ASSIGNED AIRCRAFT AND T/O&E EQUIPMENT AS AUTHORIZED BY APPROPRIATE TABLES INDICATED IN PARAGRAPH 1 ABOVE PD AIRCRAFT WILL BE FLOWN TO DESTINATION CMA ENROUTE KITS WILL BE ESTABLISHED FOR THE FLIGHT ECHELON

B. PRECEDENCE III-15 IS ASSIGNED IN ACCORDANCE WITH OPU-52-2 VOL I AUG 51 PD

C. AUTHORITY IS GRANTED TO REQUISITION ALL SHORTAGES OF EQUIPMENT IN ACCORDANCE WITH PARAGRAPHS 13 AND 18 A PD

5. MOVEMENT OR DEPENDENTS CMA PRIVATE AUTOMOBILES AND HOUSEHOLD GOODS WILL BE IN ACCORDANCE WITH PRIORITY AND POLICIES AS ESTABLISHED BY CINCUSAFE AFTER ARRIVAL AT DESTINATION PD END

THIS IS A TRUE COPY

Christian K. Madison Jr.

CHRISTIAN K. MADISON, JR.
Captain, USAF
Adjutant

The road from Pichey to the Bordeaux back gate 1951.
Pichey is now a suburb of greater Bordeaux and the road is a busy commercial street.
Dale Peotter

Appendix 6.2 Notice to Airmen 1956 (NOTAM) - USAF-CIV Bordeaux-Merignac

Elevation 163 feet, 44° 50'N - 00° 43'W. Two paved runways: 045°/225° is 9,900 feet long and 110°/290° is 7,800 feet long. Airport has rotating beacon light, boundary lights, runway flood lights, runway strip lights, approach lights, and airport obstruction lights. Runway 045°/225° supports 70,000 pounds per single aircraft wheel, safe for jet aircraft take-off and landings. Expect fifteen minute delay in landing due to heavy civilian aircraft traffic. Airdrome facilities available 24 hours daily. USAF operations 0600-2000 hours daily and during pre-planned jet aircraft movements. Limited transient aircraft storage with minor aircraft and minor engine repairs available.

AF Form #15(C), contract aircraft fuel (115-145 and 100-130 octane) and JP4 jet fuel with single point refueling service available. Jet assist starting units, C-21, C-26 electrical and MA-1A pneumatic carts. 3,500 psi high pressure air available. High and low pressure oxygen service available. Customs, Health and Immunizations agencies available.

Appendix 6.3 Notice to Airmen 1957 (NOTAM) - USAF-CIV Marseille-Marignane Airport

Elevation 65 feet, 43° 26'N - 05° 13'E. Two paved parallel runways: 14L/32R is 7,900 feet long, supports 132,000 pounds per single aircraft wheel. Runway 140°R / 320°L is 6,500 feet long, paved with approach lights but supports only 40,000 pounds per single wheel. Runway 14R/32L unsafe for jet aircraft take-off and landings.

Expect thirty minute delay in landing between 0800-1100 hours due to heavy civilian aircraft traffic. USAF operations 0700-1600 hours daily and during preplanned jet aircraft movements. During other hours, pilots will close or file flight plans and obtain weather briefings via direct phone line to the Paris Flight Service Center. Alert crew available 0800-1700 hours. Jet aircraft operations daylight hours only.

AF Form #15(C), contract aircraft fuel (115-145 and 100-130 octane) and JP4 jet fuel with single point refueling service available. Jet assist starting units, C-26 electrical and MA-1A pneumatic carts. 3,500psi high pressure air available. 500psi low pressure oxygen service available. Customs, Health and Immunizations agencies available.

Bordeaux-Merignac Air Base Assigned Aircraft

USAF History Office

Jerry McAuliffe

126th Bomb Wing, Light, B-26Bs & Cs, 21 November 1951 - 24 May 1952
Sixteen aircraft per squadron. These Invaders were flown from Langley AFB, VA to Bordeaux AB, France by 126th LBWg pilots; aircraft flown to Laon AB, France on 17-24 May 1952 by 126th LBWg pilots.
Aircraft Marking:
108th Light Bomb Squadron - Black, yellow, blue bands on vertical stabilizer and rudder.
168th Light Bomb Squadron - Black, yellow, red bands on vertical stabilizer and rudder.
180th Light Bomb Squadron - Black, yellow, green bands on vertical stabilizer and rudder.

TB-26B

44-34593	108th
44-34597	108th
44-34671	168th
44-34692#	168th
44-34702	180th
44-34729	180th

B-26B

41-39324	168th
41-39504	180th
43-22405	180th
44-34196	180th
44-34202	108th
44-34435	108th
44-34443	108th

B-26C

43-22657	180th	44-35264	168th	44-35732#	108th		
43-22662#	180th	44-35358	180th	44-35738	180th		
43-22676	108th	44-35365	168th	44-35750	108th		
43-22692	168th	44-35493	168th	44-35761	168th		
43-22717	180th	44-35506#	180th	44-35778	180th		
43-22724	108th	44-35513	168th	44-35817#	108th		
		44-35527	168th	44-35836#	108th		
44-35208	168th	44-35549	180th	44-35883#	180th		
44-35215	108th	44-35554#	168th	44-35890#	180th		
44-35219#	108th	44-35585	180th	44-35900	180th		
44-35221	108th	44-35588	168th	44-35937#	108th		
44-35222#	180th	44-35697	168th				
44-35262	168th	44-35702	168th				
		44-35714#	168th				

Modified black B-26C for Korean War

Received after 20 APR 52 Flown to Bordeaux AB by MATS ferry crews.

43-22440	168th	43-22496	180th	44-35540	108th	44-35790	180th
43-22442	108th	43-22714	180th	44-35641	108th	44-35856	180th
43-22456	180th	44-34102	168th	44-35763	108th	44-35857	168th
43-22457	180th	44-34104	108th	44-35784	180th	44-35868	168th
43-22470	108th	44-34105	108th				

Aircraft Losses: NONE
Returned by 24 May 1952 to Hill AFB, UT; OOAMA for DIR rework.
126th Air Base Group: Wing Support Aircraft C-47: 42-108922, 43-15315 (and 43-15158 on loan from 12th AF).

7413th Air Base Group: May 1952 - December 1958
C-47Ds: 43-48503, 43-49349, 44-77012
L-20: 1 each - 52-6059

81st, 82d and 83d Air Rescue Squadrons, 12th Air Rescue Group:
81st Air Rescue Squadron November 1952 - July 1953
SA-16A-GR: 51-473, 51-475, 51-476
C-47D-1-DL: 43-16376
82d Air Rescue Squadron November 1952 - September 1953
C-47B-50-DK: 45-1090
83d Air Rescue Squadron December 1952 - July 1955
H-19B-SI: 51-3898Δ 51-3900Δ 51-3901Δ 51-3899 52-7493 52-7500* 53-4456 52-7509

* Losses: 52-7500 - Crashed, rotor blade separation, 3nm SW of La Teste, France, 3 JUN 54, 4 fatalities.
Δ Three H-19Bs assigned to Cazaux AB, France.

ACKNOWLEDGEMENTS

I would like to thank the following people who contributed to this chapter:

Frank Casale was a heavy equipment operator with the 862d U.S. Army Engineer Aviation Battalion preparing Bordeaux AB for the arrival of the 126th LBWg in 1951.

Paul Douglas was an aircraft crew chief in the 108th LBSq, 126th LBWg. He opened up Bordeaux AB in 1951 and Laon AB in 1952.

Ray DuCasse was an airborne radar repairman in the 108th LBSq, 126th LBWg. He opened up Bordeaux AB in 1951 and Laon AB in 1952.

Bob Gertner was an aircraft engine mechanic in the 126th Field Maintenance Squadron at Bordeaux AB in 1951.

Dale Peotter who was a crew chief on #44-35215, one of the airplanes that made the unscheduled stop on the Isle of Tiree. Dale opened up Bordeaux in 1951 and opened up Laon AB in 1952.

George Spencer was an avionics technician in the 108th LBSq, 126th LBWg. He opened up Bordeaux AB in 1951 and Laon AB in 1952.

Norwood Thompson was in Det #2, 7413th Air Base Gp stationed at Marignane Airport. He provided valuable information on this operation and his experiences there.

St. Jean d'Iliac 1998.
Jerry McAuliffe

7

CHAMBLEY-BUSSIERES AIR BASE

Chambley is located in the Meurthe-et-Moselle Department on the plain of Lorraine in northeastern France. This area has seen violent battles from Roman times to the end of World War II. In the last few centuries Lorraine has seesawed between French and German control. It was annexed by Germany after the Franco-Prussian war in 1870, then returned to France in 1919 after World War I, occupied once more by Germany during World War II, and finally returned to French control after liberation by the U.S. Third Army in September 1944. City names, architectural styles and foods of the area retain a German flavor.

Chambley Air Base (49° 02'N - 05° 53'E, elevation 864 feet) is located 190 miles (310 km) east of Paris and 14 miles (22 km) southwest of the city of Metz. Originally, during the 1950 site selection meetings the area around Mars-la-Tour was proposed for an air base. Both the FAF and USAFE immediately agreed that it would make a good fighter base, but the final site selection was closer to the village of Chambley, about two miles south of Chambley, and five miles south of the town of Mars-la-Tour. The chosen site of 1,600 acres was well-drained, fairly flat, open farmland readily available for development. While site problems were noted, such as lack of potable water and access roads, an important plus was railroad service within one mile. Initially the base was known as Chambley-Bussieres but was later shortened to Chambley. It was designated as a single step base, to be constructed with permanent buildings, shops, and hangars over a two-year period. A small tent camp for the support group would be required only during the first year of construction. Originally the Air Force planned that a fighter wing would arrive in spring 1954.

Preliminary surveys were conducted in November 1951. The Corps of Engineers gave site approval after finding sufficient potable water by drilling deeper wells. Construction began about 1 March 1952 with the building of access roads and a railroad spur to the base. Runway grading began in May and one northeast/southwest, 7,800-foot long concrete runway was poured. This was followed by taxiways, parking hardstands, hangar floors and aprons. Trenching for underground water and heat pipes left piles of earth throughout the base. The heavy winter rains turned the piles into flowing mud, slowing all other construction. You will note from the base photos that each one was scraped clean of all vegetation prior to construction. This resulted in one common denominator as each base opened—mud, mud, everywhere!

During the initial construction period, the 73d Air Depot Wing at Chateauroux sent a five-man team to establish Flight A, 73d Support Group, Depot, Chambley. Flight A was sent to receive, store, and issue USAF supplies as needed by air force personnel or the contractors. This team of supply specialists, consisting of one officer and four airmen, arrived on 30 January 1953. Its number was increased to twenty-five in the summer of 1953. The men lived near the main train station in Metz on the French economy. They used USAF trucks to commute to the site and at least one man was always present at Chambley to provide storage site security. They continued working at the base until March 1955.

Construction had progressed enough by the beginning of 1954 that the 7002d Air Base Squadron was activated in February to provide a larger organization to prepare Chambley as each building was completed by the contractor. The 7002d ABSq also set-up the hospital, provided site security, transportation, supply support, and communications operations.

Chambley was dedicated and formally turned over to the U.S. on 12 June 1956 and accepted by the USAF on behalf of NATO. Gen. Robert M. Lee, commander of the Twelfth Air Force and Fourth Allied Tactical Air Force attended this ceremony. The newly formed Joint Construction Agency had managed construction at Chambley, and six different French contractors had worked on the base. Chambley was estimated to be only 85 percent complete in 1956, four years after construction began, but construction had cost $28 million! It was among the last of the main bases completed in France.

Chambley Air Base did not reach the configuration envisioned in 1953 until December 1957. At completion the base area was 1,582 acres with seven and one-half miles of paved roads. The concrete runway, taxiways, parking ramps, and aprons covered 450,000 square yards. Chambley had three fighter-size hangars, sixty permanent buildings and thirty-three temporary buildings. The base had two million cubic feet of warehouse storage space in five buildings with railroad access. Chambley's water system held 149,100 gallons in four underground storage tanks. It had three heating plants to produce and distribute heat throughout the base. Its underground electrical system had a 17,000-volt primary feeder with a capacity of 950,000 watts. Eleven two-story airmen's dormitories housed 146 men each in different layouts to also accommodate NCO quarters. Three two-story BOQ buildings could hold sixty-four officers each. Two one-story dining halls were configured for 500 men each, and a third for 300 men. In addition, the hospital mess could feed 150. The main entrance was south of Chambley off the west side of highway D952, south of highway D901. A second (back) entrance was south of D901 across from the tiny village of Hageville, (more commonly known as Hogville by Chambley's airmen).

On-base underground fuel storage could hold 886,500 gallons of JP4, 30,000 gallons of AVGAS, 205,000 gallons of MOGAS vehicle fuel, and 206,000 gallons of DIESEL fuel. This fuel storage field was later connected to the NATO pipeline system. Munitions storage was located one-half mile southeast of the base and one mile north of highway D131. This Mont Tonnerre Ammo Weapon Storage Annex (#3966) with twelve igloos on a forty-one acre site was constructed in the les Cotes farmland. It was used by Chambley until returned to the MLS in March 1967.

Estimated real estate value (excluding land) was $29 million. Equipment value (excluding aircraft) was approximately $6 million. Total base supply inventory was $5 million. Its mailing address was APO 247 until January 1965 when APOs became five digit zip code numbers, and Chambley changed to 09247.

The base was located in a remote area of northern France that had a housing shortage but neither Guaranteed Rental Income or Commodity Credit housing was constructed for Chambley. The housing shortage persisted until the base closed in 1967. The only provision made for housing families was construction of a large on-base trailer park for 248 trailers by the 843d and 862d Engineer Aviation Battalions. Trailer park construction took place during 1954 as part of Project Caravan. This project included installing all utilities,

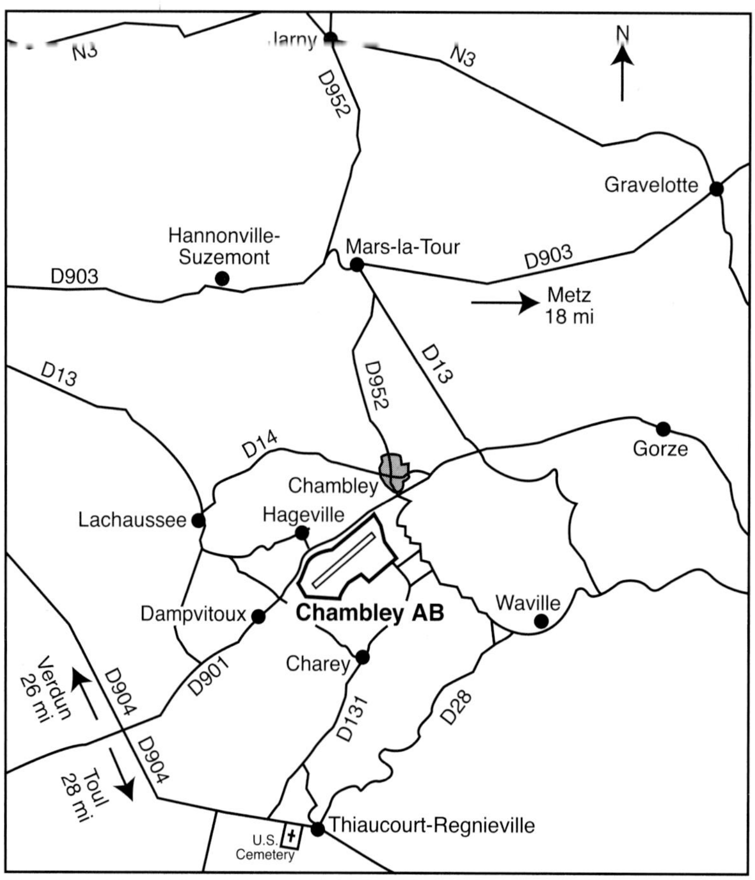

Map 7.1 Chambley AB and Surrounding Area

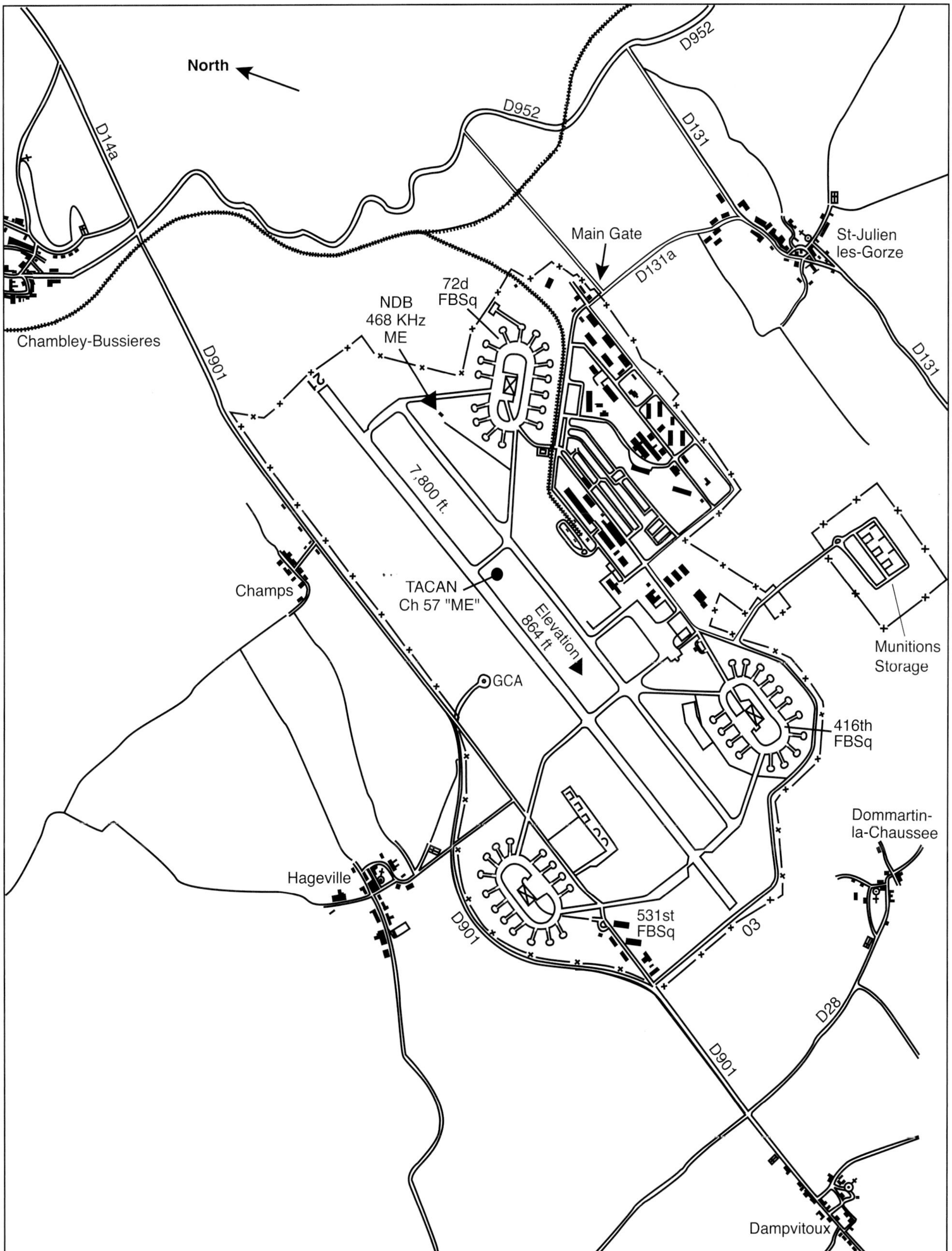

Map 7.2 Chambley Air Base

Trailer park on left, 72d FBSq hangar, marguerite and barracks on the right, Chambley, 1956.
Al Christensen

Chambley's trailer park under construction, 1954. Note the Quonset hut wash house, rear. At this stage of construction it would have been challenging to bring clean laundry back to one's trailer.
National Archives

Newly completed trailer park at Chambley AB. 1954.
Harold F. Watt, 862d EABn

Trailer interior at Chambley AB.
National Archives

21st Fighter-Bomber Wing over Chambley, 1956.
Al Christensen

building roads, concrete pads, and six portable buildings for family laundry facilities.

21st Fighter-Bomber Wing

The 21st Fighter-Bomber Wing was activated on 1 January 1953 at George AFB, California, with the mission, equipment, F-51Ds, and approximately 170 officers and 1,130 airmen that had belonged to the 146th Fighter-Bomber Wing the previous day. The three fighter-bomber squadron designators were changed to: the 72d, 416th, and 531st Fighter-Bomber Squadrons.

The 21st Fighter-Bomber Wing designation evolved from the WWII 21st Fighter Group activated on 21 April 1944 at Wheeler Field, Hawaii. It flew P-51Ds from Iwo Jima, conducting fighter sweeps across Okinawa and Japan as part of the USAAF Seventh Air Force. A DUC was awarded to the 21st Fighter Group for their noteworthy long-range escort of the B-29s that bombed Tokyo. The 21st Ftr Gp was inactivated on Guam in November 1946.

By 1 November 1954, after twenty-two months of training, the 21st was ready to depart southern California for Chambley Air Base in northern France. The F-51Ds they inherited had been replaced between August and October 1953 by F-86F-35-NAs from North American's Los Angeles factory. These block 35 Sabres had increased internal fuel, were equipped with ARC-27 UHF radios, the latest A-4 gunsight system with an APG-30 range radar set, and an M-1 low altitude bombing (LABS) computer for toss bombing. This computer produced accurate special weapon delivery. These F-86s had two additional underwing pylons for tactical nuclear weapons. The 21st Wing brought seventy-eight F-86F Sabres, four T-33As, and two C-47s to Europe in December 1954.

Commanders of the 21st Fighter-Bomber Wing during the three years it was stationed at Chambley were COL Robert R. Rowland who became commander on 27 April 1953 and COL Robert N. Baker who took command in June 1956.

The ADVON, commanded by COL John H. Stokes, departed George AFB on 5 November, flew to McGuire AFB, New Jersey, then traveled by bus to Staten Island Terminal, New York. The next day it began an eight-day voyage on the troopship USNS GEN Geiger to Bremerhaven, West Germany. On 16 November 1954, the 15 officers and 135 airmen arrived at Chambley after a long train ride from Bremerhaven to Metz and a jostling military truck ride to Chambley.

The air echelon followed shortly thereafter. COL Rowland led the air echelon; he departed George AFB with the 72d FBSq on 12 December. The 416th FBSq departed on the 13th, and the 531st followed on the 14th. Three C-124C transports carried each squadron's twenty-man enroute support team, support equipment, and spare parts. Future astronaut

21st Fighter-Bomber Wing Commander F-86F #52-5222 showing tail colors of the three squadrons, 72d-red, 416th-blue, and 531st-yellow, Chambley 1956.
Al Christensen

Lt. Michael Collins, of the 72d FBSq, participated in this record-setting, dangerous Atlantic crossing. Each fighter wing's deployment of aircraft to Europe was given a "Fox Able" designator. The 21st Fighter-Bomber Wing (Fox Able 34) held the Fox Able long distance record by flying from southern California into northern France.

Aircraft moved in flights of four F-86Fs spaced ten minutes apart, with one squadron at a time at each enroute air base. They flew the same route described in chapter 2 with additional stops at Clovis AFB, New Mexico; Alexandria AFB, Louisiana; Shaw AFB, South Carolina; and Dover AFB, Delaware. At Dover the 21st entered the MATS control system and received their North Atlantic route briefings. After leaving Dover the F-86s flew to Loring AFB, Maine, their foreign clearing station, then on to Goose Bay, Labrador. Considerable time was lost because of weather delays—twelve days at Goose Bay, five at Narsarssuak, Greenland, six at Keflavic, Iceland, and seven days at Prestwick, Scotland were common. The MATS commander was very unhappy to have his C-124s and crews obligated for eighty days.

It took two-and-one-half months to move the wing's aircraft to France, but these delays resulted in only one F-86 loss. The aircraft crashed near Toul AB enroute from Prestwick due to bad weather forecasting and communications; the pilot ejected safely after fuel starvation. Another Sabre sustained a damaged nose gear caused by main wheel chocks losing traction on ice during engine run-up; this aircraft was left behind in Greenland for a depot team to repair. It was so cold that ground "Herman Nelsons" (gasoline heaters) had to be used to pre-heat the cockpits and J-47 jet engines for easier starting. The Sabres functioned very well in this extremely cold environment except for a problem in the pilot's oxygen control panel. A small rubber valve would shrink because of the cold, and oxygen would leak out. A quick solution was found—after servicing, the control panel main shut-off valve was turned off to prevent oxygen loss; then after cockpit warm-up it was turned on again. This was a quick but dangerous solution. If anyone forgot to turn on the main valve prior to taxiing, lack of oxygen after take-off could result in a fatal accident.

After departing Prestwick, Scotland, the aircraft had to divert to other bases because Chambley's runway was still not completed! The 72d FBSq operated at Chateauroux-Deols AD, 220 miles southwest of Chambley, and the 416th and 531st FBSqs flew from Toul-Rosieres AB, 17 miles to the south. All squadrons eagerly began flying operations upon arrival since many flying training requirements had slipped during their extended Fox Able movement.

The main body of the wing, approximately 1,150 men, boarded a troop train on 26 November at George AFB and traveled for two-and-one-half days to their port of embarkation, Houston, Texas. Within a few hours they marched aboard the MSTS GEN LeRoy Eltinge with about 1,100 men from the 388th FBWg from Clovis AFB, New Mexico, also enroute to France. They set sail on 29 November for their fourteen-day voyage to La Pallice. They arrived on 12 December. Everyone stayed aboard ship overnight and debarked

F-86F #52-5258, 531st Fighter-Bomber Squadron flown by Lt. Davy Coombs. Chambley AB 1955.
Al Christensen

F-86F #52-5206 416th Fighter-Bomber Squadron. Chambley AB 1956.
Gene White

F-86Fs on the ramp at Wheelus AB, Tripoli. Quonset huts used for squadron maintenance.
Gene White

Airmen Holmes and Farmer doing brake and wheel maintenance on the ramp at Wheelus AB.
Gene White

at 1000 hours the next day to board an awaiting SNCF troop train that took them to Chambley. They arrived at Gare de Chambley near midnight in a cold, heavy rain. A short truck ride brought them to their new barracks. It was a depressing introduction to their stay in France, even though the ADVON had done a good job getting the billets and mess halls ready for their arrival. Officers and airmen assigned to the fighter squadrons were routed on trains to Toul and Chateauroux. This sealift movement of a wing would be the last of such fourteen-day trips.

After the main echelon departed, the Rear Detachment, of one officer and twenty-one airmen, had the job of making sure all wing property had cleared the base for the east coast port, all back-ordered requisitions were canceled, and all base supply accounts were closed. This small team left George AFB on 15 January 1955, flew by commercial and military air to Westover AFB, Massachusetts, then on to Rhein-Main, and arrived at Chambley five days later.

Except for its three fighter squadrons, the 21st FBWg was together again at Chambley on 20 January 1955. It was the first USAFE tactical wing to operate at Chambley where it would remain for the next three years. Its primary mission was to, "prepare for and conduct special weapons tactical air operations as directed by higher headquarters." Its secondary mission was, to prepare for and conduct non-atomic tactical air operations and other missions as directed by Twelfth Air Force.

Because of its remote location, on-base recreational activities at Chambley were particularly important. The 843d EABn built a movie theater for base personnel using a prefabricated steel building. Indoor and outdoor team sports became one of many tools used to maintain troop morale. The 416th hangar was used for basketball until the gym was completed. Chambley's inter-base teams were known as "The Desert Rats," a name derived from the wing's days at George AFB when they were located in California's high desert. Chambley had an excellent baseball team and fielded a soccer team, swim team, and a ski squad

Det #10, 31st Weather Squadron briefing room. Very familiar to the Chambley pilots.
Al Christensen

that competed at Garmisch-Partenkirchen.

The three flying squadrons were finally able to return to Chambley in June and July 1955. The 72d FBSq operated at Chateauroux-Deols from 18 February until 2 July 1955. The 416th and 531st FBSqs flew at Toul-Rosieres from 22 February through 19 June 1955. But, frustration set in when the Sabres returned to Chambley and the new runway's first 2,500 feet of concrete began breaking up, causing concern about damage to the jet engines.

The 72d Squadron was located in the hangar on the east side of the runway north of base operations, the 416th on the east side south of base operations, and the 531st on the west side of the runway near the Hageville entrance. Since the 531st Squadron was located away from the main facilities, it had its own living area and mess hall in the southwest corner of the base. Hangars included the fighter squadron operation section as well as all squadron aircraft maintenance shops. The 21st Air Base Group operated four T33As, one L-20A, and three C-47s. Support aircraft maintenance was conducted in the 72d and 416th FBSq hangars. The aircraft firing-in butt located near the 72d FBSq was in frequent use to boresight the guns prior to range firing missions.

One aspect of maintaining a busy flying schedule was getting accurate weather briefings. Finding humor when dealing with the inadequate facilities helped. Weather officer Al Christensen remembers his briefings at Chambley.

> The weather station had windows from which to actually see what was going on in the atmosphere. When the pilots came to get briefed and cleared, I would boldly stand with my back to the window and tell them if I looked it would make it too easy. I also had a crystal ball/light fixture bulb stashed beneath the briefing dais that I would bring out on occasion when the weather seemed confusing. This was all humorous fun and pay back for all the smart-ass I got from them. The radio fax room was connected to the weather rooms. Yes, it gave us that burnt smell. It was run by AACS. It was lousy reception and the maps were sometimes almost useless. I would sometimes have to call other weather stations directly using the rather unreliable French telephone system. It was quite a sight in the station on a marginal weather day with pilots perched all over inside the station, and myself with phones hanging over my shoulders, peering at smirched fax's and incomplete weather codes, trying the make a call on when the weather would break.

The 21st Fighter-Bomber Wing, like all other fighter wings in USAFE, enjoyed their flying days on the Wheelus ranges in North Africa. The ranges were

FAIRWEATHER aircraft standing alert at Landsberg, West Germany.
Al Christensen

excellent, with very little local commercial air traffic and few concerns about range safety. The desert was an ideal location for aircraft armament training, plus North Africa was a nice respite in the middle of a long French winter! While everyone was enthusiastic about winter deployments to Wheelus, ground crews hated the 115 and 122 degree Fahrenheit summer temperatures. Fighter pilots worked on air-to-air gunnery, toss bombing special delivery, rocket firing, and dive bombing at least twice a year. The 21st deployed F-86Fs to Wheelus for weapons training, using ranges south of Tripoli for air-to-ground gunnery and bombing. Later the wing used a new air-to-ground range northwest of Tripoli. Air-to-air gunnery training was conducted about thirty miles offshore over the Gulf of Sidra; targets were banners with radar reflectors that were towed by the F-86Fs. The 416th FBSq was assigned a special weapons delivery mission that required extra toss bombing range time.

During this time the 416th was getting the best scores in air-to-air shooting! The three squadrons deployed to Wheelus twice a year in 1955, 1956, and 1957, plus two trips to the range at Cazaux AB. Typically during the three-week gunnery trips, the wing would fly 800 hours for 1,000 range sorties. In July 1956 the 21st Wing won the USAFE Special Weapons Delivery Meet held at Wheelus. The same team then went on to the All USAF Worldwide Gunnery Meet at Nellis AFB, Nevada, and won second place in the Special Weapons Delivery event. There was great rivalry between the 21st and the 388th FBWg from Etain AB to see who would have the best range scores.

Another favorite pastime of 21st FBWg pilots was flying simulated air-to-air combat over northern France and Belgium. While officially illegal, all fighter outfits really enjoyed this activity whenever weather permitted. This flying was real airmanship compared to standing nuclear alerts for days on end. The greatest sport was maneuvering from 35,000 feet on down among the trees with the Canadians from Grostenquin and Marville. On a sunny day this air battle would last for six to eight hours of repeated engagements. The primary concern was that the pilots would get so engrossed in the fight they would let the F-86 run out of fuel. Some pilots even made 16mm films with the gunsight aiming-point (GSAP) camera to impress their squadron mates. The Canadian Sabre Mk-6s used the Orenda 14 engine producing an additional 1,500 lbs of thrust with better wing slats that gave them superior high altitude performance. The Mk-6s would do loops at 35,000 feet whereas the F-86Fs were struggling just to reach that altitude. As the Detroit auto engineers used to say, "There is no substitute for cubic inches." A few of these fighter pilots used this dogfight experience ten years later over North Vietnam.

The wing's "real" mission, FAIRWEATHER, was executed at different locations. It was standing nuclear alert with low drag external weapons while deployed at forward operating bases in West Germany. Detachment #1 stood alert at Bitburg, and Detachment #2 performed similar duty at Landsberg. Other forward bases were Furstenfeldbruck and Hahn. The alert fighters had to be airborne within five minutes after receipt of the dispatch message. Pilots had to be prepared for take-off twenty-four hours a day, seven days a week. Weapon load crews practiced loading MK-12 weapon shapes. At times the F-86Fs stood alert without special weapons, but they were available for rapid uploading within the minimum NATO warning time. Alert times and weapon locations varied with the defense condition as determined by SACEUR. Fre-

Flightline operations, 21st FBWg, Chambley, 1956.
Gene White

Aircraft ground servicing unit (MA-1), Chambley, 1956.
Gene White

Preparing to start the F-86F jet engine, 416th FBSq Chambley, 1956. Gene White

Crew chief Gene White and assistant Larry Hawkins fueling #52-5205, Chambley AB, 1956. Gene White

quently between 1956 and 1958, the alert teams flew in C-123Bs dispatched from Dreux. The nuclear alert mission continued from 1955 until a few weeks prior to wing deactivation.

Chalons-Vatry DOB was assigned to Chambley for bare base exercises with the F-86Fs. The 21st was one of the first fighter units to test the dispersed operating base concept. During the summer of 1955 the wing received twenty-one Mercedes 5-ton tractors and Henschal shop semi-vans for DOB operations. The shop vans had five-ton capacity and were thirty feet long with eight windows. Vans were fabricated with different interiors for specific shop functions and support equipment. No additional support equipment was authorized for DOB operations, so it was important to practice rapid loading and movement of vans from the main base to the DOB since these exercises were often part of an operational readiness inspection. These shop vans proved an excellent concept and remained in use for several years after disposal of the DOBs. The wings found that good, preplanned packing lists were the secret to successful dispersed aircraft maintenance.

All bases in Europe constantly tried to improve their defensive security, but security at Chambley was a greater concern because of its special weapons mission. In addition to the usual air police function of on-and-off base traffic control, vehicle registration and pass control, town patrols, and guard duty on base, the 21st Air Police Squadron greatly increased its base defense training and capabilities after the aircraft arrived. The wing's fighters and weapons had to be protected from armed attack and sabotage. All the air bases required extensive policing because their size made them vulnerable to attack with miles of possible entry points. There was particular concern for aircraft security while the planes were deployed at forward operating bases and dispersed operating bases. Air police manning was never considered sufficient to accomplish all these tasks. Mobile sabotage alert teams were created for rapid response to any detected threats; these teams consisted of at least five heavily armed men driving an M-20 armored truck. Teams were on duty twenty-four hours a day, and were augmented when threat warnings were received from French or USAFE sources. Eventually sentry dogs were added at Chambley to improve intruder detection.

In the early 1960s there was unrest in this northeast area of France because of the Algerian revolt. This was another reason base defense was extremely important. Bob Blessington, who arrived at Chambley in 1961 with the 523d TFSq remembers driving into Metz and seeing French paratroopers with machine guns stopping and searching cars looking for Algerian gun runners. One night he was asked to get out of the car. Ahead was a machine gun nest and a nail board in case anyone decided to run the blockade.

A base defense school was set up at Chambley; basic infantry training was conducted including firing of 50cal machine guns, 75mm and 57mm recoilless rifles and 60mm and 80mm mortars! This advance training took an exceptional amount of time away from ordinary duties.

Chambley had two Air and Airways Communication Service Squadrons attached to the base, the 1270th and 1283d. The 1270th AACS Squadron operated the control tower, navigation radio aids, and ground control approach radar system. During spring 1955 the USAFE, French Air Force, and Royal Canadian Air Force established the Moselle Radar Control Center. This tactical control center networked with Belgian, French, and German air traffic control radar and radio systems. The 1283d AACS Squadron worked at the Moselle Control air traffic control facility in an old fort on the west side of Metz. The control center was located in Maginot Line underground facilities near Verdun. The 1283d lived on base and commuted to Metz daily. Moselle Control's primary mission was ground radar control interception (GCI) air defense. GCI was practiced across eastern France. Search and height-finding radar sites were built in France, Belgium, and Netherlands. Collected information was sent into Moselle Control for evaluation, identification, and interception if necessary, and also used to avoid conflicts with commercial air traffic. This radar center was responsible for saving many aircraft during its years of service; most saves were related to jet aircraft running low on fuel because of winter navigation problems. A base T-33A was saved twice after engine flameout caused by fuel system icing.

In August 1956, the 531st FBSq flew twelve F-86Fs to Daharan AB, Saudi Arabia during the Suez Canal Crisis. These aircraft remained with the Saudi Air Force as they upgraded from their Hawker Hunters. The 531st received replacement F-86F-35s from Etain's 388th Wing as it converted to F-100Ds.

The 21st continued to be a very busy fighter-bomber wing providing air defense, a nuclear alert force, and close air support when the USAF suddenly decided it was no longer needed and cut it from the USAFE structure. In October 1957 the wing was informed that it would be shut down in February; the fighter pilots had earlier suspected something was wrong because there were no plans for conversion to F-100Ds. When inactivated, it was the only wing to fly the same fighter aircraft during its three years in France. Personnel reductions began in October; many airmen were transferred to Etain and other bases in France. Families completing their three years in France were returned to the United States. By December 1957 all squadrons were reduced to one officer and one airman except the 416th FBSq and the hospital. The 416th was still committed to its FAIRWEATHER tasking that required 36 officers and 255 airmen. It continued to stand alert until the middle of January. Aircraft from the other two squadrons were flown to Chateauroux Air Depot, and contract depots at Torrejon (CAFMS), Torino (FIAT), and Madrid (CASA) for equipment changes and inspection, and then transferred to MDAP nations. The 21st FBWg was inactivated at Chambley on 8 February 1958 and the base became a standby base for the 49th TFWg based at Etain.

Detachment #3 of the 49th TFWg at Etain AB was assigned the caretaker job at Chambley after deactivation of the 21st, but one year later the 49th had to depart Etain due to RED RICHARD. Support for Chambley was then assigned to Detachment #2, 7514th Support Group at Toul AB. In 1960 the 7514th was reorganized into the 7544th Support Group, which continued the task of maintaining the base and all equipment. Chambley was little used from March 1958 until August 1961. By March the only tenants were Det #13, 8th Radio Relay Squadron; Det #202, 7135th School Group; Company D, 249th Army Engineers; 1270th AACS Squadron (MATS); 1283d AACS Squadron (MATS); Det #10, 31st Weather Squadron (MATS); and Det #8, 12th Air Postal Squadron. This serene standby status would suddenly change as Western Europe and NATO were about to face the second Berlin Crisis.

Operation TACK HAMMER sent the 429th and 523d Tactical Fighter Squadrons TDY from Clovis

AFB, New Mexico, to Chambley on 12 September 1961. These TAC reflex units and their F-100Ds were Operation CHECKMATE's quick response reinforcements to USAFE in case war developed over a Berlin "settlement."

That same day it was announced that Chambley would reopen, and its status would change from standby to main operating base. The 7132d Support Group was activated on 7 September to prepare the base until the new tenant's advance detachment arrived to assume command responsibility for base preparation. After three years of idleness there was some deterioration of the building interiors, runway, and vehicle fleet. Support personnel initiated large base restoration programs including sealing the joints of all taxiways, marguerites, and the runway. Building interiors were examined, and heating, plumbing, electrical, and fire protection defects were logged and repaired if parts were available. USAFE had established base maintenance contracts with French companies to maintain the standby bases. Compagnie Generale de Chauffe performed day-to-day facility maintenance, freeing the Civil Engineer shops to support new construction and design new project plans for bidding.

122d Tactical Fighter Wing

The 122d Tactical Fighter Wing, Indiana Air National Guard; consisting of approximately 210 Officers and 1,140 Airmen, was ordered to federal active duty on 1 October 1961 for a period of twelve months for the Berlin Crisis and assigned to Twelfth Air Force. ANG units were activated to strengthen NATO defenses in Operation STAIR STEP as described in chapter 5. When activated, the 122d wing consisted of three fighter squadrons: the 112th Tactical Fighter Squadron (Special Delivery) based at Toledo Express Airport, Ohio; the 113th Tactical Fighter Squadron (Special Delivery) at Hulman Field, Terre Haute, Indiana; and the 163d Tactical Fighter Squadron (Special Delivery) at Baer Field, Fort Wayne, Indiana. Its three fighter squadrons had been flying Republic F-84F Thunderstreak fighters since 1957.

The 122d Tactical Fighter Wing originated as the WWII 358th Fighter Group, flying P-47 Thunderbolts on close air support missions with the Ninth Army Air Force in England, France, and Germany, earning three DUCs. The 358th Fighter Group was redesignated the 122d Fighter Group and allotted to the Indiana Air National Guard on 24 May 1946 as part of the postwar reserve forces. The 122d Fighter Group was expanded into the 122d Fighter Wing in November 1950.

When the 122d ADVON, consisting of 18 Officers and 95 Airmen, arrived on 19 October 1961, there were more than 1,500 men at Chambley. Just a few days prior to their arrival base personnel still did not know which new wing would arrive or what its mission would be. TAC reflex units departed the middle of November, but 1,100 men were still on base prior to arrival of the main body of 122d TFWg personnel and aircraft.

At the last minute prior to departure of the flight echelon, the wing was instructed to deploy only a portion of its total strength and one fighter squadron, the 163d TFSq, to France due to DOD budget cuts. The 112th and 113th TFSqs and support units remained on extended active duty at their ANG home stations, ready to reinforce the wing at Chambley. On 7 November the 122d TFWg was redesignated the 7122d Tactical Wing due to its reduced force structure. Its primary mission was to provide close air support to the Seventh Army in Europe, Operation HENNY PENNY.

The 122d Deputy Commander for Operations, COL Erwin H. Bucher, was assigned Wing Commander for the 7122d Wing. A reduced Headquarters, 122d TFWg remained at Baer Field to command the two fighter units remaining in the U.S.

By 6 November 1961 the 163d Tactical Fighter Squadron with twenty-six F-84Fs, all from Baer Field, had arrived at newly reactivated Chambley AB. The wing's C-47 and two T-33As arrived on 19 November after flying the North Atlantic route. On 1 December the Rear Detachment arrived, and all guardsman assembled for an estimated stay of ten months. The personnel at Chambley now consisted of regular air force and air guard officers; enlisted men from the regular air force, air guard, and air force reserve selective assignees; and local French employees. Selective assignees are mobilization augmentees; individuals recalled from the Air Force Reserve to fill specific jobs. All units and personnel coalesced into a smoothly working organization to make the air base operational and comfortable for the forthcoming damp winter season in France.

The 7122d Wing was manned at an overall 83 percent level with primary shortages being air policemen, aircraft mechanics, armament, and supply specialists. (Table 7.1) The major personnel problem was finding sufficient local wage rate (LWR) French civilian employees. Eighty-nine were authorized but only thirty-nine were employed on 31 December 1961. The isolated location of the air base and uncertainty about the length of its operation exacerbated this situation.

Table 7.1
7122d Tactical Wing Manning as of 31 December 1961

	Officers	Airmen
HQ 122d Wing	20	86
163d Tactical Fighter Sq	33	46
122d Armament & Electronics Sq	3	58
122d Consolidated Aircraft Maintenance Sq	3	144
HQ 122 Air Base Gp	24	104
122d Operations Sq	5	66
122d Air Police Sq	3	44
122d Civil Engineering Sq	5	90
122d Transportation Sq	4	75
122d Supply Sq	8	153
122d Tactical Hospital	9	35
Total authorized manning of a F-84F STAIR STEP wing 131 officers and 1130 airmen.		

During November supplies and equipment began arriving by the tons. Equipment had been surface-shipped from Indiana, ordered from CONUS depots, and purchased locally by base supply. A supply nightmare began with the arrival of vast quantities of conventional munitions that greatly exceeded storage capacity. By February 1962, about 8,000 tons had arrived and posed a hazard to base personnel because the ammunition had to be stored outdoors on base. At the same time 109 railroad freight cars arrived with aircraft drop-tanks. After observing incorrect stock numbers on the shipping boxes, a quick inspection revealed the drop tanks were the wrong type for the F-84F fighters. It took frustrating persistence and reams of paperwork to return the 109 freight cars of unusable drop tanks to the Chateauroux Depot.

When the USAFE received notice that Chambley would be reactivated as a main operating base, it allocated $800,000 for new construction and property renovation. The 7544th Support Group gave the job of deciding how to use these funds to the 7122d Tactical Wing. Twenty-four STAIR STEP projects were begun and 75 percent were completed by 1 July 1962. Projects included construction of eight Butler type hangars, a large outdoor supply storage area with security fencing, improved munitions storage igloos, a liquid oxygen plant, repairs to aircraft hangar doors and roofs, runway approach lights, GCA radar turntable and standby motor-generator set, airfield pavement repairs, six aircraft maintenance docks, and base electrical system repairs. These projects greatly improved the war capability of Chambley AB. Some of these projects had been started by Company D, 249th Engineer Battalion to improve Chambley prior to arrival of the 122d Wing. The GCA turntable was one of the 249th's projects. It had to be eighteen feet above grade to match the high ends of the runway. This permitted night and bad weather radar landings from either direction and improved touchdown precision for the fighters. Many buildings were improved in "self help" projects performed by the occupants. The civil engineering squadron provided tools and supplies and monitored their progress. Civil engineers were also busy during the winter of 1961-62 keeping the runway, taxiways, and roads cleared of snow and ice so alert aircraft could respond to scramble orders.

The practice of rotating pilots to Europe from the wing's stateside squadrons was very successful. On 6 January 1962 seven F-84F pilots arrived from the 112th and 113th, flew local orientation missions, reviewed war plans, and were integrated into the 163d TFSq. After thirty days at Chambley they returned to their squadrons to teach this war tasking. Because of this training, their units would have been ready to support combat operations immediately upon arrival in France if deployed. It also allowed the 163d to maintain 100 percent manning, relieved the boredom of the pilots on active duty at their CONUS base, and kept them connected to their overseas wing. Later in March and April, twenty more pilots arrived for this theater indoctrination, and each pilot flew ten or more hours in French and West German airspace.

The first major exercise of 1962 was a no-notice Tactical Evaluation conducted by a Seventeenth Air

Force team on 29 and 30 January. This Tac Eval began with an intelligence buildup and proceeded into a Simple Alert, State Orange, and then General Alert with Automatic Aircraft Launch Program. After the General Alert Announcement the four Sierra Alert F-84Fs were launched in less than fifteen minutes, followed by eight more F-84Fs prepared and launched within thirty more minutes. As would have happened in a real alert, not all the F-84Fs were at Chambley. Eight aircraft were at Wheelus for gunnery training. When notified of the alert they were immediately reconfigured and were ready to launch within three hours. Fragmentary Orders were executed both days, testing the wing's reaction capability and weapons loading and delivery ability. Armament load crews were evaluated on various weapons' load configurations and rapid weapons rearming of the returning aircraft. Aircraft maintenance personnel were tested on aircraft turn-around times and their ability to keep aircraft in commission for sustained combat launches. The 7122d Wing passed this evaluation with an excellent score.

The 7122d's second major test was the ORI conducted on 6 March 1962 by HQ USAFE. It passed this inspection on the first evaluation since it had practiced operational readiness during December as required by KEEN KNIFE, a Seventeenth Air Force operations plan.

The wing was tasked to support Seventeenth Air Force and NATO exercises throughout its stay at Chambley. Exercise RED EYE required twenty target sorties to penetrate the Spanish air defense area to test the 65th Air Division response time, and test the capabilities of the intercept controllers. CABIN CRUISER was a continuous air defense exercise conducted within West Germany. The 163d flew up to eight F-84F sorties a day. For GUNTALK, the Central Europe air defense exercise, the squadron furnished fourteen target sorties. It flew fourteen more sorties in COLD TURKEY, another air defense exercise. GRAND SLAM II was a Fourth Allied Tactical Air Force exercise between 9 and 13 April. This was a simulated test of wartime Disaster Control, the Non-Combatant Evacuation Order and Hospital Evacuation, plus the Automatic Aircraft Launch Program. One problem was obvious immediately as the 4ATAF Operations Center began requesting more aircraft support than the 7122d possessed. The 7122d Wing quickly realized that 4ATAF thought three squadrons of F-84Fs were available at Chambley instead of just one! Seventeenth Air Force promptly informed 4ATAF that only one squadron was based at Chambley. Fortunately it was only a test, not a real emergency. Overall the wing Combat Operations Center (COC) functioned very well and much was learned by all players.

To accomplish the wing's primary mission of close air support, up to thirty sorties a day were flown by the squadron when weather permitted. Usually four sorties daily were scheduled against Seventh Army ground targets under the direction of Ground Forward Air Controllers (GFAC). GFAC training was a repetitive task with one fighter pilot rotating every fifteen days with Army units in West Germany. During 1962, the 163d TFSq flew a total of 208 sorties for 425 hours to develop its close air support skills. Four pilots found time to attend the two-week Air Ground Operations School conducted by the Seventeenth Air Force at Ramstein Air Base.

A more interesting exercise was the exchange of four pilots and four airmen from the 163d TFSq with four pilots and airmen of the West German Air Force's 32d Fighter-Bomber Wing. These fighter pilots successfully flew training missions with each other's squadrons from 3 through 15 April. This exchange greatly increased understanding of NATO air integration and terminology.

The 163d TFSq flew a total of 3,625 hours during the first six months of 1962. Of these, 910 hours were actual weather instrument flying. Two gunnery exercises were conducted at Wheelus AB. It was the only place where air-to-air gunnery could be conducted since there was insufficient space for an air-to-air range in continental Europe. Approximately three hundred square miles are required for range safety. Air-to-ground gunnery, rocket firing, dive bombing, and LABS delivery was conducted at the Suippes range in France and the Siegenberg range in West Germany. All squadron pilots were qualified in conventional weapons delivery and 50 percent maintained special weapons delivery qualifications. Up to a dozen sorties were flown daily to accomplish this training. One F-84F was lost locally to engine failure, and one T-33A was lost on base in a landing accident.

These flying hours were possible because of the high quality support provided by the top-notch aircraft maintenance, armament, and electronics maintenance squadrons; in 1962, F-84F in-commission rates averaged 80 percent except for one month. In March an aircraft grounding technical order TCTO 1F-84F-802 directed replacement of all aileron control rods. This cut flying to 450 hours for the month. The wing's eight-year-old Thunderstreaks had an average total airframe time of 1,280 hours each and J-65 engine total time averaged 220 hours. All shops had greatly improved facilities and received their necessary equipment and tools since their arrival the previous November, which increased maintenance production.

All personnel were constantly involved in training to upgrade job-skill levels among the airmen. This training was made necessary by the four Unit Manning Document changes the wing had undergone as it transitioned from ANG, to TAC, to USAFE, then to a partial wing structure. Some job changes were very slight and some were total reassignments. As of 1 July 1962 the 7122d Wing had 541 airmen in job training. Approximately 220 passed tests and had their skill level upgraded. Schools were set-up on base, beginning with OJT Orientation and OJT Administrator-Supervisor courses to train the trainers. In addition to job training the wing conducted General Military Training for all personnel; the subjects were small arms marksmanship, first aid, interior guard duty, and NATO organization and mission. The wing also set up its own schools for aircraft armament loading, aircraft maintenance data collection, annual instrument flying and F-84F check-out courses for pilots.

Throughout all these hectic flight operations, the 122d Air Police Squadron faced a very serious base security problem. France was in political turmoil because of the Algerian uprising and terrorist's threats were made against the base. From January to April 1962 the air police had to increase security at the ammunition dumps, POL storage area, and supply warehouses. In January they were short thirty-two men from their authorized strength, but they were able to augment their strength with air policemen from Dreux AB during this emergency. Fortunately there were no attacks directed at the base.

By April 1962 the Berlin Crisis appeared to be settled and rumors began to spread that an early release plan was being discussed for all reserve personnel prior to their obligated date of 31 September 1962. The Kennedy Administration was interested in saving money on this emergency call-up and wanted to spend the funds on its limited war programs instead. All spring the 7122d Tactical Wing received a number of conflicting movement orders from Seventeenth Air Force. Finally on 7 June it was directed to return to CONUS with all personnel, but without its twenty-five F-84Fs. All F-84F support equipment and spare parts were to remain on base. These were to be transferred in place to the next flying unit to occupy Chambley. The support C-47 and T-33s were to be flown back to Baer Field, Indiana. All personnel were to return to Baer Field by MATS airlift for separation from the USAF by 20 August 1962. Planning began at once by wing staff agencies to assist the smooth transition of Chambley to a new fighter organization.

Immediately the 7122d Tactical Wing began by preparing a tentative airlift schedule for all personnel. An ADVON would be needed at Baer Field to set up a system to process certain ANG and Air Force Reserve personnel. All Air Force Reserve selective assignees would fly to Ft. Wayne, then be released from active duty and dispatched to their individual homes of record. At this time, the wing had ANG personnel assigned from Arizona, Missouri, South Carolina and Tennessee. Plans had to be coordinated with the STAIR STEP wings from these states for transportation of personnel to their states and units for proper release from active duty. The main body of the wing would return and be separated as a group from active duty and reassigned to ANG reserve status. Many individuals still had a reserve obligation and wished to stay in the ANG rather than chance being drafted into the Army for another year. To add to the mix, two airmen wished to separate at Chambley, tour Europe for several months, then return home. This out of the ordinary request required many messages to Seventeenth Air Force but was solved after both men obtained passports and agreed to pay their own airfare home!

The ADVON departed on 20 June on one MATS air lifter. The main body of troops departed between 5 and 25 July, usually taking two days to return to Baer Field via MATS airlift. The F-84Fs that had belonged to the 7122d TWg were transferred in place on 1 July 1962 to the 366th Tactical Fighter Wing. Their C-47 and T-33As returned to CONUS across the North Atlantic without incident. On 16 July 1962 the 7122d Tactical Wing turned a much improved air base over to the 7367th Combat Support Group and departed Chambley.

390th Tactical Fighter Squadron
366th Tactical Fighter Wing

On 8 May 1962, the 7367th Combat Support Group, consisting of the HQ Squadron, 7367th Air Police Sq, 7367th Material Sq, and the 7637th USAF Dispensary was activated to operate Chambley after departure of the 7122d Wing. The 7367th reported to the newly formed 366th Tactical Fighter Wing at Chaumont AB and supported its 390th Tactical Fighter Squadron that would fly F-84Fs from Chambley. The 390th had twenty F-84Fs and was manned by twenty-seven officers and seven airmen. The 7367th had one officer and one airman on 8 May, but by January 1963 it

Jet engine repairs, 21st FBWg, Chambley, 1956.
J-47-GE-27 engine removed from F-86F.
Gene White

Jet engine repairs, 25th TRWg, Chambley, 1966.
New jet engine repair shop overhauling J-71s from RB-66s.
National Archives

had grown to 36 officers, 392 airmen and 123 French LWR employees. In addition, Chambley's real estate was being maintained by seventy-five employees of the French O&M contractor. Three tenant units still operated the weather station; post office; and control tower, GCA, and radio beacon. Company D, 249th Engineer Battalion, Construction, continued base improvements and assisted in construction of a depot at Verdun. By this time the ammunition storage expansion, GCA turntable and access road had been completed.

The mission of the 390th while at Chambley was close air support to army ground forces and air defense. The 366th TFWg had four squadrons, with Headquarters and one squadron based at Chaumont and squadrons based at Chambley, Etain, and Phalsbourg. The 366th is covered in detail in chapter 9.

The 390th TFSq occupied hangar 110 and the base operations facilities previously used by the 163d TFSq. In February they were informed that the 10th TRWg would be moving to Chambley for four to six months while the runway and taxiways at Toul AB were being rebuilt for the fourth time. The pavement was still disintegrating! NATO was paying for this rework. The 390th Squadron had to move across the runway to hangar 810 on 12 April, as soon as it was vacated by the 249th Bn. Hangar 110 was given to the 42d TRSq and its RB-66B/C aircraft. Hangar 110 had also been the base gym, but with the RB-66s, there was no space, so Chambley no longer had a gym. In this game of "musical hangars" the 249th moved on to Toul to once again repair its buildings and hangars. The 10th brought 850 additional officers and airmen to Chambley, which filled all available quarters and placed an increased workload on the 7367th.

On 15 July 1963, when the 366th Tactical Fighter Wing left for CONUS, the 390th Squadron departed Chambley. The 10th TRWg was still at Chambley standing Ecco Alert while waiting for completion of Toul's runway repair. The base returned to standby status and continued to be managed by the 7367th CSGp until 1 July 1965 when the same RB-66s and squadrons returned, assigned to a new combat wing.

25th Tactical Reconnaissance Wing

The 25th Tactical Reconnaissance Wing, manned by 155 officers and 870 airmen, was authorized to the USAFE on 19 April 1965, and activated on 24 September 1965 at Chambley AB. It was the third reconnaissance wing in France and the fourth in USAFE. The other tactical reconnaissance wings were the 10th at Alconbury in the UK; and the 26th at Toul and 66th at Laon AB in France, flying RB-66s, RF-101s, and new RF-4Cs.

The 25th had been a WWII reconnaissance group activated on 9 August 1944 at Watton, England, to perform special missions for the USAAF Eighth Air Force. This group flew a variety of aircraft; B-17s, B-24s, and P-38s to conduct weather reconnaissance, night photography, radar chaff screens, and electronic countermeasures missions throughout Central Europe and the Atlantic Ocean, and earned four Campaign Stars. The 25th Reconnaissance Group was inactivated at Drew Field, Florida, on 8 September 1945 as WWII ended. The 25th Wing remained inactive until 19 April 1965.

Only two flying squadrons were assigned to the 25th Tactical Reconnaissance Wing at Chambley and each flew different models of the Douglas RB-66 Destroyer. On 1 July 1965, the 42d Tactical Recon-

RB-66C with direction finding antennas installed in wing tip antenna pods.
Ted Bailey

naissance Squadron was transferred from the 10th TRWg to the 25th Tactical Reconnaissance Wing, and became the first flying unit at Chambley since the departure of Det #1, 10th TRWg in 1963. The 42d flew RB-66Cs that had a seven-man crew. Its primary mission was electronic reconnaissance, commonly called "Ferret" operations; the ECM operators were known as "Ravens." The 42d TRSq's mission statement was "active and passive electronic countermeasures, visual, radar, and tactical weather reconnaissance both day and night." On 1 October the 19th Tactical Reconnaissance Squadron was transferred from the 26th TRWg at Toul to the 25th Tactical Reconnaissance Wing. The 19th TRSq flew RB-66Bs with a three-man crew and the mission of day and night photography.

Both the 19th and 42d were familiar with their missions and aircraft. But the wing was kept busy training newly assigned support personnel to operate and maintain the base. Several major construction projects were necessary to accommodate the Destroyers. Hangar shops had to be altered to make space for larger maintenance test fixtures and hangar wiring was upgraded to distribute the increased electrical power required by the B-66 aircraft systems. A larger jet engine shop, Building #619, was constructed to maintain the J-71 engines. The base operations building was modified to house the B-66 crew trainer and the usual C-11B instrument trainer. Here again electrical service had to be increased.

One major drawback of the B-66 was pilot training. It was always a problem because the B-66 was a single pilot aircraft and dual checkout was impossible. Douglas proposed a dual control version but it was never purchased by the USAF. A large B-66 analog electronic flight-crew simulator built by Curtis Wright was very useful for checkout of the flight deck crew: pilot, navigator/camera operator, and gunner. Training the RB-66C ECM operators was more difficult since the USAF had not purchased a comparable electronic warfare simulator for their ground training.

Thorough training in the RB-66B camera system was critical to accomplish the mission. The system was complex, involving three cameras, camera compartment temperature and pressure controls, flash bomb and camera shutter intervalometers, a universal camera control unit, a stabilized camera mount, and flash bomb bay operation. Later electronic warfare jamming transmitters were added to the RB-66s, increasing the mission workload.

Day and night photographic training was hindered by the 1965 ruling made by the French government that prohibited photography over their country. This forced photo missions to West Germany and Great Britain. Night photography was limited since suitable ranges for dropping the photo flash bombs, M-120, and M-122 were not available after the close of our Moroccan air bases.

USAF and TAC had considered phasing-out the B-66 and RB-66 in 1962 after about six years of service. TAC was unhappy with the Destroyers from the beginning because of its many airframe, systems, and engine problems. Especially irritating was the early decision forced on TAC to use the J-71 engine in place of the J-57. This caused the loss of 4,000 pounds of thrust on the 80,000 pound take-off weight. But since USAF had no other aircraft suitable for the special reconnaissance missions the Destroyer could perform, the RB-66 was kept in service. As it turned out, it was needed for another ten years in the Vietnam War.

The need to have tactical electronic reconnaissance capability in Southeast Asia required USAF to take six RB-66Cs and crews from Chambley in TDY status to this new theater of operations. As the war in Vietnam continued to expand so did the need for tactical electronic warfare. Detachment #1, 25th TRWg USAFE was established half way around the world from France, in Thailand on 10 October 1965. The Air Force Outstanding Unit Award (AFOUA) was presented to the 25th TRWg for their efforts in SEA. The AFOUA Citation is a masterpiece of obfuscation, "...distinguished itself by exceptionally meritorious service in support of military operations against an opposing armed force in Southeast Asia, from 13 October 1965 to 8 June 1966. During this period, the accomplishment of difficult operations under extremely hazardous conditions was an instrumental factor in the successful interdiction effort conducted by the United States Air Force."

The 25th Tactical Reconnaissance Wing was the last USAFE wing to operate at Chambley Air Base. On 22 August 1966 the 42d TRSq was deactivated at Chambley and the majority of the aircrews, including sixteen EWOs and ten RB-66Cs were sent to the 432d TRWg based at Takhli, Thailand. A few 42d TRSq aircraft were flown to Douglas Aircraft, Tulsa, Oklahoma, for additional ECM equipment and camouflage paint before going to Southeast Asia. About 1 August 1966 the 19th TRSq (Photo) was ordered to move its twenty RB-66Bs to Shaw Air Force Base, South Carolina, and was assigned to the 363d TRWg. It flew RB-66Bs from Chambley to Moron AB, Spain, then flew non-stop to Shaw with the aid of three air-to-air refuelings. Offically the 19th TRSq was to became another of USAFE's dual-based units (units based in the U.S. but available for operations in Europe). Actually the squadron and its RB-66Bs were needed to train aircrews for the expanding combat operations in SEA.

On 15 October 1966 USAFE deactivated the 25th Tactical Reconnaissance Wing at Chambley as part of FRELOC and reactivated the 7367th Combat Support Group to close the base. On the same date Chambley changed from a main operating base to a standby operating base. The 7367th immediately began to pack and ship all U.S. property off base. Chambley's value as of August 1966 was $14,247,396.07. The NATO property account was slightly over $15 million. These numbers include all structures and other real property, but do not include aircraft or spare aircraft parts. Chambley was transferred to the Liquidation Office in Paris and deleted from USAF property records in March 1967. On 1 April 1967 USAFE discontinued the 7367th Combat Support Group as part of FRELOC and the last USAF airplane, a T-33A, departed Chambley for West Germany.

The French military used Chambley for helicoptor flight operations and airborne forces parachute drop exercises for many years, but the old base is currently accessible to tourists. Attempts have been made to develop Chambley for commercial use. In 2001 the old supply warehouses were occupied by a lumber yard, mill, and building materials company. The railroad siding through the base was busy. The parachute shop building housed the commercial development office and restaurant. Hopefully its commercial use has increased and more of the buildings have been renovated. The remaining buildings may be viewed but not entered because of safety concerns.

Chambley is also used by recreational aviation groups. It has hosted hot air balloon meets every other year for many years, and was the site of a French homebuilt and antique restoration group fly-in for a week in July 2005. Chambley can be found on Michelin map #307 Local. It is located 16 km (10 mi) south of Jarney and 18 km (11 mi) south of Autoroute 4, or it can be reached by train from Paris' Gare de l'Est station.

Chambley Air Base 1992

Top left: Base Ops building with new tower cab. Top right: One of two hangars being maintained and used by the FAF.
Middle left: PE Shop now an office/restaurant. Middle right: Base chapel.
Bottom left: Base shops building. Bottom right: Remains of base auto cnter.
Considerable development and restoration has occurred since these photos were taken in 1992.
Jerry McAuliffe

Chambley Air Base Assigned Aircraft

Gene White

21st Fighter-Bomber Wing, F-86Fs, 12 December 1954 - 8 February 1958
Twenty-six aircraft per squadron. These Sabres were flown from George AFB, CA to Chambley, France by 21st Fighter-Bomber Wing pilots.
Aircraft Marking:
- 72d Fighter-Bomber Squadron - White stars on red bands on nose and tail.
- 416th Fighter-Bomber Squadron - White stars on blue bands on nose and tail.
- 531st Fighter-Bomber Squadron - Black stars on yellow bands on nose and tail.

F-86F-35-NA

52-5165	72d	52-5183	416th	52-5202	531st	52-5221~	416th	52-5244	72d
52-5167	72d	52-5184	416th	52-5203	416th	52-5222~	72d	52-5246*	531st
52-5168	72d	52-5185	416th	52-5204	416th	52-5223	531st	52-5248	531st
52-5169	416th	52-5186	416th	52-5205	416th	52-5224	531st	52-5249*	531st
52-5170	416th	52-5187	72d	52-5206	416th	52-5225	531st	52-5250	531st
52-5171	416th	52-5188*	72d	52-5207	416th	52-5227	531st	52-5254	416th
52-5172	531st	52-5189	531st	52-5208	416th	52-5228*	531st	52-5255	531st
52-5173	531st	52-5190	531st	52-5209	416th	52-5229	72d	52-5258*	531st
52-5174	531st	52-5191	531st	52-5210	416th	52-5231	72d	52-5262	531st
52-5176	531st	52-5192	531st	52-5211	72d	52-5232	72d	52-5263	531st
52-5177	531st	52-5193*	531st	52-5212	72d	52-5233	72d	52-5268	531st
52-5178	416th	52-5194	531st	52-5213	72d	52-5235	72d	53-1090	416th
52-5179	72d	52-5195	531st	52-5214	72d	52-5236	72d	53-1097	416th
52-5180	416th	52-5196	531st	52-5215	72d	52-5238*	72d	53-1098	531st
52-5181	72d	52-5197*	416th	52-5216	72d	52-5239	72d	53-1144	416th
52-5182	416th	52-5198	416th	52-5218	72d	52-5240	72d	53-1146	416th
		52-5200	531st	52-5219	72d	52-5242	72d	53-1147	531st
		52-5201	416th	52-5220	416th	52-5243	72d		

* Losses:
52-5188 - Crashed, fuel exhaustion/bad weather, near Jaillon, France. 13 JAN 55, no fatalities, ejected.
52-5193 - Crashed in France, 30 MAR 56, fatalities unknown.
52-5197 - Damaged at BW-1, Greenland, 31 DEC 54, no fatalities. Returned to Squadron October 1955.
52-5228 - Crashed, engine failure, near Herford, West Germany, 5 APR 57, 1 fatality.
52-5238 - Crashed, bad night landing at Chateauroux AD, France, 12 OCT 57, no fatalities.
52-5246 - Crashed, cockpit fire, weather, 9nm N of Bitburg AB, West Germany, 25 SEP 56, 1 fatality, ejected.
52-5249 - Crashed at Chambley AB, France, 15 SEP 55, fatalities unknown.
52-5258 - Crashed, cockpit fire, weather, at Ehekirchen, West Germany, 31 MAY 56, no fatalities, ejected.

~ Wing CO's a/c

21st Air Base Group: Wing Support Aircraft
C-47A: 42-23643, 42-92643, 43-15222, 43-16039
L-20A: 51-16536
T-33A: 52-9833, 52-9834, 52-9835, 53-5819

Chambley AB tail numbers continued next page

Chambley AB tail numbers, continued

USAF Museum

7122d Tactical Wing, F-84Fs, 6 November 1961 - 20 June 1962
Twenty-six aircraft assigned to squadron. These Thunderstreaks were flown from Baer Field, Ft.Wayne, IN to Chambley AB, France by 163d Tactical Fighter Squadron pilots. These F-84Fs transferred to the 366th Tactical Fighter Wing and remained in France.
Aircraft Marking:
163d Tactical Fighter Squadron - Red band on vertical stabilizer tip.

F-84F-25, -30, -35, -40, -RE and -25, -40-GK

51-1628	51-1676	51-1699	51-9385	51-9540	51-17080	52-6404	52-6475	52-7021
51-1657	51-1689	51-1781	51-9400	51-9542	51-17086	52-6426	52-6520	52-7023
51-1673	51-1695	51-9383	51-9518	51-17077		52-6458	52-6543*	52-7043

* Losses: 52-6543 - Crashed, engine failure, near Saint Marcel, France, 15 MAR 62, no fatalities.

7122d Operations Squadron: Wing Support Aircraft
C-47A: 42-93701 (on loan)
C-47B: 44-76566 from ANG
L-20A: 51-16533, 51-16536
T-33A: 2 ea. from ANG, 52-9732*
*Losses: 52-9732 - Crashed, bad landing on Chambley AB, France,19 MAR 62, no fatalities.

Detachment 12, Atlantic Air Rescue Center Europe (AARCE) 1963 - May 1966
HH-43B-KA: 6 ea. 62-4521, 62-4523, 62-4536, 62-4537, 62-4538, 62-4551

390th Tactical Fighter Sq, 366th Tactical Fighter Wing F-84Fs, 8 May 1962 - 15 July 1963
The 390th TFSq was based at Chambley AB. Markings: 390th TFSq - Yellow band.
Twenty aircraft per squadron. These Thunderstreaks were flown from Chambley to Holloman AFB, NM by 366th Wing pilots.

F-84F-25, -30, -35-RE, and -25, -35, -40-GK

51-1628	51-1673	51-1689	51-1699	51-9383	51-9400	51-9540	52-6404	52-6458	52-7023
51-1657	51-1676	51-1695	51-1781	51-9385	51-9518	51-9542	52-6426	52-7021	52-7043

Ted Bailey

25th Tactical Reconnaissance Wing, RB-66B/C, 1 October 1965 - 15 October 1966
Aircraft assigned to 19th TRSq, 20 ea RB-Bs, Aircraft assigned to 42d TRSq, 12 ea RB-Cs. These Destroyers were flown from RAF Alconbury, England and Toul AB to Chambley AB by 25th TRWg pilots. 42d TRSq crews delivered all RB-66Cs to CONUS or Thailand in August 1966. 19th TRSq delivered all RB-66Bs to Shaw AFB via Moron AB, Spain and Lages AB, Azores in October 1966.
Aircraft Marking: 19th Tactical Reconnaissance Squadron - Red band on engine nacelle.
42d Tactical Reconnaissance Squadron - Blue band on engine nacelle.

RB-66B-DL 19th TRSq

53-423	53-447	53-450	53-453	54-438	54-440	54-509	54-515	54-527	54-545
53-426	53-449	53-451	54-434	54-439	54-441	54-510	54-524	54-533	54-546

RB-66C-DT 42d TRSq

54-459	54-462	54-464	54-466	54-468	54-470
54-461	54-463	54-465	54-467	54-469	55-386

Loses: NONE

25th Operations Squadron: Wing Support Aircraft
C-47A: 43-49208
L-20A: 51-16533, 51-16536, 52-6132 (10th TRWg Toul to Chambley)
T-33A: 53-5132, 53-5830, 57-540

Appendix 7.1 Notice to Airmen 1959 (NOTAM) - USAF-Chambley

Elevation 864 feet (263m), 49° 02'N - 05° 53'E. One paved runway 7,800 feet long, 030°/210°. Rotating beacon, light on airfield, with runway and obstruction lights. Aircraft storage available. No transient aircraft maintenance facilities. Aircraft fuel, 100-130 octane and JP4 jet fuel with single point refueling. Jet aircraft starting units available, low pressure oxygen servicing and high pressure compressed air available.
Emergency use only, prior permission required for flight operations, aerdrome closed until further notice. (Chambley was in standby status at this time).

ACKNOWLEDGEMENTS

I would like to thank the following people who contributed to this chapter:

Ted Bailey was a propellor specialist in the 1616th Support System (MATS) at Chateauroux from February 1959 through March 1962. He was also assigned to the squadron's Mobile Maintenance Team and flew to many countries to perform "unscheduled" aircraft maintenance. This took him all over Europe, as well as to Turkey and Ghana.

Bob Blessington was part of a Mobile Alert Force at Clovis, New Mexico in 1961 and was sent to Chambley with the 523d TFSq as part of Operation TACK HAMMER.

Al Christensen was a Weather Officer in Detachment 10, 31st Weather Squadron, MATS, stationed at Chambley AB, 1955-1957. Al has provided excellent photos and information.

Charles "Chuck" Timms was an Air Policeman at Chambley AB from 1954 to 1958. Before his death he was the driving force behind Chambley Air Base reunions and composed the first Chambley Air Base history. He provided much encouragement for the preparation of this book.

Gene White was crew chief of F-86F #52-5206 in the 416th FBSq at Chambley, October 1955 to January 1958. From there he moved on to Etain AB. Gene has contributed not only his photos but his recollections as a crew chief at Chambley.

A familiar sight to Chambley airmen that has changed little. Hageville, 1992.
Jerry McAuliffe

8

CHATEAUROUX-DEOLS AIR DEPOT

Chateauroux, located in the Indre Department of France, developed around its 10th century castle as so many cities in France have. It is located 145 miles (230 km) south of Paris and 72 miles (120 km) east of Poitiers. In 1950 it was a small city with a population of 42,000 inhabitants. Deols was a small northern suburb adjoining the Chateauroux commercial airport. La Martinerie military airfield was located three miles (5 km) north of Chateauroux's center, and about five miles (8 km) east of Deols. The USAFE Chateauroux-Deols Air Depot (46° 51'N - 01° 43'E, elevation 532 feet) consisted of two separate pieces of real estate about five miles apart; the La Martinerie military airdrome and the Chateauroux airport. This complex was also known as "CHAD," "Chat," and some unprintable names by the USAF personnel assigned there.

La Martinerie was established in 1916 as a pilot training school far removed from the WWI battlefields. During WWI many American Army Air Service pilots were trained by the French in this region. The airdrome continued in use as a fighter and training base up to May 1940. The FAF used La Martinerie late in WWII as a bomber airfield, and after the war's end as a storage depot. The Chateauroux-Deols airport was started about 1929 and grew into a busy airfield by 1937 providing air transport service to Bordeaux and Paris. Runways at both airports were not paved but were grass fields as was common in Europe at that time. Both airfields offered radio aids, lighting, fuel, and repairs. During 1944 the American Army stayed north of the Loire River valley and there were no U.S. military stationed in the Chateauroux area during or immediately after WWII.

Avions Marcel Bloch constructed a large aircraft factory on the Chateauroux Airport during 1935-36, on the west edge of the airport parallel to highway N20. This was in addition to its factories at Courbevoie and Bordeaux. It was needed to increase production of Bloch Model 131, 200, and 210 bombers to aid the rapid expansion of the Armee de l'Air during 1938-40. The factory was a very modern, 1934 art deco design, and included two large administration and engineering design office buildings that served as the main entrance to the airport. The airport control tower was constructed on top of the southern administration building. The primary high-bay aircraft assembly building was a quarter mile long and built to assemble large, two and four engine airplanes having 150-foot wingspans. In 1936, France nationalized their aircraft industry and the Bloch-Chateauroux factory became a portion of the production group known as the Societe Nationale de Constructions Aeronautiques de Sud-Ouest Works (S.N.C.A.S.O.). After the fall of France in May 1940, the factory was used to produce sub-assemblies for German aircraft and for aircraft repairs. Both the La Martinerie airfield and the Chateauroux aircraft factory were bombed by the RAF and USAAF during WWII. After WWII this aircraft factory was returned to production by Dassault Aircraft, the new name of the Bloch Company, but work ceased in 1950. By 1951 the aircraft factory, with two administration buildings, six smaller engineering laboratory buildings, and one large air freight warehouse were available for long term lease.

During the 1950 initial meetings for U.S. air base site selection, choosing the location of a large air depot was a primary concern. If a site wasn't found in Europe, this depot would have to be located near Newark, New Jersey. Moving the Erding Air Depot and all its war material stocks out of Germany into France as soon as possible dominated all planning. Some consideration was given to locating the air depot in England, but France was the most logical location, since the U.S. Army logistical system was centered in France. The Army had only a minor logistical support system in the UK. Several locations were proposed: Bordeaux-Merignac airfield and port facility, Lorient and Lann-Bihoue airfield and port, Lyon-Bron airfield, Metz-Frescaty airfield, Nantes-Reze airfield and port, and the St. Nazaire-Donges airfield and port facility. The airfields at all these sites were under civilian jurisdiction and would require extensive negotiations to obtain operating approvals. Also, expanding commercial air traffic might cause future problems. The former commercial and military airfield site, Lyon-Bron, located in mideastern France on the Rhone River was the best location proposed in September 1950. The Air Force team was agreeable to a joint use

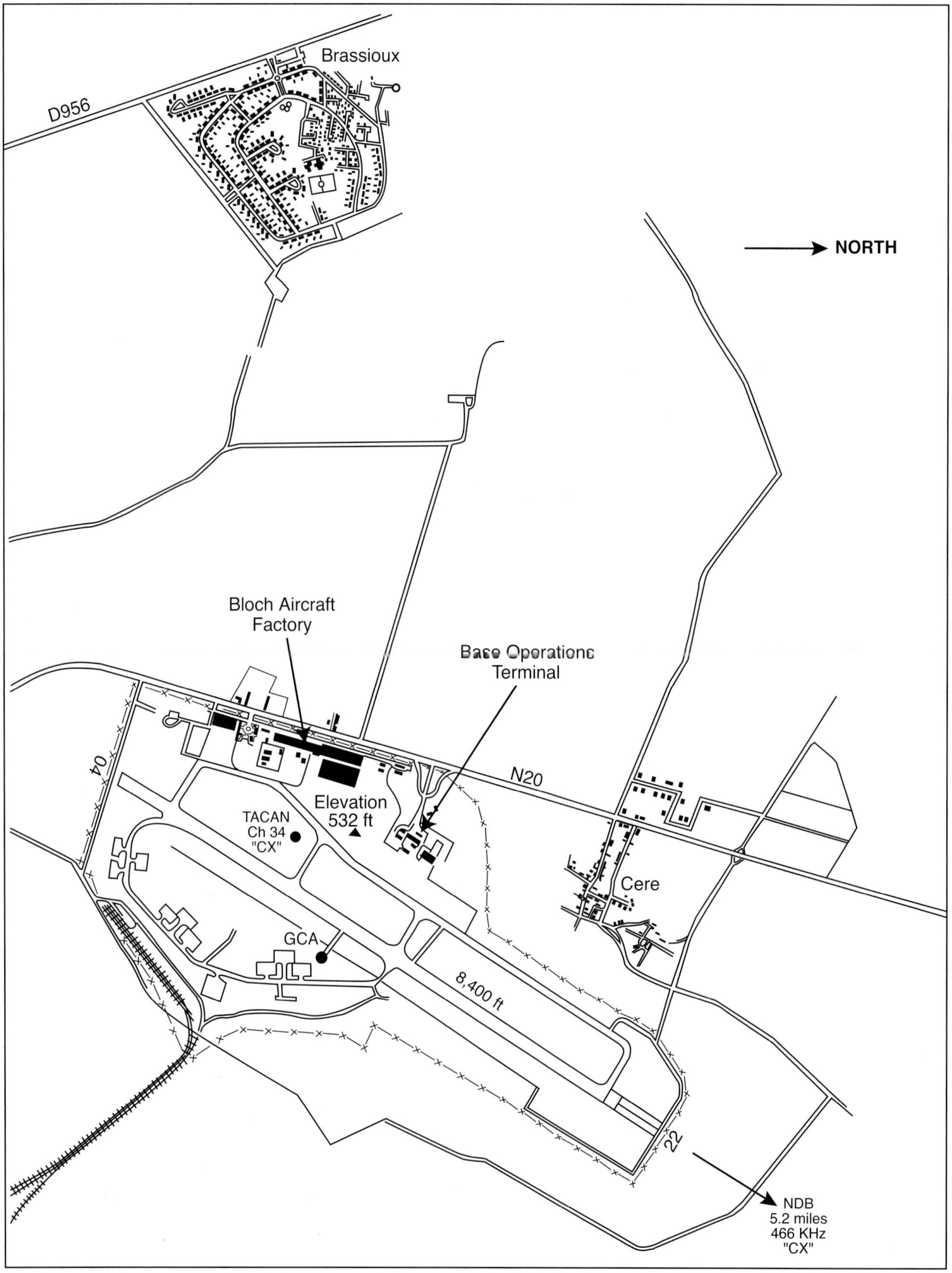

Map 8.1 Chateauroux-Deols Airfield layout in 1956 and Brassioux in 1960

Chateauroux-Deols airfield 1956. Old art deco buildings and new runway.
"History Central Air Materiel Area, Europe" via William Adamek

(civil and military) airfield operation.

The proposed air depot would be the largest depot in Europe in order to support the USAFE and all NATO air forces, and air forces of other nations receiving Military Defense Assistance Program (MDAP) aid. There was disagreement between DOD and the Department of State over the size and cost of a large depot, and uncertainty if France would agree to the presence of an MDAP depot on its soil. There were also questions about what portion of the MDAP depot would be paid by NATO nations since the depot would be supporting non-NATO aircraft also.

The mission of this proposed depot in France would encompass these tasks:

1. Provide all necessary depot logistical support to USAFE and assistance to all NATO countries.
2. Issue and control shipments of supplies to new USAFE bases and wings in France.
3. Prepare USAFE & MDAP requirements and requisitions to CONUS AMC depots.
4. Provide maintenance beyond the capabilities of the European nations.
5. Provide supply and maintenance training for foreign personnel.
6. Provide and supervise technical representatives requested by the various countries.
7. Assist Military Assistance Advisory Groups to compute detailed logistical requirements.
8. Maintain stocks for emergency issue and routine requirements for all MDAP countries.

Department of State gave final approval on 3 February 1951 for a depot somewhere in France that would serve Europe and the Near East. A USAF General could select the final location. General Hicks was specifically ordered to "exercise the greatest care so that State Department operations would not be prejudiced by premature exposure of American plans with regards to France." This was his guideline for location selection! The USAF had decided that it would pay for what it wanted immediately, which did not please the State Department. It still hoped to persuade France to pay for most of the depot's construction costs. About 17 February, the French Air Force offered the Chateauroux location as a depot installation and quick agreement was reached, with the USAF requesting two facilities for immediate use: the Chateauroux-Deols Airport and the La Martinerie Airdrome.

The French government had been very slow in reaching a decision; it always feared the communists would actively oppose the large American presence required by an extensive depot anywhere in France. Radio Moscow already had broadcast the news about the Chateauroux location, and that General Hicks would command the new depot. In addition, Moscow stated that all current French employees would lose their jobs when the Americans took over the facilities! The final agreement was signed on 27 February 1951 to permit the USAF to construct the Chateauroux Air Depot. General Hicks now became the driving force to get CHAD operational as quickly as possible for USAFE. It would be the only air depot established in France, and eventually replace both Erding Air Depot in West Germany and the Burtonwood Air Depot in the UK.

The Chateauroux location in central France was

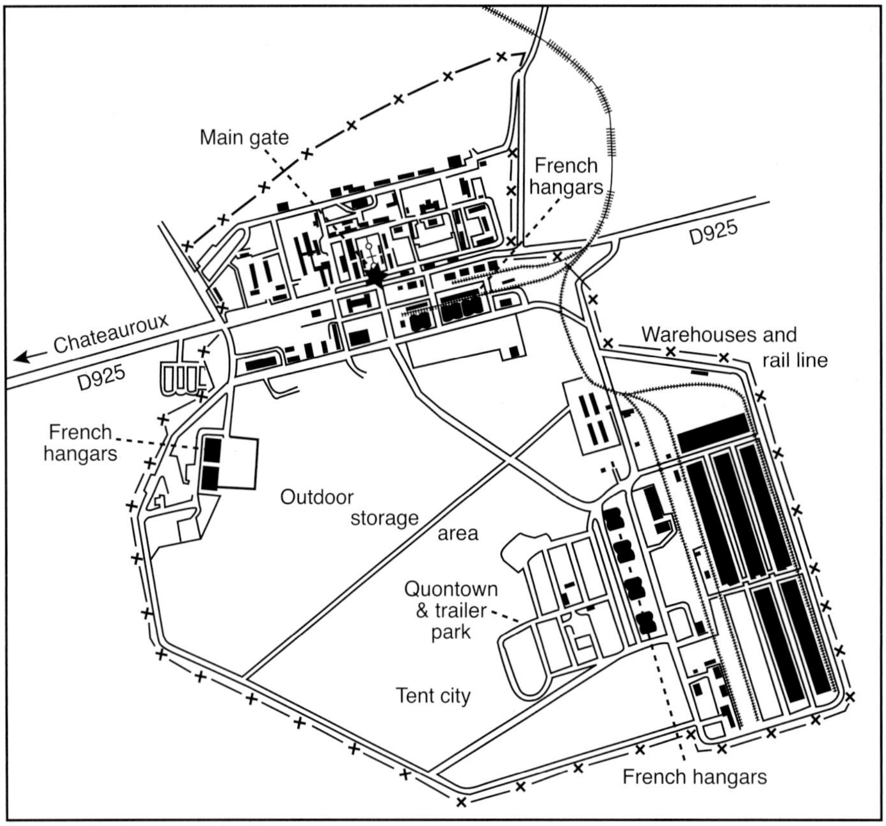

Map 8.2 La Martinerie in 1957

well south of the planned NATO air defense fighter barrier. It had a limited but trained civilian work force for hire, open land for expansion, and good year-round flying weather. This location had quick access to six national highways; the nearby deep water seaports of Bordeaux, La Rochelle, Rochefort, Royan and St Nazaire; and very good railroad service in four directions—all prime criteria for a large air depot. The location also had many deficiencies that would have been encountered anywhere else in France, or on the continent, at that time. The urgency to establish this air depot was so great that these limited facilities would be expanded as an interim air base and then later developed into a permanent air depot. Chateauroux AD, therefore, would be a two step base, first a bare base with a tent camp and leased buildings, followed in about four years with permanent buildings, warehouses and shops, and an improved airfield. The aircraft repair depot could be enlarged around the aircraft manufacturing plant that was available for lease. An 8,400-foot concrete runway 040°/220° was built in 1952, and extended to 12,000 feet in 1957. It took much money, manpower, and time to eventually solve most deficiencies.

Quick studies determined that La Martinerie was worth $10 million. The French government would lease it to the USAF for $1 per year; but the cost of relocating its occupants would be $4,285,714. La Martinerie consisted of fourteen small aircraft hangars, ten warehouses, a hospital structure, eight three story barracks, and many other small structures. Unfortunately La Martinerie was divided in half by a highway. This road provided access to the Deols aircraft maintenance factory located five miles away, and into Chateauroux's city center.

Since the Deols aircraft factory was privately owned, it would rent for $100,000 per year after an initial cost of $600,000 to displace its occupants. When operating and repair costs were estimated, the depot facility would spend $6,997,334 for fiscal year 1951. When the USAF team visited the proposed depot buildings at Deols and La Martinerie they were shocked at the amount of construction and repairs that would be required to set up the air depot. Much WWII bomb damage still remained, and the structures' interiors had deteriorated badly, needing extensive repairs. Many additional real estate parcels were leased around the region for indoor and outdoor storage, offices, and maintenance shops. This was accomplished as rapidly as possible to avoid new construction. These proper-

Aerial view of La Martinerie. Open area in center is old airfield where supplies were stored until warehouses were built.
"History Central Air Materiel Area, Europe" via William Adamek

Old control tower, La Martinerie airfield 1951.
"History Central Air Materiel Area, Europe" via William Adamek

ties are listed in Table 8.1 with their dates of removal from USAF records.

The USAF team told the French representatives in February that a half-strength air depot wing could arrive from CONUS as soon as 1 April 1951 to begin operations. The 73d Air Depot Wing was activated on 9 January 1951 at Kelly AFB, Texas, Air Material Command, and assigned the impossible mission of rapidly establishing a major air depot in France. Approximately 1,500 standby and ready Air Force Reservists were mobilized and assigned to four 73d Depot groups and ten squadrons, and moved to France as rapidly as possible. This was a small portion of the 146,000 Air Force Reservists called to active duty for the Korean War.

Individual officers and airmen began arriving at Chateauroux after 10 January 1951. The post office, APO #10, was established by one airman on 28 March. The first large shipment of depot personnel arrived on 14 April, consisting of twelve officers, eighteen airmen, two wives, and one child. Two more increments followed on 13 and 21 July until, by 1 August approximately 165 officers and 1,480 airmen were based at La Martinerie. A C-47 was the first aircraft assigned to the depot on 10 May. The 73d Air Depot Wing was transferred from HQ AMC to HQ USAFE on 21 July 1951. The final large group of 59 officers and 693 airmen arrived 23 August. This included personnel of the 7300th Material Control Group.

The 7300th Material Control Group (MDAP) was organized at Wright-Patterson on 17 January 1951. Its mission was to support all the aircraft and equipment going to foreign nations receiving our military aid.

The numbers of depot civilian personnel were also increasing rapidly. By 1 October 1951 a total of 123 Department of Air Force civilians and 979 French civilians were working at Chateauroux. On 1 January 1953, Chateauroux Air Depot personnel numbered 8,304: 462 officers, 5,472 airmen, 346 DAF civilians, and 2,024 French civilians.

Almost every airman and officer who served in France during the 1950s heard stories about Chateauroux and the horrible living conditions encountered by its troops—and were pleased that they were based elsewhere in France. Not only were living conditions bad, but the working conditions and depot facilities were near impossible. The depot was an absolute USAF command-wide failure that produced chaos, and required over four years before it became a smoothly functioning air depot. Of course the 73d AD, the real workers, received all the blame for the initial failures. How anything was accomplished during the first two years, 1951-53, is a testimony to the officers' and airmen's determination to accomplish the job in spite of the USAF's gross mismanagement. Surprisingly there are no records of airmen desertions, riots, or suicides during this period at Chateauroux! The whole depot started badly and degenerated from there. Here is a brief overview of the initial operation.

The first problem was that there was no high ground for camping out at La Martinerie, the entire site was flat, without drainage, and the soil did not readily absorb water. Two-hundred-eighty GP medium tents—without floors—were arranged in a lower portion of the airfield, which became a vast sea of mud in fall, winter, and spring 1951-52. Later in 1952, wood floors and frames were constructed along with a hot water and sewer system. Officers were initially housed in the Sainte Catherine Hotel and later moved to the Renovex Warehouse in the city. There were insuffi-

Table 8.1 Chateauroux Air Depot Property Listing and Disposal Dates

Property	Number	Date Returned
Chateauroux-Deols Airfield and La Martinerie Airdrome	**Annex #2703**	**March 1967**
Chateauroux/Bourse de Commerce Administration	Annex #3783	November 1960
Renovex Storage Station and Quarters	**Annex #3771**	**August 1955**
Mellottee Storage Station	Annex #3780	June 1957
Bitray Service Station	**Annex #3781**	**November 1966**
Rue Blanqui Depot	Annex #3787	April 1957
Chateauroux/AF Exchange Warehouse	**Annex #3782**	**November 1960**
Chateauroux/AF Exchange Auto Parts Storage Warehouse	Annex #3785	November 1960
Chateauroux/Chateau Beauregard Housing	**Annex #3784**	**November 1960**
Chateauroux / Ste. Catherine Hotel Housing	Annex #2764	October 1955
St. Maur/Chateau les Planches Housing	**Annex #3768**	**June 1960**
Neuillay/Chateau les Bois Robert Housing	Annex #3785	March 1960
Arthon/Chateau les Crubliers Housing	**Annex #3788**	**April 1957**
Chateauneuf Sur Cher Housing	Annex #3886	December 1956
Chateauroux Brassioux Family Housing	**Annex #6696**	**March 1967**
Touvent Apartment Housing and Dependent School	Annex #5306	September 1966
Villefranche-sur-Allier Storage Station	**Annex #3779**	**June 1957**
Community Toulon sur Allier Storage Station	Annex #3797	October 1961
Moulins Air Station	**Annex #2687**	**October 1958**
Bordeaux Bacalan Storage Depot	Annex #2690	June 1961
SNCASO Factory, Bordeaux	**Annex #2703**	**June 1961**
Chize Ammunition Storage Area	Annex #2688	July 1961
St. Mihiel Ammunition Storage Area	**Annex #2689**	**March 1967**
St. Mihiel Administration Area	Annex #8446	March 1967

cient buildings and covered storage for personnel, vehicles, supplies, and depot workshops. Chateauroux requested construction help from USAFE. HQ USAFE replied that, "Only German nationals from Air Installations are available, and we consider it inadvisable to use these people in Chateauroux." Aircraft maintenance was far, far down the depot's work priority at this time.

There was always a shortage of vehicles to lift, transport, and off-load all types of supplies that had to be moved from the railroad siding in Chateauroux's main train yard to La Martinerie, five miles away. Once the shipments reached La Martinerie, many off-road Army M-series trucks were needed to plow through the mire in the outdoor storage area, but they were not available.

USAFE ordered the newly arrived 73rd Air Depot Wing to send small detachments to each new air base in France to guard, inventory, and store U.S. property when it was delivered from the depots. Large quantities of aircraft support equipment and parts were shipped directly from CONUS as the air bases were started. Flight "A" 73rd Warehouse Squadron was one of the first detachments sent to Chambley AB to set up base supply. These men were usually fed and quartered in local hotels.

On 26 April 1951, prior to arrival of any depot trucks and opening of the Depot Transportation Office; rail car shipments of large bulky items began to appear in the Chateauroux city rail yard; to this day no one knows where these first shipments originated. Throughout West Germany and in northern France there still existed vast stocks of material from WWII that were in the way. Once the rumor started that a depot was to be established at Chateauroux, off went this stuff, and good riddance! There was such concern that, in the event of war, the Russians would capture this "vital material" and use it against us, therefore, it was rushed off to CHAD. The Transportation Office was unable to keep records of all this material since

Outside storage on the old airfield, La Martinerie. Aircraft engines in the foreground boxes, April 1954.
National Archives

Quartermaster equipment - tents and stoves - in outdoor storage, La Martinerie, April 1954.
National Archives

Forklift stuck in the mud, La Martinerie 1951.
"History Central Air Materiel Area, Europe" via William Adamek

Aircraft parts and engines stored outside under tarps, La Martinerie, 24 April 1954.
National Archives

it arrived so rapidly, and most identification data had disappeared while setting outside for years. The only thing everyone could really identify was many tons of pierced steel planking as it arrived out of nowhere! The city rail yard could only hold forty-five SNCF freight cars at a time (about 225 tons), and had to be emptied immediately because other trains were waiting with more "valuable stuff." The supplies were hauled by truck to La Martinerie and stacked outdoors as rapidly as possible with no identification, inventory, or location data. A rail spur track into La Martinerie was started in July, and in usual fashion it required ten months rather than three months to complete the two miles of track so freight cars could be unloaded on the depot. A similar spur track was added later in the opposite direction to bring railcars into the southeast edge of the Deols airfield. Smaller crates and packages that were recognized as fragile or higher value items were placed inside the ten, small, old hangars on La Martinerie. These hangar floors broke up as forklifts brought in the pallet loads for storage. Concrete floor repair then became an urgent project. There was a critical need for pallets, and depot employees began building pallets for both indoor and outdoor storage. Thousands of pallets were also fabricated at Erding Air Depot and shipped to La Martinerie. The 73d AD Wing sent a message to HQ AMC asking them to inform all depots to stop large shipments into Chateauroux until after 15 August since the railroad facilities were saturated, but the shipments of supplies increased. A rough estimate was that about 175 to 200 tons of supplies were arriving every day! The concept of storing like items together or grouping by stock classes broke down, and all material was now being stored outdoors in neat columns all over the airfield grounds. La Martinerie's airfield was filled by 1 October 1952; flight operations ceased in December and moved to Deols airfield. The 1951 summer brought

Construction at La Martinerie, February 1954. Rain still left ponds of muddy water throughout the base.
National Archives

Outdoor storage on old airfield, 1920 French hangars in foreground used for storage, La Martinerie, April 1954.
National Archives

Old French hangars and railroad siding on left, high value items in foreground crates, La Martinerie, April 1954.
National Archives

New warehouses completed! Material being transferred to indoor storage, La Martinerie, October 1954.
"History Central Air Materiel Area, Europe" via William Adamek

Newly completed warehouse complex with railroad siding adjacent to buildings, October 1954.
National Archives

Interior view of new warehouse, October 1954. Recessed center portion of isle is for "towveyer" system of moving items in and out of storage.
National Archives

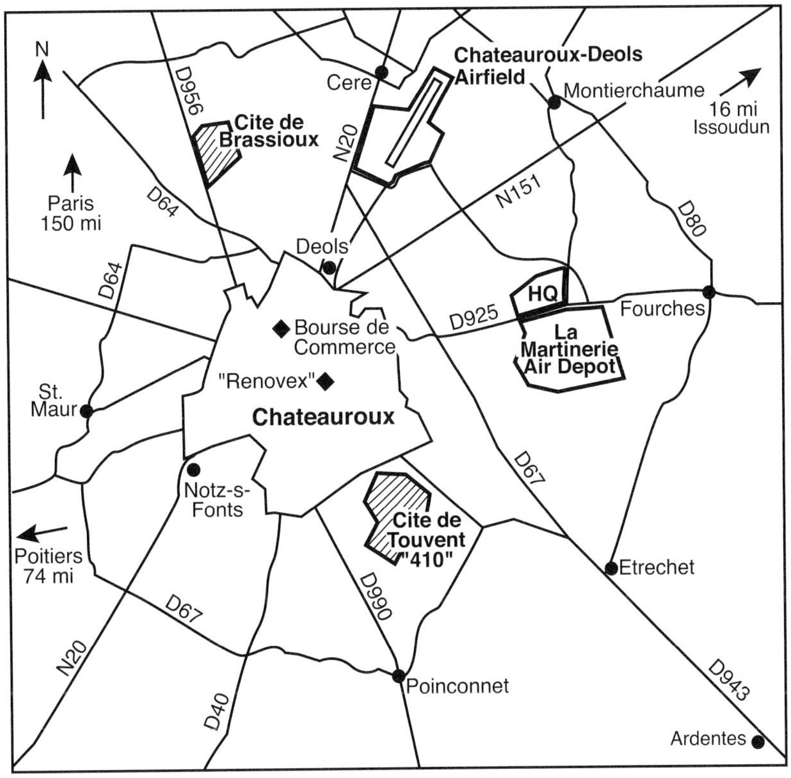

Map 8.3 Chateauroux Air Depot and Surrounding Area

little relief. It set records for low temperatures and rainfall, which was the final straw in the effort to stop the chaos unfolding at La Martinerie. Then the real winter rainy season hit in December through March, turning the outdoor storage fields into impassible quagmires. Tents and tarps were used to protect items such as aircraft engines, electrical equipment, and office equipment. Many man-hours were expended attempting to hand dig trenches on the airfield to drain the ponds of standing water. Trucks and forklifts could not work in the mud between supply stacks. This situation persisted for three years. Most material had to be left outdoors until 1.2 million square feet of new warehousing was completed during late 1954.

The 866th Engineer Aviation Battalion arrived at Chateauroux on 21 July 1952 with 27 officers and 760 soldiers to provide much needed construction skills to improve conditions at La Martinerie as described in the Engineer Aviation Battalion section of chapter 18.

By summer 1955, after a huge effort, all the supplies that had been outdoors, had been retrieved, opened, cleaned, inspected, repacked, and stored in very organized fashion in new warehouses. Some items had been destroyed or had corroded to scrap during this outdoor storage fiasco.

The 44th Statistical Services Squadron set up its IBM punch-card accounting equipment in 1952. It began operation after a delay caused by electrical power incompatabilities. By 1954 CHAD functioned using the punch-card inventory control system. In January 1955, after all warehouses were built, a material conveyor "Towveyer" system was installed throughout the complex to save time and labor. The electrical motor-driven endless chain system moved up to 200 four-wheel material carts through the sixty-eight storage sheds into the packing-shipping-receiving buildings. This system cost $247,389 and was the first in Europe.

La Martinerie handled all classes of USAF supplies. Six sub-depots were set up and commanded by the Chateauroux Air Depot during 1951-52. These Sub-Depots at Bordeaux-Bacalan, Niort-Chize, Metz-Frescaty, St. Mihiel, and St. Nazaire specialized in specific supply categories. Their locations and functions are covered at the end of this chapter.

On 2 August 1955, Chateauroux AD established daily bus service to both Chize and Bacalan/Bordeaux AB Sub-Depots to move personnel between these busy activities. Chateauroux had finally achieved an operational capability to support all its customers, and became a comfortable base that was comparable to a CONUS air depot. The CAMAE Air Depot was very busy throughout its remaining years receiving, procuring, and issuing supplies and parts, contracting logistical services, and maintaining all USAF aircraft and systems.

While this story was unfolding at La Martinerie, five miles away at Deols airfield all facilities were being repaired, improved, and expanded to accommodate aircraft depot maintenance. All construction work was performed by French contractors; there were some self-help projects for the aircraft shops and management offices performed by the troops. The Dassault aircraft factory was in superior condition compared to La Martinerie's buildings. Much of the bomb damage had been repaired by 1951, though some still existed. Therefore, new construction proceeded along with damage repairs. An 8,400-foot long concrete runway, 220 feet wide, with a full-length parallel taxiway was completed by 14 December 1952. This runway was extended to 12,000 feet during 1957. Aircraft operated by the depot grew from three C-47s in 1952 to a fleet of thirty aircraft by 1956; these were ten C-47s, two C-54s, six C-118s, six L-20As, and six T-33As. These aircraft were needed for liaison, transport, and inspection flights by CHAD managers. The C-118s were used as USAFE emergency airborne command and control posts called "SILK PURSE." The L-20As and T-33As were used to maintain flying proficiency by rated officers assigned to the depot in non-flying jobs.

The large structural steel 480-foot wide by 160-foot deep airfreight terminal was repaired. A 250,000 square-foot aircraft apron was added adjacent to the southern airport administration building. This airfreight facility became the major MATS European terminal with air delivery service from Dover AFB, Delaware. The 4th Aerial Port Squadron (MATS) operated this terminal around the clock to move air cargo throughout Europe and the Middle East. MATS airlift aircraft seen at Chateauroux were: C-97s, C-118s, C-121s, C-124s, C-130s, C-133s, and C-135s. USAFE cargo aircraft seen moving freight in and out of Deols were; C-47s, C-54s, C-119s, C-123s, C-130s, and C-131s. These served Europe, Africa, and the Middle East.

C-54G #45-481 on the field at Chateauroux-Deols AD 1959.
Ted Bailey

C-133A #56-2005-20-DL, Chateauroux-Deols AD 1959.
Ted Bailey

Two squadrons of C-124s flew from Dover AFB, Delaware to Chateauroux-Deols in July 1960 to participate in Operation Safari / New Tape, the humanitarian airlift to the Congo.
Ted Bailey

Chateauroux control tower atop the Dassault factory administration building, 1952.
"History Central Air Materiel Area, Europe" via William Adamek

Main entrance to the Chateauroux-Deols Air Depot, 1959. Structures are part of the old 1935 Marcel Bloch (Dassault) art deco factory buildings.
Ted Bailey

C-124C #52-1054
on the ramp at Chateauroux-Deols AD, 1960
Ted Bailey

Airfreight terminal building, Chateauroux-Deols AD. This facility became the major MATS airfreight terminal in Europe.
"History Central Air Materiel Area, Europe" via William Adamek

Airfreight terminal, Chateauroux-Deols AD.
National Archives

C-119 being loaded with cargo, Chateauroux-Deols AD airfreight terminal, October 1954.
National Archives

Table 8.2 Chateauroux Air Depot Organizations	
73rd Air Depot Wing	HQ Sq, CAMAE
73rd Supply Group	Directorate of Procurement and Production
7373d Supply Service Gp	Directorate of Personnel
7373d Supply Services Sq	Directorate of Transportation
7373d Medical Material Sq	Directorate of Supply and Services
7333d Material Sq	Directorate of Maintenance Engineering
7373d Aircraft Maintenance Sq	Directorate of Base Services and Production
73d Aircraft Repair Sq, Depot	HQ Sq, 3130th Air Base Wing
73d Aircraft Equipment Repair Sq	HQ Sq, 3136th Air Depot Gp
7373d Air Depot Group	HQ Sq, 3134th Supply Gp
Det #5, 7333d Air Base Gp	3134th Stock Sq
7322d Communications Sq	3134th Warehouse Sq
7322d Air Police Sq	3130th Air Base Wing, Communications Gp
44th Statistical Services Sq	3130th Air Police Sq
7322d CAM Sq	3130th Food Service Sq
7373d USAF Hospital	3130th Installations Sq
7300th Material Control Gp	
7029th Base Complement Sq	HQ Sq, 3131st Maintenance Gp
73d Warehouse Sq	3131st Aircraft Repair Sq
73d Transport Sq, Depot	3131st Aircraft Equipment Repair Sq
73d Stock Control Sq, Depot	3133d Transportation Gp
73d Clothing & Textile Cleaning & Repair Sq	3136th Motor Vehical Repair Sq

In 1955 another two-story steel hangar was built adjacent to the high bay aircraft assembly building, providing another 150,000 square feet of floor space for aircraft repair. Large employee parking lots and a dining facility were constructed on the west side of highway N20 near the aircraft factory. An underpass was installed to allow workers to walk safely under N20 from the parking lots to their workshops. An airmen's dining hall was completed at Deols in 1954.

During the runway extension program in 1956 a new air terminal area was developed about a half mile north off route N20, south of Cere. This area included twelve buildings and a 1,280,000 square-foot aircraft parking apron. This apron area could accommodate up to twenty-four C-133A-size cargo transports. Included was a new seven story control tower, base operations building, air passenger terminal, fire station, transient billeting, mess hall, warehouses, and large lots for long term auto parking. All flight operations were moved from the factory administration area into this new complex. At the same time, the southeast side of the airfield was expanded with a 3,000-foot long curved taxiway having ten large rectangular aircraft parking hardstands, plus two large metal hangars for hazardous cargo storage and handling. This area was used as a specialized repair activity for the depot. Electrical service at Deols and La Martinerie was increased to 2,500 KW during 1956. In 1957 the badly needed interconnecting road between La Martinerie and Deols was completed, reducing the drive by three miles and avoiding Chateauroux and Deols city traffic. This road was expanded and is now part of the route N20 bypass around the east side of Chateauroux. Additional construction at La Martinerie was required in 1957 to provide facilities for receiving the parts, supplies, and vehicles from the Moulins, Villefranche, and Bacalan sub-depots that were closed in 1958. Vehicle repair shops were expanded to accommodate the increased workload resulting from phase-out of Moulins vehicle shops. By 1957 Chateauroux had become the largest and best equipped overseas USAF air depot. The French were becoming very concerned that we would pave most of their Indre Department!

From the very first days, French nationals were employed to assist the depot operations. An employment office was leased in downtown Chateauroux in the Bourse de Commerce building. Citizens of the Indre Department welcomed the opportunity for employment. By December 1954 there were 3,450 French employees at the depot as approved by "Operation Native Son." Depot employment reached a maximum of 3,950 French civilians in July 1961. During the sixteen years of depot operation, military personnel decreased from about 3,200 down to 1,800, but mili-

Table 8.3 Tenant Units Located at Chateauroux-Deols Air Depot

Flt "K" 2d Air Postal Squadron	Det #3, 11th Communications Maintenance Squadron
Det #3, 12th Air Postal Squadron	1616th Support Squadron - MATS
Det #59, 18th Weather Squadron	7120th Airborne Command Control Squadron
1992d Air and Airways Communications Squadron	Det #14, 1602d Air Transport Wing - MATS
55th Air and Airways Communications Squadron	322d Air Division - MATS
610th Communications Construction Squadron	Det #1, 513th Consolidated Aircraft Maintenance Sq 1966
12th Communications Construction Squadron	Headquarters, 7th Radio Relay Squadron
Det #6, 7th Radio Relay Squadron	Headquarters, 2058th Comm Squadron, Radio Relay
583d USAF Band	1884th Electronics Engineering and Installations Sq
Det #6, 4th Aerial Port Squadron	European Area - GEEIA
4440th Aircraft Delivery Group	Upon closure of Merignac AB and the Bacalan and Moulins Sub-Depots, tenant units were relocated to the Chateauroux Air Depot

tary dependents increased dramatically from 250 in 1952 to about 3,900 in 1965. Civilian salaries averaged about 35 to 45 percent higher than local wages, which was resented by the local business owners. Common starting wages in 1955 were $1.00 to $1.70 per hour depending upon skills. CHAD provided its employees with transportation to and from work from all around the Indre; seventy bus routes were operated to serve all the workers needed at the depot. French employees were welcomed into the base community's activities, and a French newspaper was published for depot employees. Many former French workers have positive memories of their work at Chateauroux, their even treatment by American supervisors, good working conditions (after 1953), and their unusual job assignments and training. Training programs were conducted for the new employees on aircraft overhaul and repair procedures.

Of course this large air depot also had the greatest concentration of U.S. personnel in France, and this caused some friction between the French citizens and Americans. The American presence in the small city was overwhelming, especially the large U.S. family automobiles. Inflation of rents was a serious problem for both groups of people. Education in French language and customs was made available on base, and later became mandatory. Military personnel were expected to acquire a basic ability to be polite and survive in France. The language difference must have improved because 452 marriages occurred between U.S. citizens and French nationals over the sixteen years. Overall international relations fared very well at Chateauroux, there were no riots by the local citizens protesting the depot, no employee sabotage on base, and no killings of American military or civilians off base, except in auto accidents. Most importantly there were no USAF aircraft crashes into the populated areas around Chateauroux even though many aircraft had just completed major depot repairs and were being test flown from Deols airfield.

The Chateauroux Air Depot was established as USAFE's primary depot and was commanded by HQ USAFE in Wiesbaden, West Germany, until 31 December 1955. On 1 January 1956 all overseas depots were transferred to the Air Material Command, and Chateauroux AD then became the primary AMC depot for Europe and the Middle East region. Its new command title became Central Air Material Area, Europe, (CAMAE). CAMAE used its new major command insignia in its patch on 18 March 1956. This transfer between major air commands had very little effect on mission or manning. Command changed again on 1 July 1962 when Chateauroux was transferred back to USAFE from Air Logistics Command. The overseas theater commander again had direct command of his logistics depot. On 1 April 1956 all 70 and 7000 series designators were changed to 3000 series designators for all assigned units at Chateauroux, but tenant unit designators were not changed. Through all the command changes its mailing address remained APO 10. Table 8.2 lists organizations assigned to the Chateauroux Depot and Table 8.3 shows tenant units located at the depot.

Aircraft Maintenance Programs April 1951 to September 1967

In addition to the depot supply function for Europe, Chateauroux Air Depot assumed the job of equipment maintenance and disposal for Europe. Aircraft depot level maintenance became a huge task. USAFE estimated that it would have a maximum of 2,500 assigned USAF aircraft and would support an

Clockwise from upper left:

Chateauroux-Deols maintenance facility, October 1954.
"History Central Air Materiel Area, Europe" via William Adamekk

1616th Support Sq (MATS) repairing a MATS C-124C engine on ramp, Chateauroux-Deols 1959.
Ted Bailey

RB-57A undergoing depot overhaul, Chatearoux-Deols, 1955.
"History Central Air Materiel Area, Europe" via William Adamek

estimated 3,500 American built aircraft assigned to NATO nations and other MAP recipient countries. European nations began receiving U.S. aircraft through MAP in 1949 when only Erding Air Depot was available to provide maintenance support. The first depot maintenance work at Chateauroux was performed in small shops and hangar at La Martinerie prior to renovation of the Deols aircraft factory. By spring of 1952 all maintenance activity moved to the Deols factory. Chateauroux Air Depot was very busy throughout its sixteen years procuring supplies and parts, contracting services, and maintaining USAF equipment.

The first concept was to have all depot maintenance performed at Chateauroux-Deols shops using a combination of USAF personnel, American civilians, and French employees. Then HQ USAFE declared that there would not be Air Force "blue suiters" and DAF civilians assigned to the depot because of personnel manning limits, costs, and shortage of trained airmen for depot level maintenance. Next, USAFE decided it did not want to fly or ship short-ranged aircraft back to CONUS for depot overhaul and modifications; the time lost in transit would reduce combat aircraft strength.

It became apparent that a depot facility about six times the size of that planned for Deols airfield would be required for the USAFE aircraft fleet. By winter 1952 it was decided that the only reasonable solution was to contract the depot maintenance workload using Western Europe's commercial airlines and aircraft manufacturers' facilities with their skilled work force. Also maintenance costs would be less in NATO countries than at U.S. depots. Chateauroux AD would perform classified modifications, quick response work, major aircraft repairs, aircraft salvage and disposal. Contractors would operate some of the Deols depot shops. The majority of Chateauroux's aircraft maintenance workload would be contract administration, monitoring work quality, test flying, and supply support. Jet engine depot overhaul was not undertaken in Europe, engines were airlifted back to CONUS to the appropriate AMC engine depot for overhaul.

Table 8.4 Contract Maintenance Providers USAFE

Contract Facility	Work Performed
Airline Shops:	
SABENA Brussels, Belgium	F-84Gs, C-119C/F/Gs - IRANs & TCTOs
KLM, Schiphol Airport, Netherlands	C-47, F-84E/F/Gs, F-100 - IRANs & TCTOs
Air France, Le Bourget, France	C-131, C-118, C-47, F-84F,Gs - inspections
Air Italia, Naples, Italy	C-119F/Gs, C-47, H-19s, F-84F/G,s - overhauls
SAS, Copenhagen, Denmark	B-57B/Cs, C-47, F-84Gs, F-100Ds - repairs & IRANs
TAI-Transports Aerians Intercontinentaux, Paris Orly, France	C-47s, C-54s, C-121s - inspections
Aircraft Manufacturers:	
AMECO - Breguet, Villacoublay, France	T-33As, F-84Gs, TF/F-102As
Avio-Diepan, Hague, Netherlands	C-47s, F-84F/Gs
CASA, Sevilla, Spain	F-86Fs, TF/F-102s - IRANs & TCTOs
CASA, Getafe, Spain	H-19Bs, SA-16As, T-33As, TF/F-102s, F-86Fs, F-100D/Fs
CAFMS Torrejon, Spain	F-86F - overhaul
Dornier Aircraft, Friedrickshaven, Germany	F-84F, F-86Ks & Mk-4 Sabres - overhaul & storage
Fairey Aircraft, Manchester, England	B-26B/C, RB-26B/Cs - overhaul & storage
Siai-Marchetti, Sestocalande, Italy	RF-84Fs, L-20Bs, C-47s - depot IRAN
FIAT, Turin, Italy	F-84Fs, F-84Gs, F-86E/Fs, F-86Ks, F-102As - MOD & IRANs
S.A.C.A., Brindisi, Italy	F-84Fs, F-86K - overhaul
SUD Aircraft, Montoir, St. Nazaire, France	F-86Ds, TF/F-102s, T-6Gs - arrival processing
Short Bros., Harland Airfield, Belfast, Ireland	F-86Ks, F-84Gs
SNCNF Aircraft, Marseilles, France	T-33As, SA-16As, C-119s
SNCASO Aircraft, Toulouse, France	T-33As, F-84E,F,Gs, F-100Ds, C-47s - IRAN & TCTOs
Verigate, Italy	F-84G, RF-84F, L-20As - depot overhauls

The major contractor to operate in the Deols aircraft factory was SERIMA-Deols "Society of Works and Industrial Repair, Aeronautical," a combination of Sud-Aviation and International Aircraft Services. SERIMA did depot production line work on F-84s, F-86s, F-100s, and F-102s in the 1950s and 1960s, and employed about 900 French aircraft mechanics. SERIMA also assisted in the aircraft component shops in addition to "Native Son" employees. Depot level aircraft instrument repairs and calibration were performed at the Deols factory by Air Precision of Chaville, France. American contractors also provided depot support on particular airframes and special components. During 1958-59, Land Air Corp. was awarded a contract by AMC MOAMA to perform depot level repairs and modifications on USAFE B-66Bs and RB-66B/Cs based in the UK and France. Land Air was a U.S. company that specialized in providing modifications and repairs worldwide on USAF aircraft. Land Air worked in the Deols high bay factory with a team of 150 employees; the team was housed and fed on La Martinerie. The B-66 fleet needed several modifications and special rework to extend its operational capabilities for six more years.

Contract maintenance to provide services on USAFE and NATO aircraft created a large workload for CAMAE personnel. The contractors obtained the vast majority of replacement parts and material needed for depot level overhauls from La Martinerie. Contract preparation and negotiations were difficult because every document had to be in two languages, English and the language of the country involved. With work coming from ten Western European nations, this required translation experts. All contracts clearly defined scope of work, even to "inspect and repair as necessary" (IRAN) depot services, to accurately control costs. It is estimated that Chateauroux Air Depot expended US $225,000,000 annually on depot level aircraft maintenance. Companies performing work for CHAD would have USAF plant representatives on-site to monitor work performance and coordinate the logistical support needed from Chateauroux AD. Contractors also supplied field modification teams that worked at the NATO air bases keeping combat aircraft in commission at their home base. Table 8.4 lists some of the contractors I uncovered during conversations at the Chateauroux Depot Reunion in September 1998.

USAF personnel continued to work in the electrical accessory shop, aircraft instrument shop, aircraft radio-radar shops, and electronic test equipment laboratory. During 1955 the combat wings began sending two to four airmen from field maintenance squadrons to Chateauroux for four-week electronic test equipment calibration and repair schools, to comply with the new USAF worldwide Precision Measurement Equipment Laboratory (PMEL) program. Every USAFE wing would then establish test equipment calibration programs at their base.

USAFE/MDAP Aircraft Procurement Programs February 1953 - September 1956

One of Chateauroux Air Depot's unusual tasks was the support of new aircraft procurement. Two fighters peculiar to NATO and not flown by the USAF were purchased with MDAP funds: 341 North American Aviation F-86Ks and 225 Dassault Mystere IV As. These aircraft programs were intended to develop NATO's aircraft engineering, manufacturing, and repair capacity. The MAP/MDAP program was paid for completely by the American taxpayer. Table 8.5 lists MAP/MDAP Aircraft in Europe.

The F-86K was designed by North American Aviation after the F-86D had started production and proved to be a useful all-weather interceptor. NATO's all-weather air defense was considered very deficient as late as 1954. The F-86K would become a simplified interceptor by eliminating some of the Hughes E-4 Radar Fire Control System and replacing it with a North American Autonetics MG-4 FCS. The newer K model Sabre would have four 20mm M-24 cannons with 132 cannon rounds per gun, and carry two AIM-9B Sidewinder infrared seeking missiles. This would provide a higher probability-of-kill compared to the two dozen 2.5-inch diameter folding fin aircraft rockets (FFAR). The first batch of 120 F-86Ks were built by North American, Inglewood, California. These 120 Sabres were supplied to four Norwegian and three Dutch all-weather fighter squadrons.

A licensing agreement was completed on 18 May 1953 between North American and Fiat Aircraft, Turin, Italy, to build the NATO F-86Ks. Production commenced on 221 F-86Ks destined for three French, six Italian, and five West German fighter squadrons. An important consideration in awarding this NATO production contract was to maintain high employment at Fiat Turin to prevent hostile Communist agitation against the Italian Government. NATO was now evolving into more of a political and economic force than a military defense power! This F-86K program was another MDAP procurement fully funded by the American taxpayer.

Chateauroux supported this offshore procurement and managed the U.S. government furnished equipment (GFE) that the F-86K program required. USAF test pilots flew the finished Fiat Ks and accepted the aircraft for the U.S., then they were transferred as an MDAP sale to a NATO nation. The F-86K program was completed by December 1955; these Sabre interceptors were flown by NATO air forces until 1977. The F-86K interceptors like the D and L models were labor-intensive weapon systems, and many NATO

Table 8.5 MAP/MDAP Aircraft in Europe

Model	Quantity	Cost per Aircraft $US	Total Costs $US
F-84E	100 ea.	$212,000	$21,200,000.
F-84G	2,236 ea.	$237,000	$529,932,000.
F-84F	852 ea.	$769,000	$655,188,000.
RF-84F	327 ea.	$668,000	$218,436,000.
F-86E	60 ea.	$219,000	$13,140,000.
F-86F	280 ea.	$211,000	$ 59,080,000.
F-86K	341 ea.	$441,000	$150,381,000.
F-100D	203 ea.	$697,000	$141,491,000.
F-100F	45 ea.	$804,000	$36,180,000.
T-33A	120 ea.	$127,000	$15,240,000.
Mystere IV-A	225 ea.	$230,000	$ 51,750,000.
		Total	$1,892,019,000.

North American F-86K Sabre at Chateauroux-Deols AD 1958.
"History Central Air Materiel Area, Europe" via William Adamek

MDAP Dassault Mystere IV-A at Chambley AB 1957.
Al Christensen

countries could not afford the personnel to operate all-weather fighters. Chateauroux depot's final role in the F-86K program was storing low flight time airplanes, or salvaging engines, guns, instruments/avionics, and then destroying the airframes during 1963-66.

The next aircraft purchased with MDAP off-shore procurement funds and assigned to NATO air forces was a French designed and produced sub-sonic single engine day interceptor and close air support fighter-bomber, the Mystere IV-A. It was assembled at the Bordeaux-Merignac Dassault factory. Chateauroux Air Depot assisted the program, but no GFE was required. The Pleven-Dunn Agreement between the U.S. and French Government on 23 April 1953 provided for the production of 225 Dassault Mystere IV-As for the French Air Force under USAF AMC Contract AF61-514-366. At this time F-86F and D Sabre production was just meeting USAF Korean War requirements, and Sabres could not be spared for NATO. Mystere IV-A fighters were flown only by French fighter squadrons based in France and assigned to the 4th Allied Tactical Air Force.

The Mystere IV-A, was a new design by Dassault Aviation that was somewhat similar to the NAA F-86H, but had two 30mm aircraft cannons with 150 rounds per gun. A small radar set with its microwave antenna mounted in the vertical air splitter supplied range and range rate to the optical gunsight. A variety of bombs and rockets could be carried for the ground attack mission. The first IV-A flew on 28 September 1952 at Melun-Villaroche Airfield. The first production aircraft was delivered on 18 June 1954 at the Bordeaux-Merignac factory, and production was completed in 1956. Two different centrifugal-flow turbojet engines were used during the production run; the first 111 IV-As used the Rolls Royce "Tay" engine, the last 114 IV-As had Hispano-Suiza "Verdon" engine built under license. Both engines had about 7,000 pounds static thrust.

Mystere IV-A fighters were easily identified by three black construction numbers on the fuselage side above the wing root or near the tip of the vertical stabilizer. When the French Air Force phased the IV-A aircraft out of its fighter squadrons, all remaining Mysteres were delivered to RAF Sculthorpe, England, where they were demilitarized in accordance with the agreement. Mystere IV-As can be seen today in several museums in France, England, and Belgium. These fighters cost about $230,000 each. Again, this program was fully paid for by the American taxpayer.

Family Housing and Schools

Family housing for the Chateauroux Air Depot was primarily located off base at Cite Brassioux and Cite Touvent, where over 900 units were built to house the large number of married officers, non commissioned officers, and Department of Air Force civilians required to operate the air depot. Additional housing was located on base in a trailer camp constructed on the south edge of La Martinerie and Quonset huts in nearby "Quontown." About seventy-five trailer spaces were constructed after removal of the tents. Quontown consisted of about forty quonset huts that were available after the 472d Engineer Aviation Battalion departed the depot. These quonset huts were divided into duplex apartments around 1958. There was a serious housing shortage in this region of France prior to arrival of the depot complex in 1951. Some families and employees did live on the French economy and drove long distances to homes that varied from substandard to elegant country chateaus. Of course all single and unaccompanied USAF personnel were quartered on base at La Martinerie.

Cite Touvent was the large dependent housing

complex consisting of fifteen apartment buildings, one large four story building about two city blocks long, and fourteen three story apartment buildings providing a total of 410 family units. Cite Touvent or City "410" was built two miles south of Chateauroux's center near highways N20 and D40. It was a seven-mile drive to La Martinerie. Off-street parking was provided for every unit. Apartments had up to three

High school buildings at La Martinerie, April 1954.
National Archives

Student dormitory at La Martinerie, April 1954.
National Archives

Cite Touvent or "410" apartments just completed, 1954.
"History Central Air Materiel Area, Europe" via William Adamek

Quantown at La Martinerie 1954.
"History Central Air Materiel Area, Europe" via William Adamek

Quontown, Chateauroux AD, 1958.
Still being used as shops, ended up as family housing.
Ed Duquette

Quontown HQ Det #3 11th COMMAINTRON 1958.
Built in 1954 by the 866th EABn.
Ed Duquette

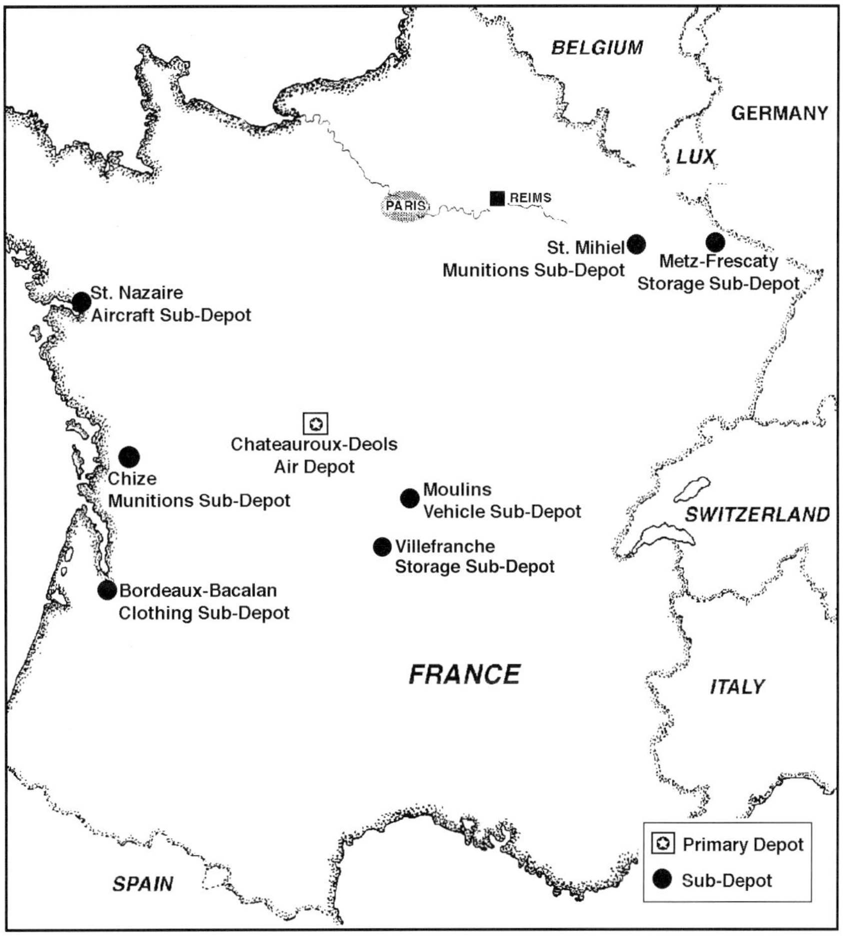

Map 8.4 U.S. Air Force Depots and Sub-Depots in France

bedrooms. A single story community center and large playgrounds were nearby as well as the base grammar school. Cite Touvent's population varied from 900 to 1,350 between 1954 and 1967. This apartment complex was unique to Chateauroux AD, nothing similar was constructed in France for the USAFE. It was funded by the Guaranteed Rental Income concept. City "410" required about twenty months to build (a record time) and was completed by October 1954. Both these apartments and the Brassioux homes were constructed with high quality materials and workmanship; all structures are still occupied today by French families.

Cite Brassioux was built on farmland three miles northwest of Deols, directly east off highway N156 (now D956) and a short drive to the Deols airfield. This large U.S. village complex of 507 single, duplex, and triplex units was funded by the Commodity Credit Housing program. The prime developer was the Marc Rainaut Company. It won the 1957 contract to build this largest housing complex in France. All homes were single story, American style design, with installed appliances and varying numbers of bedrooms. Most homes had off-street parking. A large community center, a small BX shopette, and seven large playgrounds were included at this site. Cite Brassioux required two years to build and was completed by August 1959. Brassioux's population varied from 1,300 to 2,150 over the years 1960-67. Air Force families enjoyed this location and have fond memories of their years at Cite Brassioux.

Chateauroux Air Depot was authorized two large schools because of the size of its base population and remote location from the main air bases in northern France. The DOD grammar school located adjacent to City 410 taught grades one through eight; and had twenty-four classrooms. Typically, a staff of forty-four teachers and administrators were employed to educate the approximately 600 grammar school pupils. Usually eight school buses were needed to transport elementary school students to and from their homes, and especially to Cite Brassioux. The first high school began on 15 September 1952 with twenty-two students at Chateau les Crubliers located in the city. A large Chateauroux DOD high school was built on La Martinerie Depot, including a dormitory for boarding students in grades nine through twelve. Chateauroux high school received students from Bordeaux, Chize, Moulins, and La Pallice. The high school was smaller than the grammar school with about 250 students and a staff of thirty teachers. Both schools employed male and female U.S. teachers who lived either on base or on the economy. Bus service was provided for local high school students.

The Chateauroux depot functioned from March 1951 until March 1967 when FRELOC closed all U.S. military bases in France. Today the Chateauroux airport is a commercial air terminal, business jet center, and jet transport aircraft overhaul facility. The author visited the old base site in 1992 and 1998. Some old USAF buildings still remain, and the Deols aircraft factory is in good condition. Entrance to the airport terminal complex is about a half mile north of the old 1935 factory entrance. Base operations and the control tower are now used for commercial flight operations. The airfield is frequently used for air transport aircrew flight training. Several old two-story office or barracks buildings are in use near the control tower, and a mess hall has become the airport restaurant. The large aircraft manufacturing buildings are still used for aircraft overhaul and painting. Much effort and money is being invested by the Indre Department and Chateauroux Chamber of Commerce to increase business on the airport. Chateauroux can be found on Michelin Map #322 Local, and IGN Series Blue #2125E. Chateauroux is accessable from Paris by train using Gare d'Austerlitz.

Chateauroux Sub-Depots

Chateauroux Air Depot commanded several subdepots. These Sub-Depots were located at Bordeaux-Bacalan, (special clothing & medical supplies); Niort-Chize (aircraft ammunition); Metz-Frescaty (vehicles & construction supplies) St. Mihiel (conventional ammunition storage); St. Nazaire (aircraft seaport); and Les Moulins (vehicle storage and maintenance) and the Villefranche (parts storage).

Bacalan Sub-Depot

Bacalan, a suburb of Bordeaux, is on the west side of the Gironde River, 344 miles (550 km) south-southwest of Paris on Autoroute A10, in the Gironde Department.

The Bordeaux-Bacalan Depot, Storage Annex #2690, was located very near the large WWII submarine pens, about four miles (7 km) north of the main train station in Bordeaux. The depot was 230 miles (373 km) southwest of Chateauroux. The closest airdrome was Bordeaux-Merignac. From June 1951 until December 1959 it was operated by the 73d Air Depot Wing, CAMAE, headquartered at Chateauroux.

Bordeaux Air Station (44° 52'N - 00° 33'W) was offered by France in March 1951. This facility included buildings constructed by the Ford Motor Company in 1934 and a SNCASO aircraft plant completed in 1936. The Ford plant consisted of four large factory structures with 118,360 square feet of space that were convenient to the harbor and immediately available for nine million francs rent (US $25,700) for five years. The buildings were well built, steel and concrete construction. This was another example of using rented facilities whenever possible in France to save time and money. An eighteen acre, 766,880 square-foot storage yard with a railroad siding was located adjacent to the buildings. The Bordelaise (SNCASO) aircraft plant was across the road from the Ford plant, providing 143,646 square feet of covered space and 568,160 square feet of open storage space. This space, annex #2703, was rented for nine years at a cost of 15 million francs (US $42,900). Some structures required repairs after WWII bombing. U.S. Army Engineers performed the repairs during the summer of 1951 to get the storage facility in operation quickly. It was needed for Bordeaux-Merignac Air Base as there was inadequate covered storage at Merignac airdrome to secure supplies delivered during interim air base construction. Bacalan was also used for equipment storage by the 126th Bomb Wing and the 7913th Air Base Group, as well as for storage of USAF supplies being shipped to the Bordeaux port. Bacalan sub-depot became operational on 4 April 1952, and both the American and French flags were raised at this facility.

In the summer of 1952, after departure of the 126th Wing from Bordeaux AB, the Bacalan storage facility had space for the needed AF Class 13 clothing depot. It was expanded from 73d Air Sub-Depot to the 7349th Air Depot Group in 1954 with the primary mission of supplying clothing items to all USAFE. This job was handled by the 7349th Supply Squadron. On 1 January 1956 the 7349th was redesignated the 3137th Air Depot Group. Depot clothing stocks consisted of all USAF uniform items, cold/wet weather clothing, individual field equipment, tents, bedding, and aircrew flight clothing.

Supply processing and storage contracts were established with the Sursol and Baronnet companies at Bacalan. The Baronnet contract cost the USAF $1,701 per month. Sursol's price was $1,875 per month, but this cost was shared with the U.S. Army.

Bacalan was manned by a mix of 14 officers, 158 airmen, 4 DAF civilians, and 289 French civilian personnel in January 1956. Three airmen from Det #2, 12th Postal Sq operated a small sub station of APO 16 at Bacalan. U.S. families lived off base in GRI housing at Pessac.

Bacalan also became a storage center for USAFE medical supplies. It was operated by Det #1, 7373d Medical Material Sq, which later became the 3134th Medical Material Sq. Three Federal Stock Classes (#6515, #6520 and #6830) requiring 40,000 square feet of indoor storage, were stocked to support the European area.

On 1 January 1959 the 7415th Support Group was ordered to support the Bacalan depot. Det.#1, 7415th provided administrative, personnel, and budget assistance. This action was required prior to shutdown of the 7413th Air Base Group and the Bordeaux-Merignac Air Base in 1958. On 28 February 1958 the official name of the Bordeaux Air Station, was changed to Bordeaux Storage Station.

As part of the 1958 USAFE budget cuts, the 3134th Supply Group closed the Bacalan Depot and moved the clothing and medical supply operation to the Chateauroux Air Depot at La Martinerie by March 1959. By then Chateauroux had indoor warehouse space available for storing all clothing stocks. This relocation saved about US $6 million per year. The property was formally returned to France in June 1961. Today most of the Bacalan depot structures remain and function as a large storage/shipping business. Anyone wanting to visit Bacalan can reach Bordeaux by train from Paris Gare Montparnasse station. See Michelin Map #335 Local and IGN Series Blue #1536 0.

Chize Sub-Depot

The Chize Sub-Depot was located in the Deux-Sevres Department, 255 miles (410 km) southwest of Paris, east of Autoroute A10, and 14 miles (23 km) south of the city of Niort. It was situated in a large forest, the Foret de Chize, 3.7 miles (6 km) west of the town of Chize. The depot's main entrance was south of route D1 at the village of Virollet.

Chize was requested from France in December 1950. It was planned and built as the primary USAF conventional aircraft munitions (AF Class 39B Combat and Training Munitions) specialized sub-depot in France. The sub-depot was operated from September 1952 until January 1961 by the 73rd Air Depot Wing at Chateauroux, 130 miles to the southeast. There was no available acreage near La Martinerie for munitions storage. The Foret de Chize, made an excellent ammunition depot since it was located in a thirty-five square mile forest (6,547 acres) remote from habitation. The forest had been used for wild game and bird hunting. It was an ideal example of a site that met the criteria for storing large quantities of munitions safely away from permanent inhabited dwellings. Chize also had the advantage of being near the seaports of La Pallice and Royan, convenient for bulk munitions shipments. The closest airdrome was at Niort. Since Niort is a larger city than Chize, the depot was also known as the Niort Ammo Depot.

Chize Ammunition Storage Annex #2688 was assigned to the USAF by France in Feburary 1951. All sub-depot facilities had to be constructed as part of the NATO/USAFE tactical air infrastructure program. Construction began in November 1952 under control of the Joint Construction Agency, Bordeaux Office, and resulted in a very high quality specialized depot facility. By 1953 the cost was US $20 million. Munitions storage consisted of approximately 220 corrugated sheet metal covered ammunition shelters with concrete floors and walls for storing aircraft bombs, rockets, flares, napalm tanks, and machine gun and cannon ammunition. These shelters were designed to direct any accidental blast upward to prevent collateral detonations. Special electrical grounding wiring was included to protect explosives from lightning strikes. Fifty-six miles of roads interconnected the storage shelters with the living area, administrative offices, motor pool yard, and munitions maintenance shops. Twenty-eight structures were well built using standard NATO concrete and block construction. Airmen and officer quarters, mess hall, base exchange, fire station, gym, dispensary, and a microwave RRL station were provided for 200 USAFE depot military personnel. Two large, 300 foot-long, hangar-like buildings housed the munitions maintenance shops. Thirty miles of double fencing was built along with a dog kennel, since dog patrol teams were used to provide security. A water tower, catch basin, pump station, and ten miles of piping were constructed to supply potable water for personnel needs as well as a ready source of water for fire fighting. A railroad siding from Beauvoir-sur-Niort into the depot was completed in 1953. The Chize property and buildings were officially accepted from France and dedicated on 12 August 1953.

Temporary facilities were used until construction was completed in 1953 as Chize began receiving hundreds of tons of surplus WWII stocks of aircraft munitions shipped from England, West Germany, Belgium,

This sight of crumbling structures greeted the 73d Air Depot Wing as they arrived at Moulins 1951.
Gerald F. Smith

73d Air Depot personnel have begun patching the old 1870s buildings at Moulins in 1952.
Gerald F. Smith

NCO barracks in a repaired building, Moulins 1954.
David Davis

Moulins Post Office - Det #3, 12th Air Postal Squadron, 1954.
David Davis

and France. The Chize Depot was operating by 1954, storing 30,000 tons of ammunition and supplying the combat wings in France and Germany with all munitions needed to conduct aircrew training. In a typical month, March 1956, Chize received 861.7 tons of ammunition, shipped 436.11 tons to users, renovated 272.5 tons, and maintained 28,520 tons of ammunition in permanent storage. Ammunition renovaton is the unpacking, inspection, cleaning, testing, painting/marking, and repacking of older munitions.

Total depot work force on 1 January 1956 reached 8 officers, 146 airmen, 1 DAF civilian, and 216 indigenous personnel.

A few U.S. families lived off base in Niort on the economy until nearby GRI housing was completed in 1956. Support facilities, such as the commissary, school, and hospital were located at the La Rochelle Army post, forty miles west of the base.

Chize grew from the 73d Air Sub-Depot Group into the 7374th Air Depot Group, with primary munitions maintenance performed by the 73d Ammunition Supply Sq.

Later the Chize Depot was operated by the 3134th Ammunition Supply Sq, Depot, and supported by 3130th Air Base Gp at the Chateauroux Air Depot. The Chize depot was connected by the USAFE microwave radio relay network into Chateauroux by 1954. A 7th Radio Relay Detachment maintained the microwave station. A very important attached unit at Chize was Det #2, 7410th Explosives Ordinance Disposal (EOD) Sq. A three man team, Det #14, 12th Air Postal Sq operated a small post office, APO #21.

As part of the 1957 USAFE budget cuts, the 3134th Supply Group transferred Chize Depot to the U.S. Army effective 15 October 1961. This transfer saved USAFE about $3 million per year. The Army began storing ammunition there in December 1961, and the transfer was completed in January 1962. Army Com Z continued operating Chize as a BASEC ammunition depot until 1966. The real estate was returned to France in January 1967 as part of FRELOC. Today the old depot buildings remain and are part of a recreational park known as Zoorama. The entire Foret de Chize has been developed as France's

Moulins vehicle storage yard in 1956.
New Chevrolet staff cars.
Jim Reilly

Moulins vehicle storage yard in 1952.
All old WWII "combat servicable" obsolete vehicles.
National Archives

Special delivery vehicle getting a speeding citation
Moulins Sub-Depot, 1953.
National Archives

French worker signing out at reworked main entrance,
Moulins Sub-Depot, 1954.
National Archives

largest national wildlife refuge and animal research center. Zoorama has become a major tourist attraction in southwestern France and Autoroute A10 Exit #33 is well marked! The park can be found on Michelin Map #322 Local and IGN Series Blue #1529 E. Train service is available to Niort from Paris's Gare Montparnasse.

Metz–Frescaty Sub-Depot

Metz-Frescaty is located in the Moselle Department, 190 miles (305 km) east of Paris and 1 mile (2 km) east of Autoroute A31 on Department Road D5. The Metz-Frescaty Sub-Depot, property #2684, was located on a WWII airdrome (ALG Y-34) near the southwest edge of Metz. The sub-depot's mailing address was APO 83.

The site, originally planned for an interim air base, was later developed into a sub-depot and used by the USAFE for vehicle storage and Project SEAWEED war material storage. Flight "B" 73rd Warehouse Sq, Depot, was activated in 1951 at Chateauroux AD and moved to Metz-Frescaty Airport to store the supplies and vehicles being shipped in from CONUS. By the fall of 1952, vehicle storage moved to Moulins Sub-Depot. All SEAWEED supplies were relocated to several main air bases and stored in base supply warehouses as they were completed. Frequent inventory control reports had to be prepared for HQ USAF by each base for Project SEAWEED material.

Metz-Frescaty was turned over to the U.S. Army as an airfield for a fixed wing aviation unit. The airfield (49° 05'N - 06° 07'E, elevation 623 feet) had one paved runway (010°/190°) 7,900 feet long. Frescaty airfield was returned to the French Army in 1959. Metz can be found on Michelin Map #307 Local and IGN

Series Blue #3413 O. It is accessible from Paris by train, using Gare de l'Est.

Moulins-sur-Allier Sub-Depot

This sub-depot was located in the Cher Department, 145 miles (235 km) south-southeast of Paris and 86 miles (137 km) east of Chateauroux. The city of Moulins is on the east side of the Allier River on National Route N7. The sub-depot (46° 35'N - 03° 19'E) was located in the city of Moulins, about one mile from the train station. The main entrance to the depot was on the east side of the city, east of the main rail line.

The Moulins Depot was operated by the 73d Air Depot Wing and CAMAE, from September 1951 until January 1958. It was initially established as the primary vehicle and electrical power unit specialized sub-depot of Chateauroux in summer 1951. At that time there was insufficient open space on La Martinerie for vehicle storage. Moulins Air Station, annex #2687, was offered by France in Feburary 1951. The Moulins facility had been a French Army Cavalry Caserne built in 1870-76 after the Franco-Prussian War. Approximately twenty large, tall, garage-like structures had housed an artillery unit and its horse-drawn guns, caissons and limbers; many buildings had been horse stables. The structures were stone and concrete construction, but most had badly deteriorated. Even so, it was leased to save time and money. The troops built up the Moulins depot as a large self-help project from 1951 until 1953. Extensive repair and some new construction was performed by USAF Moulins troops to get the sub-depot in operation. They built new roads, a large gym, improved all office and vehicle shop buildings, and installed a large base sewage system. Beginning with living quarters and progressing through the vehicle shops, the troops did an excellent job building their own depot. Moulins became a comfortable air station with a theater, gym, AFEX snack bar, airmen's club, commissary, and a small base exchange. About $300,000 USAF construction money was saved, but airmen manpower was diverted from rebuilding old vehicles that were needed to support the new air bases and wings. The Moulins property and buildings were officially accepted from France and dedicated on 25 October 1953.

Moulins grew from eighteen officers and airmen coming from Chateauroux's 73d Air Depot into the 7374th Air Depot Group, with vehicle maintenance performed by the 73d Motor Vehicle Sq. In August 1952 the 75th Vehicle Repair Sq, Depot, arrived at Moulins to supplement the 73d Vehicle Repair Sq. The depot workforce on 1 January 1956 was 25 officers, 275 airmen, 6 DAF civilians, and 512 indigenous personnel, (minus the 12th Comm Construction Sq).

Many U.S. families lived off base in Moulins in rented apartments. An elementary school was established on the depot that provided grades one through eight, but there was no high school.

No sooner had the depot been announced than hundreds of surplus WWII trucks, trailers, power units, and vehicle spare parts were shipped from West Germany, Belgium, and France. Many of these vehicles were thoroughly worn out, requiring major repairs, and should have been scrapped in 1946. Extensive depot level maintenance shop space was developed in the old caserne structures. The depot performed all vehicle and power unit repairs that were beyond the capabilities of the air base motor vehicle squadrons. Moulins had an extensive salvage and reclamation yard that sold obsolete vehicles and scrap parts. Supplying vehicle repair parts to all USAFE activities was the primary duty of the 7374th Supply Squadron. The most critically needed parts were for fire/rescue trucks, aircraft refueling trucks, and fork lifts. Forty-three different AF Stock Classes were stored to support the vehicles and power units. Over 72,000 line items valued at US $19 million were stocked, and 3,500 items were shipped every month to support 17,500 USAFE vehicles. The term "line item" is a USAF expression referring to one item description and part number entered on a CARDEX card line along with the quantities due-in, due-out transactions, plus item location within the storage complex. One card could contain eight or more items. The CARDEX card was one of the most important pieces of paper in the whole USAF!!

On 1 April 1956, the 7374th Air Depot Gp designation was changed to 3136th Air Depot Gp, the 7374th Motor Vehicle Repair Sq became the 3136th Motor Vehicle Repair Sq, the 7374th Supply Sq was changed to the 3136th Supply Sq, and the 7374th Support Sq became the 3136th Support Sq.

Community Toulon sur Allier Storage Station, a large, thirty-acre, vehicle storage yard was located four miles southeast of the depot off highway N7. The yard could hold up to 1,200 vehicles in outdoor storage and had 186,360 square feet of covered storage for large vehicle parts. A small airstrip south of Moulins was suitable for cargo aircraft operations.

The 2d Communications Sq at Moulins operated a communication center and radio station into the Twelfth Air Force logistics net. The microwave radio relay system was not extended southeastward to Moulins due to budget cuts. Detachment #3, 12th Postal Sq operated the Moulins Depot Post Office, APO 10.

Another Air Force unit located at the Moulins Sub-Depot was the 12th Communications Construction Squadron. The 12th Comm Const Sq mission was heavy construction required for all USAFE communications/electronics installations beyond a combat wing's capabilities. This squadron had personnel, vehicles, and equipment to build telephone pole lines, bury telephone cables, install and splice large telephone cables, erect antenna towers, and install telephone switching systems. The 12th Comm Const Sq was activated at Moulins on 1 February 1953 with personnel and equipment from the 610th Signal Light Construction Company (Aviation), a SCARWAF reserve unit activated on 19 October 1951 from the Washington Air National Guard. The unit had 125 vehicles assigned. About forty of this fleet were special purpose trucks and trailers for handling telephone poles, hole digging, cable reels, and splicing tools. Upon activation the squadron was manned by 7 officers and 163 airmen.

The officers and airmen spent much of the time TDY at construction jobs far away from the Moulins depot. The 12th Comm Const Sq applied their skills to virtually every USAFE facility across Europe, North Africa, and Saudi Arabia; installing, repairing, and replacing outside and inside telephone plant systems. Work ranged from initial site surveys to final circuit testing and customer sign-off. Most new air bases in France required total telephone system installation requiring six to ten miles of buried and pole mounted multi-pair phone cables on base. Cable splicing had to correctly interface with the commercial French Post Telephone and Telegraph (PT&T) system running off base.

A very special construction project began on 15 February 1955. This was the construction of microwave antenna towers in France to assist the 7th and 8th Radio Relay Squadrons. Fifty-three 80-foot towers were constructed at the rate of one per week and two towers had to be increased to one hundred feet. Work involved not only tower erection, but tower concrete bases, anchors, guys, reflectors and microwave antenna dishes. No on-the-job accidents or injuries occurred through careful planning and training. This project was completed in March 1956.

On 1 January 1956, the 12th Comm Const Sq at Moulins consisted of 6 officers, 142 airmen. Fifty-five family dependents resided in the Moulins area.

With the planned closure of the Moulins Sub Depot, the 12th Comm Const Sq was ordered to relocate to the Bordeaux Bacalan Sub-Depot. This movement started on 28 March 1957 and the unit moved all 250 tons of equipment, supplies, and project material 280 miles west to Bacalan using its own vehicles. This move was completed by 10 April and the unit was fully operational on 15 April. No construction schedules were interrupted by this relocation. Of course, the squadron found it had less storage space and inadequate facilities at Bacalan (SNCASO) compared to Moulins Air Station. The 12th moved again, this time to Chateauroux, in June 1958 because of additional USAFE budget cuts that closed the Bacalan Storage Station. It operated at La Martinerie until deactivated in May 1965.

As part of the 1957 USAFE budget cuts, the 3136th Air Depot Group closed the Moulins Vehicle Depot. It was moved to the Chateauroux Air Depot and immediately reestablished at La Martinerie. The well planned movement occurred over six months, from 10 January through 20 June 1957, and vehicle support was uninterrupted. By 1957 Chateauroux had space available for the vehicle shops, and after 1958 the vehicle fleets in France decreased as many air bases were reduced to standby status. Also, as the vehicle fleets were modernized they needed fewer repairs. This relocation saved USAFE about $9 million per year. Most of the French employees were transferred to other U.S. sites in France and continued their employment until 1967. Moulins real estate was returned to France in October 1958. Today portions of the old depot buildings remain and the site is operated as a business park. Moulins is accessible from Paris by train from Gare D'Austerlitz station, and can be found on Michelin Map #326 Local and IGN Series Blue #2627 O.

St. Mihiel Sub-Depot

St. Mihiel, located in the Meuse Department, is 172 miles (274 km) east of Paris and 18 miles (29 km) south of Autoroute A4 on Department Route D964. The St. Mihiel Sub-Depot (48° 53'N - 05° 34'E) was located in a French Army Caserne on the southeast edge of the city on route D907.

St. Mihiel was established in summer 1951 as the aircraft munitions specialized sub-depot of Chateauroux Air Depot to support the fighter air bases in northeastern France. This sub-depot was operated by 73d Air Depot Wing, CAMAE, from September 1951 until January 1967. St. Mihiel Air Station, Annex #2689, was offered by France for our use in February 1951. This facility had been the French Infantry Caserne de Senarmont built in 1887. Approximately eighteen large structures had housed an infantry battalion and its horse drawn wagons. This caserne was used by the U.S. Third Army in its drive east to the Moselle River in the fall of 1944. The structures needed repairs and new construction to get the sub-depot in operating condition. Depot personnel operated in temporary facilities until the warehouse, offices, motor maintenance shop, and munitions training buildings were finished in June 1954. A munitions repair building with 3,800 square feet of shop space was constructed in 1956. Finally twenty-two buildings comprised the sub-depot. A second annex was developed as part of the sub-depot, the St. Mihiel Ammunition Storage Annex #8446, a conventional ammunition storage site. The St. Mihiel property and buildings were officially accepted from France and dedicated on 18 September 1953. In January 1953 the 75th Ammunition Supply Sq arrived from CONUS to operate the new sub-depot. Later this unit changed designation to the 7372d Ammunition Supply Sq.

The mission of the 7372d Ammunition Supply Sq, as stated in Twelfth Air Force Regulation 23-49 was: "To receive, store, issue, inspect, renovate, and dispose of base level ammunition stocks and explosive items of Air Force Stock Class 39B; and to assist other ammunition sites as directed in the handling, movement, and storage of ammunition." In 1956 the 7372d Ammunition Supply Sq was redesignated the 3139th Ammunition Supply Sq with the same mission.

The St. Mihiel depot manning on 1 January 1957 consisted of 6 officers, 159 airmen, 2 DAF civilians, and 212 French personnel. The ammunition squadron also provided logistical support to three attached units. Det #14, 12th Postal Sq operated a small post office, APO #188, Detachment #27, 8th Radio Relay Squadron maintained the, OL G-11, microwave station, and Detachment #1, 7410th EOD Squadron disposed of outdated explosive bolts, pylon ejectors, and aircraft seat/canopy charges, as well as removing aircraft ordnance from accident sites. From 1954 to 1966, the St. Mihiel sub-depot received logistical support from Toul AB located twenty-five miles to the east. The 465th TCWg, the 50th FBWg, and later the 7544th Combat Support Gp provided all required services. This support was always coordinated with Chateauroux Air Depot Base Services, located 360 miles away.

The St. Mihiel Sub-Depot, as well as the other sub-depots, were transferred between the USAF Air Material Command (AMC) and USAFE during their operations in France. These transactions were primarily done to switch the operational costs to different major air command budgets. For instance, the St. Mihiel sub-depot was initially built and operated under the direction of AMC Europe. Then it was assigned to Twelfth Air Force, effective 1 January 1956, under authority of General Order #94, Headquarters USAFE, Wiesbaden, West Germany, dated 12 December 1955. Then on 1 January 1958, St Mihiel was transferred by USAFE back to the USAF Air Material Command, Central Air Material Area Europe. On 1 November 1962 the USAF Logistic Command, formerly AMC, transferred St. Mihiel back to USAFE. In mid 1961, USAFE offered the sub-depot to the U.S. Army for its use, but USAFE was directed to maintain ownership and control of this sub-depot. Det #1, 7374th Ammunition Supply Sq remained at the St. Mihiel depot to assist the Army.

On 31 January 1967, St. Mihiel Administration Annex #2689 and the St. Mihiel Ammunition Storage Annex #8446 were transferred to the Military Liquidation Section in Paris. These were the first major USAFE installations to be turned over to the MLS and returned to France as part of Project FRELOC. As of 1997 the former caserne and surrounding real estate are in commercial use. St. Mihiel is accessible from Paris by train from Gare de l'Est. It can be found on Michelin Map 313 Local, and IGN Series Blue #3214O.

St. Nazaire Sub-Depot

St. Nazaire is in the Loire-Atlantique Department, 284 miles (457 km) west of Paris and 18 miles (29 km) south of Autoroute A11. It is a port city on the Atlantic Ocean that was heavily bombed during WWII in an attempt to destroy submarine pens constructed there in 1941. The St. Nazaire Sub-Depot (47° 18'N - 02° 09'W) was located at the civil-military Montoir Airfield on the east edge of the city of St. Nazaire, with port access south of route D100.

St. Nazaire is located thirty-four miles (55 km) west of Nantes, France. Initially the Nantes-Bougon Airport was proposed as a secondary air depot to be operated by the 85th Air Depot Wing from Erding AB, West Germany. Nantes was deleted after site survey determined that airfield improvements would be very expensive. USAF desired a seaport air depot be built to accommodate ship delivery of tactical aircraft, but the primary delivery method became flying most single engine and multi engine aircraft across the North Atlantic ocean year round.

During the 1930s, the SNCAO Breguet Aircraft Company had its primary aircraft factory on the St. Nazaire-Montoir airport, and these hangars and shops were available in 1951. This resulted in occasional use of the St. Nazaire port facility for the shipment of

Cocooned F-102A being off-loaded from USNS Crotan in St. Nazaire. National Archives

A TF-102A just unloaded. Note special hoisting bridle. National Archives

F-102A after stripping off plastic coating. Delta Dagger will be towed to depot shops in St. Nazaire. National Archives

F-86D #52-4222 being inspected by USAF airmen at SUD Aviation, St. Nazaire, prior to test flight. National Archives

aircraft, decocooning, and depot maintenance prior to fly-away to USAFE tactical units. Sud Aviation was located on the Montoir Airdrome and performed the depot function at St. Nazaire under contract from Chateauroux Air Depot. The USAF operated two escort aircraft carrier delivery ships, USNS Tripoli TCVU-64 and USNS Crotan TCVU-66, from Brookley AFB, Mobile, Alabama. These ships delivered hundreds of MDAP aircraft: T-6Gs, F-84Gs, RF-84Fs, and F-86Ks; plus USAFE aircraft: F-86Ds, F-102As, and H-21Bs. The fighter aircraft were off-loaded by cranes and towed about one mile to the Sud Aviation shops. All the factory-new F-86Ds in 1954 and the overhauled F-102A/TF-102As in 1959 were prepared for shipment to USAFE by spraying the whole aircraft with a white plastic coating "cocooning" to prevent corrosion. The Sabre Dogs and Duces were shipped on the flight deck as cargo and exposed to sea air. They required a large amount of corrosion control work after arrival and were processed by the 7485th Air Depot Group. All fighters were inspected and test flown at Montoir Airport, then delivered to USAFE fighter interceptor squadrons in England, West Germany, and Spain.

The 2d Air Postal Sq sent two airmen to operate Det #9, APO #203. This APO was discontinued in November 1954 and a new APO was operated by the Army.

The St. Nazaire-Montoir sub-depot was not used for aircraft shipments after 1963 and the 7485th Air Depot Group was discontinued in 1961. Portions of this facility were turned over to the U.S. Army and no USAF controlled real estate remained at St. Nazaire.

The St. Nazaire-air depot facility is now used as an aircraft sub-assembly plant. The city of St. Nazaire is served by train from the Paris Gare de Montparnasse station, and is found on Michelin Map #316 Local and IGN Series Blue #1123 O.

Villefranche-sur-Allier Sub-Depot

Villefranche, located in the Cher Department, is 147 miles (243 km) south of Paris on Autoroute A71 exit #10. The town of Villefranche is on the east side of A71 on Department Route D16. The Villefranche Sub-Depot (46° 19'N - 02° 52'E) was located in the city of Villefranche, 73 miles (118 km) southeast of Chateauroux and 24 miles (39 km) southwest of the the Moulins Sub-Depot.

The Villefranche Sub-Depot, Annex #3779, was operated by the 73d Warehouse Squadron, Depot, from January 1952 until June 1957. It was established as a parts storage sub-depot of the Chateauroux AD in fall 1951. There was insufficient covered space at La Martinerie for parts storage. Villefranche had an existing commercial storage warehouse complex of eight warehouses with 80,000 square feet each. Buildings #5 and #6 were immediately available and were leased for ten years in October 1951. In July 1952 buildings #7 and #8 became available and were also rented. These warehouses were well built of stone and concrete block and required no repairs prior to use. Only twenty military personnel were authorized by USAFE to operate the Villefranche Air Station complex.

Villefranche is accessible from Paris by train using Gare d'Austerlitz. It can be found on Michelin Map #326 Local.

North La Martinerie under construction, old French buildings border the square. Quonset huts in front of them contain latrines and showers. Route D925 in foreground.
National Archives

Main entrance to La Martinerie 1959. This is the same area shown during construction on the left. Quonset hut latrines are no longer lining the lawn.
Ted Bailey

Temporary wooden building used as NCO Open Mess,
La Martinerie, April 1954.
National Archives

New airmen's dining hall nearing completion,
La Martinerie, 1954.
National Archives

French hospital building being refurbished at
La Martinerie 1954. Note 3/4-ton ambulances.
National Archives

Bachelor officer quarters in reworked
French buildings at La Martinerie, 1954.
National Archives

Standing in line at the movie theater.
La Martinerie,1958.
Ed Duquette

Euclid MB2 aircraft tractor, Chateauroux-Deols AD 1959.
This robust vehicle could tow a C-124.
Ted Bailey

Military Police HQ building looking at the entrance square bounded by old French buildings, La Martinerie 1959.
Ted Bailey

Old French buildings in background, snack bar on the right, power station in dark building.
Ted Bailey

Entrance to snack bar at La Martinerie, 1960.
Ted Bailey

Chateauroux-Deols Commercial Terminal.

Former Marcel Bloch aircraft factory.

Art Deco former base entrance.

Blacktop apron.

Former USAF cargo terminal.

Chateauroux-Deols aviation facility, 1990.
Chateauroux-Deols Chamber of Commerce

Appendix 8.1 Notice to Airmen June 1959 (NOTAM) - USAF Chateauroux-Deols

Elevation 532 feet (162m), 46° 51'N - 01° 43'E. One paved runway 040°/220° is 12,000 feet long. Runway supports 84,000 pounds per single aircraft wheel, safe for jet aircraft take-off and landings. Airport has rotating beacon, boundary lights, runway-taxiway lights, and approach lights. Major aircraft and major engine repairs. Aircraft storage.

Aircraft fuel (115/145 octane) and JP4 jet fuel with single point refueling service available. Jet assist starting units, C-21, C-22, and C-26 available. MA-1A and MA-2 air and electrical starting available. Low pressure oxygen and liquid oxygen service available. Jet barrier for runway 22 only available on 30 minute request. High pressure air service available. Airdrome facilities available 24 hours daily.

Appendix 8.2 Notice to Airmen 1951 (NOTAM) - USAF Chateauroux-La Martinerie

Elevation 511 feet, 46° 49'N - 01° 46'E. CAUTION - Sod field with PSP ramp. Use only for C-47 and lighter aircraft. Aircraft fuel, 115/145 octane only. Two hangars and control tower. Limited storage and repairs.
(This airfield closed after 1952.)

Chateauroux Air Base Assigned Aircraft

73d Air Depot Wing July 1, 1951 - March 25, 1967

7322d Air Base Group.
Aircraft Marking: Aircraft had "CAME" patch on both sides of fuselage.

C-47 - 10 ea

VC-47A	42-2397	C-47A	42-24304
VC-47A	42-93091	C-47A	42-93820
VC-47A	43-15204	C-47A	43-15199
VC-47A	43-15992	C-47A	43-16048
VC-47A	43-15996	C-47A	43-47981
VC-47B	45-1125	C-47B	44-77030
VC-47D	43-48686	C-47D	43-48715
VC-47D	43-48959	C-47D	43-48343
VC-47D	44-77204	C-47D	44-76920
VC-47D	45-1131		

C-54 - 2 ea

VC-54E	44-9046
C-54G	45-481

T-33A - 6 ea

51-8820	53-5826*
52-9867	53-5850
53-4921	53-5852
53-4961	55-4415
53-4964	57-690
53-5569*	

SILK PURSE
C-118A - 5 ea

53-3273
53-3283
53-3287
53-3294

C-118A

53-3274

L-20A-DH - 6 ea

52-6060
52-6132
52-6139

* Losses:
53-5569 - Salvaged, bad landing at Chateauroux AD, France, 19 OCT 56, no fatalities.
53-5826 - Crashed, bad landing at Chateauroux AD, France, 1 JULY 64, no fatalities.

NOTE: Support aircraft were frequently interchanged among users when aircraft were placed into major depot overhaul.

ACKNOWLEDGEMENTS

I would like to thank the following people who contributed to this chapter:

William A. Adamek was a Chief Warrant Officer at Chateauroux AB from July 1957 to June 1960 and October 1962 to June 1966. He provided me with the pictoral history of the Chateauroux Air Depot, "History Central Air Materiel Area, Europe."

David Davis was stationed at Moulins from February 1953 until April 1955. After a TDY in Paris, he managed the Moulins NCO club in 1954 and early 1955.

Ed Duquette arrived at Chateauroux March 1958 and was assigned to Det #3, 11th COMMAINTRON. He was then assigned to 7th RRL as a microwave technician/radio relay operator at the Chateauroux and Chize sites until his return to CONUS in 1960.

Ted Bailey was a propellor specialist in the 1616th Support System (MATS) at Chateauroux from February 1959 through March 1962. He was also assigned to the squadron's Mobile Maintenance Team and flew to many countries to perform "unscheduled" aircraft maintenance. This took him all over Europe, as well as to Turkcy and Ghana.

Jim Reilly was at Moulins from 1955 to 1957 until it closed, then moved to Chateauroux. He worked as a clerk at the Motor Vehicle Storage Area and later, in the orderly room. Special thanks to Jim for providing an excellent Moulins photo CD and facilitating contacts with other Moulins veterans.

Gerald Smith was transferred from Chateauroux to Moulins where he served from September 1951 to December 1952. Besides being a part of the construction crew rebuilding the base, he was the purchasing and contracting officer, and for a short period, base supply officer.

9

CHAUMONT-SEMOUTIERS AIR BASE

The city of Chaumont is the capital of the Haute-Marne Department. It's position at the confluence of the Marne and Suize rivers made it a natural location for early settlements. Roman artifacts from the first century B.C. have been found in the region. The Haute-Marne is best remembered by Americans for the bloody battlefields of World War I. Headquarters of the WWI American Expeditionary Force was located in Chaumont. A bronze tablet at the entrance to Damremont Barracks in downtown Chaumont commemorates the efforts of the more than two million American soldiers under the command of General John J. Pershing. In a strange coincidence, one of Chaumont's commanders, GEN A.P. Clark, was the son of COL Clark who served in Chaumont on the staff of General Pershing. During WWII the American Third Army, XV Corps, 2d French Armored Division liberated Chaumont while destroying a German counter-attack in the area on 13 September 1944.

Nearby are the towns of Colombey-les-deux-Eglises, the burial place of Charles de Gaulle, and thirty miles east is Vittel, home of the natural spring water spa and a bottling plant begun in 1854.

Chaumont-Semoutiers Air Base (48° 05'N - 05° 03'E, elevation 1,018 feet) is located 150 miles (245 km) southeast of Paris, and four miles (6.5 km) southwest of Chaumont. It is on the west side of D10 immediately north of the village of Semoutiers. The main entrance to the base is south of Villers-le-Sec off highway D65.

Between 1935 and WWII, Chaumont Air Base was a grass airstrip used by the FAF for operational exercises. Later, in 1940-41, this airstrip became a German Air Force fighter training base, and a few small buildings were constructed. The field was not used by the RAF during the Battle for France in 1939-40, or as an auxiliary landing ground by the Allies in 1944-45.

During the 1950 initial meetings for air base site selection, Chaumont-Semoutiers airfield was proposed. The airfield was not in operation and no commercial aviation service was planned. The FAF and USAFE concurred that it would be ideal for an interim tactical airfield to be developed into a fighter air base. Chaumont would be a two step base, first a bare base with tents and temporary buildings, and all permanent NATO buildings following within three years. This site was chosen because of the good flying weather around Chaumont—about 300 days a year. Also, very good highway and rail transportation was available nearby. The Corps of Engineers gave approval after determining a limited source of potable water could be obtained from Chaumont city and sufficient commercial electrical service was immediately available. The site had a good solid base of level limestone and drained well. All base roads were made of crushed stone.

Land surveys were conducted in December 1950 to determine property limits and acquisition. Quick approval by Ponts et Chaussees enabled construction to start 25 January 1951. Much effort was devoted to getting the base ready for arrival of a fighter wing by 1 November 1951, an optimistic date! Chaumont contractors, selected from throughout France, were very capable and produced a good interim base. The A&E company Frank Grad & Sons, Seelye, Stevenson, Value, & Knecht located in Paris opened an on-base office. Having a "Chaumont Resident Engineer" allowed design problems and changes to be quickly resolved. Trenching to install base utilities underground and road grading were quickly completed. A rail spur was started from Villers-le-Sec into the base to expedite deliveries of building materials. MAJ Lloyd Miller, USAF was assigned as project engineer, and upon arrival at Chaumont he was greeted by thirty French farmers intent on stopping base construction. He exercised great diplomacy, and construction was able to continue. Another unusual construction delay was encountered when many foreign aircraft bombs were uncovered and had to be removed. The bombs were later destroyed, one at a time, by 48th Wing armament personnel who used explosives in deep pits to safely detonate them. There were no EOD experts available in France at this time.

Chaumont's water needs quickly overtaxed local capacity, even the limited requirement during construction. The water problems were solved by digging wells on base with great success. A1C Coleman Montero relates his story about working at Chaumont early in 1951.

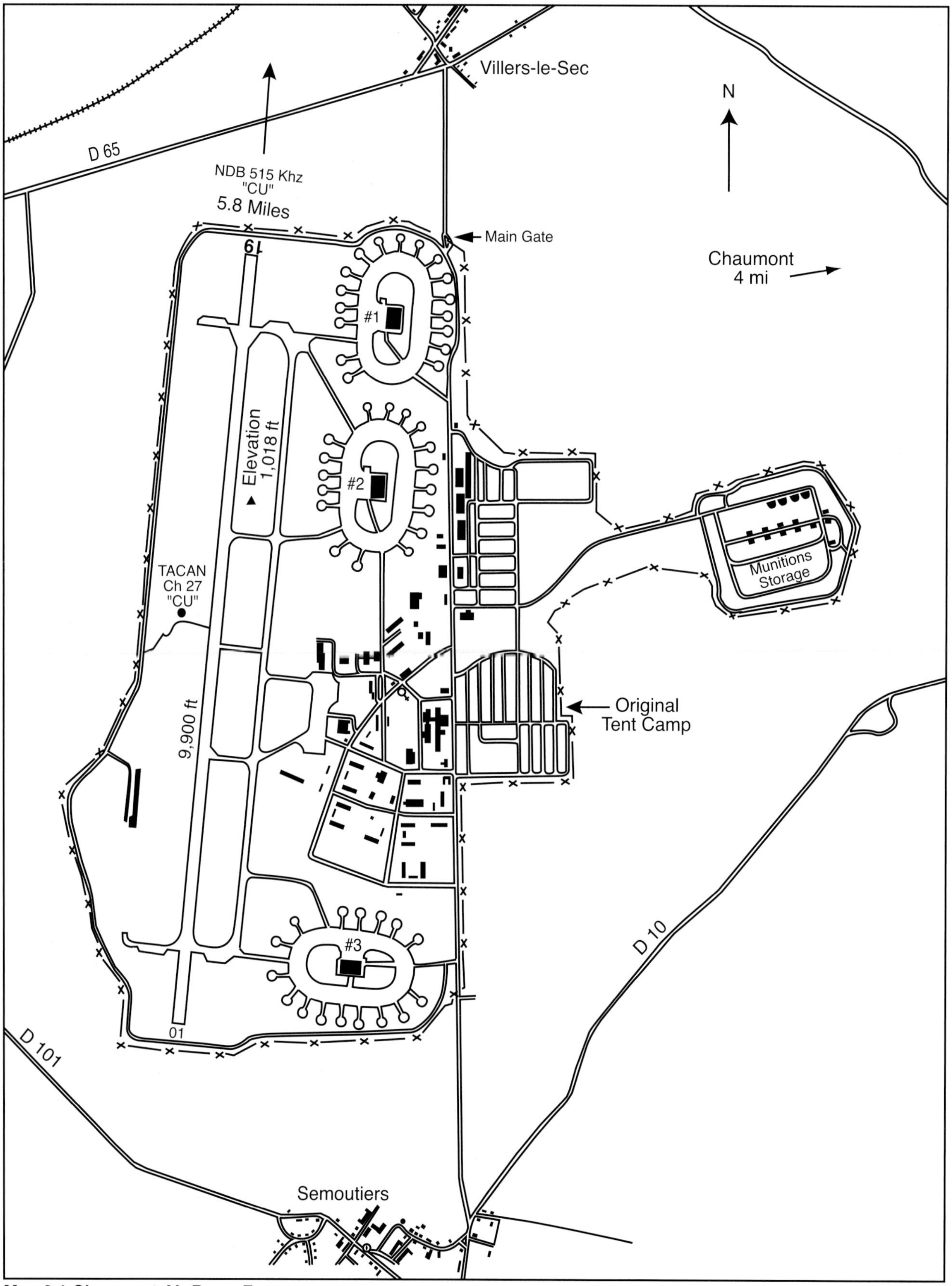

Map 9.1 Chaumont Air Base, France

Chaumont AB from the air 1954. Permanent construction well underway.
John Ibsen

Three wells were dug on base, and these supplied all base needs. The first well we dug on Chaumont was 1,450 feet deep (450m) and produced 250,000 gallons of fresh cool water per day. A huge storage tank was constructed to hold three day's supply of water in case the electrical power was cut off by inclement weather. Unfortunately in the mid 1950s one well became contaminated with jet fuel and could only be used as fire fighting water supply.

Down the road from the base, the town of Villiers-le-Sec had no water, and had to haul in water from Chaumont city daily. The Air Force agreed to drill a well for this town as a sign of goodwill. We made a wager (a case of pink champagne) with the French Engineers in town that we could find water there, and we did reach water! A survey of previous drilling showed they had always stopped about 50 meters from the source! There was a great celebration in town when we brought in the well.

Main runway construction began on 30 October 1951, immediately after the final agreement between the U.S. and France was obtained for the use of Chaumont, though site preparation had been ongoing since the beginning of the year. The contractor laid a good quality macadam runway about eight inches thick over the old runway. Concrete runway extensions, 800 feet long and 9 inches thick, were added at each end of the macadam runway, resulting in a total of 7,900 feet. Next macadam taxiways and access roads were installed. Large, 400,000 square foot, aircraft parking areas were built on a rock bed, bound with tar, and covered with PSP. All this paving was temporary because the plan was to remove and replace it with high strength concrete within three years in the final base configuration. By 1 April 1952, the interim tent camp was completed and ready to provide minimum housing for a fighter wing; 255 tent frames were built on concrete floors, and 24 prefabricated wood buildings were erected. Chaumont was superior to the interim air base at Toul, but many limitations still

Tents and heating plant under construction, November 1951.
Coleman Montero

Winterized tents after the December windstorm, January 1953.
Charles Radloff

remained. Much additional construction was necessary to provide the offices, shops, and storage space needed for wing functions.

In October 1952 the wing began a tent winterization program to prepare for the coming cold weather. Tent occupants did all the work on off duty hours, primarily weekends. They added boards to the roof and sides, installed windows, and then sheets of Celotex on the inner walls. Later the tent canvas was removed, and the whole exterior was covered with tar paper. Plywood sheeting was added on the interior. The insulated "tents" could be heated with only one stove. These structures were occupied until fall 1955; some airmen spent their complete three-year tour of duty housed in these winterized tents. In November 1952, Company B, 843d EABn arrived at Chaumont to improve the base roads and set up additional tents. On 12 December 1952, record high winds hit northeastern France and destroyed many temporary shop tents and structures, and the wing's L-5B that was parked outdoors. Fortunately most of the tents had already been "winterized" and withstood this extremely rare storm.

Chaumont, like Laon and Toul airbases, did not have a discernable stop-start gap between the interim base and permanent base construction. These bases were continuous "projects in progress" or "seas of mud" from 1951 until 1956. By the summer of 1953, the whole east side of Chaumont AB, from the main gate near Villers-le-Sec almost to the village of Semoutiers, was a construction site with an airport somewhere in the middle where new jet fighters were attempting to fly.

During the fall of 1952, four large 35-foot by 150-foot supply tents were built by the French contractor to solve the supply warehouse shortage. There were no warehouses available off base for lease. Also two unusual French tent hangars were built on the PSP aircraft parking ramp to provide some aircraft shelter during major repairs. Additional temporary German-made prefab buildings and sheet metal Fillod buildings were assembled and occupied by squadron shops and supply functions, a vast improvement over the tents on the PSP ramps. These temporary buildings were in use over the following twelve years. The prefab German buildings were used for many different functions and were moved around the base over the years. During 1964, several old prefab latrine buildings in the trailer park were finally destroyed by using them for structural fire fighting training.

Permanent buildings were gradually completed and accepted by JCA engineers. During 1953 the new base theater, a 350-man officer's mess hall and club, a jet engine test cell building, base heating plant, base gym, and the pass and ID office were accepted.

In May 1954, three BOQs and eight airmen's barracks, wing headquarters, three hangars with marguerites, and the base aircraft shops were accepted. In July the 2,000-airmen mess hall and new service club building were completed. November saw completion of the communications center building, four very large supply warehouses, and the firing-in butt. Ninety old "hutments" were dismantled and the lumber salvaged for other base needs. By December 1954 service contracts were let for building maintenance, plus O&M of base electrical and water systems, and the heating and refrigeration plants. In March 1955, contracts were approved for maintaining the base railroad, sewage

Chaumont's Post Office 1954.
Charles Radloff

Chaumont's Post Office staff. 1954.
Charles Radloff

systems, roads, and grounds. These contracts greatly reduced military manning, and were in addition to Native Son employees.

The new library building was completed in June, and the permanent BX and base operations/fire station in August 1955. The new NCO club building, a new officer's club, air installations shops building, base photo lab, six more airmen's barracks, and personal equipment building were also ready for use by August. Chaumont was the first air base in France to have all its base services located in permanent buildings by spring 1955.

A telephone system had been installed throughout the base in 1951, using WWII Signal Corps field phone equipment. Telephones were model EE-8, with a hand cranked magneto to ring down the manual switchboard operator. Three BD-96 manual switchboards were installed in the temporary Comm Center building by June 1952. Two French civilian operators were hired, and worked with twenty-four airmen to keep the phones interconnected on base and into the French long-distance lines. Eight French PT&T switchboards were delivered in October 1952, but remained inoperative until June 1953 when correct interconnect cables were received. During fall 1953 the complete automatic dial French phone system supplied by NATO was installed, eliminating Signal Corps equipment and ten military operators. Six French women operators were now employed round the clock.

The base long distance radio station was operating in May 1953 using a WWII SCR-499 Halicrafters radio set employing Morse code for all messages. A much improved radio set GRC-26C was finally received, and employed radio teletype for all radio messages increasing traffic by a factor of twenty. The 48th Comm Sq solved its Morse code operator training problem by having the students listen and record a Russian low-speed code training net that covered Western Europe at night. High speed proficiency was developed by copying Associated Press news service reports. By 1956, Chaumont was tied into the USAFE radio relay system and hosted Det #24, 8th RRL Sq personnel.

A vital tenant unit was the Air Postal Squadron. Det #4, 12th Air Postal Squadron at Chaumont consisted of one postal officer and ten airmen. It had more duties than just receiving mail, sorting and issuing it to the squadron mail clerks; money and classified military documents moved by U.S. mail. APO mail had to be handled and transported by U.S. military personnel only. Outgoing mail had to be delivered to the main station and incoming mail picked up. Chaumont's main station was 107 miles north, in the city of Metz. In good weather it was a four-hour drive in a WWII three-quarter ton Dodge weapons carrier, or a six-hour drive in rain, sleet, snow, or fog. In 1951 the main postal station had been in Paris, 170 miles away, but after 1952 Metz became the primary station. A two-man team departed Chaumont at noon with the outgoing mail, spent the night at the Metz Army depot, and returned to Chaumont with the incoming mail before noon the following day. The trip was made six days a week to provide good mail service to the troops. The weapons carriers were in poor mechanical condition, which made the trip exciting when a front or rear wheel would break off, or have total electrical failure at night, or the steering wheel would lock up. Several times trucks went off the narrow roads and down hillsides, but no postal personnel were injured. In December 1953, 103,630 pounds of Christmas mail arrived and 15,840 pounds departed through Chaumont AB. In a usual month, February 1954, the small post office had 23,390 pounds of mail arrive and 10,265 pounds trucked to Metz. Local foreign mail was processed through the French PT&T system in Chaumont.

Another important support unit, assigned to every air base was an Air Weather Service (AWS) detachment usually consisting of one to three officers and six to twelve airmen. The first weather men, one officer and six airmen, arrived at Chaumont AB on 3 May 1952, just prior to arrival of the 137th FBWg, and continued operations until February 1967. This small team set up portable equipment and was operational in the prefab communication center building within 24 hours after arrival. As the mission of Det #8 expanded, so too did its personnel increase until in 1955, six officers and forty-two airmen were assigned. Chaumont AB was unusual in that Det. #8 had the largest number of personnel in France. Det #8 had the unusual job of providing Rawinsonde observations, Pilot-to Forecaster Service, dual observation sites, and weather support to the Seventh Army.

In late 1953, Chaumont was selected as the site for a ground station in France for Pilot-to-Forecaster Service (PFSV) on special VHF and UHF radio channels. This service allowed pilots to talk directly by radio to weather forecasters in a central weather station and obtain the most current and forecasted weather picture at their destinations. European-wide hourly weather observations were provided to the Chaumont station by radio, teletype, and facsimile circuits from Rhein-Main Weather Central. This weather information was immediately available to pilots via their radio set. Weather communications equipment at Chaumont was maintained by the AACS Det #2.

A dual observation site was established in 1953 near the runway for more accurate runway weather. The communication center building was about a half-mile from the runway. Another small hut was set up near the runway so a weather observer could provide current information to the control tower, GCA van, and the weather station. Det #8 Airman First Class Bob Schmid relates his story about working weather observation in the runway position at Chaumont.

> The runway position was a little shack on skids set back 150 feet from the runway with phone-speaker lines into GCA and the weather station for reporting weather. I would monitor GCA transmissions and got very concerned when jets were told by the final controller that they were 150 feet left of centerline. That would have the fighter heading right for the shack but final corrections always put the airplane back on the runway centerline. The weather shack was never hit while I was serving at Chaumont. If it had been hit, I wouldn't have been in it, cause I was headed east across the taxiway in a big hurry. Feet don't fail me now!

The Rawinsonde operation involved launching a hydrogen filled weather observation balloon lifting a radio telemetery transmitter package that provided temperature, pressure, relative humidity, and altitude. The GMD-2 provided automatic tracking of the balloon, giving a winds-aloft profile across France. During 1955, Det #8 Rawinsonde Section set USAFE records for average weather data collections at 94,000-foot altitude; one of their observation balloons reached 141,000 feet!

During 1954-55, the 48th Air Installations Squadron planted 3,200 trees and grass seeded the dirt over the entire base to control the mud during the rainy seasons. The 843d EABn constructed a large athletic field; the big job was installing a good drainage system for football and baseball fields. By summer 1955, a skeet range was also constructed and operating for fighter pilots' training. The severe 1955-56 winter halted almost all outdoor work though interior improvements continued.

A larger 100-bed base hospital was constructed to care for dependents as well as military personnel. This hospital was about double the size of other hospitals found on U.S. air bases in France. It was authorized because USAFE considered Chaumont remote from other major Army and Air Force medical units. The hospital was completed in May 1956.

In 1956 the base chapel, a ten-chair dental clinic, AFEX service station, new base motor pool, the AFEX commissary, and base laundry were accepted by the JCA inspectors, completing most of the major NATO and USAFE construction projects. There were many small projects remaining and these continued until 1959, when all unfinished projects were canceled by Project RED RICHARD. Additional building took place in 1960-61 to meet new Seventeenth Air Force requirements for STAIR STEP users.

Local housing around the Chaumont area was in short supply since this area of France was sparsely populated. Family housing and elementary schools became a serious problem because many officers and NCOs brought their families to Chaumont in 1952 and afterwards.

Project Caravan built the first family housing, 128 on-base trailer sites and six laundry buildings west of the old tent camp in 1955. In addition to the trailer

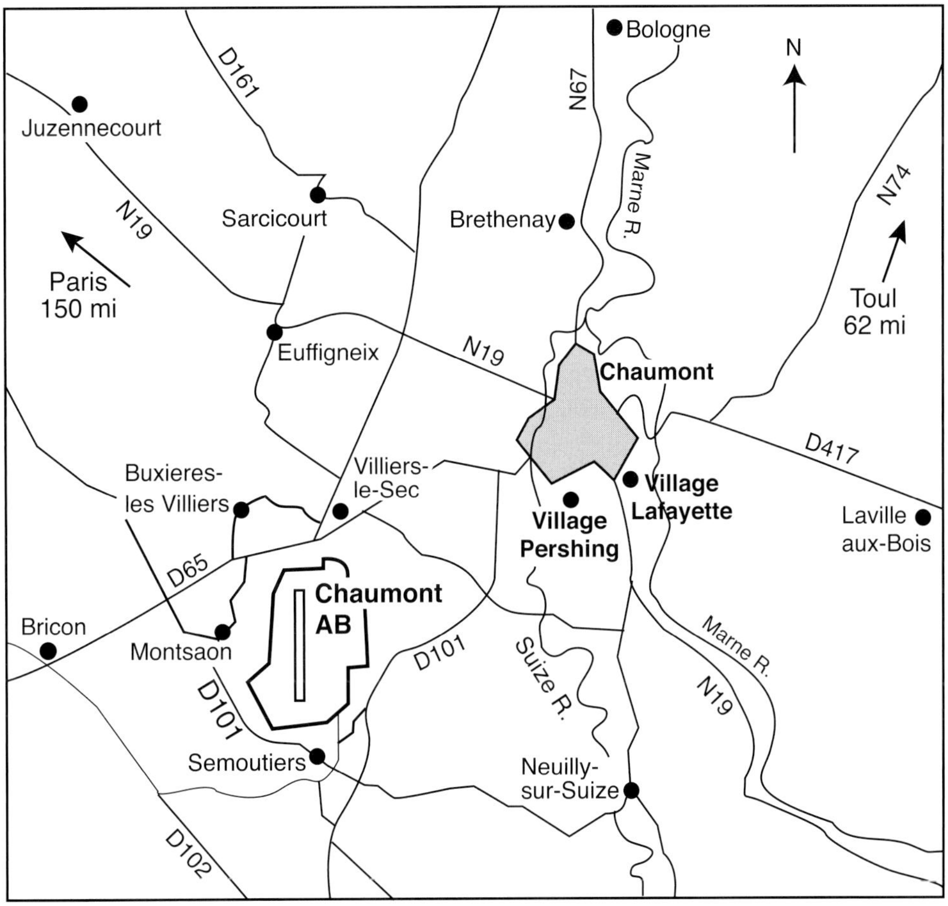

Map 9.2 Chaumont Area

camp, a large Guaranteed Rental Income housing development, Village Lafayette, consisting of 300 single, duplex, and a few triplex units, was constructed in 1955-56. This housing tract is five miles east of the base, east of highway N19, and two and a half miles south of Chaumont city center. A large Commodity Credit family housing project, Village Pershing, consisting of 108 units, was constructed in 1958-59, four miles east of the base, west of highway N19 and one mile southwest of Village Lafayette off D16B. This also consisted of single, duplex, and triplex family units. This CCH program provided adequate housing for Air Force families based at Chaumont. Both Village Lafayette and Village Pershing are in very good condition and still used by French families.

The first grammar schools were facilities leased for two years in Chaumont, Bourbone, and Vittel. Four elementary school teachers arrived from CONUS in August 1952 in time for the fall semester. The school in Chaumont city was located near the Beausejour Hotel. It had one large and one small room for twenty-five to fifty children. The Bourbone school used the downtown Grand Hotel of Bourbone, twenty-eight miles east of the base. This building had one large room with sliding partitions and could accommodate forty to fifty students. The Vittel school, thirty-two miles east, used one room of a French elementary school building for twenty to thirty children. Air Force buses were used to transport the students to these distant schools.

An eight-classroom grammar school was constructed on base in summer 1953, using two prefabricated single story buildings. This temporary school was located near the base trailer park. Later it was replaced with a permanent grammar school built off base in the Village Lafayette housing complex. Chaumont never had a high school.

In 1957 Chaumont had a base area of 1,582 acres with seven miles of paved roads. The runway was 9,900 feet long by 150 feet wide. There were 550,000 square yards of taxiways, aprons, parking ramps, etc. Chaumont had three NATO fighter-size hangars, each surrounded by a marguerite with sixteen pads. The base had seventy-six permanent and thirty-seven temporary buildings. It had 2.5 million cubic feet of warehouse storage space adjacent to a two-track siding, and 266,700 square feet of temporary storage space. The water system consisted of three wells and five 48,500-gallon tanks. Chaumont had one heating plant with a backup electrical generating plant. Fourteen dormitories, each with a capacity of 120 airmen, were in one central area. Three BOQ buildings housed 64 officers each. There were three dining halls, a 2,000-airman mess, one for 350 officers, and the hospital dining hall that could feed 300. Eight underground storage tanks provided fuel storage for 705,500 gallons of Jet fuel, 130,000 gallons of AVGAS, 70,500 gallons of MOGAS, and 200,000 gallons of DIESEL fuel. Munitions storage was located a half mile east of the main base, but enclosed within the base fencing. Twenty igloos, located on fifty-two acres, were constructed in the Bois de Villers-le-Sec. Since this munitions storage was connected to the air base it did not receive a separate real estate number. Additional storage igloos were constructed on this site during 1961-62 as part of STAIR STEP base improvements. Estimated real estate value in 1957 (excluding land) was $22 million. Equipment in use (excluding aircraft) was approximately $6 million. Total base supply inventory was $8.5 million.

137th Fighter-Bomber Wing

Upon its arrival in May 1952, the 137th Fighter-Bomber Wing became Chaumont's first combat wing. It flew the first USAF fighters in France. The wing's mission at Chaumont, as assigned by Twelfth Air Force, had two statements: first, to develop and operate efficient tactical units that would be combat ready in their new F-84Gs in the event of war; second, to continue developing air base facilities to house the troops and supplies for winter 1952-53.

The 137th Fighter-Bomber Wing originated as the WWII 404th Fighter-Bomber Group flying P-47D Thunderbolts on close air support missions with the Ninth Air Force in England, France, Belgium, and Germany, earning a DUC. The 404th FBGp was inactivated at Drew Field, Florida, on 9 November 1945. The 404th Fighter Group was redesignated the 137th Fighter Group and allotted to the Oklahoma Air National Guard on 24 May 1946, keeping the heritage, insignia, and lineage of 404th units. The 137th Fighter-Bomber Group was expanded into the 137th Fighter-Bomber Wing in September 1950.

The 137th Fighter-Bomber Wing, Oklahoma ANG, consisting of approximately 190 officers and 1,040 airmen, was called to federal active duty on 10 October 1950. The three assigned fighter squadrons were flying two different aircraft types, but during 1951 the 137th changed its mission and aircraft. When activated, the wing consisted of three fighter squadrons: the 125th flying F-84Bs at Will Rodgers Airport, Tulsa, Oklahoma; the 127th flying F-84Cs at Wichita Municipal Airport, Kansas; and the 128th at Dobbins AFB, Atlanta, Georgia, flying F-47Ds; and eleven support squadrons. Both the 125th and the 127th had converted from F-51D Mustangs between March and May 1950. Consequently they were still new to the Republic F-84s when activated. The 128th first changed to F-84Ds at Alexandria AFB. They were very sad to see their Thunderbolts go to the salvage yard. By 27 November 1950, the 137th Wing assembled at the newly reactivated Alexandria Municipal Airport, Louisiana, for eight months of intensive combat training and conversion to new Republic F-84G Thunderjets. They were also given the responsibility of restoring an air base that had been closed since 1946. (Alexandria Municipal Airport was renamed Alexandria AFB in December 1950 and later changed to England AFB in June 1955)

During training at Alexandria, the wing was often tasked to transfer pilots and skilled airmen to Korea. This necessitated repeating the complete wing training cycle twice during 1951. Deliveries of F-84Gs, the final straight wing model Thunderjet, slipped several months due to late deliveries of its uprated Allison J-35-A-29 engines. Extra aircraft technical training was required for the new jet engine, A-1C gunsight, APG-30 range radar, autopilot, in-flight refueling, and special weapon controls. Rumors persisted during this period that the wing would deploy somewhere in France to expand NATO even though a serious need existed for additional F-84 wings in Korea. Finally, after receiving sixty factory new F-84G-1s between November 1951 and February 1952, the wing had completely changed into the G model and began practicing long range fuel endurance missions. One F-84G #51-882 was damaged in an accident at Alexandria on 25 November 1951 and went to Kelly AFB for depot repairs. Later, on 3 September 1952, #882 arrived at Chaumont to serve with the 48th FBWg. By late April, the 137th Fighter-Bomber Wing was ready to fly to their new home at Chaumont AB, France. It avoided having to spend the 1951-52 winter in a tent camp and escaped the serious personnel turnover problem in France created by the early release of activated reserve airmen. Most of the 137th air reserve and air guard airmen remained in CONUS and were released from active duty before 9 July 1952.

The 137th's deployment to France followed the procedures described in chapter 2. The ADVON departed Alexandria AFB on 20 March by C-124, and arrived at Chaumont 24 March 1952. On 5 May the 137th flight echelon departed with three squadrons, flying fifty-nine F-84Gs on this Fox Able-15 movement. The air base group flew six T-33A and two C-47 support aircraft. The F-84Gs had air-to-air refueling capability installed, but it was not used because there were no tankers available. The aircraft had an impressive ferry range of 1,900 miles if all four external tanks were installed. The route was from Alexandria to McGuire AFB, New Jersey, then across the northern route to Prestwick, Scotland, and then into Germany instead of France. A five-day weather delay at Goose Bay, and a four day delay at Keflavik, Iceland, slowed the squadrons. Unexpectedly their final destination was changed from Chaumont to Landstuhl and Neubiberg air bases. The 125th and 127th Squadrons went to Landstuhl AB (Ramstein) and the 128th was ordered to Neubiberg. The squadrons arrived in Germany on 13 May 1952. Runway and taxiway repairs at Chaumont were the official excuse provided by USAFE, but there was still French political opposition to basing nuclear weapon capable F-84Gs in France! Pressure was applied to the French government, and final approval was obtained on 25 June 1952 to move the 137th into France from Germany. This was a major NATO milestone—the 137th Fighter-Bomber Wing was the first USAF fighter wing in France and only USAFE wing in France to fly the Republic F-84Gs. COL Chesley G. Peterson was commander of the 137th, from 8 August 1951 to 10 July 1952.

Sixty-three of the sixty-five 137th aircraft had arrived in Germany. One T-33A and one F-84G were damaged on 3 June and remained at Keflavik. The 137th enroute maintenance team made repairs to fly them to a USAFE depot for final repairs. The T-33A joined the wing after repairs but the F-84G #51-873 went from the Burtonwood depot to SABENA, Brussels, where it was used as a depot training aid until 7 January 1954!

The 137th was officially transferred from TAC to USAFE at Chaumont AB on 13 May 1952. The main body of the wing traveled 190 miles by air-conditioned buses from Alexandria to the New Orleans Port of Embarcation. The USNS GEN Patch troopship departed New Orleans on 14 May 1952, headed for La Pallice, France, arriving on 26 May. The men were then taken by train to Chaumont, arriving the next day. The troops were amazed that their F-84Gs were not at the base! Squadron aircraft maintenance personnel were moved to Germany for one month to support their aircraft. While operating in Germany, the primary flying was orientation flights, instrument approaches, and formation tactics.

Three small support units had set up their operations prior to the 137th's arrival at Chaumont; Det #2, 1952d AACS Sq manned the control tower; Det #8, 31st Weather Sq the base weather station; and Flt. "Q" 2d Air Postal Sq operated the post office, APO 119.

The rear echelon closed all supply accounts and turned their buildings at Alexandria AFB over to the newly arrived 132d Fighter-Bomber Wing. The rear detachment's seven officers and twenty-six airmen moved to Chaumont by C-124.

When the fighter squadrons arrived on 26 June 1952, the complete wing was finally together at Chaumont, just two weeks prior to deactivation! The three fighter-bomber squadrons set-up their flight operations and aircraft maintenance tents at Chaumont. The wing was becoming operational and began supporting NATO flying exercises. Prior to deactivation, it flew its first air-to-ground support training with the U.S. Army in West Germany.

After arrival of the 137th, no additional combat wings moved into France for two years until the permanent air bases were approaching completion.

Prior to its arrival in Europe, the 137th had been tasked to support USAF Project 7019 that affected all combat wings in the USAF. The 137th rotated combat ready fighter pilots to gain experience in FEAF's F-84D/Es. During the summer of 1952, fighter pilots deployed to Wheelus AB, Libya, to maintain air-to-air and air-to-ground bombing and gunnery proficiency prior to departure for the Far East.

Redesignation

At midnight on 9 July 1952, the 137th Fighter-Bomber Wing was redesignated the 48th Fighter-Bomber Wing as of 10 July 1952, with the same mission, fifty eight F-84Gs, two T-33As, one L-5B, one T-6D, two C-47s; 211 officers and 1,314 airmen, and equipment at Chaumont AB. The three fighter-bomber squadron designators also changed: the 125th became the 492d FBSq, the 127th became the 493d FBSq, and the 128th became the 494th FBSq. The Air National Guard wing, group, and squadron designators were returned to the states of Georgia, Kansas, and Oklahoma. The very few ANG enlisted personnel left in the 137th, primarily aircraft maintenance NCOs, had departed for CONUS by 7 June, and had been released from active duty by 9 July 1952. A few reserve officer personnel had to serve for six to twelve additional months.

The redesignation procedure was simple, HQ, 137th FBWg prepared one special order with fifteen different paragraphs, one paragraph for each squadron. For example: Special Order No 86, 3 July 1952, Paragraph 3 read, "The following named officers and airmen, USAF, are relieved from assignment and duty with 125th Fighter-Bomber Squadron, APO 119, this station and assigned to 492d Fighter-Bomber Squadron, APO 119, USAFE, without change in duty status. Officers and airmen will depart on or about 2400 hours, 9 July 1952 reporting to Commander not later than 0001 hours on 10 July 1952. No travel is involved." All the assigned squadron officers and airmen are listed by their grade, name, and serial number without any errors or missing names! This command action is always required when a unit designator is changed.

48th Fighter-Bomber Wing

The 48th Fighter-Bomber Wing was reactivated on 10 July 1952 at Chaumont. Its wing designator was mandated by the Matheny Board directive of 1946 that determined the numerical designators assigned to groups or wings in the postwar regular Air Force. Designators of deactivated groups were assigned to newly activated units in order of historical precedence. The 48th became the premier fighter wing in France, serving the longest, from 10 July 1952 through 15 January 1960. The wing worked hard to develop Chaumont into one of the best air bases in France. Its three assigned squadrons, the 492d, 493d, and 494th, remained unchanged while flying three different fighters, the F-84G, F-86F, and F-100D, and maintaining the capability to fight a conventional or nuclear air war.

The 48th Fighter Wing had been a WWII fighter-bomber group activated in January 1941. It moved across France earning five Campaign Stars as part of the USAAF Ninth Air Force flying P-47s, and ended its European campaign in Kassel, Germany. A DUC was awarded to the 48th FBGp for its excellent close air support in adverse weather to aid ground forces in the capture of Julich, Germany. It returned to the U.S. in August 1945 to prepare for deployment to the Pacific, but was inactivated suddenly on 7 November 1945 with the termination of WWII, and remained inactive until 10 July 1952. Since then it has continued as an active USAFE wing to the present day.

Table 9.1 48th TFWg Commanders at Chaumont

COL Joseph H. Moore	10 July 1952
COL Chesley G. Peterson	27 May 1953
COL William I. Leverette	1 June 1955
BGEN Albert P. Clark, Jr.	1 August 1955
COL Stanton T. Smith, Jr.	12 December 1956
COL Edward F. Roddy	24 June 1959
COL Victor E. Warford	4 August 1959
COL Emmett S. Davis	1 May 1961

Base support unit designators remained unchanged when the 48th was activated: Flt "Q" 2d Air Postal Sq; Det #8, 31st Weather Sq (MATS); and Det #2, 1952d, AACS Sq (MATS). During July 1953 the postal unit changed to Det #4, 12th Air Postal Squadron.

The 48th FBWg changed fighter aircraft models and versions often during its eight years at Chaumont. After activation, sixteen F-84Gs were delivered to bring the wing up to its authorized strength of seventy-five fighters. Then, early in February 1953, the block -16 and later block -26 F-84Gs began to arrive, and the 48th began its first aircraft change. These newer F-84Gs were some of the last Thunderjets delivered to the USAF by Republic Aviation. The 48th transferred two dozen of its F-84G-1s to the 36th FBWg at Bitburg and a few to Denmark under MDAP. During November-December 1953, new F-86F-25 Sabres built in Columbus, Ohio, arrived to replace the Thunderjets. These were the first North American Aviation Sabres in France. Their guns, gunsight, and radar equipment were identical to the late model F-84Gs, but all equipment had much easier service access. Then in November 1954, the 48th received ninety-eight later model F-86F-35-NAs to replace the -25s. These were the last block -35 models from NAA Inglewood. With a very good engine and a reliable airframe, the easy to maintain Sabre was the favorite even after fall 1956 when the 48th began conversion into F-100Ds.

The wing continued to support 7019 requirements until October 1953. One F-84 pilot from the 494th Squadron was lost to enemy action in Korea while TDY in February 1953.

The 48th was constantly training their fighter pilots in air-to-air gunnery, and air-to-ground gunnery and bombing. Beginning in July 1952 a large portion of each fighter squadron deployed to the range for two or three, three-week periods every year to support this training. The air-to-air firing was badly needed to improve accuracy using the A-1C(M) gunsight and the APG-30 radar set. Targets were A-25 banners and A-6A sleeves with radar reflectors towed by the F-84Gs and TB-26s over the Gulf of Sidra. A B-26C #41-39303 was received from the 38th LBWg on 24 February 1953 for use as the wing's tow target tug. It made a very good target tug, carrying eight to ten banner or sleeve targets internally with an on-range duration of four hours. Air-to-ground gunnery was conducted at the Siegenberg Range, at least six weeks every year. The F-84s, usually staged from Furstenfeldbruck AB. They flew thirty-six gunnery sorties per day using .50cal API ammunition, 100-pound practice bombs, and five inch HVAR rockets with live warheads.

This gunnery program was accomplished while overcoming acute shortages. In 1952 no squadron had a complete collection of test sets and operable test mock-ups for the radar set and gunsight, and repair parts were in short supply. There was no firing-in butt to conduct test firings after the aircraft guns were bore-sighted. There was no munitions storage facility; it had been delayed as other construction costs escalated. Aircraft operations were limited by insufficient fuel storage facilities, and aircraft arming and maintenance was a growing fire hazard because the aircraft were parked very close together on the PSP ramp. Until a metal fire station was constructed in April 1953 by the 843d EABn, fire trucks had to be kept outdoors where their water tanks froze in the winter.

The 48th had the same personnel problems all the wings in France were experiencing. People would depart for CONUS after completing their tour of duty and no replacements would appear! Personnel forecasting procedures proved to be of no value. The sixty airmen assigned to the 48th Air Police Sq were insufficient for base security. By late 1952 every airman was required to perform four or more hours of guard duty every six days. Air police authorizations were increased, but no police arrived at Chaumont. In March 1953 Twelfth Air Force issued the first personnel reductions for the 48th Wing; 10 officer and 144 airmen positions were eliminated from the wing's table of organization. This came as the wing was undermanned for its basic job of developing the air base and training for new aircraft. This was the first of many austerity measures the 48th would experience. In the summer of 1954, married unaccompanied officers and NCOs began rotating back to CONUS after their two years at Chaumont creating shortages of skilled people, including pilots. Armament personnel rotated so often that continuous training programs were required for radar and gunsight maintenance. The retention rate of these armament electronics technicians in USAFE was never over 5 percent. As rotation continued, shortages of skilled aircraft, electronic maintenance, supply, and administrative support airmen developed, requiring extensive OJT programs.

Though aircraft operations were kept at a high pace of 550 to 900 hours per month per squadron, flying was limited by the continued difficulty of obtaining aircraft and engine parts. Technical supplies were critical during the 1950s. Chateauroux Depot was not capable of supporting the F-84Gs until 1955. Throughout 1953 about 50 percent of the aircraft parts requisitioned, such as instruments, tires, brakes, radio sets, and oxygen regulators were back-ordered for 90 to 120 days; this indicated they had to be shipped from CONUS depots. Twelfth Air Force added to the 48th flying load by tasking the wing to train fourteen Yugoslavian, and later, Belgian, Danish, and Norwegian pilots to fly the Republic F-84Gs that were being supplied to many NATO and MDAP nations.

During summer each fighter squadron flew 1,025 hours; consequently the accident rates increased and a total of eleven F-84Gs were lost, with five fatalities.

The 48th FBWg discovered a new problem with their -16 and -26 Thunderjets; the perforated dive brake outer aluminum skin began to develop a large number of small cracks. This faster model F-84 was experiencing ultrasonic skin vibrations that could lead to eventual speed-brake failure. The outer skins had to be replaced with .032-inch thick stainless steel sheet to withstand the vibrations. New skins were fabricated by Chateauroux AD and installed at Chaumont. Every late model F-84G had to be modified during 1953, requiring many extra man hours. This type of TCTO work increased rapidly during spring 1953 since 1,153 TCTOs applied to the F-84G fleet. Many TO kits were required, but by the end of 1953, 343 kits had not been received, and aircraft had to be grounded.

Serious Foreign Object Damage (FOD) problems developed with the J-35 engine; all ramps, taxiways, and the runway had to be improved. Nose intake screens were used at all times while taxiing from parking ramps to the runway on take off and on return after landing. The fighters had to stay 500 feet apart while taxiing on the runway. J-35 engine maintenance presented many special problems with FOD and bleed-off line failures; about twenty-five engines had to be removed for engine shop work every month. The Allison tech rep presented training lectures to assist engine shop personnel. Minor repairs could be performed at Chaumont, but about ten to twelve engines had to be returned to CONUS depots. Even after minor repairs, every engine had to be vibration checked in an approved engine test cell. Chaumont did not yet have a test cell so the engines were transported to Furstenfeldburck AB for a complete vibration test using their calibrated test cell.

The F-84Gs faced the same flying limitations in France as did the B-26 and RF-80s because they only had the eight channel VHF radio sets. Plans were made

Repairing jet engines outside on PSP, 1953.
John Ibsen

F-84G engine maintenance outdoors on PSP, 1953.
Charles Radloff

to replace the VHF radio set with the new twenty channel UHF radio, ARC-33, but delivery of this radio set fell behind schedule. A few F-84Gs did receive the sixteen-channel modification similar to the B-26s. The F-86Fs had factory installed ARC-27 UHF radios that solved this problem.

In April 1953 the 494th Squadron modified two F-84Gs to carry the new APN-60 radar beacon in place of the IFF set, the -60 beacon worked with the MSQ-1 bombing radar sets in Germany to improve tracking range and bombing accuracy. The IFF set and bombing beacon required the same fuselage space.

The Skyblazers, USAFE's aerobatic team, was reorganized at Chaumont in June 1953; the five F-84Gs had an excellent paint scheme that included their WWII group insignia on the vertical stabilizers. The Skyblazers had been part of the 36th Fighter Wing at Furstenfeldbruck since 1950. HQ USAFE decided to move them out of Germany into France because of better flying weather and more open airspace around Chaumont. After arrival of the F-86Fs, the Skyblazers converted into the Sabres and performed their first Sabre airshow in April 1954. After September 1954 the new Statue of Liberty wing insignia was added on both sides of the fuselage. Many observers felt the F-86F was the best show aircraft flown by the Skyblazers. The team continued flying five F-86F's until 30 October 1956 when they departed France and moved back to the 36th Fighter Day Wing at Bitburg AB, and changed into F-100Cs. They continued aerobatic demonstrations at air shows across Europe until disbanded on 15 January 1962.

Chaumont held an open house once a year, and the French citizens attended in great numbers. In 1954 over 15,000 attended the Armed Forces Day event to see static aircraft displays, flight demonstrations, hear a French Army band, watch movies in the new base theater, and of course, watch the Skyblazers perform. Many people walked the four miles from Chaumont city or farther from outlying towns, to see the base. Their common reaction was surprise at all the buildings constructed in what they considered such a short period of time. Chaumont AB had become an important part of the Haute-Marne region.

To improve Franco-American relations in the region, the 48th Wing Staff came up with the idea of

Statue of Liberty monument in 1958.
Jack Callanan

Statue of Liberty monument in 2002.
Paul Hammond

changing the wing insignia. The competition for a new 48th Fighter-Bomber Wing insignia was won by Captain G. N. Winkler, and was displayed to base personnel on 4 July 1954. The design incorporated the Statue of Liberty, and throughout Europe the wing became known as the "Statue of Liberty" wing. In 1956 a replica of the Statue of Liberty was planned for the base. The fifteen-foot high statue was cast from Frederic Bartholdi's molds for the working model of our Statue of Liberty. It was fabricated by the French artist Durene of Paris and cost $1,752. The statue was installed on a stone base with a brass dedication plaque in the triangle in front of Wing/Base Headquarters. A special dedication ceremony was conducted on 4 July 1956, attended by MAJ GEN Robert M. Lee, Commander 4ATAF; many USAF and FAF distinguished visitors; and 3,000 French and American spectators. This event was covered nationwide by the French press, radio, and television. On 8 July, an Open House was held and over 18,000 people came to Chaumont to see the statue. It is still in its original position and appears in excellent condition after almost fifty years!

Delivery of the first F-86Fs, model -25-NH, began in November 1953. An F-86F Mobile Training Unit was on base for eighteen months conducting classes on the Sabres for all pilots and maintenance personnel. Then in summer 1954, the 48th received ninety-eight later model F-86F-35-NAs with improved nuclear weapon delivery capability using toss bombing. The extra twenty Sabres were maintained by the 48th as USAFE spares. These jets were a great favorite of the fighter pilots, very responsive, fast, and excellent for close formation flying, with a longer range. The -35s were flown non-stop from Chaumont to Wheelus without air refueling.

The 48th found the F-86 the easiest jet fighter to maintain, with accessibility to the six machine guns and ammunition being a leading factor, especially compared to the F-84. The F-84 had two .50cal guns buried in the wing roots that were difficult to remove and replace for service. The fuselage ammunition boxes were hard to refill and feed the rounds down to these guns, so they were rarely fired in training. The four nose guns were accessible through the nose armament bay door, but workstands or ladders were always needed to remove and replace a sixty-four pound M3 machine gun. The four removable ammunition cans were heavy when loaded with 300 rounds each, therefore, they were loaded in the F-84 and the ammo belts man-handled up and down ladders. Testing and replacement of the APG-30 radar required removal of the four ammunition cans.

Individual squadrons regularly deployed to Wheelus for air-to-air and air-to-ground gunnery proficiency in their F-86Fs. In June and July 1954, the complete wing spent forty-five days in Libya, concentrating on air-to-air gunnery as part of a new Twelfth Air Force standardization program. Air-to-air gunnery is the favorite flying time of all fighter pilots since they seldom get enough gunnery hours vs. all the time spent on routine flying schedules. During this extended shooting, over 90 percent of the pilots qualified in F-86F gunnery, and 75 percent achieved expert level. Aircraft maintenance kept about 85 to 90 percent of the F-86Fs in commission every day. Most firing was done on an F-86 towed, nylon sleeve, thirty-foot long target, at 25,000 feet and 400 knot airspeed. The sleeve included a radar reflector so the APG-30 range radar could assist gunsight range computations. This target was much more realistic than the B-26 towed banner at 10,000-foot altitude traveling at 225 knots. Intense squadron competition made the time pass very quickly;

Engine test cell building completed in 1953 allowed Chaumont engine mechanics to complete overhaul on base.
John Ibsen

the 492d Squadron ended the meet in first place. During this long stay at Wheelus, 3,483 hours were flown in 3,400 sorties, and 265,000 rounds of .50 caliber ammunition were fired. Oh yes, 47,000 feet of 16mm gun camera film was exposed to verify the scores! Since rocket firing and bombing had been added to the weapons delivery syllabus for all pilots, five hundred practice bombs were dropped on the ranges for scoring in low and high angle dive-bombing sorties. This 1954 range exercise was accident free.

The great concern of wing commanders in France was keeping their fighter pilots proficient in both combat operations and instrument flying in bad weather. After intense work on the part of 48th Air Base Group airmen, the Link C-11A jet aircraft instrument trainer was finally put into operation at Chaumont in April 1954. The trainer had been delivered in late 1952 and was placed in storage until the simulator room was completed, and a proper electrical generator (60Hz) was delivered. The trainer deteriorated while in storage; excessive corrosion developed in the electrical terminal boards. After finding proper technical manuals and electronic test equipment, and fabricating special tools, two airmen spent many hours correcting electrical and mechanical troubles to get the C-11A into service. Its operation was a vital part of Chaumont's new base instrument flying school program to provide additional training for its fighter pilots. The six T-33As, audio-visual training aids, C-11A trainer, and lectures were employed to improve pilots' flying ability and reduce winter flying accidents.

New ground power units, GPUs A-3A and C-22, were finally received in 1954. These GPUs were essential for starting the F-86Fs, but the wing experienced a very high failure rate, and a parts shortage developed since no parts were available from Chateauroux. Many man-hours were required to keep these units operational. One fighter squadron had thirteen GPUs assigned but only three in commission. Three GPU mechanics were authorized, but none were assigned for nine months. MA-2 truck power units were on order, but were not delivered because they did not appear on the 48th's authorization list. The Unit Authorization List did not allow the special test equipment needed for the gunsight and radar. Also, the three FBSqs and the field maintenance squadron had a grave shortage of test equipment for UHF Comm, IFF, and -60 radar beacon sets. The -60 radar beacons had to be trucked to Laon AB for calibration. Once again, supply directives prohibited maintaining the unit's mission equipment. When new aircraft support equipment arrived from the depots, some critical parts were missing, such as drive belts, high pressure valves, switches, and gauges, making equipment unusable. New electronic test equipment was received from the depot damaged and inoperative. Maintenance personnel suspected sabotage but no investigations were conducted by the OSI. No one seemed to care about technical problems. The Wing Material Officer was extremely frustrated with operating conditions at Chaumont.

The wing's ground power unit problem was finally solved in 1956 with arrival from CONUS of the MA-1 self-propelled starting trucks to replace the older A-3As and C-22s. After transmission modifications the MA-1 proved to be an excellent GPU and aircraft prime mover.

In October 1954 the 389th FBSq arrived at Chaumont; it was a TAC rotational squadron from the 366th FBWg at Alexandria AFB, Louisiana, flying F-86Fs. The 389th departed six months later, on 26 March, after completing theater and country familiarization flying. Next, in May 1955, the 613th FBSq arrived from the 401st FBWg at England AFB, Louisiana, flying F-84Fs. It remained until 25 September 1955 when replaced by the 612th FBSq from the same wing. Supporting these TDY squadrons put an extra workload on the under-manned 48th Wing. Twelve to fourteen C-124s were used to move one squadron with minimum personnel and equipment to support this rotational concept. This was the first test of rotational fighters to evaluate the concept for France, and it was considered a success. What USAF leaders forgot was that these squadrons arrived at a fully active air base with a fighter wing present, not an air base that was in standby status!

The 48th had an extremely busy year in 1955; each squadron had thirty F-86Fs and thirty-six pilots assigned, and a large amount of flying time programmed for training. One 2d LT pilot flew 83 hours during one month. Total wing F-86 flying time for the first half of 1955 was 1,203 hours in January, 1,453 in February, 2,927 hours in March, 2,933 hours in April, and 2,415 hours in May and June. Over the six months, 73 percent or more of the ninety F-86s were kept in commission.

In January 1955, four pilots in F-86Fs were detached to RAF Prestwick to brief and lead the 21st and 388th FBWgs to their new bases. All 21st and 388th pilots ended up going to bases in France and Germany other than their original destinations. These diversions, described in chapters 7 and 11, were caused by Chambley and Etain Air Bases not being ready for jet aircraft.

Also in January, the Suippes Gunnery Range in France was made available to the 48th for air-to ground gunnery, and low altitude glide bombing only. This very convenient range was located northeast of the town of Suippes, about 27 miles east of Reims and 60 miles north of Chaumont. It was used by all USAFE fighter wings based in France. During February and March, the 48th began using another air-to-ground gun and rocket range at Epigny, near Dijon, France, but very poor winter weather reduced firings because of limited visibility. Range visibility had to be excellent for live firings; USAFE did not want a French farm and its livestock destroyed because of mistaken landmarks. This would not cement good relation with our NATO host! At 1,000 feet and 350 miles per hour, most French real estate looks very similar, even on a clear day, so many dry runs were made on the ranges prior to live firings.

Intensive armament training commenced in January 1955; the on-base F-86F Mobile Training Unit began teaching the MA-3 FCS to newly arrived gunsight mechanics. Additional technical training on the A-4 gunsight was presented at Chaumont by a tech rep from AC Spark Plug Division, General Motors. A second tech rep at Chaumont from Minneapolis-Honeywell Regulator Corp conducted lectures and hands-on training for the M-1 LABS toss-bombing computer. A special weapons school was set up on base for training armament personnel in F-86F/Mk-7 bomb handling and loading; a two-week bomb loading course was taught for load crewmembers. Each squadron formed four to six load crews and extensive loading practice was conducted when F-86Fs and Mk-7 shapes were available. Special weapons delivery training was conducted at Wheelus in May and June for the wing fighter pilots in addition to air-to-air gunnery. Both low and high altitude toss bombing was practiced using the bombing computer. In late 1954, all fighter squadron personnel had begun the process of obtaining Top Secret clearances and flight line badges to be associated with the F-86F Special Weapons (nuclear) program. The process required about four months. The 48th began the Zulu Alert program in September 1955 deploying to Furstenfeldbruck AB.

On 29 March 1955 at Wheelus, the 494th FBSq set a USAFE record of one hundred air-to-air gunnery sorties in a single day. Some pilots, including the squadron commander, flew five gunnery missions on that day. The squadron logged 1,001 hours of flying on a total of 898 sorties, averaging forty flying hours per pilot over the twenty days from 11 to 31 March. F-86F failures were minimal; armament systems, including the A-4 gunsight, functioned extremely well. This was considered excellent squadron training for the wartime mission surges required of a fighter-bomber wing.

Chaumont became the host base for the AFCENT Weapons Meets held in 1955, 1957, and 1959. Many NATO nations entered fighter and bomber teams to compete for the title of Best Gunnery Team in Central Europe. Chaumont was busy hosting a wide variety of fighters: F-84s, F-86s F-100s, F-104s, Canadair Sabres, Swifts, Hunters, and Canberras. This was the 'best of times' for fighter pilots based in Europe!

Escape and evasion exercises were conducted for Chaumont's fighter pilots; a few pilots attended USAFE's special E&E school at Bad Tolz, Germany. The attendees passed on this training to their fellow pilots. In May 1955, the 493d Squadron traded places with an RCAF fighter squadron from Grostenquin for two weeks; vital operational and maintenance ideas were traded.

June, July, and August 1955 saw the 48th participate in two NATO exercises CARTE BLANCHE and VAPOR TRAILS. CARTE BLANCHE was a maximum flying effort with 4ATAF and included the wing's first deployment to its DOB at Chenevieres, and the 494th's flying their first field exercise at Sechault DOB. VAPOR TRAILS was an air defense exercise to defend SAC air bases in Spain and required the 48th and 50th Fighter-Bomber Wings to deploy to Bordeaux-Merignac AB for three weeks and operate from a bare base. Detailed after action reports were prepared and forwarded to USAFE; many lessons were learned about the DOB concept and how the fundamental shortage of vehicles, equipment, and personnel affected such deployments.

Fighter and reconnaissance wings in France had a 7th Army Ground Liaison Officer (GLO) assigned to coordinate air-ground tactical air support missions with army ground forces. The GLO team based at Chaumont had one Major and five soldiers during 1954-56. The Army's 97th Signal Battalion supplied the necessary long-range radio TTY sets to communicate with combat Corps or Divisions in Germany for air support requests and post strike reports.

All eight T-33As were transferred from the 492d FSq to the 48th Air Base Group's Base Flight along with all support equipment and trained T-33 mechanics.

Bombing training was slipping in fall of 1955. The squadrons had a problem with T-1 bomb racks. All were badly worn, and many were inoperative, with no replacements or repair parts available in USAFE; 70 percent of COM/NAV radio repair parts were back-ordered and not available for 120 days. During the last half of 1955, severe shortages of maintenance personnel and aircraft parts forced the three squadrons to place twelve F-86s in flyable storage for five months. Many Sabres were grounded throughout USAFE because of a shortage of J-47-GE-27 jet engines. Flying time for each fighter squadron during this time varied from 420 to 680 hours per month.

All the budget and personnel reductions across USAFE finally rendered the wing almost incapable of performing its mission. The wing had learned to do "more and more with less and less," until it was expected to do everything with nothing. The most important wing function, delivery of nuclear weapons, was being degraded by lack of training aids, test equipment, publications, and handling equipment for the Mk-7 and Mk-12 weapons. None of this material required for combat and for training pilots and load crews was delivered from Chateauroux, everything was on back order from the CONUS depot with no estimated delivery dates. The Mk-12 was the first supersonic special weapon shape, and was lighter and smaller than the Mk-7 weapon. But, the Mk-12 training shapes were so badly damaged and worn from excessive handling that load training had to cease until depot repair was available. Each fighter squadron had conducted about thirty special loading drills every month to maintain its teams' proficiency. Special weapons tool kits were finally issued to all teams as required by safety regulations, and the F-86Fs had S-3 weapon racks installed to allow rapid aircraft rotation with those on alert at Sembach AB.

Detachment #1, 48th FBWg was established in February 1956 at Sembach AB to support its Zulu Alert mission, replacing Furstenfeldbruck AB. "Fur-

Table 9.2 F-86 Flying Time and In-Commission Rates Jan-June 1956						
	JAN	FEB	MAR	APR	MAY	JUN
Flying Time (hrs)	811	480	1,703	1,843	1,900	1,869
% In Commission	48%	48%	58%	74%	81%	77%

Note: January and February flying hours reflect winter weather and snow removal problems.

sty" was being turned over to the new Luftwaffe. Det. #1 was manned by a team of one hundred officers and airmen selected from the three fighter squadrons, serving in TDY status from Chaumont. This translated into many long periods of absence from families in France. Bomb Commanders and eight F-86Fs were on continuous stand-by alert. The F-86Fs were combat configured with three drop tanks and the special stores pylon installed. At various times the Mk-7 or Mk-12 weapons would be installed on the pylon. These alert facilities were located in Germany because the 1952 diplomatic agreement with France limited nuclear weapons being maintained in alert condition within France. By spring 1956, all fighter wings and the light bomb wing based in France had to set up detachments in Germany to stand Zulu Alert. This negated the fundamental concept of rearward deployment of tactical aircraft into France for survival! Permission was received from National Command Authority (NCA) to fly special weapons on the F-86F under very limited conditions, but very few flights were ever made in Europe with weapons on tactical aircraft.

At this time the new term "Bomb Commander" emerged. A Bomb Commander was an operational-ready pilot who had qualified in gunnery; toss bombing; night MSQ bombing; night low level, no radio, long range cross country flights; and passed written and oral quizzes on six to ten primary and secondary target folders. One interesting aspect of Zulu Alert was the continuing primary and secondary target changes in Eastern Europe. Targets often changed once or twice a month as the Warsaw Pact air forces moved east and west.

The weapon school at Chaumont was training Mk-12 Bomb Commanders and load crews, but attendance was sparse because pilots and airmen were very busy standing Zulu Alert at Sembach or deployed to Wheelus to maintain proficiency in gunnery and toss bombing.

The 492d FBSq deployed twelve F-86s, for three days beginning 18 June, to its DOB Chenevieres with no notice. The wing had developed its mobile shop A3A semi-trailers and was ready to move to a DOB within four hours. This squadron also deployed to Lechfield, West Germany, for twenty days at yet another DOB, 380 miles away. The 48th had gained considerable experience in DOB field operations over the past eighteen months. The wing also began to furnish air police to its new DOB being completed at Brienne-le-Chateau.

After two years of flying F-86Fs it became time for the F-100Ds to arrive in Europe. In January 1956 the wing was notified that conversion to F-100 Super Sabres would begin during the year. Wing Operations prepared a conversion plan; an early step was modifying an old mess hall for an F-100 ground school that began after 1 July. USAFE directed that all F-100C/D conversion training would be conducted in North Africa at Boulhaut AB, Nouasseur AB, and Sidi Slimane AB. Conversion training was conducted at these bases because of their excellent weather and 11,000-foot long runways.

In mid-September 1956 the 48th Fighter-Bomber Wing began converting from their F-86Fs into the F-100D Super Sabre, one squadron at a time. MATS ferry pilots delivered the F-100Ds to the 45th Fighter Day Squadron, Project HI FLIGHT, at Sidi Slimane AB, French Morocco. The F-100s were then transferred to the 48th FBWg as each squadron arrived for training. Ninety-two early model, -10 and -15-NA, Super Sabres were eventually received by the 48th. The extra eighteen Huns became USAFE spares, and some were consumed during conversion training. Conversion required about five months with much of that time spent at Wheelus in gunnery and bombing training. To assist with the conversion, twenty civilian tech reps were assigned to the 48th Wing by Twelfth Air Force. Hun deliveries were behind schedule through December 1956, delaying conversion. Within fourteen months all three F-86 Sabre wings in France, the 48th, 50th, and 388th upgraded to the supersonic F-100D Super Sabre. Squadron maintenance personnel also deployed to Boulhaut to receive more training and maintain the F-100Ds during pilot checkout. The training was conducted by F-100 Mobile Training Units, unfortunately most of the training aids and handouts applied to the F-100C.

Prior to arrival of the F-100 at Chaumont, the wing

commander began an excellent public relations campaign to inform the French citizens about the importance of upgrading NATO's capability with this new fighter. The noise problem was openly described and what procedures would be instituted to mitigate its impact on the communities around the base. When the first F-100D was available, the local political leaders, news media, and general public were welcomed to come on base and witness the aircraft's performance as well as the noise levels. This introduction greatly reduced noise complaints for the next three years; in fact the local French people were not pleased with the 1960 departure of their Statue de la Liberte Wing from France.

While the F-100D conversion was proceeding in North Africa, many activities were taking place in France between July and December 1956. In September, Det #1 moved from Sembach to Hahn AB to fly from a safer airfield for the winter season, and prepare Hahn to receive the F-100Ds for Zulu Alert since the F-100Ds could not operate from Sembach. At Chaumont, the runway had two 1,000-foot extensions added during late 1956, providing 9,900 feet of pavement needed for the F-100. Jet aircraft arresting barriers were added at both ends of the extended runway for safe winter operation. During runway construction the parallel taxiway was used for flight operations, but flying was restricted to daytime flying only, on dry pavement, with less than 10 knots crosswind. The runway extension was completed on 13 December. Meanwhile, both the 493d and 494th Squadrons were training new pilots in the F-86Fs and conducting bombing and gunnery training in France and at Wheelus. These squadrons were flying about 650 hours a month while switching aircraft to and from Det #1 so periodic inspections could be performed. A major workload was the turn-in of all F-86F support equipment, tools, and shop equipment to base supply and then to the depot, so that by the first of the year there would be shop space for all the F-100D equipment. This process left the 48th Wing with no capability to support F-86 operations after 1 February 1957. Bench stocks had to be inventoried to remove all F-86 repair parts. These had to be packed and turned into base supply. Then over 17,000 items had to be stocked for the F-100D. Only 10,560 line items had been needed for routine F-86F maintenance. A new liquid oxygen plant, a larger firing-in-butt, a new relocated engine test cell, and three engine trim pads with proper tie-downs had to be constructed. These projects were being developed by the 48th AI Squadron design engineering and being procured by the Wing Contracting Office. Two more escape and evasion exercises were conducted that included prisoner interrogation after capture, about two thirds of the pilots evaded capture during the four days. In the middle of all this activity, forty-seven freight carloads of PSP runway matting appeared at the rail siding and had to be unloaded without a crane. Storing PSP on base took considerable effort from the Installations and Transportation Squadrons. Some of the PSP was used to make two 1,000-foot overruns at the Brienne DOB.

The 492d Squadron was first to deliver its F-86 Sabres to the Chateauroux depot. During 1958, many F-86Fs from the 48th, 50th, and 388th FBWgs delivered to CAMAE were sent to Dassault Aircraft at Bordeaux for depot IRAN, but no record remains of these Sabres. It appears they were salvaged at Merignac.

Throughout the conversion program the wing had to keep eight F-86Fs on Zulu Alert in Germany. But, by 1 January 1957, eight F-100Ds were in place at Hahn AB standing Zulu Alert with qualified Bomb Commanders. The F-100Ds had new radios and armament systems including four M-24 20mm cannons; but had the same A-4 Gunsight and APG-30 Radar Set, now known as the MA-3 Fire Control System. The major upgrades were the new MA-2 toss bombing computer, an improved autopilot, a new lighter UHF radio set, and enhanced IFF/SIF transponder.

Next in 1957, the 48th received twenty block -25-NA and -45-NHs with improved nuclear delivery capabilities. Its older block -10s and -15 Huns were cycled through depot overhaul in Spain and delivered to France, Denmark, and Turkey to upgrade their air forces.

Eighteen months later, forty newer block -85-NH and -90-NA Super Sabres were delivered to the 48th Wing. This final version of the F-100D was retained for sixteen years until 15 April 1972 when replaced with F-4Ds Phantoms at RAF Lakenheath. The last delivery of Huns was thirteen new two-place F-100F-15-NAs in 1958. These were much needed for new pilot training and instrument flight checkouts. The F model was capable of being placed on Zulu Alert but seldom used for that mission, as training was always its primary duty.

World events during this time required additional security measures at all 48th Wing locations, first the Suez Canal Crisis, and then the Hungarian Revolt which could have resulted in WWIII. Even the base school busses were assigned an armed guard when traveling about the countryside picking up and dropping off children at the American School in Village Layafette. Terrorism against dependents was a great

F-100D from 48th Tactical Fighter Wing Chaumont at V-E Day airshow at Chambley AB, 1957.
Al Christensen

concern of the wing commander.

As directed by USAFE, Headquarters, 48th Fighter-Bomber Group was inactivated on 8 December 1957 to reduce military manpower. Direct operational control of the three fighter squadrons was now the responsibility of the wing's Director of Operations. Seven months later on 8 July 1958, the 48th Fighter-Bomber Wing was redesignated the 48th Tactical Fighter Wing and its three squadrons changed to tactical fighter squadrons. This worldwide change was directed by Headquarters, USAF affecting all tactical fighter squadrons and wings.

Nuclear weapon toss bombing training predominated at the Wheelus ranges, and air-to-air gunnery was greatly reduced. Air-to-air air defense operations are not even mentioned in the wings mission statement. Toss bombing scores continued to improve as the Bomb Commanders set records; typically the 48th pilots were coming within a circular error of 1,400 feet in the LABS mode and 900 feet error in the HABS mode at near sonic deliveries. This may appear as a large distance from the target to most readers, but with the Mk-7 or Mk-12 having a 20,000 Ton or greater yield this miss distance is very acceptable. The toss bombing computers were now doing their job, when maintained by trained airmen using proper support equipment. The squadrons, with twenty-four F-100D/Fs and thirty-two assigned and six attached pilots, were now averaging 1,300 hours of flying per month over the whole year. Attached pilots from Wing and Group HQ jobs were also Bomb Commanders and stood alert duties at Hahn.

On 1 August 1958, the 48th Tactical Fighter Wg reported the following personnel strength: Officers 263, Airmen 1,807, Indigenous Civilians 281, for a total of 2,351 men and women. These numbers do not include the base support units, Det #4, 12th Air Postal Sq; Det #8, 31st Weather Sq (MATS); Det #2, 1952d AACS Sq (MATS); and the F-100D Mobile Training Detachment (Air Training Command).

The wing was reorganized for the new AFM 66-1 Maintenance Management Program in 1958. On 20 October the 48th Maintenance and Supply Group was deactivated and all aircraft maintenance was shifted to wing level. The 48th Field Maintenance Squadron was also deactivated and reorganized as the 48th Consolidated Aircraft Maintenance Squadron, CAMRON. The 48th Armament and Electronics Maintenance Squadron was activated on 15 November and all airborne electronics, autopilot, and aircraft armament specialists from the fighter squadrons were assigned to this A&E MATRON. It was authorized 6 officers and 183 airmen. The fighter squadrons lost all aircraft maintenance specialists; engine, hydraulic, electrical, instrument, and fuel technicians to CAMRON. All aircraft periodic inspections were now conducted by the 48th CAMRON's 9 officers and 332 airmen. The three tactical fighter squadrons were reduced to thirty-four officers (pilots) and fifty-five airmen (a line chief, four flight chiefs, thirty-six crew chiefs, and clerks). AFM 66-1 resulted in many accounting reports and tons of IBM punch cards; data collection and reporting dominated the maintenance shops. This reorganization of aircraft maintenance was USAF wide and affected all combat wings in France.

A B-45, #47-054, was flown into Chaumont in summer 1958 from RAF Sculthorpe. After many parts were removed it was designated a Class 26 (Training Aids) airframe. The Tornado was burned on base for fire fighter training. Many photos were taken which leads people to believe B-45s were based at Chaumont but none ever were.

Det #1 at Hahn was redesignated 48th Tactical Fighter Wing Operating Location #1 on 11 April 1958. It was manned by three officers and fifty-two airmen with eight to sixteen TDY Bomb Commanders standing alert duty. Det #1, 48th ABGp was activated on 1 August 1958 to maintain and operate Brienne-le-Chateaux DOB which was 80 percent completed. It had three officers, eighty airmen, and eight LWR civilians. Det #2, 48th ABGp operated Chalons-Vatry DOB with three officers, seventy-five airmen, and four LWR civilians. Thus the 48th Wing became responsible for two of the four completed DOBs.

All flying moved to Brienne-le-Chateaux from September through December while Chaumont's runway and taxiways were repaired and resealed for a third time. Runway lighting equipment and wiring was replaced, and new high intensity approach lights were installed for Runway 01. As fighter squadrons returned from Wheelus or Hahn they flew into Brienne and returned home for the holidays on 15 December 1958; this was the first time the wing was together at Chaumont since starting the F-100 conversion program in September 1957. Many pilots were in TDY status for over 210 days during 1958; the wear and tear on families was beginning to affect morale in the fighter squadrons. Over these sixteen months; twenty F-100Ds, one L-20A, and one T-33A crashed. Only seven lives were lost, four of them in the L-20A. Well maintained ejection systems and parachutes saved seventeen pilots, a few of whom ended up in the Mediterranean Sea. During 1958, approximately 80 officers and 730 airmen rotated back to CONUS, 44 airmen reenlisted to remain longer in France.

The use of the DOBs increased during 1959. The 493d TFSq was dispatched to Brienne in March and April 1959 where it conducted operations during additional runway resurfacing at Chaumont. The 492d and 494th deployed to Chalons-Vatry during this same period. Base civil engineers were convinced that the complete runway must be removed and replaced by a new twenty-inch thick concrete runway and project funds were requested, to no avail. The squadrons returned to Brienne and Chalons DOBs in May for ten days so that the runway and taxiways could be marked and painted completing the repair project. All deployments to the DOBs and Operating Location #1 placed wing personnel in TDY status requiring the 48th Air Base Gp Comptroller to process over 2,000 travel vouchers for payment. Fiscal year 1959 Operations and Maintenance Funds for Chaumont AB and the two DOBs were $4,547,900.00.

Each fighter squadron continued flying an average of 700 to 800 hours per month through 1959, but only a detachment of each squadron deployed to Wheelus rather than the complete squadron. This reduced the total annual TDY days and kept Bomb Commanders available for alert duty. The 493d TFSq achieved its goal of having every pilot including the commander, operations officer, and maintenance officer qualified as operationally ready Bomb Commanders. Summer saw the introduction of the new Mk-28 nuclear weapon for the F-100D; the Mk-28 was carried on a centerline fuselage pylon. This allowed increased range because a fourth external fuel tank had been added. The greatest Mk-28 improvement was its nuclear yield; it was three or four times greater than the Mk-7. Usually a squadron had two or three Huns at CASA, Getafe AB, Spain for depot TCTO work, two or three on Zulu Alert at Hahn, and four at Wheelus to maintain pilot bombing qualifications. The 494th TFSq achieved 100 percent of their F-100s in commission for the first time, and flew more than 800 hours in the month of March during an ORI. CAMRON completed twenty-five periodic dock inspections in the month of April for a new record of support to the fighter squadrons. Each squadron possesssed a mix of F-100 fighters, blocks -10s, -45s, -85s, -90s, and four F models.

The new Armament & Electronics Squadron was developing rapidly to support the wing, especially its Special Weapons Section. It designed a bomb sling that permitted safe ground test of the emergency jettison of a loaded special weapon. This procedure had to be tested periodically on the aircraft. It performed exactly as intended and the design was submitted for USAF approval. Operational flying made F-100Ds scarce for load crew training, so the section obtained a left wing from a crashed Hun and developed it into a training aid, including all electrical circuits. The section had all its weapon load crews trained without tying-up an in-commission F-100D.

Emphasis was placed on getting the new APW-11 MSQ beacon into operation, a ground test system was fabricated, and every system could be tested prior to an Applecore mission. This resulted in 97 percent of the MSQ missions accomplished, a new ORI record in USAFE. Several radio repairmen and armament electronics repairmen were requested to cross-train into the new USAF Test Equipment Repair and Calibration career field to meet current USAF test and measuring equipment improvement programs. The new test equipment repair and calibration section began its work in June and produced results immediately. Several items of equipment arrived with parameters that were in error by 10 to 15 percent. Their test equipment work was rated "excellent" by a USAFE inspection team. By the summer of 1959 the new AFM 66-1 maintenance reorganization was functioning very well, the F-100Ds were flying their authorized time allocations, 80 percent of wing pilots were rated as "operationally ready Bomb Commanders," and the base had achieved its best condition for all personnel, including family housing off base. The last units in Village Pershing were accepted in September. The only major problem on base was JP4 jet fuel detected in the water system; engineering teams from Seventeenth Air Force and civilian companies from France and Germany could not identify the source of fuel leakage and isolate the fault. Finally, by October 1959 the experts agreed the problem was occurring off base, which meant it went unsolved.

But a greater problem was developing for Chaumont Air Base and the 48th. The Wing Commander was informed on 1 July 1959, that Project RED RICHARD was activated. France would not permit the U.S. to store nuclear weapons on their soil, therefore all nuclear capable fighter wings had to relocate. After eight years of operations at Chaumont-Semoutieres AB, the 48th TFWg had to leave. USAFE first considered deactivating the wing in place on 31 December 1959. Next, some consideration was given to moving it to Spain. The 48th would have preferred to move into West Germany, but there was no space in Germany because the 49th TFWg had been ordered to Spangdahlem AB, and the 50th TFWg was going back to Hahn. Sembach was useless for F-100D operations. It was finally decided to relocate the wing to RAF Lakenheath, UK. It was unoccupied, and its 9,000-foot runway had been repaired in 1956. On 7 August, USAFE issued a movement order to the 48th to proceed to RAF Lakenheath by 15 October, but this order was canceled on 25 August. CAMRON and A&E MATRON had sent advanced parties and equipment to Lakenheath, but in order to provide minimum aircraft support, equipment was airlifted back to Chaumont and the airmen retuned to Chaumont in TDY status. Later, orders were received delaying the move ninety days until 15 January 1960. Organizing such a move in ninety-days was difficult enough, but the 48th also had to maintain full alert capability at Operating Location #1 until the current crisis in Berlin was resolved.

The first actions taken were stopping the arrival of new personnel, freezing dependent travel from CONUS, terminating all base improvement plans, canceling existing contracts, reducing the French workforce, and halting local routine procurements. Each unit provided estimates of its shipping requirements to the 48th Transportation Sq. All equipment, supplies, and vehicles were removed from both DOBs and returned to Chaumont. The 48th began moving personnel and supplies to England in September. By 1 October about 1,850,000 pounds were moved by military airlift, and 1,000,000 pounds by surface carriers; these quantities doubled by 1 January 1960.

On 12 November the 48th TFWg supported OPERATION SPEARHEAD, another show of force during the ongoing Berlin tensions. This was the arrival of seventy-two F-100Ds, a TAC Composite Air Strike Force from Clovis AFB, New Mexico, and Myrtle Beach AFB, South Carolina, for a stay of three weeks. The strike force required twenty vehicles from the 48th during their stay, in addition to forklifts and flat bed trailers, to unload sixty-five cargo aircraft arriving with all the CASF support equipment. The same support was needed three weeks later when the squadrons departed. Even the 48th Wing Commander was surprised by this F-100 deployment. One F-100D squadron had GAR-8 Sidewinder air-to-air missiles, and requested support on these missiles even though no one at Chaumont had ever seen one before!

Not all the 48th Wing personnel were needed at Lakenheath because some SAC people stayed there to complete their overseas tours of duty. The ABGp and squadrons moved only some personnel until the precise requirements at Lakenheath were known. Many support troops remained at Chaumont until their three-year tour of duty was completed. A few single airmen were offered early separation from the USAF and departed for CONUS. Some airmen were transferred to other bases in France to fill vacancies.

The Armament and Electronics Squadron historian summed up this period from 1 July until 31 December 1959 as, "one of intense confusion and almost complete disruption as far as personnel and supplies are concerned, with little relief in immediate sight."

Responsibility for Detachment #1, HQ, 48th Air Base Group at Brienne-le-Chateau and Detachment #2, HQ, 48th Air Base Group at Chalons-Vatry was assigned to the 7544th Support Group at Toul. USAFE directed that the DOBS would not be maintained and would be returned to France during 1960.

The 48th Wing consisted of three tactical fighter squadrons, the 492d, 493d, and 494th, flying seventy-four F-100D/F Super Sabres plus seven T-33As and two C-47A support aircraft when officially transferred on 15 January 1960 from Chaumont to RAF Lakenheath, APO 179, and assigned to the Third Air Force. Project RED RICHARD had forced the movement, and wing personnel were not happy to relocate to England and into substandard facilities compared to those finally achieved at Chaumont, but the Statue of Liberty Wing was destined for an unbelievable stay of forty-four years flying fighters at RAF Lakenheath, and still resides there in 2005.

After departure of the 48th TFWg from Chaumont, the base reverted to a standby operating base reduced to minimum manning. All real estate improvements and communications upgrades were stopped. About two hundred French employees had to be terminated as operating costs were reduced. French contractors continued to maintain the base infrastructure, but at reduced levels. Chaumont became a satellite base of Toul, and was supported by the 7544th Combat Support Group. It remained idle for twenty months with only an occasional transient aircraft visitor. But, the 1961 Berlin Wall Crisis demanded its immediate operational use, and Chaumont became a busy USAFE installation for two more years.

108th Tactical Fighter Wing

The 108th Tactical Fighter Wing (Day) (Special Delivery), New Jersey ANG, based at McGuire AFB, since 1954 was ordered to federal active duty for one year on 1 October 1961 in response to the Berlin Crisis. Approximately 235 officers and 2,280 airmen were assigned to the wing. When activated, the wing consisted of three fighter squadrons and supporting units: the 119th TFSq based at Atlantic City Airport, New Jersey; the 141st TFSq at McGuire AFB, New Jersey; and the 149th TFSq at Byrd Field; Sandston, Virginia. All three fighter squadrons had been flying Republic F-84F Thunderstreaks since the summer of 1958.

The 108th Tactical Fighter Wing began on 30 September 1942 as the WWII 348th Fighter Group. It flew P-47 Thunderbolts on long-range shipping interdiction missions with the Fifth Air Force in the Southwest Pacific earning, two DUCs in New Britain and the Philippines. The 348th Fighter Group was redesignated the 108th Fighter Group and alloted to the New Jersey Air National Guard on 24 May 1946 during the creation of the ANG. The 108th Gp inherited the insignia, and lineage of the 348th Fighter Group. The 108th Fighter Group expanded into the 108th Fighter-Bomber Wing in November 1950.

Only a portion of the 108th Tactical Fighter Wing moved to France in 1961 because of defense budget limitations. This consisted of 118 officers and 905 airmen, with one fighter squadron, the 141st TFSq. A reduced HQ, 108th TFWg remained at McGuire to command the 119th and 149th Squadrons and support units remaining on extended active duty at their ANG bases, ready to reinforce the 7108th TFWg at Chaumont within five days.

Since the overall concept of Project STAIR STEP was provided in chapter 5, only a brief description of the activities of the 7108th Tactical Wing operating at Chaumont AB should be necessary. The wing took twenty-six F-84Fs, two T-33As and one C-47 to Chaumont. In addition to the normal activity required to prepare for deployment to France, TAC decided that all STAIR STEP squadrons' F-84Fs and RF-84Fs would gather at McGuire AFB, a foreign clearing station, and move as one large wing. The 108th Wing at McGuire provided maintenance support for all 104 F-84Fs and 20 RF-84Fs as they arrived on 25 October, prior to departure for Europe.

The first element to depart McGuire was the 108th ADVON consisting of twelve officers and ninety-nine airmen; they departed on 16 October and arrived at Chaumont the next day. By 27 October 1961, all F-84Fs departed McGuire for Harmon AB, Newfoundland. Departing Lages AB, the 141st TFSq flew into Moron AB, near Sevilla, Spain. Then on 3 November, twenty Thunderstreaks flew direct to Chaumont; the last six fighters arrived on 6 November. Immediately upon arrival, the Thunderstreaks were inspected and loaded with .50 cal ammunition for their air defense alert mission.

The main body of troops moved by MATS aircraft, arriving between 12 and 15 November. The wing's C-47 and two T-33As flew the North Atlantic route arriving at Chaumont on 17 November. By 19 November 1961, the 108th Tactical Fighter Wing had assembled at the newly reopened Chaumont AB for an estimated stay of ten months. The 108th TFWg Deputy Commander for Operations, COL Joseph B. Zink was assigned as the 7108th Tactical Wing Commander at Chaumont from 20 October 1961 to 17 August 1962. On 23 November, the 108th TFWg

F-84F conventional weaponry on display at a Chaumont Open House, 1962
NIcholas Scafidi

was redesignated the 7108th Tactical Wing due to its reduced strength in France.

The STAIR STEP move was very rapid because there were no dependents or privately owned vehicles allowed to move with these activated reservists. The wing organization included: HQ, 108th Tactical Fighter Wing; 141st Tactical Fighter Sq; 108th Armament & Electronics Maintenance Sq; 108th Consolidated Aircraft Maintenance Sq; HQ, 108th Air Base Gp; 108th Operations Sq; 108th Air Police Sq; 108th Civil Engineering Sq; 108th Supply Sq; 108th Transportation Sq; and the 108th Tactical Hospital.

The tenant units on Chaumont AB when the 108th Wing arrived were: Det #3, 7544th Combat Support Gp from Toul AB; Det #4, 12th Air Postal Sq; Det #8, 31st Weather Sq; Det #2, 1952d AACS Sq; Flt "D" 8th Radio Relay Sq; and Company "C" 62d Engineer Bn (Construction) from the Toul Army Depot.

On 31 December 1961, the 7108th was manned by 120 officers, 955 airmen, and 68 French civilians. Total authorized manning of a USAFE F-84F STAIR STEP wing was, 131 officers and 1,130 airmen. The 7108th Wing was manned at an overall 86 percent level with primary shortages being air policemen, civil engineers and supply specialists. This was a common USAF manning level for combat wings in the late 1950s. Officer personnel in the 7108th now consisted of ANG officers, and Regular Air Force and Air Force Reserve officers. Enlisted ranks were made up of Air Guardsman, Regular Air Force, and Air Force Reserve selective assignees, plus local French base employees. All units and personnel merged into smoothly working squadrons and sections to make the air base operational and comfortable for the forthcoming winter season. Hiring local French civilian employees was a not a problem at Chaumont; eighty-nine positions were authorized and sixty-three LWRs were employed by 1 December 1961. These civilians were primarily former base employees that had worked for the 48th TFWg as late as December 1959. The city of Chaumont was only four miles away so the workers had few problems reaching their jobs. These employees brought a large amount of job knowledge back with them, and all could speak English, which was of great assistance.

By 16 November the first F-84F flying commenced, and aircraft maintenance began setting up their shops preparing for inspections and repair work; most shop equipment was still enroute but limited capability was available to support flying. During late November supplies and equipment began arriving by the trainload; 440-tons of equipment had been surfaced shipped from New Jersey to France. Many tons that had been ordered after 1 October 1961 also arrived from CONUS depots. Army trucks delivered vast quantities of conventional munitions that greatly exceeded base storage capacity. By February 1962, about 6,000 tons had arrived and posed a hazard to all base personnel. Munitions storage construction started on 15 August 1961.

The 7108th passed its USAFE Tactical Evaluation on the initial try, 6 to 8 February 1962, and earned an excellent rating from the Seventeenth Air Force inspection team. The wing's second major test was their no notice ORI conducted on 8 to13 March 1962 by HQ USAFE. They successfully passed this inspection on the first evaluation also.

The 7108th Tactical Wing and 141st TFSq air operations at Chaumont AB were almost identical to the other three F-84F STAIR STEP Wings in France. The wing was continually tasked to support Seventeenth Air Force and NATO exercises throughout its stay at Chaumont, and met every air tasking order when weather permitted. Flying safety was paramount when conducting low level missions. During its eleven months of active duty, the 141st TFSq flew 2,811 F-84F sorties for 5,938 hours, and lost one pilot and two F-84Fs in France.

Operations GUN TALK, COLD TURKEY, and CABIN CRUISER were continuous air defense exercises conducted in Central Europe. The 141st would furnish up to twenty F-84F sorties a day to support these exercises. Operation INDIAN SUMMER tested Seventeenth Air Forces air defenses in northern France; F-84Fs based in Spain flew north into the Laon, Metz, and Saarbrucken areas to simulate a strike force.

Operation BIG STICK developed the control and coordination skills of the 152d Tactical Radar Stations in southern Germany with fighter-bomber units flying close air support missions. The 152d command skills improved rapidly with this realistic training.

GRAND SLAM II was a Fourth Allied Tactical Air Force exercise between 4 and 16 May. This was a simulated wartime test of Disaster Control, Non-Combatant Evacuation Order and Hospital Evacuation plus the Automatic Aircraft Launch Program. Overall the new 108th Wing Combat Operations Center (COC) functioned very well and every exercise improved command and control proficiency. The only problem was the shortage of people to man the COC around the clock; some men had to work fourteen-hour shifts. New communications systems proved successful after expansion.

The 7108th's primary mission was to provide close air support to the Seventh Army in Europe under the direction of Ground Forward Air Controllers. To accomplish this mission of close air support, Operation HENNY PENNY, sometimes thirty sorties a day were flown by the squadron when weather permitted. Usually four sorties daily were scheduled against Seventh Army ground targets. One fighter pilot rotated every fifteen days with Army units in Germany for FAC training. U.S. Seventh Army division commanders were very pleased with the close air support training provided by the 141st during LONG THRUST II in Germany. During 1962, the tactical wing flew a total of 228 sorties for 445 hours to develop its close air support skills. Six pilots found time to attend the two-week Air Ground Operations School conducted by the Seventeenth Air Force at Ramstein.

The 141st Squadron flew a total of 4,261 hours in 2,121 sorties the first six months of 1962; of these, 694 hours were actual weather instrument flying. There were two deployments to Wheelus, the first 17 February to 31 March, to escape the poor winter flying conditions of France and accomplish air-to-air gunnery, as well as meeting other flying requirements. A second trip during 13 May to 23 June 1962 concentrated on conventional weapons bombing and air-to-ground gunnery. Twenty-seven out of thirty 141st pilots became qualified in weapons proficiency for the year. Air-to-ground gunnery, rocket firing, and dive bombing was conducted at the Suippes range. Two armament airmen went to Suippes Bomb Range to act as bomb spotters for scoring.

On 9 January 1962 eight F-84F pilots arrived from the 119th and 149th CONUS based fighter squadrons to fly local orientation missions, review war plans, and integrate into the 141st TFSq. Some of the fighter squadron pilots had to serve in wing positions to meet all the exercises and alerts. Most importantly, the pilots took these thirty days of experience back to their squadrons at Atlantic City and Richmond to teach them USAFE operational procedures. It was important that these fighter units would be ready to support operations immediately upon arrival in France if needed. Later in March and April twenty more pilots from CONUS arrived for this theater indoctrination and each pilot flew ten or more hours in French and West German airspace.

The 106th Tactical Reconnaissance Squadron from the 7117th Tactical Wing at Dreux AB spent all of its time in France flying from Chaumont. The 7108th TWg supported the 106th in an outstanding manner. The 7117th was another ANG wing called to active duty for the Berlin Wall crisis, but was prevented from flying its RF-84Fs at Dreux. A detailed description of the 106th TRSq activities at Chaumont AB is contained in chapter 10. The support provided by the 7108th was equivalent to having a second flying squadron in the wing. Det #1, 117th Tactical Wing and 106th TRSq had 32 officers and 260 airmen with twenty RF-84Fs at Chaumont. The 117th did supply additional troops whenever possible to assist operations at Chaumont while keeping Dreux active. The 106th remained at Chaumont until its departure for CONUS in July 1962.

The 108th Transportation Squadron operated the 324 vehicles in use on base. The 48th Wing had left a fleet of many new vehicles that were delivered just prior to their departure for RAF Lakenheath. The 108th Wing brought a well trained vehicle repair section from ANG status, and had the lowest Vehicle Deadlined for Parts (VDP) rates of all air bases in France. The only vehicles that presented problems for alerts and exercises were the F-6 and F-7 aircraft refueling units. These units were frequently out of commission due to a serious shortage of repair parts from depot sources. During the first six months of 1962, F-6 and F-7 refueling units transferred 3,600,000 gallons of fuel received from the NATO pipeline on base to the F-84Fs and transient aircraft. The Transportation Sq was also busy during the winter 1961-62 keeping the runway, taxiways, and roads cleared of snow and ice so that the alert aircraft could respond to scramble orders.

The 7108th Tactical Wing acquired the job of managing $850,000 new construction and property renovation from the 7544th Support Group. USAFE authorized funds for Chaumont upon receiving notice that it would be reactivated as a main operating base. Twenty-two STAIR STEP projects were begun, and 75 percent were completed by 1 July 1962, to improve the conventional war capability of Chaumont. Most of this major construction was accomplished using French contractors. Some projects were completed by Company "C" 62d Engineer Battalion that was working on base prior to arrival of the 7108th Wing. These projects consisted of construction of six Butler type hangars, a jet engine shop, a large outdoor supply storage area with security fencing, sixteen improved munitions storage igloos and ammunition shop building, a liquid oxygen plant, repairs to aircraft hangar doors and roofs, airfield pavement joint sealing, six aircraft maintenance docks, and base electrical system repairs. A few of the 1961 improvements had been designed by the 48th Civil Engineer but were canceled in 1959. A total of $730,000 dollars was committed in 1961 because the project packages had been saved and were ready to be submitted immediately. Many buildings were improved by their occupants through "Self Help" projects; the civil engineering squadron provided tools and supplies, and monitored progress.

Two base problems defied civil engineering solutions, first, the ongoing problem of jet fuel contamination of water well #1, where all efforts failed. Next, the very poor operation of the main base voltage regulator. It was causing over-voltage throughout the base and could not be corrected, even after repeated contractor repairs. Major repairs of the heating plant boilers were long overdue, the tube and valve replacement work was done by a contractor.

A very productive aircraft maintenance squadron and A&E maintenance squadron provided high quality support for the F-84Fs; in-commission rates in 1962 averaged 80 percent except for one month. In March an aircraft grounding technical order cut flying to 465 hours for the month. All shops had greatly improved electrical power distribution and installed all shop machinery, which improved aircraft maintenance. Aircraft maintenance data collection was almost zero due to the lack of IBM accounting machines or electrical converters.

Continuous training was required to upgrade wing airmen in their Air Force jobs. Approximately 275 airmen were upgraded in their job skill levels by passing written tests. Finding classroom space was the greatest problem in this training. General Military Training was conducted for most base personnel; small arms marksmanship training for all personnel was only possible after rework of the base firing range. The A&E Sq established an excellent school for aircraft armament loading teams that resulted in the F-84Fs being loaded, with a wide variety of munitions in record times during exercises and alerts.

Serious base security problems were addressed by the 108th Air Police Squadron. From January through April 1962 they had to work many extra hours because the political turmoil in Algeria created unrest in this area of France. Security was increased around the forty-five aircraft, the POL storage area, and ammunition dump because of terriorist threats to U.S. installations. On two occasions unknown people were sighted at 0200hrs close to the ammo dump, but they escaped. Additional air policemen were obtained from Dreux because the 108th APSq was short thirty air police from their authorized strength.

By April 1962 the Berlin Crisis appeared to be settled and rumors spread throughout the base that an early release plan was being considered by DOD for all reserve personnel prior to their obligated date of 31 September 1962. On 7 June, the 7108th Tactical Wing received its first movement order from Seventeenth AF directing the wing to return to CONUS with all personnel, but without their twenty-four F-84Fs. The support C-47 and T-33 aircraft would be flown back to McGuire AFB. The wing would assist in the smooth transition of Chaumont to the newly activated 366th Tactical Fighter Wing. All F-84F support equipment and spare parts would remain on base. All personnel would return to McGuire using MATS airlift for separation from the USAF. Planning began at once by the

Forces of many NATO nations together for the AIRCENT Weapons Meet at Chaumont 1963.
Paul Hammond

wing staff agencies. The 7108th Tactical Wing had to maintain its air defense alert capability until 15 July 1962. Twenty-four F-84Fs assigned to the 7108th Tactical Wing were transferred in place at Chaumont on 15 July to the 366th TFWg, 389th TFSq, USAFE. All tenant units remained in place and were supported by the 366th Wing.

The 7108th Tactical Wing began the movement by preparing a tentative airlift schedule for all personnel; an ADVON would be required to set up a personnel processing system at McGuire AFB and assist the Central Base Personnel Office (CBPO) to process ANG and Air Force Reserve personnel. All AFR selective assignees would fly to McGuire, then be released from active duty and dispatched to their individual homes of record. The main body of the wing would return and be separated as a group from active duty and reassigned back into ANG reserve status. Many individuals remained in the ANG to complete their six year reserve obligation.

The ADVON departed on 3 July on one MATS transport. The return crossing of the North Atlantic with the C-47 and T-33As was a routine operation. The main body of troops departed between 15 and 25 July to return to McGuire via MATS airlift, usually taking two days, stopping in the Azores. Only thirteen tons of equipment were returned to McGuire. Replacement equipment and F-86H Sabres were delivered to the 108th Wing in the six months following their return. On 15 July 1962, the 7108th Wing turned an improved air base over to the 366th Tactical Fighter Wing and departed France. All organizations and personnel from the 108th TFWg were released from active duty by 20 August 1962 and returned to New Jersey and Virginia ANG status.

366th Tactical Fighter Wing

The 366th Tactical Fighter Wing was activated on 8 May 1962 at Chaumont with four tactical fighter squadrons, the 389th, 390th, 391st, and the 480th as part of the Kennedy Administration's expansion of conventional tactical air power to change our national strategy away from "Massive Retaliation" to "Graduated Response." HQ USAF ordered that the 366th TFWg would emerge, after three years of inactivation, from the four STAIR STEP F-84F fighter squadrons about to depart France. France agreed to allow the fighter wing to be based in France using conventional tactical weapons only; no nuclear weapons operations would be permitted. Therefore, the mission of the 366th Wing would be tactical air operations, counter air, interdiction, and close air support using typical fighter ordnance—guns, rockets, bombs, and napalm. USAFE decided that the 366th TFWg would have the additional mission of keeping four fighter air bases: Chambley, Chaumont, Etain, and Phalsbourg in active status ready to receive CASAF forces in the event of another Berlin Crisis.

The 366th Fighter Group was activated on 1 June 1943 as a WWII fighter group that moved through France and Belgium flying P-47s while assigned to the USAAF Ninth Air Force. The 366th Gp earned a DUC while providing close air support near St. Lo, France, and ended their air campaign in Germany as part of the USAFE occupation force. It was inactivated in Fritzlar, Germany August 1946 as part of the post WWII reductions. The 366th Fighter-Bomber Wing was reactivated on 1 January 1953 with F-51Ds at Alexandria AFB, Louisiana. The 366th Tactical Fighter Wing flying F-100Ds was inactivated again on 1 April 1959 as part of the tactical air forces reduction.

The 366th Tactical Fighter Wing was unique in that it was the only tactical fighter wing in USAFE with four squadrons at four different air bases, Chaumont, Phalsbourg, Chambley, and Etain. Wing HQ and the 389th TFSq were based at Chaumont. The 480th TFSq operated at Chaumont until runway and taxiway rebuilding was completed at Phalsbourg on 20 December 1962. The 390th TFSq was based at Chambley, while the 391st TFSq flew from Etain. The 366th was the only USAF fighter wing activated, equipped, and trained in USAFE. It was the last fighter wing to operate in France, and the last USAF wing to fly F-84Fs in Europe. Each fighter squadron flew twenty F-84Fs left to them by the departing ANG units. The wing received twenty-five F-84Fs from both the 166th and 162d TFSqs, the 141st left twenty-four Thunderstreaks, and six were given up by the 110th TFSq. The departing STAIR STEP units left all their F-84F support equipment, spare parts, and shop facilities for immediate use by the 366th. The four STAIR STEP air bases were officially transferred to the 366th TFWg on 16 July 1962.

The 366th was assigned a Combat Support Group to operate each air base and support the fighter squadron. The Combat Support Groups and Material Groups and attached Squadrons were also activated on 8 May 1962. The Deputy Commander for Operations set up three Wing Operations Detachments at each air base: Det #0100 at Chambley, Det #0200 at Etain, and Det #0300 at Phalsbourg. The same activation order established three detachments of the Material Sq and Assistant Chiefs of Maintenance at Chambley, Etain, and Phalsbourg.This action was in agreement with the Dual Deputy organizational concept and AFM 66-1 Maintenance Management. This Dual-Deputy organization produced four independent organizations on each base. The wing commander had to talk with sixteen different unit commanders to determine what problems and solutions were affecting his wing's performance.

This decision to organize, train, and equip a new tactical fighter wing at four separate air bases in France was total stupidity and a waste of resources on the part of HQ USAF and Seventeenth Air Force. All combat wings had well documented, in over ten years of official histories, their loss of combat potential after arriving in France due to poor logistics, personnel shortages, bad flying weather, and inadequate base facilities. The first major problem was logistics, all the supplies and services needed to operate in France were very difficult to obtain. Deliveries had always taken months not weeks. The second major problem was personnel to staff a new wing in France. The USAF had a serious shortage of trained F-84F pilots and mechanics; the plane had been phased out of the USAF inventory since 1958. Married personnel avoided assignments in France with its housing problems. Most troops arriving in France would be first-term enlistment airmen having no, or elementary, job skills. The third problem was the generally poor flying weather for developing new fighter pilots. The fourth problem was the still inadequate living and working facilities at our air bases in France, and the major effort required to keep the bases in operational condition. Air base operation and maintenance required more money, manpower, and management than the aircraft and tactical squadrons. By 1 January 1963, the 366th TFWg had 384 officers, 3,465 airmen, and 446 indigenous French employees, plus French base contractors; more than double the numbers required in the usual tactical fighter wing. This manning was still inadequate to accomplish the wing's mission in France. HQ USAFE never improved the manning levels. All this labor was employed to fly eighty obsolete F-84Fs, that in 1953 were considered to be inferior to the F-86Fs or Hs. The 366th's major limitation was that it would not be trained to, or be capable of, delivering a nuclear weapon while based in France. It is a great tribute to the 366th Wing Commander and NCOs that in spite of all these obstacles this tactical fighter wing survived one year in France.

COL James S. Coward commanded the 366th from 8 May 1962 until 1964. His first task was getting the wing flying and developing some combat proficiency. To accomplish this he needed people. Only thirty officers and sixty NCOs had arrived by 15 June; so when the 3,600 STAIR STEP personnel departed between 12 and 17 July, the wing's combat capability was eliminated. Thirteen operationally ready F-84F pilots and ten NCOs elected to remain on active duty and serve with the 366th. Ninety-five percent of the

Table 9.3 366th Tactical Fighter Wing Units in France	
366th Tactical Fighter Wing, Chaumont AB, APO 119 HQ Squadron, 366th Tactical Fighter Wg Deputy Commander of Operations Deputy Commander of Material 389th Tactical Fighter Squadron 480th Tactical Fighter Squadron (before 12/62) 7366th Material Squadron 7366th Combat Support Gp 366th Tactical Hospital	**7368th Combat Support Gp, Etain AB, APO 87** Det #0200, Wing Operations Det #0200, Material Sq 391st Tactical Fighter Squadron HQ Squadron Section, 7368th Combat Support Gp 7368th Air Police Sq 7368th Material Sq 7368th USAF Dispensary
7367th Combat Support Gp, Chambley AB, APO 247 Det #0100, Wing Operations Det #0100, Material Sq 390th Tactical Fighter Squadron HQ Squadron Section, 7367th Combat Support Gp 7367th Air Police Sq 7367th Material Sq 7367th USAF Dispensary	**7369th Combat Support Gp, Phalsbourg AB, APO 115** Det #0300, Wing Operations Det #0300, Material Sq 480th Tactical Fighter Squadron (after 21 DEC 1962) HQ Squadron Section, 7369th Combat Support Gp 7369th Air Police Sq 7369th Material Sq 7369th USAF Dispensary

arriving pilots had no experience with the F-84F, and many had no fighter aircraft flying time. Personnel were drawn from USAFE and CONUS; some were from the deactivated 47th Bombardment Wing, Tactical, in England and a few were excess troops from Germany. The primary source of manpower was CONUS; it slowly supplied the bulk of officers and airmen on a three-year PCS tour of duty with concurrent dependent travel. Full authorized manning was never achieved while the 366th was based in France. Many people were still arriving in PCS status long after the wing was told by USAF that it would depart France for CONUS.

Development of the 366th's combat capability was planned for C-3 (25 percent operationally ready) by 31 October, C-2 (51 percent operationally ready) on 20 November, and C-1 (75 percent operationally ready) by 26 December 1962. Aircraft systems training was conducted at Chaumont by an Air Training Command F-84F mobile training detachment that was assisted by six Republic Aviation and two Curtiss-Wright tech reps. Training aids, primarily handbooks and manuals were in short supply, but the wing operated one C-11-C Jet Instrument Trainer and one MF-3 (F-84F) Cockpit Procedures Simulator at Chaumont. The wing deployed a permanent training detachment to Wheelus on 27 August and maintained twenty pilots in continuous air-to-ground and air-to-air weapons training. Beginning on 15 October all F-84F transition flying and water survival training was conducted at Wheelus due to the onset of poor flying weather in France. The 366th TFWg flew its first close air support mission on 25 September with two F-84Fs, one flown by the Wing Commander, the second by a former ANG pilot who stayed on active duty. Over the next six months about 300 close air support missions were requested by Seventh Army but at least half were canceled because of bad weather in southern Germany.

In the middle of this intensive pilot upgrade training, the 366th had to respond to the Cuban Missile Crisis, for two weeks on 23 October. The wing was declared "operational ready" by Seventeenth Air Force; over 50 percent of the F-84Fs were placed in alert posture for air defense or interdiction sorties. All aircraft and personnel were recalled back from Libya to their bases in France and prepared to fight WWIII. Targets in Eastern Europe changed rapidly during the Cuban Crisis, requiring the F-84F pilots to attend mission briefings two or three times a day. Two KB-50 tankers deployed to Chaumont, ready to refuel the fighters after they struck their distant targets, though none of the F-84F pilots had practiced a refueling hook-up! On 5 November, after two weeks of alert, wing training and operations returned to normal. F-84F weapons training at Wheelus resumed on 9 November.

USAFE and Seventeenth Air Force did not provide the 366th with a definite mission statement; the wing continued to build on the 7108th Tactical Wing's missions. These were expanded to include the capability to receive and support dual based tactical squadrons from CONUS "additive forces," and be prepared to support Project SHOWBOAT, the USAFE theater-wide dispersal plan. Hangar #5 became the SHOW-

BOAT facility at Chaumont after departure of the 480th Squadron for Phalsbourg on 21 December.

From September through December 1962, 366th War and Emergency operational plans were rewritten to include four fighter squadrons and three additional air bases. These plans were required prior to an Operational Readiness Inspection and Tactical Evaluation. Another important task began—preparing Combat Mission Folders and Target Planning Folders. About fifteen folders for every pilot in a fighter squadron resulted in over 1,200 classified folders requiring continuous updating. The monthly flying hours steadily increased from 71 hours in July to 1,144 hours by December for all four squadrons. The squadrons averaged about 300 hours per month. A lack of trained aircraft maintenance personnel was the main reason for the low flying hours. Maintenance training became more urgent than pilot training.

By 31 December, the 366th had participated in sixteen exercises with Seventeenth Air Force, Seventh Army, and 4ATAF, but the Combat Operations Center at Chaumont was inadequate to control the eighty fighters at four air bases. An expansion project was approved but never funded. A self-help project by the wing greatly improved the COC. The remaining obstacle was poor communication within the COC!

USAFE expenditures were reduced to extremely critical projects, especially after the final STAIR STEP construction bills came due during late 1962. The Gold Flow problem restricted any improvements to the base structures. The classic problem faced by Chaumont civil engineers was that O&M French contractors costing $520,000 per year were only partially employed because requests for building repair parts costing $40,000 were refused. The bases were told to order the parts from CONUS, but all the systems had been procured in Europe, and nothing from the U.S. was interchangable (the old metric system problem).

As 1962 ended, and the 366th TFWg achieved C-1 OPS READY status, a prior notice walk-through ORI was conducted by Seventeenth Air Force at all four 366th Wing air bases on 3 to 5 December. Many discrepancies were noted, primarily: many Ops Ready pilots did not have TOP SECRET clearances, no sidearms or ammunition were available to the fighter squadrons, and some quick reaction F-84Fs did not meet required take-off times; a few F-84Fs required thirty-two minutes to scramble after receiving orders.

In January and February 1963 pilots completed F-84F transition and qualification training. The last 391st TFSq pilot reached OR status on 18 April; the Wheelus detachment closed, and all F-84Fs and personnel returned to France. Water survival training was stopped at Wheelus due to budget cuts; instead the fighter squadrons used the indoor swimming pool at RCAF Grostenquin. They filled these training squares during February and March! Winter weather made the Suippes and Siegenburg ranges unusable 90 percent of time.

In January 1963 the 366th was placed on alert to supply a squadron of F-84Fs to the United Nations Command in Leopoldville, Congo. Operation SHORT SPEAR would provide close air support to UN ground troops and air defense for the airlift transports during the Congo emergency, but this deployment was canceled by 27 January. The 366th participated in exchange programs with the Royal Danish and Italian Air Forces. On 4 March, Squadron 725 from Karup AB, Denmark, flying F-100Ds, exchanged places with six pilots and their F-84Fs. This program was repeated from 20 to 28 April at Ghedi AB, Italy, with the 6th Aero Brigata. These exchanges were very helpful to all personnel, especially to learn close air support procedures.

The Seventeenth Air Force conducted its first Tactical Evaluation of the 366th TFWg on 4 to 7 March; the wing received an unsatisfactory rating; bombing scores were deficient. On the second visit, 12 to 15 May, the wing was satisfactory in all areas except weapon load crew proficiency and weapons delivery. Many high angle bombing and low angle strafing scores were unsatisfactory. A no-notice Operational Readiness Inspection was never conducted on the 366th during its twelve months in France. All the mandatory TDY assignments for the fighter pilots were keeping 50 percent of them away from their home bases during fall 1962; developing into a morale problem by January 1963. Many TDY days were consumed at the USAFE Air Ground Operations School at Ramstein AB and the Forward Air Control School; both were mandatory for all fighter pilots. About 70 percent of the 366th's pilots had attended both schools by 1 March. On 11 March this mandatory training was terminated; no TDY travel funds were available! On 7 June all close air support missions with the U.S. Army ceased for lack of funds; only 1,070 missions were flown in 1963. It became obvious that the 366th TFWg, with conventional weapons only, was really not needed by USAFE.

Additional aircraft maintenance personnel arrived in France during spring 1963 to fill many shortages that had existed since the previous July. Many were "three" skill level airmen who immediately began upgrade OJT. Also, about 130 "Short Spurt" airmen helped fill shortages in the 366th. These were airmen who had twelve months or less remaining on their overseas tour of duty, and had agreed to serve in France rather than completing their service in CONUS. Unfortunately, with their long duty hours they found little time to tour France.

Each 366th squadron was now flying its F-84Fs about 400 to 450 hours per month, the high time was reached in May when 525 hours were flown by each squadron. The 391st TFSq received its last squadron Tactical Evaluation from 12 to 14 May and passed; they were declared OPS READY on 14 May 1963. During the 366th's yearlong stay in France, only two F-84Fs were lost in accidents with no injuries. Maintenance personnel were being upgraded to "five" skill levels and inspection dock production increased. There were still problems in some shops; the 480th at Phalsbourg reported a lack of radio comm/nav mock-ups, and test equipment shortages. The A&E section was not performing maintenance on the A-4 gunsights or APG-30 radar sets because of no mock-ups, test equipment, or trained personnel! Two HH-43B crash rescue helicopters, Det #5 AARC, arrived at Chaumont in April 1963, and were fully operational in May, including full fire fighting equipment.

The 366th's Chief of Maintenance often complained about the different F-84F configurations the ANG had left him. These presented unusual training and repair problems. Also his QC inspectors accused the ANG of making unauthorized changes to their F-84Fs. Of course they did have configuration problems because the wing acquired F-84F blocks -25, -30, -35, -40, -50, -55-RE (Republic-Farmingdale) and blocks -25, -30, -35, -40-GK (General Motors-Kansas City). Six different blocks of Thunderstreaks from two different assembly plants may have seen a few changes over three years of production! Apparently no one from the 366th TFWg looked at the tail numbers to see what they were getting into.

During 1963 the Chaumont AB Hospital was 80 percent staffed with fourteen officers, forty airmen, and five civilians to serve 1,422 military personnel, 1,220 dependents, and 28 DAF civilians. In addition to the usual medical, dental, inpatient/outpatient, veterinary and sanitary services, they were also tasked to maintain, and practice operating an air transportable thirty-six bed infirmary. The tactical hospital operated ten hours a day, five and one half days a week; a two-man emergency team was always available. The hospital had one metropolitan and two field ambulances. Most ambulance runs were to Toul and Verdun Army medical facilities with obstetrical cases. Forty-nine active duty inpatients were transferred by air or surface to USAF Hospitals at Wiesbaden or Evreux during 1963. The Chaumont Hospital needed some updating after ten years, but denial of funds postponed the approved projects.

The on-base elementary school was located in a converted airman barracks. Classrooms were small and over-crowded because the school was short three teachers. Enrollment at the end of the 1962 school year reached 331 pupils. The elementary school located in Village Lafayette remained closed. High school students were attending Toul AB High School; it was close enough for them to be bussed home on weekends.

Late in November 1962 the wing commander was informed that the 366th would move to CONUS by summer 1963. In February, Seventeenth Air Force informed the Wing Civil Engineer that Chambley, Chaumont, Etain, and Phalsbourg would be returned to standby status. No further real estate improvements were allowed, but contract O&M of the four bases would be continued, at $1.7 million for 412 man years of service! Total confusion developed because information about the move had various classifications, from unclassified to secret. The announcement by DOD on 24 April 1963 to the world media, that the wing was relocating, was a classic example of communications failure. The wing commander had not been informed by USAFE or Seventeenth Air Force about this Information Release, and the French locals knew about the base closures from their TV news before the commander!

On 26 April 1963, the 366th Wing was officially alerted to move to Holloman AFB, departing France on 15 July and arriving in New Mexico on 18 July 1963. Wing planning began at once, and the move became Project DAILY DOUBLE. No personnel planning or actions could proceed until DOD made the official announcement about the relocation. Personnel programming was chaos and unresolved until 25 May. Personnel fell into four categories, (a) return PCS with the wing to New Mexico, (b) remain at their various bases when they were placed in standby status, (c) be listed as surplus to remain in Europe, or (d) returned to CONUS for separation.

COL Coward dispatched a reconnaissance team to Holloman AFB and HQ TAC to gather information about the facilities to pass on to his planning team; this was an outstanding decision. The team discovered that Holloman TAC personnel were setting up another disaster scene for the wing with unsatisfactory facilities from aircraft parking ramp space to

Former Chaumont AB, 2003. It is now home of the 61st Regiment d' Artillerie.
61st Regiment d' Artillerie

airmen quarters. This reconnaissance visit prevented many problems arising after the wing's arrival.

Preparation for the move to CONUS proceeded on schedule while newly arrived personnel were still being trained. The wing's advanced party departed France on 4 June. Seventeenth Air Force informed the 366th to stop all operational and alert commitments on 15 June, and to reduce flying; this allowed maintenance thirty days to prepare F-84Fs for the trip to New Mexico. From 1 January through 15 July 1963, the 366th flew 8,386 hours on 4,796 sorties in France, a monthly average of 350 hours per squadron.

The 366th Wing moved 155 officers, 810 airmen, and 1,365 dependents, with 233 POVs and 1,500,000 pounds of household goods to Holloman AFB. The majority of the personnel remained in Europe and were reassigned throughout USAFE. The 389th and 390th TFSqs departed France on 15 July, followed by the 391st and 480th Squadrons on 16 July. All squadrons flew the North Atlantic east to west crossing as described in chapter 2, stopping at Sonderstrom (BW-8) Greenland, and clearing through McGuire AFB. Air-to-air refueling was not employed. After departing McGuire, one more stop at Little Rock AFB, Arkansas, saw them off to their new home at Holloman. All seventy-eight Thunderstreaks arrived at Holloman by 21 July, completing an uneventful journey. USAFE officially transferred the F-84Fs to TAC on 22 July 1963. In 1965, the 366th TFWg converted to F-4C Phantoms and their F-84Fs were returned to the ANG.

After twenty-two months as a very active main base, Chaumont was returned to standby status, and the 7544th Combat Support Group once again became its caretaker, supervising French base maintenance contractors. The base was finally in good condition; the only problem remaining was the jet fuel contamination of #1 water well. Fortunately the other two base wells did not suffer the same fate. The 1239th AACS Sq and the 2148th Communications Sq based at Chaumont had detachments at Chambley, Etain, and Phalsbourg in the 1962-64 period. Chaumont was used for a few exercises and small deployments in 1964-65, but no combat wing moved into the base.

Base support detachments at this time were Det #3, 7544th Combat Support Gp from Toul AB; Det #2204, 7025th Air Postal Gp operating APO 09119; Det #8, 31st Weather Sq; Det #2, 1952d AACS Sq; and Flt "17" 2059th Radio Relay Sq.

Project FRELOC began in July 1966 at Chaumont AB with the 7544th CSGp being the primary agent to remove all property and close the base. Chaumont took less effort to close because of its three years in standby status, there was no inventory of aircraft spare parts, shop equipment, and ground support equipment since all had been removed in 1963. A thousand tons of aircraft munitions existed in the ammunition storage site, and this had to be moved to Germany. Excess material such as office equipment, furniture, civil engineering equipment, tools and vehicles could not be sold locally on the French economy without having to pay import duties. Instead it was transported to Germany, where most of it ended up in salvage yards. The large office buildings, hospital, warehouses, and hangars were closed as soon as equipment and supplies were removed.

The base contracting officer, Mr. Robert Marusiak, arranged to move troops into Chaumont city as barracks and mess halls were shut down in October and November 1966. Airmen were billeted in Hotel de-France and officers in Hotel Etoile. He arranged for quarters and meals, including the noon meal. This was usually sandwiches for the troops, delivered on base.

By 31 December 1966 all equipment was removed and total base personnel numbered about seventy men. Again the most difficult job was termination of the French employees, many of whom had worked ten, twelve or more years on the base and were a vital part of the USAFE team. Chaumont Air Base was transferred to the French government on 26 March 1967 through the Military Liquidation Service in Paris. Chaumont served the USAF and NATO as a very good fighter base for twelve years. Most former USAF personnel and their families have fond memories of their service and touring in the Haut-Marne region, the Viaduc, and Le Centre-Ville de Chaumont.

After Chaumont was closed and returned to the French Government, the French Army moved into the facility in 1967 and used it to house regimental sized units. The base name was changed to Quartier General d'Aboville. The 403d Regiment d'Artillerie operated there from 1967 until 1998. It is currently used by the 61st Regiment d'Artillerie, which has the mission of battlefield reconnaissance and fire direction control. The regiment uses helicopters, unmanned aerial vehicles (UAV), and several types of digital communications/computer systems to direct artillery firing units. The regiment works very hard to keep the old base in good condition. The 61st Regiment conducts an annual Open House on one June weekend where civil and military aviation displays and demonstrations draw large crowds to tour the base. The area also has a Franco-American Association; many of its members previously worked on the air base for the U.S. Air Force. Tours of the base can often be arranged through them.

Chaumont is found on Michelin Map #313 local and IGN Series Blue #3118-O. The city can be reached by train from Paris using Gare de l'Est.

Appendix 9.1 Notice to Airmen 1959 (NOTAM) - USAF-Chaumont

Elevation 1,018 feet (310.4m), 48° 05'N - 05° 04'E. One paved runway 9,900 feet long, 010°/190°. Supports single-wheel landing gear up to 80,000 pounds. Jet aircraft runway barriers at both ends of runway. High intensity approach lights for runway 01. Rotating beacon light on airfield, with runway, taxiway, and obstruction lights. Aircraft storage available, major aircraft and engine repairs available. Aircraft fuel, 115-145 octane and JP4 jet fuel with single point refueling. Jet aircraft air turbine and electrical starting units available. Low pressure oxygen and liquid oxygen servicing available. High pressure compressed air service.

Chaumont Air Base Assigned Aircraft

John Ibsen

137th Fighter-Bomber Wing F-84Gs, 13 May 1952 - 9 July 1952

Approximately twenty aircraft per squadron. These Thunderjets were flown from Alexandria AFB, LA to Neubiberg AB and Landstuhl AB, West Germany by 137th Fighter-Bomber Wing pilots. Later moved into Chaumont AB, France.

Aircraft Marking:

- 125th Fighter-Bomber Squadron - Red bands on nose and tail.
- 127th Fighter-Bomber Squadron - Blue bands on nose and tail.
- 128th Fighter-Bomber Squadron - Yellow bands on nose and tail.

F-84G-1, -10-RE

51-692	127th	51-759	127th	51-801	127th	51-861	127th	51-880	125th
51-693	127th	51-760	127th	51-802		51-862	128th	51-882*	
51-706	128th	51-762		51-813	128th	51-863	127th	51-883	127th
51-707	125th	51-763		51-824	127th	51-864	127th	51-884	127th
51-712	125th	51-765		51-826	127th	51-866		51-885	125th
51-714		51-766		51-830	128th	51-868	127th	51-887	127th
51-721*	125th	51-772		51-836		51-869	128th	51-888	
51-726		51-774	125th	51-839		51-870	125th	51-889	
51-728	125th	51-775		51-840		51-872		51-890	127th
51-737	127th	51-786	127th	51-845	127th	51-873*	125th		
51-742		51-787		51-847	125th	51-875			
51-751	127th	51-788*	125th	51-848		51-876*			
51-752		51-792		51-854		51-877			

* Losses:

51-721 - Damaged, mid-air collision near Landsthul AB, Germany, 1 JUN 52, no fatalities.
51-788 - Damaged, mid-air collision near Landsthul AB, Germany, 1 JUN 52, no fatalities.
51-873 - Damaged at Keflavik AB, Iceland,13 MAY 52, no fatalities, (arrived Chaumont 7 JAN 54).
51-876 - Damaged, bad landing at Toul AB, France, 22 JUN 52, no fatalities.
51-882 - Damaged at Alexandria AFB, LA, 25 NOV 51, no fatalities (arrived Chaumont 3 SEP 52).

137th Air Base Group: Wing Support Aircraft

C-47A: 2 ea.
T-6F: 44-81795 (from 36th FBWg, Furstenfeldbruck AB, West Germany)
T-33A: 51-4171 (125th), 51-4172* (128th), 51-4173 (127th)
* Loses: 51-4172 - T-33A Damaged, ground accident at Goose Bay AB, Labrador, 11 MAY 52, no fatalities.

48th Fighter-Bomber Wing F-84Gs, 10 July 1952 - April 1954

Approximately twenty-five aircraft per squadron. These Thunderjets were transferred in place from the 137th FBWg on 10 July 1952. Eighteen more F-84Gs were added during 1952.

Aircraft Marking:

- 492d Fighter-Bomber Squadron - Blue tail & tip tanks.
- 493d Fighter-Bomber Squadron - Yellow tail & tip tanks.
- 494th Fighter-Bomber Squadron - Red tail & tip tanks.

F-84G-1, -10, -16, -26-RE

51-692	493d	51-726		51-759	493d	51-774	492d	51-802	492d	51-840	
51-693	493d	51-728	492d	51-760*	493d	51-775		51-813	494th	51-845	494th
51-706	494th	51-732		51-762		51-786	493d	51-824*	493d	51-847	492d
51-707*	492d	51-737*	493d	51-763		51-787		51-826	493d	51-848	
51-712	492d	51-742		51-765		51-788	492d	51-830	493d	51-854	
51-714		51-751	493d	51-766	492d	51-792		51-836		51-861	493d
51-721	492d	51-752		51-772		51-801	493d	51-839		51-862*	494th

Chaumont Air Base Assigned Aircraft, continued

48th Fighter-Bomber Wing F-84Gs, -1, -10, -16, -26-RE continued

51-863	492d	51-880		51-1042		51-11175		51-11231~	
51-864	494th	51-882*	492d	51-1043		51-11190	492d	51-11245	
51-866		51-883*	494th	51-1044		51-11199		51-11248	
51-868	493d	51-884*	494th	51-1045		51-11203+	494th	51-16643	492d
51-869	494th	51-885	493d	51-1076		51-11212		51-16651+	494th
51-870	493d	51-887*	494th	51-10397*		51-11216		51-16654+	494th
51-872	492d	51-888		51-10440		51-11219		51-16667+	494th
51-873	492d	51-889*	494th	51-10461		51-11222		51-16669+	494th
51-875		51-890	494th	51-10468	492d	51-11223	494th	51-16672+	494th
51-876		51-1041		51-10469	492d	51-11226	492d	51-16674	493d
51-877						51-11228	492d		
						51-11229			

+ Indicates F-84Gs assigned to the Skyblazers aerobatic team
~ Wing commander's aircraft
* Losses:
51-707 - Salvaged, bad landing at Dijon Airport, France, 26 JUN 53, no fatalities.
51-737 - Salvaged, bad landing at Chaumont AB, 16 FEB 53, no fatalities.
51-760 - Crashed, bad landing at Wheelus AB, Libya, 23 AUG 53, 1 fatality.
51-824 - Crashed, midair collision near Chaumont AB, France, 13 JUL 53, no fatalities, pilot ejected.
51-862 - Salvaged, midair collision near Chaumont AB, France, 13 JUL 53, no fatalities.
51-882 - Crashed, letdown/bad weather, near Chaumont AB, France, 4 DEC 52, 1 fatality.
51-883 - Salvaged, bad weather landing at Furstenfeldbruck AB, West Germany, 9 AUG 52, no fatalities.
51-884 - Crashed, bad weather/emergency landing, at Chaumont AB, France, 14 JUL 53, 1 fatality
51-887 - Crashed, hit ground in simulated attack, near Bitburg AB, West Germany, 23 JUN 53, 1 fatality.
51-889 - Crashed, hit embankment on take-off, Chaumont AB, France, 14 AUG 53, 1 fatality.
51-10397 - Crashed, bad landing/weather, at Chaumont AB, France, 5 APR 53, no fatalities.

Wing Support Aircraft: 48th Air Base Group
B-26C: 41-39303 (tow target aircraft)
C-47A: 42-23355, 43-15653, 43-48088
T-6F: 44-81795
T-33A: 51-4171 (492d), 51-4172 (494th), 51-4173 (494th), 51-4413 (493d)
L-5B: 44-17323*
Losses:
44-17323 - Destroyed, bad wind storm, at Chaumont AB, France, 12 DEC 52, no fatalities.

Gene White

48th Fighter-Bomber Wing F-86Fs, November 1953 - December 1955

Twenty-five aircraft per squadron. These Sabres were flown from Columbus, OH to Chaumont AB by MATS pilots. During 1956 these aircraft were processed through Chateauroux AD and transferred to NATO and MAP nations, some were returned to CONUS.
Aircraft Marking - Vertical stabilizer, rudder: 492d - blue, 493d - yellow, 494th - red.

.

F-86F-25-NH

52-5279*	494th	52-5301	493d	52-5329*		52-5340	494th	52-5349	
52-5282+		52-5304		52-5331	494th	52-5341		52-5351	493d
52-5291	494th	52-5306		52-5333		52-5342		52-5353*	492d
52-5292		52-5319		52-5335		52-5345		52-5354	
52-5294		52-5321		52-5336		52-5346	494th	52-5355~	492d
52-5295+	493d	52-5323	494th	52-5338	494th	52-5347		52-5356	493d
52-5297	492d	52-5324		52-5339+	494th	52-5348		52-5358	

48th F-BWg tail numbers continued next page

Chaumont Air Base Assigned Aircraft, continued

48th Fighter-Bomber Wing F-86F-25s, continued

52-5359		52-5368		52-5377	492d	52-5391		52-5410	
52-5360		52-5369		52-5378		52-5392		52-5412	
52-5361*	493d	52-5370+	492d	52-5379		52-5395		52-5435	
52-5362		52-5371	492d	52-5380		52-5396		52-5436	
52-5363		52-5372		52-5382		52-5397		52-5437	
52-5364		52-5373		52-5385		52-5400		52-5439	493d
52-5365		52-5374		52-5386	494th	52-5401		52-5494	
52-5366		52-5375+	492d	52-5387		52-5402	494th		
52-5367		52-5376*		52-5388		52-5403	493d		

\+ Indicates F-86Fs assigned to the Skyblazers aerobatic team.
~ Wing commander's aircraft.
* Losses:
52-5279 - Crashed, landed short at Wheelus AB, Libya, 27 MAY 54, 1 fatality.
52-5329 - Salvaged, ran off runway at Wheelus AB, Libya, 26 MAY 54, no fatalities.
52-5353 - Salvaged, bad landing on Wheelus AB, Libya, 6 MAY 54, no fatalities
52-5361 - Crashed, hit target area at Siegenburg Range, West Germany, 14 JULY 54, 1 fatality.
52-5376 - Salvaged, bad landing at Furstenfeldbruck AB, West Germany, 1 MAY 54, no fatalities.

48th Fighter-Bomber Wing F-86F-35s, June 1954 - December 1956

Twenty-five aircraft per squadron and twenty-three spares for USAFE. These Sabres were flown from Inglewood, CA to Chaumont AB, France by MATS pilots.
Aircraft Marking - Vertical stabilizer, rudder: 492d - blue, 493d - yellow, 494th - red.

F-86F-35-NA

53-1077		53-1144		53-1164	494th	53-1181*		53-1197		53-1213	494th
53-1081		53-1147		53-1165*	492d	53-1182		53-1198	494th	53-1214+	494th
53-1082		53-1148		53-1166		53-1183*	494th	53-1199		53-1215	
53-1083		53-1149		53-1167	492d	53-1184*	494th	53-1200~	494th	53-1216	
53-1084		53-1150		53-1168		53-1185		53-1201+		53-1217	
53-1086		53-1151		53-1169		53-1186+		53-1202		53-1218	
53-1088		53-1152		53-1170+		53-1187		53-1203*	494th	53-1219+	
53-1091		53-1153		53-1171		53-1188		53-1204		53-1220	
53-1093		53-1154		53-1172	494th	53-1189		53-1205*		53-1221	494th
53-1094		53-1155		53-1173		53-1190	492d	53-1206		53-1222	494th
53-1107+	494th	53-1156		53-1174+		53-1191		53-1207		53-1223	
53-1123		53-1157		53-1175		53-1192+		53-1208*	494th	53-1224	494th
53-1126	492d	53-1158*	494th	53-1176		53-1193		53-1209		53-1225	
53-1138		53-1159		53-1177		53-1194		53-1210		53-1226	
53-1139		53-1161	494th	53-1178		53-1195		53-1211		53-1227	
53-1140		53-1162+		53-1179	492d	53-1196		53-1212		53-1228	
53-1143		53-1163		53-1180							

\+ Indicates F-86Fs assigned to the Skyblazers aerobatic team.
~ Wing commander's aircraft.
* Losses:
53-1158 - Crashed, fuel exhaustion, 19nm SE of Langres, France, 15 SEP 55, no fatalities, ejected.
53-1165 - Crashed, landing/ jet turbulance on Cazaux AB, France, 21 NOV 54, no fatalities.
53-1181 - Crashed, letdown/bad weather, 5nm W of Chaumont AB, France, 8 JUL 55, no fatalities, ejected.
53-1183 - Crashed, take-off, engine and barrier failure, on Sembach AB, W. Germany, 27 APR 56, 1 fatality.
53-1184 - Crashed, engine explosion, near Wheelus AB, Libya, 5 JUL 56, no fatalities, ejected.
53-1203 - Crashed, near Chaumont AB, France, 8 JUL 55, 1 fatality.
53-1205 - Crashed, engine failure at take-off, on Chaumont AB, France, 29 DEC 54, no fatalities.
53-1208 - Crashed, hit by leader's drop tanks, near Sembach AB, W. Germany, 18 DEC 56, no fatlaities, ejected.

48th Air Base Group: Wing Support Aircraft

C-47A: 42-23355, 43-15653, 43-48088, 44-76207
L-20A: 51-16529, 51-16531
T-33A: 51-4172, 51-4173 ,52-9337*, 52-9810, 52-9868
*Losses:
52-9337 - Crashed, letdown/ bad weather, 2nm N of Chaumont AB, FR, 30 JULY 55, 1 fatality

Chaumont Air Base Assigned Aircraft, continued

Al Christensen

48th Fighter-Bomber Wing, F-100Ds, September 1956 - 15 January 1960

Thirty aircraft per squadron. These Super Sabres were flown from Inglewood, CA to Boulhaut AB, Nouasseur AB and Sidi Slimane AB, French Morocco by MATS pilots. During 1956 many of these aircraft were processed through Chateauroux AD and transferred to NATO nations.

Aircraft Marking:

492d FBSq - Blue band. 493d FBSq - Yellow band. 494th FBSq - Red band.

F-100D-1, -5, -10, -15-NA

54-2128 494th	54-2155*	54-2176	54-2193	54-2216	54-2255*
54-2132	54-2157	54-2177 493d	54-2194	54-2219	54-2257
54-2134	54-2158	54-2178*	54-2196 492d	54-2220	54-2258*
54-2136	54-2159	54-2179 494th	54-2197*	54-2221	54-2265
54-2140	54-2160	54-2180*	54-2198	54-2222~	54-2266
54-2141	54-2161 492d	54-2181*	54-2201	54-2225*	54-2270
54-2142*	54-2162 492d	54-2182	54-2202	54-2226	54-2271
54-2143	54-2164	54-2183	54-2203	54-2227	54-2272
54-2146	54-2165 494th	54-2184	54-2205	54-2231	54-2273
54-2147	54-2166 493d	54-2185	54-2206	54-2232*	54-2275
54-2148	54-2167	54-2186	54-2207	54-2236	54-2277 494th
54-2149	54-2169	54-2187	54-2208	54-2238	
54-2150	54-2171	54-2188	54-2209*	54-2247 494th	
54-2152	54-2172	54-2189	54-2210	54-2251	
54-2153*	54-2173	54-2190	54-2212	54-2253	
54-2154	54-2175	54-2192	54-2213	54-2254	

* Losses:
54-2142 - Crashed on Sidi Slimane AB, Morocco, NOV 56, no fatalities.
54-2153 - Crashed at Chaumont AB, France, APR 57, no fatalities.
54-2155 - Crashed, approach/bad weather, 3nm NE of Hahn AB, West Germany, JUN 57, 1 fatality.
54-2178 - Crashed, fuel/exhaustion, 13nm E of Chaumont AB, France, AUG 58, no fatalities, ejected.
54-2180 - Crashed, bad night landing on Boulhaut AB, Morocco, DEC 56, no fatalities.
54-2181 - Crashed, engine failure, 6nm S of Chaumont AB, France, SEP 57, no fatalities, ejected.
54-2197 - Salvaged, ran off runway on Chaumont AB, France, DEC 58, no fatalities.
54-2209 - Crashed, engine failure, 22nm E of Wheelus AB, Libya, DEC 57, no fatalities, ejected.
54-2225 - Crashed, engine failure, 9nm SW of Boulhaut AB, Morocco, DEC 56, no fatalities, ejected.
54-2232 - Crashed, bad landing at Chaumont AB, France, JULY 57, no fatalities.
54-2255 - Crashed, bad landing at Chaumont AB, France MAY 57, no fatalities.
54-2258 - Crashed on Sidi Slimane AB, French Morocco, JUN 57, no fatalities.
~ Wing commander's aircraft

48th Air Base Group: Wing Support Aircraft

C-47A: 43-15653, 43-48088
L-20A: 51-16529, 51-16535*
T-33A: 51-4172, 51-4173, 51-6525, 52-9810, 52-9868*

*Losses:
51-16535 - Crashed, hit hill/weather, 1.3nm SE or Herrenwies, W. Germany, 20 MAY 57, 4 fatalities.
52-9868 - Salvaged, emergency landing at Chaumont AB, France, 22 JAN 59, no fatalities.

48th Fighter-Bomber Wing F-100D/Fs

Twenty-five aircraft per squadron. These Super Sabres were delivered by MATS pilots. In January 1960 these F-100s were flown to RAF Lakenheath, UK, by 48th TFWg pilots.

F-100D-45-NH and -25-NA

55-2794	493d	55-2809	492d	55-2822	493d	55-2838	494th	55-2841	493d	55-3678	494th
55-2797	493d	55-2810	494th	55-2830	492d	55-2839	493d	55-2844	492d	55-3683	493d
55-2800	494th	55-2818	492d	55-2834	492d	55-2840	494th	55-3658*	494th	55-3685	494th

48th F-BWg tail numbers continued next page

Chaumont Air Base Assigned Aircraft, continued

48th Fighter-Bomber Wing F-100D/Fs continued

F-100D-80-NH and -90-NA

56-3200	493d	56-3212		56-3225		56-3250	494th	56-3313	494th
56-3202*	494th	56-3213	494th	56-3226	494th	56-3251	493d	56-3315	492d
56-3203	493d	56-3214	494th	56-3228	492d	56-3253	494th	56-3316	493d
56-3205	492d	56-3217	492d	56-3231		56-3254	493d	56-3317	492d
56-3208	494th	56-3219		56-3236	493d	56-3262~	494th	56-3319	492d
56-3209	494th	56-3221	494th	56-3239	492d	56-3284	494th	56-3321	494th
56-3210	493d	56-3222		56-3240	492d	56-3288	493d	56-3381	494th
56-3211	493d	56-3223		56-3241	493d	56-3310	494th		

F-100F-10-NA

56-3807	492d	56-3832	493d	56-3851	56-3883	492d	56-3890		56-3903	
56-3822	493d	56-3850		56-3876	56-3884	492d	56-3895	494th	56-3907	494th
56-3824*	494th									

Losses:
55-3658 - Crashed, landing/bad weather, at Chateauroux AD, Fr, 11 NOV 56, no fatalities.
56-3202 - Crashed, engine failure, near Wheelus AB, Libya, 5 JULY 56, no fatalities, ejected.
56-3824 - Crashed, engine explosion near Wheelus AB, Libya, 19 OCT 58, no fatalities, ejected.
~ Wing Commanders aircraft.

Nick Scafidi

7108th Tactical Wing, 141st Tactical Fighter Squadron, F-84Fs, 3 November 1961 - 15 July 1962

Twenty-six aircraft assigned to squadron. These Thunderstreaks were flown from McGuire AFB, NJ to Chaumont AB, France by 141st TFSq pilots. All F-84Fs transferred in place to 366th TFWg and remained in France until July 1963.

F-84F-25, -30, -35, -40, -50-RE and -25, -30, -35, -40-GK

51-1631	51-1818	51-9437	51-9516	51-9547	52-6365	52-6405	52-6490	52-6609	52-7019
51-1651	51-9404	51-9445	51-9530	51-17061	52-6391*	52-6414	52-6495	52-6847	52-7066
51-1721*	51-9405	51-9457	51-9546		52-6392	52-6415			

* Losses:
51-1721 - Crashed, engine failure, weather, near Chaumont AB, France, 16 MAY 62, no fatalities, ejected.
52-6391 - Crashed, hit mountain, bad weather, 5nm W of Clermont Ferrand, France, 28 JAN 62, 1 fatality.

Wing Support Aircraft: 7108th Operations Sq
C-47A: 1 ea. on loan 43-15661
L-20A: 51-16538
T-33A: 2 ea from ANG - 52-9408, 53-5362, 53-5852

366th Tactical Fighter Wing, 389th Tactical Fighter Squadron, F-84Fs, 15 July 1962 - 15 July 63

The wing's four squadrons were based at different bases: the 389th Sq was based at Chaumont, 390th - Chambley AB, 391st - Etain AB, 480th - Phalsbourg AB. Twenty aircraft per squadron. Seventy-eight Thunderstreaks were flown from France to Holloman AFB, NM by 366th TFWg pilots. Aircraft Marking: 389th - blue band, 390th - yellow band, 391st - red band, 480th - green band.

F-84F-25, -30, -35, -40-RE and -25, -30, -35, -40-GK

51-1631	51-1818	51-9405	51-9457	51-9530	51-9547	52-6405	52-6415	52-6495	52-7019
51-1651	51-9404	51-9445	51-9516	51-9546	52-6392	52-6414	52-6490	52-6609	52-7066

No Losses

Wing Support Aircraft: 366th Operations Sq
C-47s: 5ea. **C-47A**: 43-15619, **VC-47A**: 43-15992, **C-47D**: 43-16387, 43-48215
L-20A/U-6A: 52-6146
T-33As: 52-9838, 53-5820, 53-5830
HH-43B: 62-4551

ACKNOWLEDGEMENTS

I would like to thank the following people who contributed to this chapter:

Jack Callanan was stationed at Chaumont from June 1958 until November 1959, and was part of the 48th Installations Squadron. His job was aircraft crash rescue.

Al Christensen was a Weather Officer in Detachment #10, 31st Weather Squadron, MATS, stationed at Chambley AB, 1955-1957.

Paul Hammond was an E-5 at Chaumont from 1962-65 who was officially assigned to fire & crash rescue but multi-tasked in supply, clerical duties, recorder for base NCO Council, Red Bird time coordinator and supervisor of Fire Prevention inspectors, and entries to NFPA & Air Force Fire Prevention contests. He met his wife at Chaumont, and is the U.S. contact for the Chaumont Air Base Assoc. He has produced a newsletter *Chaumont Friends* since 1988.

John Ibsen was a jet engine mechanic with the 48th Field Maintenance Squadron at Chaumont AB from February 1953 to January 1956. His photos were kindly provided by his widow, Mauricette Ibsen.

Coleman Montero was in air force installations at Chaumont from October 1951 to November 1953. He acted as interpreter to coordinate activities with the French Ponts et Chaussees.

Charles Radloff was in the 2nd Air Postal Squadron at Chaumont AB 1952-54, and in Paris 1954-56.

Nicholas Scafidi was in the 108th Supply Squadron in the 108th Tactical Fighter Wing of the New Jersey Air National Guard that was activated for the Berlin Crisis in October 1961. He was stationed at Chaumont AB as part of Project STAIR STEP from 1961 to 1962.

Gene White was an F-86F crew chief in the 416th FBSq at Chambley, October 1955 to January 1958.

10

DREUX-LOUVILLIERS AIR BASE

Dreux Air Base is located eighteen miles (25 km) southwest of the city of Dreux in the Eure-et-Loir Department in the Centre region of France. It is fifty-nine miles (95 km) west of Paris and twenty-three miles (37 km) northwest of Chartres.

Dreux was the capital of the Gaulish tribe Durocasses until Paris and the surrounding area was conquered by Julius Caesar circa 52 B.C. Over the centuries its geography made it a well-traveled crossroad. During WWII, on 15 August 1944, the American Third Army, XV Corps, 5th Armored Division rapidly passed through this area. It was headed east on highway N12 for the upper Seine River line.

During the initial meetings for air base site selection, the Dreux area was proposed. Both the FAF and USAFE agreed that it would be a good location for a troop carrier air base. The field at Dreux-Vernouillet was suggested as a possible site in 1950. It was a prewar airfield that had been used by the USAAF Ninth Air Force in WWII (Designator A-41). The French selection committee quickly rejected that location because of anticipated future airspace traffic conflicts with Paris-Orly, and the planned commercial expansion of the Vernouillet airport. By summer 1951 another site was agreed upon. Dreux Air Base (48° 39'N – 01° 06'E, elevation 602 feet) is located close to the village of Dampierre, about 6 km south of the town of Brezolles. Initially named Dreux-Louvilliers, the town name of Louvilliers was deleted in 1954 because it was fifteen miles away, and too many USAF personnel were getting lost around Louvilliers looking for the base.

The chosen site of 2,000 acres was well-drained, flat, open farmland that was immediately available for development. As usual, the four common site problems existed: limited potable water, insufficient commercial electrical service, very limited road capacity, and railroad service over ten miles away. Preliminary surveys were conducted in February 1952, and the Corps of Engineers gave approval after identifying a sufficient source of potable water and determining the limited commercial electrical service would be workable.

TAC and USAFE planned that a troop carrier wing would arrive in the spring of 1954. Therefore, Dreux was to be another single step base constructed within three years, with permanent buildings, shops, and hangars. All structures would be standard NATO design, but expanded for the larger base population required for a troop carrier wing. Buildings directly funded by the USAF, such as service club, officer's club, elementary school, chapel, and base exchange would be standard Corps of Engineer designs. A support detachment from Chateauroux Air Depot set up a tent camp during the first two years to receive and store incoming property. Construction started in September 1952 with the building of access roads and a base railroad spur. In November runway grading began, and one 7,900 foot-long concrete runway was poured, northeast/southwest. The runway was followed by taxiways, parking hardstands, hangar floors, and aprons. Here again all base utilities were installed underground: electrical, water, heating, and fuel storage system, and the required trenching produced a sea of mud during the winter season. The new Joint Construction Agency managed base construction, which by July 1956 cost $37 million. Seven different French contractors performed work at Dreux.

From March 1954 until May 1957 the U.S. Army, Companies B & C, 821st Engineer Aviation Battalion constructed two separate trailer parks on the south side of the runway adjacent to the main base, as part of Project Caravan. They built 100 sites for officers and 200 sites for airmen. The 300 trailers began arriving in the fall of 1954 and were occupied by winter. The EABn had arrived prior to completion of the base barracks and set up Quonset huts as living quarters before beginning work on the trailer park. The troops found winter living conditions difficult at Dreux. The Quonset huts were heated with smelly kerosene-fired potbelly stoves and there was only one latrine for every five huts. These Quonset huts were later converted into laundry rooms for the trailer courts.

The 821st EABn provided invaluable help at Dreux because the unusually cold 1955-56 winter caused frozen water pipes in many buildings. Though original construction had to be done by French contractors, the EABn found there was much to keep them busy repairing all the leaking pipes.

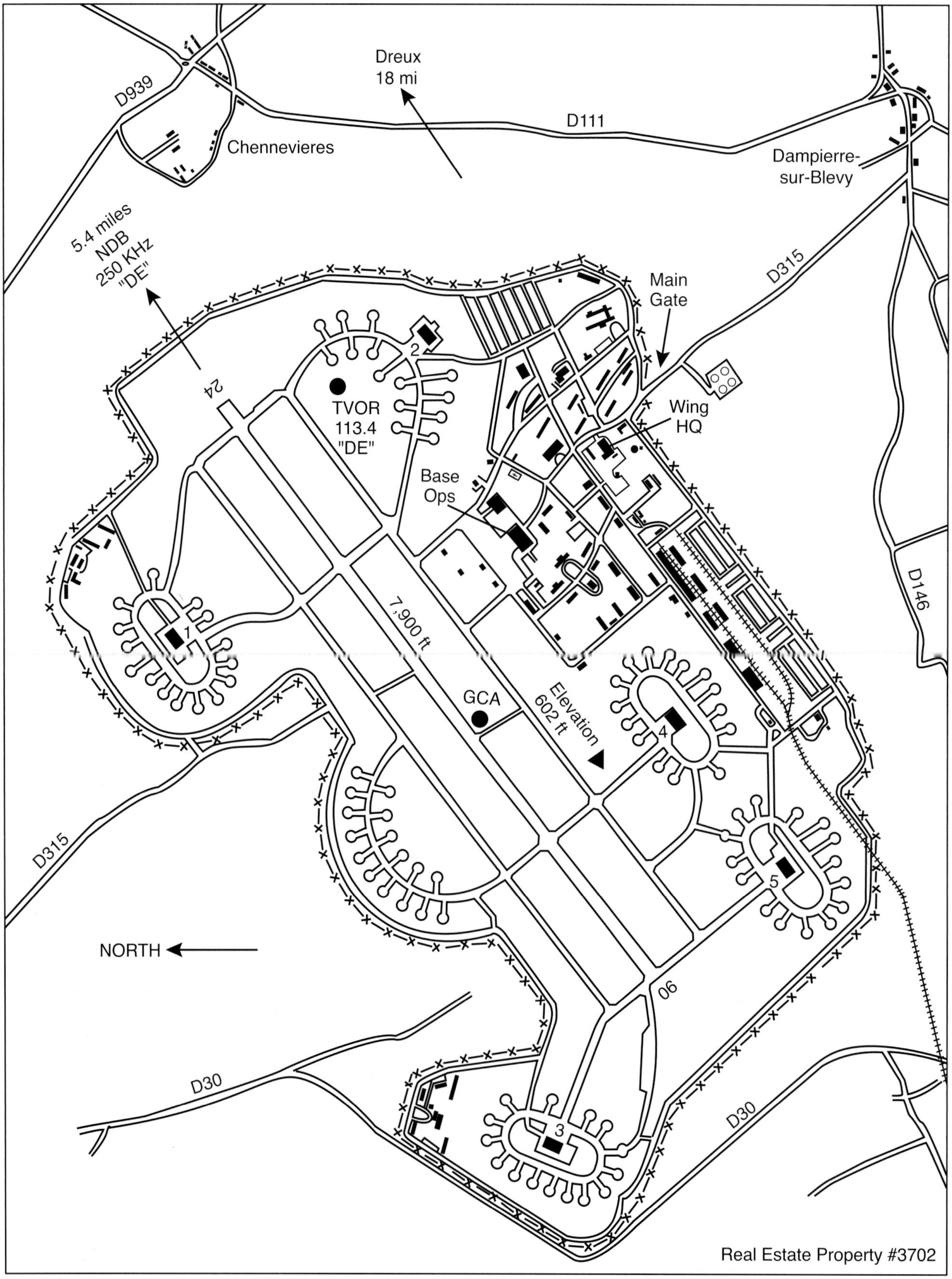

Map 10.1 Dreux Air Base

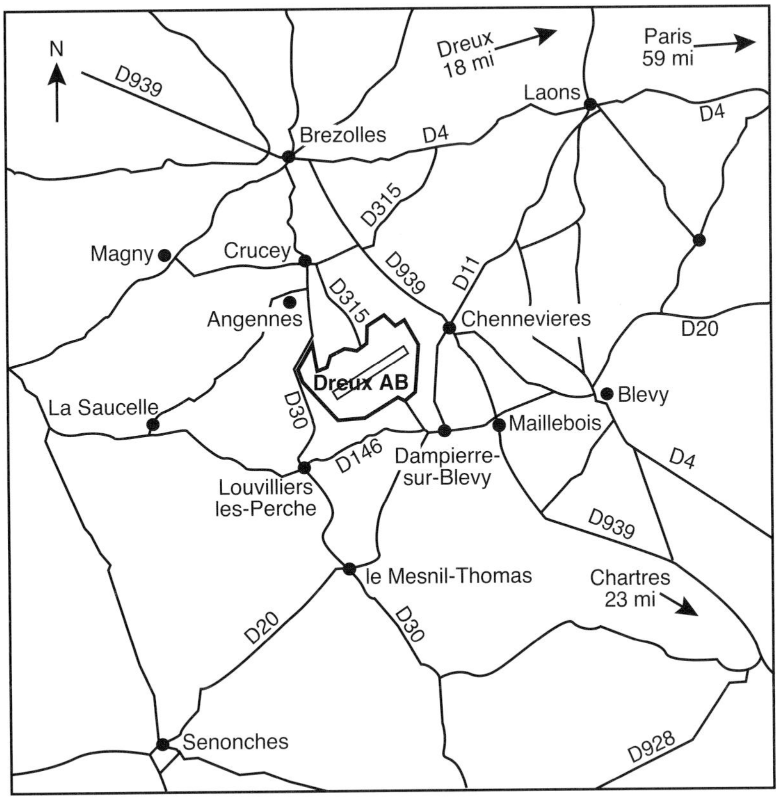

Map 10.2 Dreux Area

In addition to the two base trailer parks, five Guaranteed Rental Income housing projects with a total of 424 units were constructed for Dreux families. The first project was Cite les Corvees (Property #7157) a 280 unit housing complex located 27 km northeast of the air base in Dreux city consisting of two, three, and four bedroom duplex homes. Another GRI housing complex at St. Remy, (Property #5945) was located 19 kms northeast of Dreux and south of St. Remy-sur-Avre, south of route N12. It had thirty-six duplex units. The three other projects were Chateauneuf, located 17 kms southeast of the base with fifty-two units; Senonches, 10 km southwest of the base, with thirty-six units; and La Loupe with twenty units located 23 km southwest of Dreux AB. All GRI houses were completed by December 1956, reducing the rental shortage for 60th TCWg families. Even after these GRI houses became available, about 125 families were still renting on the local economy. All housing projects were returned to France in March 1967 and are now privately owned.

By 1958 Dreux Air Base (APO 84) extended over 2,070 acres with fifteen miles of paved roads. Taxiways, aprons, parking ramps, etc., covered 710,000 square yards. The runway was 7,900 feet long by 180 feet wide and was 26 inches thick. Building it required 98,600 cubic yards of concrete. Dreux had five hangars, three large 37,000 square-foot transport size hangars and two fighter-size hangars that were 31,000 square feet each. The larger hangars provided the space and necessary shops to accommodate two C-119s for periodic inspections. These hangars could also hold two C-130 aircraft. The base had sixty-three permanent buildings and nineteen temporary buildings. Dreux had four million cubic feet of warehouse storage space served by two railroad sidings. Dreux did not have a weapons storage annex or weapons storage site on base. The water system consisted of five underground storage tanks holding 188,500 gallons. Three heating plants supplied building heat and hot water service. Twelve airmen dormitories that had a capacity of 146 men each, and four BOQ buildings, with a capacity of 60 officers each were constructed in three separate areas. Four dining halls: a 1,000-man, two 500-man, and a 250-man hospital dining hall were located near the three living areas. Underground fuel storage could hold: 850,500 gallons of AVGAS, 150,000 gallons of Jet fuel, and 140,000 gallons of vehicle fuels. In June 1958 the estimated value of real estate (excluding land) was $41 million. Equipment in use (excluding aircraft) was approximately $8.5 million. Total Base Supply Inventory was $6 million.

C-119C #51-2612 from the 12th TCSq, 60th TCWg over France, 1955.
John Traficante

By 1959 the base had added a chapel, theater, large library, bowling alley, youth center, gymnasium, golf driving range, small arms range, and four baseball and softball fields. An elementary school was built on base that could accommodate 300 students in grades one through six. Some high school students attended Chateauroux High School and returned by bus on the weekends.

Dreux was well constructed compared to our other bases in France, with an excellent runway and sound buildings. There is no history of the runway breaking or cracking, causing an operational shutdown after its completion in 1955. But in conclusion, Dreux must be considered a poor investment since it was operational for only seven of its twelve years, and when needed for the 1961 Berlin Crisis it could not be used for jet aircraft operations because of French objections. The base spent a total of five years in standby status between 1955 and 1967.

60th Troop Carrier Wing

By September 1955, the 60th Troop Carrier Wing, Medium, was ready to depart for Dreux AB in western France, after five years at Rhein-Main AB, West Germany. The 60th Wing had three troop carrier squadrons: the 10th, 11th, and 12th, flying fifty-four C-119G Boxcars, plus two C-47s assigned to the air base group. The 60th TCGp and the flying squadrons moved all personnel and C-119Gs from 12 September through 29 September to Dreux AB as a routine mission. The 60th Air Base Group and its five support squadrons followed on 30 September making Dreux operational on 1 October 1955. Table 10.1 shows personnel strength by 30 November 1955.

The 60th Troop Carrier Wing began as a WWII air transport group activated on 1 December 1940 with four squadrons: the 10th, 11th, 12th, and 28th. The 60th Group moved their C-47s to England in June 1942 and then on to North Africa as part of the invasion force, dropping airborne forces into Oran, Algeria. It participated in eight major air campaigns in the Mediterranean Theater, primarily airborne paratroop invasions while assigned to the Twelfth Air Force. A DUC was awarded for outstanding support to Balkan partisans and for the rescue of escaped AAF aircrews. After Victory in Europe, the 60th Air Transport Group moved to Trinidad where it was inactivated 31 July 1945.

It was reactivated 30 September 1946 at Munich-Riem Air Base, West Germany, with three squadrons flying C-47s. It converted to C-54s in October-November 1948. The 60th served in the Berlin Airlift from the beginning on 26 June 1948 until the end, 30 September 1949. The group was expanded to the 60th Troop Carrier Wing, Medium, on 5 November 1948. The wing continued to provide airlift support throughout Europe while based in West Germany at Kaufbeuren AB, Wiesbaden AB, and Rhein-Main AB, where it flew C-82s then upgraded into new Fairchild C-119C Boxcars.

It was very difficult for the personnel to transition from the comforts of U.S. air bases in Germany to the primitive new bases in France. The following is an amusing tale told by Les Bradford of his encounter

C-119G #53-8145.at Dreux AB, 1956.
John Traficante

in May 1955 with the stark reality of just how much contrast there was:

One morning my boss LT COL McConnell said, "Brad, I'm sending you down to (somewhere that sounded like Droodge) France, as a member of the advance party. You'll be getting the base set up for our wing when it moves there. How soon can you pack? They are cutting your orders now." Next day I was wheeling my new ′54 Ford V8 through central Europe. I did quite well finding my way until I came to the city of Dreux. I spoke no French and after several attempts at asking for instructions 'on the economy' as it was called in those days, I started to drive in ever widening circles until I came to the main gate of *Droodge*. Dreux was a one-day drive from Rhein-Main but now it was late at night.

This was memorable! No one was manning the gate, which looked like an outhouse. In the glare of my headlights I could see a very muddy road that led to some vague black shapes on the horizon. It was a little scary! Had there been an uprising? No lights! Were the Messerschmitts attacking? I tooted my horn. "Wake up everyone, 2d LT Bradford is here to advance your primitive butts!" Then I noticed that a single wiggling dim light was probably coming up that mud road, headed for me. As it drew nearer I could see the grill of a very beat-up '53 Dodge pickup truck, and it had the paint scheme of an Air Police vehicle. I couldn't believe that the police were allowed to run with one very dim headlight.

An Airman climbed out and saluted me and went on to explain there was a power failure. He said if I followed him I would not get stuck. He led me to headquarters, and with a flashlight he helped me sign in to the 7305th Air Base Squadron. The CQ was sound asleep on a cot and we didn't wake him. Then with the same instructions to follow his wheel ruts, the patient AP led me to the BOQ which was a new building but lacking supplies. With his flashlight we found a cot and a striped mattress. "I guess there are no blankets sir," he said. He didn't mention there was no pillow either, or sheets. But I was dead tired and used my issue overcoat as a blanket and rolled up something I dragged from my B-4 bag as a pillow, and slept as an advanced party member should—soundly.

The 60th Troop Carrier Wing became the first tactical wing to operate from the still unfinished Dreux AB. The majority of wing personnel moved to France; only those whose overseas tours of duty were within six months of completion remained at Rhein-Main. After three years of construction the base was becoming habitable for men and aircraft, but was still a far cry from the facilities in Germany. Family housing was very substandard compared to Rhein-Main AB and off base German family quarters.

On 1 January 1956 the 11th Troop Carrier Squadron reported a strength of 40 officers and 120 airmen, though it was authorized 43 officers and 145 airmen.

12th TCSq C-119G-FA #53-8152 at Dreux AB.
John Needam

12th Troop Carrier Squadron loading a jeep into a C-119 at Dreux AB, 1956.
John Needam

12th TCSq shops line the back of maintenance hangar, Dreux AB 1956.
John Needam

Interior of transport size hangar, C-119 in for maintenance and squadron mascot at Dreux AB, 1956.
John Needam

C-119 / R-4360 engine repair, 60th Troop Carrier Wing.
John Needam

Airshow at Dreux, 1956. C-119 inside large transport size hangar, note door clearance.
John Needam

Table 10.1 60th Troop Carrier Wing Manning 30 November 1955

	Authorized	Assigned		Authorized	Assigned
Officers	244	250	FR Civilians	364	313
Airmen	1.523	1.363	DAF Civilians	17	17
Total	1,767	1,613	Allied Officer	1	1
			Total	382	331

In May 1956 Dreux was assigned its first female WAC, a Captain serving at HQ, 60th TCWg with the job of Personal Affairs Officer.

Commanders of the 60th TCWg while it was stationed in France were: COL Clyde Box, from 1 August 1955 to 13 February 1956; COL Randolph E. Churchill, from 22 May 1956 to 24 September 1958; and COL James W. Ingram who took command 25 September 1958.

The primary mission of the 60th was to transport U.S. Army and other NATO airborne and ground forces throughout Europe. The wing always maintained its ability to drop airborne forces into a combat operation, but intra-theater airlift support became its primary operation. The majority of the missions were short-haul air logistics support trips to support U.S./NATO forces, such as transporting equipment and spare parts between air bases. Surface transportation in Europe was extremely slow, even ten years after the war, plus damage or loss of surface shipped material was much too common. Aircraft spare parts usually had such high value that the cost of airlift was reasonable. Another very important airlift mission was the transport of personnel and equipment to support aircraft weapons training on desert ranges in Libya and Morocco, North Africa. Eight to ten C-119s were required to move each fighter squadron to and from Wheelus or Nouasseur Air Bases for this extremely important pilot proficiency training.

Table 10.2 shows the mission symbols used by the C-119 units and crews in France indicating different catagories of flight operations and aircraft utilization.

The tempo of C-119G operations slowed from 850 flying hours a month per squadron down to about 700 per month during August and September 1955, as equipment and supplies were moved from Germany to France. By October each flying squadron again built up to 850 hours per month on the fleet of eighteen Boxcars. A heavy workload of periodic inspections was required to maintain this flying rate. At this time a Curtiss-Wright tech rep was assigned by Twelfth Air Force to assist the wing with their R-3350 engines; he conducted numerous lectures to air crews and engine mechanics to improve engine reliability.

After arrival at Dreux the 60th reorganized its aircraft maintenance system from squadron crew chief to the Consolidated Specialized Maintenance Program. The concept was to have a centralized maintenance organization at wing level with a single manager rather than three separate maintenance units at the squadron level. The flying squadrons lost maintenance capability and the majority of their maintenance men. In January 1956 this program was officially adopted with the transfer of most maintenance troops from the 10th, 11th, and 12th Troop Carrier Squadrons to the 60th Field Maintenance Squadron. The 60th FMSq grew to a strength of 14 officers and 490 airmen. All scheduled aircraft inspections and maintenance, and most unscheduled repairs were now performed by the enlarged maintenance squadron. Flying squadrons retained a crew chief for each C-119 to do routine flight line servicing and to fly with his airplane. Many meetings, much personnel reorganization, movement of equipment/supply, and new offices were required to accomplish this change. A C-119 periodic inspection was required after every 100 hours of flying, so five periodic inspection docks were constructed to meet the flying schedules.

Also at this time, the 60th Wing was supporting the first TAC rotational troop carrier squadron, the 62d TCSq flying C-119Gs, that moved to Dreux for 120 days from the 314th TCWg, Sewart AFB, Tennessee. The 62d was testing the dual basing concept of troop carrier aircraft for USAF. Dual basing was tested during 1954-55 by three fighter squadrons, one reconnaissance squadron, and the troop carrier squadron. This was the first study of reducing USAFE units in France.

Flying hours declined in spring 1956 due to the worst winter weather in France in eighty years, a shortage of air crews, a critical shortage of aircraft engines, and a French air traffic controllers strike. The 60th was flying approximately 500 hours per squadron per month, down from a scheduled 800 hours per month.

Table 10.2 C-119 Mission Symbols

Symbol and Name		Mission
FLS	Fleetline Special	Non-scheduled special missions on a directed itinerary.
JT	Joint Training	Joint Army and NATO training maneuvers or exercises.
UT	Unit Training	Formation, parabundle drops, low level navigation training flights.
TA	Tactical Airlift	Airlift of USAFE units to/from operational locations.
ALS	Air Logistic Service	Scheduled air cargo movement flights.
US	Unit Support	Maintenance test flights, equipment calibration, wing and squadron administrative support.
TR	Transition	Flight tests, proficiency flight checks, and standardization checks.
AD	Air Division	322d Air Division support flights

The 800-hour flying schedule became standard for the three C-119 wings based in France. "Project Athena" required the 60th to keep five C-119s based at Athens, Greece, to immediately provide airlift support for contingencies in Turkey and other Middle East countries. The 60th was suddenly tasked in February 1956 to support Project SNOWBOUND a disaster relief mission hauling food and medical aid to Italy and northern Greece. Some relief aid (food, clothing, and animal feed) had to be air dropped into small isolated mountain towns. Several months flying exceeded the 2,400 hours programmed for each wing, depending on the European theater crisis of the week. The airlift crews seldom had a one to one ratio with their assigned Boxcars; crew shortages were commonplace. It is a great tribute to the aircrew's stamina and the maintenance crew's skills that more C-119s were not lost while operating from France.

Each of the large hangars could accommodate two C-119s at once, and they typically needed three days in the inspection docks. With a wingspan of 110 feet and height of 26 feet, the Boxcar was larger than a B-17 Flying Fortress! If aircraft parts were not available, the scheduled inspection time would be delayed and the aircraft placed in Aircraft Out of Commission, Parts (AOCP) status. A shortage of Wright R-3350-89 compound aircraft engines in Europe caused frequent AOCP groundings. The fundamental parts shortages were created by limiting base aircraft spare parts inventories to quantities "estimated" in 1950, and never revising these quantities to support typical flying schedules. As flight hours increased, aircraft aged, and some parts failed more frequently than predicted; there was no in-depth stock available in USAFE resulting in C-119s being grounded. C-119 in-commission rates in France normally varied between 55 and 70 percent. A good example of the aircraft parts problem was C-119G #53-7854. It was placed in AOCP status after inspection on 10 March 1956 for wing flap actuators. On 20 April its nose gear axle was removed to keep another C-119 in commission and the axle immediately ordered ACOP. Several messages were exchanged with CONUS depots, and on 6 June the supply officer at Dreux was informed that the parts were "Warehouse Refusal" meaning they were not authorized. Further messages revealed the problem was that the supply clerks did not know the 60th TCWg had moved from Rhein-Main to France with the same C-119 aircraft. More messages finally resulted in the required parts being shipped and #7854 was returned to operations on 17 July, after five months sitting on the ground. Unfortunately this was a common problem that drove aircraft maintenance men to drinking Cognac, Calvados and Pernod. Another ongoing task was repairing damaged aircraft cargo floors.

Many other problems had to be overcome by the 60th Troop Carrier Wing to maintain this flying schedule. Aircraft refueling trucks, model F-1A, had high rates of engine and pump failures, and this limited flight operations. A C-119 squadron consumed 215,000 gallons of 115/130 octane aviation fuel and 2,150 gallons of engine oil a month so refueling trucks were extremely important vehicles. At one period, half the F-1A fuel trucks at Dreux were out of service! Frustrated, the wing maintenance officer took the initiative and arranged through the Chateauroux Depot to pick up the needed parts at Moulins Sub-Depot. MSGT Girard, 60th Motor Vehicle Sq was dispatched in a

C-119 from the 60th Troop Carrier Wing loading equipment crates at the CHAD depot.
"History Central Air Materiel Area, Europe" via William Adamek

blue USAF pick-up truck on a 500-mile round trip to hand carry 36 requisitions for F-1A parts. He returned with 24 filled requisitions and within eight hours, two refueling trucks were returned to service. The following day three more F-1As were pumping fuel into C-119s. The 60th Wing found the primary reason for inoperative vehicles was the total lack of repair parts, not the lack of skilled manpower. A few days later MSGT Girard was sent to Brussels, Belgium to pick-up of parts from the Ford Motor Company, General Motors, the Chrysler Corporation, and International Harvester. In July he made another trip and returned with 1,000 pounds of Ford truck parts.

An unusual action was suddenly required in January 1956. General Lee, Commander, Twelfth Air Force ordered all wing/base commanders to personally conduct an inventory of base vehicles on the last day of every month! There is no record of what created this unusual inspection requirement. It was unconcerned about operational status, just the number of vehicles. Could there have been a black market for USAF vehicles in Germany?

Ground electronic systems were improved over the years the 60th operated at Dreux. On 20 January 1956, a new automatic dial base telephone system was put into operation. A French manufactured system purchased by NATO replaced the old manual WWII vintage Signal Corp TC-10 telephone switchboards. Off-base phone calls still required a manual operator. Base funded contracts for telephone maintenance were made with Compagnie Generale de Constructions Telephoniques, Paris, reducing USAF manning. During July 1956 the new MPN-11C GCA radar set was installed, replacing the original WWII model MPN-1. A ground direction finder (DF) station was constructed off base near the village of Dampierre-sur-Blevy (Site Annex #5310). An on-base TACAN ground station was scheduled for 1959, but installation of this new navigation facility was canceled to save funds.

A serious shortage of C-119 airborne radio operators developed in USAFE, requiring the 60th TCGp Headquarters to set-up an on-base training program. The USAF Air Training Command school had been closed because aircraft radio operators were not required. Radio operators were to be eliminated after 1955 because the new high-frequency single sideband (HF SSB) voice radio sets could be operated by the pilot or copilot. Since European airways required Morse Code for communication range and clarity, and did not have money to convert to HF SSB until the 1960s, the troop carrier wings had to train radio operators to accomplish their missions. Prospective C-119 radio operators were drawn from the 60th Comm Sq and aircraft radio repair sections. Candidates had to achieve a capability of twenty words per minute to operate in Europe, and learn proper radio procedures. This required many hours of classroom training using an EE-94 code tape training machine and highly skilled instructors.

Charles Lunsford, in his excellent book *Departure Message* tells of his experiences as a radio operator flying with the 12th Troop Carrier Squadron, 60th Troop Carrier Wing in the 1950s. He gives us a picture in this excerpt of some unusual hazards faced in the line of duty:

> There was a story about a small GI fire truck that was picked up by a crew in Tripoli. I don't recall who it happened to, but I remember the story.
>
> Those pieces of GI equipment were easy to load because most of them were designed to be airlifted by the C-119. All that had to be done was to put on the loading ramps, drive the vehicle up to the airplane, line up the center of gravity mark on it with the one painted on the floor, tie it down securely and drive up in the air with it. No problem of arranging a bunch of small boxes by weight and balance—vehicles were easy.
>
> At Wheelus, a detachment of loadmasters did the loading and all we had to do was inspect it before takeoff. At most other places we had to supervise the loading and sometimes we had to do the loading, working like coolies. But at Wheelus, we went to lunch.
>
> During the preflight inspection, the radio operator checked to see that the CG markings were lined up and checked the fire truck to make sure its fuel had been drained. The engineer checked the tie-down chains, found them secure and the two enlisted men pronounced the load ready to fly.
>
> All was well, the engines were started and the aircraft taxied out and got takeoff clearance. Full military emergency takeoff power (METO used for all takeoffs) was applied and the C-119 began its roll down the long runway with all instruments in the green. The pilot felt this airplane was slow to accelerate and appeared to be heavy. When he finally reached 130 knots, he pulled the nose wheel off—and it went right back down. This airplane did not want to fly. He was a smart pilot, so he reached up and chopped the throttles while telling the tower that he was aborting his takeoff.
>
> There was more than enough room to stop on the long runway at Wheelus and he taxied to the end of the runway, pulled off on the taxiway, and stopped. Everybody looked at everybody else. "This son-of-a-bitch didn't want to fly. What the hell's the matter?"
>
> "You see anything, Sarge? Was there a power loss?" The engineer shook his head, as did the co-pilot. The pilot called the tower and told them he was going to do a run-up, which was done with everybody peering at the engine instruments, looking for a telltale problem. Nothing. Everything checked out as it should, both engines running perfectly and delivering full power.
>
> The pilot asked the tower for permission to do a taxi check back down the runway and found a second time his airplane didn't want to fly. Again, he aborted and taxied off the runway. He turned to the radio operator. "Go back there and check the damn fire truck and see if there's something wrong with the loading." The radio operator rechecked everything, climbed all over it, and found nothing. It was the right fire truck and the weight was right—what the hell was the matter? He got down and looked under it and noted a small pool of liquid. He thought it was gasoline until he smelled it. It was water, dripping slowly under the truck.Water!?
>
> He climbed back to the flight deck and told the pilot, "There's nothing wrong with the load, Sir, but I think that bastard is full of water!" The pilot looked at him for a moment. "Water?" he said, disbelievingly. "Well, I'll be a dirty..." He slammed the throttles up and taxied back to the loading ramp and cut the engines. Everybody piled down to the cargo compartment and looked at the growing puddle underneath. Then they went out the door and did a walk around. The pilot walked over to the left main landing gear strut and peered at it, his face getting redder by the second. "Look at that damn oleo strut." He pointed to the big shock absorber on the gear. "It's all the way down." He ran around to the other landing gear, livid by this time, and that oleo strut was also completely compressed. The only thing that could do that was great weight; the airplane was grossly overloaded. It was a wonder the gear hadn't collapsed on those two runs down the runway.

They all looked at each other, knowing that if that airplane HAD come off the ground, it probably wouldn't have stayed there very long, they would all be burning in a ball of scrap aluminum wrapped around a GI fire truck down near the end of the runway.

"I'm going to have somebody's ass for this," roared the pilot and stalked off on a course for the loading area. The crew watched him stomping off and a poor unfortunate loadmaster happened to be in his way. They couldn't hear him, but could see him put the man at a brace and tear a strip off, waving his arms and gesturing toward his airplane. When he finished with that man, he went into the loading office and in about 30 seconds a large number of loadmasters came spilling out, running in all directions with the pilot following, yelling and waving his arms. From there he went toward base operations and was lost to sight. "Looks like he's a little pissed," the grinning co-pilot remarked.

Very soon, some 40 loadmasters converged on the aircraft, running this way and that, bumping into each other. There were even a couple of officers, a rarity around any kind of work like loading an airplane, and everybody was giving orders to everybody else. It looked like the New York Stock Exchange at 2:30, but somehow, the fire truck was off loaded and driven over to the edge of the ramp and cranked up. The pump was started and 19,000 pounds of water, about 3,000 gallons, was hosed out onto the Libyan Desert. The aircraft had been overloaded by about 10,000 pounds. It was very fortunate it wouldn't fly. It would probably have crashed. The pilot, we all heard, went all the way up to the base commander, barged into his office and tore a strip off him, too.

The end of the 60th Troop Carrier Wing is historically confusing. On 12 March 1957, Headquarters, 60th Troop Carrier Group, which directly supervised the three flying squadrons, was deactivated and the squadrons were then supervised by 60th Wing Headquarters. This reduction of tactical group headquarters was implemented at bases in Europe to reduce personnel. The 322d Air Division then decided that the wing level of command could be eliminated, and the air division could command directly down to the squadron level. The 60th Wing was deactivated on 25 September 1958, and the base and flying squadrons were assigned directly to the 322d Air Division at Evreux. Thirty months later additional USAFE budget cuts eliminated the 10th, 11th, and 12th Troop Carrier Squadrons. These were deactivated in place on 8 January 1961 at Dreux. All 60th Wing support units were also deactivated and the base reverted to standby status. Support personnel were assigned to the 317th Air Base Group and remained at Dreux or transferred to other USAFE bases. Evreux became the caretaker of Dreux from 1 January 1958 until November 1961.

309th Troop Carrier Group, Assault

The 309th Troop Carrier Group, Assault, flying C-123Bs, became Dreux's second combat airlift unit in May 1956. Upon arrival in France it was the first and only USAFE wing in Europe to fly the C-123B Providers. It had two important missions at Dreux, to increase its tactical airlift operational experience in the factory-new C-123Bs and to assist USAFE in improving dispersed operating base deployment support concepts.

COL William C. Bentley commanded the 309th TCGp during its service in France.

The 309th designator had been assigned to a WWII Medium Bombardment Group that flew B-25s while training replacement crews. The 309th Troop Carrier Group (Assault, Fixed Wing) was not an activated Air Force Reserve organization. It was a regular Air Force unit activated on 8 July 1955 at Ardmore AFB, Oklahoma and assigned to the 463d Troop Carrier Wing, Medium. Upon activation the 309th was equipped with factory-new Fairchild C-123B Providers.

The 309th departed Ardmore with fifty-four C-123B transports on 6 May 1956, arriving at Dreux from 22 May to 14 June. The wing moved in four separate flights across the North Atlantic, island hopping as described in chapter 2. It flew from Ardmore to McGuire AFB, New Jersey; then on to Goose Bay AB, Labrador; Narsarssuak AB (BW1), Greenland; Keflavik AB, Iceland; Prestwick, Scotland; and into Dreux AB, France. The wing supplied enroute maintenance teams to care for their unusual aircraft. The first flight led by the wing commander COL Bentley skipped the stop at Keflavik and flew from BW1 to Prestwick. With a no-load range of 1,700 miles, additional ferry tanks were not required. Even in May, the first flight encountered a five-day weather delay at Goose Bay.

The 309th Troop Carrier Group, Assault, consisted of approximately 120 officers and 460 airmen when ready to deploy to France. It had three flying squadrons: the 376th, 377th, and 378th, and direct support units. The group level organization implies a requirement to be assigned to another wing-base

C-123 #54-579 from the 309th TCGp at Dreux, transporting troops from Chambley AB to West Germany for bare base exercises, 1957.
Al Christensen

structure; it did not have the personnel manning to operate an air base. So, the 309th became an assigned unit of the 60th Troop Carrier Wing while based at Dreux, and was operationally controlled by the 322d Air Division. It was officially transferred to USAFE from Tactical Air Command effective 2 June 1956. This was exactly the idea of the Hobson Wing-Base plan adopted in 1949, that called for the rapid addition of combat flying squadrons or a combat group at an air base that already had a combat wing with all the necessary support units and personnel. The 309th was located on the west corner of the base in hangar and marguerite number three.

The Provider used two very reliable Pratt & Whitney R-2800-99W engines. Two 450-gallon long range drop tanks were added to provide a 1,400-mile operational range when loaded with a 5-ton payload. The C-123B did not have air-to-air refueling capability installed. Normally a three-man crew, pilot, co-pilot, and engineer/crew chief was needed for most airlift missions. Occasionally missions would require a loadmaster when an unusual or oversized load was scheduled, or when dropping airborne forces and cargo. The airframe was designed for rough, short-field operation that USAFE considered very important for wartime DOB operations. Also the Providers carried a radar interrogator set that worked with portable drop zone beacons to measure range and azimuth for bad weather or night delivery of airborne forces.

On 23 May 1956, five C-123s flew their first scheduled ALS mission from Dreux AB to Chateauroux AD as directed by the 322d Air Division. Initially the C-123 was prohibited by the 322d AD from carrying passengers, and limited to a maximum take-off gross weight of 52,000 pounds. The 60th and 465th TCWg provided experienced air route check-pilots to check out the 309th pilots for European flying. The 322d demanded a minimum of twenty-five hours of route flying and two trips over the scheduled air routes to ensure safe operations. The 309th was programmed to fly 2,400 hours per month on their fifty-four new Providers, which was a real test for its maintenance crews. The C-123B's periodic inspection interval was seventy-five hours, which required an inspection cycle of one and a half days. The 309th set up four periodic inspection docks manned by forty airmen to meet this flying schedule. The wash rack where three aircraft were thoroughly cleaned every day prior to dock inspections was manned by two airmen and four French "Native Son" civilians. After fifty years it is hard to remember how much 100-weight oil and dirt had to be washed off engines and nacelles to see what troubles could be lurking deep inside these areas.

The 309th flew its C-123Bs in ALS and special missions (SAM) throughout France, Germany, Italy, Spain, and England. The longer missions were left to the C-119 fleet. The 309th participated in several airlifts of equipment and personnel from Chambley, Chaumont, and Etain Air Bases into their respective DOBs at Chalons, Brienne, and Vouziers during exercises. The C-123s clearly demonstrated their ability to quickly move the fighter squadron recovery teams to their DOBs and arrive prior to the fighters' return from their simulated strike mission. The recovery teams could then meet the one-hour window allowed to refuel and rearm their fighters for a second combat mission. The Providers could load, fly, and unload at the DOB before the road convoy's arrival. It reduced

378th Troop Carrier Squadron C-123 #54-585.
USAF Museum

378th TCSq, 309th TCGp C-123 #54-577.
National Archives

the need for a large truck motor pool at each base and concerns for convoy safety while on the rural roads of France. There were insufficient air police at the bases to provide convoy protection in case of war. C-123Bs proved their design was viable for this type of wing support. One USAFE study proposed basing six C-123Bs at each tactical air base to directly support DOB movements and other tactical deployments, thus eliminating the two C-47s at each base. The operating costs of both aircraft types were very similar.

But, USAFE decided the capabilities versus limitations of the C-123B was not worth the expense, and agreed to its elimination from the budget after two years at Dreux. The Providers had limited all-weather capability, reduced range, and smaller payloads than the C-119; but operated at about half the cost. It was obvious though, that three C-119 wings were capable of providing all required theater airlift. Also, the DOB concept was proving too costly (as described in chapter 17), therefore, the need for the C-123s to support the DOBs evaporated.

USAFE did not inactivate the 309th in France, but alerted it on 20 April 1958 to return to CONUS with all aircraft and equipment. All C-123Bs at Dreux returned to Ardmore AFB during July and August, flying back across the North Atlantic route. The 309th Troop Carrier Group was once again assigned to Tactical Air Command on 25 September 1958.

During the period the 60th Wing and the 309th Group were operating at Dreux, there were several tenant units on the base. These were the Defense Area Communications Control Center, Europe (DACCCE); Det #14; 8th Radio Relay Squadron; Det #5, 12th Air Postal Squadron (APO 84); Det #13, 18th Weather Squadron (later changed to Det #12, 31st Weather Sq); 1274th Communication Squadron (AACS); 7650th Aero Chart and Information Squadron; 7135th School Group; and HQ 5th Aerial Port Squadron. Also the U.S. Army HQ 29th Signal Battalion, and later Headquarters of the 8th Radio Relay Squadron were based at Dreux. DACCCE was an unusual tenant unit; it provided Defense Communications Agency (DCA), communications switching and technical control services to and from Europe for the U.S. Command and NATO Military Command. Later DACCCE relocated to Camp des Loges, near Paris, to be closer to EUCOM Headquarters.

Headquarters, 5th Aerial Port Squadron moved to Dreux from overcrowded Evreux AB with six officers and seventy airmen in October 1958. It was located at marguerite number three and was supported by the 60th Troop Carrier Wing. The squadron received additional personnel and equipment while at Dreux. In October 1960, as space became available, the 5th Aerial Port Squadron returned to Evreux. A complete description of the 5th can be found in chapter 12, Evreux AB.

7305th Combat Support Group

After deactivation of the 60th, Evreux Air Base supplied base support at Dreux for the 10th, 11th, and 12th Squadrons until their deactivation. From September 1958 through 1 November 1961, Dreux was classified as standby; the air base and tenant units were supported by the 7305th Combat Support Squadron and 317th Air Base Group from nearby Evreux. Insufficient manning in these organizations prevented adequate caretaking at Dreux, and serious deterioration of buildings, utilities, and its vehicle fleet resulted. There were few flight operations into Dreux during its three years as a standby base. From November 1961 through July 1962 Dreux was operated by the

7117th Tactical Wing, 117th Air Base Group, and then returned to the 7305th Air Base Group.

A serious civil engineering problem and interesting solution occurred during 1962 with a base underground POL fuel-storage tank. POL tanks were underground and fed by underground pipelines to protect the base fuel supply from air attacks. The 7117th Civil Engineering Squadron was inspecting and cleaning all POL tanks to improve fuel quality. After removal of fuel from a 106,000-gallon steel tank, a welded seam on the bottom near the sump pit burst open and inward during cleaning. The seam failure was caused by hydrostatic pressure buildup of accumulated fuel and water on the exterior of the tank bottom, between the tank and concrete encasement. The decision had to be made to repair or replace. Repair would require re-welding the seam. This was most economical but very dangerous because of explosive vapors. Replacement would require excavation, tank removal, installation of a new tank, plumbing hookup, and pressure tests. All this would take about three months and be very expensive. A POL specialist, Mr. Wills, was sent to Dreux from HQ USAFE to assist in making the decision whether or not to repair the tank. After the decision was made to repair, they began by drilling a hole in the bottom of the tank. Fuel and water from around the tank rapidly drained into it and was pumped out. Mr. Wills and a civil engineering shop welder went into the tank, welded the damaged seam and vent hole. While this welding was being performed a gas vapor detection test set monitored the vapor levels. Tank repair was accomplished without incident; obviously the fuel vapor test set worked properly! The author does hope that the civil engineering squadron welder was awarded a three-day pass to Paris!

Dreux Resident High School

Another important activity on Dreux was the American Dependent Resident High School begun in September 1960 with capacity for five hundred pupils in grades nine to twelve. For several years U.S. high school students had attended the American High School in Paris. At that time the French Algerian problem was causing unrest, and Paris was frequently the site of demonstrations. If rioting occurred in Paris that resulted in casualties among the American students, it could create serious diplomatic problems. Most students were dependents of U.S. Government civilian and military personnel stationed in twenty-six different countries across Europe, Africa, and the Middle East. To reduce costs and improve student safety, USAFE directed that the high school be relocated to Dreux Air Base. These students boarded at Dreux for the entire school year. Students from nearby Evreux AB were bussed to Dreux and lived there from Sunday night through Friday afternoon. Day students were dependents of fathers assigned to Dreux AB. In December 1962, the boarding students paid $1.60 per day for meals, bed linen, and laundry service, but there was no tuition fee. The 322d Air Division became the primary agency to operate the on-base school, including selection of the principal and teachers from the United States. Mr. Ross Tipton was selected as Supervising Principal for this high school. The school was provided a very good budget and operated with some autonomy from the DOD school system. The base's 1,000-man mess hall was divided in half to separate the airmen and students. Students were accommodated in six former, two-story airmen barracks buildings, three for the young men and three for the young women.

A Community Service Center was opened on 10 April 1961 to provide for the recreational needs of the 360 high school students and 220 airmen stationed at Dreux. The 7305th Personnel Services Section, located on base, processed all passports and visas for these students with the American Embassy in Paris and various foreign consulates. Medical support was supplied by the Evreux base hospital since the small hospital at Dreux was closed. Most importantly, the high school accomplished its mission of providing an excellent education to its students over the six years it operated at Dreux until it had to relocate to Kaiserslautern as part of Project FRELOC in 1967.

117th Tactical Reconnaissance Wing

The 117th Tactical Reconnaissance Wing, Alabama ANG, consisting of approximately 240 officers and 1,440 airmen, was called to federal active duty on 1 October 1961 for a period of twelve months during the Berlin Crisis. This was the second tour of duty for the 117th TRWg in France; the wing had opened Toul-Rosieres AB in January 1952. When activated, the wing had four tactical reconnaissance squadrons and supporting units assigned: the 106th based at Sumpter Smith Airport, Birmingham, Alabama; the 153d at Key Field, Meridian, Mississippi; the 160th based at Dannelly Field, Montgomery, Alabama; and the 184th at Fort Smith Municipal Airport, Arkansas. Its four squadrons had been flying Republic RF-84F Thunderflashes since 1957. The 117th moved only a portion of its total strength and one reconnaissance squadron, the 106th Tactical Reconnaissance Squadron, to France. The 106th had twenty-three RF-84Fs upon activation but not all were operational; three of the aircraft were cannibalized, and the parts brought the remaining twenty aircraft to fully operational status. The three RF-84s left at Birmingham were later repaired and transferred to other squadrons.

TAC briefings conducted for wing personnel in Birmingham, Alabama, were totally erroneous in their description of conditions at the standby bases. The TAC briefer had not set foot in France, and was using information supplied by USAFE people based in Germany. First elements of the 117th ADVON arrived at Dreux, on 24 October 1961, and within four hours after arrival the ADVON Commander immediately realized the base was barely usable! He was briefed on several serious problems in the vehicles, buildings and telephone system and realized that severe shortages of vehicle parts, fuel stocks, and office equipment existed in base supply.

The 106th deployed their twenty RF-84Fs from Birmingham, Alabama, to Dreux AB, France, on 27 October 1961 as part of Operation STAIR STEP. The deployment consisted of five days of island hopping from McGuire Air Force Base to Argentia, Newfoundland; to Lajes, Azores; to Moron, Spain; and then on to Dreux. Wing Commander, BGEN George R. Doster, Jr. led the squadron to France. Sixteen RF-84Fs arrived at Dreux on 3 November; bad weather and minor repairs delayed the last four aircraft until 9 November. The trip took about 10.5 hours of flying time. This was the first time RF-84F aircraft had flown the Atlantic; previously they had been shipped to Europe. General Curtiss Le May praised the 117th for this rapid deployment.

In addition to the twenty RF-84s, the 117th was also tasked to deploy two T-33s and one C-47 in a separate move to Dreux. The T-Birds joined ten others from STAIR STEP units at Langley AFB, Virginia, and flew one leg a day across the Atlantic. The route took them to Loring AFB, Maine; Goose Bay, Labrador; Sondrestrom, Greenland (BW-8); Keflavik, Iceland; Prestwick, Scotland; and finally to Dreux. The C-47 was equipped with several extra fuel tanks and flew from Langley, to Goose Bay, to Lajes, to Dreux. The C-47 trip took twenty-nine hours and forty minutes flying time.

By 11 November, 948 officers and airmen had arrived, plus 377,000 pounds of air cargo. The rear detachment arrived from CONUS ten days later. Most of the wing's equipment was still enroute by surface shipping, which required about three months of movement time.

By 22 November 1961, the wing had assembled at newly reactivated Dreux AB for an estimated stay of ten months. On 28 November the 117th Tactical Reconnaissance Wing was redesignated the 7117th Tactical Wing because of its reduced force structure in USAFE. LTC James E. Hardwick became the 7117th Commander. The 153d, 160th, and 184th Squadrons and their support units remained on extended active duty at their ANG home stations ready to reinforce the 7117th at Dreux. The wing headquarters at Birmingham, Alabama, and the three CONUS based squadrons remained the 117th Tactical Reconnaissance Wing while assigned to TAC. As 1961 came to an end, the 7117th Tactical Wing had still not received their property sent by ship from CONUS, or any equipment requisitioned, or supplies ordered after 15 October.

After arrival at Dreux, the 106th learned the French Government would not allow jet aircraft flight operations from the base! French Air Traffic Controllers had decided that Dreux was too close to Paris airports. The controllers alleged that jet aircraft flying from Dreux would cause hazardous air traffic flow problems in the Paris airspace. The 106th TRSq was grounded! On 3 November the commander of the 117th TRWg received the following teletype message from HQ USAFE; Lindsey Air Station, West Germany,

"AIR OPERATIONS, DREUX AB, FRANCE. 117 TAC RECON WING WILL NOT CONDUCT JET OPERATIONS FROM DREUX AB UNTIL PROPER ARRANGEMENTS ARE COMPLETED WITH FRENCH AUTHORITIES. NORMAL CONVENTIONAL OPERATIONS IN THE DREUX-EVREUX COMPLEX WILL BE CONTINUED."

Needless to say this was not well received by wing personnel after being called to active duty, risking the winter Atlantic crossing, having to restore a rundown air base, and then end up only flying one C-47 to solve the Berlin crisis! The Kennedy Administration and State Department would not force this operational issue with the French government, and Headquarters USAFE would not relocate the wing and close Dreux. On 18 November, Seventeenth Air Force sent a message to the 117th stating the French government authorized the movement of six RF-84Fs on 28 November to Chaumont AB in TDY status for theater indoctrination training and operational flying. Another fourteen RF-84Fs and two T-33s were allowed to fly to Chaumont on 8 December. The airspace control problem was never resolved, resulting in the Thunderflashes making one landing and one takeoff at Dreux during the Berlin crisis. The sixty miles separating Dreux and

RF-84F #52-7425 from the 106th TRSq, 117th TRWg, Alabama ANG, at Sumpter Smith Airport, Alabama, prior to activation.
Alabama Air National Guard

the Paris Orly or Le Bourget airports were not enough to overcome the raw political power of the controller's union over the de Gaulle government and NATO. The 117th TRWg leaders wondered if the French controllers would have prevented their use of Dreux in the event of WWIII?

This divided operation required the 7117th to solve many difficult management problems to meet operational tasking at Chaumont—two hundred miles away from the Wing's Combat Operations Center at Dreux! This span of control would have been impossible without the USAFE microwave radio relay system maintained by the 7th and 8th Radio Relay Squadrons.

The first action of the wing staff was to write-up operational and contingency plans, and compose wartime reconnaissance mission target folders as required by Seventeenth Air Force war plans. The 7117th received invaluable assistance from the 66th TRWg at Laon Air Base so that one man—the plans officer—was able to prepare all plans by 23 December. These were difficult to write because they had to include the 106th now deployed to Chaumont AB.

The scope of the necessary 7117th Tactical Wing plans were as follows;

Combat Alert Plan (CAP)
Tactical Alert Plan (TAP)
OPLAN 155-61 KEEN KNIFE
OPLAN 170-61 HENNY PENNY
OPLAN 180-62 Wing Employment Plan
DCP 290-62 Disaster Control Plan
Emergency Defense Plan (EDP)
Base Security Plan
Base Defense Plan
Base Demolition Plan
Non-Combatant Evacuation Plan
Tactical Hospital Evacuation Plan

These war or contingency plans were prepared and revised by all combat wings based in Europe. Most importantly, they had to be studied and understood by all officers and airmen required to perform duties directed by these plans. Intelligence section personnel had to prepare and update as many as fifteen different wartime target folders for each combat pilot/aircrew assigned to a squadron. Much of this material was classified TOP SECRET and required special handling procedures and storage. All plans were approved by 14 January 1962, and intense training began throughout the wing to satisfactorily pass the forthcoming tactical evaluation and operational readiness inspections.

The 7117th Wing Commander attempted to alleviate the serious morale problem that existed by having the Plans Officer present a special "Why We Are Here" briefing to all wing personnel during December. The subjects presented and discussed were:

- Review of the very successful movement to France.
- Russia's Cold-War, limited wars, and general war objectives.
- Russia's Berlin and East Germany objectives.
- America's Cold-War objectives.
- The 7117th Tactical Wing's role in accomplishing

America's objectives.
• France and the French people's objectives.

The Plans Officer even had the courage to conduct a question and answer period for all attendees that would be very interesting to present here if the sessions had been recorded. This officer was able to eliminate many misunderstandings and rumors with his presentations; and wing morale noticeably improved after these briefings.

The first real tactical mission undertaken by the 106th Squadron after setting up at Chaumont was Operation EYEBALL, conducted in late December. This operation exercised the Army and Air Force communications networks by requesting target photo missions and rapid reporting of photo results. Every mission was a precision photo run on small targets in West Germany that the army requested during a war game. Photo results were very good; camera film magazines were downloaded within three minutes after jet engine shut down, and sixteen minutes later the film was developed, dried, and being viewed on Army Photo Interpreters' light tables for intelligence analysis. This first small exercise greatly improved morale of the troops deployed at Chaumont.

Three Unit Manning Document (UMD) changes during October and November changed many airmen's job codes (AFSCs) and resulted in many of the recalled filler Air Force Reserve airmen being untrained in their new jobs. These men now felt that they were illegally recalled to active duty if they did not serve in their primary AFSC. They proceeded to aggressively petition their Congressional Representatives about their job changes and demanded early releases! The UMD changes required 524 airmen out of the 998 assigned to undergo extensive on-the-job training and earn new AFSCs.

Another misuse of manpower occurred in the 117th Reconnaissance Technical Squadron manned by fifteen officers and ninety-eight airmen. Their mission was to produce reconnaissance technical data and intelligence reports for a numbered air force command level operations staff. Upon activation, the complete squadron moved to France and surface-shipped their equipment. Before their departure TAC inspectors required that four hundred supply-line items be ordered immediately from the Mobile Air Depot. But, by 1 February 1962, none of this equipment had arrived in France! Consequently, this unit had no equipment, no work facilities, and no mission in USAFE. Squadron morale became alarmingly low. Personnel were loaned out to all other squadrons for menial tasks, which only aggravated the situation.

Fortunately, Seventeenth Air Force requested sixty men be sent for ninety days in TDY status to the 497th Reconnaissance Technical Squadron at Wiesbaden for classroom and on-the-job training. The 117th Recce Tech Squadron integrated well into the 497th and augmented their work sections. This was an excellent program that provided a small bright spot in the 117th's discouraging story.

After its arrival the squadron had submitted detailed plans to convert a supply warehouse at Dreux into a reconnaissance technical facility, but these plans were disapproved by USAFE, DSC/Civil Engineering on 31 January. This scheme was changed into modifying eight new A3A thirty-five-foot cargo vans that had been delivered to the base. Again detailed plans were prepared and submitted on 19 March 1962 for approval. Unit equipment had finally begun arriving in March, so the 117th Recce Tech Squadron was eager to find a work facility. No information on the status of the proposal was received from Seventeenth Air Force until 5 June. At this time Seventeenth Air Force informed the squadron that the van project was canceled due to the squadron's early departure from USAFE. So the 117th Reconnaissance Technical Squadron history ends with statements that $150,000 in equipment lay idle for five months and over 3,500 officer man-days plus 25,500 airman man-days were expended without a single tasking of their assigned mission!

Upon arrival in France the 7117th Tactical Wing listed the following mission equipment in its historical report: twenty RF-84F Thunderflashes with eighty each, .50cal., M3 machine guns (four per aircraft). Airborne photographic equipment available for installation consisted of: twenty-six Cameras, Type K-17C with 6" lens cones; twenty-five Cameras, Type KA-22 with 12" lens cones; fifteen Cameras, Type KA-22 with 24" lens cones; and twenty Cameras, Type KA-38 with 36" lens cones. These aerial cameras required film magazines of different film sizes and capacities depending upon photo mission assignments.The wing possessed forty-six Film Magazines, Type A-9B; twenty-three Type A-8; and twenty Type LA-12. All their RF-84Fs had an A-17VF vertical viewfinder installed to improve aircraft/camera track-line positioning. This assemblage of camera systems provided 100 percent operational capability for typical daytime tactical photo reconnaissance to meet air and ground forces intelligence collection requirements. The major deficiency that had to be solved was the construction of a photo laboratory; Dreux Air Base was not built to house a tactical reconnaissance wing, therefore, no building was available for film development and

106th Tactical Reconnaissance photo lab trailers at Chaumont AB.
USAF history Office, Maxwell AFB.

printing. The base had been selected for the 117th Tactical Reconnaissance Wing because it had parking spaces and five hangars for its four assigned RF-84F squadrons in then event all flying units were moved to France if the Berlin crisis escalated. The photo laboratory problem was solved by converting two A3A cargo vans into a mobile lab. The 106th TRSq built this lab facility and moved it to Chaumont AB.

On 10 January 1962, Det #1, 7117th Tactical Wing was organized at Chaumont as a tenant unit of the 7108th Tactical Wing. A host-tenant agreement was made with the 7108th to support the squadron of four hundred officers and airmen, and the 7108th provided outstanding support. The 7117th realized that permission to fly their RF-84Fs at Dreux would never be forthcoming from the French government, so they planned a minimum stay at Chaumont of at least nine more months. The wing's Chief of Maintenance and staff also moved to Chaumont to manage the RF-84F work force. The wing next realized it needed additional pilots to meet this divided operational tasking. A call went out for volunteer pilots from the wing's three CONUS based reconnaissance squadrons. The response was overwhelming and the pilot shortage was quickly solved. The new wing Combat Operations Center remained at Dreux and maintained effective control at both locations. Similar to the other combat wings based in France, the 7117th participated in many NATO and Seventeenth Air Force exercises to maintain proficiency and operational standards. Some of these exercises were:

GRAND SLAM	INDIAN SUMMER
GUN TALK	KEEN KNIFE
MAKE HASTE	MARNE ROCK
QUICK TRAINS	ROUND ROBIN
SHARP EYES	SKI JUMP
SUPER CHIEF	TEMPO BELLO
REDEYE	COLD TURKEY
LONG THRUST	SUN BASE

Tactical Evaluation
Operational Readiness Inspection
General Inspection.

The RF-84Fs were also tasked to provide air defense and close air support because they were equipped with four .50cal. machine guns.

The first deployment exercise was Operation SUN BASE, tasking the RF-84Fs to conduct photography missions in North Africa, flying from Ben Guerir AB, French Morocco. Day photo practice was almost impossible over France's winter skies. Six Thunderflashes at a time operated in Africa. All aircraft were rotated through the exercise, flying a total of 209 sorties for 320 hours in one month. C-130s provided airlift for support teams and equipment. Excellent weather allowed all 106th pilots to complete their tactical upgrade check flights. Photo mission quality contests were held with the 66th Tactical Reconnaissance Wing that also deployed to Ben Guerir. The 106th lost by a small margin against the RF-101C Voodoos.

A four-man photo maintenance team was dispatched to Morocco to support this photo training. They were kept busy loading 3,500 feet of aerial film

Table 10.3 7117th Tactical Wing Manning June 1962

	Officers	Airmen	French Civilians	Total
Authorized:	134	1,122	60	1,416
Assigned:	128	995	39	1,152

in magazines while changing 311 different camera configurations. The team found after arrival at Ben Guerir that there was no camera repair shop space, and more importantly no darkroom for downloading exposed film. The team improvised by reworking a large wooden packing crate found in the base supply-shipping section into a darkroom. This worked very well and was shared with the 66th Detachment. Excellent preventive maintenance resulted in only two recorded camera malfunctions during the thirty days. SUN BASE provided refresher training that paid off later during the wings' tactical evaluation in March; seventy-one successful photo missions were completed without camera malfunctions. The photo intelligence section maintained "excellent" ratings throughout all exercises and inspections.

In May, Detachment #1 participated in NATO exercise SQUADRON EXCHANGE in which 106th pilots and crews traded places with Royal Netherlands Air Force RF-84F pilots and crews from Deeland, Netherlands. This exercise was considered to be very effective in establishing common terminology and standards for photo reconnaissance missions. The maintenance personnel were very impressed with the excellent quality of the RNAF aircraft. The Norwegian Air Force also sent three F-84Fs to Chaumont for orientation flights. Total flying time showed a steady increase in 1962; 1,350 hours were flown in the first quarter of 1962, and the second quarter resulted in 1,650 hours accumulated during fourteen to sixteen sorties a day. Flying hours in the first quarter were lower than usual due to aileron control rod inspection and replacement. The RF-84F and F-84F airframes were almost identical, therefore, both types developed similar faults.

A long delayed logistical problem was solved during March and April by STAIR STEP and other NATO units flying F-84Fs; the RF/F-84F Fly Away Kits (FAK) had incorrect parts, insufficient critical parts, and overstocked parts. Several meetings led to a complete rewrite of FAK stock listings that resulted in changes to 2,600 line-item parts. Maintenance personnel were required to correctly identify parts versus part numbers. By going through this exercise, approximately 1,500 excess and incorrectly numbered line-item parts were identified and deleted from the FAKs. These parts became base supply assets and were issued when needed by maintenance. This listing was used over the following ten years with only slight revisions.

During June 1962, the manning of the 7117th Tactical Wing, including Detachment #1 at Chaumont is shown in Table 10.3. These numbers do not include the ten base tenant units. The wing's payroll was approximately $240,000 per month.

It was practically impossible to maintain the desired level of local civilian employment at Dreux due to the base's remoteness and the common knowledge that it would not remain active after the 7117th Wing's departure. Airman manning was also dropping due to the lack of new filler personnel from USAFE. Also, airmen departing on emergency leaves to CONUS did not return to France after DOD announced its early release program in March 1962.

In March notice was received from Seventeenth Air Force outlining the plans for early release of the activated reserve forces during August 1962. Extensive planning was necessary to coordinate the transfer of Dreux back to the 7305th Support Squadron and 317th Air Base Group at Evreux before the 7117th Wing departed Dreux. The base would again revert to standby status, all tenant units would remain, and the high school would be kept in operation. The resident high school became the only reason why Dreux was not closed and returned to the French government in 1962 .

The 7117th's complex departure plan was submitted to Seventeenth Air Force by 8 June 1962. Redeployment planning included advance party, aircraft enroute teams, main echelon, and rear detachment movement orders; surface and airlift transportation requirements; and base phase-down schedule.

All Detachment #1 personnel, aircraft, and equipment would move directly from Chaumont Air Base back to Birmingham, Alabama. Initially RF-84Fs were to redeploy to the U.S. with their peculiar support equipment and spares. This directive was changed by USAFE to ensure all maintenance shop equipment would be left in France to support the F-84Fs being assigned to the new 366th Tactical Fighter Wing. Many logistics meetings were necessary to develop the mission equipment lists, and to determine where this support equipment and spare parts should be delivered. Planning a four squadron wing at four different locations was extremely challenging for the 366th representatives.

Flying was reduced during June as the aircraft were prepared for return across the North Atlantic route on 16 July. Only profile missions and proficiency flying were conducted. Periodic aircraft inspections were increased, so that the average aircraft fleet time would be 125 hours before the next required inspection when they departed France. This would ensure flyable aircraft after return to reserve status, while waiting for support equipment to arrive in Alabama.

The east-to-west crossing of the North Atlantic by nineteen RF-84Fs, one C-47, and two T-33As was accomplished without incident. One RF-84F had been lost in France in January. The ADVON departed on 11 June aboard one MATS C-135A transport. The main body of troops was airlifted home between 6 and 15 July, requiring two days to return to Sumpter Smith Field, Alabama. On 16 July 1962, the 7117th Wing returned an upgraded air base to the 7305th and departed Dreux. All units and personnel assigned to the 117th Tactical Reconnaissance Wing were released from active duty on 20 August 1962. The wing continued flying its RF-84Fs until 1971.

7305th Combat Support Group

The 7305th Combat Support Group commanded by the 322d Air Division took over Dreux and continued to operate the American High School and maintain the base in standby status. LTC Bill Ridding was base commander from 1962 to 1964. Dreux had no further flying units assigned and no support aircraft, therefore there was little flying activity except for C-119 and C-130 training missions. The U.S. Army used the base as a parachute training drop zone. An Army parachute demonstration team frequently practiced drops that were enjoyed by the high school students. Jet aircraft operations were still prohibited all during this 1962-66 period, but Dreux had to be kept ready to immediately receive fighter or cargo aircraft from CONUS as part of the dual basing scheme. Three barracks were prepared for aircrews' arrival; rooms and lockers were cleaned weekly. Approximately 450 beds were kept made and then covered with paper dust covers. Fire and crash rescue trucks were operated daily. Airfield lighting was tested every evening; navigation radio aids and control tower communications evaluated every morning. The quality of stored aircraft fuels was monitored weekly. Building maintenance required a large amount of labor plus materials, resulting in a budget one third that of an active air base. All defects had to be reported to Evreux and repairs made at once. About 350 trailers were still in use on base as family quarters.

The 2d Mobile Communications Squadron moved into Dreux in 1962 and supported USAFE's TALKING BIRD (Silk Purse) with highly mobile long-range radio sets. It remained at Dreux AB until it relocated to Sembach AB, West Germany, in July 1966 as part of FRELOC.

Project FRELOC began in May 1966 at Dreux with the 7305th Combat Support Squadron being the primary agent to remove all property and close the base. Dreux required less effort to close because of its standby status—there was no inventory of aircraft spare parts and there were no aircraft munitions to move. By November 1966 virtually all equipment had been removed, the high school closed, and total base personnel numbered about sixty men. Dreux Air Base was transferred to the French government on 24 March 1967 through the Military Liquidation Service in Paris.

Today the base appears on flight charts as Dreux-Senonches, and French civilian pilots refer to this former air base as Dreux-Crucey. It is currently inactive, gates secured, with four large hangars still standing but apparently there are no flight operations. The main entrance is still north of the village of Dampierre-sur-Blevy. A large radio astronomy antenna field is installed in the southwest corner at the approach end of runway 06. The city of Dreux may be visited by rail from the Paris Gare de Montparnasse. See Michelin Map #311 Local and IGN Series Blue #20150.

Appendix 10.1 Notice to Airmen 1959 (NOTAM) - USAF-Dreux

Elevation 602 feet (184m), 48° 39'N - 01° 06'E. One paved runway 7,900 feet long, 060°/240°. Rotating airdrome beacon, high intensity approach lights, runway - taxiway lights, and airfield obstruction lights. Transient aircraft storage with major aircraft and major engine repairs available. Airdrome facilities available 0700 hrs to 1900 hrs daily. Aircraft fuel, 115-145 octane and JP4 jet fuel service available. High and low pressure oxygen service available. Jet aircraft starting units, C-21 and C-26 available. Customs.

Above:

top row left: Closed main gate, Dreux Crucy Base in 2002. Jerry McAuliffe
top row right: 10th Squadron HQ building, Dreux AB 1960. Jimmy Register

middle row left: Dreux AB hangar, 1999 Jimmy Register
middle row right: Base supply warehouse in use by French AF, 1998. Jimmy Register

bottom row left: Dreux auto center in 1999. Jimmy Register
bottom row right: Street sign for the Dreux air base on side of house 2002. Jerry McAuliffe

Juli's Bar in Dampierre sur Blevy, 1957.
A spot for a "sandwich au jambon" and beer.
John Traficante

Gatehouse at Dreux AB, 2002.
It is now called Base de Crucey.
Jerry McAuliffe

C-119s in formation over Dreux AB.
John Needham

Above:
top left: The canals of Dreux, 1956 John Traficante
top right: Street sign at entrance to village of Chennevieres, 2002 Jerry McAuliffe
bottom left: Turn here for base road, 2002. Jerry McAuliffe
bottom right: Town of Louvillers-sur-Perche in 2002, on highway D30 south of the air base Jerry McAuliffe

Crumbling windmill from 1600s along highway D315 near Crucey, 1998.
Jerry McAuliffe

Dreux Air Base Assigned Aircraft

John Traficante

60th Troop Carrier Wing, C-119Gs, 1 October 1955 - 8 January 1961

Eighteen aircraft per squadron. These Boxcars were flown from Rhein-Main AB, West Germany to Dreux AB, France by 60th TCWg pilots.

Aircraft Marking: 10th Troop Carrier Squadron - Red swatch on top third of vertical stabilizer and red nose cone.
11th Troop Carrier Squadron - Green swatch on top and bottom third of vertical stabilizer and green nose cone
12th Troop Carrier Squadron - Blue swatch on middle third of vertical stabilizer and blue nose cone.

C-119G-FA

53-3218	12th	53-7832	10th	53-7843	10th	53-7854	11th	53-8148	12th
53-3219	11th	53-7833	11th	53-7844	12th	53-8138	12th	53-8149	12th
53-3220	10th	53-7834	10th	53-7845	12th	53-8139	11th	53-8150	10th
53-3221*	11th	53-7835	11th	53-7846	11th	53-8140*	12th	53-8151+	12th
53-3222*	10th	53-7836	10th	53-7847	11th	53-8141	10th	53-8152*	12th
53-7826	12th	53-7837	11th	53-7848	11th	53-8142	10th	53-8153	10th
53-7827	10th	53-7838	11th	53-7849	12th	53-8143	12th	53-8154	10th
53-7828	11th	53-7839	12th	53-7850	11th	53-8144	12th	53-8155	10th
53-7829	11th	53-7840	10th	53-7851	11th	51-8145	12th	53-8156	12th
53-7830	12th	53-7841*	10th	53-7852	11th	53-8146*	10th		
53-7831	12th	53-7842	10th	53-7853	10th	53-8147	10th		

+ 53-8151 On display at Musee Royal de l'Armee, Brussels, Belgium

* Losses:
53-3221 - Crashed, propeller failure on take off, Athens Airport, Greece, JULY 57, no fatalities.
53-3222 - Crashed, formation mid-air, near Edelweiler, West Germany, 11 AUG 55, 20 fatalities.
53-7841 - Crashed, formation mid-air, near Edelweiler, West Germany, 11 AUG 55, 46 fatalities.
53-8140 - Damaged, ground collision with B-26 at RAF Prestwick, Scotland, 14 OCT 55, no fatalities.
53-8146 - Damaged, landing gear failure at Athens, Greece, 2 APR 55, no fatalities.
53-8152 - Crashed, engine failure near Nova Siri, Italy, 13 MAR 60, no fatalities.

60th Air Base Group: Wing Support Aircraft
C-47A: 43-16379, 43-49264
C-47B: 43-49346
L-20A: 51-16531
T-33A: 53-5839

Dreux Air Base Assigned Aircraft, continued

National Archives

309th Troop Carrier Group, Assault, C-123Bs, 2 June 1956 - 25 September 1958

Eighteen aircraft per squadron. These Providers were flown from Ardmore AFB, OK to Dreux AB, France and returned to Ardmore AFB by 309th TCGp pilots in September 1958.

Aircraft Marking, stabilizer/rudder & nose cone:

376th Troop Carrier Squadron - red   377th Troop Carrier Squadron - green   378th Troop Carrier Squadron - blue

C-123B-FA

54-576	378th	54-588	377th	54-600	376th	54-611	378th	54-622	378th
54-577	378th	54-589	378th	54-601	376th	54-612+	378th	54-623	376th
54-578	378th	54-590	377th	54-602	376th	54-613	377th	54-624	376th
54-579	378th	54-591	377th	54-603	378th	54-614	377th	54-625	376th
54-581	377th	54-592	376th	54-604	376th	54-615	376th	54-626	376th
54-582	376th	54-593	377th	54-605	378th	54-616	378th	54-627	376th
54-583	378th	54-594	378th	54-606	378th	54-617	376th	54-628	377th
54-584	376th	54-595	378th	54-607	376th	54-618	377th	54-629	377th
54-585	378th	54-596	378th	54-608	377th	54-619	377th	54-630	377th
54-586	376th	54-597	376th	54-609	377th	54-620	377th	54-632	378th
54-587	376th	54-599	378th	54-610+	377th	54-621	377th	54-633	377th

No Losses, No Fatalities

+ 54-610 On display at Hill AFB Museum, Utah

+ 54-612 On display at March Field Air Museum, California

Al Christensen

7117th Tactical Wing, 106th Tactical Reconnaissance Sq, RF-84Fs, 3 November 1961 - 22 July 1962

These Thunderflashes were flown from Birmingham, AL, to Dreux AB, France by 106th TRSq pilots. Then deployed to Chaumont AB for all operations. Aircraft returned to CONUS during July 1962 by 106th TRSq pilots.

Aircraft Marking: 106th Tactical Reconnaissance Squadron - Red band

RF-84F-35, -40-RE

53-7530	53-7544	53-7558	53-7599	53-7610*
53-7532	53-7549	53-7594	53-7601	53-7612
53-7533	53-7553	53-7596	53-7602	53-7613
53-7536	53-7554	53-7597	53-7603	53-7616

* Losses:

53-7610 - Crash landed, hydraulic failure/weather, on Chaumont AB, France, 12 DEC 61, no fatalities.

7117th Operations Squadron: Wing Support Aircraft

C-47A: 43-48586 from ANG, 43-48132 from 12th AF

L-20A: 51-16531

T-33A: 2 from ANG 52-1261, 52-9539

Spare RF-84s left at Birmingham: 52-7423 to 184th TRSq.
52-7425 to 160th TRSq.
52-7432 to 153rd TRSq.

ACKNOWLEDGEMENTS

I would like to thank the following people who contributed to this chapter:

Les Bradford was trained as a fighter pilot who came to love the C-119. He was stationed at Rhein-Main and Dreux AB in the 12th Troop Carrier Squadron.

Al Christensen was a Weather Officer in Detachment 10, 31st Weather Squadron, MATS, stationed at Chambley AB, 1955-1957. His aircraft photos were shot at a Victory in Europe Day open house held at Chambley in 1957.

Chuck Lunsford was a Radio Operator in the 12th TCSq stationed at Dreux from 1956 to 1959. Tales of his adventures flying in the C-119s is related in his very enjoyable book *Departure Message*, available on line from BookSurge.com.

John Needam was in the 60th Field Maintenance Squadron at Dreux AB from 1955 to 1958. He remembers the challenge of repairing the floor sections after damage from loading heavy cargo during the 100 hour periodic inspections for the 10th, 11th, and 12th TCSq.

Jimmy Register was a C-119 crew chief at Dreux from 1960 to 1961 and moved to Evreux AB until 1963.

John Traficante, was a Flight Engineer/Crew Chief in the 12th TCSq, 60th TCWg at Dreux AB from 1955-57. His airplanes were C-119C #612 and C-119G #8145.

11

ETAIN-ROUVRES AIR BASE

Etain-Rouvres Air Base is located on the Lorraine Plateau in northeastern France, 180 miles (290 km) east of Paris and 12 miles (20 km) east of Verdun. This airfield began in 1937 for use by the French Air Force and was named Rouvres airdrome. It has been in continuous use since 1938. A tactical reconnaissance group flying Bloch 131s were located there when WWII started. Next, RAF 72 Squadron moved in with Hurricanes in the 1939 "phony war." In early 1944, JG-26 arrived flying long-nose FW-190Ds

On 1 September 1944 the American Third Army, XX Corps,7th Armored Division, drove through Etain and Rouvres heading east down highway N-3 for Metz and beyond. The tankers radioed HQ Third Army that the air base appeared useable as a fuel supply point by flying in C-47 and B-24 cargo flights from England. The Ninth U.S. Army Air Force arrived at the Etain airfield about 6 September, and after engineers repaired the damage, it became A-82, Verdun/Etain ALG. The 47th Liaison Squadron operated there from 10 September 1944 through May 1945. After runway improvements, the 362d Fighter Group with P-47Ds, and the 425th Night Fighter Sq and Det# 2, 416th Night Fighter Sq with P-61C Black Widows flew from Etain until April 1945, when they all departed for air bases in Germany. The airfield was idle for seven years until May 1952, when the first survey teams arrived to begin the new NATO air base for USAFE.

Etain-Rouvres Air Base (49° 14'N - 05° 40'E. Elevation 766 feet) had a layout similar to Chambley, sixteen miles to the southeast. Both Etain and Chambley began as fighter bases in May 1952, but in 1953 construction at these bases was delayed for about one year by DOD budget reductions. NATO phase 1 construction was nearing completion; the runway, taxiways, and three marguerites had been completed but not the buildings, because USAF structures were not funded. After much redesign several buildings were eliminated and utilities rerouted. Etain did not have a large theater, base gym, base aircraft shops, or an elementary school. It had two less airmen barracks and one less BOQ building than the other bases. The primary living-work area was on the east side of the runway, near the village of Rouvres. The spur railroad from Etain onto the base was not completed until June 1955, three years late. Underground fuel storage was delayed until 1956; tank cars on the base rail siding provided a very limited POL storage system.

The first unit on Etain was Flight "C" 73d Support Gp, Depot, with one officer and five airmen, arriving from Chateauroux Air Depot on 1 February 1953, to control USAF property. USAFE also activated the 7005th Air Base Sq to operate Etain for eighteen months prior to arrival of the 388th FBWg. Its personnel were absorbed into the 388th Wing.

Since the 388th had to be in place at Etain by the end of 1954, vital areas of construction were rushed in order to accommodate the unit. When the Wing arrived at Etain on 13 December 1954, the base was in the last stages of the Phase I and the beginning of Phase II construction. The barracks, mess hall, wing headquarters, supply warehouses, hangars, and heating plants were still incomplete! Even the heating pipes had not been installed. The hard surfaced roads had been completed, but they had to be cut in many places to dig utility trenches, consequently, even the paved roads became muddy trails. About one more year of construction was needed to have a livable base. Aircraft hangars and the operations building fell behind schedule, causing the three fighter squadrons to operate longer than expected at air bases in Germany. The base was not ready for full acceptance by the Air Force until summer 1956.

As soon as he arrived, the 388th Civil Engineer began construction of twenty-nine prefabricated buildings; twenty feet by eighty feet on concrete floors, to provide office and storage space for the squadrons. Company C, 843d EABn built the floors and constructed the buildings. The base had a BX, small theater, and chapel. Hangar #110 was modified into a base gym and could be used when aircraft were not present. Base personnel used the Army's gym in Verdun for team sports. In July 1955, the construction budget of $500,000 to build minor facilities and complete major alterations was cut to zero.

Airfield facilities were delayed until the summer 1954; two old WWII K-53 radio vans on 2.5 ton trucks were set up by the 2d Mobile AACS Sq. By 1955 this

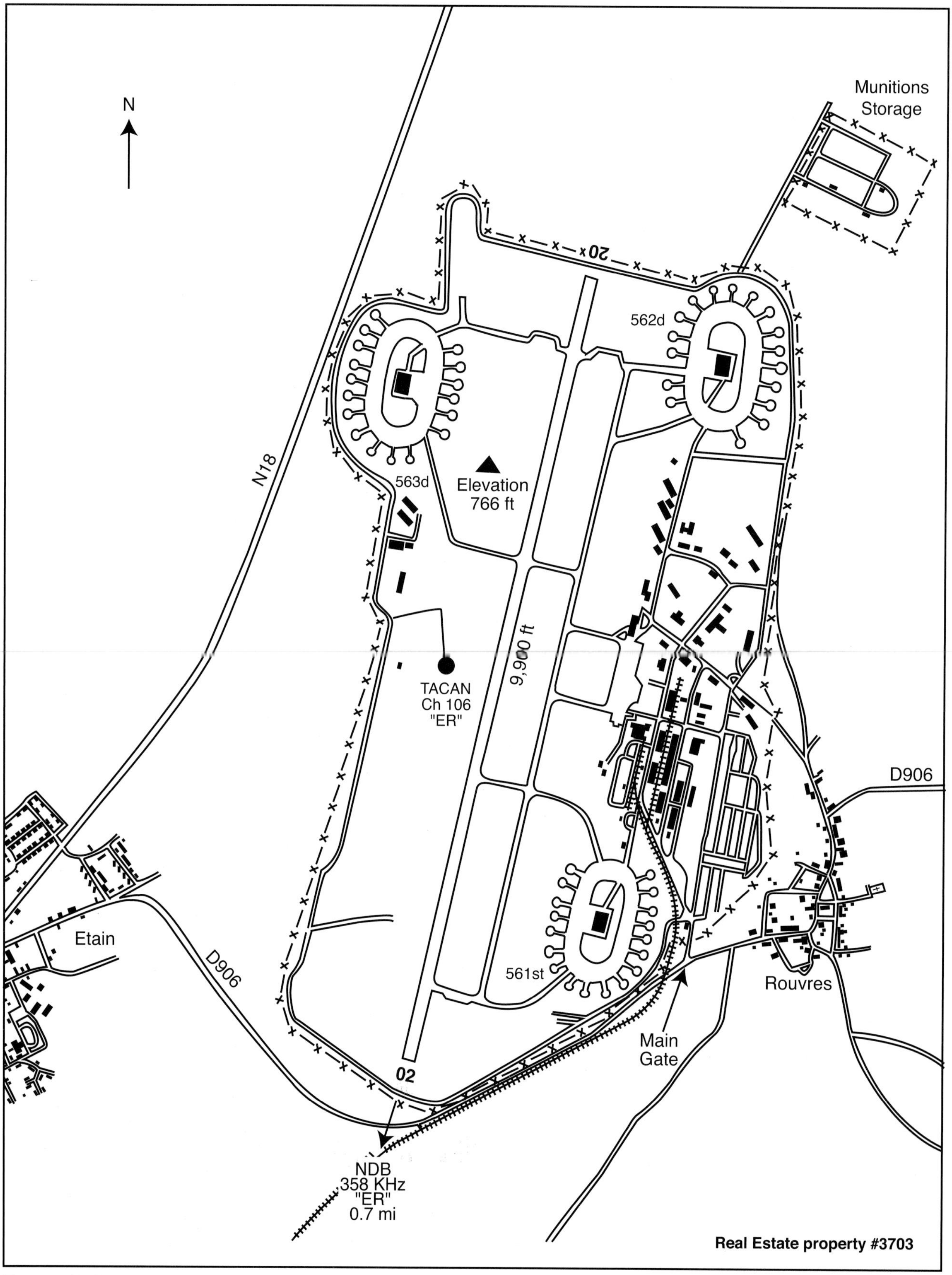

Map 11.1 Etain-Rouvres Air Base

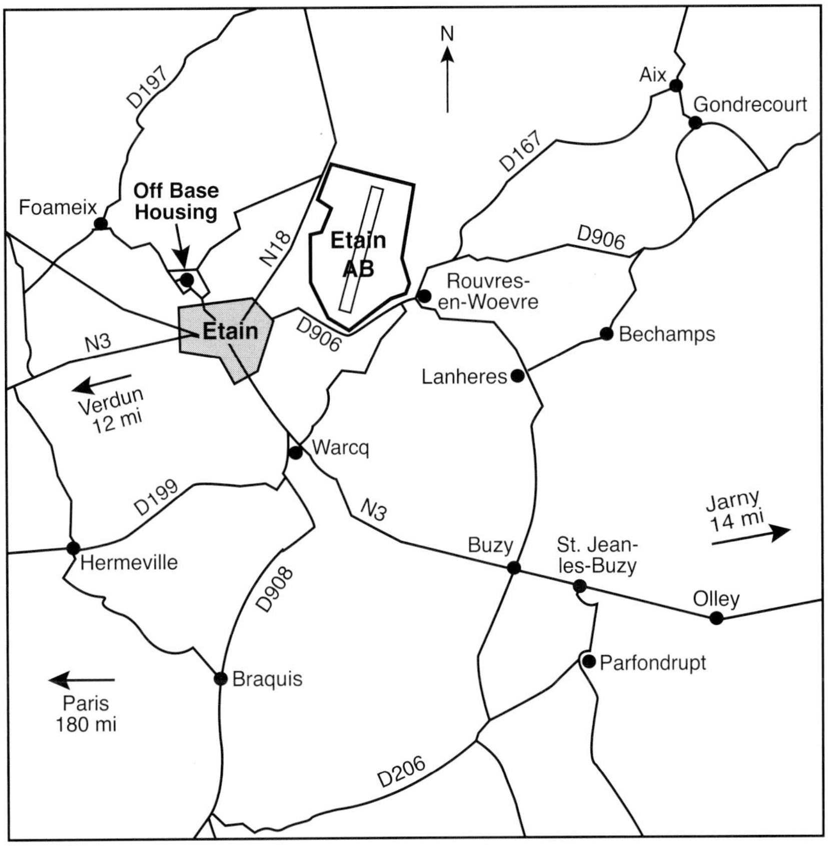

Map 11.2 Etain Area

equipment was over ten years old and approaching museum status. One van was set-up as the base low frequency 50-watt non-directional radio beacon near the north end of the runway. The off-base permanent radio beacon station was not installed until late 1956. The second van was configured as the control tower and located on west side of the runway. The tower van had both VHF and UHF radio sets and a small observation cab for one operator. In August 1955, the Base Ops Control Tower was placed into "test operation" and proved to be an excellent facility. The base UHF/DF radio set was installed in the new tower and flight checked to specifications. The programmed construction of an off-base Direction Finder site was canceled.

An antique MPN-1 GCA system arrived in February 1955, and after minor repairs was ready for operation by May. The MPN-1 was the first GCA radar designed and built in 1944. The first test flights on the GCA began on 28 June 1955. The final controller was presented with a large amount of "scope clutter" south of the runway, and would loose the F-86 on final approach in the clutter about two miles from touchdown. Finally a much newer GCA MPN-11B was received. It had a moving target indicator (MTI) that eliminated the stationary clutter problem. The -11B radar set was set up and all was fine except it arrived without its UHF and VHF radio sets needed to talk to the pilots. The new GCA was finally operational in May 1956.

An aircraft gun firing-in abutment was constructed on west side of the runway north of the 563d hangar and put in frequent use to boresight the 50cal. and 20mm aircraft guns prior to range missions.

Etain's six-position NATO telephone switchboard was installed in the base communications center in April 1955, and old Signal Corp tactical equipment was removed. The base had over 380 telephones connected into the Comm Center by the end of 1955. Twenty-two telephone and six teletype trunk lines ran off base into the French PT&T long distance lines. Etain's typical monthly off-base phone bill was $1,400.00. Telephone operator manning was critical; there were only two Air Force and three civilian operators. They had to be augmented with teletype operators and radio repairmen to keep the phone system going twenty-four hours a day. A base Military Amature Radio System (MARS) was set up by the 388th Comm Sq, and was a great morale booster because it allowed families at Etain to talk to the men TDY at

Wheelus AB and the three fighter bases in Germany.

The trailer park at Etain was constructed under Project Caravan in 1955. Roads, concrete pads, seven Quonset buildings, and all utilities to accommodate 270 trailers were installed by Company C, 843d Engineer Aviation Battalion. The trailer park was immediately south of the main base gate, on the east edge of base property. It was a short walk for the wives and teenagers into the town of Rouvres for shopping. The trailers were used for family housing until 1966 when Operation FRELOC necessitated their transfer or disposal.

Both GRI and CCH housing units were built around Etain but the base shared them with Chambley AB. One-hundred-ten Guaranteed Rental Income units, Cites St. Pierre, were completed in 1956-57. A larger 382 unit Commodity Credit development, les Clairs Chenes, was completed in 1959 just as Project RED RICHARD was announced. These CCH homes were primarily duplex units constructed (5 km) west of the base, west of highway D197 and (2 km) north of Etain city.

By 1957 Etain Air Base covered 1,205 acres and had ten miles of paved roads. The runway was 7,900 feet long by 150 feet wide. In late 1957, 1,000-foot paved extensions were added, and arresting barriers were installed at both ends of the runway. Three arm/de-arm pads were provided on the taxiways adjacent to the ends of the runways. Taxiway, aprons, parking ramps, etc., covered 460,000 square yards. It had three NATO fighter size hangars, 37,000 square feet each. The base had fifty-eight permanent buildings and thirty-nine temporary buildings. Eight airmen dormitories held 130 men each. Three BOQ buildings for 50 officers each were located near the wing-base headquarters building. There were three dining halls, one for 1,000 men, one for 350 men, and the smaller hospital dining hall that accommodated 130 men. Two of the barracks and the 350-man dining hall were built on the west side near the northwest hangar. Five base warehouses had 2.6 million cubic feet of storage space located on a railroad spur from Etain's main rail line. One warehouse was allocated to Project SEAWEED emergency stocks. Water was stored in six underground storage tanks holding 270,000 gallons supplied by two base wells and a water main into the Etain city system. The base had two heating plants. Etain was connected into the NATO POL pipeline, and had on-base fuel storage for 886,000 gallons of jet fuel, 45,000 gallons of AVGAS, 200,500 gallons of MOGAS, and 250,000 gallons of DIESEL. Munitions storage was located adjacent to the northeast corner of the base in the Bois de Saulx. Sixteen igloos located on forty acres were constructed on the east side of the service road, two tenths of a mile into the woods. This munitions storage site was connected to the air base property. Estimated value of real estate (excluding land) was $28 million. Equipment in use (excluding aircraft) was approximately $8 million. Total Base Supply Inventory was $6.5 million. Because it was developed during lean budgets, Etain Air Base never approached the complete permanent facility achieved by Laon or Chaumont. On 28 February 1958, HQ USAFE changed the name of Etain-Rouvres Air Base to simply Etain Air Base, because local government and citizens objected to the old name.

388th Fighter-Bomber Wing

The 388th Fighter-Bomber Wing was activated on 23 November 1953 at Clovis AFB, New Mexico, with three fighter-bomber squadrons, the 561st, 562d, and the 563d. These were the same designators as the 388th Fighter Wing's WWII B-17 bomb squadrons.

The 50th Fighter-Bomber Wing had departed Clovis for Germany during October-November 1953, making space for another fighter-bomber wing to be activated there. The lack of USAF bases and associated gunnery ranges was a limiting factor in the development of combat wings during the Korean War.

The 388th Fighter Wing had been a WWII B-17G bomb group that fought in the European Theater as part of the Eighth Air Force, and was awarded two DUCs. In August 1945, at the end of WWII, the 388th BGp (H) was inactivated at Sioux Falls Army Airfield, South Dakota.

The 388th Wing worked hard at Clovis to convert into new F-86F-35-NA Sabres and train many newly assigned first term airmen to achieve combat capability. Its seventy-five F-86F Sabres were later production numbers than the 21st FBWg's Sabres. The 388th would be the third F-86F-35 wing in France with nuclear weapons delivery capability. North American Aviation, Inglewood, California, on today's Los Angeles Airport, produced 264 F-86F-35 Sabres over a twenty-seven month contract; at the peak rate of three per day. By 15 October 1954, after completing all required tactical training in eleven months, the 388th Wing was considered ready to depart Clovis for Etain Air Base in northeastern France. The wing commander knew it would be very difficult to operate at Etain since it was not yet ready for the wing's arrival, so he made arrangements to fly the F-86Fs from other air bases in Germany or France. HQ USAF insisted that the 388th FBWg must immediately deploy to

Troops of the 388th Fighter-Bomber Wing exiting the troop train and preparing to board the USNS GEN Eltinge for their trip to Etain.
USAF photo via Ben Bagwell

Etain and help get the base operational. The wing pilots flew seventy-five F-86Fs Sabres, five T-33As, plus two C-47s to Europe, departing New Mexico from the 22d through the 28th of November. The flight movement was numbered Fox Able 33 (FA-33). They followed the 21st FBWg, island hopping across the Atlantic northern route during December 1954 and January 1955 as described in chapter 2. No aircraft were lost enroute. The three fighter-bomber squadrons flew directly from RAF Prestwick into Germany. The 562d Squadron arrived at Spangdahelm AB on 31 December 1954, the 563d reached Bitburg AB 1 January 1955, and the 561st flew into Hahn AB on 4 January 1955.

The 388th Wing Advance Detachment, consisting of 14 officers and 145 airmen, arrived at Etain 17 November 1954. They found it hard to believe the base was so primitive after two years of construction! The main body of troops was enroute eighteen days on train and troopship. On 27 November, approximately 1,100 officers and airmen boarded a train at Clovis for a two-day ride to Galveston, Texas, where they marched aboard the USNS GEN LeRoy Eltinge along with 1,150 men of the 21st FBWg from California who had arrived on the same train. The troops watched Galveston fade away, and settled down for a fourteen-day, 6,517 mile voyage to the port of La Pallice, France. The GEN Eltinge arrived at La Pallice late in the afternoon on Sunday, 12 December 1954. All troops remained aboard the ship overnight and debarked at 1000 hours the next day. They boarded a SNCF troop train on the rail siding next to the dock for their ride to Etain. They somehow detoured Paris and did not have to change train stations. The fighter squadron officers and airmen were routed on trains to Germany to meet the wing's aircraft. The main body arrived at Gare d'Etain in a cold rain which was an appropriate welcome to the dreary sight that greeted them when, after a short truck ride, they reached their new home on 13 December 1954.

The 388th FBWg consisted of 192 officers and 1,199 airmen. Its primary mission as part of Twelfth Air Force was to train for and conduct tactical special (nuclear) weapons delivery; its secondary mission was to conduct non-atomic tactical air operations. Additional missions were to train its wing support units and

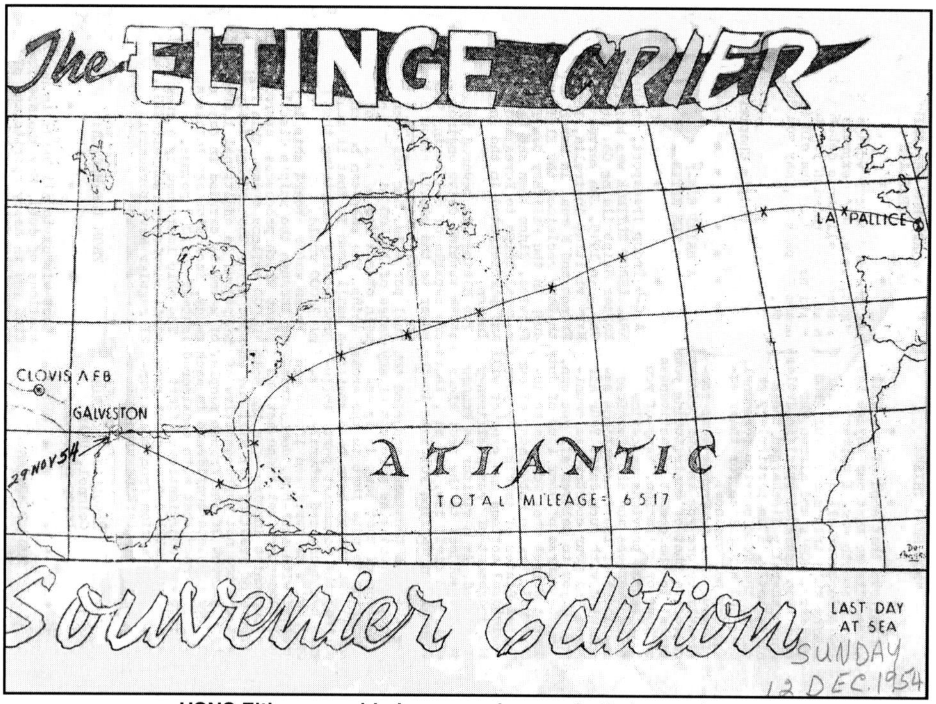

USNS Eltinge provided a souvenier map in their newsletter on the last day of the voyage to France.
Sam Roberts

operate the installation to maintain combat readiness. The numerous problems caused by weather and construction delays seriously hampered its ability to perform these missions. The 388th Wing Commander, BGEN Whisenand, was disgusted with the condition of Etain and frustrated by the inability to forecast wing operational status. The general knew he had lost combat capability after arrival at Etain. His request for an investigation into the construction program was ignored. (Appendix 11.1 GEN Whisenand's letter) The U.S. Government never conducted investigations into the construction delays and costs of the new NATO airbases in France during 1952-58. A thorough investigation was done by the U.S. Senate of the delays and excessive costs of new air bases in French Morocco. It ranted, raved and generated many headlines about the performance of Atlas Constructors, the Corps of Engineers, and the USAF in 1952-53; but completely avoided the larger problem in France out of fear of disturbing NATO cooperation.

In April and May 1955, the three fighter squadrons flew to Wheelus for their first bombing and gunnery training since arriving in Europe; 1,686 hours were flown on 2,290 sorties on the ranges. A problem developed —gunnery scores were poor, but this was quickly solved. The armament troops found and corrected defective test equipment, voltmeters, and range calibrators that were the cause of large gunsight range errors. The 388th Wing's first exercise was CARTE BLANCHE in June, flying for 4ATAF. The fighter squadrons enjoyed the summer operations after little flying in January and February. During the last half of 1955 the three fighter-bomber squadrons transferred from Germany to Etain-Rouvres Air Base. The 563d left Bitburg on 7 July, the 562d departed Spangdahlem on 15 September, and finally, the 561st reluctantly left Hahn AB on 23 November, after almost a one year "temporary" stay in the State of Rheinland-Pfalz. The fighter squadron pilots and maintenance personnel were not eager to leave their crowded but comfortable facilities in Germany. The 561st was assigned the hangar on the east side of the runway, south of base operations, near the base main entrance. The 562d Squadron occupied the hangar on the east side of the runway north of base operations. The 563d hangar was on the west side of runway near highway N18; with its own living area and mess hall in the northeast corner of the base. The 388th Air Base Group operated three C-47s, five T-33As, and two L-20As. Support aircraft maintenance was conducted in the 561st and 562d hangars.

An aircraft fuel shortage developed at Etain during exercise CORDON BLEU when rail tank cars went missing! They were found in a nearby town, so F-6 refueling trucks were driven to the tank cars, fuel was pumped into the trucks, and the F-86s were ser-

Etain AB main gate 1956. "Home of the 388th Fighter-Bomber Wing." Family house trailers located just to right of entrance.
Tom Malinowski via Etain Pioneers

viced. This type of misrouting was a constant concern of logistics officers in the event of war in Europe.

Etain's tenant units as of 1 March 1955 were: Det #10, 12th Air Postal Squadron; 1271st AACS Squadron (MATS); Det #13, 31st Weather Squadron (MATS); Det #55, Office of Special Investigations; Company D, 843d EABn (redesignated the 833d Engineer Bn [Construction] after SCARWAF was disbanded); Det #14, 8th Radio Relay Sq; 133d and 134th AACS Squadrons, Det #1, 1952 AACS Sq; and the 866th EABn Well Drilling Team from Chateauroux.

During spring 1955 the base operations/fire station was ready for occupancy; the flight planning room was finished, control tower opened, interior painted, and fire station access roads completed. By summer many of the base service functions were operating; the library had about 4,000 books and 600 registered borrowers. The Silver Wings Service Club held its grand opening on 13 July 1955, the club's interior was still unfinished, but the stage and large lounge were used for live entertainment and shows, freeing the base theater's limited facilities. Club staffing was a problem after the 1956 budget cuts, but many volunteers helped keep this badly needed club going for families as well as the lower grade airmen.

Etain's base newspaper VAPOR TRAILS began publication in 1955. It provided base news and chronicled Etain's very active sports programs. Sports were an important morale booster to counteract the dismal base conditions and T/Sgt Barney Baxter, NCOIC of Special Services, immediately developed a variety of programs. Etain competed vigorously in football, baseball, basketball, track and field, boxing, and soccer. Within fifteen months of opening the primitive base, Etain had a first rate football field with bleachers to seat 800 and an enviable baseball field. Its teams won many awards, and in 1957, Etain AB won permanent possession of the Commander's Trophy for sports excellence.

As winter 1955-56 approached, the 388th organized a base Instrument School for all pilots to improve flying skills in the expected bad weather as required by AFR 51-3. The program was a mixture of lectures, instrument flight simulator work, and T-33A or C-47 check flights. A new Link Aviation instrument flight trainer, C-11B, was unpacked, assembled, calibrated, and began operations on 10 August. A Link Aviation Corp. factory representative assisted two NCOs to get this vital training aid into operation. The C-11B operated about 165 hours a month. Lectures were presented the first week, and flight training and check rides filled the second week. Approximately sixty pilots completed the school by 31 December.

A Twelfth Air Force inspection team visited Etain in November after the fighter squadrons had moved into their new base, and found many discrepancies. Most of the problems related to not receiving equipment and repair parts from CONUS. Throughout the 1955-56 winter, lack of aircraft and vehicle parts limited flying, for instance, crash/fire truck parts were back-ordered for up to six months. Aircraft parts were typically on 150-day back-order from the depots; some T-33A and C-47 parts weren't delivered until nine months after a priority request! All F-86F Sabres in France were sent to Toul AB for a TCTO modification to the wing spar to fuselage attachments; a special repair team was set up and the rework proceeded rapidly.

F-86F #52-5266 388th Fighter-Bomber Wing.
Bill Posey

The 388th FBWg F-86Fs on the ramp, Etain AB 1956.
Courtesy of Etain Pioneers

C-119 transported Etain personnel to Wheelus AB, Libya to support gunnery training.
Courtesy of Etain Pioneers

F-86F #52-5271 388th Fighter-Bomber Wing.
Bill Posey

The 388th Wing had its first escape and evasion exercise SWEET LORRAINE from 14 to 18 November 1955. Trucks dropped the pilots off somewhere southeast of Etain, and they had to navigate and evade twenty miles through "enemy lines" to reach the Meuse River line south of Verdun. French Gendarmes and Army troops were the enemy, patrolling the entire region. Ten pilots escaped, thirteen pilots were rescued by helicopters. Thirty-nine pilots were captured and interrogated by Twelfth Air Force Teams in the Verdun "Interrogation Center." This was considered excellent training, but the wet, chilly November weather made hiding and camping anything but pleasant!

On 22 November, Detachment #1, HQ, 388th Fighter-Bomber Group was activated at Hahn AB, and was authorized six officers and forty-six airmen to stand nuclear alert in the wing's F-86s. Det #1 was established but no unit list of equipment was approved, therefore the equipment was supplied from scarce resources at Etain. People, aircraft, and supplies primarily came from the 561st Squadron. It supplied the necessary aircraft equipment at Hahn, and at Etain the 562d and 563d supplied equipment to the 561st. This saved transportation costs. Support for Det #1 was supplied by the 50th FBWg based at Hahn. Two years after being activated in CONUS, the 388th Wing placed ten F-86F-35s on Zulu Alert with nuclear weapons and qualified Bomb Commanders.

During 1955 the three fighter squadron averaged 600 hours per month and maintained 65 to 75 percent of their Sabres in commission while operating at Wheelus and the three bases in West Germany. Flying was further reduced by another French air traffic controller strike in November. Flying was limited to the local area, day VFR only, below 19,700 feet. Etain's GCA was still not working correctly, so local flying was risky. Sabres were sent to Germany, England, and Spain to meet minimum required proficiency flying. Had the French air controllers remained on strike for more than three months, and made the USAF pilots loose their flight pay, it would have been the immediate end of our stay in France—regardless of NATO, world peace, democracy, or freedom!

388th Fighter-Bomber Wing F-100D #56-3290 newly arrived at Etain AB 1956.
Grant Mobley

The 388th Wing's Intelligence Section and the fighter squadron's intelligence officers were very busy conducting briefings, lectures, and maintaining tactical target data. The wing kept current Tactical Target Materials on 15,000 targets within USAFE aircraft range. Targets were segregated into five categories; airfields, rail yards, rail and road bridges, and POL storage. Each target file had a collection of maps, photos, checkpoints, Information Sheets, Weapons Recommendations Sheets, and Special Data Sheets. The Special Data Sheets provided pilots with planning data for the desired ground zero, burst altitudes, and recommended yield settings, and the probability of kills for various types of aircraft nuclear weapons. The fighter squadrons maintained about 1,500 target folders at any given time. All this material required a very large storage vault that was finally completed in the Base Ops building in September 1955. The squadrons also had to organize all their target materials for immediate transport to a DOB. Safeguarding of all this classified information required extensive work by intelligence personnel in Europe during the Cold War.

On 1 February 1956, Detachment #1, HQ, 388th Fighter-Bomber Group moved to Spangdahlem AB from Hahn; it had more space and a better runway was available. Eight or more F-86Fs were maintained on continuous Zulu Alert at Spangdahlem.

An unusual training mission was accomplished by the 388th from April through June 1956; four officers and twenty-two airmen from the Pakistan Air Force were assigned to Etain for F-86F training. F-86Fs and later Sabre Mk 6s were supplied to Pakistan. This team was assigned to Pakistan Air Headquarters, Karachi after the OJT was completed.

In May 1956, the 563d FBSq participated in an Inter-Allied Exchange Program with the RAF 118th Fighter Sq, Jever, West Germany. Four Sabres spent five days at RAF Jever while 118th Squadron's Hawker Hunters visited Etain AB. The exchange was of great value to both teams, all support went exactly as planned with no difficulties encountered; the 563d pilots were amazed that the RAF fighter pilots had almost no additional squadron duties and flew about thirty five hours a month. "The RAF has much less paper work floating about the fighter units." The 563d Commander highly recommended that this program continue with all other NATO fighter units, especially with the non English speaking squadrons.

The 388th FBWg began planning for conversion into F-100Ds from F-86Fs starting in fall 1956, after the 48th FBWg completed its conversion. The F-100D Mobile Training Detachment arrived at Etain in August and began pilots' ground school. The 388th followed the same process in North Africa for pilot conversion training, and then weapon system training at Wheelus that began in November 1956. The 388th, like the 48th Wing, did not operate the F-86H Sabre but went directly into the Hun from their Sabre Fs.

The fighter pilot conversion training was typical of that time; pick some high time pilots in each squadron, have them read the -l Pilot's Handbook, pat them on the back and watch them take the Hun around the traffic pattern! Hundreds of fighter pilots made that well remembered first checkout flight, and crashes were very rare. The F-100Fs were just beginning down the production line, and were not in France until 1958. Also, there were no F-100 flight simulators. Some squadrons' training aids consisted of full-size cockpit photographs for the prospective pilot to stare at for a few hours! The 388th completed its conversion into F-100Ds by May 1957. Some of its F-86Fs went to the 7244th Air Base Sq, Dhahran, Saudi Arabia, via Chateauroux Depot and CAFMS in Madrid, Spain, where they underwent inspection and overhaul. By February 1957, the 388th had acquired seventy early block F-100Ds and placed eight Huns on Zulu Alert at Det #1, Spangdahlem. After a year, the newer block F-100D-90s arrived and replaced many of the original F-100Ds.

During this important period of aircraft conversion, in December 1956, the 388th Wing had to undergo a large rotation of officers and NCOs who had completed their two years of unaccompanied duty in France. The loss of experience was difficult because for every three NCOs that departed, only one replacement was received from CONUS. Most incoming officers were Lieutenants, new to the USAF. The wing was disappointed in the quality of replacement airmen; some were substandard performers who should have been separated from the USAF rather than sent to France. Most of the airmen were castoffs from SAC and Air Defense Command units; a few had courts martial records. The combat wings complained to HQ USAFE, but were told nothing could be done to improve airmen quality because it was an Air Force-wide problem! The personnel problems degraded further during fall 1957 as many single airmen completed their three years of overseas service and returned to CONUS. Airmen manning dropped to 65 percent in the 388th as the wing was about to be redesignated.

On 8 December 1957, HQ USAFE inactivated Headquarters, 388th Fighter-Bomber Group to reduce military manpower, and cut ten officers, and nineteen airmen positions. At midnight 9 December 1957, the 388th Fighter-Bomber Wing was redesignated the 49th Fighter-Bomber Wing.

49th Fighter-Bomber Wing

On 10 December 1957 the 49th FBWg designator was transferred from Pacific Air Forces (PACAF) by HQ USAF to replace the 388th designator at Etain. The financial reductions of Project CLEARWATER affected PACAF as well as USAFE, and the 49th Fighter-Bomber Wing based in Japan had to be deactivated. The 49th Pursuit Group had been activated on 15 January 1941, and the 388th Bomb Group, Heavy, on 24 December 1942, twenty-three months later. Therefore, the 49th was the older wing, and would remain an active USAF wing. Also, the 49th had produced MAJ Richard I. Bong, the leading American ace of WWII, with forty kills. Now USAFE had the 48th, 49th and 50th Fighter-Bomber Wings based in France. The 48th and 50th Pursuit Groups were also activated on 15 January 1941. The air base tenant units remained unchanged. The 49th transfer was only a designation change and no personnel, equipment, or aircraft were moved from Japan to Etain-Rouvres AB, France. All 388th FBWg units, personnel, equipment, and F-100D fighters were redesignated the 49th FBWg. The fighter squadrons were changed to the 7th, 8th, and 9th Fighter-Bomber Squadrons. Concurrent with the transfer, FEAF inactivated HQ, 49th Fighter-Bomber Group. The 49th had been associated with the Far East since 4 January 1942 when it arrived at Melbourne, Australia, so it was a strange designator for Europe.

The wing's mission and operations stayed the same; the Wing Commander did not change. Commanders of the 49th Fighter-Bomber Wing were COL Joseph L. Dickman, 10 December 1957 - 7 July 1958 and COL Wilbur J. Grumbles, 7 July 1958 - 15 June 1962.

On 8 July 1958, while flying its F-100Ds at Etain, the 49th Fighter-Bomber Wing was redesignated the 49th Tactical Fighter Wing. Its three squadrons became the 7th, 8th, and 9th Tactical Fighter Squadrons. Its F-100D aircraft colors and markings remained the same. The 49th received nine F-100Fs during spring of 1958; the fighter squadrons now had twenty-one F-100Ds and three F-100Fs. Beginning 1 February 1958, selected USAFE wings in France, the 48th, 49th, and 50th TFWgs, started keeping twelve of their aircraft on fifteen minute alert so a portion of USAFE's tactical force could react in an emergency. USAFE named this program Victor Alert in October 1958.

On 15 February 1958 the 49th Wing HQ activated Detachment #3, Headquarters, 49th Air Base Group at Chambley AB. It had become a standby air base after deactivation of the 21st FBWg. Det #3 was manned by three officers, ninety airmen, and eight LWR French employees to housekeep the closed base and maintain the trailer park used to house personnel from Chambley, Etain, and Toul.

On 1 January 1958, Detachment #2, Headquarters, 49th Air Base Group was activated to operate and maintain the Vouziers-Sechault DOB and the Suippes Gunnery Range. Det #2 was manned by two officers, fifty-eight airmen, and twenty-eight LWR French employees to keep the bare base ready for immediate operation of F-100D fighters. This job included housing, messing, communications, vehicle, and supply support.

Nuclear weapons load crew training progressed

Etain AB front gate, 49th Fighter-Bomber Wing, May 1958.
Courtesy Etain Pioneers

Typical fighter firing-in butt, still standing October 1997.
Jerry McAuliffe

well as new replacement armament specialists arrived from CONUS in 1958. After the individuals completed loading qualification, the load crews maintained proficiency through load competitions. The 49th Wing held F-100D Mk-7 and Mk-43 weapon load competitions among the three squadrons. Weapon loading time was not the most important criteria; correct use of all equipment, precise checklist procedures, and absolute safety were factors that controlled the team scores. The 9th TFSq won this loading event several times.

The 49th Field Maintenance Sq set up a ground transmitter station to preflight test the F-100D bombing radar beacon APW-11. This test procedure would assure that the Hun could receive all MSQ-1 commands and the correct preset frequencies were in use. This pre-takeoff test improved mission success rates with very good bombing scores. Correct alignment of aircraft radar beacons prior to a mission, when operating with a ground radar station several hundred miles away, has always been a critical problem in tactical radar bombing operations.

In August the 49th reorganized its aircraft maintenance organizations to meet the new AFM 66-1 Maintenance Management concepts; maintenance officers and NCOs were transferred to the Maintenance Sq to build up periodic inspection docks and prepare bench stock lists, supply documents, and requisitions.

Etain had a separate simulator building completed in May 1958. All flight training devices were installed during July, August, and September. First the Link Corp. C-11B instrument flight simulator was moved from Hangar #1 into the new simulator building. Next, an F-100D Cockpit Procedures trainer was received from Chaumont and installed in the building. On 6 August, a new training device, an F-151 Visual Gunnery Trainer, was received from CHAD. This new F-151, manufactured by the Rheem Mfg. Corp., attached into the F-100D simulator. It was so large its parts filled two tractor trailers. Some shipping damage occurred, but the Rheem Mfg. Corp. Technical Representative assisted with the repair, assembly, and checkout of this device, and it was installed in the new building.. By 1 October, the F-151 Trainer was being used for air-to-ground gunnery and bombing training; it could simulate special weapons delivery. Several electrical power problems were overcome to get all simulators working; 50Hz power had to be converted to 60Hz power for the U.S. built systems. The simulators were then scheduled by squadrons; every pilot operated the Link C-11B twenty-four hours per year, and the F-100D/F-151 aircraft procedures-gunnery trainer sixteen hours a year. By 1 November, the 49th Air Base Gp, Flight Simulator Section had the best F-100D training program in France. These simulators were well used during the winter months when bad weather reduced flying hours.

During 1958 a serious political problem arose within France over control of Algeria, its North African colony. As a result of the unrest, USAFE personnel were threatened in the cities of Nancy, Metz, and Toul. USAFE was very concerned about terrorist attacks on personnel off base and even possible attacks on Etain AB. The base commanders took several measures to prevent international incidents. As many families as possible were moved from off base rentals into government housing or into on-base trailers. The 49th Air Police Sq assigned one air policeman to each school bus on every trip to prevent possible kid-

Etain base chapel in 1955.
Tom Malinowski via Louis Bufkin

Chapel and base buildings, Etain AB 2005.
Pierre Baar

Guardhouse, Etain AB 1955. The base was still covered with large pieces of rock and red earth.
Tom Malinowski via Louis Bufkin

Official dedication and acceptance by the USAF, Etain AB .
USAF photo via Ben Bagwell

Rock strewn red earth, barracks and marguerite in the background, Etain AB 1955.
Tom Malinowski via Louis Bufkin

Etain AB in 1956. Some concrete but lots of red mud that marked an Etain AB car wherever it went.
Courtesy of Etain Pioneers

nappings. A/1C Grant Mobley, a 49th air policeman carried a loaded .45cal M3 Submachine Gun (grease gun) while riding to and from elementary and high schools. In Metz on several occasions American autos were hassled and threatened. USAFE personnel from Etain as well as Toul and Chambley were told to stop immediately for roadblocks manned by French Gendarmes or Army troops; these men had orders to shoot to kill any checkpoint runners. Fortunately no USAFE personnel were injured or killed during the Algerian uprisings.

A large portion of the 49th operated with all its F-100D/Fs and four T-33As from Chalon-Vatry DOB from September through December 1958, while the runway at Etain was undergoing major repairs and resurfacing. The DOBs were becoming very useful while runways were being repaired at the main bases. Det #2, 48th ABGp assisted the 49th with base maintenance, fire/crash rescue service, communications, and refueling trucks.

USAFE General Order #143 activated the 49th Armament and Electronics Maintenance (A&E) Squadron at Etain AB on 15 November 1958. This order assigned all wing A&E troops and support equipment to one squadron, and the fighter squadrons had their manning reduced as their A&E specialists were transferred to the 49th A&E MATRON. The 49th Field Maintenance Sq was redesignated the 49th Consolidated Aircraft Maintenance Sq by the same order.

The wing's three squadrons averaged over 715 flying hours per month from 1 January through 31 December 1958. Excellent aircraft, armament, and electronics maintenance supported this busy flying schedule, and the aircraft systems performed very well, producing outstanding gunnery and bombing results. All F-100D pilots maintained operational ready status. At the same time a minimum of eight F-100Ds were always ready on Zulu Alert, and later, fifteen fighters were ready on Victor Alert; all at Spangdahlem AB.

On 1 July 1959, the 49th Wing Commander was informed that Project RED RICHARD would force his Wing to depart France about 1 September, after five years of operations at Etain. Local routine procurements were stopped, base improvement plans terminated, existing contracts canelled, and the French work force reduced. France would not permit nuclear weapons in their country, and the nuclear capable fighters had to go. After five years of operations, Etain could no longer be used for USAFE fighters. HQ USAFE decided the 49th TFWg would move to Spangdahlem. It was home to its Det #1 and full alert capability could be maintained during the new Berlin crisis. The 10th TRWg and its RB-66s were moved from Spangdahlem to RAF Alconbury, UK, creating space for the entire 49th Wing. On 10 July, USAFE issued a movement order to the 10th to proceed to England and be officially transferred on 25 August. It vacated Spangdahlem by 1 September 1959. Personnel of the 49th were happy to relocate to Germany and into better facilities. The aircraft hangars and shops, offices, storage facilities, and living conditions were superior to Etain's.

The wing was authorized to remove from Etain all equipment and supplies required to operate in Germany. The 49th began moving personnel and supplies to Spangdahlem. The ADVON left on 18 August. Most of the people and material moved on 25 August 1959, using 49th Transportation Sq vehicles, and maintained combat capability in their one-day move. During this relocation the 7th and 9th TFSqs were deployed to Wheelus to qualify pilots in the delivery of nuclear weapons and upgrade a few new pilots to Bomb Commanders. The fighter squadrons were flying over 650 hours a month and toss bombing scores were excellent over this period. The three fighter squadrons now had 95 percent of all pilots qualified as Bomb Commanders, which reduced the Zulu Alert duty days. The relocation to Germany did not interrupt this training schedule.

As the 49th prepared to depart France it discontinued its responsibility for two nearby bases. On 1 September 1959 Wing HQ deactivated Det #2, Headquarters, 49th Air Base Group at Vouziers-Sechault DOB and Det #3, Headquarters, 49th Air Base Group at standby Chambley. These were turned over to the 7514th Support Group that was activated on the same day at Toul AB. Det #6 of the 7514th would be stationed at Vouziers-Sechault DOB, Det #2 at Chambley, and Det #1 at Etain AB. When Det #1, 7514th Support Group was activated, it gained 49th Air Base Group personnel to maintain Etain. All equipment, supplies, and vehicles were removed from Sechault DOB and returned to Etain. USAFE directed that Vouziers-Sechault would not be maintained; it was returned to France during 1960.

Not all 49th Wing personnel moved to Spangdahlem. Some 10th TRWg personnel stayed at Spangdahlem to complete their overseas tours of duty. USAFE did not want to pay for a second change of station for married personnel. Sufficient 10th personnel remained to support the 49th TFWg and keep it at full manning. Therefore, many 49th personnel were transferred to RAF Lakenheath to keep the 48th Air Base Gp at full strength in the UK, and some were transferred to other bases in France to fill vacancies.

The 49th TFWg still consisted of three tactical fighter squadrons, the 7th, 8th, and 9th, flying seventy-four F-100D/F Super Sabres, plus seven T-33As, two C-47As, and one L-20A support aircraft when officially transferred on 25 August 1959 from Etain AB to Spangdahlem AB, APO 123, West Germany. Unfortunately the fall and winter weather in the Eiffel region was no better than France. On 29 December 1959, the 49th was awarded the USAF Flying Safety Plaque for outstanding flying safety during the period, 1 January through 30 June 1959. The wing flew 29,731 hours total, with 23,463 hours in F-100D/F fighters. The 49th stayed at Spangdahlem for nine years flying fighters.

After departure of the 49th TFWg, no USAFE wings occupied Etain, and it remained in standby status for the next twenty-two months. The U.S. Army requested HQ USAFE to allow a few units to be stationed there to relieve overcrowding in the ADSEC Nancy-Verdun area. In June 1960, the 582d Transportation Company, (Army Aircraft Heavy Maintenance & Support) moved from Orleans to Etain. In 1961 it moved on to Brienne la Chateau after the U.S. Army received the former DOB from USAFE.

The 249th Engineer Construction Battalion, stationed at Kaiserslautern, West Germany, was a general construction unit, especially needed for wartime repairs of bridges, roads, and rail lines. During 1961, the 249th arrived at Etain and dispatched Engineering Companies D to Chambley, B to Phalsbourg, and A to Toul for base maintenance work, which included erecting twenty-seven small metal Butler buildings at the STAIR STEP bases. These extra hangars were built on existing parking hardstands, and each accommodated two F-84-size fighters while undergoing periodic inspections or radar maintenance. HQ Company and Company C remained at Etain while working on an Army depot at Verdun.

Tenant units at Etain during 1960-63 were Det #1, 7544th Combat Support Gp; Det #10, 12th Air Postal Sq; Det #8, 31st Weather Sq; Det #1, 1952 AACS Sq; 249th Engineer Bn (Construction) with HQ Company and Company C; and 582d Transportation Company, for one year, 1960-61.

Etain had been without USAFE flying units for two years, from September 1959 until 5 September 1961 when F-100D fighters arrived from CONUS in Operation TACK HAMMER, in response to the Berlin Wall Crisis. During October 1961 Etain was being prepared to receive an Operation STAIR STEP fighter wing and change its status from a standby into a main air base.

121st Tactical Fighter Wing

The 121st Tactical Fighter Wing (Special Delivery), Ohio ANG had been located at Lockbourne AFB, Ohio, since January 1947. Its 240 officers and 1,390 airmen were called to federal active duty for a period of twelve months on 1 October 1961 for the Berlin Crisis. Special Order G-34, dated 1 September 1961, issued by Headquarters, Tactical Air Command, Langley AFB, Virginia, assigned the wing to Twelfth Air Force. When activated, the wing consisted of three fighter squadrons and supporting units, the 162d TFSq based at Springfield Municipal Airport, Springfield, Ohio, the 164th at Mansfield-Lahm Municipal Airport, Mansfield, Ohio, and the 166th at Lockbourne AFB, Ohio. All three fighter squadrons had been flying Republic F-84F Thunderstreak fighters for more than four years. The support units included:

HQ, 121st Tactical Fighter Wing
121st A& E Maintenance Squadron
121st Consolidated Aircraft Maintenance Sq
HQ, 121st Air Base Group
121st Air Police Squadron
121st Civil Engineering Squadron
121st Operations Squadron
121st Supply Squadron
121st Transportation Squadron
121st Tactical Hospital Group

The 121st Tactical Fighter Wing originated on 1 December 1942 as the WWII 357th Fighter Group. It flew P-51 Mustangs on bomber escort missions from England with the Eighth Air Force, earning two DUCs. The 357th Fighter Group was redesignated the 121st Fighter Group on 24 May 1946 and allotted to the Ohio Air National Guard. The 121st kept the heritage and lineage of this former USAAF group. In October 1950, the 121st Fighter Group expanded into the 121st Fighter-Bomber Wing and was redesignated the 121st Tactical Fighter Wing in 1958.

The activated ANG flying units moved to their individual air bases in France in Operation STAIR STEP; this deployment is described in chapter 5. The 121st TFWg moved only one of its three fighter squadrons, the 166th, to Europe due to DOD budget cuts. The 166th Squadron brought twenty-six F-84Fs to Etain, arriving in a fierce rainstorm on 8 November. Wing HQ pilots flew one C-47 and two T-33As via Sondrestrom, Greenland on the northern route. The first T-33A arrived on 4 November, and the C-47 arrived last, on the 30th. On 16 November 1961, the 121st Tactical Fighter Wing commanded by LT COL Paul E. Hover had assembled at newly reactivated Etain AB for a stay of ten months. The 162d and 164th Squadrons and support units remained on extended active duty at their Ohio ANG stations ready to fly to France and reinforce the 7121st Wing at Etain. On 11 December 1961 the 121st TFWg was redesignated the 7121st Tactical Wing due to its reduced force structure in USAFE. By January 1962, the surfaced shipped equipment had arrived from Ohio, and routine operating supplies had been received from stocks at Chateauroux AD, so the 7121st Wing was ready to operate at its new home. Also, 1,200 tons of conventional munitions arrived and were placed in the base munitions storage site. The 7121st Wing at Etain was costing U.S. taxpayers approximately $616,000.00 per month in personnel pay and base operating expenses. Wing manning of 120 officers, 974 airmen, four DAF civilians, and 74 LWR French civilians cost $351,600.00 per month. Total authorized manning of an F-84F STAIR STEP wing was 131 officers and 1,130 airmen.

The mission of the 7121st TWg was the same as the other three F-84F wings in France, therefore, most of its activities were the same as those described in the Chambley, Chaumont and Toul chapters. Alert began immediately upon arrival; four F-84Fs were loaded with specified armament and maintained on twenty-four hour continuous launch status. Air defense alert from sunup to sundown was also a requirement, with a five-minute scramble time; the F-84F was a day fighter only. Two rotational gunnery exercises were conducted at Wheelus AB. The excellent weather and ranges provided pilots with the opportunity to re-qualify in air-to-air and air-to-ground weapons delivery necessary to maintain combat ready status. The 166th Sq fired 990 rockets and dropped 1,500 practice bombs while training at Wheelus. Weapons training was also conducted at the nearby Suippes Range, forty miles west of Etain. Armament section load crews had to learn to handle conventional bombs and rockets after being trained to load nuclear weapons for several years. Daily simulated close air support missions were flown, weather permitting, throughout West Germany in support of U.S. Army forces. This was the only area of their mission in which ANG pilots needed more experience; it was uncommon in CONUS to have large Army units constantly on field exercises requesting air support. Several fighter pilots were detached as Forward Air Controllers and as Air Liaison Officers to the Seventh Army units in Germany. Two pilots from the 162d TFSq were assigned to the 166th for a four-month tour of duty to keep the squadron at full pilot strength while several pilots were away at schools. Many fighter pilots from the 162d and 164th TFSqs wished to fly in France with the 166th Sq to gain overseas experience, but were refused because of limited travel funds.

A very interesting exchange program was conducted to better acquaint the 166th personnel with their allies in the German Air Force. Four F-84Fs with pilots and crew chiefs moved to Hopsten AB, West Germany, while an equal number of German personnel and aircraft came to Etain and flew missions with the 166th.

From 15 November 1961 to 1 July 1962, the 166th TFSq flew 4,482 hours in the F-84Fs, on 2,778 sorties while based in France. Many of these flying hours were in instrument conditions; 765 flights had to be canceled due to abnormal weather. Etain had five inches of snow on the runway one day in March. Only one F-84F was lost while the 166th was based at Etain, the pilot ejected safely after encountering J-65 engine seizure near the base.

In July 1962 it was time for the 7121st to prepare for return to CONUS. The ADVON departed 2 July on a C-118A for Lockbourne AFB, Ohio. The wing's return from France began on 18 July and required fifteen C-97 flights, one flight a day carrying fifty-five passengers, to move the main body of 7121st troops by 1 August. The last C-97 with the rear echelon arrived at Lockbourne on 9 August. The return was made much easier because all the aircraft support equipment, aircraft parts, and all F-84Fs stayed at Etain to equip the new 366th TFWg. The men from Ohio departed with only their personal property and unit personnel records. They said a sad farewell to their faithful F-84Fs that had served very well for five years. Upon return to ANG status the 166th TFSq began conversion into F-100C Super Sabres and remained at Lockbourne for the following six years until activated again for the Pueblo Crisis in January 1968.

391st Tactical Fighter Squadron, 366th Tactical Fighter Wing

The 366th Tactical Fighter Wing was a USAFE basing experiment attempted only once. It was activated at Chaumont on 8 May 1962, with four squadrons equipped with the aircraft left behind by the STAIR STEP wings. Headquarters and one squadron operated at Chaumont. The other squadrons operated at Chambley, Phalsbourg, and the 391st Tactical Fighter Squadron at Etain. The 166th had transferred twenty-five F-84Fs at Etain for the 366th on 15 July. Only twenty aircraft were flown at each base. Five F-84Fs from each STAIR STEP squadron were assigned to the 480th Squadron at Phalsbourg. Three pilots from the 166th TFSq remained on active duty in France and performed instructor duties for the new 391st TFSq pilots as they checked out in the F-84Fs at Etain. Refer to Chaumont AB, chapter 9, for the complete story about the 366th TFWg.

On 8 May 1962, while the 7121st Tactical Wing was operating at Etain, the 7368th Combat Support Group was activated to operate the base after its departure. The 7368th reported to the newly activated 366th Tactical Fighter Wing at Chaumont and supported the 391st TFSq at Etain. The Combat Support Group consisted of the HQ Squadron, the 7368th Air Police Sq, 7368th Material Sq and the 7368th USAF Dispensary. It began with one officer and three airman, but by 1 January 1963, the Group had grown to 73 officers, 439 airmen, and 96 LWR French employees. A French O&M contractor with seventy-eight men maintained Etain's real estate, i.e., buildings, roads, and fences, under the direction of the 7368th base civil engineer.

Etain's COC was operated by 366th Wing Operations, Det #0200, and staffed by nine officers, five airmen, and one LWR civilian. It operated and supervised the 391st Squadron, manned by twenty-eight officers and six airmen. Aircraft maintenance was provided by Det #0200, 7366th Material Sq, comprised of 14 officers and 344 airmen. In addition; three tenant units still supported the air base; the weather station, post office and aviation radio aids. Other tenants were HQ Company and Company D 249th Engineer Battalion, Construction, who were stationed at Etain to perform base improvements, but their primary job was constructing a large atomic blast resistant depot near Roselier and Verdun. The 7368th maintained very good relations with the Engineering Bn and provided support when needed. The 7368th Civil Engineer gave them their own area including a hangar for indoor storage of trucks, equipment, and tools in the northwest corner of the base.

The 391st TFSq used the same hangar and base operations facilities the 166th TFSq had used. Its primary mission during 1962-63 was close air support for Seventh Army ground forces and the Emergency War Plan, (Automatic Launch). The wing air defense mission involved keeping four fully armed F-84Fs on 24-hour alert. Each pilot had four or more primary targets committed to memory, and was frequently tested on how to execute the Automatic Launch Plan. The 391st began sending eight F-84Fs down to Wheelus for bombing and gunnery training immediately after pilots were checked out in flying the aircraft. The 391st pilots achieved very good high and low angle bombing scores on the range. The squadron was also fully involved during the Cuban Missile Crisis in October 1962; it assumed a total alert posture at Etain with eighteen fully armed F-84Fs on round-the-clock alert for the two weeks. Close air support during GRAND SLAM II in May 1963 saw the 391st flying excellent support missions with the First French Army, the 1st and 3d Corps German Army, and the U.S. Seventh Army. The squadron flew 2,385 hours on 1,463 sorties from 1 January until 15 June 1963.

Maintenance training continued throughout this flying program in order to upgrade aircraft repairmen; a Republic Aircraft tech rep was assigned to Etain in October to assist in this training. The 391st lost one F-84F in February; the pilot ejected safely from an uncontrollable spin, and no property was damaged. During this period the F-84F engines were being improved into J-65-7D models; this -7D engine was reworked at the Curtiss-Wright factory, and in-flight engine failures were reduced. In April, the F-84Fs were grounded for ten days due to cracked tailpipes; new tailpipes were flown to France, and the Streaks were back on alert by 15 April. Twenty 391st pilots completed their water survival training in RCAF Grostenquin's swimming pool prior to flying the North Atlantic. The 7368th CSGp continued to operate the base and support the squadron and assigned tenant units during the twelve months the 391st was based at Etain.

The 391st TFSq departed Etain on 16 July 1963, when the 366th Wing moved to Holloman AFB, New Mexico. The 7368th CSGp manning was reduced, as Etain changed into a standby base, and additional support came from the 7544th Support Group at Toul. A French contractor continued to maintain base real property.

RCAF 1 Wing at Marville Air Base moved twenty-one miles south to Etain for a temporary stay of four weeks, from 1 to 27 May 1965 in "Operation Blacktop," while their runway was being repaired and resurfaced. Two squadrons of CF-104As operated from Etain for routine training. An open house was held to let the local population see the CF-104 Starfighter up close. Most people were surprised that such a small fighter produced such a great amount of noise across the French countryside.

Base support detachments designators at this time were the 7368th CSGp; Det #2205, 7025th Air Postal Gp operating APO 09087; Det #8, 31st Weather Sq; Det #2, 1952d AACS Sq; and Flt "26" 2059th Radio Relay Sq.

Etain was maintained in standby status by the 7368th until 1 July 1966 when the first FRELOC directives were followed to prepare for removal of all

Base OPS 2002. Refurbished and in use by French 3d Regiment d'Helicopteres De Combat, Etain AB.
Pierre Baar

Base Ops building with new tower cab in place. Three fire truck bays boarded up, Etain AB 2005.
Pierre Baar

trailers from the base. The 7368th CSGp was the primary agent to remove all U.S. property and close the base. All airways radio aids and control tower equipment were removed by 1 September, and Det #8, 31st Weather Sq departed. Etain still had 5,600 tons of general supplies, even after three-and-one-half years in standby status. There was a small inventory of support aircraft spare parts, some aircraft shop equipment, aircraft ground support equipment, and many vehicles remaining after the 1963 departure of the 391st TFSq. One thousand tons of conventional aircraft munitions still stored in the ammunition storage site were moved to air bases in Germany. After removal of all equipment and supplies, each building was inspected by a team of USAFE and French officers then closed and sealed. All the metal prefab buildings were disassembled by U.S. Army troops and moved to Germany to store depot supplies. Officers and airmen were moved into hotels in Etain city after 15 October, when the base heating plant was shut down.

By 15 November 1966 all equipment was removed and total base personnel numbered about forty men. French civilian employees numbered about thirty, many of whom were terminated on 31 December 1966. The last to leave was the radio relay detachment after removing its equipment on 10 March. Etain Air Base was transferred to the French government on 15 March 1967. Etain served the USAF and NATO for seven years so it must be considered only a fair investment.

The former air base has been used by the French Army since 1969 as an air base for helicopters. Today the 3d Regiment d'Helicopteres de Combat, Etain operates the base and flies SA 341 Gazelles and Canons plus the large SA 330 Pumas. The base is well maintained; four large aircraft hangars have been added over the last twenty years. One hangar, obtained from the former RCAF Marville, was dismantled and moved to Etain. It is erected next to the old NATO hangar on the northeast complex, primarily for small observation scout helicopters. Three very large modern hangars have been constructed next to original NATO hangars. The Base Operations/Firehouse building is in excellent condition completely reworked with new hardwood floors. A new larger aluminum control tower cab has been installed replacing the original tower cab that corroded away.

Etain Air Base has an open house about once a year in May to display the helicopters and vehicles. Arrangements to visit can be made by contacting Etain Office of Tourism. The city is accessible from Paris by train using Gare de l'Est. It can be found on Michelin Map #307 Local, and IGN Series Blue #3212 E.

Appendix 11.1 Notice to Airmen 1956 (NOTAM) - USAF-Etain

Elevation 766 feet (234m), 49° 14'N - 05° 40'E. One paved runway 7,900 feet long, 020°/200°. Rotating beacon, light on airfield, with runway and obstruction lights. Aircraft storage and minor repair available. Aircraft fuel, 100-130 octane and JP4 jet fuel with single point refilling. Jet aircraft starting units available, low pressure oxygen, liquid oxygen, servicing, and high pressure compressed air available.

Caution, final approach runway 02. End of runway lies on crest of hill after approach over valley causing errors in judgement.

Appendix 11.2 GEN Whisenand's letter to Commander Twelfth Air Force (3 pages)

HEADQUARTERS
388TH FIGHTER BOMBER WING (USAFE)
APO 87, USAF

CO INS 1 — 21 February 1955

SUBJECT: Misuse of United States Resources

TO: Commander
Twelfth Air Force
APO 12, USAF

1. The misuse of the American tax payers resources in the construction of Etain Air Base is so flagrant that, as Installation Commander, I would be remiss in my duties if I did not report the facts. My examination of the complex relationship which exists between the French contractors, the Ponts et Chausses, the Joint Construction Agency, the local departmental Sous Prefet and Prefet, the French Laison Mission, NATO infa-structure, and USAFE has indicated to me that the problem cannot be solved solely within this theater. It appears that basic policy decisions by the Department of Defense and the Department of State, together with derivative Governmental Agreements must be changed if the American tax payer is to avoid the swindle now being perpetrated. The complex relationship now existing permits buck passing vertically and laterally and renders the Installation Commander powerless to influence the needless waste of American Resources. The Base Commander in the United States can control the contractor's performance by stopping construction, by rejecting substandard work, or by invoking penalty clauses. He has no such authority under arrangements in this theater.

2. The major areas in which the United States Government does not receive value commensurate with expenditures are as follows:

a. Contract items essential to making the base operational are far behind established schedules.

b. The construction is grossly substandard, both as to the base utilities system and as to structural composition of the buildings, for example:

(1) The concrete floors of warehouses are failing already, even before exposed to heavy loads.

(2) Walls and floors throughout the entire establishment are developing large cracks.

HQ 388TH FITBOMWG, APO 87, USAF, CO INS 1, SUBJ: Misuse of American Resources

(3) So called waterproof basements leak badly, and at times emergency pumping can barely keep ahead of the water pouring through the walls.

(4) Fixtures and pipes are attached to the walls with inadequate anchorage and are falling off as a result of limited legitimate use.

(5) Practically all the doors on all the buildings will have to be taken down and refitted because of flimsy hinges and inadequate anchorage.

(6) The road system is a sea of mud and the contractor refuses to properly repair deep ditches which he has cut across the road subgrade at various places. Government vehicles operating on these roads are deteriating rapidly.

(7) Large areas of the base were without hot water for five days and without cold water for two days because of defective workmanship and failure for the main water line.

(8) There have been thirteen interuptions of power service to the base, and the installation of emergency generators was far behind schedule. Consequently, on Christmas Eve, I had 1000 men sitting in the barracks with no heat and no lights. How many of these men were writing letters to their Congressmen by candle light I can only surmise.

(9) The railroad spur into the base, which is absolutely essential in order to support jet operations properly was to have been completed in November 1954 and the best estimate I can give now is completion by 1 July 1955.

3. As a result of failure to complete construction on time and as a result of generally poor construction practices, my organization is now spread out on four bases. Upon arrival of this Wing in the theater it was not possible to move the air echelon onto the base. Consequently, my three fighter squadrons are based in Germany and my support elements are based in Etain. This organization had achieved a high level of combat readiness when it left from the United States. Under present circumstances, I estimate it to be no more than forty per cent combat ready. After the Wing is assembled, possibly sometime in July, it will take at least four months to regain the level of combat readiness and

2

HQ 388TH FITBOMWG, APO 87, USAF, CO INS 1, SUBJ: Misuse of American Resources

effectiveness which we had upon departure from the Zone of Interior. Therefore, the American tax payer, is not only being swindled by the direct waste associated with these construction practices, but also through the loss of combat readiness and capability which has been bought and paid for. I estimate that the direct cost of this Wing, in terms of equipment and people, to be about $40,000,000. This $40,000,000 investment is largely paralized through the construction practices which exist in this area.

4. The Air Force is suffering a direct loss in still a third way in that the circumstances that exist here, work directly against our program to retain trained people. The American Airman and Company Grade Officer will cheerfully bear almost any hardship if there is a war going on, or if clear military necessity exists. However when they are moved into substandard conditions and they cannot see the fruits of their efforts in terms of functioning of the primary mission group (the jet fighters) they have a tendency to become cynical and disgruntled. I am morally certain that the Air Force, despite all the personal indoctrination and orientation by myself and subordinate commanders, will lose a number of trained people as a result of the current exercise.

5. Because I believe that the problem cannot be solved solely within this theater, it is recommended:

a. That this correspondence be forwarded through channels to the Chief of Staff, USAF.

b. That the Inspector General, USAF, dispatch a qualified team to inspect the construction on Etain Air Base.

c. That, to protect Air Force interests and resources, the Secretary of the Air Force investigate the complex procedures which now exist and initiate action to the Secretary of Defense to obtain American control of American Resources, and USAF control of USAF resources.

d. That the functioning of the Joint Construction Agency be investigated by the Secretary of Defense.

JAMES E. WHISENAND
Brigadier General, USAF
Commander

Etain Air Base Assigned Aircraft

Bill Posey

388th Fighter-Bomber Wing, F-86Fs, December 1954 - November 1956

Twenty-six aircraft per squadron. These Sabres were flown from Clovis AFB to Bitburg, Hahn, and Spangdahlem Air Bases in West Germany by 388th FBWg pilots. Later flown to Etain, France in July, September, and November 1955.

Aircraft Markings:

561st Fighter-Bomber Squadron - Yellow Vertical Stabilizer/rudder, with black lightning bolt.
562d Fighter-Bomber Squadron - Blue Vertical Stabilizer/rudder, with white lightning bolt.
563d Fighter-Bomber Squadron - Red Vertical Stabilizer/rudder, with white lightning bolt.

F-86F-35-NA

52-5164	562d	52-5264	562d	53-1085	563d	53-1110	562d	53-1128	563d
52-5166	563d	52-5265	562d	53-1087	562d	53-1111 ~	562d	53-1129	563d
52-5199	562d	52-5266	563d	53-1089	562d	53-1112	562d	53-1130	563d
52-5214	563d	52-5267	563d	53-1092	562d	53-1113	562d	53-1131	563d
52-5230	561st	52-5268	562d	53-1095	561st	53-1114	562d	53-1132	561st
52-5234	561st	52-5269	563d	53-1096	562d	53-1115	562d	53-1133	561st
52-5237	561st	52-5270*	561st	53-1097	562d	53-1116	561st	53-1134	561st
52-5245	561st	52-5271	563d	53-1098	562d	53-1117	563d	53-1135*	561st
52-5247*	561st	53-1072	561st	53-1099	562d	53-1118	563d	53-1136	561st
52-5252	561st	53-1073	561st	53-1101	561st	53-1119	563d	53-1137	561st
52-5256	563d	53-1075	561st	53-1103	562d	53-1120	563d	53-1141	561st
52-5257	563d	53-1076	563d	53-1104	562d	53-1121	563d	53-1142	562d
52-5260	561st	53-1078	563d	53-1105	562d	53-1123	563d	53-1146	562d
52-5261*	563d	53-1079	562d	53-1106	561st	53-1125	563d		
52-5262	562d	53-1081*	563d	53-1109	561st	53-1127	561st		

*Aircraft Losses:
52-5247 - Crashed, engine failure, 2nm E of Verdun, France, 23 JULY 55, 1 fatality.
52-5261 - Crashed, hydraulic system failure, 2.5nm NNE of Dover AFB, Delaware, 27 NOV 54, no fatalities.
52-5270 - Crashed, mid-air collision, 15nm WNW of Hahn AB, West Germany, 26 FEB 55, no fatalities, ejected.
53-1081 - Crashed, bad weather letdown, 0.5nm E of Combres, France, 11 DEC 55, 1 fatality.
53-1135 - Crashed, bad weather letdown into city of Bitburg, West Germany, 15 JAN 55, 1 fatality.
~ Wing Commander's aircraft

Wing Support Aircraft: 388th Air Base Group
C-47As: 3 ea. 42-24130, 42-92643, 43-15222, 43-16090
C-47D: 43-49295
L20A: 51-16530
T-33As: 5ea. 52-9583

Grant Mobley

388th Fighter-Bomber Wing, F-100D, October 1956 - 10 December 1957

Twenty-two aircraft per squadron. No F-100Fs were delivered to the 388th FBWg. These Super Sabres were flown from Inglewood, CA and Columbus, OH to French Morocco by MATS ferry pilots.

Aircraft Markings:

561st Fighter-Bomber Squadron - Yellow vertical stabilizer/rudder with black lightning bolt.
562d Fighter-Bomber Squadron - Blue vertical stabilizer/rudder with white lightning bolt.
563d Fighter-Bomber Squadron - Red vertical stabilizer/rudder with white lightning bolt.

F-100D-5, -10, -15, -25, -30-NA and -35, -40-NH

54-2137	562d	54-2170	561st	54-2200	54-2214	54-2223	54-2229*	54-2237	54-2241
54-2156	562d	54-2174	561st	54-2204	54-2217	54-2224	54-2230	54-2239	54-2242
54-2163	563d	54-2195		54-2211	54-2218	54-2228	54-2235	54-2240	54-2243

Etain AB Assigned Aircraft, continued

388th Fighter-Bomber Wing, cont.

F-100D-5, -10, -15, -25, -30-NA and -35, -40-NH continued

54-2244	54-2259	54-2269	55-2763* 563d	55-3659	55-3695
54-2245	54-2260* 562d	54-2276	55-2777 561st	55-3660* 562d	55-3697
54-2246	54-2261	54-2278	55-2778	55-3661 562d	55-3700 561st
54-2247 563d	54-2262	54-2282	55-3596	55-3667	55-3701 563d
54-2248	54-2263* 563d	55-2743 562d	55-3652	55-3674	55-3724 563d
54-2249	54-2264*	55-2748*	55-3654	55-3678 563d	55-3743
54-2250	54-2267	55-2756 562d	55-3655	55-3691 562d	
54-2252*	54-2268*	55-2760	55-3658	55-3693	

*Aircraft Losses:
54-2229 - Crashed, engine failure,13nm South of Wheelus AB, Libya, 7 OCT 57, no fatalities, ejected.
54-2252 - Crashed, bad landing, on Wheelus AB, Libya, August 57, no fatalities, ejected.
54-2260 - Crashed, engine failure,13nm S of Wheelus AB, Libya, 1957, no fatalities, ejected.
54-2263 - Destroyed, severe ground fire, on Etain AB, France, 26 MAR 57, no fatalities.
54-2264 - Damaged, take-off engine failure, on Wheelus AB, Libya, NOV 57, no fatalities.
54-2268 - Crashed, bad landing, 1nm S of Etain AB, France, SEP 57, 1 fatality.
55-2748 - Crashed
55-2763 - Crashed
55-3660 - Crashed into sea, engine fire, 120nm S of Cagliari, Sardinia, 20 OCT 57, no fatalities, ejected.

Wing Support Aircraft: 388th Air Base Group
C-47As: 2 ea at a time, 42-24130, 42-92643, 43-15222, 43-16090.
C-47D: 1 ea. 43-49295
L-20A: 51-16530
T-33A: 7 ea: 52-9583

49th Tactical Fighter Wing, F-100D/Fs, 10 December 1957 - 25 August 1959

Twenty-four aircraft per squadron. Newer Super Sabres were flown from Inglewood, CA to Etain AB, France by MATS ferry pilots. Most Super Sabres were transferred in place from the 388th FBWg on 10 December 1957.
388th Aircraft marking retained.

7th Tactical Fighter Squadron - Blue vertical stabilizer/rudder with a white lightning bolt and blue nose band.
8th Tactical Fighter Squadron - Yellow vertical stabilizer/rudder with a black lightning bolt and yellow nose band.
9th Tactical Fighter Squadron - Red vertical stabilizer/rudder with a white lightning bolt and red nose band.

F-100D-10, -25, -90-NA

54-2137 8th	55-3654	55-3695	56-3215	56-3242	56-3294	56-3304
54-2156 8th	55-3655	55-3697*	56-3216	56-3244	56-3295	56-3305
54-2163 9th	55-3658	55-3700 7th	56-3218	56-3247	56-3296	56-3306
54-2247 9th	55-3659	55-3701* 9th	56-3220	56-3252	56-3297	56-3308
54-2250* 7th	55-3661 7th		56-3224	56-3255	56-3298	56-3309
54-2278 7th	55-3667	56-3201	56-3229	56-3257	56-3299	56-3311
55-2743 7th	55-3674	56-3204	56-3230	56-3289	56-3300 7th	56-3312
55-2756 8th	55-3678 9th	56-3206 8th	56-3232	56-3290	56-3301	56-3314 7th
55-3596	55-3691 7th	56-3207* 8th	56-3238	56-3291	56-3302	56-3318
55-3652	55-3693	56-3208	56-3241	56-3292	56-3303	56-3322
				56-3293		

F-100F-10-NA

56-3819 9th	56-3843 8th	56-3858 7th	56-3877* 9th	56-3904 8th
56-3828 7th	56-3854 8th	56-3861 7th	56-3879 9th	

*Aircraft Losses:
54-2250 - Crashed, into sea, engine failure, near El Uotia range, Libya, MAR 58, no fatalities, ejected.
55-3697 - Crashed, let-down/bad weather, near Etain AB, France, AUG 58, 1 fatality.
55-3701 - Crashed, gyro failure/weather, 6.7nm NNE of Etain AB, France, 18 JAN 58, 1 fatality.
56-3207 - Crashed, hit ground, simulated air support, 30 JUL 58, 1 fatality.
56-3877 - Crashed, into sea, engine failure, near Wheelus AB, Libya, AUG 60, no fatalities, ejected.

49th Air Base Group: Wing Support Aircraft
C-47A: 2 ea: 42-100631, 42-92643, 43-15222, 42-92832 (on loan)
L-20A: 51-16530
T-33A: 7 ea 52-9583

Etain AB Assigned Aircraft, continued

USAF Museum

7121st Tactical Wing, 166th Tactical Fighter Sq, F-84Fs, 5 November 1961 - 15 July 1962

Twenty-six aircraft assigned to the squadron. These Thunderstreaks were flown from Lockbourne AFB, OH to Etain AB, France by 166th TFSq pilots. These F-84Fs transferred to 366th TFWg and remained in France until July 1963, then were flown to Holloman AFB, NM.

Aircraft markings: 166th Tactical Fighter Squadron - Red band.

F-84F-25, -30, -35, -40, -55-RE and -25, -30, -35-GK

51-1654	51-1739	51-1757	51-1810	51-9433	51-17073	52-6418	52-6629	52-6963
51-1672	51-1744	51-1785	51-9403	51-9490	52-6379	52-6493	52-6924	52-6993
51-1725	51-1750	51-1791	51-9415*	51-9501	52-6381	52-6526^	52-6936	

* Aircraft Losses:
51-9415 - Crashed, engine failure, 6nm SE of Etain AB, France, 30 JAN 62, no fatalities, ejected.

^ 52-6526 now at USAF Museum

Wing Support Aircraft: 7121st Operations Squadron
C-47A: 1 each from ANG, 42-92095
L-20A: 51-16538
T-33A: 2 each from ANG, 52-9624, 52-9838

366th Tactical Fighter Wing, 391st TFSq, F-84Fs, 15 July 1962 - 16 July 1963

Twenty aircraft assigned to the 391st Squadron. These Thunderstreaks were flown from Etain AB, France to Holloman AFB, New Mexico by 366th TFWg pilots.
Aircraft markings:
391st Tactical Fighter Squadron - Red band.

F-84F-25, -30, -35, -40, -55-RE and -25, -30, -35-GK

51-1654	51-1725	51-1744	51-1757	51-1791	51-9403	52-6379	52-6418	52-6526^	52-6963
51-1672	51-1739	51-1750	51-1785	51-1810	51-9433	52-6381	52-6493	52-6936	52-6993

* Aircraft Losses:
one accident - crashed, spin, no recovery, near Etain AB, FR, 22 JAN 63, no fatalities, ejected.

^ 52-6526 now at USAF Museum

ACKNOWLEDGEMENTS

I would like to thank the following people who contributed to this chapter:

Ben Bagwell was the base sports reporter at Etain from 1954-56.

Pierre Baar is a Belgian who has just completed a definitive book on the RCAF base at Marville, France.

Louis Bufkin was in the 388th Air Police Squadron stationed at Etain from 1954 to 1958. He was a member of the Etain Pioneers football team from 1955-57 and was team captain in 1957. Louis was the driving force behind the Etain Pioneer reunions until his death in 2002.

Tom Malinowski was a member of the 388th Air Police Squadron stationed at Etain from 1955 to 1958. Tom was a member of the Etain Pioneers football team.

John Marcott was a pilot at Etain with the 388th FBWg's 563d FBSq and the 49th FBWg's 9th FBSq flying both the F-86s and F-100s.

Grant Mobley was an A/1C with the 388th Air Police Squadron.

John McBee was with the 249th Army Engineers in 1960-62, working at the STAIR STEP bases preparing them for arrival of the ANG squadrons.

Bill Posey was a crew chief in the 563d FBSq at Etain.

Sam Roberts was assigned to the Operations Section as a Survival Training and Personal Equipment Specialist at Etain AB with the 563d Fighter-Bomber Squadron, 1954-58. He is active in the Etain Pioneers reunion group. Sam has provided extensive photos, clippings, and information on Etain, particularly the sports programs.

Road sign on D906 just outside the town of Rouvres en Woevre, 1998.
Jerry McAuliffe

Rouvres en Woevre 1998, located just east of Etain AB.
Jerry McAuliffe

12

EVREUX-FAUVILLE AIR BASE

The city of Evreux, capital of the Eure Department, is located twenty-six miles (46 km) south of Rouen in Haute (Upper) Normandy. Founded by the Romans, it has been devastated and rebuilt many times in the course of its history. It suffered extensively in World War II, but was rebuilt once more, and today is a busy industrial city.

It was half destroyed by Ninth Air Force bombing as part of the pre D-Day transportation plan to destroy rail yards and bridges. After breakout from the Normandy beaches in July 1944, the U.S. Army, XIX Corps, 30th Infantry Division overcame light resistance south of Evreux and liberated the city on 23 August 1944. Fortunately there was very light opposition, eliminating any further destruction within the city. The region was then turned over to the Canadian Army because it lay within their zone of operation.

The Civil Aerodrome began in the early 1920s as a typical, small, east-west grass strip for sport flying. It was located 4 km east-southeast of the city of Evreux, at that time a long walk or drive on the weekend from the city's center. In 1930 an Aero Club de l'Eure was flying from the Aerodrome, which by now had hangars with repair and fuel service. By 1938 the runway was lengthened and lighting installed. France was improving all their airports, civil as well as military, as part of their pre-WWII military preparations. In September 1939 the French Air Force dispersed Dewoitine 501 fighters to the expanded airfield, and early in 1940 added Potez-63 bombers. New Curtiss H75-1 Hawk fighters, and Martin 167 Marylands and Douglas DB-7 light bombers also operated from Evreux during 1940. These aircraft were built by the U.S. for sale to our allies in President Roosevelt's "cash and carry" plan. Previous to our entrance into WWII, allies who had not paid their WWI debt could buy aircraft for cash but could not receive loans to purchase them. This prewar production and influx of cash was a boost to our expanding aircraft industry in 1939 and 1940.

The Luftwaffe flew Ju88 bombers and Me109 fighters from Evreux during the Battle for Britain, after the fall of France in June 1940. In 1942 they built two 4,800-foot concrete runways with approach lighting and large dispersal areas. Later in 1943 and 1944, Fw190 fighters operated from here. After liberation, Evreux Aerodrome (designated B-28) was used by RAF fighter units of the Second Tactical Air Force until the war ended.

It is rumored that during the German occupation, large underground hangars and aircraft dispersal areas were built one or two miles north of the base. This virtually hidden air base was supposedly located west the village of Cerisey and south of Sassey. The underground complex was reportedly seen by USAF people in the early 1950s but its existence remains a mystery.

During the initial site selection meetings in 1950, the existing Evreux airfield was proposed and the FAF, and USAFE immediately agreed upon its use as a troop carrier air base and combat cargo command headquarters. This airfield was under local civil jurisdiction, so further negotiations were necessary to gain approval for U.S./NATO use. Other possible sites were investigated further north and west at the Cherbourg/Maupertus and Nantes/Chateau airfields to determine if they met the requirements of an air transport base. The Nantes airfield was also evaluated as a possible air depot site. But, final approval was obtained during 1951 from the City of Evreux and the Department of l'Eure to convert their civilian airport into a U.S. military air base.

Evreux-Fauville Air Base (49° 02'N - 01° 14'E, elevation 461 feet) is sixty-one miles (98 km) west of Paris on N13 and twenty-nine miles (46 km) south of Rouen. The site, located four miles (5 km) east of Evreux, was a flat plain of 2,150 acres. Its clear approaches were ideal for a large all-weather airfield. The acreage could accommodate a single runway up to 10,000 feet long and was readily available for construction. A few tenants and the Evreux Aero Club had to be relocated, but no industrial activity was located on the airport.

This excellent location presented a minimum of problems; it had good road capacity, very good rail service from Paris, and better flying weather than eastern France. A railroad spur to the base could be easily laid from about two miles away. The problems noted by the survey team were the usual—limited potable

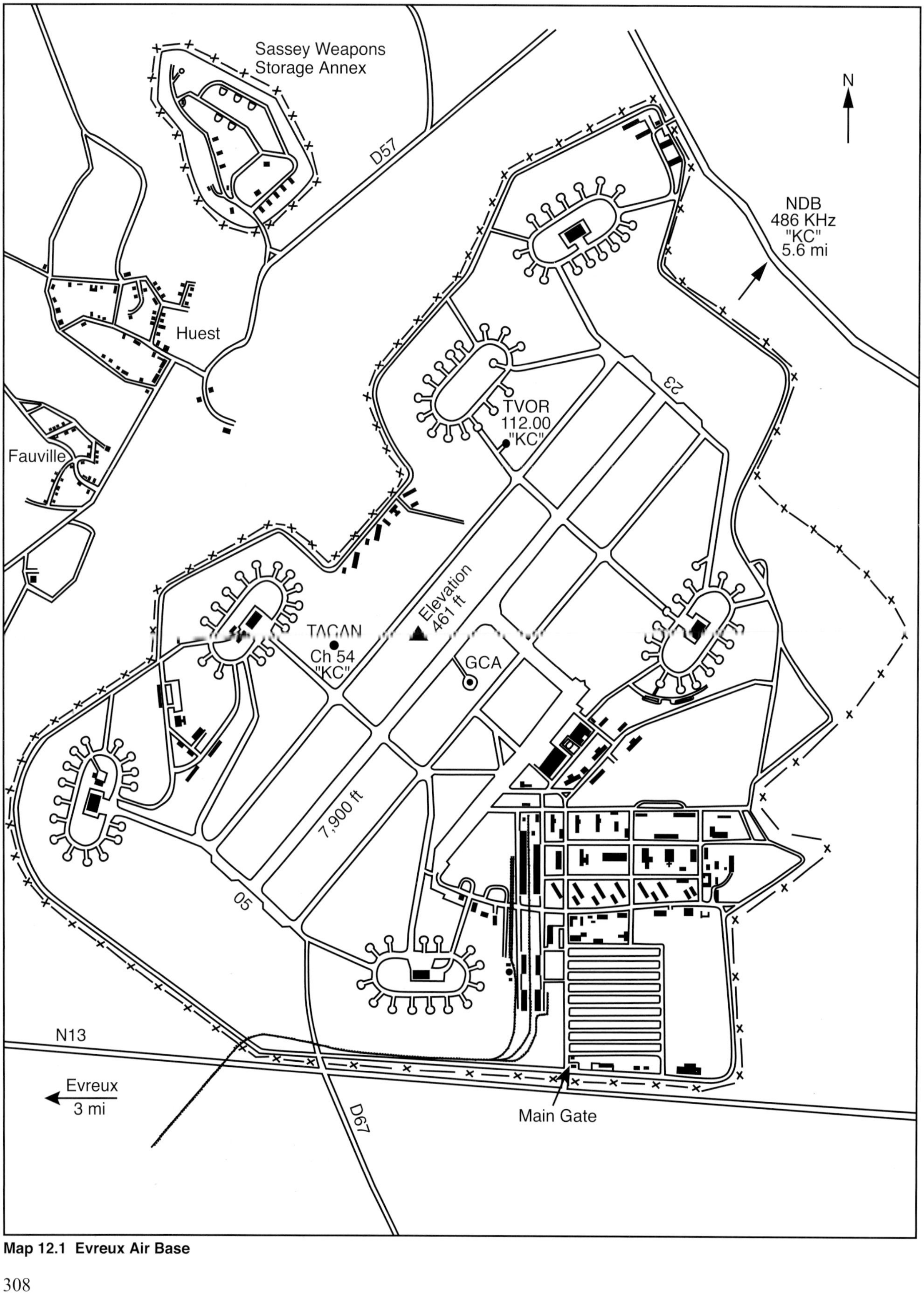

Map 12.1 Evreux Air Base

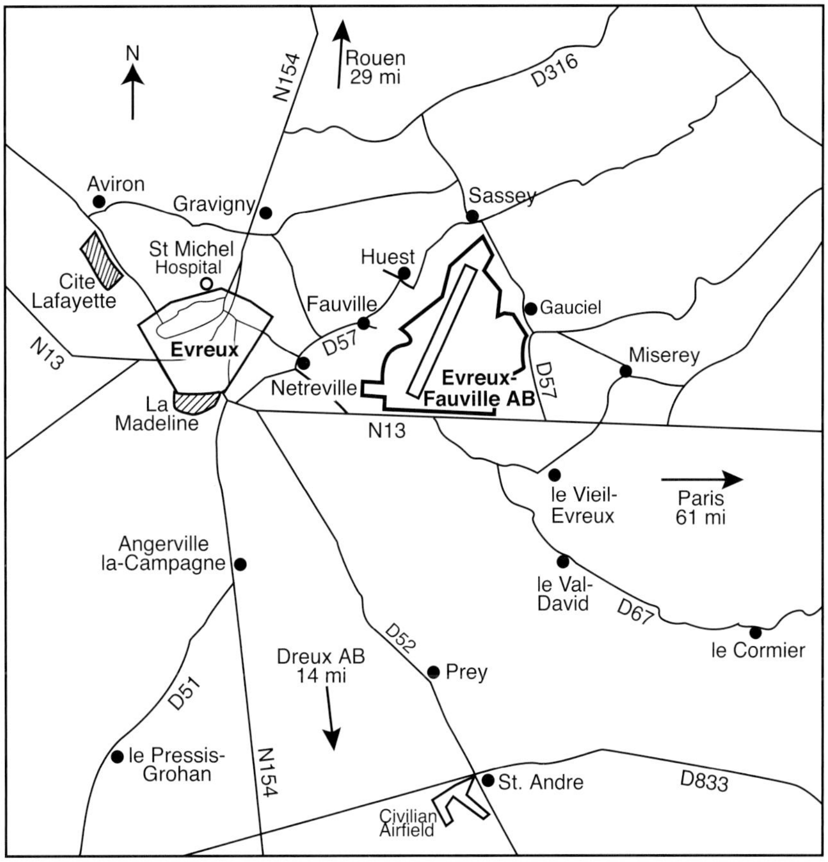

Map 12.2 Evreux Area

water and marginal commercial electrical service. There were also several small towns in close proximity to the base site.

TAC planned that a troop carrier wing, flying C-119s, would arrive by the fall of 1954. This would make Evreux a single step base, to be constructed within three years with all permanent buildings, shops, and hangars. All structures would be of standard NATO design but expanded for the larger base population required by the mission. USAF directly funded buildings such as the service club, officers and NCO clubs, elementary school, commissary, and base exchange that would be standard Corps of Engineer designs.

Preliminary surveys were conducted in April 1952 and the Corps of Engineers gave approval after determining a sufficient source of potable water. Construction started the following June with access roads and fences; the original runway was removed because of WWII bomb damage and multiple repairs. Runway grading began in July, and one concrete runway was poured, 7,900 feet long by 150 feet wide, northeast/southwest. This was followed by taxiways, parking hardstands, hangar floors, and aprons. Evreux's layout was unusual because it had six aircraft parking marguerites. The sixth marguerite was intended for transient cargo aircraft parking. Its layout was almost identical to Dreux AB, twenty-eight miles (43 km) south, except for the living areas. One living area was constructed on the north side of the base to house squadron personnel close to their hangar. Two additional living areas and an NCO club were built on the west side for the other two flying squadrons.

The 7306th Air Base Squadron detachment from Chateauroux Air Depot arrived on 22 April 1952 and set up a small tent camp to provide administration and logistics support during the first two years of base construction. The Joint Construction Agency managed the construction. Assistance was also received from Laon and Dreux air bases as Evreux neared completion. The airdrome was known as Evreux Air Base for three years, then changed to Evreux-Fauville Air Base on 1 July 1955 to clarify its location.

No permanent housing could be built on base, therefore, a large trailer park was built on the east side of the main gate as part of Project Caravan. During 1954 and 1955 three hundred trailer sites with utilities and laundry huts were constructed by the 821st

Memorial to PFC Roger J. Boender, 821st EABn at Evreux AB, 2002.
Jerry McAuliffe

Engineering Aviation Battalion, a SCARWAF unit. One soldier, PFC Roger J. Boender, from C Company, 821st EABn was killed in the line of duty while working on this construction job. This family trailer park was named "Boenderville" shortly after its completion in March 1956, and a monument still exists on Evreux in his memory. These trailers were in use as family housing until the base closed in 1967.

A twenty-two acre POL storage site was located on the western edge of the village of le Vieil-Evreux, one km south of the base on the west side of road D67. This storage site had seven buildings and was connected to the U.S. pipeline and controlled POL deliveries to Evreux and Dreux air bases. The Vieil-Evreux Petroleum Products Storage Annex (property #9592) was returned March 1967.

To meet munitions safety requirements, the Sassey Weapons Storage Site was constructed off base, midway between the towns of Sassey and Huest, away from populated areas. This ninety-six acre site provided storage for aircraft munitions awaiting air transportation to fighter airfields. This weapons storage site (property #5285) was also closed and returned to the Military Liquidation Service, Paris, in March 1967.

Two additional very large construction projects were located seven miles west of the base, on a hilltop north of the city of Evreux. The first was Cite Lafayette (property #7157), a large Commodity Credit Housing complex of 175 units consisting of two, three or four bedroom duplex homes in a park-like setting. The Evreux-St. Michel grammar school (property #5946) for 500 students in grades first through fourth was built immediately east of this housing area.

The second was a very large hospital, St. Michel (property #5945), with a 1,000-bed capacity and major medical treatment facilities, that opened in 1960. It was the largest USAFE medical facility in France. This hospital was intended for wartime use to provide initial treatment of casualties before their air evacuation to safer locations in the UK. This facility, occupying about one-half square mile, consisted of a core hospital building with nine wings. Twelve additional buildings spaced on a large circular drive surrounded the hospital. These buildings provided officer and airman quarters, a small service club, a six-bay ambulance and fire station, a vehicle shop, a small BX, two warehouses, and a heating plant. By 1962 annual operation and maintenance costs of this hospital complex were $200,000.

La Madeline, a Guaranteed Rental Income housing development of 152 units, was located five miles west of the air base, south of route N13 and south of the main rail line. All these properties were returned to France in March 1967. The housing and hospital are still in use by the local French people and the hospital now includes a medical school. Today the entire setting is covered with pine trees and appears much like a western U.S. town; all homes are occupied and kept in very fine condition.

By December 1957 Evreux-Fauville Air Base (APO 253, later 09253) occupied an area of 2,150 acres with thirteen miles of paved roads. Taxiways, aprons, parking ramps, etc. required 640,000 square yards of concrete. The base had seventy-five permanent buildings and twenty-six temporary buildings. It had four million cubic feet of warehouse storage space and two railroad sidings. The base chapel had been enlarged and was considered one of the finest military chapels in France. An elementary school for grades fifth through eighth was built on base. Water storage tanks held 290,000 gallons. Four heating plants furnished hot water for all building heat and wash water via under-

Barracks and Mess Hall, Evreux 1956.
Cletus "Frank" Mebane

Evreux AB main gate 1965.
Harry W. Foulds

ground ducting. Ten airmen dormitories with a capacity of 140 men each and two 220 airmen barracks were built in four different areas. Five BOQ buildings were constructed to hold sixty officers each. There were four dining halls, a 1,000-man facility on the main base and three 400-man units in the three squadron areas. Underground fuel storage held 960,500 gallons of aviation gas, plus 140,000 gallons of gasoline and diesel for vehicles. All base utilities and storage tanks were installed underground. Estimated value of real estate (excluding land) was $60 million. Value of equipment in use (excluding aircraft) was approximately $9 million. Total Base Supply Inventory was $7.5 million. Four different French contractors performed work at Evreux, and overall the quality was excellent, but completion of the base slipped about fourteen months. By 1959 many amenities had been added to the base: two theaters, a large library, a bowling alley, an American Youth Activities center, a gymnasium, a golf driving range, small arms range, and six baseball and softball fields.

In conclusion, Evreux-Fauville Air Base can be considered a good investment since it was used operationally for a total of nine years. After completion in 1955 the base was in standby status for only two years. It was well constructed compared to our other air bases in France, with an excellent runway and well built buildings. There is no history of the runway breaking or cracking and causing an operational shut down after completion.

465th Troop Carrier Wing Medium

The first tenant scheduled for Evreux-Fauville was the 313th Troop Carrier Wing based at Mitchel AFB, New York, but it did not pass its port-of-embarkation inspections and remained in CONUS. Instead, the 465th Troop Carrier Wing Medium, which had been activated on 1 February 1953 at Donaldson AFB, South Carolina, was chosen to occupy Evreux. Unfortunately, construction of Evreux was well behind schedule, so initially they had to be stationed at Toul Air Base. Toul was not complete either, but it was more ready to accept troops than Evreux in January 1954.

Commanders of the 465th during its time at Evreux were COL James A. Evans who commanded the wing until July 1956 and COL Robert D. Forman who was commander from 15 August 1956 to 8 July 1957.

The 465th moved with its subordinate units from Toul-Rosieres to Evreux-Fauville in May 1955; there was no change in mission, aircraft, or commander. By 23 May, the wing had moved about 95 per cent of it's aircraft, personnel, and equipment from Toul to Evreux. Everyone was happy to leave the damp, cold environment of Toul and was very optimistic about the new location. The wet, overcast winters in the woods were ended! At Evreux there was not a single tree on the whole base in the summer of 1955, and no grass either! Evreux was still not completed; living and working conditions were crowded, but as quickly as facilities were accepted by JCA from the contractors the units moved into superior buildings compared to Toul. Aircraft parking was remote from squadron operations and maintenance shops, so flight scheduling was difficult during the first year due to a shortage of vehicles and ground communication systems. But, the milder weather around Evreux and its proximity to Paris improved morale considerably.

The 465th was still flying fifty-four C-119C Boxcars and consisted of the 780th, 781st, and 782d Troop Carrier Squadrons, plus the usual supporting groups and squadrons. It was the only airlift wing in France and was the first USAFE tactical wing to operate from the partially completed Evreux-Fauville. Evreux continued for the next nine years as a main operating base.

By 1 June 1955 the non-flying units had also moved to Evreux. The 465th Troop Carrier Wing took command of HQ, 465th Troop Carrier Group; HQ, 465th Maintenance & Supply Group commanding the: 465th Field Maintenance Supply and Motor Vehicle Squadrons; the 465th USAF Tactical Hospital; the HQ Squadron; and 465th Air Base Group. Under jurisdiction of the Air Base Group were the Air Police, Communications, Food Service, and Air Installations Squadrons.

The wing also provided logistical support to the following agencies assigned at Evreux:

- Detachment #6, 12th Air Postal Sq (APO #253)
- Detachment #1, 1272d Air & Airways Communications Sq (MATS)
- Detachment #15, 31st Weather Sq (MATS)
- 2d Aeromedical Evacuation Group
- 5th Aerial Port Squadron, Detachment #3
- 6th Aerial Port Squadron, Detachment #13
- 8th Radio Relay Squadron
- 7416th Aeromedical Evacuation Group
- 4th Forward Aeromedical Evacuation Flight
- U.S. Army 557th QM Aerial Support Company.

Later, in 1957 the C-130 Mobile Training Detachment (Air Training Command) was added.

The 557th Quartermaster Company (Aerial Support), 1st Aviation Detachment, was a new U.S. Army unit in France. It joined the 465th Wing at Evreux in October 1955 and remained on base until December 1965. The mission of this 140-man company was to prepare army equipment and supplies for combat air drops in support of airborne operations. Combat vehicle and explosive loads had to be carefully prepared for aerial movement to eliminate any hazards to the cargo aircraft. Weight and center of gravity computations were a critical task performed by this unit prior to aircraft loading. They were tasked with delivering loads to the aircraft and assisting loadmasters. This quartermaster company also owned a fleet of vehicles to transport ground forces' equipment from a rail yard onto the base and directly to the aircraft cargo ramp.

Each squadron was scheduled to fly 750 to 800 hours per month to meet tasking for Air Logistical Support (ALS), Special Air Logistics Missions (SALM), Tactical Airlift (TA), Unit Support (US), Joint Training (JT), and Training Flights (TR) requirements. Some months the squadrons approached 900 hours of flying even though the 465th had personnel shortages during 1955 and 1956. Enlistments of skilled personnel were expiring and many replacements were three-level apprentices. Five-level aircraft flight engineers, airborne radio operators, engine mechanics, technical supply personnel, skilled clerk typists, and airborne COM/NAV radio repairmen were very much in demand. This resulted in many C-119s being out of commission for lack of maintenance and required intensive individual training. The solution was to consolidate maintenance shops by function. Instead of each flying squadron having its own maintenance people, technicians from all three squadrons were combined. Individual squadron integrity could not be kept, and this was hard for the squadrons to accept. Depot maintenance on the C-119s was performed for the 465th by SABENA Airline under contract. They performed Inspection and Repairs As Necessary (IRANs) and Technical Order Compliance (TOCs).

Emphasis on training continued with the acquisition of a transportable ground drop zone radar beacon TPN-2, that was set up as a fixed installation and worked with the C-119's radar interrogator set APN-12. This beacon served as a very good training device for new pilots and navigators. The 465th changed to C-119Gs beginning in May 1956, and was surprised to receive its first C-119 flight simulator. Other unusual items received by the squadron intelligence section from USAFE were gray plastic aircraft scale models to be used by aircrews for recognition training. Pilots hadn't seen these since WWII and didn't even know they were still being procured.

The 780th and 781st Squadrons were awarded the Air Force Outstanding Unit Award for extraordinary operations over the period 29 October to 16 December 1956. The wing airlifted United Nations' Troops, evacuated U.S. and other nations' personnel from the Middle East, and flew Red Cross emergency supplies to Hungarian refugees, while conducting all their routine airlift missions.

The 465th Wing was reorganized on 12 March 1957. Headquarters, 465th Troop Carrier Group was deactivated and the wing deputy commander for operations assumed direct command over the three troop carrier squadrons. This action eliminated approximately fifty personnel slots. Group level support functions were now folded into wing staff agencies. Most group headquarters' personnel were moved to vacancies within the wing. Elimination of the flying groups was implemented throughout all USAFE wings to reduce costs. At this time most wings were operating at 75 to 80 percent of authorized manning levels; unfortunately most manpower shortages were of operational combat aircrews and aircraft maintenance technicians.

C-119 #53-3213
National Archives

On the weekend of 19 May 1957, an open house and air show was conducted on Evreux for the first time; a very large French civilian crowd enjoyed their base tour. The large collection of military aircraft from five nations attracted people from Normandy, Brittany, and Paris. It created a new phenomenon for France - traffic congestion was beginning to be a problem in post war France!

An unusual aircraft accident occurred near Evreux in 1957 when a U.S. Navy AD-5N Skyraider ran out of fuel and landed gear up about fifty miles west of the base. The AD-5N was repaired by base mechanics and the pilot flew it out of the barley field back to its carrier! Not all mishaps ended so happily. Aircrews flying in Europe during the cold-war years got the message that these were truly "war years" when they lost friends in aircraft accidents and when they personally encountered Soviet treachery and almost became a cold-war casualty themselves. Roger Misgen's story of his experience follows:

I was based at Evreux, France with the 465th from 1955 to 1957 flying C-119 Flying Boxcars as part of NATO's air logistics service. We had a motto "tons for Tunner." General Tunner was Twelfth Air Force commander at the time. He had acquired fame as the commander who made the Berlin Airlift successful during the Russian blockade in 1947. During my time in France, the 465th flew everything from C-rations and cots, to bombs and ammunition. I once was Courier Officer for an atomic bomb as it was transported! We carried supplies to the fighter bases throughout Europe and delivered munitions, crews and supplies of all types to Mideast bases such as Tripoli, where our fighters staged for gunnery practice. We went as far east as Turkey where we could see the Russian border.

On this particular flight we were delivering top-secret cargo to Stockholm, Sweden. Whatever it was, was in crates and was covered with a canvas tarp. We never found out what it was, but the Russians must have known about it and all about our flight.

Our flight took us up the Berlin Corridor,

which was a route through and over the Russian controlled area of Germany. Although the route was in agreed space through the five-mile-wide corridor, the Russian's frequently buzzed and harassed NATO aircraft as they transited. It was the only air corridor for the west into West Berlin and north, where we were headed. This, of course, added to the excitement of our trip. Our flight across Germany allowed us to survey the very cities that our bombers of the mighty Eighth Air Force had destroyed ten years earlier. After crossing Germany we headed out over the Baltic Sea which separates Germany from Sweden. The flight had been without incident so far. As we approached the Swedish coast, we contacted Stockholm Control. We were given a heading in preparation to being picked up on radar by Stockholm. We flew this heading, which was not exactly toward Stockholm. We tuned in Stockholm radio beacon that was the only nav aid available to us. It came in loud and clear. The radio beacon was indicated on a direction-finding needle or pointer on our instrument panel. The needle indicated that we were flying to the beacon; it was on our nose.

Everything seemed normal except that we were flying over clouds, over an undercast and could not see the ground or in this case the sea for visual navigation. Suddenly our navigator shouted, "Turn around! Make a 180 now!" indicating a complete reversal of course. "We are about to enter the Polish FIR," meaning we were about to enter Polish controlled air space which the Russians really controlled. We immediately turned and contacted Stockholm control. "Oh yes, now have you on my radar. Take a heading of 350 degrees." This was now a heading toward Stockholm. Why we had been given the earlier heading I don't know. What had happened was that the Poles had "jammed" the Stockholm radio beacon. By overpowering it with a stronger signal on the same frequency. We almost fell for it. We almost flew into Russian controlled air space. I'll bet the MIGs were orbiting, ready to force us to land at a Polish air base or shoot us down. We must have had some really hot cargo that the Russians wanted. I am sure they didn't want an old C-119 cargo plane or its sweaty crew.

A couple of years later a C-130 was shot down on the Turkish border under very similar circumstances of radio jamming.

The remainder of the trip was uneventful and I had a pleasant time for my first and only visit to Stockholm, Sweden.

During September 1957, the first C-130A Hercules was introduced into the USAFE inventory. As their reliability and productivity improved, the projected need for three airlift wings in Europe was reduced. Also the U.S. Army projected a decrease of airborne units in Europe, so the need for troop practice drops would decline. It was determined that the 465th would be deactivated.

The 465th Wing had one of the longest deactivations in France, perhaps anywhere. Flying group headquarters had been deactivated 12 March 1957. Four months later in July, wing headquarters and all support squadrons were deactivated. As the 465th support squadrons were deactivated, personnel were transferred into 317th Wing vacancies, transferred to other bases within USAFE, or returned to CONUS as excess. The three flying squadrons continued to operate for another six to nine months. All personnel, aircraft, equipment, and supplies were assigned to the 317th Troop Carrier Wing, which now had six flying squadrons. At this time the 317th shared Evreux with the 465th Troop Carrier Wing. The end of the 465th occurred on 8 July 1957, when it was deactivated at Evreux-Fauville by the 322d Air Division. The 465th designator was later assigned to a Strategic Air Command bombardment wing that was activated in 1963 and based in the U.S., flying B-52s and KC-135s until 1968.

The 780th and 781st Squadrons, now under control of the 317th, had been programmed to receive C-130As prior to deactivation of the 465th, and continued to prepare their C-119s for return to Air Force Reserve troop carrier wings in CONUS. All C-119s were readied for departure by conducting the normal transfer inspections. The reserve units required that the aircraft be delivered to them in excellent condition, which delayed their departure. Each C-119 had to be reconfigured by adding Benson fuselage fuel tanks for flying across the Atlantic, as well as the usual collecting, tagging, and packing of flyaway equipment. Thirty-seven C-119Gs had departed for delivery to the U.S. Air Force Reserve by 31 December 1957. This exceptional maintenance workload was very difficult when added to the C-130 conversion training and reduction of personnel. For instance, 780th TCSq manning as of 1 January 1958 had been reduced by eleven men. It was authorized forty-seven officers but had forty-one, and of eighty-seven airmen authorized, it had eighty-two. The one warrant officer authorization stayed the same.

In September 1957 after completing instructor pilot and instructor flight engineer training at Ardmore AFB, Oklahoma, a three-man crew from the 780th returned with the first C-130A in USAFE. As the 780th and 781st Squadrons began conversion training, total operational flying time was reduced from 800 to 400 hours a month per squadron. By 31 December 1957, the 780th had seven C-130As and only five C-119s on hand. The 781st received their first C-130 in October and began aircrew checkout and maintenance training. All C-130 operational and training flying was hampered by the shortage of spare parts and high failure rates on the new aircraft, which delayed phase-in. Fuel leaks and leak repairs were the biggest problem at that time.

On 20 December 1957, USAFE inactivated the 782d Squadron, which was stationed TDY at Neubiberg Air Base. The 782d had not received C-130s prior to deactivation. Next, the 780th and 781st Squadrons were deactivated, but in a manner that seems as illogical as it is confusing. It is their convoluted deactivation that has confused historians and the airmen involved as well. On 6 January 1958, all personnel, aircraft and equipment of the 780th TCSq were transferred to the 39th TCSq of the 317th Wing. All personnel, aircraft, and equipment of the 39th TCSq were transferred to the 780th TCSq. This was primarily a "paper" switch in squadron designations with the 39th now the unit with C-130s. This same action also occurred on 6 January to the 781st TCSq and the 40th TCSq. Now all C-119Gs belonged to the 780th and 781st Squadrons, and they flew the aircraft back to the U.S. as soon as weather and crew availability permitted. The 780th and 781st Squadrons were inactivated on 8 March 1958 at Evreux-Fauville, thus ending any remnant of the 465th Troop Carrier Wing's time in France. After 8 March, all C-119Gs remaining at Evreux were assigned to the 41st TCSq until all 103 Boxcars had returned to CONUS. By mid April 1958, approximately ninety C-119Gs had departed and the rest followed as soon as they were overhauled.

In 1958 Evreux became host to Detachment #1, 66th Tactical Reconnaissance Wing, a very small tenant unit consisting of one officer, five non-comissioned officers, and two T-33As. The T-33s at Laon Air Base had supported the many rated USAF officers assigned to SHAPE HQ in Paris, but when MGEN Glen Barkus was assigned to SHAPE in 1958, he or his aide did not like the long drive across Paris and north to Laon. After some negotiations it was decided that a detachment with two T-33's would relocate from Laon to Evreux. Here the T-33 flying supported the SHAPE officers and the detachment commander conducted annual and instrument check rides with these pilots to maintain their flying proficiency. CAPT Richard B. Goebel was the first commander of Detachment #1 and the T-33 Instructor Pilot at Evreux. The rest of the detachment consisted of an AF Form 5 clerk and four T-33 mechanics led by MSGT Robert Gary.

317th Troop Carrier Wing

The 317th designator originally belonged to a WWII air transport group activated on 22 February 1942, with four squadrons: the 39th, 40th, 41st, and 46th. The group moved its C-47s to Australia in December 1942 and was assigned to the Fifth Air Force. The 317th Group airlifted men and equipment throughout the Southwest Pacific Theater of Operations from New Guinea to Japan. It participated in five major air campaigns, earning two DUCs for outstanding flying in New Guinea, and later, for precisely dropping paratroops on Corregidor Island. After Victory in Japan, the 317th remained in Japan until 21 September 1948. The 317th TCWg (Heavy) then flying C-54s was subsequently transferred to USAFE and participated in the Berlin Airlift. It was inactivated 14 September 1949 due to reduced DOD budgets.

The 317th Troop Carrier Wing, Medium, manned by 145 officers and 890 airmen, was reactivated on 14 July 1952 at Rhein-Main AB with the C-119Cs, mission, and personnel that had belonged to the 433d Troop Carrier Wing. The 433d had completed its twenty-one months of extended active duty and was returned to Air Force Reserve status at Cleveland Municipal Airport, Ohio. The 317th, with its three original squadrons: the 39th, 40th, and 41st Troop Carrier Squadrons, was again assigned to USAFE Twelfth Air Force, flying Fairchild C-119C Boxcars. On 21 March 1953, the 317th Wing moved to Neubiberg AB, West Germany, and upgraded to C-119G Boxcars. Its primary mission was paradropping airborne forces and their equipment, but due to the very few airborne troops in Germany, intra-theater airlift support became the primary operation. A very important airlift mission was supporting fighter aircraft weapons training on the desert ranges at Wheelus AB. Libya. Every USAFE fighter squadron moved its maintenance personnel, aircraft support equipment, spare parts, tools, and test sets by C-119 to assure maximum range flying time for all assigned pilots.

The new West German Air Force wanted Neubiberg returned for their use as a fighter base, but demanded the air base be restored to the best possi-

Loading a C-119, Evreux AB 1958.
Wolfgang Peters - www.shoeboxphotos.net

Unloading U.S. Army M-35 truck from C-130, Evreux AB 1959.
Wolfgang Peters - www.shoeboxphotos.net

C-119 being towed to the hangar using a Coleman tractor.
Wolfgang Peters - www.shoeboxphotos.net

ble condition before taking possession. This required a large sum of money and time to complete repairs; the 317th's budget for fiscal year 1957 was $6 million for operation and maintenance of Neubiberg.

By late March 1957, the wing was ready to depart West Germany after four years at Neubiberg AB. It received orders on 17 April 1956 to relocate to Evreux AB where it would join the 465th Troop Carrier Wing. The 317th was in no hurry to go to France! Relocation extended over eighteen months as hangars became available at Evreux for C-119 maintenance. Six large C-119 maintenance docks were disassembled and moved overland to France, then reassembled in the hangars at Evreux.

Relocation began on 3 June 1956, when the 39th Squadron moved to Evreux and flew C-119s under operational control of the 465th. Next, on 15 March 1957, the 41st Squadron arrived with the 465th providing operational control. By spring 1957, wing headquarters and subordinate units arrived. The 317th Wing was officially considered moved to Evreux on 16 April 1957. Finally, the 40th Squadron arrived on 6 December 1957. A rear detachment remained at Neubiberg until early 1958 to complete base improvement

C-119 Cargo Extraction, 1956.
Charles Spicka

317TCWg 780th TCSq C-119s in formation 1956
Charles Spicka

317TCWg 780th TCSq G-12 chutes 1956
Charles Spicka

projects. The majority of 317th personnel moved to Evreux except those members whose overseas tours of duty were within eight months of completion. These men were transferred to Rhein-Main. Personnel shortages were filled by 465th personnel as it was deactivated. Once again, most shortages existed in aircraft maintenance technician and combat aircrew positions.

The 317th Troop Carrier Wing continued flying its C-119G Boxcars until the end of 1957 but converted into C-130As in January 1958 with the transfer of Herks from the 780th and 781st Squadrons. Delivery of new aircraft continued from CONUS, so that by 1 July the wing had received forty-eight C-130As, and by 1 September 1958 it had a full complement of fifty-four planes with each squadron having eighteen aircraft.

The 317th, along with the 465th and other USAFE wings, had been restructured in March 1957. With the deactivation of 317th Troop Carrier Group Headquarters, wing operations assumed direct command over the three troop carrier squadrons. This USAFE-wide action eliminated approximately fifty group personnel to reduce costs.

On 25 September 1958 the two troop carrier wings, the 317th at Evreux, and the 60th at Dreux were deactivated, and their flying squadrons assigned directly

C-130 #57-453 maintenance being performed by 317th CAMS in Evreux hangar, 1958.
Wolfgang Peters - www.shoeboxphotos.net

Left, propellor removal in preparation for a Post Dock engine change on C-130A # 57-0460. Right, after propellor is removed engine is lifted out by an M62 crane truck, 317th CAMSq, Evreux AB 1958. The Smithsonian National Air and Space Museum has selected #460 as representative of the first production version of the C-130s.
Wolfgang Peters - www.shoeboxphotos.net

Aerospace Ground Equipment "MD-3" power unit in front of C-130 #57-0455. It provided AC/DC electrical power to start and service a/c electrical and electronic systems, Evreux AB 1958.
Wolfgang Peters - www.shoeboxphotos.net

C-130A-LM #55-0014 on snowy taxiway, Evreux AB.
Wolfgang Peters - www.shoeboxphotos.net

to the 322d Air Division. The 317th Air Base Group continued to operate and maintain Evreux and support attached units and off-base real estate. The 7333d Air Base Group was activated to support flying operations from 1959 to 1962 after inactivation of the wing. Next the 7305th Support Squadron was activated at Evreux to support the base and nearby Dreux AB from 1958 until 1967.

By 1963 USAFE decided that a wing structure was again necessary to command the three C-130 troop carrier squadrons at Evreux, and reduced 322d Air Division manning accordingly. The 317th Troop Carrier Wing designator was reactivated at Evreux-Fauville on 13 March 1963 and was reassigned its 39th, 40th, and 41st Squadrons. This action caused little change in European airlift operations that were still directed by the 322d, but there was an increase in aircraft availability as the wing improved both maintenance and supply management procedures.

A year later in 1964, USAFE was faced with additional force reductions as DOD Project CLEARWATER was being implemented throughout the Air Force to reduce expenses. USAFE Commander, GEN Gabriel P. Disosway lost all his assigned organic tactical airlift. The 322d Air Division was transferred to the Military Air Transport Service (MATS) and the last troop carrier wing returned to CONUS on 20 June 1964, when the 317th Troop Carrier Wing with its three C-130A squadrons, the 39th, 40th, 41st, plus wing support units was transferred to Tactical Air Command. After twenty years USAFE no longer had any troop carrier squadrons authorized.

Throughout May and June 1964, the 317th moved itself from Evreux-Fauville to Lockbourne AFB, Ohio, using its fifty-two C-130As to fly 4,100 miles across the North Atlantic. The wing airlifted all 2,722 personnel and dependents, and 1,853 tons of support equipment, supplies, and household goods. Only the 450 French civilian base employees were left behind. The 317th Troop Carrier Wing was back in the U.S. after twenty-two years, and remained at Lockbourne for the following five years.

The departure of the 317th and 322d reduced Evreux to standby status for the next two years. The 7305th Combat Support Group became the primary caretaker since there was no flying wing assigned. Now Evreux and Dreux were both without airlift units.

5th Aerial Port Squadron, USAF 1957 - 1965

Aerial port squadrons were "wing level" units that were based with troop carrier wings and provided direct support to airlift operations. They reported directly to the 322d Air Division. In the fall of 1957, as Evreux began receiving its first C-130s, HQ 5th Aerial Port Squadron moved from Neubiberg along with the 317th squadrons. Detachment #3 of the 6th Aerial Port Squadron, a Combat Control Team consisting of one officer and thirteen airmen, all C-130 jump qualified, was already based at Evreux. Nine months later, the 5th absorbed the 6th Aerial Port Squadron's personnel and moved to Dreux from overcrowded Evreux. The 5th returned to Evreux in October 1960 when more space became available after departure of the C-119 aircraft and 465th personnel.

The 5th Aerial Port Squadron had three missions:

1. Operate twelve airfreight terminals within USAFE area of operations in Europe and around the Mediterranean Sea from Morocco into eastern Turkey. Small detachments at each airfield will provide loading and unloading service, both passengers and freight, to the cargo aircraft.

U.N. troops boarding C-130 #457 of the 322d Air Division, for airlift to Leopoldville, Congo, July 1960.
USAF via Greg Devejian

Congolese unload flour delivered by 322d Air Division, C-130 #70465, Leopoldville, Congo, July 1960.
USAF via Greg Devejian

2. Provide qualified loadmaster/dropmasters for cargo and troop parachute drops, air mobility, and joint tactical airlift training with the U.S. Army. Assist with classified clandestine special operations at remote landing sites.
3. Provide three parachute-qualified Combat Control Teams made up of air traffic controllers and radio operators responsible for setting up, marking, and providing air traffic control over airborne forces drop zones and bare bases.

Approximately 30 officers and 240 airmen comprised the 5th APO Squadron assigned to Evreux. They operated aerial ports at Evreux and throughout the USAFE theater. The squadron was a self-sufficient unit organized into the following sections: Headquarters, Administration, Personnel, Operations, Combat Control Teams, Air Terminal Operations, and Support.

The Operations Section had approximately sixty loadmasters and five officers. Operations furnished loadmaster teams for movement of unusual or oversized loads and aerial delivery of personnel and equipment. These APO loadmasters were air-drop qualified and, when needed, flew in addition to the usual loadmasters found in the troop carrier aircrews. Later, after a few years of operations, all the C-130 loadmasters became air drop qualified.

All loadmasters and officers assigned to an aerial port squadron had to undergo training for aerial delivery of personnel and equipment from the C-119, C-123, C-124, and C-130s at the aerial delivery school operated by the 5th APO Squadron at Evreux. Selected officers trained at a special school operated by NATO at RAF Old Sarum, very close to Salisbury, England. Training in accurate load weight-and-balance computations was a vital, ongoing program.

The section provided augmentee loadmasters for the C-124s that were assigned temporarily to 322d Air Division air assault missions. Three Combat Control Teams consisting of one officer and thirteen airmen were assigned to the CCT Section. These "Pathfinders" were equipped with portable radios, portable radar beacons, identification panels, weather sensors, and drop zone lighting kits. The CCT air controllers had to maintain parachute-jumping proficiency in order to be the first to arrive at the drop zone and report surface wind velocity and direction. Several practice drop zones were established around Dreux and Evreux for realistic training.

The Support Section had sixty-five airmen assigned to the motor pool, with automotive maintenance and special equipment operators, a parachute packing and repair shop, a carpenter shop, cooks, medical technicians, and security police. The 5th APO Squadron motor pool had about seventy Army M-series tactical off-road vehicles such as forklift trucks, 1/4-ton trucks (Jeeps), 3/4-ton weapons carriers, 2-1/2 ton 6X6 trucks, 5-ton 6X6 tractors with their 40-foot long flatbed trailers, and 2-1/2-ton 6X6 wreckers. All this equipment was necessary for rapid loading and off-loading aircraft, and for recovery of drop zone equipment. The airhead had to be quickly cleared of supply loads and vehicles to prevent destruction of follow-up air drops.

The small carpentry shop had facilities to fabricate equipment platforms, bridging, and shoring for air dropping special loads to ensure they survived ground impact. Of course, they could also repair their drop platforms after an exercise. The parachute shop had large industrial grade sewing machines and strong fans for repairing and drying large-sized cargo parachutes. The 5th security police had a special collection of heavy infantry weapons including grenade launchers, 50cal. heavy barrel machine guns, and 60 mm mortars for local defense of the tactical airheads or drop zones. These weapons were also available to the combat control teams.

The 5th APO Squadron was involved in many of the humanitarian airlift operations and demonstrated its capabilities in two major airlifts. On 29 February 1959, Agadir, Morocco, was hit by a severe earthquake followed by a tidal wave that killed several thousand people. The 5th set-up a complete air terminal at Rabat. Here it unloaded tons of relief supplies and U.S. Army Engineering units to aid rescue and recovery. Ten vehicles were airlifted into the terminal. The following year in 1960, the Congo airlift occurred. This required 5th APO Squadron resources for more than a year to set-up two air terminals for evacuation of civilians, then receive fourteen million pounds of cargo and 38,000 incoming U.N. troops. Airhead security was a serious issue because of the civil revolution; USAFE was very concerned about the targets the C-130s and C-124s presented while on the Congo airport ramps.

Another aerial port squadron, the 2d APO, is associated with Evreux and mentioned in 322d Air Division reports. The 2d was part of the rotational C-130 squadrons sent to Evreux between 1961 and 1965. It was the fourth airlift squadron in the 322d Air Division. The 2d had C-130A loadmasters assigned to a pool. They flew with the 314th and 463d Troop Carrier Wings at Sewart AFB, Tennessee. When a C-130 squadron rotated on temporary detached duty from Sewart to Evreux, it had 2d Aerial Port Squadron loadmasters among the aircrews.

322d Air Division

The 322d Air Division began its history as the 322d Troop Carrier Wing on 4 December 1944 when activated in New Guinea. The wing was inactivated in Manila, Philippines, on 15 February 1946. The 322d Air Division (Combat Cargo) was reactivated at Wiesbaden AB, West Germany, on 1 March 1954, then moved within the month, on 22 March, to Ramstein AB as the new USAFE headquarters' buildings were completed. The 322d finally relocated to Evreux-Fauville on 12 August 1955, after arrival of the 465th Troop Carrier Wing. Evreux had been designated since the planning stages in 1951 to receive a Combat Cargo Air Division Headquarters. The air division offices were first located across the street from the wing base headquarters building, and after 1959 they relocated into the wing base headquarters building.

Commanders of the 322d Air Division were BRIG GEN Franklin Rose from March 1954 to May 1956, COL Clyde Box from May 1956 to 1958, and COL Tarleton H. Watkins from 1959 to 1961.

The 322d Air Division was a command element activated in USAFE to control all airlift units assigned to the European area of operations, but it did not have command and control over the inter-theater MATS aircraft, cargo, or routes. The 322d directed the three troop carrier wings based in France; the 317th and 465th at Evreux, and the 60th at Dreux; the USAFE headquarters squadron; a medical evacuation squadron; and two separate troop carrier squadrons located in the UK.

The 322d did not have any directly assigned aircraft, but had operational command over the troop carrier wings, groups, and squadrons assigned to the Third, Twelfth, and Seventeenth Air Forces. It could make requests for airlift assistance directly to HQ USAF and MATS. The Air Division was a large organization with many detachments located on airdromes across Western Europe, and as far east as Afghanistan. These detachments, known as Combat Airlift Support Units (CALSUs), varied in size depending on the scope of the required airlift operations. The 322d became responsible for the operation of Evreux and Dreux as the headquarters and troop carrier wings were deactivated. Air base groups continued to operate and maintain the two air bases for the troop carrier squadrons.

A Transport Control Center room was set up at Evreux. It operated around-the-clock to support routine and emergency airlift needs. Airlift operation had to be carefully managed to prevent the waste of flying assets. Air cargo movement was very expensive compared to surface movement, and excessive demands for air movement would often develop because of poor planning for surface delivery.

The missions of the airlift squadrons remained the same after assignment to the 322d: air drop and support of airborne forces, air logistics support (ALS) to U.S./NATO forces, theater air medical evacuation (EAV), and special air missions (SAM) such as evacuation and humanitarian airlift. By 1957, the 322d Air Division directed the airlift efforts of 11,000 personnel and 260 aircraft.

Humanitarian airlift became the major unscheduled workload of the 322d; frequent, very serious natural and political disasters within USAFE operational area required immediate aid. Any type of assistance involved air transportation of food, clothing, tents, blankets, medical supplies, and medical and rescue personnel. This operation began with the great Berlin Airlift in 1948-49 and continues to the present day. The 322d Air Division and its flying units supported so many of these emergencies that it would be impossible to present a complete list. A few of the well remembered are found in Table 12.1. This is only a partial listing of our efforts across Europe and the Middle East. The 322d Air Division and its personnel were awarded the Air Force DUC for its Congo airlift mission.

Another large air division effort was directed toward planning emergency evacuation of U.S. citizens and government personnel from countries throughout the USAFE area of responsibility, which included Africa and the Middle East. Country teams were organized in each nation, and they assisted in the evacuation planning. They would direct extraction efforts when required for U.S. and foreign personnel as ordered by the State Department. This type of airlift always involved flying long distances, operating into primitive airports, and sometimes encountering questionable reception committees. Constant updating and improvement of these plans required continual effort by the plans officers. Some of these operations had to be executed by the 322d in the Belgian Congo and Lebanon crisis.

Medical air evacuation aircraft were upgraded in 1955 with two C-54Ms to provide long-range service to Turkey and North Africa. In 1957, new Convair C-131D Samaritans replaced the C-47 on medical evacuation missions. They stopped at all the U.S. air bases in France. After deactivation of the 60th and 317th Troop Carrier Wings in 1959, flying units of the 322d were now the 10th, 11th, 12th, 39th, 40th, and 41st Troop Carrier Squadrons, and the 42d Troop Carrier Squadron (Special).

An unusual Special Air Mission (SAM) was conducted in 1959, when a 322d C-130A hauled a gift of cattle from President Eisenhower to Premier Khrushchev. A Russian crew boarded the C-130 at Copenhagen, and assisted the Evreux 317th crew flying into Moscow. The cattle were delivered on schedule but no one knows what became of these animals!

One maintenance support aircraft, initially a C-54, then a C-119, and eventually a C-130A was set-up to fly anywhere in the operating area to an aircraft that

Table 12.1 322d Troop Carrier Wing Humanitarian Airlift

1954	Provided assistance during Syrian and Iraqi earthquakes and floods, and Austrian avalanche.
1955	Provided humanitarian airlift during Rhineland flooding, hail storm in Lyons, France, and the Valles-Greece earthquake.
1956	Earthquake, fires and floods in Turkey, and record snowstorms in Greece, Sicily, Sardinia and Italy. Medical support provided in Lebanon, Saudi Arabia and French Morocco after calamitous earthquakes.
	Operation SAFE HAVEN provided emergency aid and airlift of about 15,000 Hungarian refugees out of Austria following the failed Hungarian revolt.
1957	322d airlifted 200 tons of insecticide to control a locust plague in Tunisia.
1959	322d rushed equipment to the Frejus Dam disaster in France that left 523 dead and missing.
1960	322d provided a major airlift of U.S. Army Engineers and heavy equipment to rescue victims of the Agadir, Morocco, earthquake and tidal waves.
1960-61	A two-year airlift of U.N. troops, cargo, and food, requiring 2,000 sorties to and from the Republic of Congo.
1962	Northern Germany received aid for coastal flooding. 322d airlifted cargo, vehicles, and a complete evacuation hospital to northwest Iran after a violent earthquake.
1963	Twenty-five C-130As airlifted 250 tons of supplies and another evacuation hospital from West Germany into Belgrade, Yugoslavia, to assist Skopje earthquake casualties.
1964-65	C-130s hauled 400 Belgian paratroopers to rescue hostages in the second Congo civil war and provided cargo airlift.
1966	Medical personnel and supplies to aid victims of severe flooding in the Florence, Italy, region.

needed major repairs. This eliminated individual squadrons having to fly-in to support their own aircraft.

The commander of the 322d Air Division, BGEN T. H. Watkins, obtained permission from HQ USAF to establish the weather minimums for cargo aircraft within the European flight operations area. C-119 and C-130 crews had extensive experience with the individual airdromes and air traffic controllers, therefore, he allowed them more decision making in difficult weather departures and arrivals. Both aircraft had better flight instrumentation and radio/radar navigation systems than other USAFE aircraft; this enabled them to make more accurate weather decisions. Another directive was instituted that required the crews to proceed to the closest airport in the event of an in-flight problem and not press on to their planned destination. This prevented a small problem from escalating into a bad landing accident or complete aircraft loss. The 322d won the USAF Flying Safety award for several years as a result of these actions. An interesting argument developed between the air division and USAFE over the loss of a C-119G that had landed safely on a beach in Italy, and then suffered considerable airframe damage later as the tide came in. USAFE wanted to charge an in-flight accident to the 322d, but the incident was finally changed to a ground accident after the C-119G was repaired and flown away.

The Air Division implemented the new USAF-wide Aircraft Maintenance Management System (AFM 66-1) in 1958 throughout its airlift units. The basic goal was to improve aircraft maintenance and personnel productivity. This program collected maintenance man-hour statistics that finally showed aircraft maintenance supervisors how much time was potentially available and then lost, wasted, or not consumed directly on repairing aircraft. Especially important was the accounting of maintenance overtime hours and man-hours lost due to parts cannibalization at the squadron level. AFM 66-1 was extremely unpopular among the troops because it involved considerable "paperwork" and standardized work procedures, but it eliminated the old USAF concept that manpower was a free commodity. The directive also transferred the C-130s to the maintenance squadrons, and aircraft scheduling from the flying squadrons to the maintenance organization. This caused severe consternation among the aircrews. The 322d demanded this program be implemented in its airlift units throughout Europe and be used to accurately justify manpower assignments.

In mid August 1959, USAFE tasked the 322d Air Division to perform one of the most unusual missions during its stay at Evreux. The Air Division was to supply C-130s and personnel to support the investigation of the B-24D "Lady Be Good" that was lost on the night of 4 April 1943 in the Libyan desert during WWII. The bomber had raided Naples harbor and was returning to its base near Bengazi, Libya, when it disappeared with its nine-man crew. It was assumed that the bomber and crew had crashed into the Mediterranean Sea and were lost forever. Fifteen years later, on 9 November 1958, the Liberator was unexpectedly discovered 455 miles south of Bengazi by a British oil exploration team. A year later, on 4 June 1959, HQ USAFE in Wiesbaden released the information that the long missing B-24D had been discovered far out in the Libyan desert, but no bodies were found near the wreckage. The Department of Defense wanted the crash site investigated and remains of the missing aircrew found.

The first 322d mission, flown by C-130A #57-0459, was to transport two U.S. Army H-13A Sioux helicopters based at Wheelus, along with an Army mortuary team and 22,000 pounds of support supplies to the Liberator crash site. This crew consisted of:

CAPT Shelton L. McConnell; Instructor Pilot, 322d Air Division
LT COL Harry S. Thompson; Pilot, 39th TCSq
1st LT Norman L. Murphy, Navigator, 39th TCSq
CAPT Ira H. Gessner; Flight Surgeon, 317th Tactical Hospital
MSGT Robert P. Madigan; Instructor Flight Engineer, 322d Air Division
SSGT Robert A. Childes; Flight Engineer, 39th TCSq
SSGT John H. Perritt; Loadmaster, 39th TCSq
SSGT Carl F. Jones; Loadmaster, 39th TCSq

This C-130 crew flew twice to the crash site; the landings and takeoffs on the desert sand were perfect at gross weights of about 100,000 pounds. Reverse pitch to decelerate was not used in order to reduce sand ingestion in the jet turbine engines. The Army H-13 helicopters were assembled and flown over a wide area to search for crew remains. Parts of the B-24D were removed and returned to Evreux for evaluation. Amazingly, the nose wheel was still fully inflated after the crash impact and setting in the desert heat for sixteen years! Maintenance personnel of the 40th TCSq removed the propellers and engine, and they are now displayed in the Air Force Museum at Dayton, Ohio. Many small souvenirs could be found in the squadron shops after subsequent C-130 trips!

A total of twelve missions were flown to the desert site by three or four different C-130As until eight bodies of the B-24 crew were recovered. The ninth man, a gunner, remains missing in action. CAPT Shelton L. McConnell wrote an excellent report, dated 25 August 1959, about the first flight to the "Lady Be Good" crash site, describing C-130 desert operations.

By 1964, the 322d Air Division had been reduced to a planning and operations staff at Evreux-Fauville. It was transferred on 1 April 1964 to MATS from USAFE, and relocated south to Chateauroux Air Station, France. With this transfer all European area airlift responsibilities were consolidated under MATS. This action was part of Project CLEARWATER cost reductions. Chateauroux was a logical location for the 322d because it was the major airfreight terminal for Europe, and had very good communications facilities.

An example of this new reorganization was rotation of two Tactical Air Command troop carrier squadrons from the 317th Wing at Lockbourne AFB, Ohio, to Evreux in September 1965. They were based at Evreux under operational control of the 322d Air Division, Military Air Transport Command, at Chateauroux. The 41st TCSq was the first squadron rotated back to Evreux where it operated for eighty-five days then returned to Lockbourne. Two C-130B squadrons from the 313th Wing at Forbes AFB, Nebraska, were deployed TDY to Evreux in December 1965. One C-130B, #0745, was involved in a bad, fuel fire, ground accident and was towed 300 miles on highways, from Evreux to Spangdahlem, West Germany, for reconstruction. Spangdahlem AB had a wing and parts from another C-130B crash to restore the plane to airworthy condition!

In September 1966, Project FRELOC forced the relocation of the 322d Air Division from Chateauroux to RAF High Wickham, UK.

513th Troop Carrier Wing

USAFE activated the 513th Troop Carrier Wing at Evreux-Fauville on 15 April 1966, a month after General Charles de Gaulle announced France's withdrawal from NATO's military structure. The 513th's C-130A and B equipped tactical airlift squadrons were loaned to USAFE in TDY status, thus the manning would not appear in USAFE authorizations. On 1 July, the wing moved to RAF Mildenhall, UK, with two TAC rotational airlift squadrons as part of Project FRELOC. The squadrons provided invaluable assistance airlifting high-value equipment out of France during FRELOC.

Project FRELOC began at Evreux Air Base in June 1966. The 7305th Combat Support Squadron was the primary agent to remove all property and close the base. More effort was required to close Evreux because of its active status. There was a large inventory of aircraft support equipment and spare parts to move. By January 1967 virtually all equipment had been removed, and about eighty men were left on base. Evreux-Fauville Air Base was transferred to the French government on 26 March 1967 through the Military Liquidation Service in Paris.

It is currently used by the French Air Force for tactical airlift aircraft. While not generally open to the public, an open house and air show is held annually in late May or early June. This has become a big event for the Normandy region and attracts a large gathering of aviation enthusiasts. Evreux can be found on Michelin map #304 Local. The city of Evreux is accessible from Paris by train from Gare St. Lazare.

Appendix 12.1 Notice to Airmen 1959 (NOTAM) - USAF Evreux-Fauville

Elevation 461 feet (141m), 49° 02'N - 01° 14'E. One paved runway 7,900 feet long, 050°/230°. Supports single-wheel landing gear up to 84,000 pounds. Rotating beacon light on airfield, with runway, taxiway, and obstruction lights. Transient aircraft storage available, minor aircraft and engine repairs available. Aircraft fuel, 115-145 octane and JP4 jet fuel with single point refueling. Jet aircraft MA-1 starting unit available. Low and high pressure oxygen available. Crash-rescue facilities available. Caution - civilian aerodrome in runway 05 approach zone.

Below are photos taken during a 2002 reunion held on Evreux Air Base.
The exception is the 1956 photo of the base chapel.
The buildings are occupied and in good repair. Evreux AB is now a French Air Force tactical airlift base, Base Aerienne 105.

St. Michel Hospital main entrance, Evreux 2002.
Jerry McAuliffe

Airmen barracks, Evreux AB 2002.
Jerry McAuliffe

Evreux base chapel 1956.
Cletus "Frank" Mebane

Evreux base chapel, 2002.
Front, and both side wall windows are stained glass.
Jerry McAuliffe

Roadmap at the entrance to the Cite Lafayette complex, Evreux 2002.
Jerry McAuliffe

Fauville restaurant and bar, 2002.
Jerry McAuliffe

Evreux-Fauville Air Base Assigned Aircraft

National Archives

465th Troop Carrier Wing, C-119Cs, 23 May 1955 - 8 July 1957

Eighteen aircraft per squadron. These Boxcars were flown from Toul AB, France to Evreux AB, France by 465th TCWg pilots.
Aircraft Marking:

780th Troop Carrier Squadron - Red.
781st Troop Carrier Squadron - Yellow
782d Troop Carrier Squadron - Green

C-119C-25 and -26-FA

51-2587	780th	51-2602*	782d	51-2630		51-2646	780th
51-2588	780th	51-2606	781st	51-2631	781st	51-2647	781st
51-2589	780th	51-2611	780th	51-2632	781st	51-2649	781st
51-2591	782d	51-2612	781st	51-2633	780th	51-2650	780th
51-2592	780th	51-2613		51-2634	781st	51-2651	
51-2593	782d	51-2615	782d	51-2636	781st	51-2652	781st
51-2594	782d	51-2617	780th	51-2637	781st	51-2653	781st
51-2595	782d	51-2618	781st	51-2638	780th	51-2654	781st
51-2596	782d	51-2622	781st	51-2639	782d	51-2655	782d
51-2597*	782d	51-2623	782d	51-2640	781st	51-2656	780th
51-2598	782d	51-2626	781st	51-2641	781st	51-2657	780th
51-2599	782d	51-2627	780th	51-2642	782d	51-2658	782d
51-2600		51-2628		51-2643	780th	51-2661	780th
51-2601	782d	51-2629		51-2644			

* Losses:

51-2597 - Crashed, gear up landing at Chateauroux AB, France, 12 FEB 56, no fatalities.
51-2602 - Crashed, Evreux AB, France, JULY 57, fatalities unknown.

C-119G-FA, May 1956 - 20 October 1958

C-119G-FA

51-7976	780th	51-7997	51-8011	51-8057	782d	53-3184		53-8091	781st
51-7877		51-7998	51-8014	51-8058		53-3188		53-8092	781st
51-7978	780th	51-7999	51-8037+	51-8061		53-3209		53-8093	781st
51-7979	781st	51-8000	51-8039			53-3213	781st	53-8096	781st
51-7983		51-8003	51-8041	53-3163		53-3217		53-8118	
51-7985	782d	51-8004	51-8042	53-3173		53-7849		53-8128	781st
51-7988		51-8006	51-8046	53-3174		53-7852		53-8129	781st
51-7994		51-8008	51-8049	53-3176		53-8087		53-8131	781st
51-7996		51-8010	51-8051	53-3178	780th	53-8089		53-8132	782d
								53-8137	782d

Losses: none
+ 51-8037 Now at USAF Museum
C-119Fs were converted to C-119Gs.

Wing Support Aircraft: 465th Air Base Group
C-47A: 43-15672
C-47B: 44-76482
VC-47A: 43-15992

Evreux AB Assigned Aircraft continued next page

Evreux Air Base Assigned Aircraft, continued

317th Troop Carrier Wing, C-119Gs, 17 June 1956 - December 1958
Eighteen aircraft per squadron. These C-119Gs were transferred from Neubiberg AB, West Germany to Evreux AB by 317th crews.
Aircraft Marking: 39th TCSq - Red, 40th TCSq - Green, 41st TCSq - Yellow

C-119G-FA

53-3179	39th	53-3192	39th	53-3201	41st	53-7858	39th	53-8110	40th	53-8120	39th
53-3180	39th	53-3193	39th	53-3202	41st	53-8101	40th	53-8111	40th	53-8121	39th
53-3181	40th	53-3194	41st	53-3203	41st	53-8102	40th	53-8112	40th	53-8122	39th
53-3182	40th	53-3195	41st	53-3204	41st	53-8103	40th	53-8113	40th	53-8123	39th
53-3183	39th	53-3196	41st	53-3205	41st	53-8104	40th	53-8114	40th	53-8124	39th
53-3185	39th	53-3197	41st	53-3206	41st	53-8105	40th	53-8115	40th	53-8125	39th
53-3187	41st	53-3198	41st	53-3207	41st	53-8106	40th	53-8116	41st	53-8126	39th
53-3189	41st	53-3199	41st	53-7830	40th	53-8108	40th	53-8117	40th	53-8129	39th
53-3190	39th	53-3200	41st	53-7852	39th	53-8109	40th	53-8119	41st		
53-3191	39th										

* Losses: None

Jimmy Register

317th Troop Carrier Wing, C-130As, 8 January 1958 - 20 June 1964

C-130A-LM

55-0004		55-0019		56-0526*	41st	56-0546*	40th	57-0458	
55-0005		55-0020*	40th	56-0527	40th	56-0547	40th	57-0459	39th
55-0006		55-0026	40th	56-0529	39th	56-0548	41st	57-0460#	
55-0007		56-0507		56-0531	41st	56-0549	39th	57-0461	
55-0009		56-0513		56-0532	39th	56-0550	40th	57-0462	40th
55-0011		56-0515	39th	56-0533	40th	56-0551	41st	57-0463*	40th
55-0014		56-0516	41st	56-0536	39th	57-0453	41st	57-0464	
55-0015	40th	56-0521	40th	56-0537	39th	57-0454		57-0465	
55-0016		56-0522	40th	56-0539	39th	57-0455	40th	57-0466	39th
55-0017		56-0523	40th	56-0544	41st	57-0456	40th	57-0470	
55-0018		56-0524	40th	56-0545	39th	57-0457		57-0494	

* Losses:
55-0020 - Crashed, low level/bad weather, 7nm N of Alencon, France, 8 MAR 62, 15 fatalities.
56-0526 - Crashed, mid-air collision with Mystere IV, near Poissy, France, 19 SEP 58, 7 fatalities.
56-0546 - Crashed, final approach/weather, 17nm from Embakasi Airport, Kenya, 17 MAY 62, 13 fatalities.
57-0463 - Crashed, final approach/weather, on Evreux AB, France, DEC 57, fatalities unknown.
- Aircraft 57-0460 is scheduled to become part of the Smithsonian Air and Space Museum collection.

Wing Support Aircraft: 317th Air Base Group
L-20A: 52-6153

Base Support Aircraft: 7333d Air Base Group 1964 - 1966
VC-47Ds: 43-49338, 44-76334
C-47Ds: 44-76657, 45-1117
T-33As: 53-5261, 53-5281 (15 December 1965), 53-5820 (1 March 1965)

ACKNOWLEDGEMENTS

I would like to thank the following people who contributed to this chapter:

Greg Devejian was at both Evreux and Dreux as a Combat Operations Officer in the Headquarters of the 5th Aerial Port Squadron from April 1958 till October 1960.

Harry W. Foulds was stationed at Evreux in 1964 until he was sent to Lockborne, Ohio due to the gold flow force reduction but he returned to Evreux often TDY. He worked in the comm shop on airborne radios, basically on C-130s.

Bill Lloyd was in the 317th TCWg, 317th Consolidated Aircraft Maintenance Squadron, Radar/Nav Aids Maintenance Shop at Evreux AB from September 1959 to September 1962. He is also President of the 317th Veterans Group (www.usaf317thvet.org) that has held frequent reunions both in the United States and in France.

Cletus "Frank" Mebane was a SSGT in the 465th TCWg stationed at Evreux from 1955 to 1956.

Wolfgang Peters was an aircraft mechanic in the 322d Air Division, 317th Consolidated Aircraft Maintenance Squadron at Evreux AB from 1956 to 1959. He worked on both C-119s and C-130s in the Post Dock section of Periodic Inspection. Copies of his photos have been provided by www.shoeboxphotos.net.

Jimmy Register was a C-119 crew chief at Dreux from 1960 to 1961 and was based at Evreux AB from 1961 to 1963. He provided "Lady Be Good" information and tail numbers as well as much information on Evreux.

Charlie Spicka was a C-119G pilot with the 39th TCSq of the 317th Troop Carrier Wing. Charlie was a member of the ADVON when the 317th moved from Neubiberg to Evreux in 1956. He flew with the 465th until the 317th completed its move to Evreux. He continued on at Evreux flying as a C-130 Hercules Aircraft Commander until his departure in March 1960.

BGEN Tarleton H. Watkins commanded the 322d Air Division from 1959 to 1961. I want to thank him for graciously sharing his experiences at Evreux with me.

Monument Dedicated at Evreux Air Base, September 2004.
This monument commemorates the sacrifice of forty-three airmen who lost their lives while stationed at Evreux AB. The dedication ceremony was with full military honors. Several hundred people were present for the ceremony, including dignitaries from the City of Evreux, the French Air Force, the American Embassy in Paris, and U.S. Air Force cadets from the Air Force Academy, Colorado Springs. The dedication reads: "In memory of all US Armed Forces personnel who served at Evreux Air Base from 1954 to 1967 and gave their lives in defense of freedom for the United States of America and its allies."
Bill Lloyd

13

LAON-COUVRON AIR BASE

The old cathedral city of Laon is in the Aisne-Oise Department, in the Picardy region of France, sixty-two miles (101 km) northeast of Paris. It is a large city with a population of 25,200. The area is rich in military history; both WWI and WWII passed through here. One of the 1917 Krupp's "Paris Gun" sites was three miles north of the city on a prominent hill in the St. Gobain forest. The huge gun successfully shelled Paris, sixty-five miles to the southwest.

Laon-Couvron Air Base (49° 39'N - 03° 33'E, elevation 263 feet) is located a quarter mile southeast of the small farming village of Couvron, and six miles (11 km) northwest of the city of Laon. The base was used by the French Air Force prior to WWII, then by the Royal Air Force for a few days in 1940 before the Luftwaffe moved in with bombers and fighters from 1940 until 1944. The American First Army, VII Corps, 3d Armored Division liberated Laon on 30 August 1944 while rushing toward Rethel and the Ardennes. The U.S. Ninth Army Air Force flew from Laon (designated ALG A-69) in 1944 and 1945. First the 366th Fighter Group; and next the 409th Lt Bomb Group operated from its runways, flying A-26B/Cs. This airfield should not be confused with Laon-Athies, 5 km northeast of the city of Laon that had the WWII designator A-70. The Laon-Couvron airfield was returned to France on 23 October 1945.

Laon-Couvron airfield was one of the first sites offered by France in 1950, and the FAF and USAFE concurred that it should be used as an interim tactical unit airfield and then later developed into a light bomber air base. It was decided that Laon would be a two-step base, with a tent camp and a few temporary buildings to support a light bomber wing, to be replaced by permanent buildings and hangars in about two years. Laon was a very good location and had the potential of developing rapidly into an operational air base. The site was on high ground with a solid base. Good drainage would permit all-weather operation. Prewar hangars and buildings had been destroyed in the 1940 and 1944 bombings, and no remnants of hangars or aircraft shelters existed, making it a bare base. It did have two serviccable concrete runways and two large dispersal areas that had been constructed prior to WWII. These aircraft dispersal hardstands for seventy-five aircraft were located about two miles to the south and provided some protection from air attack, but this dispersal area was not included in the new base boundaries.

There had been no flight operation since 1945 and no commercial aviation use was contemplated. The airfield was farmed from 1946 until December 1951, even after major construction had begun! There was a good road network around Laon and the Laon-St. Quentin main rail line was 1,500 feet south of the base. Building a short spur rail line into the base would provide good rail service. A large rail yard existed in Laon for rapid off-loading of vehicles and heavy equipment. The Corps of Engineers gave site approval after determining it could find sufficient potable water, and that limited commercial electrical service was immediately available from Couvron. Being an old WWII site, Laon air base was developed in half the time of a new site.

The first airfield surveys were conducted in March 1951. Quick approval of interim base construction by the French agency, Ponts et Chaussees, allowed construction of base roads to start 15 June 1951. One deep well was dug to provide water, and new water lines and sewage pipes were laid. A completely new base electrical system was installed with good street lighting. A new sewage treatment plant was constructed and concrete roads were extended from the main roads to the base. Concrete tent pads were poured in August 1951.

The two old runways, the north-south was 4,000 feet long by 200 feet wide, and the east-west runway was 3,800 feet long by 200 feet wide, had been quickly patched in fall 1944. They could be used by B-26 and C-47 aircraft, but were not suitable for jet fighters. Construction of the new 7,900-foot long N-S runway started on 10 October 1951. USAFE and NATO had planned that the new N-S runway would be completed by spring 1952, but in November 1951 progress was not sufficient for the 126th Light Bomb Wing to move into Laon AB, so it spent the winter at the Bordeaux interim base instead.

The new 7,900-foot runway was built on the existing short N-S runway. Earth moving was kept to a minimum to save time and money on runway construction. This resulted in a runway that had a twenty-foot drop-off on each end! Freezing weather delayed progress during January and February 1952 because it slowed curing of the newly poured concrete but the runway was completed by late March 1952. A new taxiway was constructed parallel to the runway. The short E-W German runway needed only minimum repairs to be used as an interim parking apron for sixty-five aircraft, and was not resurfaced until 1957. A very small, fifteen-foot high, temporary control tower was

East-west German runway used as a parking ramp Laon AB, July 1952.
Ray Ducasse

B-26s on German parking ramp,Laon AB, May 1952. Black spots on apron are patched bomb damage.
Jerry McAuliffe

15-foot high temporary control tower, Laon AB, June 1952.
George Spencer

French contractor's son helping to build tent frames, Laon AB, June 1952. George Spencer

108th Bomb Squadron living area. Construction still underway as troops arrived at Laon 24 May 1952. Moving a multitude of rocks brought order just a few months later, as seen here in September 1952.
Jerry McAuliffe

installed far from the runway and was operational in January 1952. By February 1952, a 2d Communications Squadron team had installed a low power non directional beacon and had it flight tested for coverage. By spring, construction was progressing rapidly, and estimates were made that the 126th Wing would arrive by 1 July 1952.

NATO Phase I air base construction began during September 1952 with earth grading and filling for taxiways, three aircraft hangars, and marguerites. Two hundred and thirty tent frames were constructed between February and July 1952 for quarters, offices, and shops. Each tent was heated with one coal burning stove. In September 1952 the large, portable BX building was dedicated, and by October the base theater building was completed. Delivery of portable buildings for two large mess halls, a twenty-five bed hospital, the base exchange, and seven 200-man latrines had been delayed by disagreement about their use in France. Three sheet-steel Fillod buildings were constructed on base, one for the field maintenance shops located on the aircraft parking ramp, a second for the base civil engineering office and shops, and the third for the base theater. These larger buildings were in use by 1 December 1952.

The U.S. Army depots at Verdun and Toul supported the 126th Bomb Wing during the development of Laon AB. Company C, 843d EABn moved on base in September and winterized the tents during October and November 1952 by adding plywood roofs and sheet insulation under the canvas. This improvement made tents comfortable for the approaching 1952-53 winter. This work was considered repair, not new construction. The tents were again improved for the approaching 1953-54 winter by removing the canvas and covering the complete structure with tar paper. This made the tents comfortable in winter but hot in the summer, and gave the camp a shanty town appearance.

After completion of the rail spur, the Army Transportation Corps sent railroad tank cars of aviation fuel directly onto the base. Six to ten tank cars made up the base fuel storage facility. This eliminated the twenty mile round trip to Chambry by the aircraft refueling trucks. Army units trucked in aircraft munitions from a new depot being set up near Chize. Transportation assistance was vital because the bomb wing continued to have a shortage of trucks and drivers.

Supplies for the wing and base construction projects were arriving at an overwhelming rate. Equipment storage sites were leased to provide 65,595 square feet of indoor storage and 692,100 square feet of outdoor covered storage adjacent to the main railroad line. From 1951 to 1954, base supply and vehicle maintenance shops were established in Chambry, about six miles east of the base on the northwest edge of Laon. They were operated initially by a small team from Chateauroux. By December 1954, the 38th Supply Squadron closed the clothing warehouse and the Motor Vehicle Squadron closed its maintenance facility at Chambry as new buildings were finished on base.

The interim tent camp was finally closed in October 1954; after three years officers and airmen moved into new buildings and occupied their long awaited quarters. One hangar, three barracks buildings, and one 500-man mess hall were located on the northeast side of the base to support one flying squadron. The men living and working in this area had a three-mile drive to reach the main gate, and a two-mile drive to use any of the major base services. This area was next to the on-base munitions storage site that had twelve igloos and four weapons maintenance buildings.

Throughout spring and summer of 1954, the 862d EABn constructed a trailer park at Laon as part of Project Caravan. Two-hundred-eighteen concrete pads were constructed and laundry centers were built. Electrical and water service was installed to each trailer site.

In addition to the on-base trailer park, a large GRI housing tract "Cite Marquette" consisting of 200 units was constructed in 1955. This housing annex was 11 km southeast of the base off highway N44, and about 4km south of the main Laon rail station. The housing consisted of duplex units with three or four bedrooms. Most homes had an unobstructed view of Notre-Dame Cathedral located high on the Laon plateau. Laon had an on-base grammar through junior high school but no high school.

By January 1958, Laon Air Base occupied 1,280 acres with twenty-four miles of paved roads. The main runway was 7,800 feet long by 150 feet wide; a secondary runway 3,800 feet long by 200 feet wide was suitable for parking only. Taxiways, aprons, and parking ramps consisted of 520,000 square yards of concrete surface. The base had three, 37,000 square-foot, bomber-size hangars encircled by marguerites with sixteen parking hardstands each, ninety-four permanent buildings, and thirty-seven temporary buildings. Five warehouses had 3.7 million cubic feet of storage space. Five water storage tanks held 750,000 gallons. Two additional storage tanks held 240,900 gallons of non-potable water for fire fighting. Laon AB had two heating plants; the primary plant could produce eighty million Btus a day. An auxiliary plant could produce

Main gate, Laon Air Base, 1954.
National Archives

twenty million Btus a day. There were eight 150-man airmen dormitories, and two BOQ buildings with a capacity of 190 officers. A large 100-bed hospital was staffed and operated by the 38th Medical Group. There were three dining halls on base: one 900-man, one 500-man, and a small 100-person hospital mess hall. There was underground fuel storage for 988,500 gallons of JP4, 122,000 gallons of AVGAS, 50,500 gallons of MOGAS, and 52,000 gallons of DIESEL fuel. The main entrance to the base is off highway D26, running between Crepy and Couvron. A secondary entrance is direct from the village of Couvron on D268. The estimated value of real estate (excluding land) was $29 million in 1958. Equipment in use (excluding aircraft) was approximately $9 million. The total Base Supply Inventory was $7.8 million.

Four light bomber bases had been proposed, but Laon was the only light bomber base built in France. It was a light bomber base for seven years, and a tactical reconnaissance base for nine years. An air division headquarters building was also proposed for Laon but later canceled.

126th Bombardment Wing, Light

A complete description of the wing's history and lineage can be found in chapter 6, Bordeaux-Merignac AB. COL William L. Kennedy was commander of the 126th Light Bomb Wing from 4 February 1952 when it was at Bordeaux, until its deactivation at Laon AB on 31 December 1952.

Soon after its arrival at Bordeaux, the 126th began preparing to support the development of Laon AB as directed by Twelfth Air Force. Beginning 12 January 1952, wing and group staff officers visited the new base to determine what support could be provided by wing personnel. On 7 February the wing dispatched the ADVON, Flight "A" Provisional HQ, 126th Wing, led by LTC Hoffman with seven officers and forty-one airmen. By 1 May this ADVON had expanded to 24 officers and 210 airmen. Personnel were selected from wing HQ, air police, air installations, food service, motor vehicle, and supply squadrons. The tenant units at Laon assisting the 126th establish this new base were Flight "P" 2d Air Postal Sq operating APO 17; Det #7, 31st Weather Sq; Det #2, 1992d AACS Sq; and Flight "B" 7480th Supply Sq.

The first primitive base exchange at Laon was a one-man operation in a tent. A/2C Paul L. Garrett was sent on special order #56 from the 7480th Supply Squadron (Exchange Service) at Bordeaux on 2 May 1952 to set-up and operate the exchange at Laon. He was attached to Flight "A" 126th Bomb Wing for rations and quarters, and operated the BX six days a week. Since a tent can't be made secure, there is an extra twist to his story,

> I was an A/2C at the time, and along with an American civilian started the Base Exchange at Laon. When I arrived, he and his wife had just completed setting up wooden shelves in one of the tents. They were selling items out of the back of a truck up to this point. A new small building was being constructed to house the BX, but was not completed. We stocked the shelves in the tent, and I stayed in the tent day and night with a carbine and ammo for about a month until we could move into the new BX building. Some-

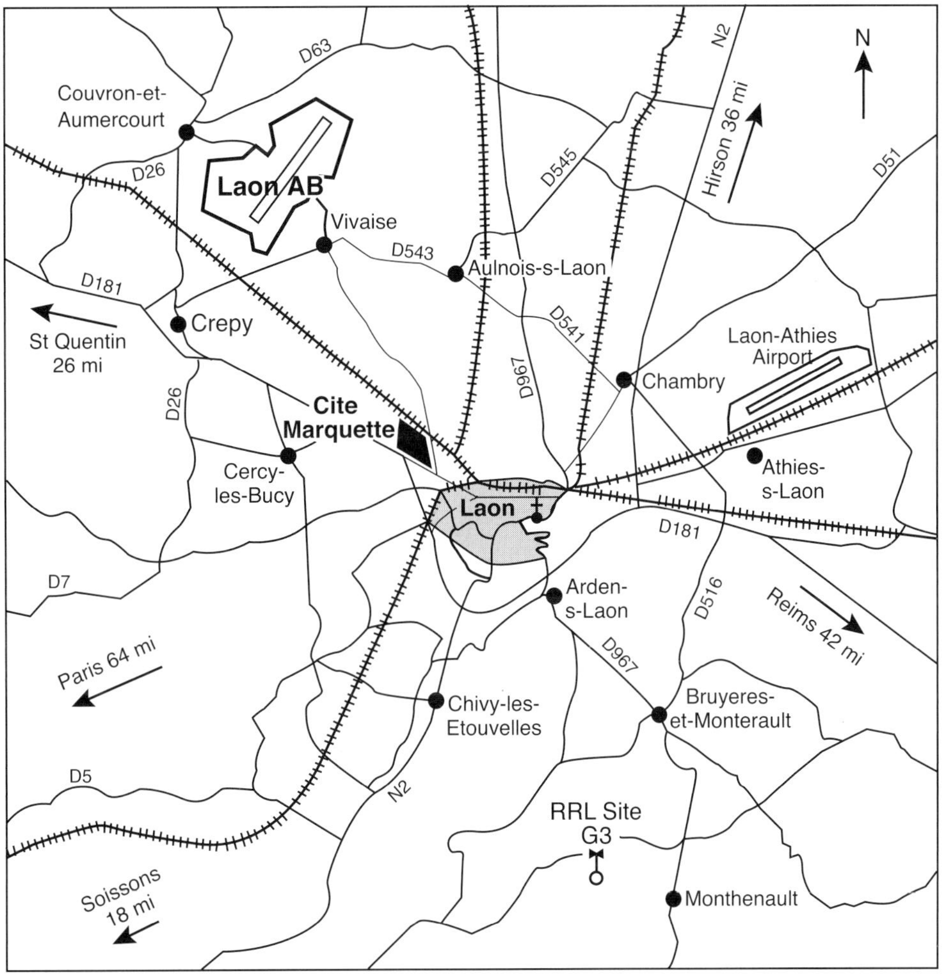

Map 13.1 Laon Area

one had to guard it and I was the only GI. I had a field phone and the Air Police would relieve me to go to the chow hall, latrine, and wash up. When we moved the BX to the building about two months later, I moved into one of the other luxury suites (another tent) with the postal service personnel."

Having someone to talk to after his two-month-long solitary confinement must have made any shared tent seem like a luxury suite!

By 10 May 1952, after six months at Bordeaux-Merignac, the 126th Wing was ready to move to Laon-Couvron Air Base in northern France. The 126th Wing still consisted of three light bombardment squadrons, the 108th, 168th, and 180th, and their supporting squadrons, flying fifty-seven B-26B/C Invaders and three C-47s. The B-26 fleet was now a mix of 40 percent modified Korean War "Black" night intruders and 60 percent original WWII daylight bombers. The older Invaders still carried three horizontal bands on the vertical stablizer/rudder of black and yellow, and either blue, green or red.

Wing personnel moved to Laon from 17 to 24 May 1952 by aircraft, troop train, and either wing vehicles or private auto. All B-26s and aircrews were on Laon AB by 24 May. The majority of wing personnel traveled on a SNCF WWII troop train that was routed around Paris and required one, very long, travel day to reach Laon. Approximately 115 men were dispatched directly to Bremerhaven from Bordeaux for early release rather than proceed to Laon. The wing's rear detachment arrived at Laon on 12 June, completing the relocation. Five supply specialists remained at Bordeaux and transferred to the 7413th Air Base Squadron that had assumed command of Bordeaux on 1 June 1952. The wing was officially moved from Bordeaux to Laon on midnight, 24 May 1952. The 126th was the first USAFE tactical wing to operate from Laon as the base began a fifteen year period of continuous operations as a USAFE main operating base in France. COL William L. Kennedy officially accepted the air base as a USAFE/NATO facility on 18 July 1952.

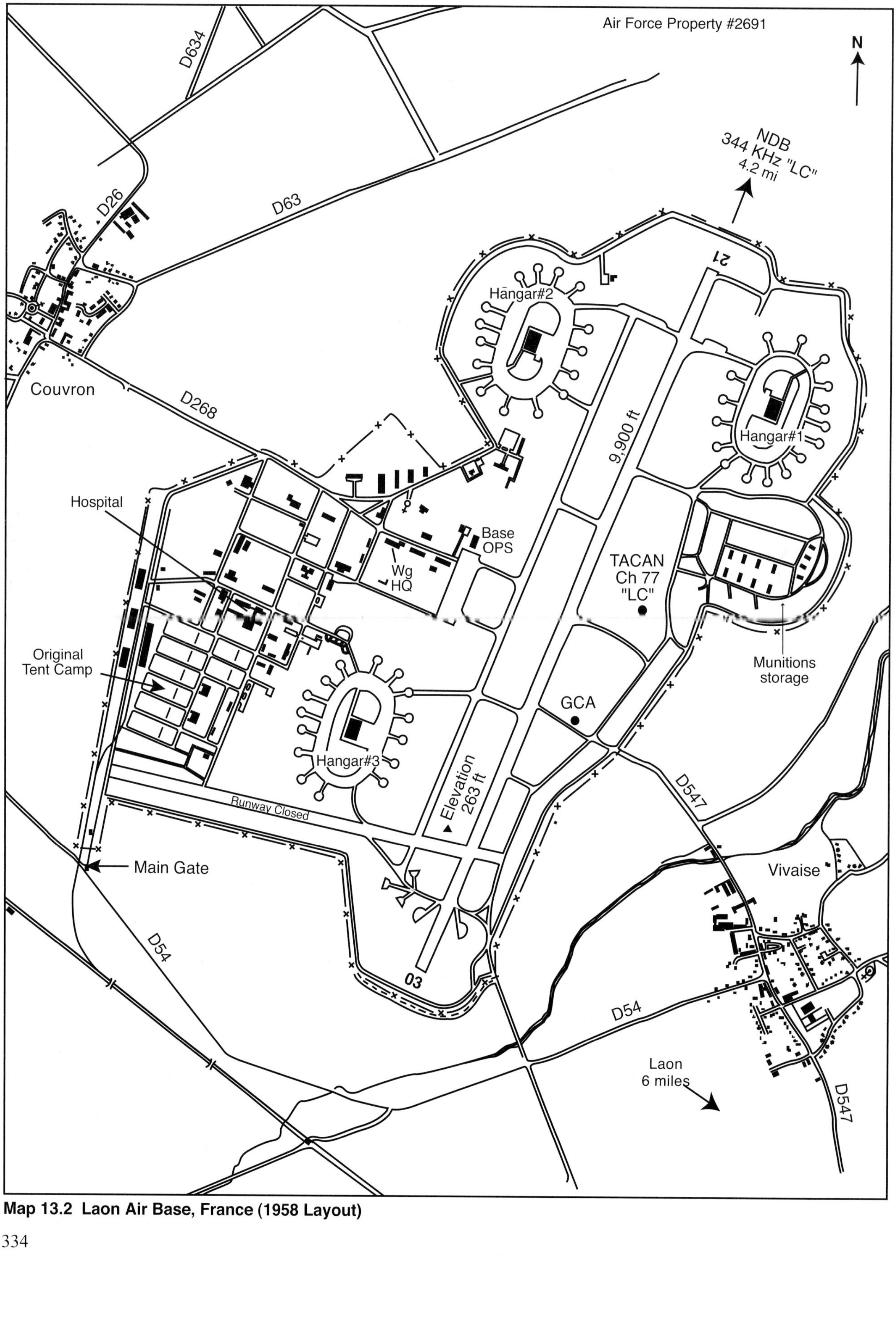

Map 13.2 Laon Air Base, France (1958 Layout)

Laon Air Base July 1952.
Ray DuCasse

The wing's problems were the same as at Bordeaux AB: a shortage of trained personnel, a serious shortage of B-26 airframe and engine parts, no maintenance facilities, no electrical power at the aircraft maintenance aprons, and aircraft fuel shortages. An aircraft fuel shortage developed in USAFE because of refinery strikes in the United States during the summer of 1952.

The tents were very comfortable living quarters in the summer. Space increased in every tent as Reserve personnel departed for early release. Most tents had five airmen, though a few had only four instead of the eight men they normally held. The portable buildings; mess halls, base exchange, hospital, and latrines functioned well, and the base was improving rapidly in July and August. Mess hall meals improved greatly compared to the food at Bordeaux AB; much of the preparation was now being done by French cooks. By 15 November 1952, the base had 245 French civilian employees working throughout the base support squadrons.

Airmen personnel strength continued to be a major problem for the 126th as large numbers of "non-essential" Air National Guard troops departed Laon during June and July 1952. By 15 July, the wing airman manning levels were at 60 percent; there was a critical lack of replacements in the aircraft maintenance sections. Many of the replacements were direct duty assignees, "Helpers," without technical training. By 1 August the bomb squadrons were manned by regular air force airmen except for thirty ANG NCOs that were retained at Laon for their full tour of active duty. The hundreds of airmen that had left for an early discharge would have been very useful for the manual tasks and guard duty needed at the new base.

The flying squadrons set up aircraft maintenance shops as quickly as possible. Their primary goal was preparing facilities to maintain aircraft to support maximum flying in the usual wet, cold winter common in northern France; there would be no hangars for at least two years. Secondary objectives were to begin on-the-job training programs for all newly assigned personnel, prepare old B-26s for return to CONUS, and conduct acceptance inspections on new B-26s. All sections' work hours were increased to nine hours a day minimum and a half day on Saturday. Most aircraft maintenance troops worked a sixty-hour week.

The first step was erecting temporary shops in

Setting up shop tents on the ground next to the B-26 parking aprons, Laon AB, May 1952.
Ray DuCasse

Line maintenance conditions upon arrival. Laon AB, June 1952.
Jerry McAuliffe

PSP laid to provide a temporary maintenance ramp, Laon AB, June 1952.
Jerry McAuliffe

A-3 aircraft engine maintenance shelters, Laon AB, October 1952. Jerry McAuliffe

Temporary shop tents (center right) and concrete blocks in position for permenant shops (right foreground), Laon AB, July 1952.
Ray DuCasse

Permanent aircraft radio maintenance shop tent with work benches designed and built by radio shop airmen. Laon AB, August 1952.
Jerry McAuliffe

GP large tents with sand floors; these tents were used for two months. Next, during the evening hours after supper, each squadron built one aircraft maintenance apron, 150 feet by 400 feet, using pierced steel planking. The summer evenings in France were perfect for this type of physical effort. About 10 June a French contractor began construction of six large tent frames per squadron for its operations, armament shop, aircrew personal equipment shop, radio/radar shop, and two aircraft repair shops. All were completed by 1 August 1952. These shop tents were within ten feet of the new maintenance apron, providing very quick access to the Invaders. The airmen then configured their shop interiors with work benches, test stands, and storage shelving, resulting in excellent maintenance facilities. Each squadron had to set up and operate its own 10Kw, 60 Hz electrical generators for all shop lighting and test equipment. Base electrical power service had not been installed out to these aircraft parking areas on the old German runway.

By 1 October, each squadron erected four engine maintenance shelters, A-3s, that completely covered the R-2800-79 engine and propeller. These shelters were on the edge of the PSP apron forming two inspection docks rigged with lights, compressed air, and work stands. Much new aircraft support equipment such as A-7 engine cranes, B-1 and B-4 maintenance platforms, C-1 engine trailers, and M-6 CLETRAC aircraft tractors had been shipped to Laon, and were in use by 1 August. The only serious deficiencies remaining were aircraft electrical generator sets such as A-3 or C-22 units, and these arrived in summer 1953. The aircraft maintenance facilities at Laon were vastly superior to those at Bordeaux, or the crowded tiny shops at Langley AFB.

Aircraft inventory increased after moving to Laon as Depot Inspection and Repair (DIR) production increased at Hill AFB, Utah. Most USAF B-26s had not been through a depot maintenance program since new in 1944-45 because of very limited budgets. B-26s were not returned to CONUS by 126th Wing aircrews but only by MATS ferry crews. Occasionally a MATS ferry crew would deliver an Invader to Laon and pick up a B-26 from a different base in Europe. Several USAFE B-26s were used as tow target tugs, and all were overdue for DIR. Fifty-four Invaders were now authorized for a light bomb wing instead of forty-eight. The wing had fifty-seven B-26s on 1 July; this increased to sixty-two on 1 August 1952. Six black B-26s arrived in October, and seven old bombers departed for CONUS rework. In October the 108th LBSq had twenty-one B-26s, the 168th had eighteen aircraft, and the 180th had twenty bombers. Three Invaders were destroyed in accidents during October and November. Winter weather in the North Atlantic stopped the flow of B-26s, and this resulted in a stable bomber fleet from November to March 1953. On 31 December 1952, the 126th owned fifty-eight B-26s, three C-47s, and one L-5 Sentinel. The B-26 fleet was now a mix of 80 percent black night intruders and 20 percent original WWII light bombers.

The 126th continued to furnish three B-26 crews every three months after arrrival at Laon to support USAF Project 7019 that started at Bordeaux. The wing conducted combat aircrew training to meet Project 7019 tasking. B-26 pilots were required to have napalm bomb practice prior to departure for Korea. The wing had no napalm experience; drops had not been conducted on Langley ranges in the fall of 1951 prior to overseas movement. Each bomb squadron sent four armament NCOs to Furstenfeldbruck AB, West Germany, for training in napalm mixing, and tank filling and arming. The problem was finding a suitable range for napalm bombing; there were no approved ranges in Europe. Amazingly, this training was done by dropping the napalm on Laon AB! The wing and group commanders decided a quick solution would be to drop napalm bombs between the taxiway and new runway. From August through October 1952, every B-26 pilot dropped four 175-gallon napalm tanks on the base. There were no problems or complaints! This is the only on-base napalm drop training conducted by the USAF that I am aware of. Many photos were taken during these drops, but this air-to-ground napalm range solution is not recorded in the 126th Wing history.

Most of the new replacement B-26 gunners had not had the opportunity to actually fire at airborne or ground targets in their CONUS training. B-26 gunner training, target tracking, and actual firing suddenly became an important requirement. Unfortunately all this training was acquired in daylight hours only, night range operation was not yet permitted in Europe. Almost all the B-26 crews participating in Project 7019 had their introduction to night gunnery and bombing on combat missions in Korea. Many B-26 bombadier/navigators acquired their first SHORAN bombing experience during night interdiction over North Korea. A shortage of airborne SHORAN equipment at Laon prevented training of all navigators.

B-26 parts shortages became acute during summer 1952. In July, a 168th LBSq crew chief heard a rumor during a visit to Erding Air Depot that there was "something for B-26s out in the yard." A senior flight chief from the 108th Bomb Sq was dispatched

Maneauvers with the French Army at Sissone, France, 1952.
George Spencer

Black B-26s on maneauvers over Italy, 1952.
Foreground aircraft is #43-22288, 108th LBSq 1952.
Paul Douglas

to Erding in August to discover what this "something" was. TSGT Edward D. Peotter ended up with two C-47 loads of B-26 replacement parts issued to him on hand receipts. He had to open crates, inspect and identify their contents, and prepare appropriate yellow tags. Sgt. Peotter found generators, starters, engine fuel pumps, carburetors, and other engine accessories. He also discovered control surfaces, cockpit canopies, and nose transparencies. All the items were well preserved. This was great find, and provided critically needed spares for the next six months to keep the wing's B-26s in commission. They had been shipped to the Chateauroux Air Depot in April 1951 as B-26 war reserve stock. Chateauroux shipped them to Erding knowing only that they were "something for B-26s." The basic problem was that the shipping crates had lost their identification tags and markings after setting outdoors since WWII. There was insufficient manpower and a serious lack of skill at the depots to properly identify and correctly document the many crates of aircraft parts that had been shipped to Europe, or remained there after the war.

During September the three squadrons flew a total of 1,300 hours. Some of the black B-26s had ILS receivers installed, and the pilots would practice approaches at Le Bourget, Rhein-Main, and Marignane civil airports whenever possible. GCA landings were practiced at several USAFE bases in Germany. Laon's GCA system, MPN-1, arrived in October and became operational in late December 1952 after repairs and calibration. Other exercises involving many hours of flying were night low-level simulated attacks on shipping in the North Sea, night intrusion missions into UK airspace to test air defense forces, and several large formation flights over major cities in NATO nations. B-26 crews began deploying to Wheelus AB, Libya to maintain air-to-air gunnery and bombing proficency.

Bomb group and squadron tasking continued to be training newly assigned squadron aircrews, bombing, rocket, and gunnery training, flying close air support exercises, and radar calibration flights. Training French aircrews in B-26 aircraft continued at Laon to prepare them to fly their B-26s being supplied under MAP. Close air support exercises involving U.S. Seventh Army and NATO ground forces were conducted at various camps in Belgium, France and Germany. Close air support missions were considered worthless by the B-26 crews because of the total failure of tactical ground-to-air communications and a shortage of forward air control teams. Frequent radar calibration missions were flown in Germany. These flights included the training of GCI plotters and intercept directors. Night cross-country navigation training flights completed a busy summer flying schedule. Several night exercises were conducted and the B-26s performed very well; but the lack of runway lights prevented many night intruder missions in marginal weather. Oil-burning road flare pots and road flares were tried, but they did not produce sufficient runway references on overcast nights. Runway lights were installed in 1954.

The 126th LBWg, 108th LBSq lost its first B-26C in France when #44-35540 flew into the ground on a clear sunny day killing both the pilot and passenger. This was the 108th's first B-26 aircrew fatality since receiving the Invaders in November 1946. It was also the first 126th LBWg B-26 lost while serving on active duty, and flying 16,200 hours since 1 April 1951. On 7 November 1952, the 168th Sq lost

Napalm drop on base, Laon AB, September 1952.
Jerry McAuliffe

Napalm drop on base, Laon AB, October 1952.
Jerry McAuliffe

two B-26s at night in very bad weather during a NATO exercise near Salerno, Italy. One B-26's nose gear collapsed on landing and was subsequently torn in half by recovery crews moving it off the runway. The 168th lost its squadron commander and his navigator when they struck a mountain in the rain on the same mission. Operational training to be combat ready was making USAFE pay a high cost in pilots and crew members.

During the fall, 126th aircrews began training for their new primary mission, night interdiction with their fleet of black B-26s. On 20 October 1952, Twelfth Air Force changed the 126th Bomb Wing's mission from Light Bombardment to Night Intruder, and directed Wing Ops to concentrate flight training towards night operations. This training was very similar to the night interdiction combat tactics used in Korea by the Third and Seventeenth Bomb Wings. Col Kennedy requested that all B-26Cs be exchanged for B models with eight-gun nose armament, but this conversion was never achieved. Therefore, the wing maintained a day bombing capability, training with the M-9 Norden bombsight.

The B-26 required radar aids for night and all weather operations; only clear nights would allow visual attacks down to low levels. The 126th did not possess any B-26s equipped with APQ-13 Bomb/Nav radar. The most common B-26 radar aid for night bombing was the SHOrt RAnge Navigation system (SHORAN), code named "RONNIE." It was developed by RCA and appeared late in WWII. SHORAN operated with two accurately located ground transponder stations, "BEACONS." The aircraft SHORAN, APN-3 interrogator set simultaneously measured the distance between the B-26 and the two ground stations. The pilot had to fly a precise radius guided by the navigator/observer to the bomb release point computed by a K-1 Bomb Computer. SHORAN required accurate pre-mission calculations and constant flight training to deliver bombs on a target. The major unknown was always the accuracy of target maps relative to both ground stations, and the distance between ground stations within plus or minus twenty-five feet! RONNIE missions began by using SHORAN beacons located in England. Later the Shoran Beacon Squadron was moved to Germany, and RONNIE training missions continued for the B-26 and B-45 wings.

A second method of conducting night bombing was using one precision automatic tracking ground radar set, with a ground controller directing the pilot by voice radio to a pre-calculated bomb release point. This bombing technique was developed in the European Theater of Operations late in WWII using the SCR-584 radar system originally designed for anti-aircraft gun fire control. This ground radar system was highly accurate, and when coupled with an analog plotting board, could direct any tactical bomber or fighter to a bomb release point. Equipment was improved during the Korean War, and became known as "TADPOLES" MPQ-2 radar sets when larger plotting boards and additional radio sets were installed. Radar equipment was again improved between 1952-55 and was designated MSQ-1 "MIS-QUE." In USAFE this bombing method was code-named "APPLECORE." The ground controllers required more training hours than the pilots. The pilots found the voice procedure similar to GCA approaches. Later an airborne radar beacon set, APW-11, would improve radar range and accuracy, plus eliminate voice transmissions to the pilot. The airborne beacon could receive pulse data from the ground autotrack radar and display commands on an APA-90 indicator, giving heading, airspeed, altitude, and bomb release time. Both RONNIE

Excellent example of the B-26 level landing attitude. 108th LBSq #44-34104 coming in for a nice even landing, Laon AB, September 1952.
Paul Douglas

SHORAN APN-3 equipped black B-26 #43-22484, Laon AB, August 1952.
Jerry McAuliffe

and APPLECORE night missions were developing aircrews' combat skills. As more APPLECORE ground stations became available in West Germany, the crews were able to make more frequent training flights.

The wing was considered combat capable at Laon in September 1952. USAFE now had two light bombardment wings; the 47th LBWg flying B-45As at RAF Sculthorpe, England, and the 126th Light Bomb Wing in France.

At midnight on 31 December 1952, the 126th Bomb Wing, Light was redesignated the 38th Bomb Wing, Light on 1 January 1953, with the same mission, aircraft, equipment and personnel. All reserve enlisted personnel had departed France by 5 December 1952 for CONUS and release from active duty. A few officers had to serve an additional six months. All Air National Guard unit designators and colors were returned to Illinois and Missouri on 1 January 1953.

38th Light Bombardment Wing

The 38th Light Bombardment Wing, consisting of approximately 205 officers and 892 airmen activated on New Year's Day, faced the same problems that had confronted the 126th LBWg. The three bomber squadrons designators changed: the 108th became the 71st LBSq "Lancers," the 168th became the 405th LBSq "Green Dragons," and the 180th became the 822d LBSq "Falcons." The 38th Air Base Group operated three C-47As and one L-5A Sentinel light courier airplane. The 38th Wing remained at Laon until deactivated in place on 18 June 1958.

The 38th Light Bombardment Wing had been a WWII combat Group flying B-25s in the Fifth Air Force. It fought across the Southwest Pacific Theater from Australia to Okinawa and compiled an outstanding war record. The Group participated in ten air campaigns over four years, earning four DUCs. One pilot, Major Ralph Cheli of the 405th Bomb Squadron earned a Medal of Honor at Wewak, New Guinea. The 38th Bomb Group, Light served in the occupation of Japan until inactivated in Japan on 1 April 1949.

Commanders of the 38th Bombardment Wing, Light during its service in France were:

COL William L. Kennedy 1 JAN 53 - 4 JUL 54
COL Albert W. Satterwhite 4 JUL 54 - 17 JUL 54
COL Wilbur W. Aring 17 JUL 54 - 20 JUL 57
COL John N. Eubank 20 JUL 57 - 18 JUN 58.

Flight operations proceeded uninterrupted during this designation change. Excess B-26 aircraft were flown to keep them in good condition, ready for return to CONUS when ferry crews would again bring black Invaders into Laon as weather improved on the North Atlantic. Air to ground rocket firing and gunnery training continued through the winter. A shortage of rocket adapter rails for two-inch rockets reduced the training missions to a maximum of six per day for the three squadrons. On 22 March 1953 twelve B-26s conducted the first practice bomb drops by APPLECORE radar control on the Hohnfels Range, forty miles southeast of Nurnberg, West Germany. The "blue devil" bombs were 100-pound M38A1, sand filled, blue bombs with spotting charges. The pilots and ground controllers had gained proficiency over the past months with many dry runs, so Twelfth Air Force approved these missions. In April the bomb squadrons began conducting day and night bombing and gunnery missions at the Siegenberg Range, thirty-five miles north of Munich. Often these missions were flown from Furstenfeldbruck AB where armament was loaded on the Invaders. It was only a short, eighty-mile flight to the range, so each bomber

B-26 in aircraft maintenance shelter, Laon AB 1953.
USAF History Office, Maxwell AFB, AL

could make three to four sorties per day. This night bombing and gunnery practice was the first for many of the wing's new B-26 pilots.

Three unusual, low cost, aircraft shelters were ordered in November 1952, and assembled during the summer of 1953 on each squadron's PSP aircraft parking ramp. Each shelter had a dual inspection dock configured for two B-26s. The engine shelters functioned well, but the cockpit was exposed to rain because of its canopy design, and this caused corrosion in the forward fuselage. The new aircraft shelters covered the majority of the B-26, but each wing protruded about seven feet, and the complete aft fuselage and tail assembly were exposed. Twelfth Air Force approved the purchase of these shelters because there was no firm date for hangar occupancy.

Another operational problem was simplified in December 1953 when all B-26 VHF radio sets were converted from eight to sixteen channels. Kits were received to upgrade all ARC-3 VHF Radio Sets to ARC-36s. Navigators still carried a bag of four to eight radio crystals to change frequencies in flight on some European trips. During the summer of 1954, the air traffic control radio communications problem was solved by installing ARC-27 UHF radio sets in all USAFE B-26s. The UHF radio set had 1,750 built-in frequencies, weighed ninety pounds, and was in addition to the ARC-36 VHF radio set.

The 38th LBWg completed the slow conversion of B-26 models from the WWII light bomber to black night intruders as more reworked B-26s arrived in late 1953. The 126th and 38th LBWgs were the only USAFE wings that required eighteen months to accomplish a change of fifty-eight aircraft. The fleet of black B-26s was a mix of models and configurations; most Invaders were shipped from the depot short of all required armament and radio/radar equipment. About 75 percent of the wing's B-26s were now equipped with gaseous oxygen systems. The 38th Bomb Wing became a repair center for B-26s in Europe. In February the 71st Sq received four new B-26Bs and transferred four C models to other squadrons. Several black B-26s were transferred to other wings; two from the 71st and one from the 822d were transferred to the 10th TRWg at Toul AB during March and April 1953. On 31 May, the 822d had three B-26Bs, fourteen B-26Cs, and one TB-26B. The flow of B-26 aircraft through the 38th LBWg during 1953 is illustrated by these 405th Squadron activities. A cracked wing spar was found on B-26C #44-35868 during a periodic inspection in April; it was transferred to Chateauroux AD for major repairs. The 405th received a B-26C #41-39303 from the 66th TRWg at Sembach on 27 April. Then it received a new TB-26B #44-34608 from OOAMA, Hill AFB on 11 June and a TB-26B #44-34156 from Furstenfeldbruck AB on 29 June. This Invader required a large amount of repair during its acceptance inspection. In August the 405th was surprised at the return of B-26C #44-35513 that had spent fourteen months at the Burtonwood Depot. It was immediately sent to Chateauroux for return to CONUS. There were no records of what repairs had been accomplished at Burtonwood, so

405th Light Bomb Squadron's TB-26B #44-34745 after a crash landing near Sezanne, France.
Jerry Black

before MATS pilots would fly it across the Atlantic, it had to be inspected at Chateauroux. The wing had fifty-nine B-26s on 1 January 1954; this increased to sixty-two on 1 August. The last four black B-26s were received during October. On 1 January 1955 the 71st had eighteen B-26s, the 405th had eighteen, and the 822d had twenty. To reduce the maintenance workload, the three bomb squadrons were attempting to decrease their B-26 inventory until the authorized quantity was reached. The wing's B-26 fleet would require fifty-two or more R-2800-79 engine changes within the next four to six months if current flying schedules continued through the winter months of 1954-55. Everyone hoped that the B-57 Canberras would arrive before these engine changes were necessary, but the bomb squadrons, with the field maintenance squadron's assistance, began planning for special work teams and ordering special tools, engine accessories, and expendable hardware.

On 10 August the base flight transferred its L-5 Sentinel to Bitburg AB, West Germany. On 1 October, the 38th Air Base Group had three C-47s, and received one L-20A Beaver to replace the L-5.

On 14 January 1954, the 38th lost its first aircraft, B-26C #43-22590, in a night accident near Mazagan, French Morocco. The pilot and navigator were killed, the instructor pilot suffered near fatal injuries, and the gunner minor injuries. Power failure on both engines at 1,000 feet resulted in a forced gear-up landing. The B-26 stayed together after ground impact, slid 600 feet, and hit a four-foot high stone wall that destroyed the Invader. The gunner climbed out of his aft compartment and walked to the nearest village where he phoned Sidi Slimane AB to report the crash.

A second 405th Squadron B-26 was lost on 10 July 1954. TB-26B #44-34745 had an unusual accident near Sezanne, France. The Invader was flying a bit low, about twenty-five to fifty feet above the terrain; suddenly one engine cut out about three times, diverting the pilot's attention. The aircraft struck the ground, bending both propellers and tearing up the engine nose case gears, and bounced back into the air. The instructor pilot immediately reduced power, made a 100 degree left turn to avoid trees, and landed straight ahead. The airplane skidded about 130 feet after a second impact. There were no fatalities or injuries; the TB-26B stayed together with no fire after it stopped. The four men abandoned the plane instantly and later the Instructor Pilot phoned Laon Base Operations from the nearby village to report the accident. Their trusty Invader was beyond economical repair.

Another unusual B-26C accident occurred on 23 October 1954 while the 71st LBSq was night glide bombing on the Tarhuna Gunnery Range, Libya. The crew of #44-34105 smelled fuel as they neared Wheelus AB, and while turning into the final approach, the right engine nacelle and wing burst into flames with a minor explosion. The pilot executed an excellent fast landing, and all three crew members evacuated safely. The fire was extinguished but the Invader was badly damaged. The accident board found the right carburetor oil dilution line fitting had failed, dumping raw 115/145 octane fuel at engine pump pressure into the accessory section. The dilution fitting had fractured due to metal fatigue. The Invaders were getting old but not easily eliminated from the inventory. B-26 #105 was repaired and returned to service for several more years.

The training of French B-26 aircrews ended on 1 August 1954 as the French Indochina War ended with a peace settlement in Geneva. B-26 combat operations were stopped, and all Invaders were returned to the USAF during 1955. The Geneva Accords divided French Indochina into four nations, North Vietnam, South Vietnam, Laos, and Cambodia, and the war was reduced to a low intensity guerilla campaign for the next six years.

On 3 August 1954, the 71st LBSq moved into the first completed new hangar at Laon. This was the first hangar for indoor B-26 maintenance since October 1951! The 822nd was in Hangar #1 on the northeast corner of the main runway with its own living area; the 405th was in Hangar #2 on the northwest side of the runway, and the 71st LBSq used Hangar #3 on the southwest side of the runway. The 38th Air Base Group base flight still worked outdoors. Base flight used Hangars #2 and #3 closest to the base operations building when major maintenace was required.

In the summer of 1954 the 38th Bomb Wing, with one squadron of B-26s, conducted its first operational deployment to a dispersed operating base at Laon-Athies DOB, located nine miles east of Laon-Couvron AB. Many valuable lessons were learned in one week of flying. The 38th carefully documented all experiences and prepared an excellent Wing Operations Plan for future exercises or war. Later the wing flew its B-26s to dispersed bases located near Peronne–Estrees, twenty-nine miles to the northwest, and St. Simon-Clasters, sixteen miles in the same direction. These deployments were repeated with the new B-57s, and an operational readiness inspection was conducted while operating from the DOB. This training, although disliked by some personnel, was the most realistic exercise conducted by a tactical wing based in France.

Det #2, 1992d AACS and Det #7, 2d Postal Squadron personnel were still going to the R&R villa in Cannes, but its use was declining among 38th Wing airmen and officers. The men preferred to visit Paris, London, and the Garmisch area. After completion of the barracks and other buildings, HQ Twelfth Air Force ended the Rest & Rehabilitation leave status, and the Moritzia Villa was closed by 1 December 1954.

All Laon personnel spent the winter of 1954-55 indoors in barracks, but the barracks were only somewhat better than the old tent shelters. Loose fitting windows and doors, and intermittent heating systems made for uncomfortable living.

As 1955 began, the 38th Bomb Wing converted to a new bomber that greatly increased tactical capability. The long delayed B-57B Canberras were being produced by Martin Aircraft at the rate of about fifteen per month. A wing aircraft conversion plan prepared in early 1954, finally began in November 1954 by requesting the loan of T-33A trainers from various USAFE fighter wings, and T-33 mechanic training at Landstuhl-Ramstein AB.

The 38th began one of the most difficult aircraft conversion programs undertaken by a wing stationed in France. This conversion affected all pilots, navigators, and aircraft maintenance personnel. Changing from its Douglas B-26 Invaders to factory new Martin B-57B Canberras involved switching from a two reciprocating engine, propeller driven airplane into a twin engine jet powered bomber with twice the weight and airspeed. The pilot sat about seven feet closer to the runway in the B-57 compared to the B-26, which made the first few landings very interesting!

Ten T-33As were used for pilot training conversion at Laon from February to December 1955. On 17 February the first two T-33A jet trainers arrived, then two more arrived in April, and the last six arrived at the base by 4 June. The jet pilot training program commenced as soon as the first two trainers became available. T-33 flying was an absolute requirement because the dual control B-57Cs did not arrive until December, after the wing's conversion into B-57Bs.

No B-57 flight simulator was available for training at Laon during or after conversion. One Link Corp. instrument flight trainer, Model C-11B, was installed on base and was busy operating 120 hours per month.

Pilots and navigators who had not operated in jet aircraft faced the greatest training challenge. Several were from WWII A-20, B-25, or B-26 vintage training programs and needed a minimum of twenty-five jet hours before flying the B-57. A few post-WWII pilots in the wing had flown T-33s during their advanced pilot training, but after graduation had only flown the B-26. Also, by this time the USAF was proceeding with more structured conversion training than in prior years when a cockpit briefing, and, "try it once around the patch, it handles a lot like an AT-9," was considered normal checkout. New B-57 pilots had to have 1,000 hours of total time flying twin-engine aircraft. The pilots were divided in three categories; those who would train in CONUS, pilots to be trained at Laon, and pilots who would continue flying the B-26 at Laon. Pilots with one year or less remaining on their tour of duty in France did not convert into the Canberra. These pilots continued flying the B-26 to participate in exercises as directed by USAFE. The second group of pilots with less than three years remaining on their tour of duty in France received their B-57 flight training at Laon. Pilots with more than three years remaining on their tour of duty in France returned to CONUS for B-57 flight training. Three groups of six pilots were sent to the 3510th Combat Crew Training Wing at Randolph AFB, Texas, for B-57 conversion training. After course completion they picked up new B-57s at Warner Robins AFB and flew them back to

Laon. These pilots had acquired twenty-five hours minimum in a T-33 to become jet aircraft qualified at Randolph, and about twenty hours of B-57 flying. The pilots staying at Laon for conversion training received about thirty to thirty-five flight hours in the T-33, as well as additional instrument training to become qualified in jet aircraft. The T-33s were also used as chase planes during initial checkout flights by pilots in the T-33A and the B-57s. Both pilots and navigators had to receive high altitude physiological training with altitude chamber certification which was not required for the B-26s. Newly graduated pilots being assigned to Laon first went to Randolph for B-57 training, then proceeded individually to Laon upon course completion.

The navigators/bombardiers also received extensive classroom training at Laon by a USAF B-57 mobile training detachment. Navigators had an improved version of the same SHORAN system as in the B-26 to operate, therefore little retraining time was required for this bombing method. A few navigators were transferred to other wings, since the Canberras had a single navigator as opposed to the two navigators authorized for a B-26.

Several airmen jobs were eliminated by the B-57, primarily in the armament sections: gunners, bombsight mechanics, and turret system mechanics. Many of these airmen changed job codes into other armament skills and remained with the wing until their overseas service ended. Aircraft and engine mechanics required a large amount of classroom and on-the-job training. Classes were conducted by Martin Aircraft Representatives and USAF field training teams. The aircraft radio and radar shop had minimum changes because the Canberras carried the same equipment as the B-26s. The armament and communications/electronics sections within the bomb squadrons were merged into one section to better use shop space, electronic test equipment, bench stocks, and OJT training classes. The 38th LBWg completed all this jet conversion flying training and combat crew transition in France in difficult weather without an aircraft accident.

The new gloss black B-57Bs were flown from Martin Aircraft's, Baltimore, Maryland factory to AMC's B-57 Depot, Warner Robins Air Material Area (WRAMA), Georgia. Here the Canberras were prepared for delivery to Europe, an internal ferry tank was added. The depot installed a 550-gallon ferry tank on the bomb bay door and flight-tested the fuel system. Some aircraft and crews had long delays at WRAMA due to tip tank leakage. The tanks required careful purging, re-welding, and then pressure testing to cure the problem. These 600-gallon drop tanks were peculiar to the B-57A/B/C aircraft, and were in very limited supply. When the repairs were completed they were flown to France by MATS crews and by 38th crews as they completed training at Randolph. B-57s were delivered by 1737th Ferry Squadron crews based at Dover AFB, Delaware. MATS and USAFE wanted all B-57s delivered during summer and fall to avoid winter delivery flights across the North Atlantic.

After departing Warner Robbins in flights of two Canberras, the flight-legs were to Dover AFB, next to Goose Bay AB, then direct to Keflavik AB, Iceland, skipping Greenland. Sondrestrom (BW-8) was an alternate airfield. After a night's rest for the crews, the B-57s departed Keflavik and flew nonstop to Laon. RAF Prestwick or RAF Manston were alternates if required. With decent summer weather enroute, some B-57s made the trip in two days. The crews had little concern about aircraft range, which was about 2,200nm. The ferry tank provided excellent range compared to the B-26. Only one B-57 was damaged enroute to Laon. B-57B #52-1565 sustained major damage while landing at Dover AFB on 28 May 1955, and was repaired by a depot team. This Canberra remained in CONUS and was not delivered to the 38th Bomb Wing. The first B-57B arrived at Laon AB on 2 June 1955, and was assigned to the 71st LBSq.

The mission of the three light bomb squadrons was dramatically changed by HQ USAFE on 1 July 1955. The new mission statement was, "To deliver nuclear weapons against pre-selected targets, day or night." Conversion was still underway and already runway alert tasking was being scheduled. Sixteen B-57Bs and two B-57Cs were now authorized for each bomb squadron at Laon. Weapons delivery training began during September. With this mission change, weapons system protection became a vital new requirement so extensive security training was conducted for all operations and maintenance personnel working in the hangars and aircraft parking areas.

An important exercise related to the mission was Operation Harvest Moon where the aircrews practiced escape and evasion over four days in September 1955. The crews made simulated parachute landings from trucks about seven miles north of Chateau Thierry. Their goal was to escape and evade the local Gendarmerie and French Army troops while making their way to a safe area twenty-five miles away. About 90 percent of the pilots and navigators successfully avoided capture by moving mostly at night. This form of E&E training was conducted about once a year across

France by all USAFE and RCAF wing pilots and aircrew members.

As USAFE converted from B-26B/Cs to Canberras, Invaders were delivered to Ringway Airport, Manchester, England, and overhauled by Fairey Aviation prior to return to the U.S. for storage. Approximately ninety black Invaders from the 38th LBWg, and the 10th and 66th TRWgs were processed through Fairey Aviation during 1955-57. Part of the depot work was inspection/repair of wing spar/fuselage attachment fittings for cracking, and engine changes. This wing spar fatigue problem was first detected in December 1949 and was a constant concern. Also, the gloss black paint and red lettering was stripped and the plane repainted with silver enamel and black lettering. Many of these reworked B-26s were later removed from storage and flown in USAF Projects FARM GATE and MILL POND.

On 30 September 1955 the 38th Air Base Group, Base Flight was assigned all remaining wing Invaders, two TB-26Bs and three B-26Cs. The five Invaders were flown only by pilots and navigators not converting into B-57s. These officers were awaiting orders sending them to new CONUS assignments. The last B-26 departed Laon on 22 January 1956.

A B-57 bomb squadron was authorized 40 officers and 158 airmen. On 30 September 1955 the 71st LBSq had 42 officers and 158 airmen, the 405th had 45 officers and 147 airmen, and the 822d LBSq had 43 officers and 151 airmen. Most personnel reassignments had been completed.

In September 1955, the 405th LBSq possessed fourteen B-57Bs. Two Canberras had .50cal machine guns and twelve had 20mm cannons. All three squadrons had a mix of gun and cannon equipped B-57s. B-57B #52-1576 and subsequent B and C aircraft had four (two in each wing) M-39 20mm cannons that replaced the eight M-3 .50cal machine guns. This was the same cannon used in the F-100Ds. The M-39 cannons were not fired during armament training in October and November because of a 20mm ammunition shortage in USAFE. Also, the cannons could not be fired until a required modification was made to wing gun-bay doors. This door modification consisted of adding hydraulically operated purge vents to increase gun gas-flow when the cannons were fired.

Late arrival of the dual-control B-57Cs slowed tactical glide bombing training; the first C models arrived in early December 1955. The squadron B-57 flying rates varied from a low of 90 hours up to 400 hours per month between July and November; the aircraft in-commission rates varied from 45 to 70 percent because of repair-parts shortages. Parts shortages always plagued the introduction of a new type of airplane. Base supply worked overtime to get these items ordered from WRAMA and out to the squadrons as soon as received. Because Laon AB was the only B-57B/C operator in Europe, Chateauroux did not establish a major parts stock for the airframe; all parts were stored at Laon. During this period, maintenance had to accomplish several TCTOs on their B-57s, fourteen on the airframe and four on the J-65 jet engines. TCTOs are also a common extra workload on new aircraft. The squadrons performed all required scheduled and unscheduled maintenance to keep aircraft available for the flying schedules. On 31 August 1955, Captain John W. Harris, 71st LBSq, 38th Bomb Wing, was the first pilot to accumulate one-hundred hours flying the B-57B. The navigators were also busy learning their new airplane's abilities; Leutenants Robert S. Bicknell and Louis F. Miserocchi developed improved B-57B/C cruise control charts for all aircrews. This became vital data in a few months, when the 38th was assigned real targets in Eastern Europe while standing nuclear weapon alert.

B-57s had the newer APN-84 SHORAN system with the Indicator and K-4 Bomb Computer installed below the instrument panel on the aft cockpit floor. This made the three-inch diameter cathode ray tube display difficult to read. The navigators developed a special sun shade to help them read the J-scope range display on bright days. Bombing training missions using SHORAN and MSQ were always scored to determine crew proficiency. The navigators needed to practice more SHORAN runs to become acquainted with the much faster Drift and Rate position changes. One C-47 with an APN-84 installation made a very good training platform for initial navigator training on this complex bombing system. The SHORAN instructor could provide hands-on training to the student, which was impossible in the B-57.

Detachment #4, 6th Aerial Port Squadron was activated on 1 September 1955 at Laon to operate a Class V Air Freight Terminal. Det. #4 officers and airmen were attached to the 38th Supply Squadron for administration and logistical support.

On 1 October 1955 while flying its B57-B/Cs at Laon, the 38th Bombardment Wing, Light was redesignated the 38th Bombardment Wing, Tactical. A new USAF regulation replaced the word "Light" with "Tactical" for all light bombardment wings, groups, and squadrons worldwide.

At this time the 38th's gloss black Canberras received their distinctive markings. The 71st TBSq had

38th Bomb Wing, 405th Bomb Squadron B-57 Canberra # 52-1581 on the field at Laon AB, 1957.
Al Christensen

red rudders with white letters, the 405th green rudders with white letters, and the 822d had yellow rudders with black letters. Letter sequence was A through S; the letter Q was not used. Special squadron insignias were painted on the side of the black tip tanks.

In December, the C-47s were finally being dispatched to the IRAN contractor at Verigate Airfield, Italy. They were long overdue for major inspections, repairs, and modifications; C-47A #42-108922 had arrived in France in November 1951 with the 126th LBWg. The 38th's T-33 fleet was reduced in December, three were returned to Ramstein-Landstuhl AB and one was reassigned to the 50th FBWg at Hahn AB. Six T-Birds were retained by the 38th for use as jet instrument trainers and for proficiency flying by the wing HQ and Paris region pilots.

In January 1956, the 38th Tactical Bomb Wing began a three year commitment to maintain a detachment of ten B-57s on nuclear Zulu Alert at Ramstein AB, twenty-four hours per day, seven days a week. Det #1 at Ramstein consisted of twenty-two officers and fifty-two airmen on thirty-day TDY assignments. The crews rotated back to Laon after thirty days in Germany. The Mk-7 nuclear weapons were kept at Ramstein and loaded in the B-57s there. The wing was also tasked to maintain six to twelve B-57s on continuous Victor Alert at Laon. The shortage of combat crews grew between June and August 1957; only about 60 percent of the aircrews were fully trained and available for this alert duty. Alert duty conflicted with the required proficiency training, but this nuclear alert duty continued up to 18 July 1958 when 38th was deactivated and the Canberras phased out of USAFE. The B-57 had excellent toss bombing capability to perform the weapon delivery mission; this reduction of tactical nuclear forces was purely the result of administration budget cuts and not a reflection of crew or aircraft performance. The B-57 wing was theoretically replaced by the TM-61A Matador.

On 5 March 1956 the 38th completed conversion into the B-57B/Cs and was fully equipped with forty-nine B-57Bs and eight B-57Cs. A B-57 acrobatic team was organized and named the "Black Knights" using five standard B-57s. The Black Knights performed at several air shows around Western Europe including the May 1957 Paris Air Show. The B-57 would demonstrate its excellent performance and stability to the crowds. The Black Knights are thought to be the only tactical bomber show team in the world.

Throughout 1957 the 38th TBWg continued proficiency training with three trips down to the ranges at Wheelus AB, Tripoli. The B-57s now had high in-

B-57 Canberra #52-1582 checkout, Laon AB 1957.
John Bissel

commission rates, exceeding 80 percent during the summer months, and over 90 percent during fall deployments at Wheelus. Maintenance man-hours were half of those required by the B-26 Invaders. SHORAN bombing missions, using an S-4 system consisting of the APN-84 and K-4 Bombing Computer, dropped live 500-pound bombs. MSQ-1 directed APPLECORES live bombing missions, using APW-11 beacons, were also conducted both day and night with excellent scores. The B-57 was proving to be an excellent, stable, long range day/night tactical bomber. The 822d TBSq won the fall bombing competition at Wheelus with excellent scores

In February 1956, the 405th TBSq configured a B-57B with a TM-61 Matador guidance system to evaluate the missile's performance on the Wheelus test range. The TM-61 Matador, the first USAF ground launched cruise missile, had a series of in-flight navigation failures during training flights at Wheelus on the El Uotia range. The B-57B evaluated the MSQ-1's initial command guidance and terrain matching navigation system. Both TAC and USAFE were attempting to find solutions to the in-flight guidance system faults, as the Matador was programmed to replace USAFE tactical bombers by 1959. This B-57 flew on several tests and contributed data to solve the problem.

After 1 March 1956, all B-57B/C depot level maintenance was being performed at the Scandinavian Airline System (SAS) aircraft repair facility in Copenhagen, Denmark. The primary work was inspection and repair of the horizontal stabilizer trim system. It became a serious problem at low altitude high speed nose pitch down. Work was also performed on avionics systems, the bomb bay door, and the fuel control system; each Canberra spent about two months at the depot. SAS provided all depot support for the B-57B/Cs under contracts from Martin Aircraft and Chateauroux Air Depot.

During 1957 the B-57 in-commission rates varied from 75 to 95 percent, the aircraft were proving easy to maintain and parts problems were minimal. J-65 engines were reliable and spare engines were readily available in the base warehouses. Bomb squadron flying rates varied from a low of 500 hours up to 700 hours per month, and like all airplanes the more they flew the more the machine stayed fixed to be flown.

As a very sucessful year of flying came to a end, the 38th Tactical Bomb Wing lost its first B-57 on 11 December 1956. The Canberra went down sixteen miles east of Laon AB near Sissonne, France after take-off from Laon-Athies DOB resulting in two fatalities.

The 583d Air Force Band was assigned to Laon as another tenant unit in November 1957 for about eight months and then moved to Ramstein. During 1957 a new tenant unit, the Joint Construction Agency office was established at Laon, but JCA was phased out in spring 1958. Laon AB tenants at this time were Det #7, 31st Weather Sq; Det #7, 12th Air Postal Sq; Det #54 OSI; and Det #2, 1992d AACS Sq.

On 8 December 1957 USAFE inactivated Headquarters, 38th Tactical Bombardment Group, to eliminate about thirty-five military personnel positions. The group command and operational functions were added to wing staff officers' functions. The Tactical Bomb Group Commander and staff offices were located in the wing/base headquarters building and after 8 December merged into the Wing Deputy Commander for Operations offices.

The 38th Tactical Bombardment Wing was deactivated in place at midnight on 18 June 1958 at Laon AB, France. On 18 June 1958 the 38th Tactical Missile Wing was activated at Hahn AB, West Germany,

Black Knights' acrobatic team's Canberra starting up, Laon AB 1957.
John Bissel

replacing the 701st Tactical Missile Wing with the same mission of operating and maintaining the TM-67A Matador missile system. This was only a wing designator change. No personnel, aircraft, or equipment was transferred from Laon to Hahn. The three squadron designators were also changed to the 71st, 405th, and 822d Tactical Missile Squadrons. All B-57B/C aircraft departed France for CONUS during 1958. Many 38th Bomb Wing personnel remained at Laon to fill vacancies in the 66th Wing.

66th Tactical Reconnaissance Wing

The 66th Tactical Reconnaissance Wing with its three squadrons, the 30th, 302d and 303d Tactical Reconnaissance Squadrons, was assigned to USAFE, Twelfth Air Force on 7 July 1953. The wing moved its RF-80As and RB-26s during June and July from Shaw AFB, South Carolina, into the nearly completed Sembach AB, West Germany. During 1955, while at Sembach, the 302d and 303d Squadrons upgraded to RF-84Fs, and the 30th Squadron converted from RB-26Cs into new RB-57As. By 1955 Sembach had become an undesirable base. The runway was too short to safely operate fighters, base facilities had been outgrown, and it lacked room for expansion. The base was divided in two parcels with the headquarters, administrative, living, and supply functions crowded on a hilltop one mile north, separated from the runway, aircraft operations, and maintenance facilities. The runway and parking aprons were built almost into the small town of Sembach. A very important support squadron, the 66th Reconnaissance Technical Sq had to be stationed eleven miles south at Kapaun Barracks because of the lack of land at Sembach. Protests over the F-84F/J-65 engine noise had grown during 1955, especially with night operations. USAFE and Twelfth Air Force wanted to move the 66th out of Sembach to a location better suited for the future RF-101s scheduled to arrive in summer 1958. USAFE officers knew that the RF-101s with their two J-57s plus afterburners would bring angry complaints from the people of Sembach and Mehlingen, and perhaps shut down flying.

The first base selected in France was Phalsbourg, but USAFE decided to move the 66th to Laon after the 38th Tactical Bomb Wing was scheduled for deactivation. The 66th TRWg was offically transferred to Laon by Twelfth Air Force on 10 July 1958; although the flying squadrons remained at Phalsbourg until runway improvements were completed at Laon, as described in chapter 15. At Laon the 66th still had the day reconnaissance mission with RF-84F Thunderflash aircraft and equipment, and was manned by 215 officers and 1,310 airmen. Laon became an excellent base for the RF-101s and the 66th TRWg remained there for a record stay of eight years until 1 September 1966 when forced by Project FRELOC to relocate to RAF Upper Heyford, England. The 66th was based in France longer than any other combat wing, only the CAME air depot at Chateauroux served longer.

The 66th Tactical Reconnaissance Wing began in September 1941 as the 66th Observation Group activated at Jacksonville, Florida for WWII. The group

66th TRWg, 32d Tactical Reconnaissance Squadron RF-84F #51-7013, prior to transfer to Laon. V-E Day Open House, Chambley AB May 1957.

Al Christensen

flew antisubmarine patrols off the Atlantic coast during spring and summer 1942, to reduce shipping losses. The group and its five assigned squadrons moved about the eastern United States supporting the Carolina and Tennessee Army Maneuvers of 1942 and 1943. The 66th Reconnaissance Group was disbanded in April 1944, but was assigned to the USAF Reserve program from 1946 until 1951. It was redesignated a Tactical Reconnaissance Wing and was activated during the Korean War expansion at Shaw AFB, South Carolina, on 1 January 1953.

The 66th TRWg went through several major changes in 1956 and 1957 prior to its relocation to France. First, the RB-57A Canberras flown by the 30th TRSq were replaced by RB-66B aircraft, while the 302d and 303d Squadrons continued flying their RF-84Fs. The 19th TRSq was assigned to the 66th TRWg on 1 January 1957 while flying RB-45Cs at RAF Sculthorpe. On 8 December 1957 HQ USAFE inactivated 66th TRGp Headquarters to reduce personnel. On 8 March 1958 HQ USAFE reorganized its two reconnaissance wings to improve logistical efficiency and reduce costs. Two squadrons, the 19th and 30th TRSq flying RB-66B and Cs, twin engine bomber type reconnaissance aircraft, were transferred to the 10th TRWg at Spangdahlem AB. Two RF-84F squadrons, the 32d and 38th TRSq were transferred from the 10th TRWg to the 66th on 8 January and 8 May 1958. The 66th TRWg now had four squadrons; the 32d, 38th, 302d, and 303d, all flying RF-84Fs. Additional information on these changes will be found in chapter 15, Phalsbourg.

The new McDonnell RF-101C Voodoos first appeared in Europe, on 16 May 1958, when three landed at Phalsbourg AB, France. The fourth Voodoo crashed near the base upon arrival. The four RF-101s had flown nonstop from Shaw AFB using air refueling enroute. During the next few months, the 32d and 38th Squadrons at Phalsbourg began training on the RF-101Cs. An RF-101 Mobile Training Detachment operated at Phalsbourg and later moved to Laon. The first RF-101Cs were delivered to Nouasseur AB, French Morocco in the summer and fall of 1958 where pilot conversion training was conducted in the excellent desert weather on the long 12,000 ft. runway. At this time there were no two-place TF-101F trainers or flight simulators to aid in this aircraft change. As thirty RF-101Cs arrived for the 66th, their RF-84Fs were phased through depot contractors and transferred to NATO or MAP countries.

The 66th TRWg had more changes during 1959. On 10 May the 17th TRSq transferred from TAC to USAFE, and the 18th TRSq followed on 1 June. Both squadrons moved their thirty-six RF-101Cs and pilots

66th TRWg RF-84Fs over Italy.
USAF Photo

from the 432d TRWg at Shaw AFB to Laon, and were assigned to the 66th TRWg. Then on 20 June, USAFE deactivated the 302d and 303d TRSq in place. By 1 October 1959 the 66th Tactical Reconnaissance Wing now commanded the 17th, 18th, 32d, and 38th Tactical Reconnaissance Squadrons, all flying eighty-four RF-101Cs at Phalsbourg and Laon. These squadrons stayed with the 66th TRWg for the following six years.

Several major construction projects were completed at Laon in the summer and fall 1958 to accommodate the RF-101 Voodoos. From August 1958 to February 1959 the main runway was repaired and lengthened. Two 1,000-foot extensions were added to the runway beyond the taxiway intersections. Arresting barriers were installed about 900 feet before the runway pavement ended. The RF-101Cs had a drag parachute and a tail hook that provided positive barrier engagements to keep the aircraft on the runway after touchdown at 160 mph. This was the first major runway repair since it was new in 1952. The bomber-size hangars were excellent for the RF-101s that were taller and longer than the B-57s they replaced. Three hangars were available for the four tactical reconnaissance squadrons; the 17th and 18th were in Hangar #1 on the northeast corner of the main runway, with their own living area. The 32d was in Hangar #2 on the northwest side of the runway, and the 38th used Hangar #3 on the southwest side of the runway. The 66th Air Base Group Base Flight worked on T-33As in Hangar #3, which it shared with the 38th TRSq. It also used Hangar #2 closest to the base operations building for C-47 maintenance. The jet engine test cell had to be modified to accommodate the larger P&W J-57 engine with afterburner, but munitions storage on base was very adequate for photo flash cartridges.

The 66th moved their RF-101C squadrons in April 1960 as part of Operation Dim View. The 17th, 18th, 32d and 38th TRSqs transferred to Toul for 120 days TDY while additional major runway resurfacing and taxiway repairs were undertaken at Laon. About 120 airmen were assigned TDY from Laon to assist the 7544th Support Group with this additional workload. A total of 601 personnel from Laon had to be fed and housed by the 7544th Gp. The runway repairs at Laon required five months, keeping Toul a busy active air base while in standby status. The 18th TRSq returned to Laon on 23 August, followed by the 17th on 27 August. The 32d and 38th returned in October. All personnel were happy to return home to Laon.

The 66th TRWg participated in a NATO tactical reconnaissance competition, Royal Flush, similiar to the AFCENT Weapons Meets conducted by the fighter wings. The annual meet began in 1956 and continued into the 1970s. Reconnaissance units from all nations could enter and represent 2d or 4th ATAF. Royal Flush exercises were held in the summer or fall at a different NATO air base each year. The meet consisted of a variety of photo runs on several specific ground objectives at low and high altitude levels over a prescribed route. Contest points were awarded on navigational accuracy, time enroute, photo quality, and visual details. Individual pilots and unit teams became winners by earning the greatest number of points. Royal Flush involved a number of different reconnaissance aircraft types and camera systems in competition. This was closely followed by NATO commanders. The 66th TRWg competed almost every year and frequently won the meet flying the RF-84F, RB-57, and the RF-101C. The RF-101 was a formidable machine when

RF-101C #56-0097 with camera equipment on display.
National Archives

seen at 500 feet running low level photos. Royal Flush exercises and other routine reconnaissance training missions in Europe produced well trained pilots to fly similar operations in Southeast Asia.

A very special mission request from Twelfth Air Force tasked the 66th to provide photo mapping support for Operation Climax during the summer of 1960 as requested by the Commander, Seventeenth Air Force at Wheelus AB, Libya. Operation Climax was the final effort to recover four missing crewmen from the B-24D "Lady Be Good" that had crashed in the desert on 4 April 1943. The Liberator had been found in February 1959, but over the following fifteen months only five crew member bodies were found in the Libyan desert. Four RF-101Cs were deployed from Laon on 6 April to strip photograph the crash area of about 10,000 square miles. The photographs were assembled into photomaps used by ground search teams in hopes of finding the four missing bodies. The photo mapping did not reveal any clues to the bomber crew members but aided the search teams. The 18th TRSq performed this mission in three weeks. Three crew members were finally found in August 1960 by ground search, but one B-24 crewman remains missing to the present day.

RF-101Cs were slowly improved during 1962-64 by adding KA-45 cameras for better low altitude high speed photography, new KS-72A cameras, a larger vertical camera, an upgraded camera control system, and flash cartridge pods for night photography. Major airframe modifications were made to the hydraulic system, main landing gear, and fuel system. The RF-101's original nuclear weapon delivery system was updated by installation of a new weapon control panel and wiring to provide low altitude retarded delivery of centerline mounted Mk-28RE or B-43 external weapons. This last improvement permitted the RF-101s to stand Zulu Alert with either nuclear or thermonuclear weapons. These modifications plus structural repairs resulted in Recce Voodoos serving in USAFE until 1970. The 66th's flying squadrons and maintenance squadron invested approximately seventy-five hours of maintenance for every flying hour at the average cost of $1,200 per hour. Each RF-101C reconnaissance squadron was typically authorized 550 hours of flying a month, but extra flying hours were made available to support special USAFE and NATO exercises.

The 66th TRWg was one of the first USAFE wings to feel the effects of the reduction of air assets in Europe to support the war in Southeast Asia. Tactical reconnaissance was badly needed throughout Vietnam and Laos to collect visual and photo intelligence to formulate a strategy to counter the insurgency. The RF-101C filled that operational requirement. HQ USAF levied ten RF-101Cs on 8 August 1965 to depart France and proceed to CONUS; then nine aircraft would proceed on to the Pacific Air Forces (PACAF) while one Recce Voodoo would be assigned to Shaw AFB to assist in a crew training program. The first flight of seven RF-101Cs departed Laon between 29 August and 3 September for Moron Air Base, Spain, then to the U.S., and on to Tan Son Nhut AB, South Vietnam. The second flight of three RF-101C aircraft left Laon on 6 October for Moron Air Base and headed for Shaw

66th Tactical Reconnaissance Wing, 18th Tactical Reconnaissance Sq RF-101C #56-0122.
USAF Photo via Nancy Brooks

AFB. Two of the Voodoos continued on to PACAF; one aircraft remained at Shaw. During 1965 and 1966 additional aircraft and personnel were being supplied to the Vietnam War.

After five years of organizational stability, the 66th TRWg lost its first flying squadron on 1 October 1965, when USAFE ordered the 32d TRSq to be moved to Toul AB without aircraft and personnel, and be assigned to the new 26th Tactical Reconnaissance Wing. Three months later on 1 January 1966 the second flying squadron, the 38th was transferred to Toul, again without aircraft, as the 26th Wing expanded with the arrival of new RF-4Cs. The 66th TRWg at Laon was reduced to the 17th and 18th Tactical Reconnaissance Squadrons still flying their RF-101Cs.

Immediately after President de Gaulle demanded that all NATO forces must depart France by 31 March 1967, the 66th began planning to move somewhere in the UK during that summer. There was no space for the wing and its sixty RF-101Cs in West Germany. USAFE reactivated its standby base at RAF Upper Heyford, England, on 1 August to accommodate the 66th TRWg as part of Project FRELOC. The 66th transferred everything possible that it could remove from Laon. Their motto was "if in doubt—take it out." On 1 September 1966, the 66th Tactical Reconnaissance Wing with the 17th and 18th Tactical Reconnaissance Squadrons was officially operational at RAF Upper Heyford located fifty miles northwest of London. Relocation was completed by November 1966. The 66th operated at Upper Heyford for four years until deactivated in place on 1 April 1970. This deactivation was part of another massive DOD reduction: Reduction of Costs and Forces in Europe (Project REDCOSTE).

On 10 June 1966 the 7379th Tactical Group was activated at Laon AB and assigned the task of clearing out and closing Laon after the departure of the 66th Wing. Tons of material were shipped as directed by Project FRELOC schedules. Between 10 and 16 March 1967 all remaining personnel were transferred to West Germany. On 17 March 1967, the base was turned over to France and the flags lowered; Laon Air Base was closed after sixteen years of continuous use. The 7379th Tactical Group was deactivated in place at Laon Air Base at midnight 31 March 1967.

The base is currently in use by the French Army for air mobility operations. Its current name is "Quartier Mangin sur l'ancienne Base de Couvron," and since 1980 has been home to the French Army 1st Regiment D'Artillerie de Marine. About half of the USAF buildings are still standing and well maintained; the three large hangars were dismantled and moved during the 1970s. Both runways remain; the main runway is used for aircraft and helicopter operations. The French Army has built several large new buildings, changing the base layout. It is possible to tour the base by making prior arrangements with the Franco-American Association in Laon. A large monument to USAF personnel has been installed in the Crepy town center by the association. Laon can be found on Michelin Map Local #306 and IGN Blue #2610E. It can be reached by train from Paris' Gare du Nord station.

By the end of 1953 and beginning of 1954 Laon AB was beginning to take shape though few permanent buildings had been completed.

38th Air Base Group base OPS and fire station in winterized tents, Laon AB 1953.
National Archives

Permanent base OPS under construction, Laon AB 1953. The base was still covered with mud when it rained.
National Archives

Base OPS nearing completion, November 1954, Laon AB. Old 15-foot tower, now 25 feet high, in foreground.
National Archives

Tar paper covered tent frames gave Laon AB a "shanty town" look, 1953.
National Archives

BX in prefab building 1953 - a step up from the first tent BX at Laon AB.
National Archives

Theater in Fillod building, November 1952.
National Archives

Squadron shops and HQ surround sides and back of hangar, Laon AB 1954. Note garage doors for truck delivery.
National Archives

Permanent supply warehouse nearing completion 1954.
National Archives

Even in 1956 grass cutting was still handled by sheep!
John Bissel

Familiar highway signs at D26 and D54 intersection, 2002.
Jerry McAuliffe

Appendix 13.1 Notice to Airmen, August 1957 (NOTAM) - USAF-Laon-Couvron

Elevation 263 feet (80m), 49° 39'N - 03° 33'E. One paved runway 7,900 feet long, 030°/210°, supports 84,000 pounds single wheeled aircraft. Second E-W runway closed, used for aircraft paarking only. Rotating beacon, approach lights. Runway and taxiway lights, and airfield obstruction lights. Transient aircraft storage with minor repairs available. Aircraft fuel, 115-145 octane and JP4 jet fuel with single point service. Jet aircraft starting units A-3A, C-21, and C-26 available. MA-MP air and electrical starting available. Type S-12 aircraft starting cartridge available. Jet aircraft barrier in operation. Airdrome facilities available 24 hours daily.

Laon Air Base Assigned Aircraft

USAF History Office

126th Bomb Wing, Light, B-26Bs & Cs, 25 May 1952 - 31 December 1952
Eighteen aircraft per squadron. These Invaders were flown from Bordeaux AB, France to Laon AB, France by 126th LBWg crews.
Aircraft Marking:

- 108th Light Bomb Squadron - Black, yellow, blue bands on vertical stabilizer and rudders.
- 168th Light Bomb Squadron - Black, yellow, red bands on vertical stabilizer and rudders.
- 180th Light Bomb Squadron - Black, yellow, green bands on vertical stabilizer and rudders.

TB-26Bs

44-34593	108th
44-34597	108th
44-34671	168th
44-34702	180th
44-34729	180th
44-34742	168th

B-26Bs

41-39324#	168th
41-39504	180th
44-34194	168th
44-34196	180th
44-34202	108th

B-26Cs

43-22657#	180th	44-35262#	168th	44-35588#	168th
43-22676#	108th	44-35264	168th	44-35697#	168th
43-22692#	168th	44-35358#	180th	44-35702	168th
43-22714	180th	44-35365#	168th	44-35738#	180th
43-22717#	180th	44-35493#	168th	44-35750	108th
43-22724#	108th	44-35513	168th	44-35761#	168th
44-35208	168th	44-35527#	168th	44-35778#	180th
44-35215#	108th	44-35549#	180th	44-35900#	180th
44-35221#	108th	44-35585#	180th		

Black B-26Cs

41-39190^	108th	43-22457	180th	44-34102	168th	44-35274^	168th
41-39263^	108th	43-22461^	180th	44-34104	108th	44-35540*	108th
41-39276^	108th	43-22470	108th	44-34105	108th	44-35641	108th
41-39288^	108th	43-22477^	108th	44-34110^	108th	44-35652*^	168th
41-39297^	168th	43-22484^	108th	44-34113^	180th	44-35742^	108th
41-39303^	168th	43-22489^	108th	44-34114^	168th	44-35763	108th
43-22268^	180th	43-22496	180th	44-34120^	168th	44-35784	180th
43-22271^	180th	43-22499^	168th	44-34121^	168th	44-35790	180th
43-22288	108th	43-22502^	168th	44-34124^	108th	44-35856	180th
43-22440	168th	43-22511^	180th	44-34128^	168th	44-35857	168th
43-22442	108th	43-22590^	168th	44-34135^	108th	44-35868	168th
43-22456	180th	43-22612^	180th				
		43-22722*^	168th				
		43-22714	108th				

B-26s returned by 31 DEC 52 to Hill AFB, UT, OOAMA, for DIR rework.
^ Black B-26s received at Laon from CONUS, 25 May thru 31 DEC 52
No black B-26Bs received in 1952.
* Losses:
43-22722 - Destroyed, nose gear collapsed, landing in rain. Torn in half by recovery crew at Capodichino Airport, Naples, Italy, 7 NOV 52, no fatalities.
44-35540 - Crashed, low level, on sunny day, near Pargnay, France 23 OCT 52, 2 fatalities.
44-35652 - Crashed, hit mountain in rain, 1nm NW of Cava de Tirreni, Italy 7 NOV 52, 2 fatalities.

126th Air Base Group: Wing Support Aircraft
C-47A: 42-108922, 43-15315
L-5A: 44-17205

Laon Air Base Assigned Aircraft, continued

Jerry McAuliffe

38th Bomb Wing, Light, B-26Bs & Cs 1 January 1953 - 31 December 1955
Eighteen aircraft per squadron. All B-26s transferred in place from the 126th LBWg to the 38th LBWg on 1 January 1953.
Aircraft Marking:
- 71st Light Bomb Squadron - Red band, white letters.
- 405th Light Bomb Squadron - Green band, white letters.
- 822d Light Bomb Squadron - Yellow band, black letters.

TB-26Bs

44-34593#	71st
44-34597	71st
44-34671	405th
44-34702#	822d
44-34729	822d

B-26Bs

41-39504	822d
44-34194	405th
44-34196	822d
44-34202	71st

B-26Cs

43-22714#	822d
44-35208#	405th
44-35264	405th
44-35513#	405th
44-35702#	405th
44-35750	71st

Black TB-26Bs

44-34608	405th
44-34742	71st
44-34745/Y*	405th

Black B-26Bs

44-34103	71st
44-34114/X	405th
44-34127	405th
44-34130	
44-34138	71st
44-34144	822d
44-34156	405th
44-34163	822d
44-35750/P	405th

Black B-26Cs

41-39190	71st
41-39263	405th
41-39276	405th
41-39288	71st
41-39297	405th
41-39303	405th
43-22268	822d
43-22271	71st
43-22288	71st
43-22415	
43-22436	71st
43-22440	405th
43-22442	
43-22456	

43-22457	
43-22461	
43-22470/Q	71st
43-22477	71st
43-22484	71st
43-22489	71st
43-22496	
43-22499	
43-22502	
43-22511	405th
43-22590/U*	405th
43-22612	822d
43-22714	822d

44-34102	405th
44-34104	71st
44-34105*	71st
44-34110	71st
44-34113	822d
44-34114/X	405th
44-34120/D	405th
44-34121	822d
44-34124	71st
44-34128	405th
44-34135	71st
44-34139/W	405th
44-35274	405th
44-35339	405th

44-35641	71st
44-35713	
44-35742	71st
44-35763	71st
44-35784	822d
44-35790	822d
44-35856	822d
44-35857	405th
44-35868/B	405th
44-35975	822d

* Losses:
43-22590 - Crashed, engine failure, 10nm SW of Mazagan, Fr. Morocco, 14 JAN 54, 2 fatalities.
44-34105 - Damaged, engine fire - explosion, on Wheelus AB, Libya, 23 OCT 54, no fatalities.
44-34745 - Crashed, low level, hit ground, 5nm NE of Sezanne, France, 10 JUL 54, no fatalities.

- B-26s returned during 1953 to HILL AFB, UT OOAMA for DIR rework.

38th Air Base Group: Wing Support Aircraft
C-47A: 42-108922, 43-15315

Laon Air Base tail numbers continued next page

Laon Air Base Assigned Aircraft, continued

Al Christensen

38th Bomb Wing, Light, B-57Bs & Cs, April 1955 - 18 June 1958
20 aircraft per squadron. On 6 June 1955 the 38th completed conversion to B-57B/C.
Aircraft Marking: (Buzz letters used were "A" through "S")

71st Light Bomb Squadron - Red rudders, white letters.
405th Light Bomb Squadron - Green rudders, white letters.
822d Light Bomb Squadron - Yellow rudders, black letters.

B-57B-MA

52-1508	71st	52-1566*	71st	52-1580/G	71st	52-1592	822d
52-1510	71st	52-1567/O	405th	52-1581/H	405th	52-1593	822d
52-1511	71st	52-1568/D	405th	52-1582/N	822d	52-1594	405th
52-1513	405th	52-1570	71st	52-1583	822d		
52-1514	71st	52-1571/L	71st	52-1584	405th	53-3859/P	822d
52-1515	822d	52-1572	71st	52-1585	405th	53-3860	822d
52-1518/D	71st	52-1573	405th	52-1586	822d	53-3861	405th
52-1519#	71st	52-1574/H	71st	52-1587/O*	822d	53-3862/F+	822d
52-1520	822d	52-1575	405th	52-1588	822d	53-3863/L	405th
52-1530	405th	52-1577/M	822d	52-1589	405th	53-3864	405th
52-1533	71st	52-1578+	405th	52-1590/C+	822d	53-3865/E	822d
52-1560/J+	71st	52-1579	822d	52-1591/G*	822d	53-3869+	405th
52-1561	71st						
52-1564/E	71st						

B-57C-MA

53-3834/A	71st	53-3841/A	405th	53-3850/C	405th	53-3852/B*	405th
53-3839/C	71st	53-3846/B+	822d	53-3851/B	71st	53-3856/A	822d

+ Indicates B-57s assigned to the Black Knights acrobatic team
# Located at March ARB, CA Museum.
* Losses:
51-1566 - Crashed, final approach bad weather, near Pouilly sur Serre, France, 2 APR 57, 2 fatalities.
52-1587 - Crashed, mid-air collision, near Otterstadt, West Germany, 26 MAR 57, 2 fatalities.
52-1591 - Crashed, climb-out/bad weather, near Sissonne, France, 11 DEC 56, 2 fatalities.
53-3852 - Crashed, cause unknown, on Laon AB, France, 14 MAR 57, 2 fatalities.

38th Air Base Group: Wing Support Aircraft
C-47A: 42-108922, 43-15315
C-47B: 44-76207, 44-76757/C
L-20A: 51-16529, 51-16536
T-33A: (9) 53-5061, 53-5132, 53-5281, 53-5339

Laon Air Base tail numbers continued next page

Laon Air Base Assigned Aircraft, continued

Al Christensen

66th Tactical Reconnaissance Wing, RF-84Fs, 10 July 1958 - August 1959

Eighteen aircraft per squadron. These Thunderflashes were flown from Sembach AB, W. Germany, Phalsbourg AB, FR and Toul AB, FR to Laon AB, FR by 66th TRWg pilots.

Aircraft markings:

32d Tactical Reconnaissance Squadron - Yellow band.
38th Tactical Reconnaissance Squadron - Green band.
303d Tactical Reconnaissance Squadron - Blue band.
302d Tactical Reconnaissance Squadron - Red band.

RF-84F-10, -25-RE

51-1841		51-17013	32d	52-7315		52-7363	
51-1862		51-17014		52-7317		52-7364	
51-1894	303d	51-17037		52-7342	32d	52-7365	
51-1911	38th	51-17038		52-7343 ~	303d	52-7368*	38th
51-1913		51-17041	38th	52-7344		52-7369*	38th
51-1923		51-17042		59-7345		52-7371	
51-1933	303d	52-7287*	302d	59-7346	38th	52-7373	38th
51-17003		52-7288	38th	52-7347	302d	52-7374	
51-17004	303d	52-7289*	303d	52-7348*	303d	52-7375	
51-17005	32d	52-7290	38th	52-7349*	38th	52-7377	
51-17006		52-7291		52-7350		52-7379	
51-17007	303d	52-7292	32d	52-7355		52-7381	302d
51-17009		52-7293	32d	52-7356		52-7391	302d
51-17010		52-7295		52-7358			
51-17011	38th	52-7309		52-7359	38th		
51-17012		52-7313	38th	52-7361	38th		

* Losses:
52-7287 - Crashed, bad landing, Sembach AB, W. Germany, 57/58, no fatalities.
52-7289 - Crashed, bad landing on Phalsbourg AB, FR, SEP 58, fatalities unknown.
52-7348 - Crashed, bad landing, on Laon AB, France 15 OCT 58, 1 fatality.
52-7349 - Crashed, take-off, fuel fire, 2nm N of Nouasseur AB, Morocco, 21 AUG 58, 1 fatality.
52-7368 - Crashed, landing/weather, on Phalsbourg AB, France, 10 APR 58, no fatalities.
52-7369 - Crashed, landing at night/weather, on Phalsbourg AB, France, 9 JUL 58, 1 fatality.

~ Wing Commander's Aircraft

66th Air Base Group: Wing Support Aircraft
C-47A: 42-92710,
C-47D: 44-77228
L-20A: 51-16537 or 51-16536
T-33A: 51-17411

Laon Air Base tail numbers continued next page

Laon Air Base Assigned Aircraft, continued

USF/Brooks

66th Tactical Reconnaissance Wing, RF-101Cs, May 1958 - 30 August 1966

17th Tactical Reconnaissance Squadron - Blue band.
18th Tactical Reconnaissance Squadron - Red band.
32d Tactical Reconnaissance Squadron - Yellow band.
38th Tactical Reconnaissance Squadron - Green band.

RF-101C-35, -40, -45, -50, -55, -60, -65, -70, -75-MC

56-0055		56-0093		56-0113*	17th	56-0131		56-0210	
56-0057		56-0095		56-0114		56-0132	18th	56-0211	32d
56-0058		56-0096		56-0115		56-0133		56-0212	
56-0060	38th	56-0097		56-0116	17th	56-0134		56-0213*	32d
56-0062*	32d	56-0099	38th	56-0117		56-0135		56-0214	38th
56-0063	17th	56-0100*	18th	56-0118*	18th	56-0180		56-0215	
56-0069		56-0101		56-0119		56-0184		56-0216	17th
56-0070		56-0102		56-0120		56-0185		56-0217	
56-0072		56-0103*	18th	56-0121		56-0196		56-0218	
56-0073*	38th	56-0104		56-0122		56-0198		56-0219	
56-0074*	32d	56-0105		56-0123		56-0199		56-0220	32d
56-0076*	18th	56-0106		56-0124		56-0200*	38th	56-0221	32d
56-0077*	18th	56-0107		56-0125		56-0201		56-0223	
56-0078	18th	56-0108		56-0126		56-0202	17th	56-0224	
56-0082*	32d	56-0109		56-0127	32d	56-0205*	38th	56-0226	
56-0089	38th	56-0110	17th	56-0128		56-0206	32d	56-0229	
56-0090		56-0111*	18th	56-0129		56-0208*	32d	56-0231	
56-0091		56-0112		56-0130		56-0209*	32d		

* Losses:
56-0062 - Crashed, gear failure, 14nm SE of Nouasseur AB, Morocco, 28 FEB 59, no fatalities, ejected.
56-0073 - Crashed, weather/go-around, on Phalsbourg AB, France, 10 MAR 60, no fatalities, ejected.
56-0074 - Crashed, on take-off, on Phalsbourg AB, France, 13 APR 59, 1 fatality.
56-0076 - Crashed, collision on night take-off, on Toul AB, France, 22 MAY 60, 1 fatality.
56-0077 - Crashed, collision on night take-off, on Toul AB, France, 22 MAY 60, 1 fatality.
56-0082 - Crashed, GCA/weather, 13nm S of Phalsbourg AB, France, 22 SEP 60, no fatalities, ejected.
56-0100 - Crashed, hit mountain in weather, 2.2nm E-SE of Treminis, France, 25 APR 63, 1 fatality.
56-0103 - Crashed, mid-air/weather, 2nm NW of Reuilly, France, 29 APR 61, no fatalities, ejected.
56-0111 - Crashed, GCA/weather, 1.5nm E of Landouzy la Cour, France, 10 DEC 61, 1 fatality.
56-0113 - Crashed, cockpit fire, 18nm SE of Toul AB, France, 17 APR 64, no fatalities, ejected.
56-0118 - Crashed, mid-air/weather, 2nm NW of Reuilly, France, 29 APR 61, no fatalities, ejected.
56-0200 - Crashed, gyro failure/weather, 10nm N of Schladern, W. Germany, 14 MAY 64, no fatalities, ejected.
56-0205 - Crashed, cause unknown, at Douzillac (Dordogne), France, 8 FEB 62, 4 fatalities.
56-0208 - Crashed, pitch-up, 9nm SE of Reims, France, 4 NOV 59, no fatalities, ejected.
56-0209 - Crashed, landing/weather, on Phalsbourg AB, France, 22 JAN 58, no fatalities.
56-0213 - Crashed, control loss, on Torrejon AB, Spain, 23 DEC 58, no fatalities.

66th Operations Squadron: Wing Support Aircraft

C-47B: 44-77228
C-47D: 43-48959, 44-76656
L-20A: 51-16529
T-33A: 53-5060, 53-5211, 53-5282, 53-5825, 53-5829, 53-5831, 53-5839, 51-6905
T-39A: 62-4476

Atlantic Air Rescue Center Europe (AARCE), 1960: **SH-19B-SI:** 52-7507, 52-7509

Atlantic Air Rescue Center Europe (AARCE), 1966: **HH-43B-KA:** 2ea 62-4532, 62-4538

ACKNOWLEDGEMENTS

I would like to thank the following people who contributed to this chapter:

John Bissel was an Intelligence Officer in the 822d LBSq, 38th LBWg. He served at Laon Air Base 1956-58.

Jerry Black was at Laon in the 38th Bomb Wing, 822d Bomb Squadron engine shop from 1955-59.

Nancy Brooks is the widow of Captian Wesley J. Brooks, a pilot in the 18th TRSq, 66th TRWg stationed at Laon AB, France, in 1962.

Al Christensen was a Weather Officer in Detachment 10, 31st Weather Squadron, MATS, stationed at Chambley AB, 1955-1957. Al has provided excellent aircraft photos and information.

Paul Douglas was an aircraft crew chief in the 108th LBSq, 126th LBWg. He opened up Bordeaux AB in 1951 and Laon AB in 1952.

Ray DuCasse was an airborne radar repairman in the 108th LBSq, 126th LBWg. He opened up Bordeaux AB in 1951 and Laon AB in 1952.

Paul L. Garrett arrived at Bordeaux in late December 1951. He was in the 7480th Supply Squadron Exchange Service Headquarters which officially opened there in January 1952. Its mission was to set up and operate the Air Force Base Exchanges in France, North Africa & Italy. He returned to the states in March 1954.

Dale Peotter was a crew chief on #44-35215, one of the airplanes that made the unscheduled stop on the island of Tiree. Dale opened up Bordeaux in 1951 and opened up Laon AB in 1952.

George Spencer was an avionics technician in the 108th LBSq, 126th LBWg. He opened up Bordeaux AB in 1951 and Laon AB in 1952.

Monument commemorating the service of U.S. Air Force personnel at Laon Air Base, dedicated November 2002.
The inscription reads: In memory of our American friends of the NATO base of Laon-Crepy-Couvron from 1952 to 1967.
Jerry McAuliffe

14

PARIS - USAF OPERATIONS

This chapter provides an overview of USAF activities in the Paris region over the years 1950-67. The North Atlantic Treaty Organization became synonymous with Paris, the "City of Light," from 1949 until its rapid departure for Belgium in 1967. Most NATO political and military activity was centered in the Paris area after its establishment in 1949. The French spelling of NATO, "OTAN," became the common name because of the numerous meetings and functions conducted in Paris. UN meetings as well as NATO ministerial and defense planning committee conferences were held here. A special temporary building, Palais de Chaillot, was constructed as the temporary home of NATO HQ. It was located in the Jardins du Trocadero facing the Eiffel Tower and opened 16 April 1952. NATO's permanent headquarters building in Paris, on Porte Dauphine, was completed 15 December 1959.

Establishment of NATOs headquarters in Paris presented the United States with an interesting situation to resolve. Since August 1945 all U.S. military forces and command facilities had been based in West Germany, but NATO meetings could not be held there since West Germany was not a member of NATO. Most of Western Europe was determined not to allow West Germany into NATO for the next one hundred years! The U.S. had to decide if it should move the Air Force and Army European theater command facilities and personnel into France, or just create a duplicate level of command in France's NATO offices. The solution was EUCOM, USAFE, and USAREUR sent duplicate command staff representatives to NATO headquarters in the Paris region. Interestingly, EUCOM HQ, HQ USAFE and HQ USAREUR never relocated to the Paris area as planned, but preferred to be forward based, and "rough it" in West Germany; i.e., Frankfurt, Wiesbaden, and Heidelburg.

Temporary Headquarters of NATO,
Palais de Chaillot in Jardins du Trocadero, Paris 1952.
NATO Photos

USAFE Headquarters did not move into its selected air base at Melun-Villaroche between Fontainebleau and Paris. Melun airfield was a substantial airdrome used during WWII by Ninth Air Force bomber and transport groups, designated as ALG A-55. Headquarters buildings were designed but not constructed at the Melun-Villaroche airfield. The proposed large MATS air terminal was scaled down and located on Orly-Paris Airfield instead. Melun-Villaroche airfield was expanded with NATO funds and used by the French Air Force. The major USAFE hospital proposed for Melun-Villaroche was constructed near the city of Evreux and supported by Evreux Air Base. As Evreux was nearing completion in 1955, USAFE proposed that it become the major air terminal for Paris. This air base could support VIP travel to Paris and accommodate all personnel being moved to and from France. Bus and train service from Evreux could provide rapid travel to Paris center, only sixty-one miles away. Evreux AB had adequate aircraft parking space and security, but would have to expand its aircraft maintenance and ramp services for VIP transports. But, the VIPs preferred Paris and demanded the Paris-Orly airport terminal operations be maintained for their convenience.

As the United States became very committed to building military facilities across France, Paris gradually became the administration center for Air Force and Army activities. Paris has been a great magnet for armies over the past two hundred or more years due to being the capital of France, with its strategic road and rail center, and comfortable living conditions and lifestyle. Paris is very similar to a black hole in space because it can absorb an infinite amount of military personnel. In WWII both German and American military leaders cautioned commanders to avoid Paris, but with poor results. By November 1944 there were over 200,000 U.S. Army troops in the Paris area! General Eisenhower and SHAEF Head-

Table 14.1 DOD, U.S. Air Force, U.S. Army, U.S. Navy in Paris and Environs, 1952-1965
AFEES Center; Air Forces European Exchange Service, 32 rue Marbeuf, Paris
AAFIC, Allied Armed Forces Information Center, 127 Champs Elysees, Paris
U.S. Military Attaches; Air, Army, and Naval, 4 avenue Gabriel, Paris
USAFE Paris Office, Liaison Representative, 51 boulevard de Latour-Maubourg, Paris
USAFE, United States Air Forces in Europe, Paris Office; 22 rue de la Tremoille, Paris
USAFE Main Post Office in France, APO 230, 41 rue d'Alleray, Paris
USAFE - OSI, Office of Special Investigation, 9 rue Weber, Paris
USAFE - PAPC, Paris Air Passenger Center, Hotel Littre, 9 rue Littre, Paris
USAFE - PCS-TDY Billets, Hotel Powers, 32 rue Francois 1er, Paris
USAFE - VIP Quarters, Hotel Pierre Premier des Serbes, 29 rue Marbeuf, Paris
AGARD, Advisory Group, Aeronautical Research and Development, Palais de Chaillot, Paris
CAA, Civil Aeronautics Administration, Hotel Perey, 5 cite du Retiro, Paris
GAO, General Accounting Office, 41 Faubourg St. Honore, Paris
MAAG, Military Assistance Advisory Group, 58 bis rue de la Boetie, Paris
MWDP, Mutual Weapons Development Program, Hotel Talleyrand, 2 rue St. Florentin, Paris
NSRE/NSLO, U.S. Navy Shipbuilding Liaison Office, 58 bis rue de la Boetie, Paris
OPC/P, Ordnance Procurement Center, Paris Office, 58 bis rue de la Boetie, Paris
PAPO, Paris Air Procurement Office, Hotel Perey, 5 cite du Retiro, Paris
U.S. Representative to OECE, 2 avenue Gabriel, Paris
U.S. Representative to NATO, 4 avenue Gabriel, Paris
USRO, U.S. Mission to NATO & European Regional Organization, Hotel Talleyrand, 2 rue St. Florentin, Paris
EMCCC, European Military Communications Coordination Committee, 51 blvd de Latour-Maubourg, Paris
FAFLO, Franco-American Liaison Office, 51 boulevard de Latour-Maubourg, Paris
JCA, Joint Construction Agency, later changed to USACAF, Boulogne-Billancourt (Seine)
USACAF, U.S. Army Construction Agency, France, Boulogne-Billancourt (Seine)
MATS Terminal, Military Air Transport Service, Orly Field, Orly
NATO, North Atlantic Treaty Organization Planning Group, Palais de Chaillot, Paris
NATO HEADQUARTERS, Porte Dauphine, Paris
NATO-DC, NATO Defense College, 21 Place Joffre, Paris
SHAPE, Supreme Headquarters Allied Power Europe, Rocquencourt
U.S. EUCOM, European Command Representative, Camp des Loges, St. Germain-en-Laye
USAREUR. U.S. Army Europe - Representative, Camp des Loges, St. Germain-en-Laye
USAREUR. Communications Center, 72 avenue Marceau, Paris
USAREUR. Finance and Accounting, 32 rue Marbeuf, Paris
USAREUR. Overseas Audit Agency, 32 rue Marbeuf, Paris
USAREUR. Seine Area Command, 2 rue de la Faisanderie, Paris
USAREUR. Communications Zone Paris Representative, 32 rue Marbeuf, Paris
USAREUR. American Hospital, 63 Blvd Victor Hugo, Neuilly
USAREUR. Outpatient and Clinics, 32 rue Marbeuf, Paris
USAREUR. VIP Billet, Hotel de Paris, 8 boulevard de la Madeleine, Paris

Permanent NATO Headquarters building on Porte Dauphine, Paris, completed in 1959.
On the left is main entrance and on the right is an aerial view (huge building in the lower foreground, arrow).
Today this building is University of Paris building IX.
NATO Photos

quarters had moved to Versailles, just outside Paris, in October 1944. A favorite joke among Ninth Army Air Force veterans during the Battle of the Bulge in late December 1944 was, "When we hear that IKE and SHAEF are pulling out of the Palace of Versailles, its time for us to scurry back to England!"

In a similar fashion, eight years later, NATO, DOD, EUCOM, USAFE, and USAREUR established many offices and agencies in and around Paris. Some of the offices in the Paris region from 1953 through 1965 that absorbed USAF assignments can be found in Table 14.1.

USAFE Postal System

This section briefly describes the second most important USAF function in France; only the 7480th Supply Squadron (Base Exchange) was more important! USAFE realized that an additional Air Postal Squadron and Mail Distribution Center would be required to provide postal service to the large number of USAF personnel and dependents scheduled to live in France. Initially the 2d Air Postal Squadron based in Wiesbaden, Germany, expanded rapidly to support the needs of the air bases being constructed in France. The first five interim bases received one officer and three or four airmen to establish a small Air Post Office (APO) in very primitive facilities. The 2d APO Squadron assigned letter designators to these detachments. Bordeaux had Flt"M," Chateauroux Flt "K," Chaumont Flt"Q," Laon Flt"P," and Toul had Flt "O." In summer 1952 these were changed to numbers. Chateauroux's APO 10 post office was run by Flt "K" 2d APO Sq. It was changed to Det #10, 2d APO Sq and finally to Det #3, 12th APO Sq. All outgoing and incoming mail for the bases in France went through Frankfurt, West Germany. During 1951, surface letters took from 25 to 40 days from the CONUS sender to our air bases in France.

A major reorganization occurred on 8 July 1953 when the 12th Air Postal Squadron was activated in Paris with six APOs, and 11 officers and 85 airmen from 2d Air Postal Sq personnel in France. Squadron Headquarters and a Mail Distribution Center, APO 230 were established in Paris at 8 avenue Kleber near the Arc de Triomphe. In 1955, to handle the increasing volume of mail and reduce expenses, a larger two story facility with 18,000 square feet was acquired and remodeled at 41 Rue d'Alleray near Gare Montparnasse. All mail arriving by train and aircraft destined for a USAFE facility in France was processed through APO 230.

On 31 December 1954 the 12th APO Sq had 16 officers and 178 airmen performing postal duties at nine APOs across France. By 1955 a typical air base APO would handle 5,100 pounds of airmail, 2,400 pounds of first class mail, 4,200 pounds of official mail, issue 2,100 money orders worth $78,000, and sell $4,200 worth of postage stamps every three months. These often forgotten small postal detachments were crucial in maintaining base morale with reliable mail services.

The 12th Air Postal Sq continued serving France until 1962 when it was reorganized into the 7025th Air Postal Group with four digit detachments, for example, Det #2100 manned APO 09010 at the CHAD AD.

Customer Liaison Section workload increased

as French Customs officials at Paris-Orly Air Mail Terminal began stopping more international mail parcels for levies. This resulted in a growing number of packages being returned to sender.

Much erroneous FRELOC information and directives were received by the 7025th Gp about APO phase-out dates, support responsibilities, and postal personnel assignments. This created an additional workload throughout the postal system, but morale remained high during this phase-out confusion. These postmen were among the last USAF officers and airmen to depart France in late March 1967.

Orly Air Base, MATS Terminal
Orly, France, April 1955.

Above:
Passenger counter
at Orly terminal.

Left:
USAF personnel in snack bar
at Orly terminal.

Below:
Civilian and military personnel
waiting room in air terminal
at Orly AB.
Note small BX counter
in background.

National Archives

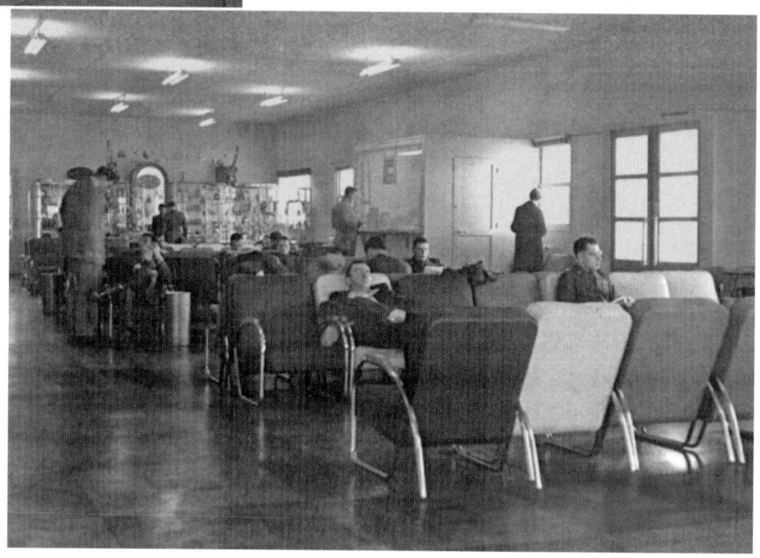

Paris-Orly Air Base

Aeroport de Paris-Orly (48° 44'N - 02° 23'E, elevation 295 feet) is nine miles (15 km) south of Paris off Autoroute A6/A10, with a highway exit directly into the terminal. It is in the Essonne Department and can be found on Michelin Map #312 Local.

Post WWII international diplomatic and military travel was changing from ship and rail to air transportation, requiring a special air terminal operation in the Paris area for NATO meetings. Le Bourget Airport, on the north edge of Paris close to the

Aeroport de Paris-Orly from the air, Orly AB facility in foreground, approximately 1955. Note the Quonset hut barracks assembled in an "x" shape with the latrine in the center.
USAF via Robert G. Evans

city center, was used by VIP transport aircraft during Western Union and preliminary NATO meetings. It had been damaged during the war but was repaired in August 1944. The USAAF Air Transport Command operated an air transport base here known as A-54. Le Bourget was used by the USAAF until May 1946 when commerical air travel resumed, and Air France reestablished its major overhaul facilities on the field. The airport was small and, as domestic air traffic rapidly increased, ramp space became very limited.

Aeroport de Paris-Orly was a newer and larger international air terminal, convenient to meet the needs of NATO political and military leaders going into Paris, or traveling southeast to Fontainebleau, or west to Camp des Loges and Rocquencourt. The airport, orignally known as the Villeneuve-Orly Airport, was located in the southern surburbs of Paris. It opened in 1932 as a secondary airport to Le Bourget. It was used throughout WWII and had been heavily bombed. Runways, buildings, and two large airship hangars were destroyed. The airfield was repaired in July-August 1944, and used by the USAAF Ninth Air Force as tactical airfield A-47. The 50th Fighter Group operated there during September 1944, and later, liaison squadrons used the airfield until October 1945. The primary operator at Orly from September 1944 through March 1947 was the 1408th Army Air Force Base Unit. The airport was returned to the French Government on 7 November 1947, and was reactivated as a commerical airport on 1 January 1948.

The first NATO tenant at Aeroport Orly-Paris was the USAF Military Air Transport Service, 1630th Air Base Squadron, activated in June 1950. Agreement was reached 10 November 1950 on a new lease to allow for the use of a small portion, namely seventy-five acres on the east edge of the airfield, primarily for aircraft parking. Also located on this parcel were five usable Quonset huts. On 1 April 1951 the Air Base Squadron was expanded to fifty-seven officers and airmen to support the air transport needs of SHAPE, which was activated on the same day. Another important mission developing at Orly Air Base was providing aircraft and facilities to maintain the flying proficiency of USAF pilots assigned to the Paris region. On 10 October 1951 Orly AB was expanded to 350 acres and personnel were increased; the 1630th AB Squadron was upgraded to the 1606th AB Group. The 7470th Headquarters Support Squadron, APO 55, was activated in April 1951 to operate the HQ USAFE Paris Office, and was attached to the 1606th ABGp.

On 1 July 1952, HQ USAFE assumed command of Orly Air Base because the majority of its work was in support of USAFE missions. A small detachment from MATS remained as a tenant unit to manage passenger traffic. The 1606th ABGp was redesignated the 7415th ABGp at Orly AB in July 1952. Orly Air Base's mailing address was APO 58.

Once again, HQ USAF insisted that no new construction should be considered, but this was impossible. Paris-Orly required major construction as offices and agencies expanded in and around Paris. A few buildings, hangar space, and air terminal space were obtained on short-term leases. The 1950 lease was expanded in 1953 to provide additional property for a headquarters building, officers club, NCO club, airmen's service club, personnel office, a new passenger terminal, billeting for 450 troops, a 500-man mess hall, motor vehicle shop, aircraft parking apron for fifteen assigned aircraft, and an expanded dispensary with twenty-five hospital beds. The personnel living at Orly were housed in the old Quonset huts that were divided into rooms and arranged in an "x" shape with a central latrine facility. After a new BOQ was built these huts were used for airmen only.

Construction proceeded rapidly using local contractors and 821st EABn troops. The thirty 821st men had a list of fourteen projects. Among these were repairing the aircraft parking area, the concrete sidewalks, and vehicle parking lots, and moving the Quonset huts. The projects at Orly were considered excellent training for the new 821st troops prior to starting work at Dreux AB. In 1954 the 843d EABn arrived to continue improving the Orly equipment storage yards, recreational areas, roads, and aircraft parking ramps. In late 1955 a 43,000 square yard aircraft parking apron was added next to taxiway #6. This work was performed by the 862d EABn.

During 1954-55 French contractors completed the largest USAF air terminal in France, a new AFEX snack bar, a large service club, group headquarters building, fire station, Air Police center, officers open mess, BOQ, VIP billets, and an excellent vehicle repair shop. They built an 18,500 square-foot equipment storage warehouse and covered 554,500 square feet of outdoor storage space. Most buildings were single story concrete masonry construction; a few portable prefab buildings were erected to save construction time and funds. In 1955 seven permanent buildings programmed for construction were eliminated by USAFE budget cuts. There were limited provisions for aircraft POL storage, but motor fuel storage was installed; all fuel was purchased from the ESSO airport fueling contractor. The capital value of facilities at Orly AB was $1,125,000.

A large 136 unit off-base GRI housing complex of single and duplex houses for 232 Orly AB families was built five miles south of the base at Grigny, west of highway N7. Building began on 20 February 1955 and they were ready for occupancy in October 1956. This project ended some long commutes throughout the Paris area.

During the years 1954 to 1957 the 7415th AB Group's mission, personnel, and facilities expanded both at Orly and in Paris as air transportation replaced the troopship as the common carrier for USAF personnel as described in chapter 2. The 7113th Personnel Processing Squadron operated the Paris Air Passenger Center (PAPC) in Paris, APO 230, with a staff of two officers, twenty-six airmen, one DAF civilian, and nineteen LWR French employees. On 25 July 1957 its designation was changed to Headquarters, 7415th Air Base Group with the same mission. PAPC processed 15,300 inbound and 21,100 outbound personnel during the last six months of 1957. Outbound Air Force troops were given a three hour time block to report to PAPC, then moved by bus to Orly AB for their flight back to CONUS. The average processing time for inbound troops assigned to France was three hours; this time was measured from aircraft off-loading at Orly to bus off-loading at a Paris train station for their trip to their new assignments in France. A small number of incoming personnel bound for duty in the Middle East or Africa remained at the Hotel Littre awaiting scheduled commerical flights direct to these destinations. Direct flights were necessary because of concerns for the safety of military personnel traveling in these regions during the 1950s. Additional PCS-TDY billets were available at the Hotel Victoria Palace which adjoined the Hotel Littre. The U.S. Army 524th Replacement Company also operated at the PAPC to process Army personnel arriving and departing France.

The 7415th ABGp at Orly had 60 officers, 450 airmen and 30 Department of Air Force civilians assigned, plus 345 LWR French national employees. By 1955 there were forty units attached to the 7415th ABGp for administrative and logistical support around France. The 7415th operated fifteen C-47As, one C-54G, one C-121A, and one C-131B aircraft based at Orly for VIP transportation within Europe (Special Air Support), and for proficiency flying. This allowed 158 pilots, 14 navigators, and 3 flight surgeons assigned to non-flying assignments throughout the Paris region to meet their annual AFR 60-2 requirements. Jet qualified

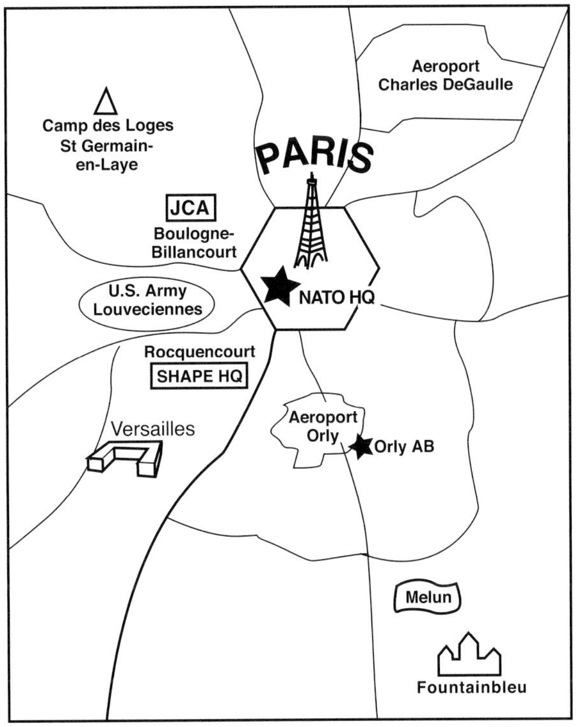

Map 14.1 NATO locations around Paris

pilots maintained their proficiency in T-33A aircraft at Evreux AB. Three flight simulators (Link trainers) were operated as part of an excellent instrument flying training program conducted by the 7415th ABGp, Operations Section.

Several special airlift operations were conducted from USAFE Orly AB, and some received very little international publicity. The first night operation was an airlift of 500 French Paratroop-Commandos and their equipment from Paris to Saigon as requested by France. Six TAC C-124s from the 62d TCWg, Larson AFB, Washington, flew the paratroopers from Paris to Saigon's Tourane Airfield (Da-Nang) Indochina. This was the longest troop movement in history. It required five days in March 1954 to fly 8,500 miles to Saigon. The troopers wore civilian clothes and departed Orly AB at 0310 hours in the morning. These men were then moved into Dien Bien Phu to reinforce the battlefield. The C-124s continued across the Pacific to their home base, making the airlift an around-the-world flight.

A second airlift, "Operation Wounded Warrior," made the longest medical evacuation flight when the first C-118Bs from Westover AFB, Massachusetts, landed at Orly on 3 July 1954. The aircraft was returning forty-seven wounded French soldiers from Saigon. These veterans had fought in the famous battle of Dien Bien Phu. After boarding the wounded in Saigon, the C-118 flew eastward to Japan, Hawaii, California, Massachusetts, across the Atlantic to the Azores, and on to Paris. Over the next two weeks a total of 500 seriously wounded men were returned by USAF-MATS. French Army nurse Genevieve de Gallard-Terraube, the "Angel of Dien Bien Phu" was among the ranking dignitaries and honor guards assembled to welcome home the last of these men on 18 July. The French Army and government officials were deeply appreciative of the airlift effort supplied by America.

From 1953 through 1958, USAFE operated "Kinderlift" flights during the months of July and August. This program flew about 2,000 underprivileged German children each year from Berlin to West Germany for a month's vacation in German and American homes. The 7415th ABGp supplied aircraft and crews for 100 of these missions in 1957, flying 160 hours between Berlin and Rhein-Main or Hanover.

Contract aircraft maintenance was performed by two companies at Paris-Orly. Air France and TAI-Transports Aerians Intercontinentaux supported transient VIP aircraft and provided periodic inspections on 7415th aircraft. This contract maintenance reduced USAF manning needs at Orly AB. The 7415th Food Service section was always busy, preparing 4,600 in-flight meals per month for passengers on outbound military flights as well as operating the base mess hall for unit and transient personnel.

The primary mission of the 7415th ABGp was meeting and greeting VIPs visiting the Paris region; VIPs were later defined as distinguished visitors (DV). DVs included President Eisenhower, the Secretaries of State and Defense, and an army of curious visitors to attend international meetings and see what was going on in NATO-Paris. From 1955 through 1959 approximately 800 DV per month passed through Orly AB; some summer months over 200 Congressmen would stop in Paris. A summit meeting in Europe could draw 1,100 to 1,350 DV guests. The 7415th protocol officers would have to provide aircraft parking, transportation and drivers, luncheons, photographers, press rooms, secure telephone communications, and security police. There are no reports of any Congressman requesting a driver and staff car to visit a main USAFE air base in France. At four summit meetings, arrangements were made with Orly Airport management to close an active runway and use it for DV aircraft parking. Space at Orly was becoming critical in the late 1950s.

Flight operations were greatly reduced from 10 November through 31 December 1955 by a French control tower operators and approach radar controllers strike, plus bad weather. Flying was relocated to Dreux and Evreux to meet minimum requirements. The 7415th ABGp was informed in November 1955 by Aeroport d'Orly officials that most of the USAFE facilities would have to be abandoned at the end of 1957 to allow for planned airport expansion. USAFE and the French Government could make no agreement for a replacement airfield near Paris. Evreux AB was considered as a replacement for the Orly operations but no decision occurred. Orly International Airport was reworked several times during the late 1950s and 1960s, but the Orly Air Base operation continued until March 1967.

Clearances for diplomatic flights were processed through Chateauroux AD prior to 1 July 1957. After that date Orly AB was designated as a foreign clearance base, thereby reducing request time for diplomatic clearances into the Middle East and Africa.

Also during the 1950s and 1960s, there were six-tenant units attached and operating at Orly AB. These were:

Det #22, 12th Air Postal Squadron
1622d Support Sq, Atlantic Division, (MATS)
Det #48, 18th Weather Squadron (MATS)
1990th Airways and Air Communications Squadron (MATS)
Det #2, 7370th Flight Service Sq (MATS)
Armed Forces Courier Service.

On 25 September 1957, the 7415th Air Base Group was redesignated the 7415th Support Group at Orly AB with no changes in mission. Personnel strength was increased a small amount to a total of 703 officers, airmen, DAF civilians and French workers. Its seven squadrons were reduced to four. These units were Headquarters, 7415th Support Group; 7415th Support Squadron; 7415th Material Squadron; and 7415th USAF Dispensary.

On 1 January 1958 the 7415th Support Gp was ordered to support two remote sites. Det #1, 7415th would support the Bacalan depot, in the suburbs of Bordeaux, and Det #2, 7415th would support Aeroport de Marseille-Marignane on the Mediterranean Sea. This additional tasking was required because Bordeaux AB, which had been responsible for these facilities, was closing over the next nine months.

On 28 February 1958, the official name of Orly Air Base was changed to Orly Airport and the Paris USAFE Office was changed to Paris Administration Office (USAFE). Some local government officials had objected to the USAFE names.

Fontainebleau

The city of Fontainebleau (48° 24'N - 02° 43'E) is located twenty eight miles (15 km) southeast of Paris, west of the Seine River. It is in the center of seven highways and is easily accessible from Paris by Autoroute A6, the "Autoroute du Soleil." Highway N37 leads directly into the city and to the chateau. Fontainebleau can be found on Michelin map #312 Local. The city is close to Paris but light years away in atmosphere. It is located in the "Foret de Fontainebleau" that has been maintained as a protected forest since 1669. The city developed around the Palace de Fontainebleau of Francis I, and the French cavalry base located there in the 1800s.

The Western Union held its early meetings in Paris and the first home of the Western Union military command structure was at Chateau de Fontainebleau. The U.S. Army 7966th EUCOM HQ Detachment was based there with the 504th Base Dispensary Company. Det #1, 7961st HQ Group, U.S. Army Europe (USAREUR), and the 8478th Administrative Area Unit, Det #1, Allied Land Forces, Central Europe were also at Fontainebleau until they moved to SHAPE HQ at Roquencourt. In 1954 EUCOM HQ was relocated to new buildings at Camp des Loges, St. Germain-en-Laye.

In 1952 a Com Z Medical Depot was organized, as well as a twenty-five bed Army Hospital to support the numerous Army personnel moving into the area around Fontainebleau. Later the 307th Field Hospital established a large 400-bed facility outside the city. The Army Petroleum Distribution Command was established to control the POL pipeline and terminal operation that was being installed across northern France.

The final activity at Fontainebleau in 1967 was formation of the Allied Forces Central Europe Termination Group, Provisional, to control the orderly withdrawal of supplies and material to properly support NATO land forces in the event the Warsaw Pact attacked Western Europe during the critical period of NATO's movement out of France.

USAFE's presence at Fontainebleau was the 7495th Headquarters Support Squadron that was stationed there from September 1951 through December 1959, and Det #13, 12th Air Postal Sq operating APO 11. Fontainebleau was the home of HQ 4th Allied Tactical Air Force for a short period in 1952-54 until it moved to Trier, Germany. To support HQ AAFCE, USAFE organized Det #2, 1141st Special Activities Squadron at Camp Guyenmer in 1954. Camp Guyenmer, just outside Fontainebleau in the city of Avon, was home to the 7th Radio Relay Squadron repair shops and three hundred USAFE personnel, as well as British, Canadian, Dutch, French, and German military. No air base was associated with Fontainebleau, though a helicopter pad was constructed near the NATO hospital.

All these U.S. and NATO military activities were closed and moved into West Germany as required by Project FRELOC during 1966-67. The U.S. Army departed the area by August 1967.

Disengagement and Departure

USAFE reduced its Paris real estate over several years. In November 1961, the lease on Hotel Powers, 52 rue Francois, off rue Champs Elysees, was terminated after seven years, and the owners returned it to commercial hotel operation. The Paris OSI Office was closed in June 1964.

On 20 June 1966 in Project FRELOC, the USAFE Paris Office on 22 rue de la Tremoille was closed upon expiration of its lease and returned to the French. All functions and personnel of the forward office were moved into the USAREUR office building on 32 rue Marbeuf. Hotel Littre, listed as housing annex #7044, was closed in January 1967 and returned in March.

During 1966-67 all these U.S. agencies were quickly closed and moved to the area around Mons, Belgium, as required by FRELOC. NATO political headquarters was relocated to downtown Brussels, Belgium. SHAPE HQ and NATO military command agencies were established at Camp Casteau, Belgium, about five miles north of Mons. The Distinguished Visitor air terminal was established at Chievres AB, Belgium, ten miles northwest of Mons. These NATO facilities are currently active. The last two USAFE activities in France, except for the Suippes Range; were the Orly Airport, property #2682, and the Paris Administration Office, #3909. Both were closed returned to Military Liquidation Section in June 1967.

Dedication of new SHAPE HQ at Camp Casteau, Belgium, 31 March 1967.
NATO Photos

Orly-Paris Air Base Assigned Aircraft

1630th Air Base Squadron, 7415th Air Base Group, 7415th Support Group, 1951 - 1967

15 ea C-47s:

VC-47A	VC-47D	C-47A	C-47D	C-54G
43-48005	43-49338	42-23336	43-16163	45-553
	45-943	42-23934	43-16250	45-555
	45-1106	42-24199	43-48809	
		43-15661	43-49328	**VC-54G**
			43-49338	45-516
			43-49375	
			43-49493	
			44-77235	

C-117B	VC-131D	C-121A	L-20A
45-2549^	54-2822	48-614	51-16128

^This may be the last USAF aircraft in France, departing 31 May 1967.

Detachment #2, 7333d Material Squadron
T-39A: 62-4460
VC-118A: 53-3303

ACKNOWLEDGEMENTS

I would like to thank the following people who contributed to this chapter:

Robert G. Evans was stationed at Orly Field, Paris, as a Base Ops dispatcher, from February 1955 until 15 November 1957.

Terry Karselis was with the 7th Radio Relay Squadron at Bordeaux in1956 and was then transferred to the 1241st SPACTRON at Fontainebleau.

Bob Strobel was assigned to the 7415th Air Base Group at Orly Airport and then the Paris Air Passenger Center in Hotel Littre between 1956 and 1960. He has contributed a great deal of information on Orly AB and the PAPC operation in Paris.

15

PHALSBOURG AIR BASE

Phalsbourg is located in the Moselle Department, on the eastern edge of the Lorraine Plateau near the Saverne Gap in the Vosges Mountains. This area, like most of France, marks its history in thousands of years. It has seen barbarian invaders, Celtic conquerers, Roman colonizers, and was part of the land given to Lothair I, one of Charlemagne's grandsons, in 854. It was called Lotharingia, which has evolved to the regional name Lorraine.

For about 50 years out of the last 130, Alsace and Lorraine have been under German control. As a result, to the outsider they seem to have a split personality with city names, architecture, and regional specialties that mix both German and French features.

Phalsbourg Air Base (48° 47'N - 07° 13'E, elevation 1,016 feet) was the most eastern of all the U.S. air bases in France. It was 260 miles (420 km) east of Paris and 29 miles (46 km) northwest of Strasbourg. Phalsbourg was the last air base completed in France. It was not completed until late 1956! It was also the smallest air base in France.

In the 1950 air base selection meetings, the FAF and USAF concurred that a base should be built in the Phalsbourg area. During site inspection the USAFE decided the prospective base should become a fighter base due to its eastern location near the Rhine River. There were no airfields in this area to create air traffic conflicts. The final site selected was close to the village of Bourscheid about one mile (2 km) west of the city of Phalsbourg, adjacent to National Route N4. The chosen airfield site was gently rolling farmland and was available immediately for construction. This site had very good road access and water sources. Four site problems were noted: highway N4 was too close to the base, the runway would be very close to the villages of Bourscheid and St. Jean-Kourtzerode, there would be operational limitations imposed by winter weather, and the area had only limited commercial electrical service. Also, there was no railroad nearby so it would be necessary to build a railroad spur of approximately eight miles from a large freight yard on the east side of Sarrebourg city.

Initially the base was known as Phalsbourg-Bourscheid Air Base, but later was shortened to Phalsbourg Air Base. USAF planned that a fighter wing would arrive in the summer of 1955. This schedule would allow Phalsbourg to be a single step base, constructed within two years with all permanent buildings, shops, and hangars completed before arrival of its first wing. In February 1952 the 7040th Air Base Squadron was activated at Phalsbourg to administer the base and control all USAF property during construction until a combat wing arrived. The 31st Air Weather Sq activated Det #18, and dispatched men and equipment to Phalsbourg on 15 October 1954. When the weather men realized that there would be no flying to support for two years, they closed up operations until June 1956. On 15 January 1955 the 12th Air Postal Squadron arrived, organized Det #12, and set up the new post office, APO 115. The post office used the building intended as the base guard house.

In preparation for base construction, highway N4 was moved a half mile to the south, around the village of St Jean Kourtzerode. The rerouting made it possible to keep the living and working areas on one east-west real estate parcel north of highway N4. During 1951-52, development was delayed when the USAF changed its plans about the type of combat wing to be assigned: light bomber, fighter-bomber, or tactical airlift? Change in aircraft type would require alteration of some buildings, ramp spaces, and would possibly require a fourth hangar. The decision was finally made to add the fourth hangar and configure the base to accommodate a fighter-type wing. Also during this period, USAFE considered halting construction at Toul AB and diverting funds to Phalsbourg construction. Instead, they decided to complete both bases.

By summer 1952 work began by grading and moving earth throughout the whole base. Preliminary grading for the runway uncovered a major obstacle—the large concrete foundation of a German bunker! The block of concrete had been the base of a WWII Luftwaffe Wasserman early-warning search radar system. This concrete mass had to be removed before building the runway. The challenge was to find a way to remove it without greatly increasing the cost of airfield grading. Dynamite proved to be the only method to finally eliminate this structure, but delayed the con-

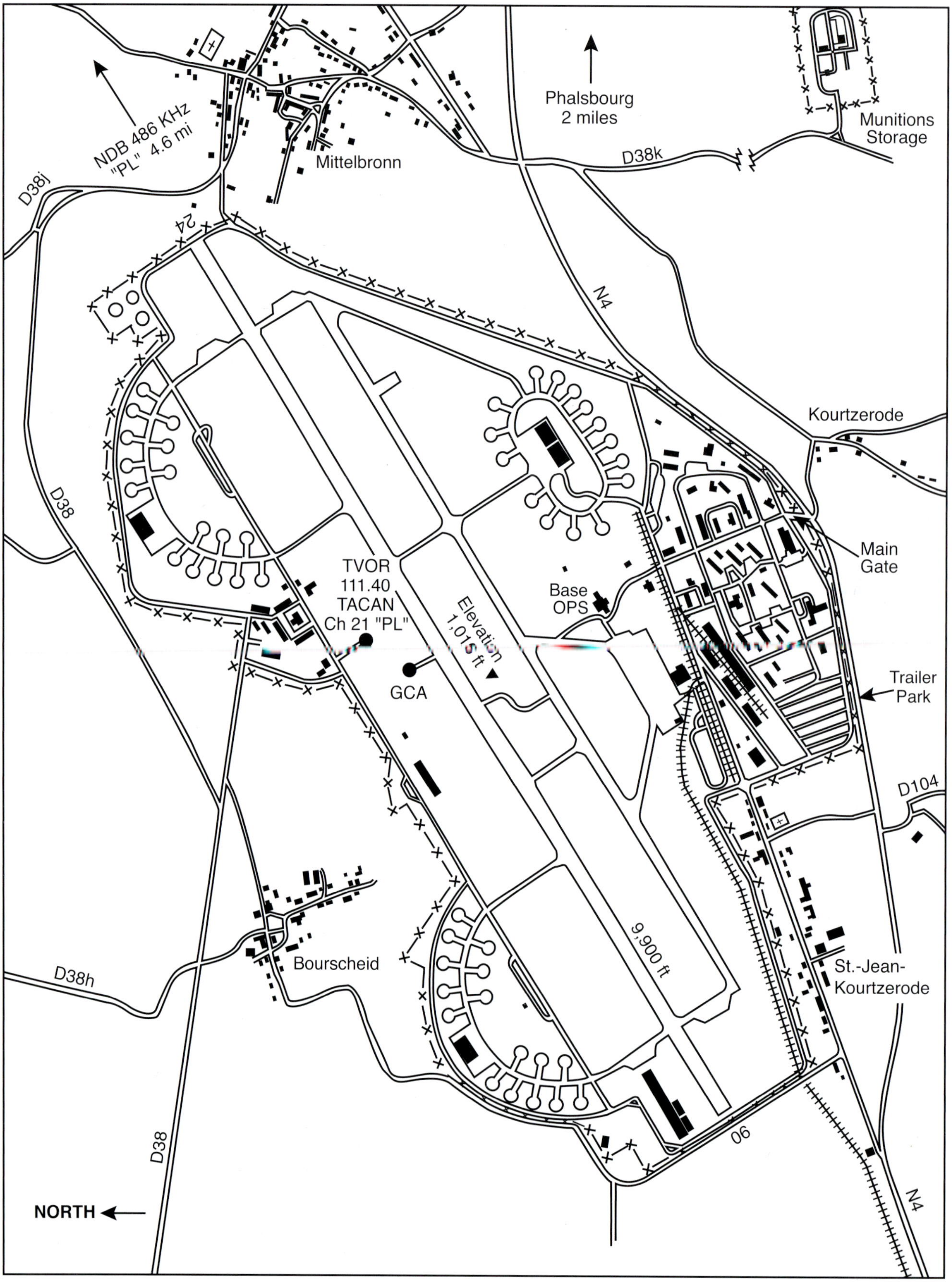

Map 15.1 Phalsbourg Air Base

Phalsbourg AB from air, approximately fall 1956.
Official USAF photo

struction schedule.

After dissatisfaction with runway construction at other bases in France, a new approach was used to build the runway at Phalsbourg. French contractors were supplied with highway concrete paving machines from the U.S. to produce a smooth, thick runway. Also, runway construction was scheduled during summer and fall 1953 to ensure higher quality by avoiding winter freezes. Even with all these precautions, problems soon developed with the runway paving job and several sections had to be replaced, further delaying this project. Two fighter-size hangars and taxiways were built on the north side of the runway and two on the southeast end of the runway close to the highway.

Good construction progress was made during 1954 when most permanent buildings were completed, including three hangars and base operations. The runway, taxiways, parking marguerites, and aprons were completed. Unfortunately by the spring of 1955 the base was still barely habitable because few roads were paved, and utilities were not yet installed. The dirt roads were mud tracks during the winter snows and thaws, and the base was a maze of wooden walkways that people had to follow or sink into the mud. Most AF property was still stored outdoors because base warehouses had not yet been accepted by the USAF.

Twelfth Air Force took possession of this base on 4 February 1955, though no combat wing or aircraft had yet been assigned. TAC advised USAFE that a fighter wing flying F-100Ds would be ready to move to France during 1956. Construction continued, and by the fall of 1955 after another good summer construction season, Phalsbourg AB was finally ready to receive its first combat wing. By this time though, 1955 DOD budget cuts forced the programmed tactical fighter wing to remain in CONUS.

As building progressed on base, consideration was given to the need for family housing since it was obvious that it would be very scarce in the neighboring small villages. A team from C Company 862nd Engineer Aviation Battalion was deployed TDY to Phalsbourg from Spangdahlem to build trailer sites on base. The engineers moved their heavy equipment,

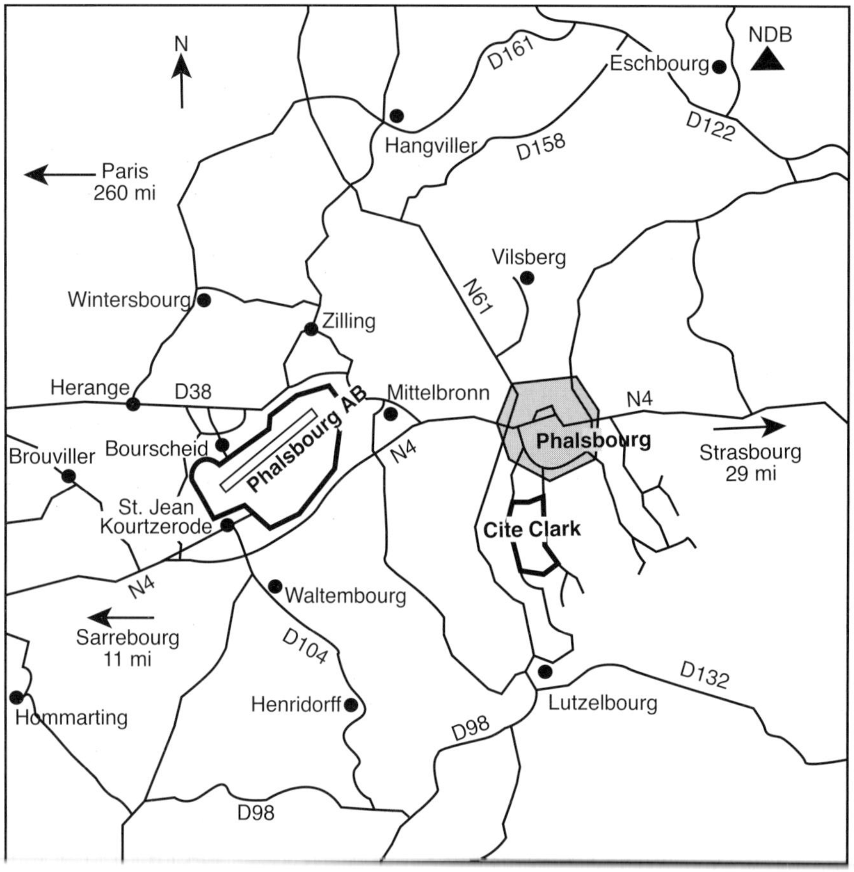

Map 15.2 Phalsbourg Area

crane, graders and bulldozer on the narrow, winding roads from West Germany, through Luxembourg, to Phalsbourg. Guiding such large loads through the little villages was an engineering feat in itself! They were joined at Phalsbourg by a team from the 843rd Engineer Aviation Battalion. Together they constructed eighty-five trailer sites, including all utilities on the southwestern edge of the base. While at Phalsbourg, during the winter of 1954-55, the engineers lived in the recently completed southeast aircraft hangar. The hangar was their mess hall, barracks and equipment storage shed. Warmth came from the little portable stoves used to cook their meals. It was very primitive duty compared to their comfortable base in West Germany where waitresses served mess-hall meals and housekeepers made their beds and cleaned their rooms!

Other housing in the area was built for the U.S. by French contractors as part of the Guaranteed Rental Income program. A small forty-unit tract known as Cite Clark, Phalsbourg Housing Annex #7953, was constructed 1.5 km south of Phalsbourg city, south of N4 towards Trois Maisons. An excellent golf course was built near Cite Clark providing recreation for military and dependents alike. Another large housing complex was constructed near the city of Sarrebourg, north of N4 adjoining the town of Grand Eich, 10 km west of the air base. This large Sarrebourg Housing Annex #7955 had 236 units and was constructed in 1956.

Cite Clark was closed and returned to the MLS Paris in November 1962, and the Sarrebourg housing annex soon followed in January 1963. This off-base housing was considered "excess to needs" after Project RED RICHARD caused departure of the fighter wings from France. These units are still in use today by French families.

By July 1957 Phalsbourg had reached its final configuration as a fighter base. It covered an area of 955 acres with five miles of paved roads. The main entrance was on the north side of N4 with a secondary entrance about 700 feet south of the village of Bourscheid. The northeast/southwest runway (060°/240°) was 9,900 feet long by 150 feet wide with overruns. Aircraft arresting barriers were installed in 1958. Concrete taxiways, parking ramps, aprons, etc. covered 150 acres. Phalsbourg had four NATO fighter-sized hangars each, that provided 12,500 square feet of clear aircraft workspace. Three marguerite net-

Airmen's barracks under construction (heating plant is dark building left foreground) Phalsbourg AB, February 1955. Construction underway, but roads not in yet!
National Archives

Duckboard sidewalks were vital in the winter of 1955. Heating plant is center rear. Base was virtually unoccupied at this time.
National Archives

Base Operations nearing completion amid the snow, Phalsbourg AB, February 1955.
National Archives

Temporary motor pool. Phalsbourg AB, February 1955.
National Archives

works adjacent to the hangars provided forty-eight fighter parking pads.

The base had fifty-two permanent buildings and twenty-one temporary buildings. The largest building was base operations, south of the runway; it housed flight operation offices, the weather station, fire station, and the control tower. A large, five-acre aircraft parking apron was located west of base operations. The two-story wing/base headquarters was located one block from the main gate. The base had 1.75 million cubic feet of storage space located in four warehouses with railroad sidings. Ten two-story airmen dormitories had a capacity of 126 men each and two BOQ buildings could house 70 officers each. One single story dining hall was configured for 1,000 men, another for 500, and the hospital mess could feed 200 men. This includes a squadron living area with mess hall and barracks that was constructed adjacent to the northeast hangar. The twenty-five bed hospital was located on the south edge of the base, close to the old N4 route which had become part of the base road network. A grammar school for dependents in grades one through eight was constructed on base; there was no high school. All buildings were constructed of concrete block with a white stucco finish. Roofs were sheet aluminum and were insulated for the colder climate.

Underground storage tanks held 215,100 gallons of water. Two heating plants provided underground central heating to all buildings, plus emergency electrical power generators. The base electrical system was totally underground with a service capacity of 900 kilowatts. On-base underground fuel storage held 810,500 gallons of jet aircraft fuel and 35,000 gallons of AVGAS. There was also underground storage for vehicle fuels: 20,200 gallons of MOGAS and 200,000 gallons of DIESEL. During 1960 the Army pipeline system extension connected into this fuel storage field.

Mittelbronn Ammunition Storage Annex #9899 was constructed in the Bois de Mittelbronn, 3 kms southeast of the base. This munitions storage facility, consisting of sixteen igloos on fifty-two acres, was in the woods south of highway N4 off D38 on the east side of the road. It was closed and returned to MLS Paris in March 1967.

Another supply storage building, Annex #7159, was leased in Saverne city. It was returned to MLS in September 1961 as space developed in on-base warehouses, and as SEAWEED emergency supplies were relocated and reduced.

As of May 1957, estimated value of real estate (excluding land value) was $13.9 million. Equipment in use was valued at approximately $3.5 million. Total Base Supply inventory was $1.7 million.

Phalsbourg AB gained the title of "The Friendliest Base in France" and is still remembered for the many open houses and air shows conducted by the various USAFE units based there from 1957 until 1963. This slogan appeared in the masthead of the "Phalsbourg Falcon" base newspaper. On Sunday, 20 May 1962, a crowd of 25,000 visitors gathered for an open house held to celebrate U.S. Armed Forces Day. Both the French and U.S. Army and Air Force participated with static displays and aerial demonstrations. These events are still remembered by the local French population. Air shows and open houses are still conducted at the base by the French Army.

The 7040th Air Base Squadron continued as caretakers after completion of the base until replaced by the 7486th Air Base Group in late 1955. Phalsbourg was assigned standby operating base status after completion, and remained so until the arrival of the 102d Tactical Fighter Wing in 1961. In the interim it had other tenants, but no combat wing. Its first tenant was the 23d Helicopter Squadron that arrived in November 1956.

23d Helicopter Squadron

The 23d Helicopter Squadron, equipped with the Piasecki H-21B "Workhorse," was the first flying unit assigned to Phalsbourg after its completion, and was the only USAF helicopter squadron in Europe. This squadron was supplied to USAFE by the 314th Troop Carrier Wing, Medium (TAC), from Sewart AFB, Tennessee. A similar helicopter squadron was dispatched to Japan.

The H-21Bs deployed to France by first flying 500 miles south to Brookley AFB, Mobile, Alabama, where they were loaded on an aircraft transport ship, TCUV-64 Tripoli. All eighteen H-21s, squadron personnel, and support equipment arrived in Bremerhaven, West Germany, on 1 November 1956, after nineteen days at sea. The 23d Sq personnel de-cocooned, inspected, tested, and then flew their helicopters across Germany and France to Phalsbourg, arriving between 7 and 15 November 1956. One helicopter was damaged enroute, requiring depot repairs.

The squadron was assigned to the 322d Air Division at Evreux AB for operational control, mission scheduling, and airlift priorities. The 23d Helicopter Squadron provided very useful general airlift support throughout France. The H-21B had a Wright 1820-103 engine driving the two rotor assemblies. It could lift 4,000 pounds and be fitted with a 250-gallon drop-tank for range extension. Standard helicopter missions included: Special Air Lift Mission (SAM), Administrative Support Mission (DC), and Emergency Air Evacuation Mission (EAE). The H-21 was ideal for transferring injured U.S. personnel and dependents that required major medical attention to full-service hospitals from remote military sites across Europe. No H-21 night flying was permitted in France.

Phalsbourg had plenty of hangar space and quarters for the 23d Squadron. It could keep all its H-21Bs indoors. But the 23d Helicopter Squadron had some difficulties operating from Phalsbourg. Neither a wing nor group operations staff was assigned to the base, and the squadron had insufficient manning to provide a complete base flight operations section. The H-21s had only a low frequency ADF (ARN-59) installed for radio navigation. The Eschbourg radio beacon, when installed in the spring of 1957, finally provided a means of finding Phalsbourg in bad weather. The 23d had no helicopter losses and no fatalities during its brief fourteen months of flying in France.

The 322d Air Division recommended that the 23d Helicopter Squadron be divided into four detachments for greater utilization. Detachments #1 and #4 remained at Phalsbourg with ten aircraft. Major maintenance was performed by teams dispatched from Phalsbourg, and all H-21B-peculiar spare parts were stocked at Phalsbourg.

Detachment #2 flew four H-21s to RAF Wethersfield, UK via Fontainebleau, Evreux AB, Lille, France, and on across the English channel. These four H-21Bs were equipped with air-sea hoist provisions for rescue flights. Their first task was to assist in the rapid assembly of a ground radar antenna structure at RAF Upper Heyford. The H-21Bs lifted large antenna segments and saved at least four weeks of time erecting these antennas.

23d Helicopter Squadron H-21B #51-15857 at Phalsbourg.
USAF History Office, Maxwell AFB, AL

Detachment #3 relocated four H-21Bs to Wheelus AB in December 1956. The H-21 was designed for rapid disassembly and reassembly for this type of air movement; both rotor assemblies were removable, and the fuselage split in half to make smaller and lighter loads. This process required eight hours work by an eight-man team at each end of the Workhorse's journey. The four H-21s were moved to Wheelus to support gunnery range operations at El Uotia and Tarhuna, and to assist the TM-61 Matador missile launches and flight test programs. This required some long range flights of 250 miles into the desert to missile target sites such as Mizda. Soon after arrival, on 22 March 1957, Det #3 recovered one injured pilot and one fatality from an RB-57A crash that occurred on the gunnery range, and then supported the crash investigation team for several days. Their mission was so successful that after the 23d HSq departed France, six of their H-21Bs continued to operate at Wheelus AB, supported by the 7272d Flying Training Wing. During 1960 the helicopters participated in an ongoing long distance rescue mission when they evacuated American and European civilians from the Congo where they were being threatened by rioting native troops.

USAFE felt the limitations of helicopter airlift were not worth the costs, and decided to eliminate the 23d Helicopter Sq from its force structure after fourteen months in Europe. During this same time, the U.S. Army in France was obtaining similar helicopter airlift capabilities, which made the 23d redundant. The squadron was inactivated on 8 January 1958, as part of USAF-wide reductions due to DOD budget cuts. Ten H-21Bs from Phalsbourg and two from RAF Wethersfield, UK, were returned to Brookley AFB, Alabama, in August 1959. They were shipped to CONUS on the aircraft transport ship, TCVU-64 Tripoli.

10th/66th Tactical Reconnaissance Wing

On 8 January 1958 the 10th Tactical Reconnaissance Wing at Spangdahlem moved their two RF-84F squadrons, the 32d and 38th TRSqs, to Phalsbourg for approximately 180 days TDY while their runway and taxiways were undergoing repairs to accommodate programmed RF-101As. Three months later, on 8 March 1958 while still at Phalsbourg, both RF-84F squadrons were transferred from the 10th Tactical Reconnaissance Wing to the 66th Tactical Reconnaissance Wing which was then based at Sembach AB, West Germany. This action resulted from the USAFE decision to create homogeneous reconnaissance wings rather than mix fighter-type and bomber-type aircraft in the same wing. To further confuse history, while the 32d and the 38th Squadrons were still at Phalsbourg, the 66th TRWg was transferred to Laon AB, France, but the two squadrons remained at Phalsbourg in TDY status during the spring and summer of 1958 until Laon completed runway rework. The other two 66th TRWg Squadrons, the 302d and 303d, which had been stationed at Sembach, also moved to Phalsbourg with their RF-84Fs while Laon's runway was being repaired. These units flew from Phalsbourg with the 513th Fighter-Interceptor Squadron which was also stationed at Phalsbourg by this time. Runway repairs at Laon required five months, so Phalsbourg remained a busy, active air base even though officially in standby status. On 31 March 1958 the base commander COL Clark and MAJ Perkins were lost in a T-33A crash very near the base.

A total of 375 personnel from the 10th Tactical Reconnaissance Wing had to be fed and housed by the 7486th Support Gp when they moved TDY to Phalsbourg. About 160 airmen were assigned temporary duty from Spangdahlem to assist the 7486th Support Gp with this additional workload. The majority

513th FISq F-86-D #51-8377 attending 1957 V-E Day Airshow, Chambley AB, while stationed at RAF Manston.
Al Christensen

of 10th TRWg support personnel were returned to Spangdahlem in May 1958. RF-84F pilots and aircraft maintenance personnel were transferred to the 66th Tactical Reconnaissance Wing after its move to Laon from Sembach on 10 July.

During its stay at Phalsbourg, the 66th TRWg's new RF-101Cs began arriving from the U.S. The first RF-101Cs were flown non-stop from Shaw AFB, South Carolina, to Phalsbourg using air-to-air refueling and were delivered to the 66th for conversion training on 16 May 1958. These reconnaissance squadrons departed Phalsbourg for Laon in September 1958, leaving the base to the 513th Fighter-Interceptor Squadron.

513th Fighter-Interceptor Squadron

During WWII, the 513th began as the 629th Bombardment Squadron, (Dive) assigned to the 406th Bombardment Group on 4 February 1943, flying A-24s and A-36s. This squadron was later redesignated the 513th Fighter-Bomber Squadron on 10 August 1943. The 513th earned a DUC serving with the USAAF Ninth Air Force in Northern Europe Air Campaigns while based in France, Belgium, and Germany. The 513th Fighter-Bomber Squadron was deactivated in Nordholtz, Germany on 20 August 1946.

The 513th Fighter-Interceptor Squadron, which evolved from the 513th FBSq, was activated at RAF Manston, England, on 10 July 1952 as a squadron in the 406th Fighter-Bomber Wing. The 513th was redesignated a Fighter-Interceptor Squadron on 1 April 1954, still assigned to the 406th which had now become a Fighter-Interceptor Wing at RAF Manston. The 406th FIWg was deactivated on 1 May 1958, and the 513th FISq was assigned to the 86th Fighter-Interceptor Wing at Ramstein AB. The 513th pilots flew their F-86Ds from RAF Manston to Phalsbourg on 12 April 1958. Maintenance personnel and support equipment were moved by C-124 and C-130 airlift on 15 and 16 April 1958.

The 513th FISq with twenty-six F-86Ds, 37 officers and 218 airmen began their new adventure in France. For the first six months it shared Phalsbourg with the 66th TRWg. The 513th had flown F-86Ds since March 1956 and continued flying this aircraft until January 1961. These F-86Ds were brought to Europe by a TCVU transport ship from late 1955 into spring 1956. They were delivered to the St. Nazaire Air Depot for inspection and test flights, and then flown to fighter-interceptor bases in Europe. The Sabre-Dog remained in the air defense of Western Europe for the next five years.

The 513th FISq stood air defense alert at Phalsbourg, but there were no air defense alert shelters, so the two Sabres on five-minute-scramble alert were kept outdoors. Alsace-Lorraine's wet winter weather was a poor environment for the G.E. engine's electronic fuel control system and the Hughes E-4 Fire Control System. As with all interceptor units, the 513th constantly practiced air-to-air radar intercepts under the direction of Moselle Control. Pilots became very proficient in instrument flying (IFR); about 60 percent of all flying was in actual bad weather conditions. They also became very experienced with real GCA landings. The ERCO F-86D analog flight simulator was installed at Phalsbourg and used to enhance instrument flying training, in-flight emergency procedures, and E-4 radar fire control system operation. Every 513th pilot was required to spend at least three hours per month "flying" the simulator. As the end of the 513th approached in the fall of 1960, the flight simulator was shut down on 26 October and eventually shipped to Chateauroux Air Depot.

While the 513th FISq stood air defense alert at Phalsbourg, five other USAFE interceptor squadrons changed from F-86Ds to Convair Delta Dagger F-102As, greatly improving NATO's all weather air defense. The F-102s began arriving in Europe during 1958 by aircraft transport ship. The 525th FISq at Bitburg AB, West Germany, was the first USAFE squadron to receive these Daggers, on 28 January 1959. The Dagger was always a favorite at air shows in France and would visit U.S. air bases often, but none were based in France. The F-102s served in USAFE from January 1959 until 16 April 1970.

On 18 November 1960 the 513th was assigned to the expanded 86th Air Division, (Air Defense) as it prepared for its deactivation on 8 January 1961.

Its aircraft left during the last two months of 1960. The first flight of eight F-86Ds departed Phalsbourg on 2 November 1960 for Chateauroux and depot processing; the remainder were flown to the depot by 22 December. These F-86Ds were scrapped at the Chateauroux Depot during 1961. The J-47 jet engines, avionics, and instruments were removed and placed in depot inventory. NATO countries were now flying F-86Ds and F-86K interceptors, and these spare components were made available for MAP issue. The last F-86D Sabre interceptor squadrons in USAFE were shut down on 8 January 1961 when the 513th at Phalsbourg AB and the 514th Fighter-Interceptor Squadron at Ramstein AB were inactivated in place. Personnel of the 513th were transferred to F-102 units.

Phalsbourg was once again without a flying unit and remained in standby status, with the 7486th Air Base Group as the caretakers. Any additional base support that was needed was provided by Toul AB. The calm was short lived, because within seven months the Berlin Crises would require Phalsbourg to host its first complete fighter wing and meet the need for which it was designed and built.

During the period the 513th FISq and the 24th Helicopter Sq were operating at Phalsbourg AB, there were several tenant units on the base. These were Det #12, 12th Air Postal Sq, Det #18, 31st Weather Sq, 1273d AACS Communications Sq, and Det #33, 8th Radio Rely Sq.

102d Tactical Fighter Wing

The 102d Tactical Fighter Wing, Massachusetts ANG, consisting of 245 officers and 1,360 airmen, was called to federal active duty on 1 October 1961 for a period of twelve months for the Berlin Crisis. When activated, the wing consisted of three fighter squadrons and supporting units: the 101st TFSq based at Logan Airport, Boston, Massachusetts; the 131st TFSq at Barnes Field, Westfield, Massachusetts; and the 138th TFSq at Hancock Field, Syracuse, New York. All three fighter squadrons had been flying North American F-86H Sabres since 1957.

The wing originated as the WWII 318th Fighter Group that flew P-47 Thunderbolts on bomber escort, interdiction, and close air support missions with the Seventh Air Force from Saipan and Okinawa. The 318th Fighter Group was redesignated the 102d Fighter Group and allotted to the post war Massachusetts Air National Guard on 24 May 1946. The 102d Fighter Group was expanded into the 102d Fighter Wing in October 1950.

During the summer of 1961, as the Berlin crisis unfolded, several reserve units were notified on 16 August that they were considered priority organizations and should "achieve maximum operational readiness in as short a period as possible." The 102d was one of these reserve fighter units. They were notified on 26 August that 1 October would be the beginning of twelve months of active duty and the gaining USAF Command would be TAC. On 20 September final orders were received, sending the 102d Wing and its three fighter squadrons to Phalsbourg AB, France, on or about 2 November. The great question throughout the three bases was, "Where in the hell is Phalsbourg." No one had heard of the air base! Most of the reserve personnel thought they were being sent to West Germany. After the usual mobilization processing and packing, ADVON from the three fighter bases departed via C-118s on 16 October, heading for Phalsbourg. Next, the enroute support teams departed on 23 October for the first three enroute stops.

For the 102d TFWg, Operation STAIR STEP meant seventy-eight F-86Hs departing Boston, Westfield, and Syracuse between 28 and 30 October, flying to Dow AFB, Bangor, Maine, joining up with sixteen T-33As, and heading to France. Because the F-86H was not equipped with an air-to-air refueling probe or receptacle, the 102d was directed to move all three fighter squadrons to Europe via the northern route.

F-86H-10-NH #53-1233 from the 102st TFWg,138th Tactical Fighter Squadron.
Roger Warren

The wing's flight to France proceeded as described in chapter 2. By 7 November 1961, the complete 102d Tactical Fighter Wing had assembled at newly reactivated Phalsbourg AB, for an estimated stay of ten months. All personnel were in place by 14 December, which allowed them to become operational almost immediately. The 102d TFWg was not redesignated during its stay in France because, unlike the other air guard units mobilized for the Berlin crisis, it was a complete wing with three squadrons and all support squadrons.

After arrival of the wing there were some local demonstrations by the French communists and newspaper articles protesting Wing Commander GEN Sweeny's role in the bombing of Nagasaki in August 1945. This never erupted into a threat to the base, and the 102d was able to carry out its mission with normal security.

The 102d TFWg's primary mission was close air support to NATO and Seventh Army ground forces, air defense, and interdiction using conventional weapons. These had been its primary training missions since 1952. The wing's air defense mission involved keeping twelve fully armed F-86Hs on 24-hour alert. Ground-radar-controlled penetration missions were practiced through the three Berlin air corridors. By 5 December the squadrons began rotating twelve F-86H Sabres down to Wheelus AB for bombing and gunnery training. The 102d TFWg had an interesting mix of aircraft; the 131st TFSq flew -1-NA Sabres with six M3 .50cal machine guns, while the 101st and 138th TFSqs flew -5-NA and -10-NH Sabres, having four M39 20mm aircraft cannons. This difference in armament prevented mixing aircraft on gunnery range schedules. Air-to-air gunnery used the early models of the dart targets that were towed by the 7272d Flying Training Wing based at Wheelus AB.

The 102d Tactical Fighter Wing was tasked by Seventeenth Air Force to participate in the same USAFE and NATO exercises as the F-84F units, such as:

GRAND SLAM	GUN TALK
INDIAN SUMMER	ROUND ROBIN
SUPER CHIEF	LONG THRUST
KEEN KNIFE	QUICK TRAIN
RED EYE	BIG STICK
CABIN CRUISER	COLD TURKEY
SQUADRON EXCHANGE	

A new wing Combat Operations Center was constructed to command all the scheduled operations and exercises; this building modification was built by wing civil engineering personnel to expedite availability. The COC was opened on 25 January 1962 and met exercise control requirements very well. During this period, Wing Intelligence Section personnel conducted five briefings from January through April for many distinguished visitors to Phalsbourg AB interested in evaluating the STAIR STEP Operation.

Exercise SQUADRON EXCHANGE consisted of pilots, ground crews and F-86s of the West German Air Force trading places with 102d personnel and their F-86Hs. The Phalsbourg squadrons traded small groups of pilots and ground crews with teams from the 72d Fighter Wing at Leck Air Base, near the Danish border. The pilots spent many hours testing different bombing and rocketry techniques, aerial combat tac-

F-86Hs from the 131st and 101st Tactical Fighter Squadrons, standing alert in the rain, Phalsbourg 1962.
Roger Warren

Canadian Canuck Interceptors, on exercise at Phalsbourg 1962.
COL Dave Watt

tics, and mission briefing/planning. The ground and support personnel from both countries learned how to service aircraft fuel and oil systems, do preflight and post-flight inspections, and minor maintenance procedures. Language differences between the groups made solving common problems challenging, but each man's effort led to rapid understanding. In all, these exchanges were very useful for NATO members. It's one thing to have diplomats, with translators, meet and plan joint operations, but it is a completely different environment to deliver close air support or change a damaged fuel drop-tank without misunderstandings when there's no one available to translate.

By 7 May 1962, Seventeenth Air Force directed that all 102d TFWg personnel, F-86H aircraft, support equipment, and spare parts would move directly from Phalsbourg back to their home bases. USAFE requested some of the repair shop machinery. Replacement machines were issued to the units after return to CONUS. Redeployment planning included an advanced echelon, aircraft enroute support teams, main echelon, and a rear detachment. Personnel movement orders, separation orders, surface and airlift transportation requirements, and base transfer schedules were submitted on 8 June 1962 to Seventeenth Air Force. A group of Air Guardsmen, thirty-four officers, and forty-nine airmen, agreed to stay on active duty with the USAF and remain in France after 20 August. Thirty-one of the thirty-four officers were fighter pilots. Another survey found that 100 percent of the full-time Air Technicians wished to return to their ANG jobs after release from active duty. Regular USAF personnel began arriving in May to form the cadre of the 480th Tactical Fighter Squadron of the newly activated 366th Tactical Fighter Wing.

In June, only proficiency flying was conducted as the aircraft were being prepared for their return across the North Atlantic. Periodic inspections were increased, so when the F-86Hs departed France the fleet average would be greater than 140 hours before the next required inspection. This would ensure flyable aircraft after return to reserve status while waiting for surface shipped support equipment and parts.

Three ADVON teams departed 2 June on one MATS C-135A transport that stopped at each ANG base. The teams quickly opened up their bare bases and obtained all vital DOD and USAF forms, office equipment, typewriters, Ditto machines, ID card camera sets, and boxes of paper needed for publishing orders to process approximately five hundred men at each air base. A very complete personnel processing plan had been prepared prior to departing Phalsbourg. The majority of equipment and individual property was packed into 1.5-ton CONEX containers and shipped by surface transportation. All items were checked by U.S. Customs representatives at Phalsbourg during packing, which allowed direct shipment to their home air bases. All cargo was shipped by train to the three seaports operated by the U.S. Army: La Pallice, Rochefort, and St. Nazaire. The Bordeaux/Bacalan port operation had shut down in 1960.

The main body of troops departed between 12 and 23 July, requiring one day to return to CONUS using C-135A transports. The east-to-west Atlantic crossing of seventy-four F-86Hs, two C-47, and six T-33As began on 16 July and was accomplished without incident as aircraft returned to Logan Airport, Barnes Field, and Hancock Field by 20 July.

On 13 August 1962, the 102nd rear detachment closed the final supply accounts, returned an improved

F-86H 131st TFSq, Massachusetts Air National Guard, open house, Phalsbourg 1962.
Roger Warren

Phalsbourg AB over to the 7369th Support Group, and departed. All units and most personnel assigned to the 102d TFWg were released from active duty on 20 August 1962 and continued flying their F-86Hs in ANG status. TAC gained all aircraft from USAFE on 31 July 1962. A few personnel desired to remain on active duty for the complete twelve-month period and were processed for separation on 30 September 1962, ending the Berlin Crisis call-up.

480th Tactical Fighter Squadron
366th Tactical Fighter Wing

The 7369th Combat Support Group consisting of the 7369th Air Police Sq, 7369th Material Sq, and 7369th USAF Dispensary was activated on 8 May 1962 to operate Phalsbourg after departure of the 102d TFWg. These new units reported to the 366th Tactical Fighter Wing located at Chaumont AB and supported one of its fighter squadrons, the 480th, also activated 8 May. The 480th TFSq remained at Chaumont until a major NATO construction project was finished at Phalsbourg—complete replacement of the runway and taxiways! When the 480th TFSq arrived on 21 December, some work remained, such as runway lighting and marking, which was completed by February 1963.

Other tenant units on base in 1962-63 were Det #12, 12th Air Postal Sq; Det #18, 31st Weather Sq; Det #3, 2148th Communications Sq; Det #22, 2059 Radio Relay Sq. Also on base was Company B, 249th Engineer Battalion, Construction, performing repair work on portable steel buildings and hangars, and improving roads. An elementary school opened on base in September 1962 with 219 pupils.

The primary mission of the 480th TFSq during its time at Chaumont and Phalsbourg was close air support to Seventh Army ground forces and air defense. The wing's air defense mission involved keeping four fully armed F-84Fs on 24-hour alert. Ground radar controlled interception missions were practiced across France and West Germany. During September the squadron began sending six F-84Fs down to Wheelus for bombing and gunnery training. During the Cuban Missile Crisis in October 1962; the squadron assumed a total alert posture with eighteen fully armed F-84Fs on round-the-clock alert. Bomb loads were frequently changed by Seventeenth Air Force as targets in the Eastern Zone were relocated in the initial days of the crisis. It was an extremely tense week for the 480th and all NATO forces who were prepared to engage the Soviets if the missiles hadn't been removed from Cuba.

On 16 July 1963, the 480th TFSq joined the rest of the 366th TFWg and flew their Thunderstreaks to Holloman AFB, New Mexico. On 20 July 1963 Phalsbourg AB was again designated a standby base; the 7369th CSGp remained to maintain the base. All activity and manning were reduced.

Phalsbourg Air Base 1963-1966

In October 1963, Phalsbourg was used as an airlift terminal for Operation BIG LIFT, as part of Exercise REFOREGER, "Re-enforcement of Forces in Germany." This was an early test of the new DOD concept of moving large numbers of U.S. Army personnel and equipment into Germany. BIG LIFT, using C-124s, C-133s, and C-135s, moved a complete army division to Europe and equipped them with pre-positioned heavy combat vehicles and war stocks from depots around Kaiserslautern, West Germany. This was proof to NATO that the United State's "dual based unit" concept was a viable strategy. The success of this exercise made greater airlift capacity a major requirement, and drove the development of the C-141 Starlifter and C-5

GRC-26B radio van, Army GLO team.
COL Dave Watt

GLO team radio station at Phalsbourg AB.
COL Dave Watt

Sherman tank, monument to French 2nd Armored Division forces who liberated the city, November 1944. On N4, 1/2 mile south of auto route A4. Jerry McAuliffe

Phalsbourg town square 1997.
Jerry McAuliffe

Galaxy. During the BIG LIFT exercise, TAC deployed F-100Ds from the 401st TFWg based at England AFB, Lousiana. They operated from Phalsbourg for about forty days, until 15 November 1963. These F-100s were the last tactical aircraft to operate at Phalsbourg AB.

The 7369th Combat Support Group maintained Phalsbourg in standby status from August 1963, when the 480th departed, until its closure in March 1967. When Project FRELOC began in April 1966, the base had 420 officers and airmen, 11 Department of Air Force civilian employees, and 105 Wage Grade and Local Wage Rate French employees. There were 620 dependents present and supported by the base. By this time the USAF had invested $18 million (excluding land value, aircraft, and supplies) and spent about $1,185,000 to operate and maintain Phalsbourg from 1955 through 1967.

Since no flying wing was present, it was a fairly simple shut-down process. The 7369th Combat Support Gp immediately began to pack and ship all U.S. property from the base. All real estate facilities, when no longer in use, were inspected, repaired, and secured for the new owner, the French Army.

The final closing ceremony was held on 15 February 1967 when the U.S. flag was lowered and presented to the mayor of Phalsbourg, France. That flag is still displayed in the city museum. The base was transferred to the Military Liquidation Office in Paris and the base and annexes were deleted from USAF property records on 20 March 1967, after thirteen years of intermittent use.

On 1 April 1967 USAFE discontinued the 7369th Group as part of FRELOC, and the final aircraft, a C-135B, departed Phalsbourg AB moving the last of the base personnel to West Germany. Anyone wishing to visit the area can find the city of Phalsbourg on Michelin map #307 Local; it can be reached by train from Gare de l'Est station in Paris.

Phalsbourg Air Base Assigned Aircraft

USAF Museum

23d Helicopter Squadron, H-21Bs, November 1956 - January 1958
Eighteen aircraft assigned to squadron. These helicopters were shipped from Brookley AFB, AL to Bremerhaven, West Germany, then assembled and flown to Phalsbourg AB, France, by 23d pilots. Dets #1 and #4 based at Phalsbourg with 10 H-21Bs. Det #2 based at RAF Wethersfield, UK. Detachment #3 based at Wheelus AB, Libya. Ten helicopters shipped back to Brookly AFB in February 1958.

H-21B-PH

51-15857+	51-15859	51-15871	51-15874	51-15880	52-8666^	52-8669^	52-8673#	52-8702#
51-15858	51-15869	51-15872	51-15878	52-8665^	52-8667	52-8671^	52-8694#	52-8704#

No losses, no fatalities
H-21Bs assigned to Detachment #2 RAF Wethersfield, U.K.
^ H-21Bs assigned to Detachment #3 at Wheelus AB, Libya
+ Now at USAF Museum

7486th Air Base Group: Support Aircraft
L-20A: 51-16528, 51-16529

A. Christensen

513th Fighter-Interceptor Squadron, F-86Ds, 16 April 1958 - 8 January 1961
Twenty-six assigned to squadron. The 513th FISq stationed at RAF Manston, England was assigned to the 86th Fighter-Interceptor Wing at Ramstein AB, West Germany in May 1956. F-86Ds flown to Phalsbourg from RAF Manston by 513th FISq pilots.
Aircraft Marking: - Red & black sunburst on vertical stabilizer/rudder with eagle emblem on both sides vertical stabilizer.

F-86D-35, -45, -50-NA

51-8336	52-3899	52-3940	52-4063	52-4130	52-4144	52-4219 ~	52-10050
51-8353	52-3900	52-3946	52-4075	52-4137	52-4208	52-4226	52-10072
51-8377	52-3901	52-3947	52-4077	52-4138	52-4209	52-4266	52-10130
51-8393	52-3921	52-3948	52-4082	52-4140	52-4210		

No losses, no fatalities
~ Squadron Commanding Officer's Aircraft

7486th Air Base Group: Base Support Aircraft
L-20A: 51-16529
T-33A: 51-8658

Phalsbourg Air Base Assigned Aircraft, continued

Roger Warren

102d Tactical Fighter Wing, F-86Hs, 7 November 1961 - 20 July 1962
Twenty-six aircraft per squadron. Sabres were flown from Logan Airport, MA, Barnes Field, MA, and Hancock Field, NY to Phalsbourg Air Base, France, by 102d TFWg pilots. Aircraft returned to their U.S. bases by 20 July 1962.
Aircraft Marking: 101st TFSq - Green, 131st TFSq - Red, 138th TFSq - Yellow.

F-86H-1, -5-NA, -5 & -10-NH

52-1983	131st	52-2046	131st	52-2119	101st	53-1304	101st	53-1391	101st
52-1987	131st	52-2055	131st	52-2120	138th	53-1308	101st	53-1392	101st
52-2002	131st	52-2057	131st	52-2122	101st	53-1314	138th	53-1403	138th
52-2007	131st	52-2061	131st	52-5732	101st	53-1330*	138th	53-1404	101st
52-2008*	131st	52-2062	131st	52-5741	101st	53-1331	101st	53-1406	101st
52-2009	131st	52-2063	131st			53-1334	138th	53-1408	138th
52-2012	131st	52-2064	131st	53-1231	101st	53-1335	138th	53-1413	101st
52-2017	131st	52-2068	131st	53-1233	138th	53-1338	101st	53-1494	138th
52-2018	131st	52-2069	131st	53-1234*	138th	53-1344	138th	53-1495	138th
52-2019	131st	52-2075	101st	53-1239	101st	53-1351	101st	53-1502*	101st
52-2028	131st	52-2079	131st	53-1274	138th	53-1358	101st	53-1509	138th
52-2029	131st	52-2085	138th	53-1279	138th	53-1365	138th	53-1512	101st
52-2030	131st	52-2090	138th	53-1281	101st	53-1366	101st	53-1515	101st
52-2033	131st	52-2092*	138th	53-1290	101st	53-1376	138th	53-1519	101st
52-2035	131st	52-2094	138th	53-1292	138th	53-1383	138th	53-1527	138th
52-2037	131st	52-2113	101st	53-1300	101st	53-1386	101st		
52-2042	131st	52-2116	138th	53-1302	138th	53-1390	101st		

* Losses:
52-2008 - Crashed, low level flight, 11nm S of Chalons-sur-Marne, France, 21 MAR 62, 1 fatality.
52-2092 - Crashed, 1nm N of Phalsbourg AB, 13 JAN 62, fatalities unknown.
53-1234 - Crashed, close air support, near Kirm, West Germany, 17 APR 62, 1 fatality.
53-1330 - Crashed, on take-off at Hancock Field, NY, 31 OCT 61, 1 fatality.
53-1502 - Crashed, Phalsbourg AB, DEC 63 (note: accident records list '63 but must be typo since 102d had departed Phalsbourg.)

Wing Support Aircraft: 102d Operations Squadron
C-47A: 2 each from ANG 42-23599 (131st), 43-15619 (138th)
T-33A: 6 each from ANG 52-9681 (131st), 52-9685 (101st), 53-5324 (138th), 53-5327 (131st), 53-5329 (138th), 53-5970 (101st).

366th Tactical Fighter Wing, 480th Tactical Fighter Squadron, F-84Fs, 21 December 1962 - 16 July 1963
The 480th TFSq was based at Chaumont, then moved to Phalsbourg. Twenty aircraft per squadron. These Thunderstreaks were flown from Phalsbourg to Holloman AFB, NM by 366th TFWg pilots.
Aircraft Marking: 480th Tactical Fighter Squadron - Green band

F-84F-30, -35, -40, -50, -55-RE and -10, -30, -35, -40-GK

51-9354	51-9490	51-9531	51-17073	51-17080	52-6365	52-6475	52-6629	52-6846	52-6848
51-9437	51-9501	51-17061	51-17077	51-17086	52-6372	52-6520	52-6631	52-6847	52-6924

No losses, no fatalities

Wing Support Aircraft: 366th Operations Squadron
L-20A: 52-6146
T-33A: 2 ea.

Appendix 15.1 Notice to Airmen 1958 (NOTAM) - USAF-Phalsbourg

Elevation 1,016 feet (310 m), 48° 47'N - 07° 13'E. One paved concrete runway 9,900 feet long, 060°/240°. Rotating beacon light on airfield, with runway/taxiway lights. No transient aircraft repairs available. Aircraft fuel, 115-145 octane and JP4 jet fuel available. Low pressure oxygen only available. Jet aircraft starting units C-26, MA-1, and MA-2 electrical power available. Jet aircraft barrier available, contact tower for instructions. Caution, sharp drop-off at end of each runway overrun. Very limited crash, fire, rescue facilities available.

ACKNOWLEDGEMENTS

I would like to thank the following people who contributed to this chapter:

Al Christensen was a Weather Officer in Detachment 10, 31st Weather Squadron, MATS, stationed at Chambley AB, 1955-1957. Al has provided excellent photos and information.

Roger Warren served at Phalsbourg Air Base, France with the 102d Tactical Fighter Wing, 1961-62. He was a SSGT in the 138th Squadron, and was a 70250 (administration) who worked at HQ 102ds TFWg as unit mail clerk, First Sergeant and whatever jobs needed to be done.

COL Dave Watt served at Phalsbourg with the U.S. Army's Ground Liaison Team during reconnaissance exercises.

Cathedral on Phalsbourg town square 1997
Jerry McAuliffe

16

TOUL-ROSIERES AIR BASE

Americans became familiar with the region around Toul and Nancy during World War I since many U.S. Army troops were stationed in the area. The famous First Pursuit Group was organized at an airfield east of Toul in May 1918. From here they supported the Meuse-Argonne and St Mihiel offensives.

Fighting occurred here again during WWII; in fact, the area was liberated by Patton's Third Army. In September 1944, immediately after combat moved eastward, an Auxiliary Landing Ground was constructed north of Toul city. It was named Rosieres-en-Haye ALG and designated A-98. The airstrip was needed for close air support during the Moselle campaign. It became operational in November 1944 and was manned by the 354th Fighter Group, flying P-47Ds until April 1945, as part of the Ninth Tactical Air Force. The Luftwaffe bombed it several times during the winter nights of 1944/45.

Rosieres-en-Haye ALG became Toul-Rosieres Air Base (48° 46' N - 05° 58' E, elevation 934 feet). It is located in the Meurthe-et-Moselle Department, 195 miles (315 km) east of Paris. Toul-Rosieres Air Base is located ten miles (17 km) northeast of the city of Toul on the west side of highway N411, and half a mile (1 km) south of Rosieres-en-Haye. Main entrance to the base is south off highway D907. Its mailing address was APO 83.

During construction of ALG A-98 in 1944, the 850th Engineer Aviation Battalion encountered a difficult problem that has plagued this site to the present day. Winter rains aggravated the severe drainage problem in the region and the entire base became a quagmire of slippery clay. Six inches of stone were laid to support the pierced steel plank runway, but this proved insufficient to prevent mud rising through the PSP. Finally the PSP had to be rolled up and six additional inches of slag laid to keep the runway operational for the P-47s. The problem was so extreme that men from the 354th Fighter Group had to assist the aviation engineers to maintain an operational runway and taxiways during the Ardennes offensive. Both the 354th Fighter Group and the 850th EABn were happy to move into Germany in April 1945.

At the initial meetings for air base site selection in 1950, Toul airfield was proposed and the FAF and USAFE concurred on its use as a tactical reconnaissance air base and a tactical control center. When it became apparent that Metz-Frescaty airport would not be available for an interim USAFE tactical unit, Toul was reprogrammed as an interim airfield and later was developed into a fighter base. Toul, therefore, was planned as another two-step base, first with tents and temporary buildings, and then within three years these would be replaced with permanent buildings and hangars. The USAF planned for arrival of a tactical wing by 1 December 1951.

This location was chosen because the site was immediately available for construction, and because there was familiarity with the area from WWII. Unfortunately, there must not have been anyone around familiar with the operational problems caused by Toul's poor drainage. Preliminary surveys were conducted in January 1951 by the Corps of Engineers. Two problems were immediately evident: the area was extremely damp and the runway site did not drain properly. There was a sufficient source of potable water, but very limited electrical service was available. The old 5,100-foot, unused runway still existed but had deteriorated since 1945 and no structures remained. No commercial aviation or industrial activity had developed here after WWII, though a good highway and rail line were not far away. An important stipulation demanded by Ponts et Chaussees meant base planning would have to "work around" the trees. It would not permit total forest clearances, so the majority of the base would have to be constructed in a thick forest.

Construction started in February 1951, with the building of access roads and a base railroad spur. On 10 November 1951 runway grading began, the PSP was removed as scrap metal, and new concrete was poured over the WWII stone and slag. Several different French contractors performed this work but, as was the case with so many of the bases, insufficient cement was used throughout the construction causing rapid deterioration of concrete surfaces. During this initial construction period, from December 1951 through mid March 1952, the 7412th Support Squad-

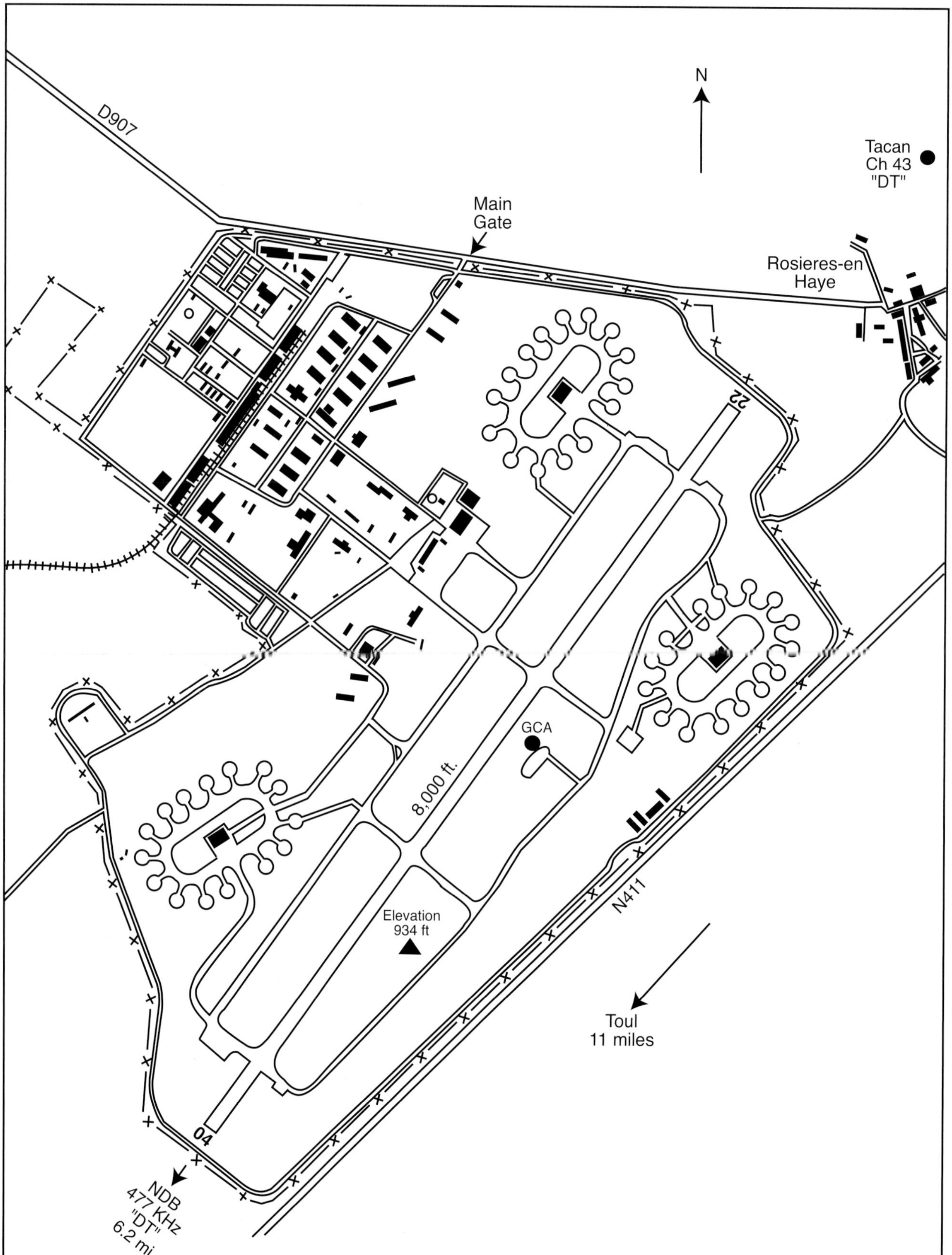

Map 16.1 Toul-Rosiers Air Base

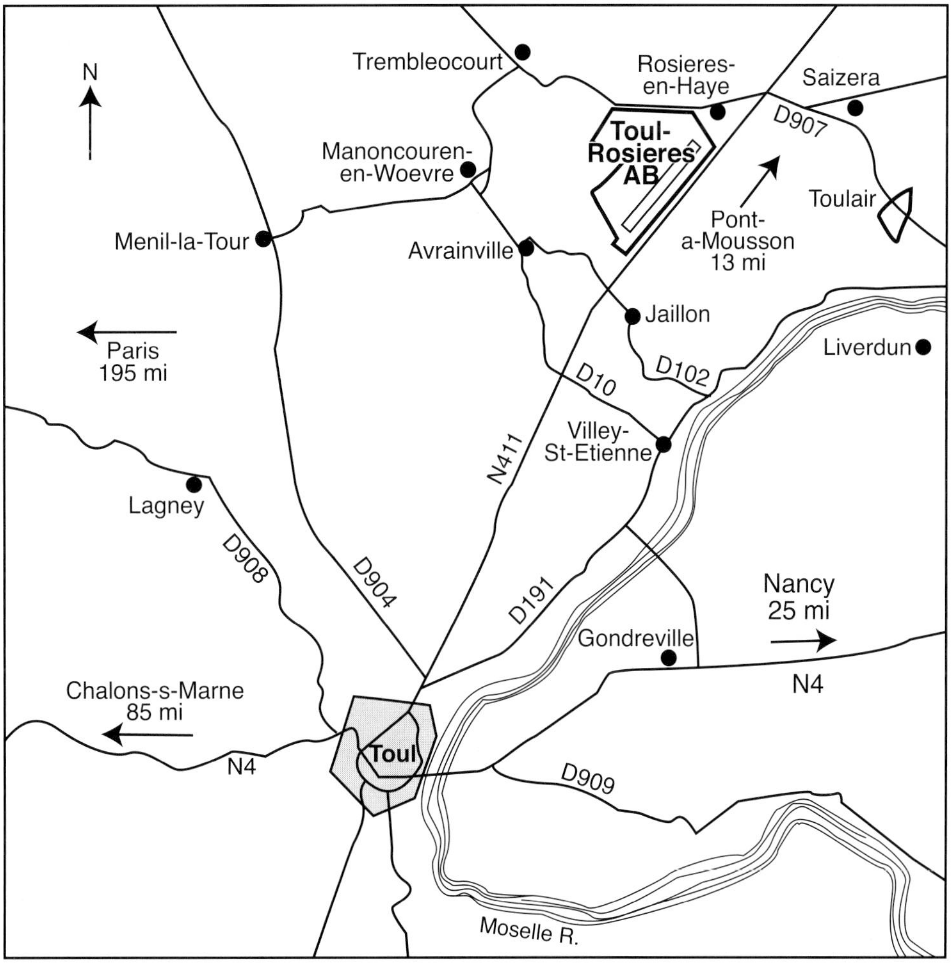

Map 16.2 Toul Area

ron provided site security, logistics support, and communications operations.

117th Tactical Reconnaissance Wing

As Toul Air Base was being constructed, the 117th Tactical Reconnaissance Wing was selected to be its first occupant. The 117th Fighter Wing from the Alabama ANG had been ordered to federal active duty on 10 October 1950 for a period of twenty-one months for the Korean War. Approximately 195 officers and 1,100 airmen manned the wing's units.

When activated, the wing consisted of three squadrons and supporting units: the 106th Light Bomb Squadron at Sumpter Smith Municipal Airport, Birmingham, Alabama; the 157th Fighter Squadron at the Congaree Air Base, Columbia, South Carolina; and the 160th Fighter Squadron also at Sumpter Smith Municipal Airport. Within weeks the 106th LBSq was transferred out to the 118th Reconnaissance Wing at Shaw AFB. It was replaced with the 112th Light Bomb Squadron based at Cleveland Hopkins Airport, Cleveland, Ohio, keeping the 117th Wing's strength at three flying squadrons.

The wing moved to Lawson AFB, Georgia adjacent to Ft. Benning on 2 November 1950 for nine months of base development, aircraft conversion, and tactical reconnaissance training. The wing had been flying both Invader light bombers and Mustang fighters since late 1946, but changed mission and aircraft type after call-up. Many of the Air Guard units called up during the Korean War were given different aircraft and assigned a completely different mission than the one in which they were proficient. These changes required considerable training and delayed their overseas movements.

The 112th LBSq initially received eighteen B-26s and flew tactical close air support training for Army units in the southern states, but then converted to a tactical reconnaissance squadron (Night Photo) and received newly depot-modified RB-26Cs between June and September 1951. In the first three months of 1951, both the 157th and 160th Fighter Squadrons,

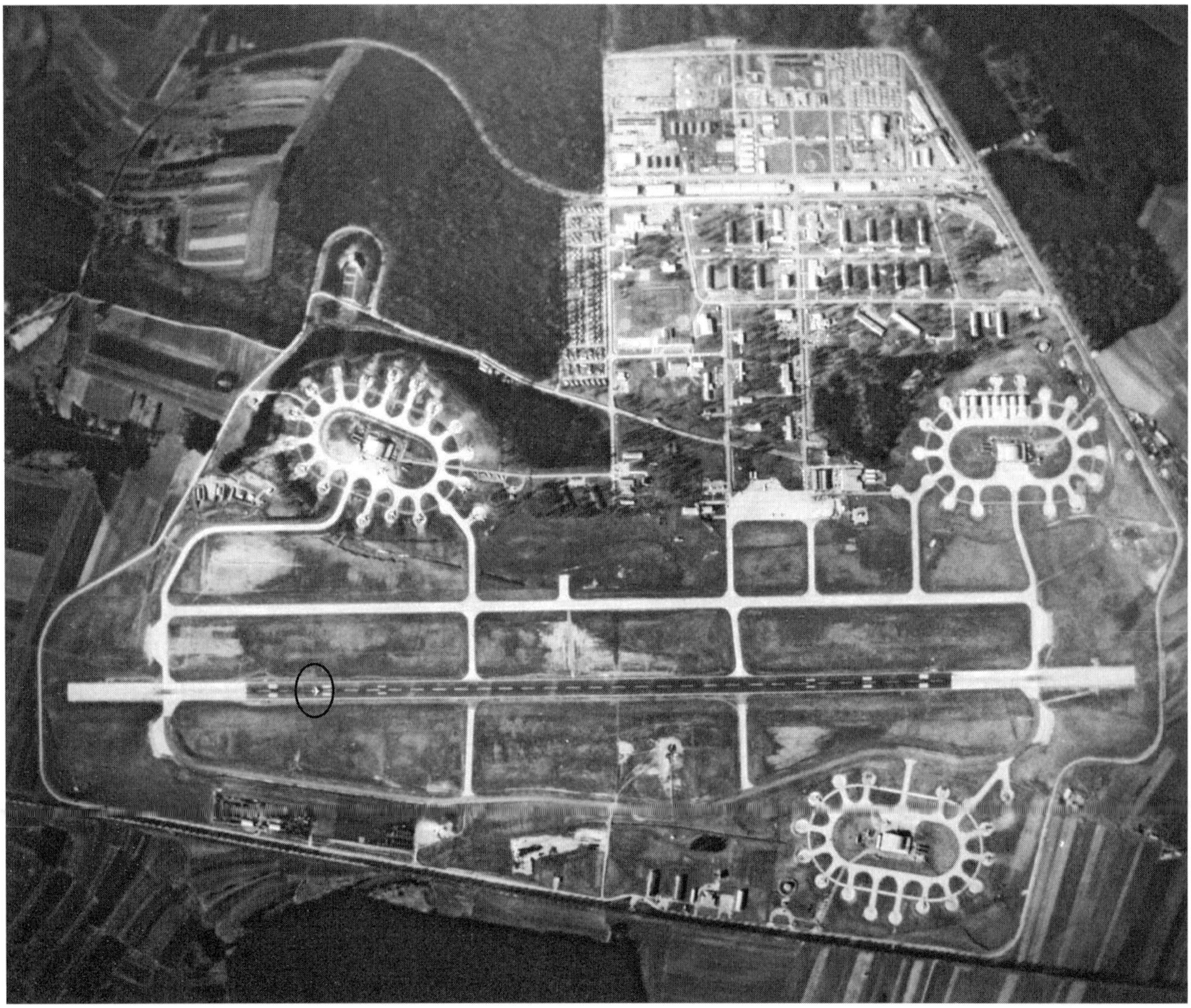

Toul Air Base circa 1964. Vertical photo from an RB-66B taken at about 25,000 feet. Note aircraft on runway (circled).
Gilbert Savona

which had been flying F-51Ds, received a few RF-51Ds and began photo and artillery spotting training. By March the 117th TRWg was flying a wide variety of aircraft, nineteen RF-51Ds, fifteen F-51Ds, nineteen B-26s, four C-47s, two C-45s, three T-11s, and six T-6s. During the summer of 1951, the 157th and the 160th were re-equipped with RF-80As. Many of these RF-80As were old FEAF F-80As returned from Japan and reworked into the photo model at Lockheed-Burbank. When they moved to Europe with their RF-80As and RB-26s the 117th TRWg had the capability to conduct visual, day and night photo reconnaissance, plus rudimentary electronic reconnaissance.

During the spring and summer there were rumors that the wing would deploy to France even though a second reconnaissance wing had been requested for Korea by the commander of FEAF. The rumors were correct, and by late October 1951 the wing was ready to depart for their new base in France. First to depart was the ADVON, which left Lawson AFB by air for Toul. Here they assisted the 7412th Support Squadron in setting up limited facilities and organizing incoming supplies.

Next the air echelon flew its fifty-two RF-80s and RB-26s across the North Atlantic, with a stop at Dow AFB, Maine to clear for overseas movement to Goose Bay, Labrador. By stopping at Dow they reduced the leg between the U.S. and Labrador by 250 miles. This movement of units flying across the ocean was given the code name Fox Able 14, as described in chapter 2. The 117th struggled with the same weather forecasting problems encountered by the 126th Bomb Wing that had flown to Bordeaux two months earlier. Bad weather caused several close calls that almost cost air-

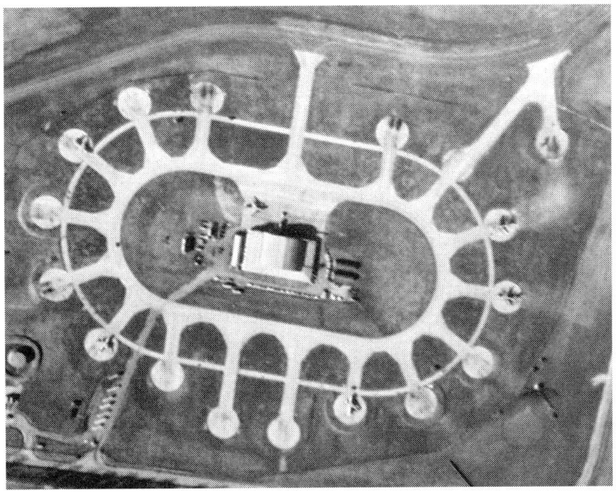

Close-up of hangar and marguerite from photo facing page, Toul AB, approximately 1964.
Gilbert Savona

craft and pilot losses, but fortunately no aircraft were lost on the crossing even though this route was considered closed for the winter season.

The surface echelon traveled by C-124 airlift from Lawson AFB to Camp Kilmer, New Jersey; then departed Brooklyn on January 16th on the troop ship USNS GEN W.G. Hahn. On 27 January 1952, 1,506 officers and airmen arrived at Bremerhaven, West Germany, after twelve days at sea. All the voyagers were relieved to have completed the crossing. Living aboard this crowded ship was very unpleasant, and worries about winter weather in the North Atlantic added to their discomfort. Though they experienced an easy January crossing, they had heard about the loss of the Flying Enterprise cargo ship in rough seas off Spain during this same period. A long train trip from northern Germany into France brought the men to their tent camp and a very difficult stay at Toul-Rosieres Air Base. Toul was the poorest site in France developed by NATO,

On 12 February 1952, after arrival at Toul of all aircraft and personnel, the 117th TRWg was transferred from TAC to USAFE. By April the following base support units were assigned to Toul: Det #3, 1992d AACS Sq; 1st Radio Relay Sq; 3d Shoran Beacon Unit; Flight "O" 2d Air Postal Sq; and Det #5, 31st Weather Sq.

The 117th had arrived at Toul about one year ahead of permanent base completion, and even before the initial construction phase was completed. Whatever discomforts they had expected as part of opening a base, they never imagined what they found! The tent camp was not ready for occupancy; mess halls were not functional, latrine plumbing was not installed, no aircraft shops were built, and there was a shortage of electrical power!

Since the tent camp was not ready, wing personnel had to be divided between two old French Army casernes constructed about 1870. Luxembourg Caserne, located in Toul, fifteen miles south of the air base, housed Wing Headquarters, 117th Tactical Hospital, and the 117th Air Base Group with its squadrons. Duroc Caserne, located in Pont-a-Mousson thirteen miles north of the air base, was home to the 117th Maintenance & Supply Group, its squadrons, and the 117th Reconnaissance Technical Squadron. These buildings were spartan when new but were now little more than dilapidated shells. The casernes were damaged during WWII and had never been repaired. The men had to put up with "small inconveniences" such as missing windowpanes, no heat, no electrical service, and antiquated latrine facilities. Winter habitation was unbearable; the casernes were always cold, drafty, and damp. There was no water for showers so the troops were trucked to Toul once a week to use the public city baths. Most of the 117th personnel felt they had lost the Korean War and somehow had become POWs. Wing morale rapidly disintegrated during the six months of depressing conditions and everyone looked forward to "real" base facilities when they reunited at Toul.

By May base construction had progressed sufficiently so that the 117th Wing could vacate the casernes and return to their air base. Living conditions in the 235 eight-man squad tents were superior to the casernes, though below U.S. standards. The tents were constructed with concrete floors. Because of the poor quality cement, clouds of dust were raised each time the floors were swept, but at least the tents could be kept warm. The shiny new latrines looked satisfactory

117th TRWg RF-80s of the 160th TRSq flying on maneuvers - in the air, life was good!
National Archives

On the ground - life was not good! 117th TRWg troops spent the 1952 winter at Luxembourg caserne.
Sam Whitworth

but were still not draining properly and couldn't be used. Slit trenches had to be dug for toilets! All of this was surrounded by the ever-present mud! Moving back to Toul didn't solve the low morale problem!

Though a runway existed upon arrival of the 117th, it was obvious that the base was not any more ready for aircraft than people. Contractors had rushed airfield construction, which resulted in a disintegrating 7,900-foot runway and incomplete taxiways. The runway was literally breaking up and presented a foreign-object-damage hazard to RF-80 jet engines. The wing commander, COL Dixon Allison, immediately decided that he had to move his aircraft from Toul to prevent aircraft losses. By 26 February the three flying squadrons had moved to West Germany. The 112th TRSq (Night Photo) moved their RB-26Cs to Wiesbaden AB, the 157th TRSq (Photo, Jet) deployed eighteen RF-80As and two T-33As to Furstenfeldbruck AB and the 160th TRSq (Photo, Jet) moved a similar number of aircraft to Neubiberg AB. This resulted in overcrowding at these forward air bases and increased the vulnerability of the only tactical reconnaissance aircraft in Europe. While in West Germany the 36th Fighter-Bomber Wing supported the 157th TRSq at Furstenfeldbruck and the 86th Fighter Bomber Wing supported the 160th TRSq at Neubiberg. The 112th TRSq was supported by the 7100th Air Base Group while operating at Wiesbaden AB.

Flying began about 1 March 1952 with area familiarization around southern Germany, particularly important because of its limited airspace. East-West border violations could result in a shoot-down by Soviet fighters. Day photographic missions by the three squadrons were conducted, but were drastically reduced by several problems. The most serious was that the wing had half its authorized aircraft cameras. Conversion of F-80s into RF-80s had been rapid, but aircraft camera procurement lagged by years. Night photo work by RB-26s was not attempted due to the shortage of Mk-20 and Mk-24 photo flares and an approved night-dropping range in Europe. A few RB-26s had incomplete SHORAN radar installations and could not fly controlled photo tracks, even after SHORAN ground stations arrived in West Germany. Aerial photo processing was seriously hindered by the lack of mineral free water needed for photo processing and no 60 Hz electrical power to operate photo enlargers, printers, and drying racks. By June the most frustrating problem was the developing shortage of aircraft spare parts, which limited flying. Shortage of F-80 parts was particularly acute because the 117th TRWg had the only F-80 type aircraft in Europe, but spare parts for both aircraft types were in worldwide short supply, in part due to the Korean War. There had been little spares procurement during 1945-50 due to the reduced USAF peacetime budget. Increased flying hours and combat damage during the Korean War caused acceleration of the problem.

The men of the 117th were not only living with the hardships of an incomplete, poorly built base, but also were unable to satisfactorily perform the mission they were sent to France to do. Most wondered at the poor planning that activated their unit, assigned them a new mission, and then sent them to France without sufficient tools to accomplish it.

Finally in late June 1952 a joint exercise, Operation JUNE PRIMER, tasked the 117th TRWg to perform its primary mission of vertical and oblique day photography of gunnery ranges and preplanned airborne drop zones. Vertical photos of Rhine and Danube River bridges and shipping tested the pilots' abilities because the RF-80s did not have a vertical viewfinder

RF-80A-LO #45-8400 of the 157th Tactical Reconnaissance Squadron, 117th Tactical Reconnaissance Wing, 1952.
National Archives

installed. Their photo processing and interpreting skills were evaluated and met the tactical needs of the air and ground forces commanders. The 112th crews were able to take night photos by dropping photo flares on the Siegenberg range. Army artillery fire control missions were flown by the RF-80s. The 157th had voice wire recorders, ANQ-1, installed in five of their RF-80s for post-mission evaluation. The wire recorders proved very helpful in visual reconnaissance mission debriefings; the pilot could record many details of real-time sightings. Another important mission given the 117th TRWg was vertical and oblique day photography of new USAFE air base construction and U.S. Army installations in France, West Germany, and United Kingdom on a monthly or semi-monthly schedule.

Army and Air Force commanders were very surprised that the 117th TRWg was able to accomplish its missions in spite of all the difficulties the wing had to overcome during the preceding six months.

On 6 June 1952 COL Allison held the first news conference conducted at Toul Air Base. His primary topic was what the U.S. and USAFE were attempting to accomplish at Toul, and in France as part of NATO. He decided to do this after hearing all the stories about "the U.S. takeover and occupation of France, including impressment of local workers." The French communist party had done a very good job of spreading totally false rumors and stories among the population of northern France. The French government was supposed to perform this public relations task but did not because it was afraid to confront its citizens with the NATO agreements it had made. French newspapers ran many columns about the information presented by COL Allison and this greatly improved Franco-American relations around the Toul region.

Aircraft parking ramps at Wiesbaden were becoming very crowded with C-47 traffic into HQ USAFE, so in July the 112th TRSq returned to Toul from Weisbaden. The wing commander felt the B-26s could fly from Toul's poor runway. Frustrated by the lack of shop facilities at Toul, aircraft maintenance personnel took it upon themselves to construct tents for aircraft shops and inspection shelters to maintain the B-26s. Both RF-80 squadrons remained in West Germany until a new runway was completed.

At midnight on 9 July 1952 the 117th TRWg was released from active duty with the USAF. Only its wing and squadron designators were returned to the states in which they were activated in October 1950.

10th Tactical Reconnaissance Wing

On 10 July 1952 the 10th Tactical Reconnaissance Wing was activated at Toul with the mission, aircraft, equipment, and the 215 officers and 1,310 airmen that had belonged to the 117th Tactical Reconnaissance Wing the day before. Its three reconnaissance squadron designators also changed: the 112th TRSq became the 1st TRSq, the 157th TRSq became the 32d TRSq, and the 160th TRSq became the 38th TRSq. The 32d and 38th Squadrons remained at Furstenfeldbruck AB and Neubiberg AB respectively, after changing their designations.

The 10th Tactical Reconnaissance Wing was the WWII 10th Tactical Reconnaissance Group activated in September 1941. It had moved to England and then

RF-80A #45-8391 of the 38th Tactical Reconnaissance Squadron, 10th Tactical Reconnaissance Wing, 1953.

Harold Wall

across northern France and into Germany, earning seven Campaign Stars as part of the Ninth Air Force. A DUC was awarded for its excellent photo coverage of Normandy invasion beaches. The 10th TRGp was inactivated in April 1949 at Pope AFB, North Carolina, in the 1949 DOD budget cuts.

The 10th TRWg continued flying the same missions as the 117th. During the summer and fall of 1952, good weather facilitated excellent day photo results. In November 1952 Operation LONGSTEP required the 1st TRSq to deploy ten RB-26s to Campodichino Airport near Naples to perform maritime day and night photo reconnaissance of the U.S. Sixth Fleet. The RB-26s had to fly some long, six-hour night missions to obtain photos. During this exercise, the 10th's photo interpretation and print quality impressed NATO Southern Command operations/intelligence officers. One RB-26 demonstrated several night drops of new paraflares over Naples Bay that caused alarm among the Neapolitans.

Flying and photo operations were reduced in the winter of 1952-53 because of Europe's exceptionally cold weather. Fog frequently grounded the RF-80s in Germany. HQ USAFE tasked the 32d TRSq to photograph air base construction progress at four French Morocco sites in North Africa. Operating from Nouasseur and Sidi Slimane was much preferable to Central Europe; the day photo conditions were excellent. This was the beginning of Operation SUN BASE that was repeated during the winter months by all tactical reconnaissance squadrons based in France and West Germany until the U.S. was forced out of Morocco in 1963. Photo targets such as isolated desert oasis and forts tested both dead reckoning navigation photo runs and camera operation.

The 10th performed its mission well but it also inherited all the fundamental problems the 117th had been unable to solve at Toul, so it looked forward to leaving when it was transferred to West Germany. On 9 May 1953 it became the first wing to enjoy the vastly superior facilities at newly completed Spangdahlem AB, West Germany. This relocation to Spangdahlem finally permitted the complete wing to live at and fly from one air base. The 10th TRWg continued to serve in Europe until 1983.

Prior to departure of the 10th, a support organization was activated by HQ, Twelfth Air Force to manage Toul until arrival of the next flying wing. This caretaker unit was the 7412th Support Squadron that had served at Toul during initial construction in late 1951. The squadron consisted of seventy-five officers and airmen. Several airmen from the 10th Wing were assigned to the 7412th because of their experience with specific functions at Toul: procurement, finance, and installations. So unfortunately, they didn't have the pleasure of joining the rest of their wing at Spangdahlem. Det #8, 12th Postal Sq; Det #3, 1992d AACS Sq; and the Det #5, 31st Weather Squadron also stayed behind to support the base.

During this time U.S. Army Aviation Engineers were assigned to Toul to rework the runway and improve facilities. Almost immediately the 843d EABn encountered Toul's ongoing problem—dampness. During the summer of 1953 the runway was unexpectedly covered in water. Since it was during a dry season, air installations crews thought an underground water line had broken somewhere on the base. After much digging and testing the SCARWAF unit determined it was just Toul's unique topography. They greatly improved runway drainage and flying resumed. The 843rd EABn worked at these projects for over twenty months. Meanwhile, French contractors started construction of the permanent NATO structures: wing headquarters, base operations, and three large hangars.

During October 1953 the 7412th Support Squadron received notice that a C-119 troop carrier wing would arrive with 1,600 personnel during the first quarter of calendar year 1954.

465th Troop Carrier Wing, Medium

The 465th Troop Carrier Wing, Medium, was activated on 1 February 1953 at Donaldson AFB, South Carolina with the C-46s, mission, and personnel that had belonged to the 443d Troop Carrier Wing. The 443d was an Air Force Reserve wing that had completed its twenty-one months of extended active duty on 31 January 1953. Its unit designation was returned to Hensley Field, Dallas, Texas. The newly formed 465th Troop Carrier Wing was manned by 165 officers and 930 airmen. It was assigned to Tactical Air Command, and had three squadrons: the 780th, 781st, and 782d Troop Carrier Squadrons. In the spring and summer of 1953, the 465th converted from C-46s to the new Fairchild C-119C Boxcars.

Originally the 465th designator was a WWII heavy bombardment group activated on 1 August 1943. The group moved their B-24s to Pantanella, Italy and conducted strategic bombing in Austria, Czechoslovakia, France, Germany, Italy, and the Balkans. It participated in eight campaigns within one year as part of the Fifteenth Air Force. Two DUCs were awarded for excellent bombing of two very heavily defended targets in Vienna and Friedrichshafen. The 465th Bomb Group was inactivated in July 1945 in Trinidad as the USAAF demobilized after Victory in Europe.

Initially another wing, the 313th TCWg based at Mitchel AFB, New York, had been alerted to move to France but it did not pass its port of embarkation inspections—equipment shortages were the primary problem. Instead, many skilled personnel from the 313th were transferred to the 465th TCWg to fill personnel shortages so the 465th could deploy overseas within one year after activation.

Each squadron was assigned eighteen C-119Cs. Several new aircraft arrived from Pope AFB. Aircraft maintenance personnel had to begin learning the C-119C aircraft since all their experience was on C-46s. The R-4360-20 engine was very different from the R-2800 type in the C-46. Also, extensive ground and flight training was required to develop the newly assigned aircrews. During late August 1953, the 465th Wing received an alert message to prepare for a permanent change of station to APO 83 and movement to Europe.

The ADVON left for Europe on the USNS GEN Patch troop ship in November 1953. The main body followed during March on the USNS GEN Butner and arrived at Toul AB on 3 April 1954.

Aircraft of the 465th departed Donaldson AFB on 1 December 1953, and began arriving at Toul nine days later. All had completed the trip by 16 January 1954. These Boxcars successfully made the winter flight across the North Atlantic from Donaldson to Toul. They were the first C-119s based in France. Construction at Toul had continued but was far behind schedule. Aircraft parking aprons, hangars, and shops were still not complete and not usable, therefore USAFE decided to temporarily base the squadrons at air bases in Germany. After arrival at Toul; the 780th moved to Rhein-Main until 10 May 1954; the 781st relocated to Wiesbaden until 3 May 1954; and the 782d was at Neubiburg until April 1954.

Airlift capabilities were in demand to meet the growing logistics needs of NATO air power. The primary mission of the 465th was dropping airborne forces and their equipment, but with very few airborne troops in Germany intra-theater airlift support throughout Europe became the primary operation. A very important mission was transporting personnel and equipment to support aircraft weapons training on desert ranges at Wheelus AB in Libya, North

Line for mess hall, Toul AB, 1954.
Culvert to drain off the frequent rains.
Norm Adams

View of the flight line from base shops, Toul AB, 1954.
Mud and construction continued..
Norm Adams

Temporary steel building housed base theater at Toul AB, 1954.
Norm Adams

Permanent construction at Toul AB 1959.
Theater on left, service club on right.
David Menard

Africa. Several C-119s were required to move each fighter squadron's maintenance and support personnel to and from Wheelus for this extremely important pilot proficiency training.

Aircraft repair facilities were still not finished when the squadrons returned to Toul in the spring of 1954, but other problems limited flying as well. Special calibration and test equipment was unavailable. Another problem involved manpower shortages. Upon arrival in Europe the wing found a shortage of airborne radio operators, so airborne radio repairmen were used after considerable training. This provided radio operators, but radio maintenance sections were then shorthanded and built-up a backlog of repairs. This left C-119s out of commission because they lacked operational communications/navigation radios.

At least building construction had made good progress during 1953 and 1954. Barracks were completed for the 465th Wing personnel, so they did not have to live in tents.

Tactical Air Command began two-month rotations of fighter squadrons into USAFE in 1954. The 366th Fighter-Bomber Wing from Alexandria AFB and later the 312th Fighter-Bomber Wing from Clovis AFB deployed to Toul. These were the first wings to test the idea of dual basing—when a wing is committed to NATO war plans but is based in the United States, thus reducing gold flow. Several aircraft losses occurred during rotation, particularly among pilots unfamiliar with Toul's unique weather conditions. Heavy fog developed frequently within the runway area and very low ceilings around the base caused some pilots to eject after running low on fuel. Three F-86Fs were lost on a flight from Marseille to Toul when they attempted to land using GCA at night in a dense fog. Repeated approach attempts left them with below minimum fuel. LTC England, commander of the 389th Fighter-Bomber Sq, was killed when his

F-86H #53-1418 of the 81st Tactical Fighter Squadron, 50th Tactical Fighter Wing, 1957.
Al Christensen

F-86 crashed in woods near the base, and his wingmen lost their two F-86s when they had to eject. Another jet crashed three miles south of Toul from fuel starvation but the pilot ejected safely. Another rotational F-86 crashed on Toul AB in March 1955.

There can be rough days that test a pilot's airmanship even in the troop carrier business. The 780th Troop Carrier Squadron lost two C-119Cs in separate accidents on 18 April 1955. The first loss occurred near Moulins, France, when an elevator trim-tab developed severe vibrations that caused loss of aircraft elevator control; fortunately the crew bailed out and all survived. Several hundred miles south another C-119 had both engines fail over the Mediterranean Sea. It made an emergency landing on an abandoned airstrip on the island of Corsica. The aircraft was badly damaged but the crew survived the landing without serious injury.

From February through July 1955, the 416th and 531st Fighter-Bomber Squadrons had to be based at Toul on temporary duty from the 21st Fighter-Bomber Wing. They were unable to fly from their new base because runway construction at Chambley was still unfinished when the units arrived in France. The 465th Wing and especially the 465th Supply Squadron supported these fighter squadrons during their extended stay at Toul.

Several U.S. Army aviation engineer units were based at Toul-Rosieres from 1953 to 1956 to train and gain experience. In addition to improving the runway, SCARWAF personnel provided much needed manpower for base projects. The 465th Motor Vehicle Squadron received assistance from the 885th Engineer Aviation Maintenance Co. and the 843d Engineer Aviation Battalion to eliminate a large backlog of inoperable base vehicles that had been awaiting parts and repairmen. Company A, 843d EABn constructed 108 trailer sites on base for family housing. Their work included pouring concrete pads; installing water, sewer, and electrical utilities; and building roads. The 359th Engineer Aviation Supply Point Company supported any logistical requirements for the SCARWAF units.

In addition to the trailer camp, a large Commodity Credit Housing project, "Toulaire," was built by French contractors during 1957. It was located four miles southeast of the base and consisted of 320 duplex and triplex units. There was a critical shortage of off base family housing in the Toul-Nancy region due to the thousands of U.S. military personnel being assigned to bases in the area. The duplex units at "Toulaire" are still in use by French families.

By May 1955, the 465th Wing was ready to leave

for the partially completed Evreux-Fauville Air Base about 200 miles west in France. The 465th, flying fifty-four C-119C Boxcars, still consisted of three troop carrier squadrons, the 780th, 781st, and 782d and their supporting squadrons. The 465th was the first USAFE tactical wing to move into Evreux. By 22 May 1955 all personnel had departed for Evreux-Fauville after sixteen months at Toul-Rosieres.

In anticipation of the 465th's departure, USAFE activated the 7430th Air Base Squadron in March 1955 to maintain Toul in standby status until the next tactical wing arrived from CONUS. But, rising costs of NATO basing prevented moving any additional USAF wings to France. For the next year the 7430th, with about 400 French employees, operated Toul as a standby base. It was assigned one C-47A and one L-20A for base support flying.

The 7430th AB Sq was organized into eight sections as follows:

Unit Administration	Comptroller
Air Installations	Material
Air Police	Operations-Flying
Chaplin	Staff Judge Advocate

Toul commissary, also operated by the 7430th ABSq, was tasked to support St. Mihiel Air Depot (Munitions), the Toul Engineering Depot, and Nancy Ordnance Depot.

On 1 June 1955, while the base was in standby status, a new, non-directional radio-beacon-transmitter frequency of 477 Khz "DT" was assigned to Toul. The NDB was moved upward in frequency to improve coverage around the base airspace. Radio engineers hoped this step would prevent aircraft losses due to bad weather navigation errors. Det #3, 1952d AACS Sq was still operating with their old WWII Ground Controlled Approach radar system MPN-1 that had arrived on base in 1952. Det #29, 8th RRL Sq maintained the radio relay station on Toul AB.

50th Tactical Fighter Wing

The 50th Fighter-Bomber Wing was transferred to Toul from Hahn AB, West Germany, on 1 July 1956. The 50th had arrived in Europe in 1953 from Clovis AFB, New Mexico, and was assigned to Hahn. While there, the wing had converted from its F-86Fs to F-86H Sabres. It consisted of three fighter-bomber squadrons, the 10th, 81st, and 417th, flying seventy-four F-86H Sabres plus two C-47s.

Later, in the summer of 1957, F-100Ds replaced the F-86Hs. The 50th FBWg was the third and last fighter wing in France to convert into Super Sabres, using the same procedures as described for the 48th FBWg in chapter 9. The 50th flew the "Hun" for the following ten years. The primary mission of this wing was the delivery of special (nuclear) weapons for interdiction; its secondary missions were tactical air support for ground forces and day air defense operations.

On 8 July 1958, while flying their F-100Ds at Toul, the 50th Fighter-Bomber Wing was redesignated the 50th Tactical Fighter Wing, with its three squadrons changing to Tactical Fighter Squadrons. This designation change occurred throughout the USAF.

The 50th Fighter Wing had been tasked to support nearby DOBs. On 1 September 1959 Detachment #2, Headquarters, 50th Air Base Group was deactivated at Chenevieres as the 7514th Support Group was created at Toul. Supporting the DOBs then became the job of the 7514th.

After three years of operations at Toul, the 50th Wing had to depart France in late 1959 as part of RED RICHARD. De Gaulle would no longer allow nuclear weapons or aircraft capable of delivering nuclear weapons to be based in France. Pferdsfeld AB, West Germany, was considered as a possible relocation site. Instead it was decided to return the wing to Hahn since it was partially occupied and the runway had recently been reworked. The wing's personnel were happy to return to Germany and better facilities. The runway at Toul had begun to disintegrate again due to the F-100's increased footprint weight of 39,000 pounds; almost double that of the F-86H. The 50th Wing and its three tactical fighter squadrons, the 10th, 81st, and 417th, flying seventy-six F-100D/F Super Sabres and two C-47 support aircraft, officially transferred from Toul to Hahn on 10 December 1959, where they stayed for thirty-two years.

As the five main bases emptied in 1959 because of Project RED RICHARD, Seventeenth Air Force activated support units to provide a minimum work force to maintain these bases in standby mode. The bases became Standby Operating Bases (SOB). This acronym didn't look too appropriate in correspondence and was soon dropped. The 7514th Support Group was created to perform this function at Toul, but was then given the additional responsibility to maintain the other four main bases—Chambley, Chaumont, Etain and Phalsbourg; and be the primary support unit for Bordeaux-Bacalan, Marseille-Marignane Airport, Suippes Gunnery Range, and St. Mihiel Ammunition Depot; plus the dispersed operating bases at Brienne, Chalons, Chenevieres, and Vouziers prior to their transfer or disposal. It was also responsible for eight radio relay sites. With the forecasted 1960 through 1963 USAFE budget reductions, it was planned that the four main air bases would remain inactive for at least five years. Small numbered detachments of the 7514th were assigned to each base to secure and maintain all equipment and facilities. At some of these locations USAF personnel had to live off base on the French economy.

Det #1 Etain AB
Det #2 Chambley AB
Det #3 Chaumont AB
Det #4 Brienne-le-Chateau DOB
Det #5 Chalons DOB
Det #6 Vouziers DOB
Det #7 Chenevieres DOB
Det #8 Bordeaux-Bacalan Storage Depot
Det #9 Marseilles-Marignane Airport
Det #10 Suippes Gunnery Range
Det #11 Paris-Orly Field Air Terminal
Det #12 Moselle Radar Control Site

These maintenance functions had previously been performed by the 21st, 48th, 49th and 50th Fighter Wings. In fact, before their move to Hahn, personnel of the 50th TFWg helped train the newly assigned 7514th airmen.

Since the 7514th was intended to be a small, simple "housekeeping unit" with limited manpower when it was activated on 1 September 1959, Seventeenth Air Force reduced its manning. The large underestimated need was for air policemen to provide security for all the air bases and remote sites to prevent property theft and vandalism. Airmen required for building maintenance were carpenters, electricians, painters, and plumbers. Supply clerks and warehouse men were needed to control and transfer stored parts, and equipment and fuel specialists were needed to maintain the large quantities of vehicle and aircraft POL stocks. Many trained mechanics were required to keep the vehicle fleets in a usable condition.

Being manager of the RED RICHARD relocation over the four-month period from 1 September to 31 December 1959 was an enormous task. The 7514th Transportation Squadron history gives the reader an understanding of the workload that RED RICHARD produced. Military trucks moved 1,502 tons of cargo; 1,130 tons were moved by the Army and 372 tons by USAF trucks. The 574th Medium Truck Company from Jeanne d'Arc Hospital, near Toul, provided their 10-ton tractor/trailers for the 120 five-day round trips to Hahn. Using commercial movers, the Household Goods Section shipped 162 tons of goods for 176 families going to Hahn and 52 families going to Ramstein, while 168 tons of goods were shipped back to CONUS for families completing their four years of duty in France. These numbers do not include the shipment of privately owned vehicles. Yet, during this period twenty-three airmen were transferred out of the transportation squadron and only six replacements arrived, illustrating the slow steady decline in manning of units stationed in France.

A major responsibility of the 7514th Headquarters Squadron was the termination of programmed construction projects at all standby bases and sites, as well as cancellation of all ground communication/electronic installations schemes. Some of these programs and projects had been waiting five years for funding as part of original base requirements and added up to millions of dollars. After stopping all new base improvements these funds had to be reprogrammed for other expenditures, primarily to pay for commercial transportation of departing people and equipment. This reprogramming required extensive overtime by limited finance section personnel to justify HQ USAFE funds transfer approvals.

On 1 January 1960 the 7514th was reorganized into the 7544th Support Group. Upon activation the 7514th had consisted of eight squadrons: headquarters, air police, supply, support, installations, transportation, communications, and food services–all designated 7514th. Reorganization changed these squadrons into sections within two squadrons, the 7544th Support Squadron and the 7544th Material Squadron.The Support Squadron had five sections: air police, support, installations, communications, and food service. Material Squadron had three sections: aircraft maintenance, supply, and transportation. By 1 July 1960, the 7544th Support Group was manned by 102 officers, 970 airmen, 348 French nationals, and 8 Department of Air Force civil service personnel for a total 1,428 men and women to keep all facilities ready for immediate occupancy in the event of NATO war mobilization.

An ongoing and time consuming duty of the 7544th Group was keeping Project SEAWEED emergency war reserve vehicles and equipment in operational readiness. Because vehicles sat idle for many months they rapidly deteriorated and required many repair man-hours.

In April 1960 the 66th Tactical Reconnaissance Wing at Laon AB moved all four RF-101C squadrons, the 17th, 18th, 32d, and 38th TRSqs to Toul for 120 days TDY in Operation DIM-VIEW while major runway rework was undertaken at Laon. About 120 airmen were assigned TDY from Laon to assist the 7544th Support Gp with this additional workload. A total of 601 personnel from Laon had to be fed and

F-84F-40-GK #51-9545 of the 110th Tactical Fighter Squadron, 7131st Tactical Wing, 1961.
USAF Official Photo

housed by the 7544th. Toul was a busy flying base for the five months required to complete the runway repairs at Laon.

As the 7544th became a trained unit, with a minimum of personnel turnover during 1960 and into 1961, and had settled into routine maintenance of its bases and equipment, a major new crisis engulfed the USAFE and Europe. In October 1961 increased Soviet hostilities and the construction of the Berlin Wall triggered the return of U.S. air power to France. Once again, Air National Guard units were activated and sent to France.

7131st Tactical Fighter Wing

The 131st Tactical Fighter Wing, Missouri ANG, consisting of approximately 220 officers and 1,350 airmen, was called to federal active duty on 1 October 1961 for a period of twelve months for the Berlin Crisis. When activated, the wing consisted of three fighter squadrons and supporting units: the 110th Tactical Fighter Squadron based at Lambert Field, St. Louis, Missouri; the 169th Tactical Fighter Squadron at Peoria Municipal Airport, Peoria, Illinois; and the 170th Tactical Fighter Squadron at Capitol Airport, Springfield, Illinois. All three squadrons had been flying Republic F-84F Thunderstreak fighters for more than four years.

Due to budget constraints the 131st Wing moved only a portion of its total strength and one fighter squadron, the 110th Tactical Fighter Squadron, to Europe. The advance detachment arrived on 19 October 1961 followed by the main group of 76 officers and 586 airmen. When they arrived, they found the base in very good condition and ready for operational use. The wing was short fifty personnel, primarily in support squadron areas that did not critically affect mission readiness.

The C-133A was used in addition to other MATS airlifters to move high priority aircraft support equipment. The 110th Squadron flew twenty-six F-84Fs and wing pilots flew over one C-47 and two T-33A support aircraft. An L-20A was assigned to the base and operated by Wing HQ as an additional support airplane. Operation STAIR STEP, the activation and movement of ANG flying units to the air bases in France in October 1961, was described in detail in chapter 5.

By 24 November 1961 the 131st Tactical Fighter Wing had assembled at Toul for an estimated stay of ten months. It was assigned to the Seventeenth Air Force, and was redesignated the 7131st Tactical Wing, which indicated a partial wing.

During this period the wing's 169th and 170th Tactical Fighter Squadrons and support units remained on extended active duty at their Illinois ANG home stations, ready to reinforce the 110th TFSq at Toul. Some of the personnel, primarily fighter pilots from these two units, rotated to Toul to gain operational experience in Western Europe.

Support squadrons quickly established working areas as their equipment arrived. The wing also received very large shipments of conventional munitions, bombs, rockets, and gun ammunition in the first two months after arrival. Pilots began European theater flying orientation and air/ground close air support procedures with U.S. and NATO ground forces. The missions assigned by Seventeenth Air Force were close air support, day interdiction, and counter air operations. Their first mission, begun on 26 November 1961, was runway alert—Sierra Alert. The pilots had acquired air defense mission experience in reserve status by working with the Air Defense Command flying their F-84Fs. Sierra Alert required four armed fighters on five-minute alert and provided air defense against attacks on airfields across France. All new STAIR STEP F-84F wings were tasked to accomplish this same alert mission. The 7131st interacted with Moselle Control that provided ground control intercept (GCI) radar service for air defense across northeast France, Luxembourg, and Belgium.

After initial move-in and set-up, the 7131st Wing was inspected and evaluated by Seventeenth Air Force and HQ USAFE in early 1962 to determine its operational capabilities. The first Tactical Evaluation conducted from 12 to 17 January resulted in an unsatisfactory report. This evaluation occurred only a month and a half after arrival. A repeat TAC Evaluation on 6 to 8 March produced an outstanding rating. A General Inspection of the units and base conducted by HQ USAFE produced very good results. An Operational Readiness Inspection on 13 to 16 March conducted by the Seventeenth Air Force resulted in another outstanding report. The wing and all its squadrons worked long hours and overcame many obstacles to develop an operationally ready combat organization after their arrival in France.

The 7131st was tasked to participate in many USAFE and NATO exercises such as:

GRAND SLAM	CO-OP
GUN TALK	ROUND ROBIN
RIXATICK	SUPER CHIEF
INDIAN SUMMER	LONG THRUST
KEEN KNIFE	RAZOR'S EDGE
QUICK TRAIN	RED EYE
BIG STICK	NUDET
CABIN CRUISER	SQUADRON EXCHANGE
COLD TURKEY.	

A wing Combat Operations Center was badly needed to manage all the upcoming exercises. This modification was put out for bid, but instead was designed and built by wing and base engineering personnel to speed construction. Experience using local labor had shown that whenever possible "doing it in-house" produced much more satisfactory and timely results. The COC was opened on 22 May 1962 and satisfied requirements very well. During this period Wing Intelligence section personnel conducted two or more briefings a week from January through March for many distinguished visitors interested in evaluating the STAIR STEP operation, including the Assistant Secretary of Defense for Manpower.

Two bombing and gunnery training deployments to Wheelus from 4 January to 6 February and from 1 April through 12 May 1962, provided an opportunity for all 110th TFSq fighter pilots to complete their six-month gunnery proficiency requirements. Maintenance personnel as well as pilots really enjoyed these deployments because it gave them a welcome opportunity to work and fly in excellent weather conditions. Another very interesting exercise was a NATO exchange program conducted with the Danish Air Force at their Skrydstrup, Denmark air station in May 1962. Four Thunderstreaks and support personnel traded places with four F-100Ds from the 730th Eskadrilleren (Fighter-Bomber Squadron). This gave both bases experience supporting different aircraft and crews. During this period the 110th also furnished Forward Air Controllers to the 3d Armored Division, U.S. Army stationed in West Germany to provide close air support training.

Also in May the 110th flew fourteen F-84Fs in a fly-by formation on an Armed Forces Day air show at Toul-Rosieres Air Base; a few days later fifteen F-84Fs flew formation at the change of Seventeenth Air Force commanders at Ramstein Air Base in Germany. Excellent comments were dispatched to the 7131st commander praising these formation displays.

That same month the 7131st Tactical Wing received orders to begin planning an efficient redeployment to CONUS for early release from active duty. Initial plans had called for all F-84Fs to remain in France to equip a new fighter wing to be activated in France. This new fighter wing would have conventional weapon capability only, to satisfy President Charles de Gaulle's requirements. All F-84F spare parts and peculiar support equipment were to remain at Toul. The wing's support C-47 and T-33s were to be flown back to Lambert Field. All personnel, except those remaining on Air Force active duty at Toul, were scheduled to return to Lambert Field by 20 August 1962 for demobilization.

On 25 May the wing was told that nineteen F-84Fs would return to CONUS along with all personnel, aircraft support equipment, and most aircraft parts. This change required plans for an enroute support team and additional MATS support. Six F-84Fs were assigned to the 366th TFWg and remained in France. The 7131st Tactical Wing departed Toul between 14 and 18 July to return to CONUS to be released from active duty. The east-to-west crossing of the North Atlantic in their F-84Fs was accomplished without incident. On 23 July 1962 the 7131st Wing returned the air base to the 7544th Support Group that had remained active, continuing its mission of maintaining various USAFE facilities in France.

Detachment #1
10th Tactical Reconnaissance Wing

After six years the 10th Tactical Reconnaissance Wing reappeared at Toul with a detachment of Douglas RB-66B/C Destroyers. The 10th had officially moved to RAF Alconbury, UK, from Spangdahlem in West Germany, on 25 August 1959 as part of Operation Red Richard. After arrival at RAF Alconbury, the 10th was directed by Seventeenth AF to forward deploy RB-66s into Toul in October 1959 to stand fifteen minute combat Echo Alert with minimum personnel to support the Destroyers. The 10th now had to operate at four locations, RAF Alconbury, RAF Bruntingthorpe, RAF Chelveston, and Toul. The forward basing allowed B-66s to quickly join up with the F-100Ds on Victor Alert in West Germany and provide electronic warfare screening as the Huns penetrated Eastern Europe's airspace. Det #1's operation solved two serious problems for the Wing. First, family housing was available at Toul, and second, the B-66 engine noise around RAF Alconbury was cut in half by the wing flying in France. Det #1 personnel were in either permanent change of station status or TDY status over the six years. This Echo Alert deployment continued at Toul until October 1965 when the 25th TRWg at Chambley received the RB-66s and the 26th TRWg was activated at Toul. From April through July 1963, Det #1 moved to Chambley while Toul's runway and taxiways were rebuilt for the fourth time. No records exist on the money spent repairing Toul-Rosieres AB from 1954 until 1967!

Det #1, 10th TRWg began operations at Toul on 15 October 1959, with a mixed fleet of approximately twenty-four RB-66s and 550 personnel. Throughout this six year stay, Det #1 was supported by organizations at Toul, i.e., the 50th TFWg, 7451st Support Group, 7544th Support Gp, and the 7131st Tactical Wing. Major unscheduled aircraft repairs were performed by the 7544th Material Squadron. Crews from the 1st, 19th, 30th and 42d TRSqs flew EB-66Bs, RB-66B/Cs, and WB-66Ds at Toul from 1959 through 1965. All these B-66 versions were not capable of carrying nuclear weapons and, therefore, were acceptable to France. The EB-66Bs were modified bombers—B-66Bs that had been coverted into electronic jamming platforms, known as "Brown Cradle" aircraft. Each contained twenty high power jamming transmitters. Their radar bombing systems, K-5, were maintained by Det #1 radar troops. The WB-66Ds were weather reconnaissance aircraft that departed Europe in June 1960.

An RB-66C from the 42d TRSq at Toul was shot down over Gardelegen, East Germany, as it crossed over the East/West border on 10 March 1964. Its crew ejected and were taken prisoner. The men were eventually repatriated. Gyro compass failure was the suspected cause of the border violation.

Det #1, 10th TRWg was deactivated at Toul on 1 October 1965 when the 19th TRSq was transferred to the 25th TRWg at Chambley AB. The RB-66Bs and Cs performed the same mission when operated by the 25th TRWg as described in chapter 7.

26th Tactical Reconnaissance Wing

The final USAFE combat wing to operate from Toul AB was another reconnaissance wing, the 26th Tactical Reconnaissance Wing, activated 1 July 1965. The 26th TRWg designator was originally assigned to a WWII Observation Group with two squadrons, activated on 1 September 1941 at Ft. Devins, Massachusetts. The group flew anti-submarine patrols along the New England coastline after the Pearl Harbor attack. They participated in one campaign, Anti-Submarine-American Theater of Defense. The group did not deploy overseas during WWII and was deactivated 11 November 1943 at Reading Army Air Field, Pennsylvania.

The 26th Tactical Reconnaissance Wing was assigned to be the lead unit in Europe to transition into the new RF-4Cs and allow the 10th and 66th TRWgs to maintain operational readiness with their reconnaissance aircraft. An extensive ground and flight training program was established at Toul. This would permit the long period of training required by the RF-4C's highly complex airframe and avionics, plus new reconnaissance sensors. Toul had sufficient facilities for personnel and aircraft, and was remote from large cities, which was important as civilian protests about the increased jet engine noise were becoming a problem

Toul AB salvage yard 1965. Some of the material that had to be disposed of before moving out of France in Operation FRELOC.
Gilbert Savona

throughout Europe. The new RF-4C Phantoms began to arrive in France on 3 October 1965. USAFE had been programmed for six RF-4C squadrons by 1967, with phase-out of the RB-66s and RF-101s by 1968; but the war in Southeast Asia and FRELOC destroyed this schedule.

Some confusion exists about which squadrons served with the 26th at Toul. The three tactical reconnaissance squadrons initially assigned to the 26th Tactical Reconnaissance Wing were the 22d, activated at Toul on 19 April 1965, the 19th, flying RB-66Bs that transferred in on 1 July 1965 from the 10th TRWg; and the 32d, flying RF-101s, that transferred in on 1 October 1965 from the 66th TRWg at Laon. Not only were the squadron arrivals staggered, but after only three months at Toul, the 19th and its RB-66Bs were transferred to the new 25th Tactical Reconnaissance Wing at Chambley. For three months the 26th operated with two squadrons, the 22d and 32d. Then on 1 January 1966, the 26th received the 38th Tactical Reconnaissance Squadron that had been assigned to Laon. This gave it three squadrons: the 22d, 32d and 38th.

But in March of 1966, as the wing was becoming operational, de Gaulle announced that USAFE must depart France within one year, resulting in Project FRELOC. The 26th was assigned to the 86th Air Division at Ramstein AB, West Germany. On 5 October 1966, as soon as facilities at Ramstein were prepared, the 26th TRWg and two of its squadrons, the 38th and 22d and their forty RF-4Cs departed Toul. About one month later, the 22d moved to Mountain Home AFB, Idaho, with its twenty RF-4Cs. It became a dual-based tactical reconnaissance squadron earmarked for the 26th at Ramstein. Later in 1969, the 26th relocated its RF-4Cs to newly acquired Zweibrucken AB about 30 miles west of Ramstein. The third squadron, the 32d was transferred without personnel and equipment from Toul to the 10th TRWg at RAF Alconbury on 15 August 1966. This was a paper transfer only as all personnel and equipment were moved to Southeast Asia to equip tactical reconnaissance units being expanded to fight the Vietnam War

All during 1966 and 1967, the 7544th Support Group that had continued to operate Toul and support the assigned combat wings and other nearby U.S. installations, was working at a hectic pace to help move the 26th TRWg to Ramstein, transfer all supplies and equipment to bases in the UK and Germany, then dispose of excess property through local sales. Toul-Rosieres AB was closed after sixteen years, assigned to the Military Liquidation Section office in Paris for return to France and removed from USAF property records the end of March 1967. On 1 April 1967, USAFE deactivated the 7544th Tactical Group at Toul, which ended U.S. presence at the base.

It has been used by the French Air Force as a tactical fighter base but was closed in 2004 and is now a munitions storage base until around 2006-07. It is not open to visitors. The base site appears on Michelin map #307 Local. The city of Toul can be reached from Gare de l'Est in Paris.

Toul-Rosieres Air Base Assigned Aircraft

117th Tactical Reconnaissance Wing, RB-26C & RF-80A, 10 January 1952 - 9 July 1952

Eighteen aircraft per squadron. These aircraft were flown from Lawson AFB, GA to Toul AB, France by 117th TRWg pilots.

Aircraft Marking: 112th TRSq - Yellow bands. 157th TRSq - Red bands. 160th TRSq - Green bands.

RB-26C-DT

44-35227	112th	44-35500	112th	44-35606	112th	44-35617+	112th	44-35846	112th
44-35343	112th	44-35512	112th	44-35607	112th	44-35621	112th	44-35858	112th
44-35385	112th	44-35599	112th	44-35616	112th	44-35822	112th	44-35889	112th

RF-80A-LO

44-85062	157th	44-85397	160th	45-8384	160th	45-8400	157th	45-8462	160th
44-85095	157th	44-85443	157th	45-8386	157th	45-8403	157th	45-8463	160th
44-85122	157th	44-85461	160th	45-8387	157th	45-8404	157th	45-8464	157th
44-85177	157th	44-85473	160th	45-8389	157th	45-8422	157th	45-8465	157th
44-85196	157th	45-85485	157th	45-8390	160th	45-8449	157th	45-8466	160th
44-85330	160th	44-85491	160th	45-8391	160th	45-8459	157th	45-8476	157th
44-85356	160th	45-8359	160th	45-8394	160th	45-8460	160th		
44-85366	160th	45-8364	157th	45-8399	160th	45-8461	160th		

No losses, no fatalities

+ On display at Hill AFB Museum, Utah

117th Air Base Group: Wing Support Aircraft

C-47A:

T-33A: 51-4415 (157th), 51-4527 (160th), 51-4455 (157th)

10th Tactical Reconnaissance Wing, RB-26C & RF-80A, 10 July 1952 - May 1953

Eighteen RB-26 aircraft per squadron. All RB-26s and RF-80s transferred in place from the 117th TRWg to the 10th TRWg on 10 July 1952.

Aircraft Marking: 1st TRSq - Black and white bands. 32d TRSq - Red and yellow bands.
38th TRSq - Green and yellow bands 42d TRSq - Red and white bands.

RB-26C-DL and DT

43-22268	1st	44-35256	1st	44-35343	1st	44-35512	1st	44-35607	1st	44-35682	1st	44-35846	1st
43-22477	1st	44-35257	1st	44-35359	1st	44-35583	1st	44-35616	1st	44-35691	1st	44-35858	1st
44-34186	1st	44-35262	1st	44-35385	1st	44-35599	1st	44-35617+	1st	44-35808	1st	44-35889	1st
44-35227	1st	44-35322	1st	44-35500	1st	44-35606	1st	44-35621	1st	44-35822	1st		

RF-80A-LO

44-85062	32d	44-85397	38th	45-8384	38th	45-8400	32d	45-8462*	38th
44-85095	32d	44-85443	32d	45-8386	32d	45-8403	32d	45-8463	38th
44-85122	32d	44-85461	38th	45-8387	32d	45-8404	32d	45-8464	32d
44-85177	32d	44-85473	38th	45-8389	32d	45-8422	32d	45-8465*	32d
44-85196	32d	45-85485	32d	45-8390	38th	45-8449	32d	45-8466	38th
44-85330	38th	44-85491*	38th	45-8391	38th	45-8459*	32d	45-8476	32d
44-85356	38th	45-8359	38th	45-8394	38th	45-8460	38th		
44-85366	38th	45-8364	32d	45-8399	38th	45-8461	38th		

Toul-Rosieres Air Base Assigned Aircraft, continued

10th Tactical Reconnaissance Wing, continued

* Losses:
44-85491 - Crashed at Erding AB, West Germany, 9 JAN 53, 1 fatality.
45-8459 - Crashed, engine fire, over Belgium, 5 MAR 53, no fatalities.
45-8462 - Crashed, engine failure, near Neubiberg AB, West Germany, 10 MAR 53, no fatalities.
45-8465 - Crashed at Bitburg AB, West Germany, 21 MAR 54, no fatalities.
+ On display at Hill AFB Museum, Utah

10th Air Base Group: Wing Support Aircraft
C-47A:
T-33A: 51-4415 (32d), 51-4527 (38th), 51-4455 (32d), 51-8624, 51-8628, 51-8693, 51-8752, 51-8754

John Traficante

465th Troop Carrier Wing, C-119C, 2 April 1954 - 22 May 1955

Eighteen aircraft per squadron. These boxcars were flown from Donaldson AFB, SC to Toul AB, France by 465th TCWg pilots.
Aircraft Marking:

780th Troop Carrier Squadron - Red.
781st Troop Carrier Squadron - Green.
782d Troop Carrier Squadron - Yellow.

C-119C-25 & -26-FA

51-2587	780th	51-2606	781st	51-2631	781st	51-2646	780th
51-2588	781st	51-2611	780th	51-2632	781st	51-2647	781st
51-2589	780th	51-2612	781st	51-2633	780th	51-2648*	780th
51-2591	782d	51-2613		51-2634	781st	51-2649	780th
51-2592	780th	51-2615	782d	51-2636	781st	51-2650	780th
51-2593	781st	51-2617	780th	51-2637	781st	51-2651	
51-2594	782d	51-2618	781st	51-2638	780th	51-2652	781st
51-2595	781st	51-2622	781st	51-2639	782d	51-2653	781st
51-2596	782d	51-2623	782d	51-2640	781st	51-2654	781st
51-2597	782d	51-2626	781st	51-2641	781st	51-2655	782d
51-2598	782d	51-2627	780th	51-2642	782d	51-2656	780th
51-2599	782d	51-2628		51-2643	780th	51-2657	780th
51-2600		51-2629		51-2644		51-2658	782d
51-2601	782d	51-2630		51-2645*	780th	51-2661	780th
51-2602	782d						

* Losses:
51-2645 - Crashed, lost elevator control near Moulin, France, 18 APR 55, no fatalities.
51-2648 - Crashed, lost both engines near Corsica, France, 18 APR 55, no fatalities.

Wing Support Aircraft: 465th Air Base Group
C-47A: 43-15115
C-47B: 44-76757, 44-76996
L-20A: 51-16537

Base Support Aircraft: 7430th Air Base Squadron
C-47A: 43-15115 on June 1955

Toul AB tail numbers continued next page

Toul-Rosieres Air Base Assigned Aircraft, continued

Al Christensen

50th Fighter-Bomber Wing, F-86H, 17 July 1956 - April 1958

Twenty-four aircraft per squadron. These Sabres were flown from Hahn AB, West Germany to Toul AB, France by 50th FBWg pilots.
Aircraft Marking: 10th FBSq - Blue band, 81st FBSq - Yellow band, 417th FBSq - Red band.

F-86H-10-NH

53-1405	10th	53-1431		53-1449	417th	53-1467		53-1485	
53-1407		53-1432		53-1450*	417th	53-1468		53-1486	
53-1412		53-1433	10th	53-1451	417th	53-1469		53-1487	
53-1414		53-1434		53-1452		53-1470		53-1488	
53-1415		53-1435		53-1453		53-1471*	417th	53-1489	
53-1416		53-1437		53-1454		53-1472		53-1490*	81st
53-1417		53-1439		53-1455		53-1473		53-1491	
53-1418	81st	53-1440*	417th	53-1456		53-1474		53-1492	
53-1419		53-1441		53-1457		53-1475		53-1493	
53-1420		53-1442		53-1458		53-1476		53-1496	
53-1421	10th	53-1443	10th	53-1459		53-1477		53-1497	
53-1422		53-1444*~	417th	53-1460		53-1478		53-1498	
53-1424		53-1445		53-1461		53-1479	81st	53-1499	
53-1425	417th	53-1446		53-1462		53-1480		53-1500	
53-1426		53-1447		53-1463		53-1481*	81st	53-1502*	
53-1427*	417th	53-1448		53-1464		53-1482			
53-1430				53-1465		53-1483			
				53-1466		53-1484			

* Losses:
53-1427 - Crashed, let-down/bad weather, 5nm W of Ulm, W. Germany, 6 JAN 58, no fatalities, ejected.
53-1440 - Crashed, final approach, weather, 7nm NE of Traben, West Germany, 16 DEC 57, no fatalities, ejected.
53-1444 - Crashed, take-off, engine failure, 0.75nm NE of Toul AB, France, 21 APR 58, 1 fatality, ejected.
53-1450 - Crashed, final approach, weather, 0.75nm E of Erlenbach, W.Germany, 6 DEC 57, no fatalities, ejected.
53-1471 - Crashed, low level, bad weather, 0.1nm SE of Oberndorf, W.Germany, 5 DEC 56, 1 fatality.
53-1481 - Crashed, range ops-engine fire, 70nm W of Wheelus AB, Libya, 7 JUL 56, no fatalities, ejected.
53-1490 - Damaged, control loss, night take-off at Landstuhl, W.Germany, 26 AUG 56, no fatalities.
53-1502 - Crashed, final approach, Dijon, France, March 56, no fatalities, ejected.
~ Wing Commander's Aircraft

50th Air Base Group: Wing Support Aircraft
C-47A: 42-100883, 42-23356, 42-24096
C-47D: 44-76656, 44-76996
L-20A: 51-16532
T-33A: 51-6876, 51-8568, 51-8573

7430th Air Base Squadron: Base Support Aircraft
C-47A: 43-15115 on June 1955

50th TFWg tail numbers continued next page

Toul-Rosieres Air Base Assigned Aircraft, continued

USAF Museum

50th Fighter-Bomber Wing, F-100D, May 1957 - 10 December 1959

Twenty-five aircraft per squadron. These Super Sabres were flown from Toul AB to Hahn AB, West Germany by 50th TFWg pilots in December 1959.

F-100D-NA								F-100F-10-NA	
54-2227		55-2937		55-2952		56-3235		56-3730	417th
54-2236		55-2938		55-2953*		56-3237	417th	56-3813	
54-2243		55-2939		55-2954*		56-3238		56-3820	
54-2253		55-2940	81st	56-3024	417th	56-3243		56-3821	
54-2275		55-2941*		56-3025	417th	56-3245		56-3823*	
54-2779		55-2942		56-3027		56-3246*		56-3826	
55-2768		55-2943	10th	56-3029		56-3256		56-3830 ~	81st
55-2779		55-2944	81st	56-3030		56-3258		56-3835*	
55-2801	10th	55-2945		56-3031		56-3260	417th	56-3847	417th
55-2816	10th	55-2946		56-3032		56-3261		56-3871	
55-2932*		55-2947		56-3041	417th	56-3305		56-3901*	
55-2933		55-2948		56-3218		56-3307	417th		
55-2934	81st	55-2949		56-3227		56-3318			
55-2935		55-2950 ~		56-3233		56-3369			
55-2936*		55-2951		56-3234	417th				

* Losses:
55-2932 - Crashed, let-down, bad weather, 2nm S of Zweibrucken AB, W. Germany, 7 MAY 59, 1 fatality.
55-2936 - Crashed, bad landing, weather, 1nm N or Toul AB, France, 22 FEB 59, 1 fatality.
55-2941 - Crashed, landing, bad weather, 5 nm NE of Toul AB, France, 9 AUG 59, 1 fatality.
55-2953 - Crashed, engine failure, 5nm E of Wheelus AB, Libya, 16 APR 58, no fatalities, ejected.
55-2954 - Crashed, take-off engine failure, on Wheelus AB, Libya, 23 SEP 59, no fatalities.
56-3246 - Crashed, 6nm NW of Toul AB, France, AUG 58, no fatalities, ejected.
56-3823 - Crashed, engine failure, 6nm NW of Toul AB, France, 27 AUG 1959, no fatalities, ejected.
56-3835 - Crashed, engine failure, near Wheelus AB, Libya, 13 DEC 59, no fatalities, ejected.
56-3901 - Crashed, let-down/bad weather, 7nm S of Toul AB, France, 18 MAY 1959, 1 fatality.
~ Wing Commander's Aircraft

50th Air Base Group: Wing Support Aircraft
C-47A: 42-100883, 42-23356
C-47D: 44-76656, 44-76996
L-20A: 51-16532
T-33A: 51-6876, 51-8568, 51-8573

Toul AB tail numbers continued next page

Toul-Rosieres Air Base Assigned Aircraft, continued

Ted Bailey

Detachment #1, 10th Tactical Reconnaissance Wing RB-66B/Cs July 1958 - April 1965

RB-66 aircraft seen at Toul AB from 1958 through 1965. Destroyers were deployed from RAF Alconbuy, RAF Bruntingthorpe, and RAF Chelveston, UK. RB-66s would stay in France two to four months and return to England.

Aircraft Marking: 1st Tactical Reconnaissance Squadron - Blue. 19th Tactical Reconnaissance Squadron - Green.
30th Tactical Reconnaissance Squadron - Yellow. 42d Tactical Reconnaissance Squadron - Red.
Plus shooting star with four-color tail on vertical staiblizer.

EB-66B-DL ^^		RB-66B								RB-66C 42d TRSq
53-482	53-492	53-423	1st	54-430*	19th	54-509		54-524	1st	54-451*
53-484	53-493	53-426	1st	54-432	1st	54-510	30th	54-525		54-459
53-485	53-495	56-434	30th	54-434	30th	54-511	19th	54-526		54-460*
53-486	53-496	53-447	19th	54-435	19th	54-512		54-527		54-461
53-487	53-497	53-449	1st	54-436	30th	54-513	19th	54-528	30th	54-462
53-489	53-498	53-450	30th	54-438	19th	54-514	1st	54-533		54-463
53-491		53-451	30th	54-439		54-515		54-534	19th	54-464
		53-453	19th	54-440	1st	54-516	19th	54-539		54-465
		53-476	30th	54-441	30th	54-518	1st	54-542	30th	54-466
		54-420	1st	54-446	30th	54-519		54-545	1st	54-467
		54-421*	19th	54-506	19th	54-520		54-546	19th	54-468
		54-424	30th	54-507	19th	54-521	30th			54-469
		54-429	1st	54-508	1st	54-522				54-470
										55-380
										55-386

^^ Converted from B-66B-DL (Brown Cradle)

* Losses:

54-421 - Crashed, take-off, engine failure, near Skeffingham, UK, 12 DEC 59, 4 fatalities.
54-430 - Crashed, lost into North Sea during Royal Flush, 16 MAR 61, 3 fatalities.
54-451 - Crashed, shot down near Gardelegen, East Germany, 10 MAR 64, no fatalities, 3 ejections.
54-460 - Crashed, take-off, engine failure, on RAF Chelveston, UK, 7 FEB 62, 4 fatalities, 3 survivors.

10th Operations Squadron: Wing Support Aircraft
T-33A: 51-8754, 52-9624, 53-5132, 53-5906

7514th Support Group: Support Aircraft
C-47As: 42-100883, 43-15221 **C-47D:** 44-76671
L-20As: 52-6140, 51-16537
T-33As: 49-1002, 51-6808, 51-6834, 51-6875

USAF

7131st Tactical Wing, F-84F, 13 November 1961 - 17 July 1962

Twenty-six aircraft assigned to squadron. These Thunderstreaks were flown from Lambert Field, MI to Toul AB, France by 110th TFSq pilots. Nineteen F-84Fs transferred back to Lambert Field, ANGB and returned by 110th TFSq pilots in July 1962.

Aircraft Marking:

110th Tactical Fighter Squadron - Red band.

F-84F-25, -30, -40-RE and F-84F-10, -25, -40GK

51-1639	51-1680	51-1730	51-9378	52-6368 ~	52-6525	52-6598	52-6631	52-7035
51-1640	51-1697	51-1817	51-9531	52-6372	52-6551	52-6604*	52-6634	52-7080
51-1644	51-1701	51-9354	51-9545	52-6413	52-6572	52-6616	52-7027	

7131st TWg tail numbers continued next page

Toul-Rosieres Air Base Assigned Aircraft, continued

7131st Tactical Wing, 110th TFSq. continued.

* Losses:
52-6604 - Crash landed, hit trees during close air support in France, 20 APR 62, no fatalities.
~ Wing Commander's Aircraft

7131st Operations Squadron: Wing Support Aircraft
C-47A: from ANG 42-23771
L-20A: 52-6140
T-33A: 2 ea 52-9671 from ANG

26th Tactical Reconnaissance Wing, RF-4C, 1July 1965 - 5 October 1966

Eighteen aircraft per squadron. RF-4Cs delivered from factory by MATS ferry pilots.

Aircraft Marking:
22d Tactical Reconnaissance Squadron - Blue band.
32d Tactical Reconnaissance Squadron - Red band.
38th Tactical Reconnaissance Squadron - Green band

RF-4C-MC

64-1060	22d	64-1073	38th	65-0821	32d	65-0839	22d	65-0857	32d	65-0878	32d
64-1061	22d	64-1074	38th	65-0823	22d	65-0840	32d	65-0858	32d	65-0882	22d
64-1063	22d	64-1075	38th	65-0824	38th	65-0842	32d	65-0859	22d	65-0883	22d
64-1064	22d	64-1076	38th	65-0825	22d	65-0845	32d	65-0861	32d	65-0885	32d
64-1066	38th	64-1080	38th	65-0826	38th	65-0847	32d	65-0865	22d	65-0888	22d
64-1067	38th	64-1081	38th	65-0827	22d	65-0848	22d	65-0866	38th	65-0893	32d
64-1069	38th	64-1084	38th	65-0831	32d	65-0851	32d	65-0867	32d	65-0894	22d
64-1070	38th	64-1085	38th	65-0835	38th	65-0853	32d	65-0868	32d	65-0895	22d
64-1071	38th			65-0836	38th	65-0854	32d	65-0873	38th	65-0899	22d
64-1072	22d	65-0819	22d	65-0838	32d	65-0855	32d	65-0877	32d	65-0901	38th

No losses, no fatalities.

Wing Support Aircraft: 26th Operations Squadron
C-47A: 42-100883, 43-16387
L-20A: 51-16537
T-33A: 51-6876, 53-5338

Appendix 16.1 Notice to Airmen 1958 (NOTAM) - USAF Toul-Rosieres

Elevation 934 feet (284 m), 48° 46'N - 05° 58'E. One paved concrete runway 8,000 feet long, 040°/220°. Bearing capacity 88,000 pounds for single wheel type landing gear. Rotating beacon light on airfield, with runway lights only. Aircraft storage with minor aircraft and minor engine repairs available. Aircraft fuel, 115-145 octane and JP4 jet fuel available with single point fuel service. Low pressure oxygen and liquid oxygen available. Jet aircraft starting units MA-1, and MA-2 and high pressure air available. Standard jet barrier and Safeland barrier installed for runway 04 only. Crash, fire, rescue facilities available.

ACKNOWLEDGEMENTS

I would like to thank the following people who contributed to this chapter:

Norm Adams was an avionics technician in the 465th Troop Carrier Wing stationed at Toul AB from May 1954 to May 1955 and then moved with the 465th to Evreux where he was stationed until December 1955.

Al Christensen was a Weather Officer in Detachment 10, 31st Weather Squadron, MATS, stationed at Chambley AB, 1955-1957. His aircraft photos were shot at a Victory in Europe Day open house held at Chambley in 1957.

David Menard served with the 50th Tactical Fighter Wing at Toul from May 59-Dec 59. He is a retired NCO and a retired USAF Museum employee (1978-99) who is an avid collector of aircraft photos and an expert on USAFE aircraft of the 1950s. He is a respected author of numerous aviation books.

Gilbert Savona is an Officer in the French Air Force who was stationed at Toul until its closure in August 2004. He provided an extensive collection of aerial photos taken at Toul, from the 50s to the present.

Harold Watt was a heavy equipment operator in the U.S. Army 862d Engineer Aviation Battalion. He constructed roads and trailer parks on the Chambley and Phalsbourg Air Bases in 1954 and 1955.

Sam Whitworth endured the winter of 1952 in the old Luxembourg barracks. He was in the 117th Wing HQ Squadron at Toul until moving to Evreux AB with the 465th in 1955.

17

DISPERSED OPERATING BASES

The concept of using Dispersed Operating Bases (DOBs) to improve air power survival was not new when NATO began planning for tactical air bases and aircraft in central Europe. Dispersal tactics and protective measures were very common during World War II and practiced by all nations. The USAAF was less concerned than its allies about base defense and dispersal because of total air superiority and unlimited resources of aircraft, aircrews, and ground personnel to replace combat losses. After D-Day as allied tactical air forces moved rapidly across the continent, investment in base and aircraft survival was impractical. Usually the allies used dispersal sites and shelters developed by the Luftwaffe. In France dispersal usually involved moving aircraft a long distance from the runway into wooded areas for concealment. By 1948 these dispersal areas had been converted back to farmland and any structures removed.

NATO faced several problems when attempting to solve the air power survival equation in France. First, planning for first strike survival in both nuclear and conventional wars had to be considered; second, the new main operating bases being built were on small parcels of land with very limited dispersal space; and third, any acquisition of real estate created enormous political problems. The first step towards force protection in France was the decision to separate the new air bases by a minimum of thirty miles (50 km). The second step was to space parked aircraft as far apart as possible by construction of a circular marguerite system of hardstands that could be revetted later with earth for added protection. Typically the marguerite consisted of fifteen to eighteen hardstands around a large central hangar. Each hardstand held one or two aircraft, and allowed the planes to be spaced approximately 150 feet (50m) apart. Each squadron was assigned to a separate hangar/hardstand complex.

As the main air bases became operational, the USAFE planners had to decide on the best dispersal of tactical aircraft in the event of enemy counter air strikes. Their goal was to have no more than one fighter squadron at each base in the event of war. The 1954 dispersal concept placed one fighter squadron forward on alert in West Germany, one fighter squadron at a DOB in France, and one fighter squadron at its main air base.

Beginning in 1953, DOBs were constructed at Chalons-Vatry, Luneville-Chenevieres, Vouziers-Sechault, and Vitry-Brienne; all sites in northeastern France. These were completed in about two years with a 7,900-foot runway, at least one hangar and parking for about thirty aircraft, and a few permanent buildings. Tent frames were constructed so the dispersed squadron could set up its tent camp on arrival. Electrical service, and water and sewage disposal systems were installed. Standard fighter-size hangars allowed the dispersed squadrons to have minimal aircraft support capability while working from their semi-trailer mobile shops.

Ten additional DOBs were listed "for emergency use" by USAFE. These bare-bones facilities were developed by the French Government. All airfields had at least a 7,900-foot standard NATO runway. These DOBs were intended for use by all NATO nations to disperse their aircraft in event of war, while Chalons-Vatry, Luneville-Chenevieres, Vouziers-Sechault and Vitry-Brienne were intended for use by the USAF wings in France. Some USAFE wings conducted exercises, at these emergency bases, for instance, the 38th Bomb Wing used Laon-Athies in 1957 during their Operational Readiness Inspection (ORI). These DOBs and their WWII designators were:

Cambrai - Epinoy 50° 13' N & 03° 09' E (A-75, B-72)
Cambrai - Niergnies 50° 08' N & 03° 16' E (A-74)
St. Simon - Clastres 49° 45' N & 03° 13' E (A-71)
Laon - Athies 49° 34' N & 03° 45' E (A-69)
St. Nazaire - Montior 47° 19' N & 02° 09' W
Beauvais - Tillie 49° 27' N & 02° 07' E, (A-61, B-42)
St. Quentin - Estrees 49° 53' N & 03° 03' E
Nancy - Ochey 48° 35' N & 5° 57'E (A-96)
Metz - Frescaty 49° 4' N & 06° 08' E (Y-34)
Mirecourt 48° 19' N & 06° 04' E (A-68)

A mobile communication system, "Project Four Wheels," was designed and produced to provide the

Chalons-Vatry DOB being used by the 21st Fighter-Bomber Wing, Chambley AB, for bare base exercises in 1956.
Al Christensen

DOB with positive command and control over the deployed tactical nuclear weapon delivery aircraft, it's wing command post, and higher NATO headquarters. Radio communications provided secure voice and teletype circuits. The "Project Four Wheels," system was a series of vans containing mobile control towers, weather data terminals, low frequency radio beacons, and TACAN beacons. These were contained in small, dual-wheel vans weighing 5,000 pounds designed to be airlifted in C-119 or C-123 transports from the main base to the DOB. The vans could be towed by 2.5-ton trucks to their operating site. Communication nets could be established within three hours after arrival. "Project Four Wheels" was fabricated by Craig Systems and were being delivered about the time the DOBs were being deactivated. This equipment was used for many years afterwards by mobile communications squadrons throughout the USAF.

Dispersal training usually consisted of one tactical squadron flying to a DOB and operating for a week or two while undergoing an ORI. The squadron maintenance sections would pack up their Henschel-built shop semi-trailers, drive to the DOB, set up the camp site and support an intensive flying schedule.

As the DOBs became operational, wing commanders soon realized they had acquired unforeseen collateral problems. Practice exercises to the DOBs made it clear that much had to be solved before this concept operated as planned. The big question was, "Where are we going to get the additional personnel and funds needed to maintain and secure these DOBs in operational condition?" The DOBs needed at least some of the same equipment and manning as the permanent bases; they could not be left without any infrastructure. A minimum of ninety Air Policemen would be required to control base access; guard fuel, munitions and supplies, prevent vandalism, and monitor alarm systems. An air installations crew of twenty-five personnel would be needed to maintain fencing, roads, runways, hangars, buildings, and utility systems. These troops would have to be billeted and fed in DOB facilities; daily commuting back to the main base would require more vehicles than were available. Extra aircraft support vehicles such as aircraft tugs, refueling trucks, fire crash rescue trucks, and munitions handling equipment would have to be at the DOB prior to aircraft arrival. Many of these vehicles were difficult to move rapidly by flatbed trailer over narrow French roads. Consequently, it was impractical to assume that they could all be brought with the dispersing squadron in a timely manner. Additional aircraft ground support equipment such as ground power units, jacks, tow bars, engine stands, and hydraulic test carts were required to be on the DOB for immediate arming and turn-around when the aircraft landed. While some squadrons trained at their assigned DOBs these problems were never completely solved due to severe manpower and funding limitations in USAFE.

The training lessons learned by operating from a dispersed base were considered by all to be worth the costs and operational hardships though the troops questioned whether the dispersal concept would actually work in event of war. One officer's reminiscences show the importance of training to make this a practical reality. Al Christensen, Det #10, 31st Weather Squadron, stationed at Chambley, has this to say about one of the exercises he participated in when deploying to a dispersed base in Germany:

> We had these large diesel trucks to transport food and living facilities when we deployed. First the fighter-bombers were launched, and then about an hour later we got off the ground in the C-123s; then the trucks and everybody else moved out from the base. We took important

items with us in the 123s, copious quantities of beer and a lot of snack food. We got to our DOB about an hour and a half later. The F-86s flew their mission and got there soon after we did. The trucks with all the tents and C rations did not get there till late the following day. So, the first night we all slept on what ever we could find in the one large empty hanger. We had a lot of little sterno fires going and cans of Vienna sausage we brought along were passed around. It looked like an encampment of Mongols. To pass the time we had a track meet around the hangar. The next day, the poor 1st Lieutenant in charge of the convoy arrived looking much worse than we did. The Air Policeman at the gate refused him immediate entry so he seized a large wrench and smashed the padlock on the gate. He was very short tempered, greasy, and tired. They had lost their way, the trucks had broken down, and there were no mechanics that knew how to fix them. It was plain to see that not a lot of thought went into this deployment business. Probably the higher ups knew quite well there would never be enough time to get anything off the base except the fighter-bombers. Most of us knew that from the beginning. Unless the Russian bombers got lost or intercepted, we were all gone.

By 1959, because of RED RICHARD and the reduction of tactical fighter and bomber wings in France, the need for these DOBs was virtually eliminated. The USAF transferred three of them to the U.S. Army to reduce the expense and manpower required to maintain them in minimum operational condition.

Following are more detailed descriptions of the four USAFE DOBs: Chalons-Vatry, Luneville-Chenevieres, Vouziers-Sechault, and Vitry-Brienne. All were built on open farmland. All were one step bases, meaning that permanent buildings were constructed and infrastructure completed before the base was useable. The Joint Construction Agency supervised construction of the airfields, which were built by French contractors. The logistics were supervised by the 73d Air Depot Wing, Chateauroux. No USAFE flying units were permanently assigned to these bases, and they were used for dispersal training only.

Vitry-Brienne DOB

This airfield has had two names; it was built as Vitry-Brienne and is currently known as Brienne-le-Chateau. The site was offered to USAFE in 1951; it was a substitute for St. Dizier airfield, which had been requested by USAFE. St. Dizier was familiar to the U.S. from WWII operations, but it was being used by the FAF. Vitry-Brienne was intended as a main base for a tactical wing, not a DOB. Construction began in 1953 but was delayed because the USAF could not decide what type of wing should be assigned: light bomber, fighter-bomber or tactical reconnaissance. In 1956 it was decided not to deploy another combat wing from CONUS into France. Instead, Brienne was assigned to the 48th FBWg at Chaumont as its DOB.

Brienne was officially activated as a DOB on 8 October 1958. It was a one step base that began with a few tents. A small eight-man team was deployed from Chateauroux to control property as it was shipped to the DOB. First, the runway was constructed parallel to highway D960. Next, three NATO fighter-size hangars were constructed. There were two hangars on the south side of the runway and a third at the northeast end of the runway. Three marguerites provided parking for forty-eight aircraft. Brienne's buildings differ from standard NATO design; the exteriors had tile roofs, multi-pane windows, more trim, and a mustard colored stucco finish. Wing/base headquarters was a one-story building. Eight long, two story barracks housed about 240 airmen each. Five large concrete POL pump-fill hydrant stations, holding 100,000 gallons each, were built south of the control tower. Three large vehicle maintenance shops and two large warehouses were constructed along the railroad siding. The gym, service club, communications center, theater, and mess hall were the final buildings completed. Three earth covered air raid shelters were built on base but the date of their construction is unknown. Having been planned as a main base, it was considerably more developed than the other DOBs. NATO and the USAF had invested about $17 million by summer 1959.

An early tenant unit, the 8th RRL Squadron, built Radio Relay Station Golf 7 on Brienne; it provided excellent communications for units using the DOB. A second tenant unit was an AACS detachment equipped with the portable "Project Four-Wheels" control tower van and portable TACAN station. Det #1, 48th Air Base Gp was activated on 1 May 1958 and was manned by three officers, eighty airmen, and eight LWR French employees to operate the base. This manning was totally inadequate. Initially Det #1 lived and worked in the northeast hangar while construction was nearing completion. Det #1 personnel assisted the JCA engineers by testing electrical, heating, and plumbing systems in the new buildings. The 48th Wing awarded a base facilities maintenance contract to a French company, but there were insufficient

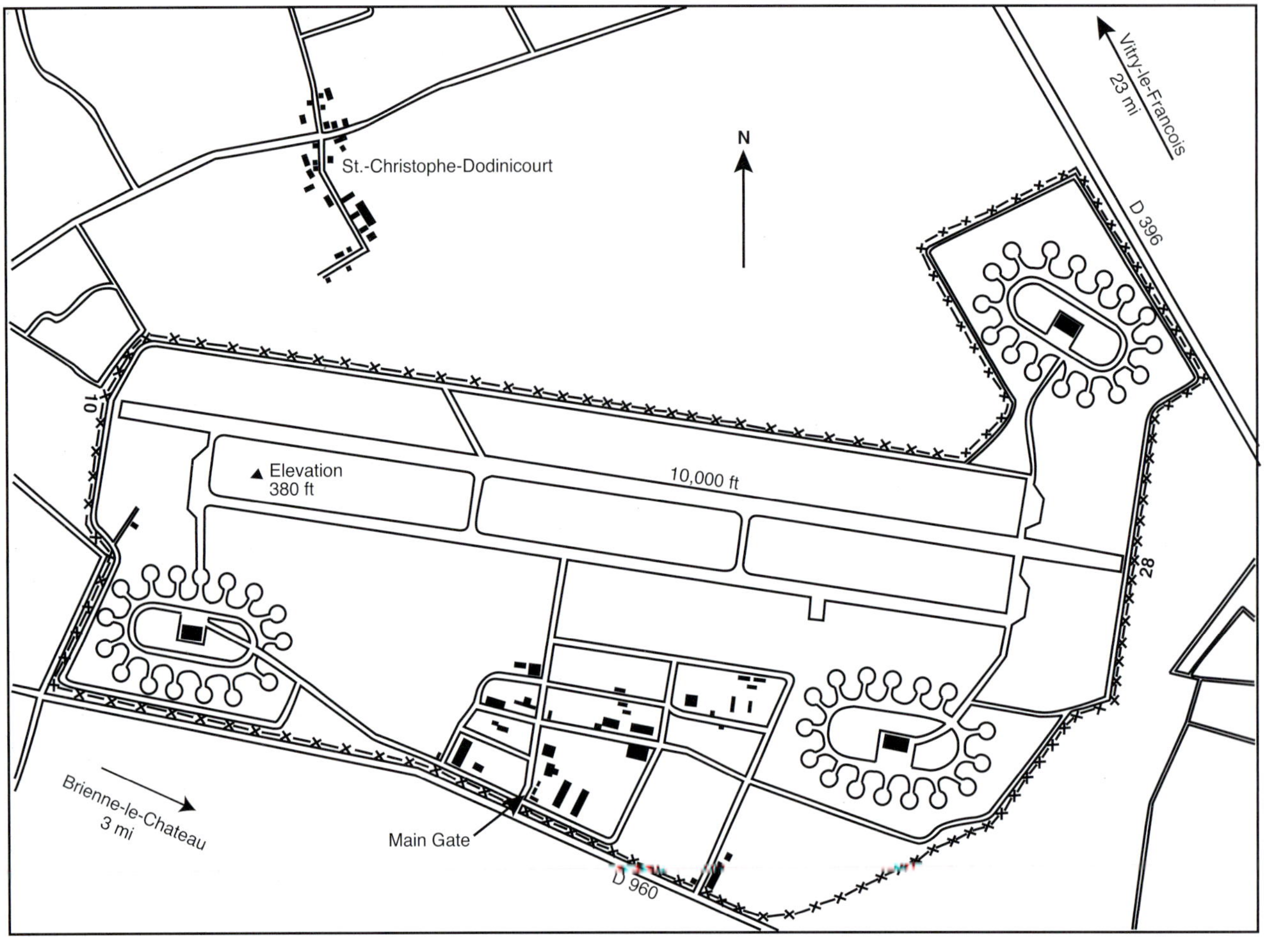

17.1 Vitry-Brienne DOB

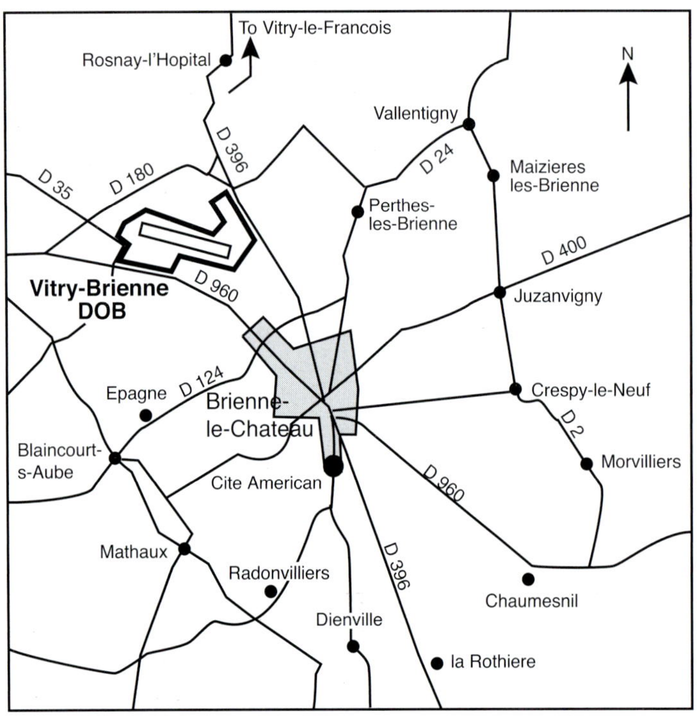

17.2 Vitry-Brienne DOB Area

Vitry-Brienne DOB: (Property #5940)

Location: Aube Department. 105 miles (170 km) east southeast of Paris, 17 miles (27 km) east of Auto Route A26 at exit 30. 23 miles (37 km) south of Vitry-le-Francois on RD396, and 3 miles (5 km) northwest of Brienne-le-Chateau. Main entrance on north side of route D960. 35 miles (56 km) northwest of Chaumont AB. Michelin Map #313 Local.

1950s Notam to Pilots -

Spare DOB. Emergency use only. 48° 26' N - 04° 29' E. Elevation 380 feet (115 m). One paved concrete runway 100°/280°, 8,000 feet long. Aircraft storage, major repairs. Airfield lighting: rotating beacon, runway, approach, and obstruction lighting. Prior permission for use required thru Chaumont base operations. DOB Instrument Letdown: Navigation aids Brienne Radio Facilities: Low frequency radio beacon, 463 KHz, "BC" 25W, on field. TACAN on Channel 45, "BC" on field. Approach Control: use Chaumont approach control. Remarks: Tower activated by "Notice To Airmen."

Control Tower: 315.90, 257.80, 243.00 UHF & 117.90, 121.50 VHF.

trained USAF personnel to monitor the contractor's performance. An IG inspection team visited in July 1958, pointed out all the discrepancies, and described better procedures to follow. By 11 August 1958 all personnel, offices and equipment were moved into the new permanent buildings. Two 1,000-foot runway extensions were added in 1959, using PSP over graded dirt. The base phone system was completed with three 120-line switchboards. Field telephone equipment and wiring was removed and stored. A forty-unit GRI housing complex, Cite American, was built south of Brienne city center. Completion of the BX, officers' club, airmen's club, snack bar, billeting office, and transient quarters in 1959 transformed Brienne DOB into a real USAF air base in less than a year.

Vitry-Brienne main gate 1962.
John Jakubic

The first major operation at Brienne was the 48th TFWg's deployment of its three fighter squadrons to the new DOB while Chaumont's runway and taxiways were being repaired. The F-100Ds operated from Brienne from 1 September through 15 December 1958. The DOB was also used for some unusual activities during 1959. In June the U.S. Army used it for truck driver training courses. The 70th Trucking Company from Vitry-le-Francois organized the twenty-day program; 225 drivers attended classes and qualified for their vehicle operator license. On 19 July, Brienne hosted the International Wakefield Cup Model Aircraft Championship, and about 7,000 spectators and model builders attended this very successful event. A French contractor operated a depot facility for aircraft drop tank repair in the southeast hangar, from February through July. CAMAE awarded them two contracts, one for work on 485—275-gallon drop tanks, and a second for 882—200-gallon drop tanks.

Vitry-Brienne DOB was phased out by Project RED RICHARD. All aircraft munitions were trucked to Chaumont. Aircraft parts and equipment were transferred back to Chaumont base supply, and then shipped to RAF Lakenheath. SEAWEED material, and supplies not required to maintain the DOB were returned to Chaumont. The 8th RRL Sq remained on Brienne to maintain the radio relay station. Det #1, 48th Air Base Group was deactivated on 25 October 1959, and military personnel returned to Chaumont AB. The forty Brienne GRI housing units were retained by the Chaumont Housing Office. The DOB was transferred to the 7544th Support Gp that maintained Brienne for a year, then turned it over to the U.S. Army.

The Army moved into Brienne in September 1961 and remained until June 1965. It put the Brienne facilities to good use, establishing the only major Army aircraft modification center in Europe. The Army operation at Brienne is described in detail in chapter 18.

The Army returned Vitry-Brienne to France on 24 June 1965. The airport was purchased in1970 by the Brienne Chamber of Commerce and later sold for private development. It has been an airport for sport aviation, sky diving, and soaring. Two hangars and several flightline buildings were used for an aviation museum. About fifteen museum aircraft were parked outdoors on old marguerites, but the museum is now inactive. The old officers' club was part of a campground complex. About twenty-five buildings still exist. Brienne airfield was considered as the site for a super air cargo airport, but the local residents objected loudly, so developers moved on to Chalons-Vatry DOB which is now being developed into the largest air cargo terminal in Europe.

Chalons-Vatry DOB

This airfield has had four names since 1950: Chalons-sur-Marne, Chalons-Sommessous, Vatry-Sommessous and now Chalons-Vatry. The site was offered to the U.S. in 1952, and construction began in 1953. It was the first DOB built for a tactical wing. A ten-man team was deployed from Chateauroux to control property as it was shipped to this site. A 7,900-foot runway, parking for fifty fighters, and three large hangars were constructed. When construction was

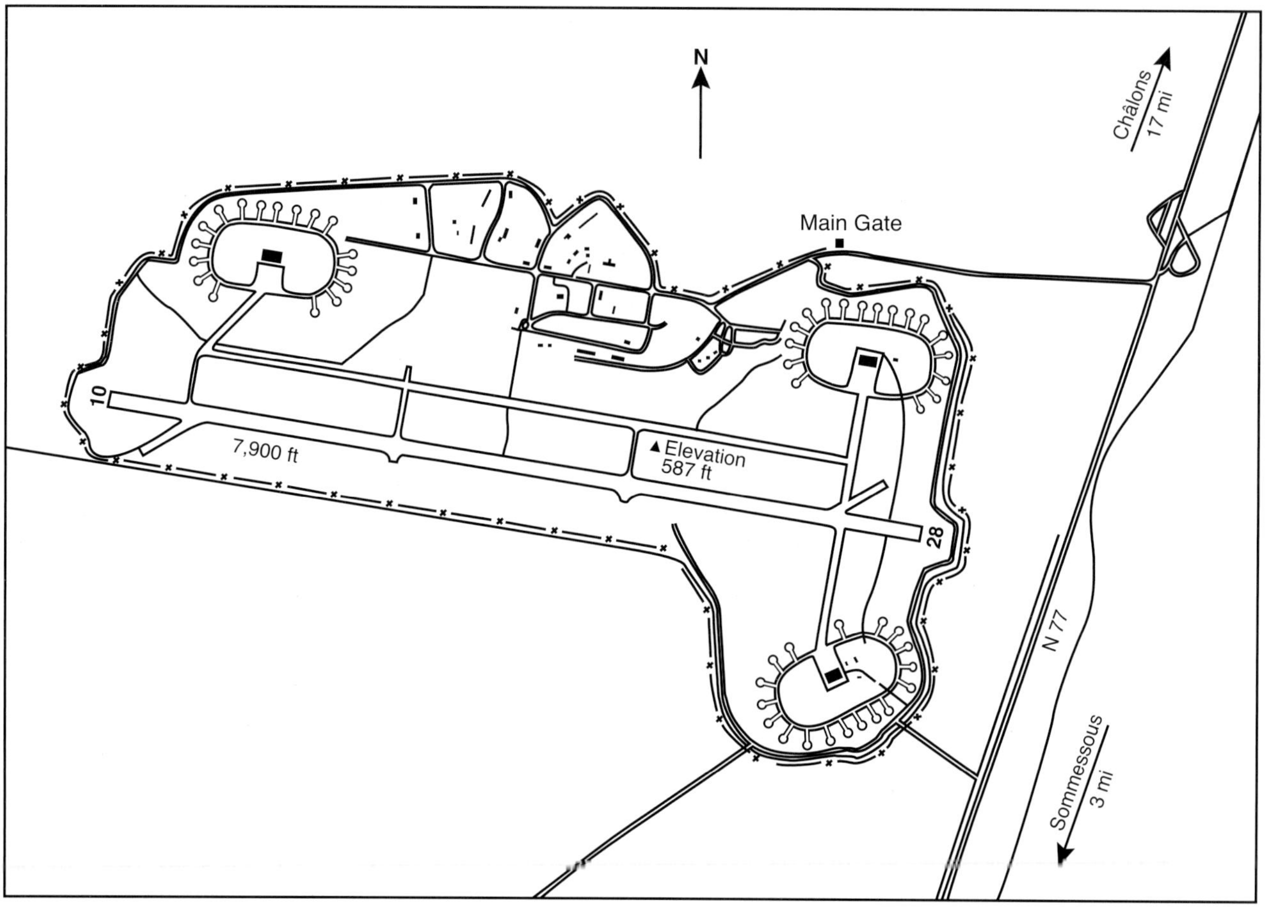

17.3 Chalons-Vatry DOB

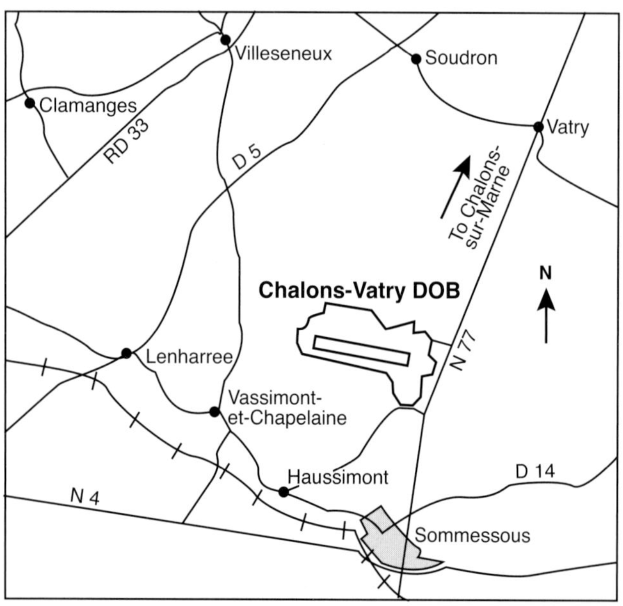

Map 17.4 Chalons-Vatry Area

Chalons -Vatry DOB: (Property #5941)

Location: Marne Department. 91 miles (145 km) east of Paris, 21 miles (34 km) southeast of Reims, 75 miles (60 km) northwest of Chaumont AB, and 17 miles (27 km) south, southwest of Chalons-en-Champagne (formerly Chalons-sur-Marne) on N77 and 3 miles (5 km) north of Sommessous on west side of route N77. Michelin Map #306 Local.

1950s Notice to Pilots -

Spare DOB. Emergency use only. 48° 47' N - 04° 12' E. Elevation 587 feet (175 m). One paved concrete runway 100°/280° 7,900 feet long. Aircraft storage, no repairs. Airfield lighting: rotating beacon with portable runway strip lights. DOB Instrument Letdown. Note: All facilities inoperative except when activated by "Notice To Airmen." Navigation Aids—Chalons radio facilities: Radio beacon, 442 KHz, "CO", 25W, on field. Approach Control: "Chalons", 380.80 UHF & 135.90 VHF. Direction Finder: 257.80 - 380.80 - 243.00 UHF. RADAR; GCA Search, 310.80 - 344.00 UHF, 135.90 VHF. GCA Final Approach, 282.30 - 385.40 UHF & 140.58 VHF, for runway 28. Control Tower; 243.90 - 257.80 UHF & 141.30 -117.90 VHF.

150th Transportation Company, Medium Truck, vehicle overhaul facility, Chalons-Vatry 1961.
James Arnold Lambert

completed in 1956, the DOB was assigned to the 48th FBWg at Chaumont. Det #2, 48th Air Base Group was activated to operate Chalons. It was manned by three officers, seventy-five airmen, and three LWR French employees. Its primary mission was, "to maintain Chalons-Vatry AB as a Dispersed Operating Base to support fighter type aircraft during exercises or emergencies; to maintain it in operationally ready status to receive a flying organization, furnish security protection for equipment and pre-stocked material, maintain the base as a housekeeping unit, take responsibility for all property, security, maintenance, requisitioning, receiving and warehousing of Project SEAWEED material, and to maintain ground and wire communications as required to support the mission." All DOB detachments had identical missions.

A Radio Relay Station, Golf 5, was built on Chalons-Vatry, and manned by the 8th RRL Sq. This RRL station was required to link Chaumont with other air bases in France and HQ USAFE in Germany. Forty GRI housing units were built in Chalons-sur-Marne city in 1957 to provide family quarters. A large quantity of Project Seaweed supplies and vehicles were stored in two large warehouses on this DOB. Arresting barriers and high intensity approach lights for runway 28 were installed by Det #2 for F-100D operations. Permanent runway and taxiway strip lights were added November 1958. A telephone system was installed within the base by September 1958. The last NATO funded construction occurred in 1959 when three miles of perimeter roads were completed. This made roving patrols possible, which greatly improved base security.

Chalons-Vatry was used by the 21st, 49th, and 388th FBWgs, as well as the 48th; usually one fighter squadron at a time. The 21st FBWg from Chambley deployed with their F-86 Fighters for bare base exercises in September-October 1957. Later, the 49th from Etain deployed to Chalons-Vatry from 1 September to 30 November 1958 while its runway was being repaired. In March, April, and May 1959, Chaumont's 492d, 493d and 494th TFSqs operated from this DOB for a total of fifty days. The squadrons lived and operated out of two hangars while maintaining their operational-ready status.

As Chalons-Vatry was phased out by Project RED RICHARD, all aircraft munitions were removed to Chaumont. All aircraft parts, and equipment were returned to Chaumont base supply. SEAWEED material and supplies not required to maintain the DOB were returned to Chaumont. The 8th RRL Squadron remained on Chalons to maintain Golf 5. Det #2 48th Air Base Group was deactivated on 25 October 1959, and military personnel returned to Chaumont. The forty GRI housing units were transferred to the U.S. Army at Vitry-le-Francois on 31 December 1959. The DOB was transferred to the 7544th Support Gp, maintained for a month, then transferred to the U.S. Army.

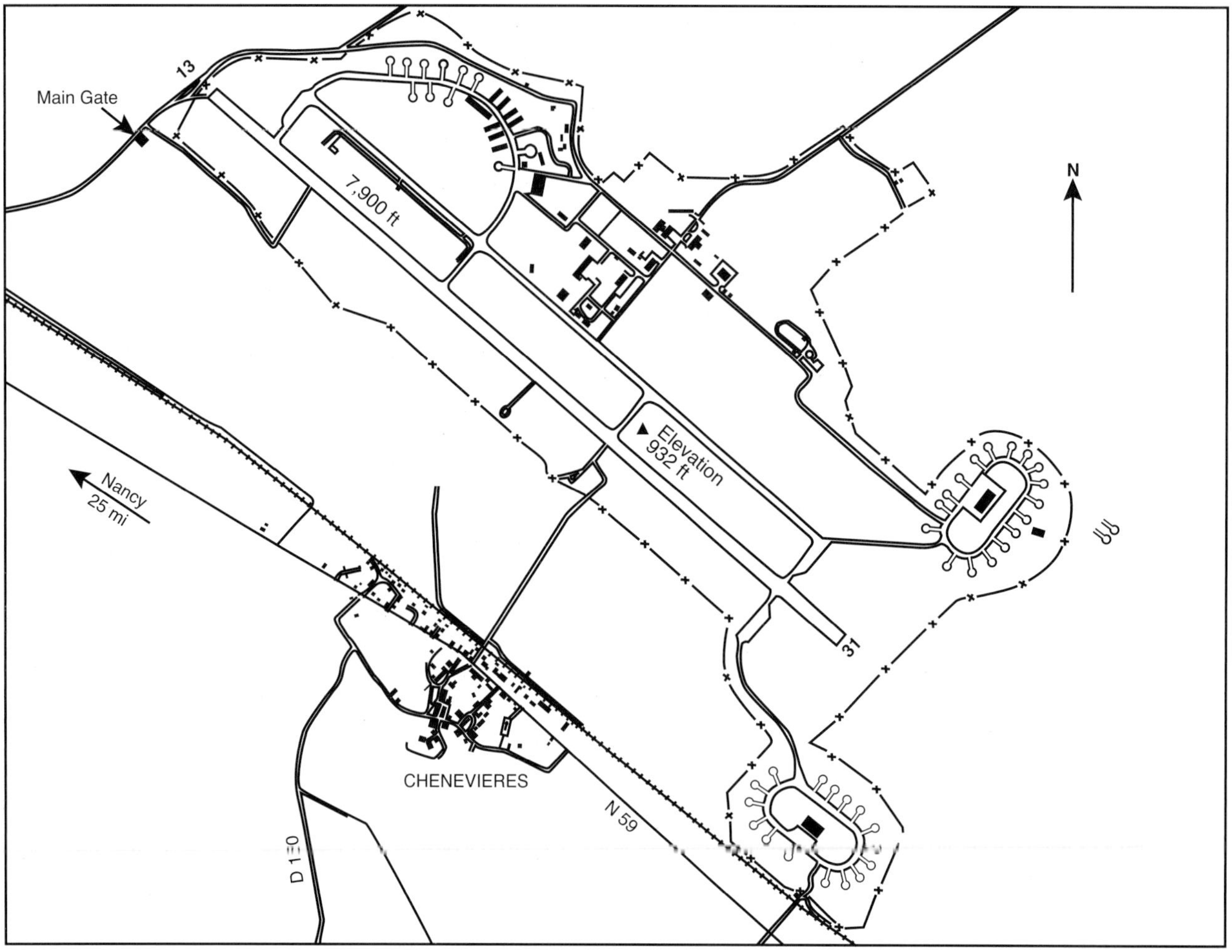

Map 17.5 Luneville-Chenevieres DOB

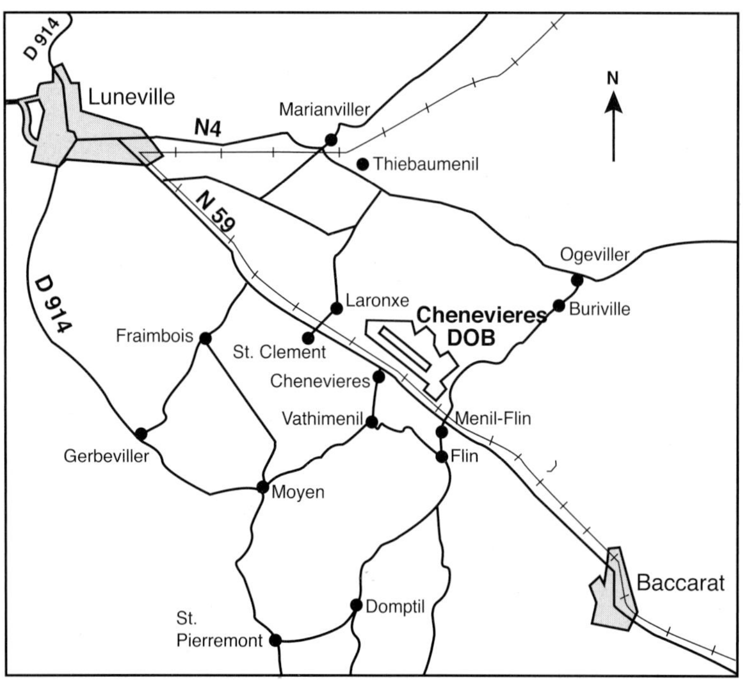

Map 17.6 Luneville-Chenevieres Area

Luneville-Chenevieres DOB:

(Property #5951)

Location:

Meurthe et Moselle Department.

225 miles (360 km) east of Paris, east of Auto Route of A31.

8 miles (12 km) southeast of Luneville on the east side of N59.

Base main entrance. 1 mile (2 km) east of N59 from village of St. Clement.

35 miles (56 km) southwest of Phalsbourg AB.

Michelin Map #307 Local.

1950s Notice to Pilots -

Spare DOB. Emergency use only.

48° 32' N - 06° 38' E, Elevation 932 feet (280m). One paved concrete runway 130°/310°, 7,900 feet long. Aircraft storage, no repairs. No airdrome lighting. No specific working hours. DOB Instrument Letdown, none. Radio navigation aids, none. Radar, none.

In 1960 the U.S. Army 150th Medium Truck Company was activated at this base. The former aircraft hangars provided excellent vehicle maintenance shops and secure parking for their trucks. This unit operated 2.5 and 5-ton trucks, and 10-ton semi trailers to haul cargo throughout France and West Germany. From 1963 through 1965 Detachment 6, 256th Signal Company, (Support) was stationed at Chalons. Approximately 450 personnel worked on the base including U.S. Army personnel and French civilian employees.

HQ USAF officially disposed of Chalons in March 1967 during FRELOC. After 1967 it was used briefly by the French Air Force for air transport flight training. It is currently being developed into Europe's largest cargo hub, named Aeroport International de Vatry offering integrated air, rail and highway cargo shipping and receiving services. Construction began on this $200 million project in 1998 and very little remains of the old DOB.

Luneville-Chenevieres DOB

Initially in 1950, the Luneville-Croismare airfield site was proposed as a DOB, but the population of Luneville and the Ministry of Agriculture opposed peacetime use of this field. France substituted the Chenevieres site in 1953, and construction began that year after USAFE accepted it as a DOB site. It was the second base built for tactical wing dispersal. A twelve-man team was deployed from Chateauroux to control property as it arrived. The Verdun office of the Joint Construction Agency supervised construction at this base. Radio Relay Station Golf 18 was built on Chenevieres in 1954 and operated by the 8th RRL Sq. It provided communications for the DOB, and connected Phalsbourg AB into Toul AB. Several barracks, a mess hall, base operations, munitions storage igloos, and vehicle sheds were completed by late 1954. Parking for thirty fighters was constructed around two standard NATO hangars. Installation of the sewage system, water supply, and electrical distribution systems exceeded projected costs, and eliminated construction of one aircraft hanger. With the completion of the runway, taxiways, and arm/de-arm pads in 1955, Chenevieres was finally operational.

Initial plans placed this DOB under control of Phalsbourg, but because Phalsbourg did not receive its combat wing to support a DOB, Toul AB was assigned responsibility for Chenevieres. Det #2, 50th Air Base Gp from Toul was activated in 1958, and manned by three officers, eighty-five airmen, and seven LWR French employees. Chenevieres was used for bare base exercises by the 50th FBWg from 1957 to 1959. This DOB, like the other three, was used for runway pattern work and "touch and go" in good weather and daylight hours.

Det #2, 50th Air Base Gp was deactivated at Chenevieres 1 September 1959 by RED RICHARD as it became another remote installation. It was turned over to the U.S. Army, but was maintained by Det #7, 7514th Support Gp from Toul. The job of this small team was base security and monitoring performance of the French maintenance contractors. The first Army units to occupy this DOB were artillery regiments. These units, the 16th Artillery Regiment, the 30th Artillery Regiment, and the 36th Artillery Regiment stayed at Chenevieres while deploying from West Germany to CONUS, using the port at La Pallice.

On 1 January 1960, Det #7, 7514th Support Gp became Det #7, 7544th Support Gp. On 25 October 1964, it's responsibility for the DOB ended when Chenevieres was returned to the French. It was renamed Quartier La Salle and used by the Armee de Terre for engineering equipment storage from 1970 to 1995. In 2002 it was home to the "53rd Regiment de Transmissions," a mobile communications unit using microwave satellite communications.

Since this former airfield is a French army camp it is normally closed to the public, but an annual open house with aircraft displays is conducted once a year during the summer months. Information about this event is available from the Luneville Office of Tourism.

Vouziers-Sechault DOB

Sechault was the last DOB built. Land was transferred to the U.S. in 1953, and work began in 1954. Chateauroux AD assigned a seven-man team to store property as it was shipped to Sechault. By 1955, the runway, aprons, and taxiways were completed. In early 1956 two NATO fighter hangars and parking spaces for thirty fighters were completed. In 1957 the DOB was a tent camp with field living conditions, with poor water supply, sanitation, and heating, and no recreation facilities. Only seven operations and supply buildings were constructed, resulting in minimum facilities. By this time USAF budget limitations were reducing the scope of all projects. The radio relay link to Vouziers was canceled in 1956. This DOB was under control of Etain and used for deployment training exercises by the 388th FBWg and later the 49th FBWg, but it was seldom used for deployment exercises. In 1958 the 49th TFWg activated Det #2, 49th Air Base Gp to operate the DOB with an authorized manning of two officers, sixty-four airmen, and eight

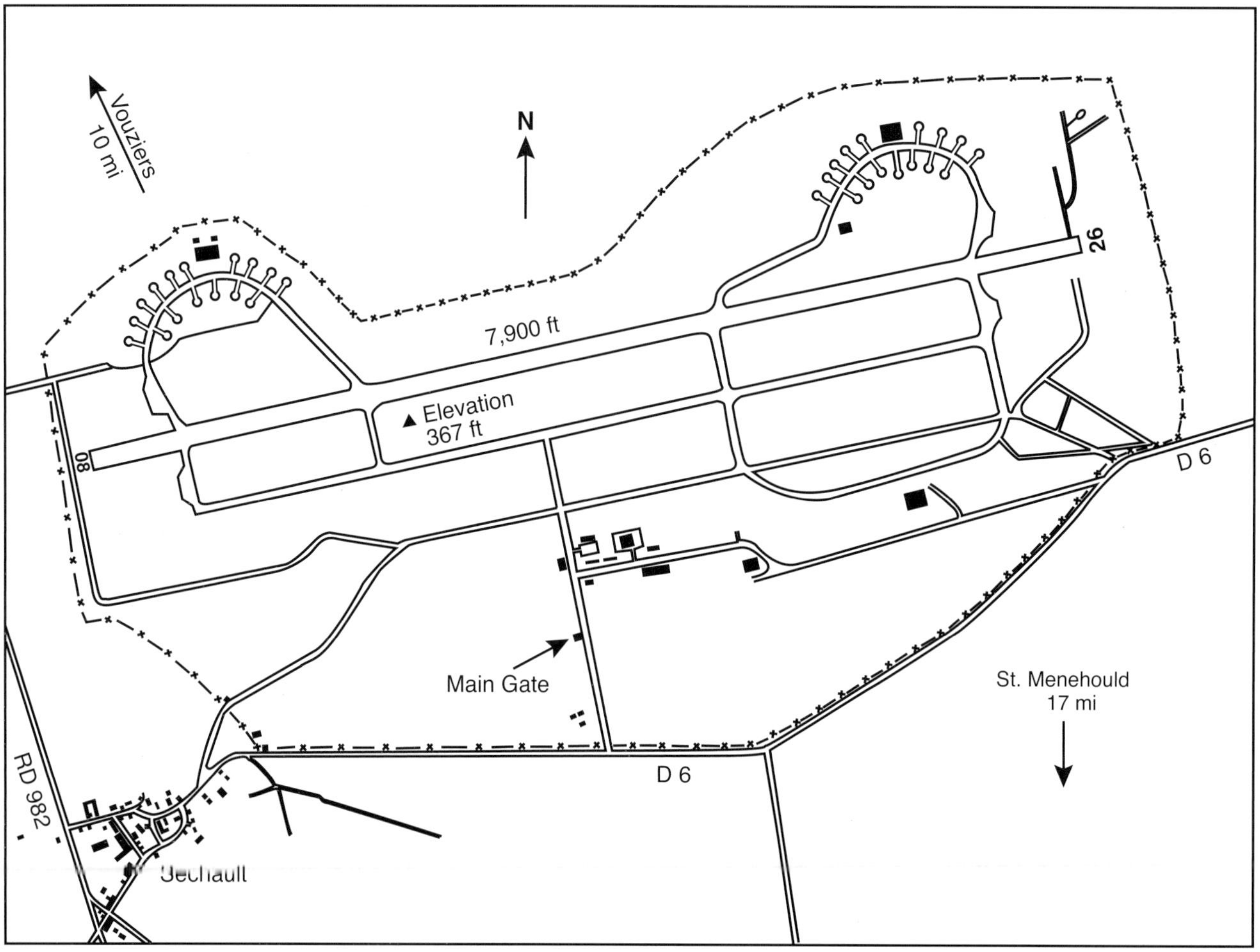

Map 17.7 Vouziers-Sechault DOB

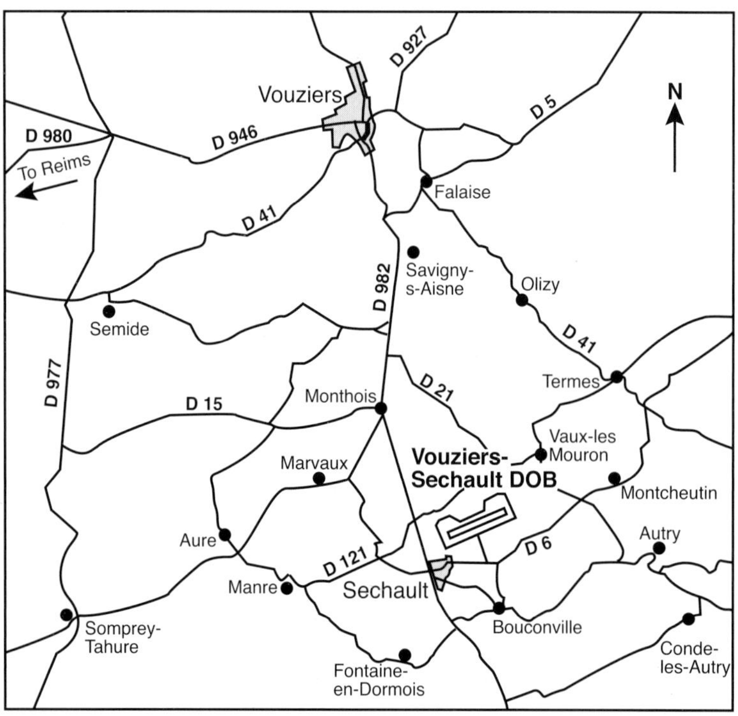

Map 17.8 Vouziers-Sechault Area

Vouziers-Sechault DOB:

(Property #5943)

Location:

Ardennes Department.
135 miles (215 km) east of Paris,
37 miles (60 km) east of Reims and north of Auto Route A4, 17 miles (28 km) north of St. Menehould on RD 982. Suippes Range is 13 miles (20 km) to the south.
The base entrance is 1 mile (2 km) east of the village of Séchault on the north side of route D 6.
43 miles (68 km) west of Etain AB.
Michelin Map #306 Local.

1950s Notice to Pilots -

Spare DOB. Emergency use only.
49°16' N - 04° 45' E, elevation 367 feet (112 m). One paved concrete runway 080°/260°, 7,900 feet long. Limited aircraft storage, no repairs. No airdrome lighting, portable runway strip lights only. No specific working hours. Prior permission required through HQs USAFE to operate U.S. military aircraft.

LWR French civilians. Its primary mission was DOB security, transportation, fire protection, emergency stock control, and maintaining radio communications with Etain.

In 1958 permanent runway over-runs were added, and the DOB was closed to F-100Ds for three months. In October 1958 the Suippes Gunnery Range resumed operations after expansion for air-to-ground bombing and gunnery. Supporting Suippes operating personnel was added to Det #2's mission. One officer and seventeen airmen were attached to Vouziers for billeting and feeding. In January 1959 Det #2 moved out of tents and into permanent buildings, and morale improved. But as the living conditions improved and summer approached, it was time to shut down and return to Etain AB as required by RED RICHARD. Det #2 moved all vehicles, equipment, and supplies back to Etain, and on 1 September 1959, Vouziers-Sechault was inactivated

It became a remote installation maintained by Det #6, 7514th Support Gp at Toul AB. The job of this very small team was base security and monitoring performance of the French maintenance contractors.

The U.S. Army did not want this DOB because it did not meet their needs. Its limited facilities did not provide the necessary troop housing and equipment storage, and the small hangars did not offer sufficient maintenance shop space. It was transferred to the French Air Force on 25 October 1960. At first, the FAF used Vouziers for flying training. But, since 1980, French Army and Air Force civil engineers use the DOB for rapid runway repair training by destroying runway sections, then laying matting or rapid setting concrete. As of 2004 it is being used as an auxiliary airfield, and access to Vouziers-Sechault is prohibited.

Vouziers-Sechault French Air Force auxiliary flight training airfield, 1997.
Jerry McAuliffe

Vitry-Brienne DOB, now Brienne-le-Chateau, 1999.

Former Base Ops. The tower cab has been replaced and is in use. Note the unusual brick buildings.

Former Officer's Club, now the campground office.

POL fill-stand remaining on the grounds at Brienne. These fill-stands are not found at any other base in France.

Sign at the entrance to the flight school on Brienne.

All photos Jerry McAuliffe

Chalons-Vatry DOB

Chalons-Vatry DOB 1999, now site of Europort, the largest cargo terminal in Europe.
Upper left: Road sign showing the new name of Chalons-Vatry, Chalons-en-Champagne.
Upper right: Sign at entrance to Europort.
Center: Europort tower on the old DOB site is located where former hangar was built.
Bottom: View of the warehouse buildings located on the field to handle cargo shipments from all over Europe.

Chenevieres DOB

Trying to extract the POL truck from the winter mud. The 50th Supply Squadron, Det #2 was TDY from Toul AB in 1957.
Ed Lasher

Shower tent in 1957,
before permanent barracks were completed.
Ed Lasher

Hangar was completed in 1957 and became the center of base life for the troops sent TDY to Chenevieres from 50th Fighter-Bomber Wing, Toul AB.
Ed Lasher

The lean-to shops attached to the hangar were used as living quarters at Chenevieres in 1957.
Ed Lasher

Chenevieres DOB

Aerial photo of Chenevieres DOB taken in 1985. Marguerites and hangars still visible. In 2004 photos the forest has overtaken the two lower marguerites.

Ren l'Ecuyer

French Army radio communications regiment stationed at Chenevieres in 2002.

Jerry McAuliffe

Road leading into town, 2002

Jerry McAuliffe

Chenevieres local restaurant/bar in 2002.

Jerry McAuliffe

ACKNOWLEDGMENTS

I would like to thank the following people who contributed to this chapter:

Al Christensen was a Weather Officer in Detachment 10, 31st Weather Squadron, MATS, stationed at Chambley AB, 1955-1957. He participated in 21st Fighter-Bomber Wing exercises at Chalons-Vatry in 1956.

Ren l'Ecuyer was in the RCAF, stationed at Grostenquin. He has devoted much time and effort to preserving the history of the Canadian effort in France through his website www.grostenquin.org.

Jack Jakubik was in the Avionics Detachment, U.S. Army Aviation Maintenance Center (USAAMC), stationed at Brienne from March 1962 to December 1963.

James Arnold Lambert was in the U.S. Army's 150th Transportation Company at Chalons Vatry.

Ed Lasher was stationed at Toul AB from July 1956 to July 1959. He TDY'd to Chenevieres for seven months in late 1956 through 1957. He was attached to the POL section of the 50th Supply Squadron.

18

U.S. ARMY IN FRANCE

During reorganization of the U.S. military after WWII, the National Defense Act of 1947 carefully defined the roles and missions of each department of the military. Duplication of effort was to be absolutely avoided. The U.S. Air Force became an independent service at this time, but continued to depend upon the Army for critical areas of support. This support was much the same as the U.S. Army Air Forces required during WWII: surface transportation, major construction engineering, combat vehicles, non-aviation ordnance, quartermaster field equipment, ground signal equipment, petroleum-oil-lubricants procurement and distribution, and medical support.

When it was decided to establish a major Air Force presence in France, Army support functions were also required. This was especially so during the early 1950s because the new independent USAF was in the throes of reorganizing and focusing on air power, its primary mission. There was little time or enough people to reinvent the wheel! The USAF would have to work very closely with the U.S. Army's Corps of Engineers, Transportation Corps, Ordnance Corps, Signal Corps, Quartermaster Corps, Chemical Corps, and Medical Corps for its logistical support.

Initial Deployment of the U.S. Army into France, 1951-1952

In Europe after World War II the Army, like the Air Force, occupied bases scattered throughout the U.S. Zone of Occupation in Germany, very close to the East-West border. These support bases, several located in large cities, were selected as the Army captured western Germany during April-May 1945. These sites served the Army of Occupation very well. In 1950, as East-West tensions grew, NATO's defensive planning required the Army to relocate its support depots west of the Rhein River in Germany, and in France and Benelux. The first step was to move existing support units westward toward the French-German border. They established bases in the region around Kaiserslautern, West Germany, as quickly as land in the French Zone of Occupation was made available. Primitive facilities were set up, then permanent facilities were constructed over the next ten years.

The second step was to establish major lines of communications across France to support U.S. forces in Germany and other NATO forces throughout Europe in the event of a war. Lines of communications, (LOCS) is a military term used to describe the infrastructure required to support a large movement of combat troops. The lines of communications developed by the Army also supported the USAFE air bases throughout France and West Germany.

The U.S. Army had completely departed France by 1946, except for small teams of its Graves Registration Service. Therefore, it had to build from zero personnel and installations in France to over 50,000 personnel and hundreds of installations by December 1954, the date NATO planners had set for completion of construction. The Army had to perform this feat in addition to increasing its combat strength in West Germany, and while fighting the war in Korea!

Units began arriving in France during the spring of 1951, at bare bases that were used as interim depots for all classes of supply. They constructed major depots, storage sites, general hospitals, and seaports across France from Bordeaux to Metz. Many of the installations began as open fields with squad tents, or in old French Casernes. Some portions of the pre-WWII Maginot Line facilities were employed for storage, command centers, and depot shops. These logistical facilities could have supported Army forces consisting of at least five corps, having twenty-four divisions. No U.S. Army combat corps or divisions were stationed in France, all Army combat units continued to be based in West Germany. In this chapter I have attempted to provide an overview of the U.S. Army activities in support of the Air Force in France.

West Germany was considered the forward or combat zone, while France was considered the logistics or communications zone (COM Z) to support the theater of operations. France was divided about in half with the eastern half defined as the Advance Section (ADSEC) and the western half the Base Section (BASEC). In the center was a small area known as Orleans Area Command (OAC). If the Soviets moved into West Germany, ADSEC would be the next zone within their strike range. Therefore, the units that had

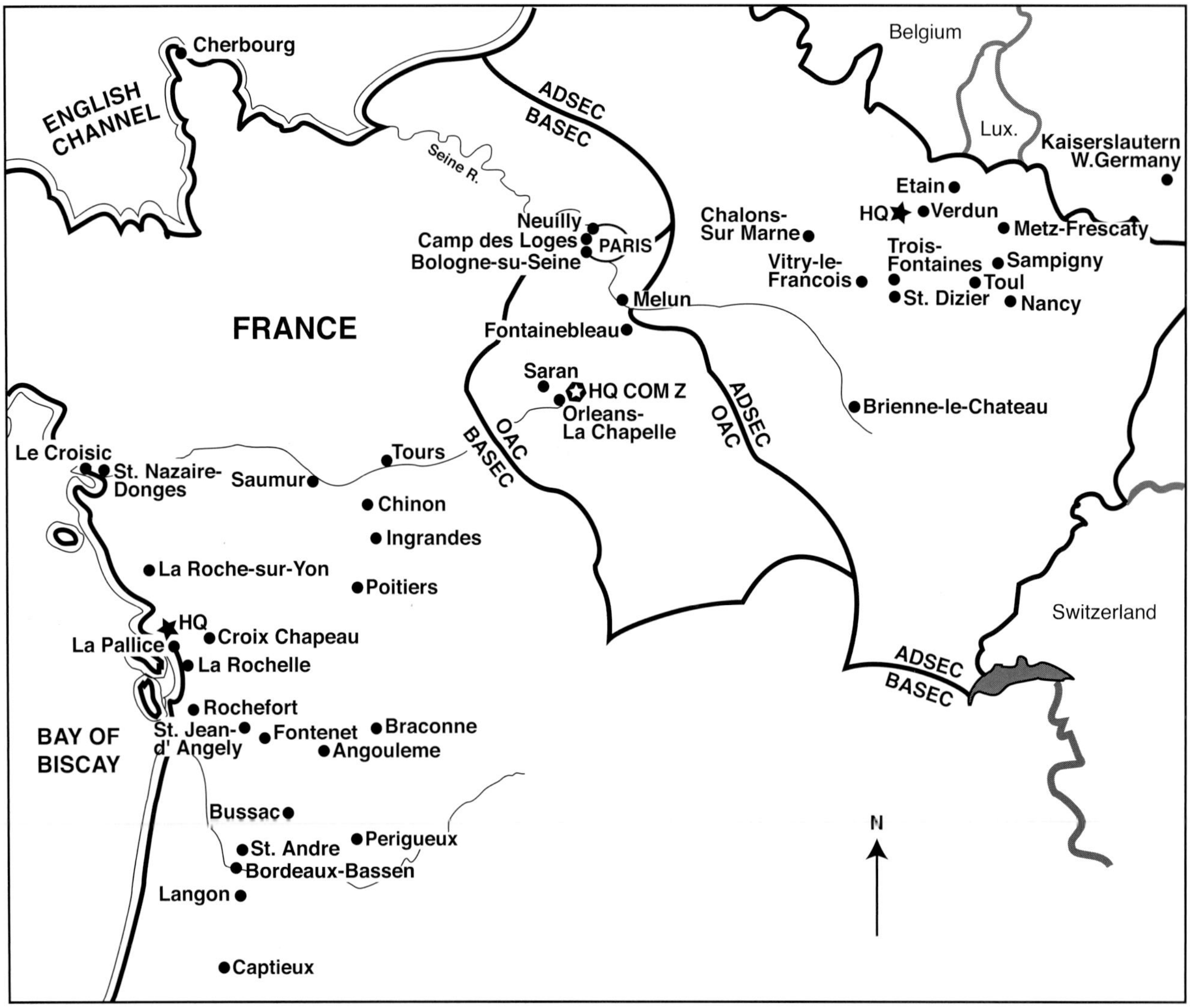

Map 18.1 U.S. Army Facilities 1955

greater capacity to defend their position and were more mobile and flexible were placed in ADSEC. More permanent, less mobile infrastructure was located in BASEC since it was considered beyond first strike range. This ADSEC/BASEC division roughly followed a northwest-southeast line from Dieppe, east of Paris to Macon, then straight east to the Swiss border. Orleans became the site of Headquarters, Communications Zone with La Pallice as BASEC HQ and Verdun as ADSEC HQ.

The lines of communication within the ADSEC/BASEC zones closely resembled the march route of GEN Patton's Third Army. LOCS flowed from CONUS toward West Germany. NATO planned to build on the Army's still recent World War II experience in France by locating its installations in familiar areas. Many of the major Army support centers were located in cities where the Army had seen combat: La Rochelle, Saumur, Tours, Orleans, Toul, Nancy, Verdun, and Metz. Army installations were located from the Atlantic ports, running across France south of Paris into the northeast corner at the West German border. Each city might contain four, six, ten, or more separate installations. The size of each installation varied from one building to many structures over hundreds of acres. Army personnel strength at these locations ranged from company size of 200 men to battalion size of 1,000 men. The primary criterion was quick access to national highways and railroad lines.

Major seaports were developed in France to eliminate the Army's dependence on the port of Bremerhaven, Germany, in the British Zone of Occupation. Bremerhaven was located 420 miles north of Nurnberg and only 85 miles west of the Soviet Zone of

Occupation. This was strategically untenable. It was assumed the Soviets could sever this logistical lifeline within the first weeks of a war. Therefore, France assigned the ports of Bordeaux-Bassen, La Rochelle-La Pallice, Nantes, Rochefort, Le Croisic-Donges on the Bay of Biscay, and Cherbourg on the English Channel for NATO/U.S. use. Most of these deep-water harbors required repairs and major construction because they had been heavily damaged during WWII. Many harbors still contained hazardous debris and sunken ships. Map 18.1 shows the major U.S. Army facilities in France as of 1955.

U.S. Army Construction Support

The most important support service the Army performed for USAFE was construction supervision and engineering. From 1951 through 1955, building Army and Air Force facilities in France became the largest and most expensive overseas, peacetime construction program. Approximately $1 billion was expended by the United States to establish the air bases and lines of communications needed to meet NATO planning objectives.

The Corps of Engineers was responsible for all construction in Europe. It set up a main office in Paris and two district offices to manage its various construction projects throughout France. On 15 January 1953, the Joint Construction Agency (JCA) was formed to coordinate Army, Air Force, and Navy construction in France. Their efforts in supporting the Air Force are described in chapter 3, in the Construction Management section.

Engineer Aviation Battalions

A USAF combat wing cannot construct its own permanent base, but it is manned and equipped to maintain its air base once built. The Army Corps of Engineers, Engineer Aviation Battalions (EABn) had done this heavy construction for the USAAF in WWII. When the USAF became a separate service, the EABn had remained Army, so the Air Force never had its own heavy construction units. In the postwar period, the U.S. Army Corps of Engineers was authorized special aviation engineering units to provide wartime construction capability for the USAF. These specialized EABn units known as Special Category Army With Air Force (SCARWAF) continued their mission of building airfields for the USAF. SCARWAF was a unique solution to the Air Forces's heavy construction needs. The Army agreed to recruit, organize, train, and equip these aviation battalions. The USAF was responsible for funding the EABn program and manning was charged against USAF authorized manpower limits. The EABn's mission was, "To construct and rehabilitate airfields, roads, utilities, buildings, structures, and other ground facilities required to exclusively support operations of the Air Force, and to defend the construction sites." The EABn Table of Organization and Equipment called for 35 officers and 720 enlisted men, over 150 vehicles, plus 170 construction machines. An engineer aviation battalion was not a "light" unit to move! Construction machinery included rock crushers, earthmovers, road graders, fifteen-cubic-yard concrete mixers, ten-ton mobile cranes, and asphalt machines.

The USAF realized in early 1950 that there were serious problems with the SCARWAF concept. There were not even enough trained units for Korea. Many enlisted personnel were drafted and only served for two years. This resulted in 45 to 60 percent personnel turnover every year in overseas battalions. USAF leaders felt the troops received insufficient construction training before being sent overseas, especially in earth moving, concrete paving, and electrical utility installation; and that time spent in combat infantry training reduced the time available for construction education. In spite of these deficiencies the EABns produced excellent results through the efforts of highly dedicated officers and enlisted personnel. Their enthusiasm, improvisation, long working hours, and ability to learn quickly accomplished very difficult missions.

In 1950-1951 there were no EABns in CONUS ready for dispatch to France; the primitive conditions of Korean airfields consumed all available battalions. Nine Engineer Aviation Battalions eventually served in Korea to keep air bases operational. USAFE had one EABn based in Germany since 1945, the 862d EABn at Rhein Main AB. The 862d was the first EABn dispatched to France in November 1951. It provided valuable assistance for three months during Bordeaux-Merignac's tent camp construction. The shortages of heavy construction equipment, replacement parts, and trained personnel limited development of new EABns. More trained men filled out the thin ranks as Army Reserve engineering units were mobilized. By 1952 the Army was able to train and move EABns to France and immediately committed these battalions to air base improvements. These units were the 843d EABn at Bordeaux, with companies at Chaumont, Laon, and Toul, and the 866th EABn at Chateauroux. The 866th deserves special mention because of its accomplishments at Chateauroux Air Depot. It literally saved the base and supplies from disappearing into the mud. The

862d EABn operations shack while building the "Operation Caravan" trailer park at Chambley AB, 1955.
Harold Watt

Operating an 862d EABn CAT-12 motor grader. Grading a road at Chambley AB, 1955.
Harold Watt

862d EABn heavy equipment mired in the mud and snow at Chambley AB, 1955.
Harold Watt

862d EABn troop repairing a truck mounted crane engine at Phalsbourg AB 1955. Ordinarily a depot repair, but done on site to save time. Harold Watt

Equipment stored outside in the rain. This sorry sight faced the 866th EABn at La Martinerie in 1952.
National Archives

Construction of the trailer park at Phalsbourg AB, 1955. 862d Engineer Aviation Battalion.
Harold Watt

battalion arrived with its heavy construction equipment at the port of La Pallice on 24 June 1952, after a 25-day trip from California. It moved initially to Bordeaux-Merignac AB, then about 17 July, the battalion began its 230-mile movement of men and equipment to Chateauroux. Getting the huge construction vehicles through the small French towns and across narrow bridges without incident was an outstanding feat. All men and equipment arrived safely at Chateauroux-La Martinerie Air Depot on 1 August.

The first task they were assigned was the construction of a 2,000 man prefabricated Quonset Hut housing area. Moving seventy-six railcar loads of Quonset kits provided excellent training for crane operators. But higher priority projects such as hardstands, supply shelters, and roads soon interrupted this housing construction. Building an all-weather road network on the base required a rock quarry operation working double shifts to produce sufficient gravel. This road network, on the north side of La Martinerie, was vital to provide the access French contractors needed to build thirty permanent buildings. This road network and the buildings were still in use in 2002.

Unfortunately, because the road project had to be completed before housing construction could begin, most of the military personnel spent a very wet, miserable, 1952-53 winter in a tent city. The heavy rain in November and snow in December 1952 had slowed construction progress by 50 percent. For many USAF troops this was their second winter in tents since their arrival. Mud infiltrated every aspect of life and made proper storage of equipment impossible. The Air Depot Commander, GEN Hicks, said of the 866th, "I have nothing but praise for the work that they have done and are doing." By 1953 an outstanding job of engineering and construction by the 866th EABn had eliminated the tent city and prevented the base from sinking into the vast quagmire of mud, while accelerating long-term base construction.

Later as more EABns were activated and trained, they were dispatched to France during 1953 to assist all air bases. The 472d EABn, and later the 818th were at Phalsbourg. The 821st EABn, then the 846th supported Dreux. The 821st moved on to Evreux and the 833d EABn assisted Etain. The 850th was stationed at Bordeaux and the 862d was at Laon AB. Though the EABn in France could not perform their primary construction missions because of the NATO requirement that only French contractors could build the bases, they were kept busy improving and repairing these facilities after construction was complete. Many projects built with sub-standard materials had to be repaired shortly after completion.

A very important construction program undertaken by these battalions was the development of trailer parks for on-base family housing. The EABn graded and built roads; installed electrical, sewage and water utilities; built utility buildings; and poured concrete pads to provide spaces for up to 300 trailers on each air base. Trailers were the only on-base housing allowed, so the EABn built the parks, and most of the trailers were provided by the USAF. Trailers were rented to families of officers and airmen. A few were privately owned. Though cramped and spartan they provided convenient on-base housing and boosted the morale of Air Force families. This construction project was known as "Operation Caravan."

The SCARWAF program was discontinued in 1955 as DOD budget cuts forced the Air Force and Army to curtail this 40,000-man aviation engineer program. Costs vs. benefits were too great for an Army facing a 500,000-man reduction. It badly needed the resources to fill combat engineer positions required in the "new look" Army.

U.S. Army POL Support Operations

The Army Transportation Corps is responsible for procurement and delivery of petroleum-oil-lubricants (POL) to the Air Force overseas. It delivers POL by tank truck, rail tank car, or pipeline to base storage tanks; then it's the combat wing's responsibility to deliver the fuel to the aircraft. Normally, Air Force refueling trucks are not dispatched off base to pick-up fuel.

Ordinarily in France, the Transportation Corps purchased bulk fuels from Western European refineries and shipped them by rail to the air bases in Army tank cars. Each base had its own railroad siding, so tank cars could remain on base for long periods while fuel was transferred into the wing's fuel trucks. Initially, the tanks cars served as base fuel storage tanks until underground tanks could be installed. (Map 18.2)

The Army laid a POL pipeline across France into West Germany to provide rapid transmission of these vital products for the combat forces. The POL pipeline also supplied aviation fuels to all air bases. The Bay of Biscay seaport of Le Croisic-Donges was chosen as the off-load terminal for the Army pipeline, with storage capacity of 1,520,000 barrels of POL products. Bulk delivery by tankers into port storage tanks provided rapid POL transfer to BASEC storage. ADSEC storage ranged from underground tanks to acres of five-gallon jerry cans. The POL storage and pipeline project began in 1953 but required ten years to achieve

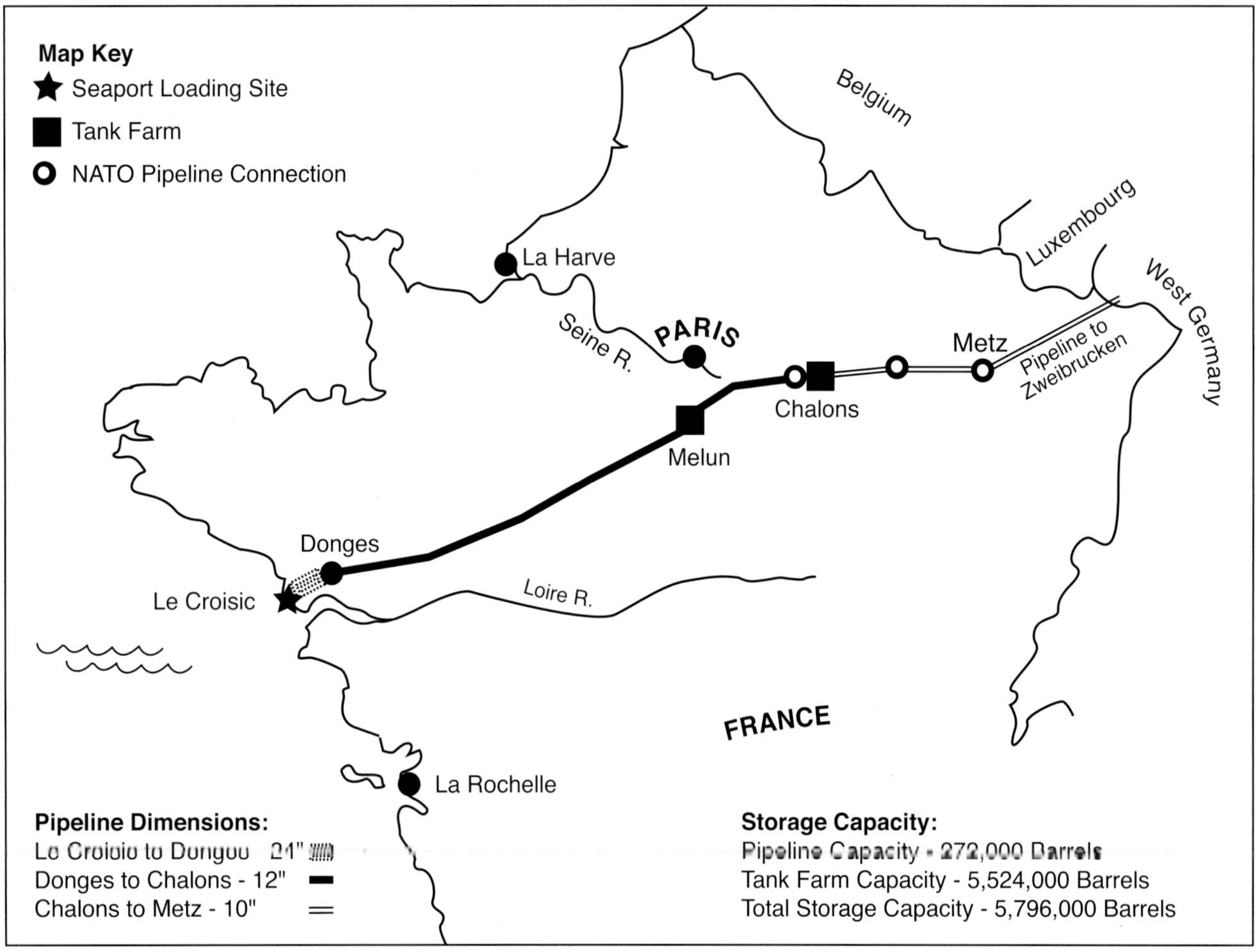

Map 18.2 POL Pipeline

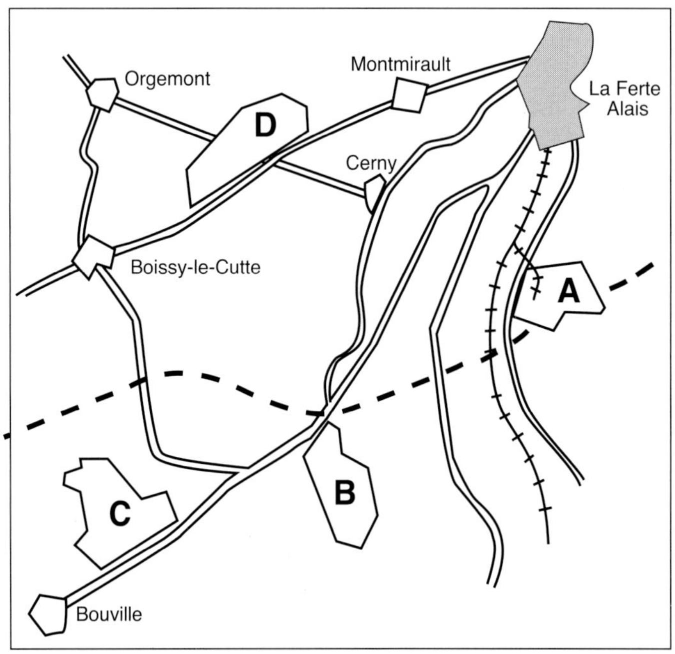

Map 18.3 Melun Tank Farms A, B, C, D. Note dispersal for survival.

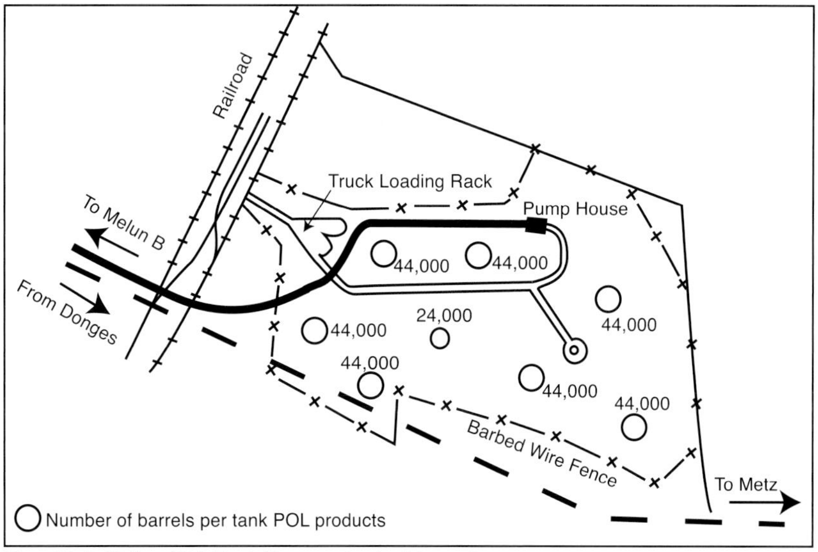

Map 18.4 Melun "A" Tank Farm, a typical layout.

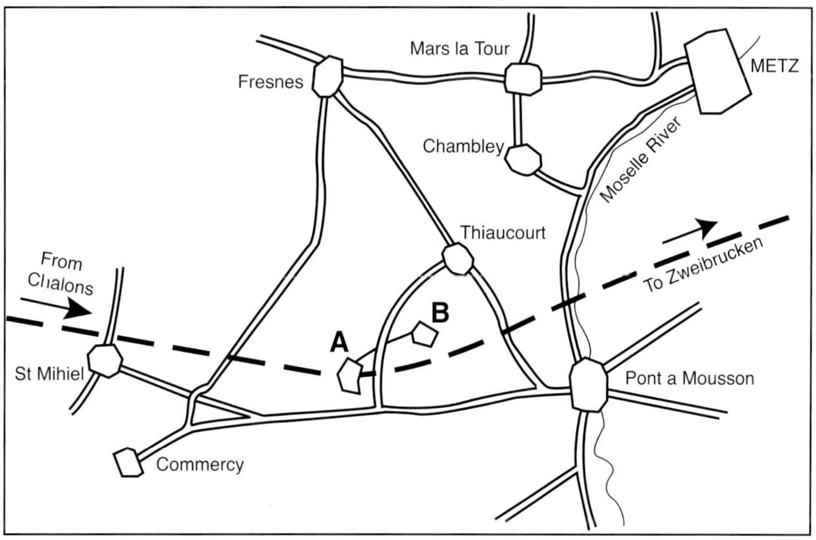

Map 18.5 Metz Tank Farms "A" and "B"

complete distribution. Within France the pipeline was constructed by French contractors under Corps of Engineers management.

Fuel requirements for an air base are provided here to give the reader some understanding of POL consumption. An F-100 wing flying each fighter three sorties per day would burn 43,700 barrels (2,352,000 gallons) of jet fuel per week. Similarly a C-119 wing, flying two missions per day per aircraft, could consume 29,700 barrels (1,638,000 gallons) of aviation grade gasoline per week.

The main underground line running east to Chalons had twelve-inch diameter pipe that reduced to ten inches as it proceeded to Metz. Underground storage tank farms holding 4,315,000 barrels, and eight booster-pump stations maintaining 1200-psi line pressure were located along the 415-mile route. Four types of fuel were pumped and stored in this system: vehicle diesel fuel, vehicle motor gas, aviation gasoline (115/145 octane), and jet propulsion fuel. Extreme care was taken to safely pump and store the aviation fuels to prevent explosions and contamination. Decanting facilities were located along the pipeline for filling fuel trucks and railroad tank cars. Smaller eight-inch pipelines delivered jet fuel and aviation gasoline to the air bases' 900,000-gallon underground tanks until it was transferred into USAF refueling trucks. The 7870th Army Unit Quartermaster, (Petroleum Distribution) headquartered at Fontainebleau operated and maintained this pipeline. Maps 18.3 thru 18.5 show the tank farm layout.

This pipeline was expanded by the addition of a

NATO system that included a north-south main pipeline running from a Mediterranean seaport near Martigues, France, up the Rhone River valley into West Germany. The two pipelines joined at Chalons-sur-Marne and Metz, France, to provide redundancy throughout the system.

U.S. Army Hospital Operations

The U.S. Army constructed general hospitals in the Base Section with 1,000-bed hospitals at Croix Chapeau, La Chapelle, and La Rochelle, and 750-bed hospitals at Bussac and Chinon. A 250-bed hospital was constructed in Paris at Neuilly, near Camp des Loges, with an excellent post exchange and commissary for the personnel assigned to SHAPE and Headquarters commands. Hospital complexes were also built in the Advance Section with 750 beds at Verdun, and a 1,000-bed hospital at Toul. In addition, the Army operated eight smaller hospitals and twelve dispensaries that were available for Air Force personnel and their dependents. The Medical Corps staffed and operated field and general hospitals to provide 7,000 beds within France to meet wartime casualty estimates. It was planned that wounded would be brought to these hospitals should the cold war become a hot war.

It was the mission of the 80th Ambulance Trains, (Rail) to move casualties across France from the eastern battle zone to BASEC hospitals, then onto hospital ships or airlift for evacuation to the United States. The 80th was headquartered at Orleans, but its eight trains were kept at Tours. Each consisted of an engine, eight ward cars, one personnel car, one kitchen-dining car, and one utility car. The ambulance trains drilled monthly by moving simulated patients from Landstuhl Hospital in West Germany to Bordeaux, France. Medical personnel from BASEC hospitals were rotated to staff these exercises so everyone would be proficient in an emergency

U.S. Army Depot Operations

Large Army depots were established throughout France for storage, issue, and maintenance of chemical, engineer, medical, ordnance, quartermaster, signal, and transportation equipment.

Table 18.1 lists the depots according to type and their location in ADSEC or BASEC. These depots in France supported the USAFE and MDAP equipment used by NATO combat forces throughout Europe. Many depots organized mobile maintenance teams to bring their services to bases across Europe.

The 294th Engineer Battalion at Etain found itself in a two-year major construction job building a large NATO munitions maintenance and storage depot between Verdun and Etain near the town of Eix-Abaucourt. The engineers commuted daily from Etain AB to the work sites. Much of the project was located on the east side of the Verdun WWI battlefield. Trenches and quantities of unexploded ordnance were uncovered. These old shells had to be cleared out by EOD teams before work could proceed. Thirteen miles of railroad track were installed, involving large amounts of earth moving to grade, cut, and fill the roadbed. Caterpillar D-8s were pushed hard to complete the job as quickly as possible; some of the old WWII D-7s and D-8s wore out and ended up in the Toul AB reclamation yard as scrap. Two dump truck companies, the 525th and 548th, assisted the 249th in hauling a large amount of fill for the roadbed. The 97th Engineer Construction Battalion joined in this project near its completion.

The 582d Transportation Company, (Army Aircraft Heavy Maintenance & Support) set up in one of Etain AB's hangars to maintain helicopters operated by Seventh Army. This aircraft maintenance company was moved in 1962 to the Army facilities at Breinne le Chateau AB. These Army units operated at Etain until 1963 when budget cuts reduced several ADSEC units and created living space closer the their depots.

U.S. Army Aircraft Operations

During the period 1952-1966, the U.S. Army operated over 300 aircraft in France. They flew a variety of airplanes and helicopters to support their units spread across Europe. They flew:

H-13 Sioux	L-19 Bird Dog
H-19 Chickasaw	L-20 Beaver
H-21 Shawnee	L-23 Seminole
H-34 Choctaw	OV-1 Mohawk
H-37 Mojave	U-1A Otter

Aircraft was based at Brienne-Le-Chateau, Dreux-Vernouillet, La Rochelle-Laleu, Melun-Villaroche, Metz-Frescaty, Nancy-Essey, Orleans-Bricy, Poitiers-Biard, Toul-Ochey, and Verdun-Rozelier. Army Aviation units were primarily located on civil airports with joint use agreements. Most bases consisted of two or three hangars, an operations building, and maintenance shops.

At Brienne-le-Chateau the Army established the only major Army aircraft avionics modification center in Europe for their fleet of over 750 helicopters and fixed wing aircraft. The center was dedicated to avionics rework and testing of aircraft. It upgraded communications, radar, autopilot, and reconnaissance sensors systems in their fleet. A retrofit program was

Table 18.1 U.S. Army Depots in France 1951 - 1967					
Depot	Advance Section	Base Section	Depot	Advance Section	Base Section
Chemical	Sampigny, Verdun	Bussac	Quartermaster	Metz	Ingrandes Perigueux Poitiers St. Andre
Engineer	Toul	Chinon			
Medical	Vitry le Francois	Croix Chapeaux Maison Forte (Orleans) La Roche Sur Yon	Signal	Verdun	Saumur
			Transportation	Frescaty (Metz)	Bussac Rochefort
Ordnance	Nancy Trois Fontaines	Braconne (Angouleme) Captieux Fontenet Rochefort	Hospitals	Toul Verdun	Captieux Fontainebleau La Chapelle La Rochelle

required because some aircraft were over ten years old. Brienne was originally intended to be a main base and had many permanent buildings and well developed infrastructure. These facilities allowed for complete airframe rework and rewiring as well as sheet metal rework for avionics installations. Major airframe, rotor, and engine repairs were handled by the 582d Transportation Company (Aircraft Heavy Maintenance and Support). Approximately 2,000 personnel worked on the base. This number included U.S. Army officers and enlisted personnel, U.S. civil service employees, and French technicians and engineers who were employed at Brienne for several years.

Army units stationed at Brienne Air Base during 1961-1963 were the 582d and Det #6, 256th Signal Support Company, as well as the U.S. Army Aircraft Field Maintenance and Avionics Center-Europe, and the U.S. Army Airfield Operations Detachment, (Provisional).

U.S. Army Communications Systems

The Army Signal Corps was tasked to install and operate the Strategic Communications (STRATCOMM) network. This system was required to provide continual secure command and control of U.S. forces in Europe by the National Command Authority in the United States. The long distance high frequency radio system required finding remote tracts of land located far away from electrical noise sources in which to construct very large antenna arrays. Saran, a northern suburb of Orleans, was selected as the terminal station. The 7784th Army Unit, Signal, (Service), whose headquarters were in Orleans, operated and maintained the SARAN Tape Relay Center. Microwave radio relay systems and commercial French PT&T telephone and teletype circuits connected into Saran, and provided international service to all U.S. and NATO users, and a backup system for USAFE.

Radio Relay Nets

A reliable telephone system connecting U.S. Army units in France to their units stationed in West Germany was unavailable until a low cost radio relay network was installed by the Signal Corps. Short distance, simultaneous, two-way radio communications similar to the home telephone became known as radio relay. Both voice and teletype messages were carried by this technique. Distances were usually limited to thirty to thirty-two miles over flat terrain but installations on hilltops greatly increased distances between radio stations. Radio relay sites formed a path across France and were maintained by twelve to fifteen-man teams at each location. This Army system was very similar to USAFE systems installed in France; they interconnected at several sites to serve all users. The 102d Signal Battalion, (Microwave and Radio Relay) with headquarters at Verdun maintained the Army radio relay system. Map 18.6 illustrates the Army microwave RRL system between Saran, France, and Kaiserslautern, West Germany.

Project FRELOC

Chapter 5 described how Project FRELOCK affected the USAF in France. Here I hope to provide a brief view of the U.S. Army's efforts to comply with project FRELOC. The Army had invested over

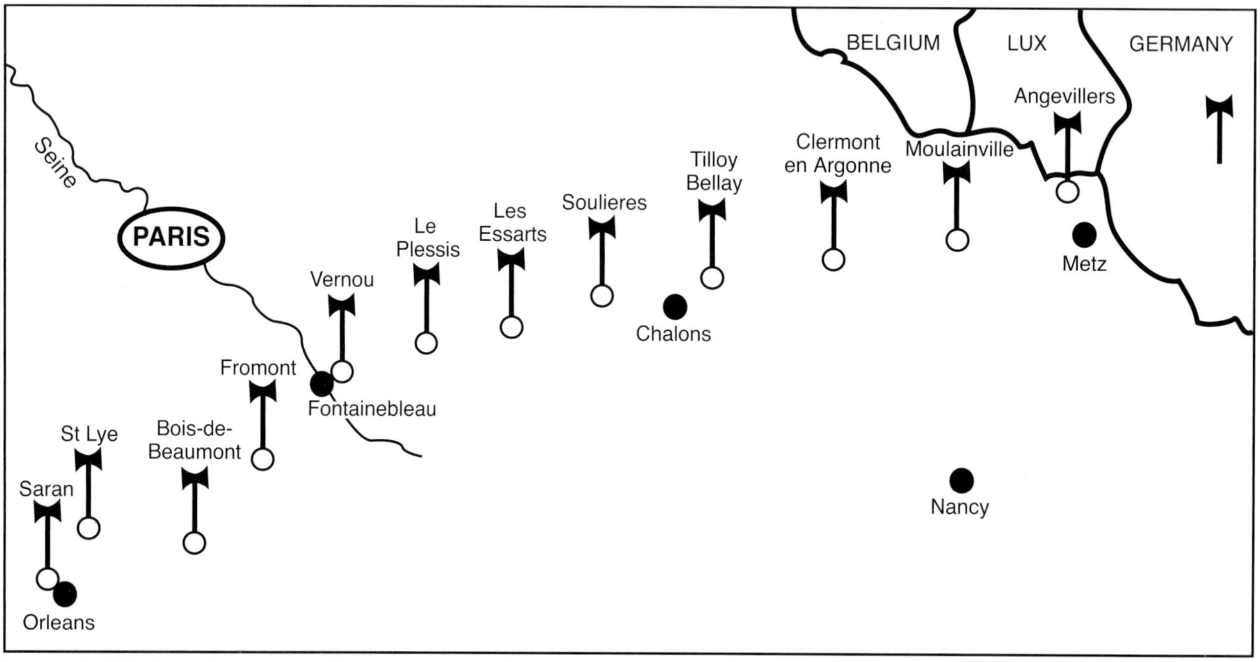

Map 18.6 U.S. Army Radio Relay Sites

$1,800,000,000 on 260 parcels of real estate in France, excluding land acquisition cost. It had developed five major seaports; constructed twenty-five depots, eighteen storage complexes, a pipeline network, a twelve-station microwave radio relay network, and improved eight small airfields. Upon completion of its FRELOC inventory, the Army found it had a giant moving project on its hands. It had 722,000 tons of material, including station property. Of this about 500,000 tons were considered vital theater reserve war stocks that were spread across France from south of Bordeaux to the French-German border near Saarbrucken. War readiness material consisted of 355,000 tons of general combat supplies Class I, II, III, IV, and 140,000 tons of ammunition, Class V. All this war reserve material was configured for immediate war support to the Seventh Army in Germany and NATO nations; and to provide combat stocks for 150,000 army personnel re-enforcements arriving from CONUS within thirty days after declaration of an international emergency. Not included in this figure were prefabricated steel buildings that were inventoried in April 1966; COM Z command found it had 1.2 million square feet of buildings within France that could be relocated to other sites after disassembly. USAREUR had 10,600 hospital beds and associated equipment in strategic storage in France. After picking up all this material, the next problem was where to put it! Only three locations were immediately available, Germany, United Kingdom, or CONUS. CINC USAREUR did not want any of this war reserve material returned to CONUS. He felt there was insufficient air and sealift available in CONUS to return this material in the event of a crisis in Europe; most CONUS air and sealift was committed to the Vietnam War.

Storage in Germany had serious limitations; no war reserve stocks were to be stored east of the Rhine River for fear it might be lost to the Warsaw Pact within days after start of WWIII. Existing depots in West Germany were insufficient for present stocks. Any new material would have to be stored outdoors on PSP brought from France. The Kaiserslautern region was the least desirable area due to hilly, wooded sites, few railroads, no roads, and limited access! Army marine equipment, used for seaport operation and maintenance, that was reserved at Rochefort and La Pellerin was relocated to the vicinity of Antwerp, Belgium. This fleet consisted of 179 vessels; one-third were unpowered and had to be towed, starting in November 1966. A large fleet of 2,000 steel pontoon cubes was moved to the southern coast of England for long-term storage.

The Army Aerial Support Center at St. Andre, near Evreux AB, was closed and the 557th QM Company, (Air Support) relocated to Camp Passchacqua, West Germany. Many Army units in France were transferred into Germany or deactivated. In eastern France, at the Abaucourt and Rozelier depots near Verdun and at the Vatry Depot, there were critical Corps survival stocks stored in specially constructed

Atomic Blast Resistant (ABREST) facilities. COM Z proposed that these stocks be moved into Germany at the Advanced Weapons Support Command (AWSCOM). USAREUR ruled out any use of these facilities due to AWSCOM's highly sensitive mission. Fourteen million dollars were required for new construction in Germany to accommodate FRELOC stocks at Einsiedlerhof, Fischbach, Germersheim, Landstuhl, Muenchweiler, Nahbollenbach, Neubrucke, and Pirmasens. On 21 June 1966, the Secretary of Defense authorized $5 million and 300 personnel for depot inspection, preservation, and maintenance functions in Germany. Additional construction was required in England at the Burtonwood General Depot for inactive storage, and at four munitions storage depots. The cost estimate for UK storage was $12,825,000 for relocation and annual recurring maintenance costs of $5,444,000. The British Minister of Defense (MOD) officials resolved all problems on the spot and cut red tape in every situation; without this outstanding support by UK officials, the FRELOC deadline for munitions removal could not have been achieved. A munitions storage complex was set up in England at Fauld, Bramshall, and Dittion Priors, and by January 1967 they were accepting shipments.

At Captieux and Chize, BASEC depots near the Atlantic ports, there were approximately 100,000 tons of Army artillery munitions and general explosives. Another 23,000 tons of ammunition, primarily tank rounds, were stored at the Trois Fontaine ADSEC depot. Munition storage in Germany was already a grave situation, for example the Miesau Ammunition Depot had a rated storage capacity of 138,000 tons, but they ended up with 238,000 tons, and over 100,000 tons of this capacity had to be covered by safety exemptions waivers! Space was leased at the port of Bassens near Bordeaux to store ammunition coming from Captieux and Chize Depots, until it could be shipped to either England or CONUS. Some of these munitions shipments from France were routed direct to Southeast Asia.

The last truck movements were completed by 28 March 1967. There were no fatal accidents associated with Project FRELOC, even while using every available Army truck and driver in France. Special mention must be made of the outstanding efforts of the 37th Transportation Motor Command units with their 10-ton semi trailer cargo trucks driving day and night across France into Germany in support of FRELOC during the winter of 1966-67. Great cooperation among all Army units made possible the maximum extraction of supply stocks from France within the time deadline.

All this Army material was removed from France by de Gaulle's deadline, but it took many years to properly sort and catalog. In the interim the material was not readily available for use in case of war. After completion of FRELOC, USAREUR evaluated its tactical logistical position, and it was far from satisfactory. The material moved out of France was theater war reserves and stocks for the forces arriving D+30 days after NATO mobilization. The 113,000 tons of material now located in four new storage sites in England were less vulnerable than French depots, but presented a transportation problem to move this war stock over to the continent in an emergency. The 277,000 tons of war supplies moved into Germany were added into existing Army facilities located in a small region centered around Kaiserslautern. These stocks were not located in readily accessible sites. The Army was left with a lucrative strategic target easily destroyed by nuclear weapons. Seventy-five percent of the Army's vital combat stocks were located within a thirty-mile radius of Kaiserslautern, Germany. Within this small space were ten major supply depots, two major combat headquarters, two major USAFE air bases, and EUCOMs primary hospital complex. Surface transportation consisted of one primary east-west railroad line and one east-west Autobahn, Saarbrucken to Mannheim. There was little strategic depth west of the Rhein River for logistical survival. There could be no advanced section or base section combat logistical support commands, due to the lack of real estate. In April 1967 after FRELOC, the U.S. Army found itself in the same tactical position that it faced in 1951, despite its great efforts and expenses during sixteen years in France.

ACKNOWLEDGEMENTS

I would like to thank the following people who contributed to this chapter:

Frank Casale was a heavy equipment operator with the U.S. Army 862d Engineer Aviation Battalion stationed at Erding AD, West Germany. He was among the first engineers in France in 1951, and has provided me with extensive information on the EABns in Europe.

Peter Darde, Jr. was a Corporal in the U.S. Army's 866th EABn stationed at Chateauroux Air Depot, 1954.

Professor M. David Egan who in 1962-64 commanded the 39th Ordnance Company at the U.S. Army Trois-Fontaines Ammunition Depot (Robert Espagne, France). He has kindly provided volumes of information on the U.S. Army and is currently writing a comprehensive book about the U.S. Army in France during the Cold War period 1950-1967.

Johnny McBee was a D-8 CAT driver with Company C, 249th Engineer Battalion at Etain and Chambley Air Bases from 1960-63.

Harold Watt was a heavy equipment operator in the U.S. Army 862d Engineer Aviation Battalion. He constructed roads and trailer parks on the Chambley and Phalsbourg Air Bases in 1954 and 1955.

Taking a break among the piles of PSP, Bordeaux 1951. 862d Engineer Aviation Battalion.
Frank Casale

Typical EABn airfield construction job, Spangdahlem AB, 1954. 862d Engineer Aviation Battalion.
Harold Watt

19

RCAF BASES IN FRANCE

This final chapter is a brief description of the contribution Canada made to the expansion of NATO airpower in France during early years of the Cold War. Very early during 1949 as force planning began, Canada agreed to supply twelve fully manned and equipped fighter squadrons to Western Europe's air defense. Canada's contribution to NATO funding was CAN $1 billion in 1953, and amounted to 8 percent of NATO's annual costs. The Royal Canadian Air Force (RCAF) moved early into France, and survived the mud and cold to became great friends with our USAF fighter pilots and squadrons in France and Germany. The RCAF participated in NATO air defense strategy by forming an air defense fighter belt about two hundred miles deep, and in an arc roughly from Brussels, Belgium, to the Swiss border to provide counter air operations to protect NATO ground forces and infrastructure. This fighter force would eventually be augmented with expanded coverage by French, Belgian, Danish, Netherlands, and later the West German day fighter units. As mentioned in earlier chapters, the USAFE fighter units' mission would be to concentrate on offensive counter air and interdiction operations by delivering tactical (small) nuclear weapons into Eastern Europe. After achieving air superiority this fighter force would change its mission tasking to tactical close air support of NATO ground forces. In 1952, air defenses were day fighters only, however by 1956, the all-weather/night fighter interceptor was introduced, improving NATO's survival. The RCAF supplied both types of fighters to NATO. It did not invest in a tactical bomber force.

In 1949 when Canada joined NATO, the RCAF had recently completed an historic accomplishment, from 1 September 1939 to 8 May 1945 when it built thousands of aircraft, trained thousands of pilots and aircrew members, and supplied dozens of bomber and fighter squadrons to the British Commonwealth's Victory in Europe. The RCAF had diminished in size during the fall and winter of 1945, but a core of competent leaders and fighter pilots remained to quickly rebuild another air force five years later.

Canada had the capability and military budgets to quickly supply a fighter air force to NATO rather than increase army divisions in West Germany. In 1950, the national goal was to establish four fighter bases in northeastern France, but during 1951 this objective changed slightly by obtaining two air bases in France (Grostenquin and Marville) and two bases located in the French Zones of Occupation in Germany (Baden-Soellingen and Zweibrucken). Each air base would house a fighter wing with three fighter squadrons flying seventy-five fighter aircraft. The two bases in France began as open farmland and required four years to complete. The two new bases in Germany were completed more rapidly and were home to two Sabre wings by 1954.

October 1952 saw the arrival of the first Sabres at RCAF Station Grostenquin, France, though the base was barely usable. From 1952 until its closure, Two Wing (F) Grostenquin flew Mk. 2, Mk. 4, and Mk. 6 Sabres. The base was home to 416 Squadron (Lynx) whose motto was "Ready to Leap," 421 Squadron (Red Indian) with the motto "They Have Sounded the War Trumpet," and 430 Squadron (Silver Falcon) that had the motto "Swiftly and Surely." In 1957, 416 Squadron was replaced by 423 Squadron (Eagle) whose motto was "We Search and Strike." The RCAF operated its fighter wing at Grostenquin, until December 1963, when it closed the air base and returned it to France.

In April 1955, One Wing (F) arrived at nearly completed Marville, flying Sabre Mk. 5s. One Wing (F) at RCAF Station Marville was the home of 410 Squadron (Cougar) with the motto "Wandering by Night," 439 Squadron (Sabre Toothed Tiger) "Fangs of Death," and 441 Squadron (Silver Fox) that had the motto "Stalk and Kill." In 1956, 410 Squadron was replaced by 445 Squadron (Wolverine) whose motto was "Strike as Lightning." Marville upgraded to Mk. 6 Sabres during the summer of 1956. RCAF Marville was an active fighter station until 1967 when Canada was required to depart because of France's withdrawal from NATO's military structure.

The RCAF set up its own fighter Ground Controlled Intercept radar facility "Yellow Jack" near Metz, France, and had its own command and control system across France to interconnect the four fighter wings.

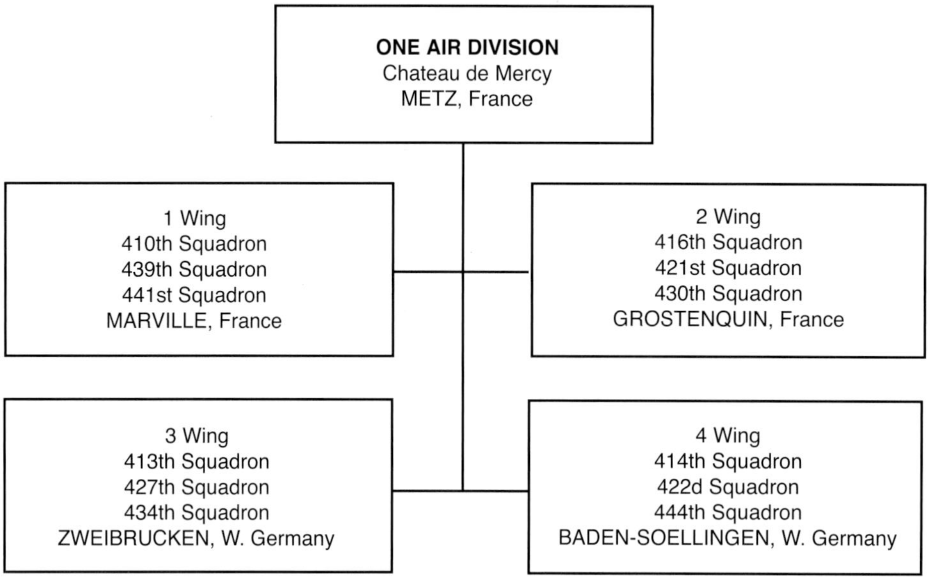

All squadrons flying Canadair Sabres

Figure 19.1 RCAF Wings and Squadrons Assigned to NATO, 1952-56

By 1957, the RCAF had approximately 3,500 officers and airmen, and 150 airwomen, operating and maintaining 150 fighter aircraft in France. The officers and airmen brought 5,300 family dependents to Europe, consisting of 2,200 wives and 3,100 children. In addition, 124 Canadian schoolteachers were employed at twelve or more different schools. Similar to USAFE, the RCAF employed French and German civilian personnel in non-combat functions to reduce military personnel expenses; 670 French citizens were hired at a total of FF480,000,000 (US $1,200,000) per year, and 700 West German citizens earning Dm3,576,000 (US $852,000) per year. The RCAF also paid the very high cost of approximately twelve fighter pilots killed in crashes in France while defending Western Europe.

RCAF Organization

RCAF organization was similar to the USAF with a wing headquarters command structure having support units that operated the air base and commanded three tactical flying squadrons. Figure 19.1 illustrates the RCAF initial command structure in Europe, 1952 through 1956, when the twelve squadrons flew Sabres. One Air Division, commanded the four fighter wings, and reported directly to HQ RCAF located in Ottawa, Canada. Within NATO command structure, One Air Division was commanded by the Fourth Allied Tactical Air Force. One Air Division initially established an administrative office in Paris, located at Hotel Violet, 35 avenue Montaigne, off the Champs Elysees. A Dakota (C-47) was operated from Orly Airport for administrative support flights to the bases. In 1954, after construction of several additional buildings, One Air Division moved its headquarters from Paris to Chateau Mercy located near Metz.

The Air Division required command and control communications systems to 4 ATAF and to its four fighter wings. Initially leased commercial circuits were used, and as usual, frequent circuit outages were common. The RCAF installed its own radio relay system across Belgium, France, and Germany consisting of eight terminals and seventeen relay sites. By 1954 a RRL system using microwave equipment was being surveyed and established by the 501st Radio Relay Squadron. The radio terminals were operated in buildings, but the relay radio sets were installed in mobile vans and trucks located on the highest hill sites; sometimes near similar U.S. relay towers such as at Dabo, France. This RCA MM-18 off-the-shelf equipment was easily identified by its ninety-foot-high towers and parabolic dish style antennas. This microwave network could convey telephone conversation as well as teletype/digital data. The RRL system was declared operational on 31 December 1954 and a great improvement in reliable phone service was immediately observed. Grostenquin became the central maintenance shop and 501st RRL Squadron headquarters. The 501st RRL Sq was redesignated the 601st Telecommunications Squadron in September 1958 to better describe its function and expanding workload. The 601st provided service as the RCAF removed its Mar-

Entrance to the USAF Dabo Radio Relay facility. Canadian RRL towers can be seen in the background, center.
Tom Simundich

ville air base, division headquarters at Metz, and its NATO aircraft warning and fighter control center near Metz during 1966-67.

The RCAF established a supply depot, No. 30 Aircraft Maintenance Base, at RCAF Langers, England, and contracted depot level aircraft special inspections, repairs, overhauls, and reclamation/salvage to Scottish Aviation at Prestwick Airport and Fairey Aviation, Renfrew Airport, Manchester, England.

On 1 July 1956, One Air Division had twelve fully equipped squadrons flying 300 excellent RCAF Mk. 6 Sabres, with highly trained fighter pilots, and very professional aircraft maintenance teams assigned to 4 ATAF that provided NATO with a formidable air defense barrier across Central Europe.

RCAF Aircraft

In 1949 the RCAF selected North American Aviation's F-86A Sabre as its standard fighter to replace all older jet powered and propeller driven fighters. Canadair Ltd. at Montreal, Quebec, obtained a license from NAA during 1950 to assemble the Mk. 1 version, the F-86A. Only one Mk. 1 was assembled and flight tested. Demands for improved Sabres in 1951 for the Korean War resulted in an NAA contract with Canadair to produce 120 F-86Es for the USAF and MDAP nations costing US$225,000 each. The second Canadair model, the Mk. 2, was the same as the F-86E and used the General Electric jet engine, J-47-GE-13. The Mk. 2 Sabre was the first Sabre model moved to France in October 1952. All Canadair Sabres were configured much like the F-86F; all armament systems were the same: six .50cal M3 machine guns, an A-1C or later, an A-4 lead computing optical gunsight, and a range computing radar set APG-30. The second version, supplied to One Air Division in 1955, was the Mk. 4, with a few small changes from the F-86F. The major change involved using a Canadian manufactured jet engine, the Avro Orenda having 6,300 to 7,200 pounds of thrust. It required a slight increase in the fuselage interior due to increased engine diameter. The final Canadair version produced was the Mk. 6 with an Orenda 14 engine producing 7,275 pounds of thrust without afterburning. This engine resulted in the best performing Sabre day fighter with a maximum speed of 710 miles per hour, and a combat ceiling of 55,000 feet, which surpassed the F-86H model!

Canada became very active in the all-weather air defense planning as part of North American Air Defense Command (NORAD), and decided to produce its own all-weather interceptor force. The first all-weather interceptor designed and manufactured was the Avro CF-100 "Canuck," affectionately renamed "Clunk" by its pilots. This aircraft was a two-place, stable, subsonic airframe powered by two Orenda jet engines, and designed for a compact radar package installed in the nose compartment. The MG-3 radar Weapon Control System was purchased from Hughes Electronics, and performance was very similar to the MG-4 radar system installed in the NAA F-86K. Armament was a fuselage belly-mounted package of eight .50cal M3 machine guns. Air to air missiles were not used. The CF-100 was ready for deployment to Europe by fall 1955; the first squadron went to Grostenquin, France. At each of One Air Division fighter wings, a CF-100 all weather fighter squadron replaced one Sabre fighter squadron; an aircraft conversion program was not conducted in Europe. The CF-100 squadrons had different designators, thus changing the RCAF order of battle in NATO. The four Sabre squadrons returned to Canada for reassignment into the air defense interceptor force.

416 Squadron Sabre Mk. 5 at Grostenquin, May 1955.
Donald M. Norrie

Sabre Mk. 5.
Department of National Defense, Canada

The last RCAF fighter that served in France was the CF-104 Starfighter, built by Canadair under license from Lockheed Aircraft. The Starfighter was a low cost solution (US$1.7 million each) to the supersonic all weather interceptor mission. The NATO mission of the CF-104s was changed from point air defense to tactical strike and reconnaissance, and unfortunately, a superior air defense fighter force for Western Europe was eliminated. The strike mission used a centerline mounted small nuclear weapon. The reconnaissance mission required a large camera pod with three to five cameras installed on the belly of the Starfighter to collect the pre/post strike photos. The Canadair Starfighters in France were based at Marville only, but did operate from Etain AB for a brief period while the runway at Marville was being reworked.

As aircraft costs rapidly increased aircraft procurement decreased, and the RCAF had to reduce its NATO fighter forces to one wing at Marville, France, and another at Zweibrucken, Germany, with each squadron flying twenty-four Starfighters. The CF-104s were removed from France in 1966 and moved to RCAF Lahr south of Baden-Soellingen, Germany.

Movement to France

RCAF aircraft, personnel, and equipment moved to France and Germany as described in chapter 2 with a few variations. All Sabres and support aircraft were flown year-round to Europe via the North Atlantic route. The fighter squadrons moved their Mk. 2 Sabres to Europe with the usual stops enroute, but from Keflavik, Iceland, usually flew into RAF Kinloss, Scotland, instead of Prestwick. The final leg of about 670 miles was direct from Kinloss to their bases in France or Germany. Total flying time was 7.5 hours from Goose Bay to Soellingen. Later replacement Sabres, models Mk. 4 and Mk. 6, were delivered by the RCAF No.1 Overseas Ferry Unit that operated from St. Hubert, Quebec. Canadair North Star transports were the enroute support aircraft. The North Star was a re-engined Douglas DC-4 powered by four Rolls-Royce Merlin engines that sounded beautiful on take-off climb out. The last fighter, CF-104s, were air lifted to Marville, France in RCAF C-130s.

The majority of RCAF personnel and their family members traveled to France by commercial passenger ships departing Halifax, Montreal, and Quebec City, and disembarking in the ports of Cherbourg or La Havre. Personnel were processed through RCAF Station Lachine, Quebec, given ship tickets and train tickets, and off they went in small groups to Europe, even though in the early days, 1951-53, they had never heard of Grostenquin and had no idea of existing living conditions. Good accommodations and food service made the crossing a pleasant experience to be remembered rather than a troop ship ordeal. The new arrivals proceeded by SNCF trains directly to Paris. An enjoyable two or three day rest in Paris was permitted, then the troops and families headed for Metz, Faulquemont, or Montmedy and their new duty stations. The first large shipment of people bound for Grostenquin arrived at Cherbourg, France, on Saturday, 25 October 1952 on S.S. Columbia. Air Division HQ arranged a two-day visit in Paris before their train trip to the Faulquemont rail station. The travelers stayed in Paris hotels on the economy for both nights. Three warrant officers and ninety-two airman, plus seven wives and eight children were in this early contingent.

RCAF Sabre Mk. 6 at V-E Day open house at Chambley AB, 1957.
Al Christensen

CF-100 from RCAF Marville at V-E Day open house at Chambley AB, 1957.
Al Christensen

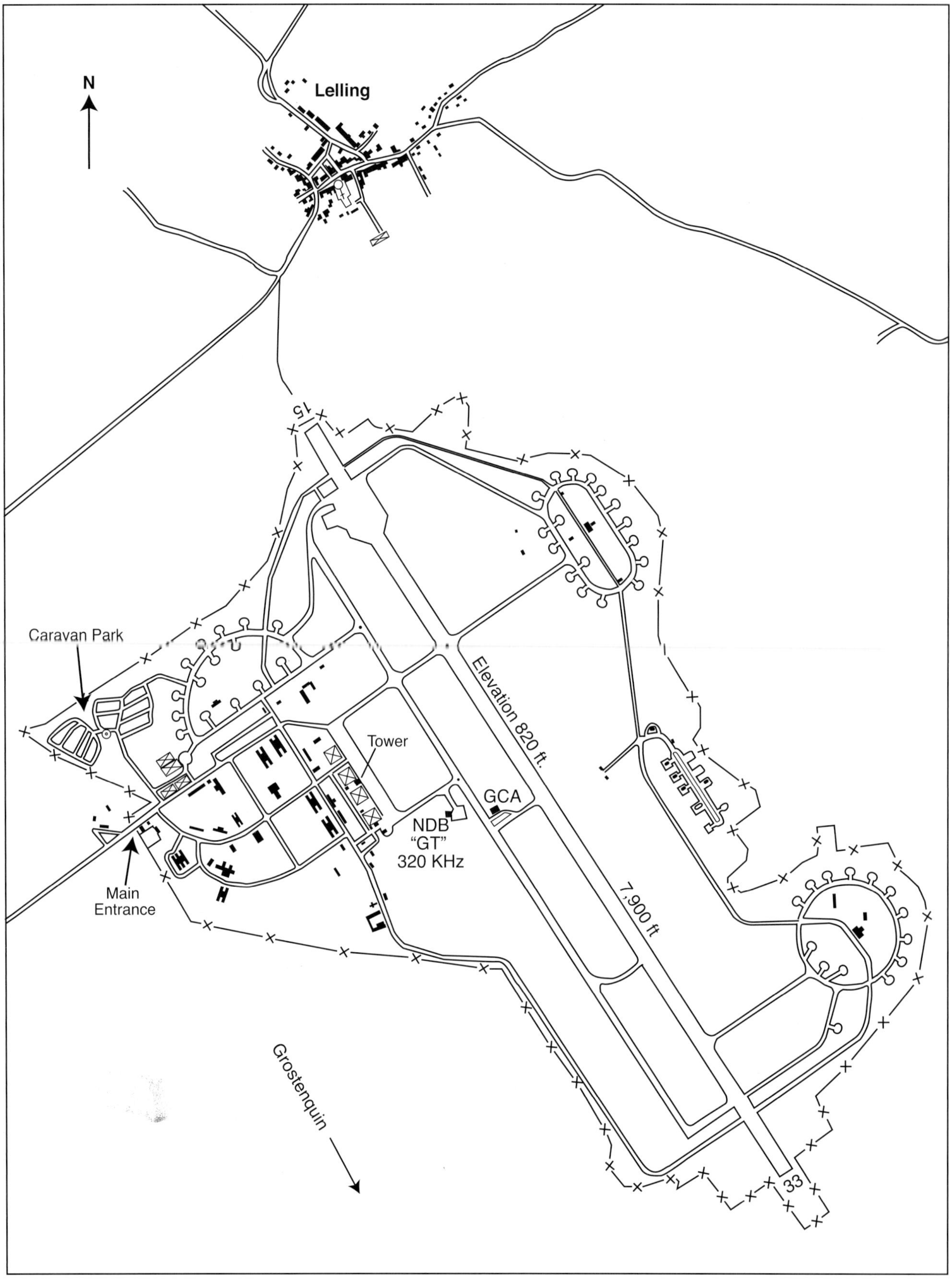

Map 19.1 RCAF Grostenquin

Former RCAF Station Grostenquin from the air, 1986.
Ren L'Ecuyer

During 1959 the RCAF began flying all military personnel and dependents to France using the new RCAF Yukon four-engine turbo-powered CL-144 transport to save travel time and cost. The usual route was from Ottawa to Marville. All personnel could be processed through French immigration and customs upon arrival at RCAF Marville.

RCAF Grostenquin

RCAF Grostenquin (Gro-ton-ken) was located in the Moselle Department, in the Lorraine Plateau region of France. It is located 207 miles (325 km) east of Paris, south of Auto Route A32, and 6 miles (10 km) south of St. Avold on highway D22. Grostenquin is a very small crossroads village located within the Maginot Line region. During WWII, the American Third Army, XII Corps, 35th Infantry Division captured Grostenquin on 20 November 1944 while heading for the Rhine River. The Grostenquin air base site was not used as a WWII airfield. No advance landing grounds were constructed in this area by the U.S. Ninth Air Force in 1944-45.

RCAF Station Grostenquin (49° 02'N - 06° 43'E, elevation 820 feet, 250m) is 3 miles (5 km) northwest of Grostenquin on D79. Main entrance to the airfield is 0.6 mile (1 km) east of highway D79. Canada and France agreed to the location near St. Avold. There were no existing airfields in this local area and there were no commercial airports within twenty miles, therefore there would be little conflicting air traffic. The initial survey team arrived in the Grostenquin-Faulquemont-Morhange valley in spring 1951, and selected Guessling and Bistroff farm sites. Prevailing winds forced a north-south runway orientation. Runway approaches at both ends were fairly clear for two miles and free of large populated areas. Final site layout north of Grostenquin village began in July 1951 to determine property owners and prepare land leases. The base real estate was purchased by France for CAN $240,000 for 805 acres of farmland, including a very large old stone farmhouse and barn. Next, construction schedules and costs were estimated for a standard NATO air base that was still being designed! The USAFE air bases being started at this time were interim tent camp layouts with an unknown final configuration. The final base layout was smaller than USAFE air bases in France, having one living/industrial site at the northwest end of the base. RCAF Grostenquin would be a unique air base because of its prefab buildings constructed with aluminum siding and roofs, no fighter squadron hangars out in the marguerites, an above-ground hot water distribution system, and no

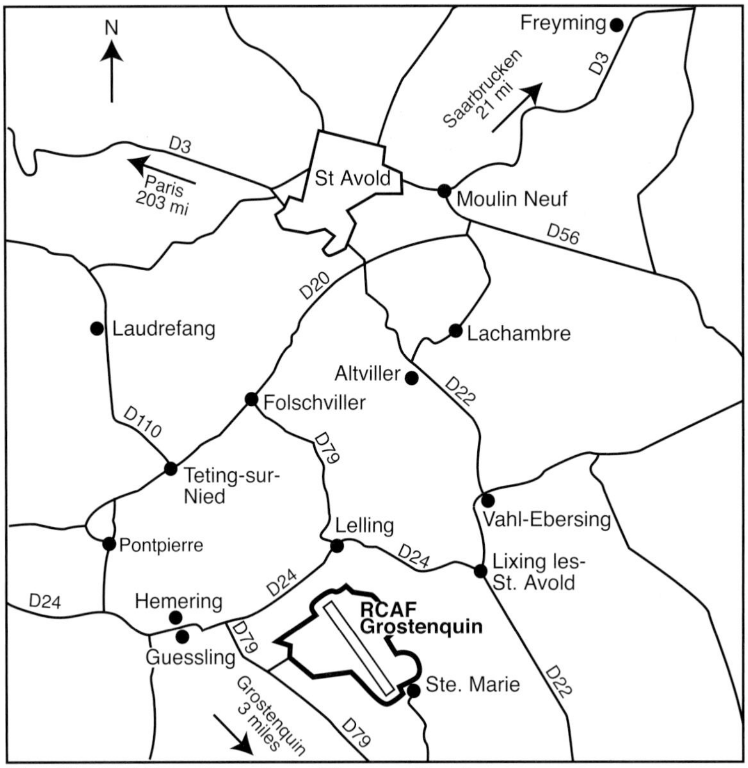

Map 19.2 RCAF Grostenquin and Surrounding Area

railroad spur track onto the base. The prefab buildings were never replaced and some still stand in 2002.

The site was an ancient sea bed and a flood plain requiring a fair amount of earth moving and compacting to produce a well drained all weather runway (including snow). A French company began earth moving in September 1951; a single 7,900-foot long, 160-foot wide concrete runway was built in eight months. In 1955, 500-foot runway extensions were added. Runway over-runs and an arresting barrier were added in 1958. Munitions storage for bombs, rockets and gun ammunition was located on base north of the runway, between the two east side marguerites. Eight standard munition igloos and four smaller shelters were constructed with revetments. The third squadron marguerite was north of, and adjacent to, the living area. Each marguerite had sixteen parking petals (buttons), with each button capable of holding three fighters. Seventy-five Sabres could be distributed around the base for survival; no aircraft revetments were constructed. One concrete parallel taxiway, 7,500 feet long, 75 feet wide that could serve as an emergency runway, was built west of the runway. Taxiway, parking ramp, marguerites and aprons, etc. required 410,000 square yards of concrete.

Four fighter-sized hangars, about 110 feet wide by 190 feet deep with 20,000 square feet of 25-foot high, clear, aircraft workspace, were built on the aircraft parking ramp west of the runway. The hangar sides and rear had one story lean-to structures supplying 6,600 square feet of repair shops. The hangar roof frame and steel sheeting were assembled on the concrete floor, then the roof was hydraulically jacked upwards twenty-five feet, and the side wall steel framing was assembled. All walls were made of bricks, filling in the steel framework. Hangar design allowed as much sunlight as possible and were heated for winter work. Each Sabre squadron was assigned a hangar; the fourth hangar was used for the wing support aircraft. A four-story-high control tower was attached to the south edge of #2 hangar. A base operations building for flight operation offices, communications, and the weather station was located behind the hangars.

RCAF Grostenquin was transferred from France to the RCAF on 13 December 1952. By June 1954 the base finally reached completion as designed in 1951. The total area was 805 acres with ten miles of paved roads. The base had forty-seven permanent single story buildings. Wing headquarters was located on the main street about one block east of the main entrance gate and three flags were flown in front of this building, the Canadian, French, and RCAF flags. Twenty-three "H" shaped buildings provided billeting for single and unaccompanied officers and airmen; one building was

416 SQ barracks Block #19, April 56. Note the overhead heating pipes unique to Grostenquin.
Donald M. Norrie

F-86F-35 from 494th FBSq, 48th FBWg Chaumont AB visiting Grostenquin, 1955.
Len Wickens

designated for female personnel. The RCAF assigned forty-eight female officers and airwomen to Grostenquin in 1952. Two dining halls were on base; one configured for 300 officers and NCOs, a second served another 700 airmen. The base had recreation service facilities for all personnel; a large service club, a hospital, two chapels, base exchange store, theater, gym, and unique to the Canadians, an indoor ice hockey rink, curling ice rink, and a large indoor swimming pool. A bowling alley was constructed below the swimming pool deck. Like the United States, Canada had to pay 100 percent of the costs to provide these quarters and service facilities for their troops in France.

A small construction setback occurred on 12 December 1952 when an unusual wind storm hit the area and tore loose some of the aluminum sidewalls and roof panels on airmen barracks, one chapel, and two warehouses. At this time the central heating plant was not finished, therefore gasoline powered Herman Nelsons (aircraft heaters) had to be run constantly to produce heat for the billets. The usual flexible fabric heating ducts were used to get the heat into the buildings making it appear as if huge yellow worms were taking over the living area.

Three large supply warehouses provided 2.7 million cubic feet of storage space. The water system was fed by underground storage tanks holding 60,000 gallons. The water came from on-base wells. In the first years this water supply was badly polluted and required continuous testing and special chemical treatment. The base's heating plant was unique to Grostenquin; hot water was piped throughout the building area in insulated distribution pipes mounted on poles. Electrical power was purchased from the local utility. Power failures were common which brought the hot water system pumps to a halt and left the buildings without heat. The base electrical system was installed underground as was common at NATO bases. Auxiliary electrical generators had to be installed near critical operational facilities to keep the base combat ready. The underground fuel storage system consisted of ten sites about the air base, each with four 10,000 gallon tanks holding a total of 360,000 gallons of aircraft fuels, and 40,000 gallons of vehicle fuels. Prior to 1958 all fuel was delivered to the Faulquemont rail yard where tank cars were used for fuel storage. Fuel was pumped from the tank cars, trucked to the air base, and transferred to underground storage tanks. It was then pumped from the underground tanks into aircraft refueling rigs to service the three Sabre squadrons. The base fuel storage system was connected into the NATO pipeline system near St. Avold in 1957. By 1958 the estimated value of Grostenquin, excluding land, was US$12 million.

Off-base housing for RCAF personnel was in very limited supply in 1952 in the Grostenquin area because of extensive WWII damage to homes across northern France, and the remoteness of the base from large cities that may have had rental housing. The first solution to this housing shortage, in 1951-52, was to prohibit bringing families to France; no funding was approved for the movement of dependents. The RCAF had a much higher percentage of married personnel than the USAF at this time. A few families did travel to France at their own expense and discovered that indeed, rental housing was very scarce plus what was available was below usual Canadian housing standards. The Lorraine region was living with 1918 era utilities: light, heat, water, and sewage services. The second attempt to solve the problem was to provide family quarters on Grostenquin. English built house trailers (caravans) were purchased and placed on the northwest aircraft marguerite as soon as it was completed. Later a large caravan park was built in the northwest corner of the base next to the marguerite. In 1954 concurrent dependent travel was approved, and many RCAF families began arriving in France.

The third solution was off-base housing. Constructed during 1954-56, it consisted of a very large rental complex on a 35-acre hilltop located 5 mi (8 Km) north of air base in St. Avold's southern suburb of Wenheck. This Permanent Married Quarters (PMQ) complex was constructed by a French company under an agreement similar to the U.S. Guaranteed Rental Income program. The RCAF guaranteed a fixed monthly income to the French company, and in turn, the officers and airmen did not receive their usual housing allowance, which was paid to the French company. This Wenheck housing complex consisted of eleven large, five story buildings, and twelve smaller, one or two story buildings. The 443 apartments, for 67 officers, 108 senior NCOs, and 268 airmen, had various floor plans of five to nine rooms. The design provided ground level laundry rooms as well as storage rooms for the occupants. About ten single-family homes were provided for the highest ranking officers. To reduce moving costs from Canada to France, the apartments were rented furnished with French manufactured furniture. A large four-story elementary school was included at the PMQ site where most of the children lived, and the Lorraine High School was established on Grostenquin using a barracks "H" building. Both schools were staffed with Canadian school teachers. An FM radio broadcast station, "CFGT" at 97.1, was set up on base and produced a wide variety of programming, some directed toward families, children, and teens. In addition to the Wenheck housing, a number of RCAF families rented quarters in the local French towns and cities of St. Avold, Faulquemont, and Merlebach.

On 31 July 1964 the RCAF closed Grostenquin and departed the facility after twelve years of fighter operations. There was some consideration of either Canada or the U.S. maintaining Grostenquin as a standby base, but defense budget realities could not justify its retention along with six similar air bases in France. Canadian defense budgets were decreasing, fighter aircraft programs were being scaled down, and the cost of European basing was increasing rapidly. Marville was considered the better of the two air bases and remained active. For a year after the RCAF returned Grostenquin to the French Government, the French Air Force used the base as a fighter dispersal field. Then it was transferred to the French Army and used for vehicle maintenance and supply storage. During the 1970s several buildings were disassembled and removed because of deterioration. There are now concerns about clean-up of fuel and chemical spills before the base can be released for civil use. The French Army was still using Grostenquin in summer 2002, and visitors were not permitted to tour the base. The PMQ apartments in Wenheck are now privately owned and are well maintained. The greatest surprise for all visitors is the size and number of trees growing on the base housing area and around the PMQ site.

Grostenquin can be found on Michelin Map #307 Local, and IGN Series Blue #3513 E. The nearby towns of St. Avold or Faulquemont are accessible from Paris by train using Gare de l'Est.

RCAF Marville

RCAF Station Marville (49° 28'N - 05° 25'E, elevation 906 feet, 276m) was located in the Meuse Department, in the Lorraine Plateau region of France, near the Meuse River; and very near the Belgian border at the west end of the Maginot Line. Marville is 204 mi (328 km) northeast of Paris, west of Luxembourg City, 26 miles (40 km) north of Verdun, and 6 miles (9 km) south of Montmedy. Marville is a very small farming village built on a sharp ridgeline in rolling hills. During WWII, the American First Army, V Corps, 9th Infantry Division passed through the area on 2 September 1944 while marching towards Luxembourg. The air base site was not used as a WWII airfield.

After agreement between Canada and France over the air base location and runway orientation in summer 1952, the initial survey teams arrived on the property in September of that year and began accurate site layout for land leases, and to determine construction schedules and costs for a standard NATO air base. The base required a real estate parcel of 780 acres. The farmland purchased for Marville cost France CAN $290,000.

One Wing (F) activated RCAF Marville on 1 April 1955. It had been stationed at RCAF Station North Luffenham, England, since February 1952. The air base became home to approximately 150 officers and 1,000 airmen, known as "other ranks," upon arrival. Arriving when construction was almost complete eliminated the usual battle of living and working in the French mud. Marville's mailing address was CAPO 5052; Canadian Armed Forces, Europe.

The final base layout provided one living/industrial site built at the west end of the base. The site required a large amount of earth moving, filling and compacting to produce a flat well drained plain for three kilometers eastward towards Marville. A French heavy construction company began earth moving in early October and a single 7,900 foot long, 160 foot wide concrete runway was built in eight months. The problem of storing bombs, missiles, and rockets on base was solved later in 1956 by acquiring an off-

Trailers on northern marguerite button, Grostenquin 1953. A RRL station is in the foreground, left.
Canadaian National Archives

Grostenquin PMQs in Wenheck, 1963.
www.Grostenquin.org

Roadsign for French base at Grostenquin on a foggy day 1997.
Jerry McAuliffe

Grostenquin base gate 1997. Entrance is prohibited.
Jerry McAuliffe

The town of Lelling, 1955.
Donald M. Norrie

Entering the town of Lelling, 2002.
Jerry McAuliffe

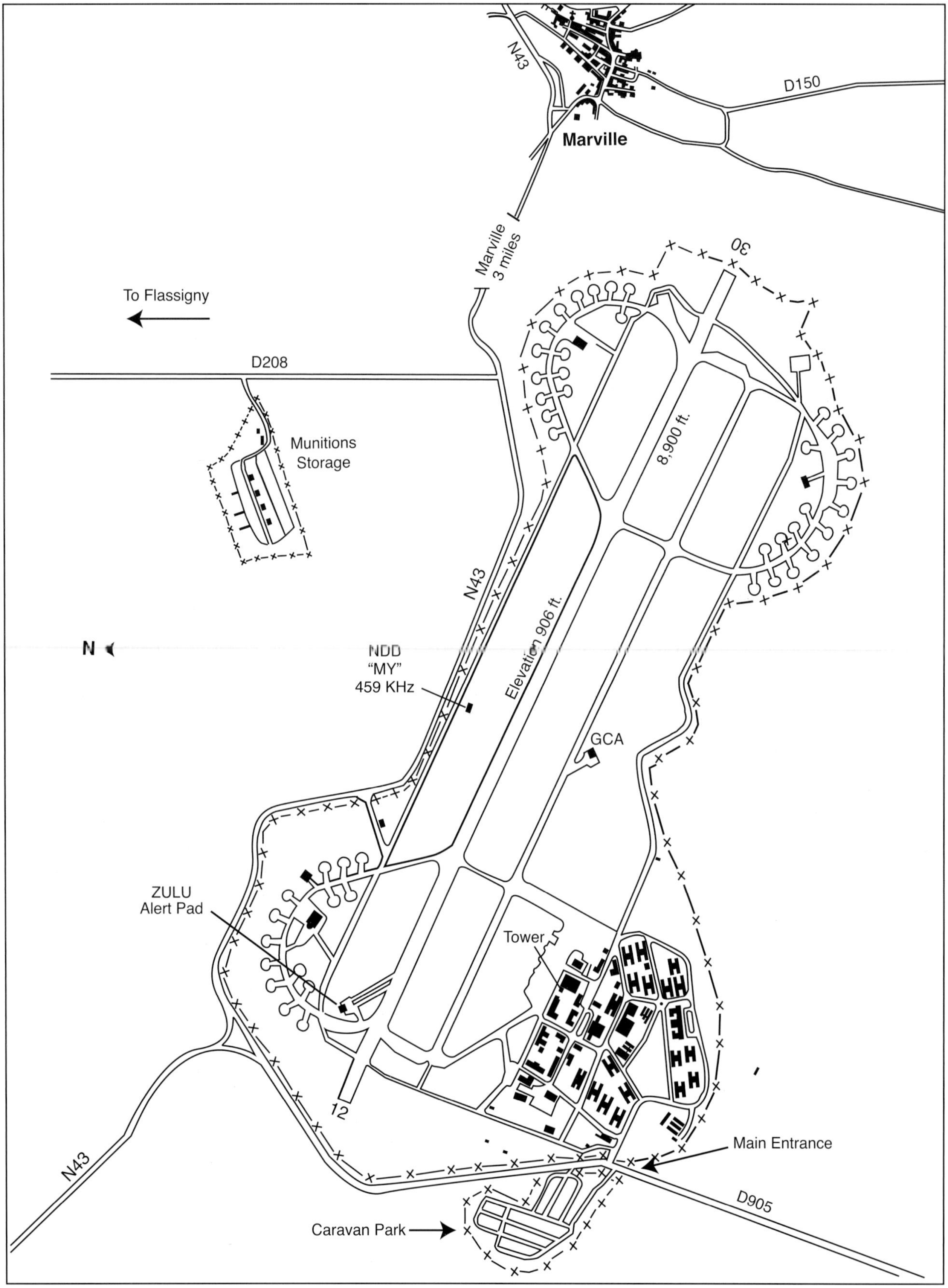

Map 19.3 RCAF Marville

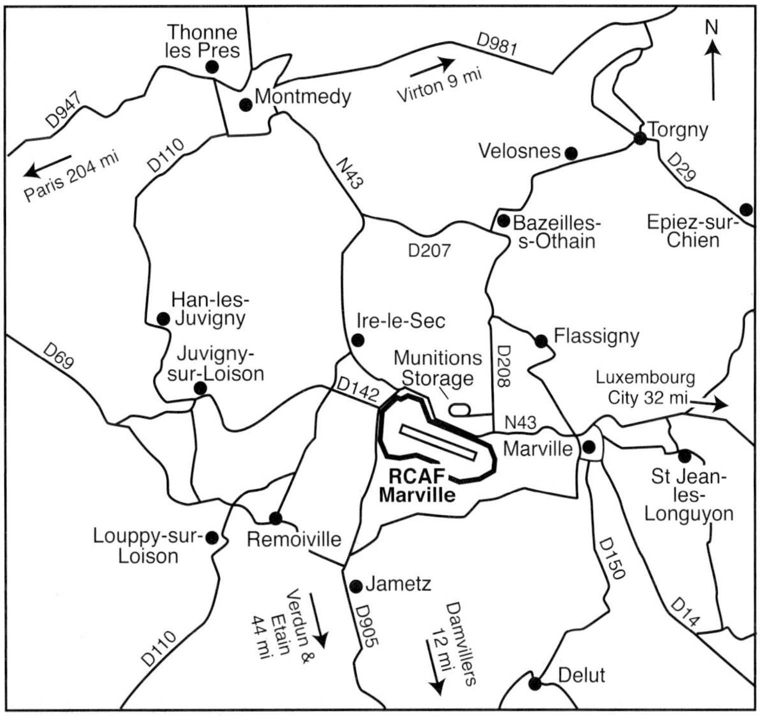

Map 19.4 RCAF Marville and Surrounding Area

base 35-acre site one kilometer north across highway N43. Four large igloos plus eight smaller shelters were constructed on this property. A 1,000-foot runway extension was added in 1956; runway over-runs and an arresting barrier were added on runway 12 in 1957.

By January 1956, RCAF Marville reached completion as designed in 1952; the total area was 840 acres with seven miles of paved roads. One concrete parallel taxiway, 7,100 feet long and 75 feet wide, was built south of the runway. Taxiway, parking ramp, marguerites, aprons, etc. used 420,000 square yards of concrete. Three fighter sized hangars, 20,000 square feet each, provided 13,000 square feet of 35-foot high clear aircraft workspace. Hangars were heated for winter work and were well lighted. Two fighter squadrons were located on the north side of the runway and one at the southeast corner of the base. Each fighter hangar was surrounded by a marguerite with fifteen parking petals. The Sabres were well spaced around the base for survival, but no revetments were installed. Two smaller, 15,000 square foot hangars were constructed for wing support aircraft (T-33s, C-45s, and C-47s) on the large aircraft parking ramp. The control tower was on the south edge of the ramp adjacent to a support aircraft hangar. A base operations building for all flight operation offices and the weather station was located next to the control tower adjacent to the transient aircraft ramp. A very large earth covered air raid shelter was constructed on the north side of the runway and had many VHF/UHF radio antenna masts rising from its top surface. This may be the only personnel air raid shelter built in France at a NATO air base in the 1950s!

The base had fifty-eight permanent single story buildings of concrete block and metal construction. Wing headquarters was located one street south of the aircraft ramp, and the Canadian, French, and RCAF flags were flown in front of this building. Sixteen buildings provided billeting for single and unaccompanied officers and airmen; one building was designated for female personnel. Two dining halls were on base; one configured for 300 officers and NCOs, a second served another 600 airmen. The base had recreation service facilities for their personnel; a large service club, a hospital, chapel, base exchange store, theater, gym, and also like Grostenquin, an indoor ice hockey rink and large indoor swimming pool. Again, Canada paid 100 percent of the cost to provide these badly needed facilities for their air base personnel and dependents.

One large warehouse provided 1.6 million cubic feet of storage space. The potable water system held 90,000 gallons in underground storage tanks. These were supplied by wells located two miles off base near Remoiville. The base had twelve dispersed heat-

Marville PMQ buildings in 2002.
Jerry McAuliffe

Grammar school at Marville PMQ, 2002.
Jerry McAuliffe

Commemorative Plaque, at former Marville PMQ, 2002.
Jerry McAuliffe

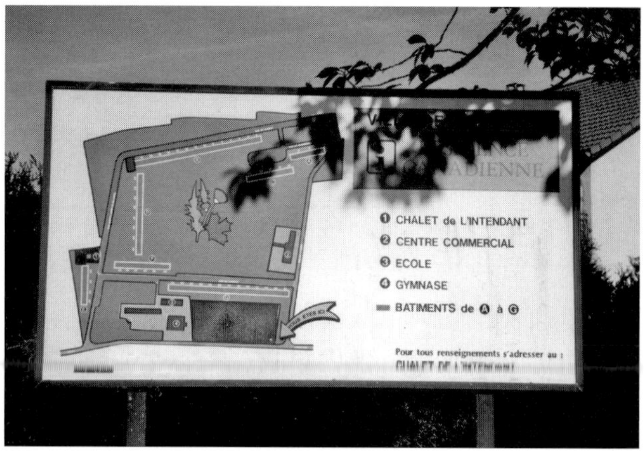

Map at entrance to former Marville PMQs, 2002.
Jerry McAuliffe

ing plants throughout the building area with underground heat distribution pipes. The base electrical system was also installed underground. Underground fuel storage capacity was 800,000 gallons of jet fuel and 80,000 gallons of AVGAS, plus vehicle fuels. Fuel was pumped underground to the three squadron marguerites. The base fuel storage field was connected into the NATO pipeline system near Metz. By 1958 the estimated air base value excluding land was CAN $16.5 million.

Here also, extensive damage to homes during WWII, made it necessary to provide housing for RCAF married personnel at Marville. Housing constructed to fill this shortage consisted of a very large Permanent Married Quarters (PMQ) apartment complex located 17 miles (27 km) east of the base in Longuyon, and a large caravan park immediately west of the base main entrance across highway D905. The PMQ was constructed during 1954-55 under an agreement similar to the Grostenquin program. This complex consisted of seven, four-story buildings having 418 apartments sited on 50 acres of land. The apartments for both officers and enlisted men were arranged with various floor plans from three to six rooms. An elementary school and gymnasium were included with "Cite Canadienne Marville."

In addition to the PMQs and trailers, a number of RCAF families rented quarters locally in the nearby cities and towns of Montmedy, Longuyon, and Longwy in France, and in the Belgium cities of Virton, Florenville and many other small towns up to 30 miles from the air base. Large Totem Poles will be found today in Longuyon and Virton town squares, a gift from Canadians to their French and Belgian neighbors in memory of their very pleasant years residing in the region.

After the RCAF turned Marville back to the French Government, the French Air Force used the base as a flight pattern training field for a short period. Afterwards, without proper security, the base was subjected to vandalism and destruction. During the 1970s two hangars were disassembled and moved to other bases;

Road sign for the French Air base at Marville, 2002.
Jerry McAuliffe

N43 entrance to north side of former RCAF Marville, 2002.
Jerry McAuliffe

Main gate at entrance to business park on site of former RCAF Marville, 2002.
Jerry McAuliffe

Hangar in use by French military on former RCAF Marville, 2002.
Jerry McAuliffe

one of the wing support flight hangars was relocated to Etain AB and is used for helicopter maintenance. Currently, the former base is an active airport for sport aviation and is owned by the town of Marville. Much effort is being invested in developing the site into an industrial zone that has been established in the hangars and old base buildings. Several buildings have been leased for small fabrication businesses. The French army was using both northern hangars as DOB deployment sites and for training exercises in 1999, but departed Marville in 2002. The PMQ apartments in Longuyon are privately owned and are in excellent condition.

Marville can be found on Michelin Map #307 Local, and IGN Series Blue Maps #3111E & #3211O. The nearby towns of Montmedy and Longuyon are accessible from Paris by train from Gare de l'Est.

Tower at Marville, 2002.
Jerry McAuliffe

Hangar now used as steel fabrication shop at Marville, 2002.
Jerry McAuliffe

Marville hangar still showing its 439 squadron number.
Jerry McAuliffe

Facing Page:
Top row (L to R)
Recreation hall, 2002.
Marville warehouse, 2002.

Upper middle row (L to R)
Base shops, Marville 2002.
Barracks building, Marville 2002.

Lower Middle Row (L to R)
Base chapel, Marville 2002
Personnel shelter, Marville 2002.

Bottom row (L to R)
Abandoned large hangar, Marville 2002.
Small hangar, Marville 2002.
All photos by Jerry McAuliffe

Right:
Highway sign in 2002 as you
exit the main gate at Marville, in 2002.
Jerry McAuliffe

Appendix 19.1 Notice to Airmen 1957 (NOTAM) - RCAF Grostenquin

Elevation 820 feet (250m), 49° 02'N - 06° 43'E. One paved runway 7,900 feet long supports 84,000 lbs, 150°/330°. Airfield operations limited: 0700 - 1600hrs, Mondays thru Fridays, all other times on request with 1 hour notice. Airfield lighting consists of: rotating beacon, runway - taxiway lights, and high intensity approach lights. Transient aircraft storage and minor engine repairs available. Aircraft fuel, 100-130 octane, and JP4 jet fuel service available. High and low pressure oxygen service available. Jet aircraft starting units, A-3, C-21 and C-22 available. High pressure air service with 3,000psi maximum. Jet aircraft arresting barriers installed. Crash and rescue facilities. Customs available.

Appendix 19.2 Notice to Airmen 1957 (NOTAM) - RCAF Marville-Montmedy

Elevation 906 feet (276m), 49° 28'N - 05° 25'E. One paved runway 8,900 feet long, 120°/300°. Airfield operations limited: 0700 - 1600hrs, Mondays thru Fridays, all other times on request with 15 minute notice. Airfield lighting consists of: rotating beacon and high intensity approach lights for runway 12; runway lights and obstruction lights only, for runway 30. Aircraft fuel, 100-130 octane, and JP4 jet fuel service available. High and low pressure oxygen service available. Jet aircraft starting units available. High pressure air service. Jet aircraft arresting barrier on runway 12 only.

ACKNOWLEDGEMENTS

I would like to thank the following people who contributed to this chapter:

Ren l'Ecuyer was in the RCAF, stationed at Grostenquin. He has devoted much time and effort to preserving the history of the Canadian effort in France through his website www.grostenquin.org.

Donald M. Norrie served as an M & W Technician with 416 (F) Squadron, Wing Armament and Wing Maintenance at 2 Fighter Wing, RCAF Grostenquin, France, 1955-1959

Tom Simundich was stationed at Dabo with the 8th RRL Sq from 1961-64. I would also like to thank him for providing much information about 8th RRL Squadron locations and operations.

Len Wickens was an avionics technican, air, in 416 (F) Squadron at RCAF Grostenquin from July 1954 to July 1956.

The town of Marville, 2002.
Jerry McAuliffe

COMMON ACRONYMS

AACS Air and Airways Communications Service; subcommand of MATS
AAFCE Allied Air Forces Central Europe
AB Air Base, a USAF overseas flying facility
A/C Aircraft
AD Air Depot or Air Division
ADC Air Defense Command
ADSEC Advance Section, forward logistics area near the battlefield
ADVON Advanced Echelon, small number of troops sent to prepare new base
AF Air Force
AFCENT Allied Forces Central Europe
AFR Air Force Regulation
ALC Air Logistics Command, new name for AMC after 1957
AMA Air Material Area, geographical logistics support region
AMC Air Material Command, major supply command of the USAF
ANG Air National Guard of the United States, part of the reserve air forces
AO, BN Aerial Observer, Bombardier/Navigator
AOCP Aircraft Out of Commission for Parts
APO Army Postal Office, overseas postal service number by unit or location
ARSq Air Rescue Squadron
ATAF Allied Tactical Air Forces
AWS Air Weather Service, subcommand of MATS

BASEC Base Section, rear logistics area distant from the battlefield

CASA Support contractor at Madrid, Spain
CASF Composite Air Strike Force
CCH Commodity Credit Housing, a method of financing family housing units
CINC Commander in Chief
CINCEUCOM Commander in Chief, European Command
CINCUSAFE Commander in Chief, U.S. Air Forces in Europe
CINCUSAREUR Commander in Chief, U.S. Army in Europe

COB Colocated Operating Base
COM Z Communications Zone, Logistical arena behind the forward combat area.
CONAC Continental Air Command .
CONUS Continental United States of America
C of Eng Corps of Engineers, U. S. Army

DAF Department of the Air Force
DCA Defense Communications Agency
Det. Detachment, small unit USAF level of organization
DOB Dispersed Operating Base
DUC Distinguished Unit Citation

EABn Engineer Aviation Battalion, U.S. Army SCARWAF construction unit
EUCOM European Command

FAF French Air Force
FB Fighter-Bomber unit or aircraft
FBGp Fighter-Bomber Group
FBSq Fighter-Bomber Squadron

FBWg	Fighter-Bomber Wing
FISq	Fighter-Interceptor Squadron
FEAF	Far East Air Force, USAF in Japan, Korea, and Guam
FOL	Forward Operating Location
FIAT	A/C support contractor
FRELOC	Code name for the fast relocation of NATO units from France, 1966-67
FRG	Federal Republic of Germany, West Germany after 1955
GCA	Ground Controlled Approach, a ground radar landing aid
GRI	Guaranteed Rental Income, a method of financing family housing units
HABS	High Altitude Bombing System
IRAN	Inspect and Repair as Necessary
JCA	Joint Construction Agency
KLM	Royal Dutch Airlines, support contractor at Amsterdam
LABS	Low Altitude Bombing System
LBGp	Light Bomb Group
LBSq	Light Bomb Squadron
LBWg	Light Bomb Wing
LOCS	Line of Communications, infrastructure to support ground combat forces
MAP	Military Assistance Program
MDAP	Military Defense Assistance Program or Mutual Defense Assistance Program after 1954
MATS	Military Air Transport Service, major command of the USAF
MLS	Military Liquidation Section, DOD real estate agency in Paris
MOAMA	Mobile Air Material Area
MOB	Main Operating Base
NATO	North Atlantic Treaty Organization
NEAC	Northeast Air Command
NDB	Non-directional beacon, a low frequency radio navigational aid
OJT	On The Job Training
O&M	Operation & Maintenance
OOAMA	Ogden Air Material Area
PCS	Permanent Change of Station, relocation of a unit or individual
POL	Petroleum, Oil, Lubricants, Class II supplies
RAF	Royal Air Force, Air Force of Great Britain
RCAF	Royal Canadian Air Force
RED RICHARD	Code name for the rapid relocation of USAF units from France, 1958-59
RRL	Radio Relay Network or System
SAC	Strategic Air Command, major command of the USAF
SAS	Scandinavian Airline Service, support contractor at Copenhagen, Denmark
SCARWAF	Special Category Army personnel With Air Force; see EABn
SDB	Standby Deployment Base
SEAWEED	SAC program to provide support to returning bombers
SHAEF	Supreme Headquarters Allied Expeditionary Forces, 1944-45

SHAPE	Supreme Headquarters Allied Powers Europe
SHORAN	Short Range Navigation System, electronic navigation system
Sq	Squadron, USAF level of organization
TAC	Tactical Air Command, major command of the USAF
TACAN	Tactical Air Navigation radio aid
TB	Tactical Bomber unit or aircraft, replaced light bomber designator
TBGp	Tactical Bomber Group
TBSq	Tactical Bomber Squadron
TBWg	Tactical Bomber Wing
TC	Troop Carrier unit or aircraft
TCGp	Troop Carrier Group
TCSq	Troop Carrier Squadron
TCTO	Time Compliance Technical Order
TCWg	Troop Carrier Wing
TDY	Temporary duty
TF	Tactical Fighter unit or aircraft, replaced fighter-bomber designator
TF Gp	Tactical Fighter Group
TF Sq	Tactical Fighter Squadron
TF Wg	Tactical Fighter Wing
TR	Tactical Reconnaissance unit or aircraft
TR Gp	Tactical Reconnaissance Group
TR Sq	Tactical Reconnaissance Squadron
TR Wg	Tactical Reconnaissance Wing
TWR	Aircraft control tower used for local aircraft operations
USAF	United States Air Force
USAFE	United States Air Forces in Europe
USCINCEUR	United States Commander in Chief, Europe
USAREUR	United States Army, Europe
Wg	Wing, USAF level of organization
WOQ	Women Officers' Quarters
WRAMA	Warner-Robbins Air Material Area
WWII	World War Two, 1939 - 1945
ZI	Zone of Interior, Continental United States of America

SELECTED BIBLIOGRAPHY

SOURCES SPANNING MORE THAN ONE CHAPTER.

BOOKS:

Cantwell, Gerald T. *Citizen Airmen; A History of the Air Force Reserve, 1946-1994.* Washington, D.C.: Air Force History and Museums Program, 1997.

Grey, C.G. and Leonard Bridgeman, editors. *Janes All The World's Aircraft.* London: Sampson Low, Marston & Co., Ltd., December, 1939.

Johnson, David C. *U.S. Army Air Forces Continental Airfields (ETO) D-Day to V-E Day.* Research Division, USAF Historical Research Center, Maxwell AFB, AL, 1988.

Knaak, Marcelle Size. *Encyclopedia of U.S. Air Force Aircraft and Missile Systems. Vol I. Post World War II Fighters, 1945-1973.* Office of Air Force History, Washington, D.C.: United States Air Force, 1986.

——— *Encyclopedia of U.S. Air Force Aircraft and Missile Systems. Vol II. Post World War II Bombers, 1945-1973.* Office of Air Force History, United States Air Force, Washington, D.C. 1988.

Mark, Eduard, *Defending the West: The United States Air Force and European Security, 1946-1998.* Air Force History and Museum Program.

Maurer Maurer, ed. *Air Force Combat Units of World War II.* USAF Historical Division, Air University, Washington, D.C.: Dept. of the Air Force, 1960.

——— *Combat Squadrons of the Air Force, World War II.* USAF Historical Division, Air University, Washington, D.C.: Dept. of the Air Force, 1969.

Mueller, Robert, *Air Force Bases, Vol I, Active Air Force Bases Within the United States of America on 17 September 1982.* Office of Air Force History, Washington, D.C.; United States Air Force, 1989.

Nalty, Bernard C. ed. *Winged Shield, Winged Sword; A History of the United States Air Force. Vol. I, 1907-1950.* Washington, D.C.: Air Force History and Museums Program, 1997.

Ravenstein, Charles A. *Air Force Combat Wings, Lineage and Honors Histories 1947-1977.* USAF Historical Research Center. Office of Air Force History, Washington, D.C.: United States Air Force, 1984.

Snyder, Thomas S. and MSGT Shelia A. Shaw. *United States Air Forces in Europe, Historical Highlights, 1942-1992.* Office of History; Headquarters USAFE, Ramstein Air Base, Germany, 1993.

REPORTS, STUDIES, AND UNPUBLISHED WORKS:

"Army and Air Force Installations Outside the Continental U.S. Inventory-France." Dept. of the Air Force and Dept. of the Army Special Report, 31 December 1953.

"Radio Facility Charts and In-Flight Data: Europe." United States Air Force, Distribution: 3 November 1958.

SOURCES OF INTEREST TO A SPECIFIC CHAPTER.

INTRODUCTION

Parish, Patricia, editor. *Forty-five Years of Vigilance for Freedom; United States Air Forces in Europe, 1942-1987.* Office of History, Headquarters USAFE, Ramstein Air Base, Germany.

Assorted papers, notes, drafts, and telegrams of President Harry S. Truman and his cabinet regarding the formation of NATO. Truman Library and Museum on line: www.trumanlibrary.org/nato/natodocs.htm.

CHAPTER ONE: HISTORICAL PERSPECTIVE

Futrell, Robert. *The United States Air Force in Korea 1950-1953.* Duell, Sloan and Pearce, New York, 1961.

Gibson, James N. *Nuclear Weapons of the United States, An Illustrated History.* Atglen, Pennsylvania: Shiffer Publishing, Ltd., 1996.

Hanson, Chuck. *U.S. Nuclear Weapons, The Secret Story.* Arlington, Texas: Aero Fax, 1988.

Harrington, Daniel F., *The Air Force Can Deliver Anything! A History of the Berlin Airlift.* Office of History. Headquarters USAFE, Ramstein Air Base, Germany, 1998.

Tusa, John and Ann, *The Berlin Airlift.* Staplehurst, Kent: Spellmount Limited; The Old Rectory, 1998.

"North Atlantic Treaty 1949" NATO On-line library, www.NATO.org.

CHAPTER TWO: BASE SELECTION AND MOVEMENT TO FRANCE 1950 -1954

Rust, Kenneth C. *The 9th Air Force in World War II.* Fallbrook, California: Aero Publishers, Inc., 1970.

CHAPTER THREE: CONSTRUCTION IN FRANCE 1951-1960

Adams, COL Gerald M. *A History of U.S. Strategic Air Bases in Morocco, 1951-1963.* The Moroccan Reunion Association: Nebraska, 1992.

Benson, Lawrence R. *USAF Aircraft Basing in Europe, North Africa, and the Middle East, 1945-1980.* USAF Historical Division, Air University, Washington, D.C.: Dept. of the Air Force. Historical study prepared April 1981.

Freeman, Dexter. *France Over Lightly.* Information and Education Branch, HQ 12th Air Force. USAFE. July, 1952.

Tulley, BGEN David H. "The Military Construction Program." *Military Engineer, No. 314* (Nov/Dec 1954).

CHAPTER FOUR: MISSION READY 1955-1958

Pottier, Olivier. *Les bases americaines en France: un outil militaire, economique et politique, 1950-1967.* France: 2004.

Unit History, 7th Radio Relay Squadron: K-SQ-RAD-7-HI, 1954-62. AFHRC, Maxwell AFB, AL.

Unit History, 8th Radio Relay Squadron: K-SQ-RAD-8-HI, 1952-62. AFHRC, Maxwell AFB, AL.

Unit History, 7480th Maintenance and Supply Group (SA): K-GP-M&S-7480-HI, 1952-67. AFHRC, Maxwell AFB, AL.

CHAPTER FIVE: REACTIVATION AND FINAL DISENGAGEMENT 1959-1967

FRELOC After Action Report, 1966-1967, Vol 1 and Vol 2. Edited by Office of Operations, Headquarters, U.S. Army Communications Zone. Heidelberg, Germany: August, 1967.

CHAPTER SIX: BORDEAUX-MERIGNAC AIR BASE

Unit History, 126th Bomb Wing: K-WG-126-HI, 1951-52. AFHRC, Maxwell AFB, AL.

Unit History, 7413th Air Base Group: K-GP-7413-HI, 1952-59. AFHRC, Maxwell AFB, AL.

Unit History, 7th Radio Relay Squadron: K-SQ-RAD-7-HI, 1952-67. AFHRC, Maxwell AFB, AL.

Miller, Jr., Edward A. *A Sojourn in France, A History of the 126th Bombardment Wing (Light) in Federal Service, 1951-1952.* n.a., 1990.

CHAPTER SEVEN: CHAMBLEY-BUSSIERES AIR BASE

Price, Alfred M. *The History of U.S. Electronic Warfare, Volume II, 1946-1964.* Association of Old Crows, Washington, D.C., 1989.

Timms, Charles R. *Chambley Air Base, France (1954-1967), The Best and Worst Place We Ever Lived.* Privately published, 1993.

Unit History, 21st Tactical Fighter Wing: K-WG-21-HI, 1954-58. AFHRC, Maxwell AFB, AL.

Unit History, 7544th Support Group: K-GP-7544-HI, 1958-63. AFHRC, Maxwell AFB, AL.

Unit History, 7122d Tactical Fighter Wing: K-WG-7122-HI, 1961-62. AFHRC, Maxwell AFB, AL.

Unit History, 366th Tactical Fighter Wing: K-WG-366-HI, 1962-63. AFHRC, Maxwell AFB, AL.

Unit History, 25th Tactical Reconnaissance Wing: K-WG-25-HI, 1965-66. AFHRC, Maxwell AFB, AL.

CHAPTER EIGHT: CHATEAUROUX-DEOLS AIR DEPOT

Cunny, Jean. *Mystere IVA, Les Avions de Combat Francais, 1944-1960.* I-Chasse-Assault: 1990.

Prot, Valerie. *The American Forces in Chateauroux, 1951-1967.* France: Editions Tarmeye, 1998.

"Air Force Pioneers Save USAFE $300,000 In Moulins Build-up." *Air Force Times, European Edition, 14* October 1952.

The History of Central Air Material Area, Europe. Edited by Office of Information Services, Chateauroux Air Station, France. Darmstadt, Germany: Stars and Stripes, 1956.

Welcome to Chateauroux Air Depot. Edited by Office of Information and Education, Chateauroux Air Station, France. Wiesbaden AS, Germany: AF USAFE, 1953.

866th Engineer Aviation Battalion, 1951-1954. Edited by Office of Information Services, Chateauroux Air Station, France. Darmstadt, Germany: Stars and Stripes, 1954.

Unit History, Chateauroux Air Depot: K-AD-CHATEAUROUX-HI, 1951-67. AFHRC, Maxwell AFB, AL.

Unit History, 12th Communications Construction Squadron: K-SQ-COMM-CONST-12-HI, 1952-67. AFHRC, Maxwell AFB, AL.

CHAPTER NINE: CHAUMONT-SEMOUTIERS AIR BASE

Davies, Peter E. with David W. Menard. *North American F-100 Super Sabre.* Wiltshire, UK: Crowwood Press, 2003.

Menard, David W. *Before Centuries, USAFE Fighters 1948-1959.* Virginia: Howell Press, Inc., 1998.

Unit History, 137th Fighter-Bomber Wing: K-WG-137-HI, 1951-52. AFHRC, Maxwell AFB, AL.

Unit History, 48th Fighter-Bomber Wing: K-WG-48-HI, 1952-60. AFHRC, Maxwell AFB, AL.

Unit History, 7108th Tactical Fighter Wing: K-WG-7108-HI, 1961-62. AFHRC, Maxwell AFB, AL.

Unit History, 366th Fighter-Bomber Wing: K-WG-366-HI, 1962-63. AFHRC, Maxwell AFB, AL.

Unit History, 7544th Support Group: K-GP-SUP-7544-HI, 1960-61. AFHRC, Maxwell AFB, AL.

Unit History, 31st Weather Squadron: K-SQ-WEA-31-HI, 1951-68. AFHRC, Maxwell AFB, AL.

CHAPTER TEN: DREUX-LOUVILLIERS AIR BASE

Lunsford, Charles L. *Departure Message, Chronicles of an Airborne Radio Operator.* greatunpublished.com. 2001.

Unit History, 60th Troop Carrier Wing: K-WG-60-HI, 1954-60. AFHRC, Maxwell AFB, AL.

Unit History, 376th Troop Carrier Squadron: K-SQ-376-HI, 1955-58. AFHRC, Maxwell AFB, AL.

Unit History, 377th Troop Carrier Squadron: K-SQ-377-HI, 1955-58. AFHRC, Maxwell AFB, AL.

Unit History, 378th Troop Carrier Squadron: K-SQ-378-HI, 1955-58. AFHRC, Maxwell AFB, AL.

Unit History, 7107th Tactical Reconnaissance Wing: K-WG-7107-HI, 1961-62. AFHRC, Maxwell AFB, AL.

Unit History, 7306th Air Base Group: K-GP-7306-HI, 1953-58. AFHRC, Maxwell AFB, AL.

Unit History, 8th Radio Relay Squadron: K-SQ-RAD-8-HI, 1953-67. AFHRC, Maxwell AFB, AL.

CHAPTER ELEVEN: ETAIN-ROUVRES AIR BASE

Unit History, 388th Fighter-Bomber Wing: K-WG-388-HI, 1954-58. AFHRC, Maxwell AFB, AL.

Unit History, 49th Fighter-Bomber Wing: K-WG-49-HI, 1957-60. AFHRC, Maxwell AFB, AL.

Unit History, 7121st Fighter-Bomber Wing: K-WG-7107-HI, 1961-62. AFHRC, Maxwell AFB, AL.

Unit History, 366th Fighter-Bomber Wing: K-WG-366-HI, 1962-63. AFHRC, Maxwell AFB, AL.

Operation Stair Step, 7121st Tactical Fighter Wing, 1961-62. Edited by 7121st TFWg. 14 July 1962.

Le 3eme Regiment d'Helicopteres de Combat. France: Etain Air Base, 2002.

CHAPTER TWELVE: EVREUX-FAUVILLE AIR BASE

McConnell, CAPT Shelton L. *C-130 Desert Operation.* Memorandum, dated 25 August 1959. HQ 322d Air Division.

Unit History, 317th Troop Carrier Wing: K-WG-317-HI, 1956-64. AFHRC, Maxwell AFB, AL.

Unit History, 322d Air Division, Cargo: K-AD-322-HI, 1955-66. AFHRC, Maxwell AFB, AL.

Unit History, 465th Troop Carrier Wing: K-WG-465-HI, 1955-58. AFHRC, Maxwell AFB, AL.

Unit History, 513th Troop Carrier Wing: K-WG-513-HI, 1966. AFHRC, Maxwell AFB, AL.

"Lady Be Good." *After The Battle, No. 25.* Fall, 1979.

CHAPTER THIRTEEN: LAON-COUVRON AIR BASE

Pierrot, Michel. *de l'Avion au Char: le Camp Militaire.* Bulletin Municipal d'Information de Couvron-et-Aumencourt. Couvron, France: 2000.

Unit History, 126th Bomb Wing: K-WG-126-HI, 1952. AFHRC, Maxwell AFB, AL.

Unit History, 38th Bomb Wing: K-WG-38-HI, 1953-58. AFHRC, Maxwell AFB, AL.

Unit History, 66th Tactical Reconnaissance Wing: K-WG-66-HI, 1957-66. AFHRC, Maxwell AFB, AL.

"Bienvenue—Welcome" Laon Air Base. Pamphlet 190-1-1, USAF. December 1963.

CHAPTER FOURTEEN: PARIS-ORLY

Unit History, 7415th Support Group: K-GP-SUP-7415-HI, 1953-59. AFHRC, Maxwell AFB, AL.

Unit History, 2d Air Postal Squadron: K-APU-2-HI, 1951-53. AFHRC, Maxwell AFB, AL.

Unit History, 12th Air Postal Squadron: K-APU-12-HI, 1953-63. AFHRC, Maxwell AFB, AL.

Unit History, 7025th Air Postal Squadron, 1953-63: K-APU-7025-HI. AFHRC, Maxwell AFB, AL.

"How to Enjoy Your Trip To Paris." Pamphlet. Edited by Armed Forces Information Center. Wiesbaden, West Germany, USAFE, 1958.

CHAPTER FIFTEEN: PHALSBOURG AIR BASE

Mauffrey, Philippe, editor. *Phalsbourg Air Base, Histoire de la Base de Phalsbourg, Periode americaine - 1953-1967.* Drulingen: Imprimerie Scheuer, nd.

Unit History, 7486th Air Base Group: K-GP-7486-HI, 1954-67. AFHRC, Maxwell AFB, AL.

"Facts About Phalsbourg." 7486th Air Base Group. AFHRC, Maxwell AFB, AL: 1959.

Unit History, 23d Helicopter Squadron: K-SQ-23-HI, 1956-57. AFHRC, Maxwell AFB, AL.

Unit History, 406th Fighter Interceptor Wing: K-WG-406-HI, DEC 1957- MAY 1958. AFHRC, Maxwell AFB, AL.

Unit History, 66th Tactical Reconnaissance Wing: K-WG-66-HI, 1956-59. AFHRC, Maxwell AFB, AL.

Unit History, 102d Tactical Fighter Wing: K-WG-102-HI, 1961-62. AFHRC, Maxwell AFB, AL.

Unit History, 366th Tactical Reconnaissance Wing: K-WG-366-HI, 1962-63. AFHRC, Maxwell AFB, AL.

CHAPTER SIXTEEN: TOUL-ROSIERES AIR BASE

Base Aerienne de Toul-Rosiers, Du Zenith au Nadir. Edited by Base Aerienne de Toul-Rosieres Active and Reserve Personnel: France, 2004.

Unit History, 117th Tactical Reconnaissance Wing: K-WG-117-HI, 1951-52. AFHRC, Maxwell AFB, AL.

Unit History, 10th Tactical Reconnaissance Wing: K-WG-10-HI, 1952-66. AFHRC, Maxwell AFB, AL.

Unit History, 465th Troop Carrier Wing: K-WG-465-HI, 1954-55. AFHRC, Maxwell AFB, AL.

Unit History, 50th Fighter-Bomber Wing: K-WG-50-HI, 1956-59. AFHRC, Maxwell AFB, AL.

Unit History, 7415th Support Group: K-GP-SUP-7415-HI, 1953-58. AFHRC, Maxwell AFB, AL.

Unit History, 7544th Support Group: K-GP-SUP-7544-HI, 1958-67. AFHRC, Maxwell AFB, AL.

Unit History, 7131st Tactical Fighter Wing: K-WG-7131-HI, 1961-62. AFHRC, Maxwell AFB, AL.

Unit History, 26th Tactical Reconnaissance Wing: K-WG-26-HI, 1965-67. AFHRC, Maxwell AFB, AL.

CHAPTER SEVENTEEN: DISPERSED OPERATING BASES

Glasstone, Samuel, editor. *The Effects of Nuclear Weapons.* U.S. Air Force Pamphlet #136-1-3, Prepared by Department of Defense, Washington, D.C.: April 1962.

Unit History, 48th Fighter-Bomber Wing: K-WG-48-HI, 1957-60. AFHRC, Maxwell AFB, AL.

Unit History, 388th Fighter-Bomber Wing: K-WG-388-HI, 1956-60. AFHRC, Maxwell AFB, AL.

Unit History, 7415th Support Group: K-GP-SUP-7415-HI, 1956-66. AFHRC, Maxwell AFB, AL.

Unit History, 7544th Support Group: K-GP-SUP-7544-HI, 1958-67. AFHRC, Maxwell AFB, AL.

CHAPTER EIGHTEEN: U.S. ARMY IN FRANCE

"Personnel; SCARWAF, ARWAF, and AFWAR." *Army Regulation AR 600-650 and Air Force Regulation AFR 35-20.* Departments of the Army and the Air Force. Washington, D.C.: 3 April 1950.

"Directory and Station List of the United States Army." *AGAO-1 461.* United States Army. Monthly, 1950-1968.

CHAPTER NINETEEN: RCAF BASES IN FRANCE

Baar, Philippe, Pierre Baar, Hugues Herr. *Marville RCAF Air Base.* Saint-Mard, Belgium: 2004.

Collin, Leon. "La Base Canadienne de Marville." *Bulletin No. 32, Racines et Memoires du Terroir.* Saint-Laurent-sur-Othain, France: November 1997.

Gunston, Bill. *Night Fighters, Development and Combat History.* New York: Charles Scribner & Sons, 1976.

Milberry, Larry. *The Canadian Sabre.* Toronto, Canada: CANAV Books, 1986.

On-line historical sources have been helpful, particularly the Truman Library online that has an excellent collection of papers dealing with the post war period and provides an inside look into the U.S. Government's commitment to the formation of NATO. This collection can be accessed at: www.trumanlibrary.org. Also, the NATO website: www.NATO.org makes not only historical material but high-quality photographs available to the public. For anyone interested in further patch research, I also highly recommend two books that are still the definitive volumes on Air Force heraldry, *Combat Squadrons of the Air Force, World War II* and *Air Force Combat Units of World War II* edited by Maurer Maurer.